The Lyrics of Prince Rogers Nelson/

C. Liegh McInnis, Jr.

Psychedelic Literature/Jackson, Mississippi

Psychedelic Literature ®

203 Lynn Lane
Clinton, MS 39056
(601) 383-0024
psychedeliclit@bellsouth.net

Copyright © 1995, 2000, 2007 by C. Liegh McInnis for Psychedelic Literature. All Rights Reserved, including the right of reproduction in whole or in part in any form without permission in writing from the author.

LCCN: 96-092619
ISBN: (13 digit) 978-0-9655775-0-2
ISBN: (10 digit) 0-9655775-0-3

Other Works by C. Liegh McInnis

Matters of Reality: Body, Mind & Soul (Poetry, 1996)
Scripts: Sketches and Tales of Urban MS (Fiction, 1998)
Confessions: Brainstormin' from Midnight 'til Dawn (Poetry, 1998)
Searchin' 4 Psychedelica (Poetry, 1999)
Prose: Essays and Letters (Social Commentary, 1999)
Da Black Book of Linguistic Liberation (Poetry, 2001)
Poetic Discussions (Interviews, DVD 2005)
Introduction of a Blues Poet (Poetry, CD 2005)

Acknowledgment

To God...It's been a gloriofantastic ride. Thanks.

To Monica, my female mirror image (Soul of my Soul). Thank you for your patience and belief. One day all our days will be yellow days.

This is for Ricki, John, George, Morris, Eric, and Albert, and all of those nights of listening to Prince until dawn. Believe it or not, it shaped our philosophies toward life.

To Kevin Taylor, I can never thank you enough for taking time from your daily grind to talk to me. Brothers like you keep the transcendental brothers rooted.

To Jeff Gibson, my original poetic mentor. Black fists pumpin'. Black expression flowin'.

To my father, C. Liegh, Sr., thanks for the music lessons. PS John didn't steal all your albums. I did.

To my mother, Claudette W, I know you don't agree with this topic, but you have continued to love and support me. That means the world to me. Love...

To Iola Fisher, thanks for reading this over and over and over.

To Nelson George, Scott Pulson-Bryant, Charlie Braxton, and Kevin Powell, your lives have been an inspiration to another young writer.

To Charlie Braxton and Mtume ya Salaam for providing insight and research of the hip hop world.

To Mrs. Bonnie Gardner, none of this would have been possible without you.

To Dr. Walter M. Hums, I know that you know, but thanks for

everything. You have been a light unto my path.

To Dr. Marie O'Banner Jackson, you listened when I wanted to whine. Your wisdom has been everything.

To Preselfannie W. McDaniels, Dr. Dilla Buckner, Dr. Jean Chamberlain, Ken Patterson, Dr. Louise Jones, Leelinda Parker, Kimberly Butler, Chevonne Thomas, LaSha Baylis, Anthony Moncreif, Karen Allen, and Nettie Ravick—my JSU Angels. Thanks for having my back when I needed it.

To Carl E., Anthony E., Tim E., Joseph S., Shun H., Robert W., Victor I., Michael E., Frederick S., Eddie M., Vincent and Pat P., Chris S., Steven P., Deshun R., Gary M., and everyone in Clarksdale, Mississippi who looked out for me.

To Dr. Jerry W. Ward, Kalamu ya Salaam, and Paulette Richards for the mini workshop.

To Mrs. Betty Lamb for lending your eyes, insight, and encouragement.

To Tony Keys at <u>Rock's Backpages Library</u> for the archival assistance (rocksbackpages.com).

Transcription of the lyrics to many of the songs have been found at the websites for the Databank Transcription Team, http://www.dttlyrics.com, Prince Lyrics at http://www.princelyrics.co.uk/, and Lyrics Directory at http://www.lyricsdir.com/prince-lyrics.html.

To DJ Brother Jules, Paul and Tim of the NPG Store, Michael B., and Mr. Hayes, time is everything, and you gave time.

And to ☥, thanks for your work. Your work kept me believing in life, Love, God, and myself when no one else believed in what I wanted to do. And that glorious night in your house (Paisley Park) was the ultimate glam.

The Lyrics of Prince Rogers Nelson/⚥:
A Literary Look at a
Creative, Musical Poet, Philosopher, and Storyteller

I.	Preface/Introduction	6
II.	Minneapolis as the Microcosm of America	37
III.	Theory: A Method to the Madness?	75
IV.	Father's Son	161
V.	The First Two Albums: Laying a Foundation	169
VI.	The Beginning of Controversy with the Breaking of New Grounds	179
VII.	The Minneapolis Genius and His Message	213
VIII.	His Purple Reign	228
IX.	Our Trip Around the World in a Day	243
X.	The Hopeless Romantic	261
XI.	Genius at Work: Poet of the Times	268
XII.	The Turmoil and Rebirth	277
XIII.	The Commercial Storyteller: The Pop Philosopher	308
XIV.	It's all about...Love!	318
XV.	One Gem of a Talent	333
XVI.	⚥	339
XVII.	The Gold Experience	352
XVIII.	The Personas	372
XIX.	Sex	397
XX.	Emancipation	457
XXI.	The Dawn of the Rainbow Children	558
XXII.	Poets' Praises for Prince	603
XXIII.	Conclusion	622
XXIV.	Bibliography	633
XXV.	Quoted or Referenced Index	665

Preface/Introduction

Literature, as a form of art, a tool of history, and a medium to convey information, has a more powerful impact when combined with the medium of music. Both literature and music are direct representations of what is occurring inside the human soul, its emotions and thoughts. Also, both have the ability to reproduce and convey the human trinity of mind, body, and soul in its primary, primitive, and original form with minimal loss in translation. This effective communication of the human condition is what creates the aesthetic pleasure and is the value of literature and music.

> "It seems possible to me that some kind of graph could be set up using samplings of Negro music proper to whatever moment of the Negro's social history was selected, and that in each grouping of songs a certain frequency of reference could pretty well determine his social, economic, and psychological states at that particular period. From the neo-African slave chants through the primitive and classical blues to the scat-singing of the beboppers: all would show definite insistences of reference that would isolate each group from the others as a social entity" (Jones/Baraka 65).

Over the past eighty years, the combined medium of literature and music as popular music has reflected, affected, impacted, changed, molded, and shaped the very essence of social, political, economic, and religious beliefs, sentiments and values, not to mention the interpersonal relationships, romantic and platonic, of mankind. One of the most influential and vivid examples of these musical poets, satirists, philosophers, and storytellers is Prince Rogers Nelson. Over the past thirty years, Prince Rogers Nelson has single-handedly affected the deviation or, in many cases, total change of the ideas and beliefs of sexuality, racism, and religion of a mass populous, not to mention his lifelong dedication to freedom, independence, creativity, and music, helping to define a place and system of lifestyle for a new generation of citizens based on individuality, cultural relevancy, and tolerance.

My interest in Prince dates back to the <u>Dirty Mind</u> album (1980) when I was ten. I knew of the first album and had danced to the second, but it was not until <u>Dirty Mind</u> that I understood that this guy, Prince, was a special talent with his finger on the pulse of the new, young African American individual. Or, as I conceived of it at age ten, this funny looking guy is really cool. I was drawn to the music and the controversy. One must understand what it was like to be a young, black male, growing up in the Mississippi Delta within a highly religious, conservative, and academic family. In this type of setting, concepts of self and society are rigid and ground into the psyche early and often. Before I had any concept of who I was, I was already quite knowledgeable in the concepts of the black southern Baptist church, Martin Luther King, Jr., the unified, unilateral politics of black America, and the belief that a good job is the goal of life. Until age ten, I had not begun to develop, to any degree, any concept or notion of what or who I was as an individual or what I truly believed for that matter. For me, God was not the God of Love, but the God of Judgment. Martin L. King, Jr., was not a man, but an archangel, untouchable and inaccessible. The black race was not a people but a movement, and all of my actions were to be scrutinized and judged according to how my actions aided in the fight for first-class citizenship. However, all of this was to change in 1980, even though I was too young to buy records or to go to the record store. Besides, Clarksdale, Mississippi, had only two or three "ma and pa" record stores that carried a very limited selection of music, mostly blues, country, and top 40. Essentially, what I knew about music was filtered to me through a white dominated playlist with limited access to black music, which would make for a unique musical experience. During the day, black folks listened to the one black station out of Memphis, the historic WDIA, but it would burn out as the evening faded into night. Then, all that was left was a white station that played mostly soft rock and light R&B pop. Of course, once I got old enough to walk downtown alone, I realized that in the Delta we breathe in the blues like most people breathe air. But even by 1980 the middle-class attitudes of the black community had delegated the blues to late night joints and very special functions where the blues is often watered down to appease middle-class white sensibilities, which ironically is how rock-n-roll is created. Adding to this musical variety or complexity, the separation of the religious and the secular had very definite and strong lines drawn. In my religious upbringing, there was a wide chasm between the sacred and the profane, the secular and the spiritual. However, this separation seemed to be arbitrary at best because the street that housed most of the churches intersected with the street that housed most of the cafes. So a walk home from choir practice down Fourth Street and Issaquena included passing cafes that smelled of barbecue, fish sandwiches, and the blues. Yet even with all of these sounds rolling through my head, I did not know that popular music was really the baby created from the consummation of gospel and the blues. And I must admit that I accepted the notion that these cafe people were going to hell, but I also must admit that sometimes hell seemed like a rocking good time. Little did I know that Ray Charles had already married the two and that Little Richard produced the offspring called rock-n-roll. So, I was left without much guidance to construct my own musical tastes through black radio in the day, white radio at night, gospel on Sunday, and the blues up and down the street. It is an interesting blend that the musicians, producers, and record companies of the nineties seem to have forgotten existed. Or, we have forgotten how to make ourselves accessible to all of them. At this stage, my musings seem to be a bit naive since I now know that I am not the original black Renaissance man. Although in 1985, I surely felt that only Prince and I were, having not a clue of Little Richard's, Chuck Berry's, Jackie Wilson's, James Brown's, Jimi Hendrix's, Sly Stone's, Curtis Mayfield's, and George Clinton's influence on popular music.

My musings are naive because I am a part of a generation that is naive in understanding how today fits into the narrative of human history. Integration has produced a generation of children who was amputated from its roots in the same manner as African descendants were disconnected from Africa during slavery. Just as second and third generation slaves lost a good part of their African selves through forced integration into a new, foreign system, black people who have been born after 1954 have lost a connection with the struggle and culture of those African Americans who lived segregated. Just as true as it is to say that second and third generation slaves were not Africans, it is also as true to say that children born after 1954 are not the same types of Negroes born before 1954. These "new" people come of age under integration, where so much of what kept African Americans afloat has been either lost or thrown aside for the riches of the new world. Culture rooted in African heritage no longer maintains the race. With the enrollment of African American students at white colleges hitting all-time highs by the mid-seventies, the importance of culture was replaced with the importance of the paycheck. Black folks had become privy to social, economic, and political opportunities like never before, and they readily accepted those new opportunities as symbols of the success of the Civil Rights Movement. However, in readily embracing the ideology of American capitalism, African Americans were forced to relinquish a good bit of their culture/Africanisms. By relinquishing so much of their culture, African Americans were putting themselves in a position of further exploitation because they were relinquishing their foundation and road map for survival and evolution, which allowed their history and culture to be colonized, co-opted, sold back to them, and even used against them. Hence, Prince could be sold to the world as a revolutionary artist, when he was really a recontextualization of American music, especially black music. And maybe being able to recontextualize styles is revolutionary. But when a people lose sight of their history and culture, they lose their identity. When they lose their identity, they are at risk of having the larger, oppressive culture assign their identity, which also assigns their self-worth. They are put in a position of accepting and internalizing notions of themselves based on somebody else's view of the world and not on their own view of the world. This allows their culture to be separated from them, taken, and repackaged in the manner that Prince was taken, allowed himself to be taken, from the bowels of the black community. When this happens, the art can be aesthetically pleasing, but its ability to empower the community from which it comes becomes severely diminished. Owen Husney, Prince's first manager attests to this:

> "When Prince was beginning with me, we worked all of the major black radio stations: Detroit, Philadelphia, Chicago, Atlanta, and Houston. When he became a mega-star, he hit the white stations. That was the worst mistake he could have made. He turned his back on black radio, and now black radio has turned its back on him. I've seen it happen so many times before. Black people still suffer from an inferiority complex that makes them want to be accepted by the larger white masses, look at Diana Ross and others. This desire to assimilate into white America affects everything from their lifestyles to their music. Maybe sometimes they think that they can't make the music or the art that they want so they try to break free of what they see as limitations on their art. Sometimes it is strictly for money and prestige. With Prince it was a bit of both" (Husney 2000).

Individual survival in the face of racial oppression is an ongoing struggle for African Americans. This is seen most specifically in the themes of black music.

> "...the insistence of blues verse on the life of the individual and his individual trials and successes on the earth is a manifestation of the whole Western concept of man's life, and it is a development that could only be found in an American black man's music...The whole concept of the *solo*, of a man singing or playing by himself, was relatively unknown in West African music" (Jones/Baraka 66).

By the time we get to Prince, this shift has gone 180

degrees, from the collective to the singular. Though Stevie Wonder was a one-man band, his images, tropes, and subject matter kept him firmly rooted in the midst of the collective as a griot. Prince becomes a one-man band under the umbrella of integration, where economic gain and individuality are as much of an influence on the art as the personal and collective need to create art. When this happens, it is the group that suffers. Prince can become a star, but his people (the place from which his talent originates) do not collectively benefit in that art's ability to document, celebrate, and uplift them. And if the art does innately and involuntarily document the collective, the documentation is so marginalized (made to seem as less important than the pleasing sounds and watered-down universal ideas) that the documentation is missed.

Art is not only for leisure, i.e., entertainment; it is also a basic component for defining, establishing, and maintaining society. Art affirms a people: their beauty, their intelligence, their essence, and their value. As poet, editor, and first black leader of the NAACP, James Weldon Johnson asserted:

> "...blacks must create literature because it is, inevitably, a fundamental aspect of their larger struggle for civil rights, and it can never escape this role because it serves as *prima facie* evidence of the Negro's intellectual potential...'The final measure of the greatness of all peoples is the amount and standard of literature and art they have produced. The world does not know that a people is great until that people produces great literature and art. No people that has produced great literature and art has ever been looked upon by the world as distinctly inferior'" (Gates and McKay xxxv).

Early in his career Prince is not creating under the notion that he is working to make life better for black folks. He is, however, under the impression that his art should work to make society better for humanity.

> "At the same time [that' you're telling kids] about wanting to be loved…you can tell them about contraception and things like that, which need to be said. No one else is going to say it. I know I have definite viewpoints on a lot of different things: the school system, the way the government's run, and things like that. And I'll say them, in time. And I think they'll be accepted for what they are" (Graustark 63).

His acceptance of integration causes him to create from the universal standpoint of all races blended as humanity rather than from the particular standpoint of one race. Though the art is aesthetically pleasing (sounds good musically and lyrically), it is seen as artificial or disposable because it seems to deal vaguely with the issues of love, hate, race, class, and oppression. Later in his career, Prince does become more tangibly race conscious, but it is viewed by the masses of African Americans as too little too late. His initial desire to be a rock icon on white America's terms separates him from the African American collective. When an African American artist is separated from his people as something other than or greater than his collective culture, it diminishes the power of his art to give voice to his people and to be an authentic record of his times. If an art form is the result of a particular socio-political condition and it is not asserted as such, then the account of the work's value is not accurate. Prince's initial ideology and journey speaks directly to the movement of African Americans acquiescing/assimilating into the larger culture and losing more of their culture/Africanisms. So then, Prince's work and career is a record of the integrated African American, the misguided struggle for place, power, and individuality, and the subsequent counter-reaction by more militant forces rooted in the black community, such as hip hop.

> "Each phase of the Negro's music issued directly from the dictates of his social and psychological

environment. Hence the black man who began after slavery to eliminate as much of the Negro culture from his life as possible became by this very act a certain kind of *Negro*. And if this certain kind of Negro still endeavored to make music, albeit with the strict provision that this music not be a Negro music, he could still not escape the final 'insult' of this music being evaluated socially, psychologically, and musically as a kind of Negro music" (Jones/Baraka 65).

Prince represented those like myself who had no real knowledge of African American history and accepted life in a vacuum with no historical road map of how we got to the eighties and no understanding of where we needed to be going. In high school, I believed that nothing like Prince had ever existed before him. I now realize that the Tom Jones album lying amongst my mother's collection of Motown, Teddy Pendergrass, Aretha Franklin, and Mahalia Jackson records should have been a sign of the marriage of white and black culture for the purpose of creating popular music.

I often ask myself if I would have been a Prince fanatic if I had really understood who Little Richard, James Brown, Jimi Hendrix, and George Clinton were. This leads me to another question. Why was Prince so popular in the eighties, and what does his popularity say about the culture and prevailing ideology of the eighties? Prince's success in the eighties speaks to five issues: his great talent, his mastery of visual imagery, the dawn of the video age, white America's continued fascination with black art and sexuality, and the successful marketing of pseudo-integration and multiculturalism. The combination of these five elements created economic opportunities for black musicians, which had not before existed. Of course, to achieve these economic benefits, African Americans found themselves having to make their work more palatable to white tastes and sensibilities. Thus, the eighties is the first time when black stars belonged to others at the same time or often before they belonged to the black community. If we examine the four most popular stars of the eighties—Bruce Springsteen, Madonna, Prince, and Michael Jackson—Springsteen and Madonna belonged to a certain segment of the white community before they belonged to the larger mainstream society. This has been their staying power. They have always had a base to which to return. On the other hand, Prince and Jackson worked to make themselves hybrids. This had never really happened before in black music. Even when Stevie Wonder was the biggest act of the seventies, he belonged to the black community. Wonder was the popular manifestation of the Black Arts Movement. Jackson and Prince are symbols of where the mass of black folks are headed in the beginning of the eighties—examples of what happens when the Black Arts Movement is co-opted and exploited: Motown songs are used to sell products for white owned companies that do little to benefit black communities or poetry from the members of the Black Arts Movement is used to sell products for white owned companies that do little to benefit black communities. To go even further, although hip hop is seen as a black medium, it is only when the acts are scaled back to one dimensional caricatures that they ascend to the heights of white star economic success. Even when the acts are rebelling against the mainstream culture, they are flattened to such a degree that they fail to truly articulate or represent the complexity, diversity, and dimensionally of black culture or the genre of hip hop. In his early work, Prince clearly has an understanding of the past, is clearly a student of the past, but his understanding is on an individualized, aesthetic level. Music, for Prince, is something that transcends or rises above particular cultures. As an artist, he believes that he has the ability and the right to amalgamate sounds at his pleasure and leisure regardless of how his amalgamation disconnects the art from the particular culture or event that produced the art that he is co-opting into his work for his own agenda. Thus, to think of oneself as a black artist, or a white artist, or a male artist, or a female artist is limiting and the very antithesis of what it means to be an artist because these categories, for Prince, are the antithesis of being human. In this, Prince was an artist in the post-European Renaissance sense, where:

"…serious Western music, except for early religious music, has been strictly an 'art' music…Of course, before the Renaissance, art could find its way into the lives of almost all the people because all art issued from the Church, and the Church was at the very center of Western man's life. But the discarding of the religious attitude for the 'enlightened' concepts of the Renaissance also created the schism between what was art and what was life. It was, and is, inconceivable in the African culture to make a separation between music, dancing, song, the artifact, and a man's life or his worship of his gods. Expression issued from life, and was beauty. But in the West, the 'triumph of the economic mind over the imaginative' as Brooks Adams said, made possible this dreadful split between life and art. Hence, a music that is an 'art' music was distinguished from something someone would whistle while tilling a field" (Jones/Baraka 29).

So Prince represents the new, integrated artists who have accepted the European notion of art and judge the value of art on its ability to be universal—which means to espouse some notion of the universality (whiteness) of mankind while selling a minimum of records. In this notion, high art or good art is not art that articulates a particular experience, but is an art that is able to make that particular experience palatable to the larger, ruling society. This often means a diluting of African American sensibilities—not that Prince is guided by maliciousness, but more an misunderstanding of what it means to be integrated. Prince is, for the most part, integrated. He grew up in Minneapolis, Minnesota, where the black population is about three percent of the entire population. Prince had accepted the notions of success on the terms of living in an integrated society, which means, as Langston Hughes asserts, that African Americans have an "urge…toward whiteness, the desire to pour racial individuality into the mold of American standardization, and to be as little Negro and as much American as possible" (Gates and McKay 1267). To get the white dollar, you must become as white as possible. This is the constant battle of popular black art; how does it make money and not lose its black essence, which is often in revolt of the larger white society?

It was not until I was an undergraduate at Jackson State University, thrust from Clarksdale into the urban setting of Jackson, Mississippi, under the now watchful eye of a father very concerned about the chemicals in his son's hair and his knowledge of his blackness, that I was given the notion that art must be studied in the context of collective history and social impact and not in a vacuum of individualized pleasure. Before this, I was under the same illusion as Prince seemed to have been in those early albums, as Nelson George states in a 1991 interview with the BBC's <u>Omnibus</u>, "Prince's work represents an African American who saw himself quite differently than African Americans of the past. Here was a man who had grown up pretty much assimilated into American culture" (George 1991). I grew up believing that the Civil Rights Movement had solved the problem of race in America. I thought that the next fight was for individuality. I needed to find and engage the struggle for individual identity. But I knew not how to interpret history. I knew black history, but I do not think I understood how to place black history in the context of American history. I knew what black people did. I just did not know why they did what they did. So, it was my lack of understanding the evolution of black culture and its essential importance to American culture which, as I now look back, caused me to cling so forthrightly to the music and wisdom of Prince. He embodied the spirit of my own, personal revolution. I was a black kid who wanted to be free from the conservative restraints of a small town and its smothering, monolithic religious and cultural ideology. Without proper knowledge of my people's history, my war for individuality was waged in separating myself from my people instead of examining and finding the true diversity and contribution to American culture of and by my people. All I knew was that I loved rock-n-roll; Elvis was king; the blues was for old, drunk people in nasty dives; Little Richard was a fag (my partners in all of their infinite machismo wisdom taught me that), and Pat Boone's rendition of "Blueberry Hill" was cool. Above all, black people dressed cool and kept a low profile. Then I am introduced to this black kid from Minneapolis who is wild and "original" to my limited scope. I did not even know where Minneapolis was. I remember one of my father's friends asking, "There ain't no black people in Minneapolis, is it?"

Prince became a hero who embodied all that I needed in a contemporary cultural figure with whom I could identify. He was a black guy with a guitar who played rock-n-roll and was not dead. For weeks after the release of Dirty Mind I kept hearing people talk about this album. I had to see it. I had to hear it. So I sneaked downtown to LaVean's Music Shop. That was quite a walk for a kid who had been only as far as three streets over. Keep in mind that Clarksdale's population is only 22,000. It is not like I walked for hours. Just the same, if my very religious, overly protective mother had known where I was going and why...Let's just say that I may not be writing this now. I remember there were a lot of people looking at and discussing the album, but very few buying it. Once I got a glimpse of it, looking at the Dirty Mind cover was a revelation. There is this skinny black kid wearing nothing but a raincoat and drawers, looking as if to say, "If you find something wrong with this picture, there is something wrong with you, not me." At that moment I realized that there were others out there attempting to find their own voices and identities, which need not be validated by a group. Even at this point, I do not believe that I was asserting the political identity of those blacks who see more to gain by ingratiating themselves to whites. I am talking about the fundamental notion that denying rights to a race is tantamount to denying rights to individuals and vice versa. I am talking about forcing both whites and blacks to deal with blacks on interpersonal levels and thus exploring the totalities of our human self, especially in the arts. This, of course, can only be achieved when African Americans are willing to remove themselves from the white controlled social and economic institutions and risk the losses of economic gains in order to retain control of their humanity, which is reflected through their art. This is essential since white Americans have a definite history of not being able to conceptualize the idea of the African American individual because we, as a country, have not yet begun to deal with Ralph Ellison's <u>Invisible Man</u> and the economic and political invisibility of black people.

The term "invisibility" refers to the fact that African Americans are seen by whites as an object to be used for the will or good of whites or in service to the maintenance of white supremacy and are rarely seen as sovereign human beings whose work and labor should be used for their own good. Thus, although everyone enjoys African American culture, only whites profit from it in a manner that allows them to control and influence the political landscape of who makes money, what subjects are discussed, and how those subjects are discussed. Ice Cube effectively identifies this invisibility and hypocrisy when he states that "It's not a problem when I'm talking about killing my own people, but it is a problem when I start talking about killing the people who oppress my people." As long as black art denigrates black people for the pleasure of a white audience, then there is no problem. But when black art proposes that black people rebel against the white power structure, then the art is denounced by the white power structure. This limiting of black voice creates or perpetuates black invisibility. Further evidence of this is that white republican conservatives are not the only ones who profit from the political silencing and fragmenting of African Americans. So called "white liberal democrats" are some of the loudest voices against the creation of black voting districts because these districts will diminish African American votes that are plentiful enough in white districts to help white democrats get elected but too small to have any real influence on policy. Any time African Americans attempt to use their culture as a base for unity to gain some power or sovereignty over their own lives, it is met with resistance from every segment of the white community, which understands that white sovereignty depends on

African American subjugation. Therefore, African Americans are invisible in relation to political and economic power even when it comes to controlling their own art. As a race they are invisible, and as individuals they are even more invisible. Furthermore, African Americans remain invisible because white America is more fascinated with African American physicality than African American intellect. In fact, white Americans view African American physicality as the African American's greatest asset and African American intellect as the African American's greatest liability. Much of the fascination that many white publishers and readers had with the Harlem Renaissance was their preoccupation with black sexuality. For many whites, the actual "renaissance" was merely a reason to be exposed to and absorbed in black sexuality. Even the terms "jazz" and "rock-n-roll" are derived from white people's notion of black sensuality and sexuality. African American art has always been equated by whites to black sexual prowess. So, the African American has yet to be truly seen or embraced by himself or the totality of American culture as human, therefore making individuality almost an impossibility to achieve. An invisible race makes for invisible individuals.

    This struggle for individuality is a risky road to travel. Black America's strength has been its unity. The black individual threatens the cohesiveness of the Black Movement, especially if he is willing to deny or destroy the collective for his own personal gain. Furthermore, no African American wants to be deemed insufficiently black, not even Clarence Thomas whom I, as many other African Americans, see as the whitest, most conservative man in D.C. This is what makes Prince's work and accomplishments so compelling and astounding. He has been able to craft a career by defying the critics, especially when playlists were as segregated as the pre-1950s. Unlike Michael Jackson who stayed closer to the traditional R&B formula, Prince was alienating himself from the commercial formula, ironically by blending the history of rock-n-roll. As George indicates, "He is literally an encyclopedia of rock-n-roll" (George 1991). Since he saw himself as a "new Negro," Prince was searching for a different fan than the usual pop audience. In Prince's own words, "They only come around to check you out when you have a hit" (Hilburn, "The Renegade Prince," 66). He was searching for the music fan who wanted to be challenged both by music and by subject matter, which also meant challenging their notions of life, which included class, race, gender, and sexuality. Jackson's music is dance oriented with the lyrics emphasizing party and romance. The beats are structured around rigid and well-regulated rhythms with the beat intervals spaced for dancing rather than thinking—no way to offend. Prince's music is designed to challenge categories by not conforming to them with lyrics that solicit the young to stand up, be noticed, and demand their rights, "Reproduction of a New Breed, leaders stand up and organize" (Prince, "Sexuality," Controversy, 1981). Yet, instead of concentrating on freeing the masses, Prince entered through the back door, attempting to liberate individuals by challenging all notions of "group" definitions: race, gender, and class. Prince is fighting racism, but he is doing so in a method that is all but foreign to the "collective" struggle and history of African Americans. Also, his plan is safe for an individual who is conflicted over wanting the white dollar but not the racism that comes with that white dollar. His strategy, in the end, becomes a double-edged sword—it gives him his freedom to create and sell various types of music, but alienates him from the group with which he shares the pain and the struggle. Still, his work and his legacy speak for themselves. Few in the eighties created music or lyrical imagery to the caliber of Prince. In the end, he is respected for his talent and his ability to stay his course even if he is seen as one who turned his back on or separated himself from his race.

In Blues People (1963), Amiri Baraka (LeRoi Jones) asserts that black music is the record of black history. He uses music "to measure this world in which we find ourselves, where we are not at all happy, but clearly able to understand and hopefully, one day, to transform" (Jones/Baraka viii). Music, as with any other art form, is not only a record keeping device, but it also serves as a catalyst for human evolution. To achieve or help along this evolution, Baraka further asserts that we, the lovers and beneficiaries of the music, must create a system which allows us "to measure [our] own learning and experiences and to set out a system of evaluation, weights, and meaning" (Jones/Baraka viii). My attempt is to shed light on why Prince's work is important as a record of history and as a voice of African American struggle and development. In studying the blues and the development of all black music, Baraka places and bases his study in the collective souls, movements, and developments of the race. My study is much more singular, not just because it is about one person, but because that person is born into a time and generation where the African American concerns, because of the shift in the emphasis of the Civil Rights Movement, shifted from the collective to the individual. Being a product of this shift myself, I began studying Prince's work as a process of measuring myself as it relates to the manner in which his music shaped my generation. In the eighties, African Americans are struggling with the symptoms of white supremacy rather than with the ill, itself. This misguided struggle creates misguided solutions, which tend to provide temporary relief but fail to liberate the mass from the umbrella of white supremacy. For instance, Prince can create a Paisley Park (both the recording studio and the ideology), which solves his physical and metaphysical problems with this society, but his Paisley Park does not cure the problems of the collective, which is suffering the same ills from which he is seeking relief. Of course, it must be noted that for millions like me Paisley Park represented a possibility that I too could break free. As he asserted, "Paisley Park is in everybody's heart. It's not just something that I have the keys to" (Karlen, "Prince Talks: The Silence Is Broken," 30). I accepted the limitations of this individuality for the hopes that I too could one day create my own Paisley Park, which would allow me some solace and sovereignty.

The notion of individuality, breaking free from the mindless, overly conservative masses, is directly related to the rebellious spirit of rock-n-roll. Little Richard's music and dandyism was a revolt against what he perceived as overly conservative music and lifestyles. And though Little Richard was only trying to liberate himself, his work spoke to millions of white kids who also felt smothered by the conservatism and hypocrisy of their parents. Elvis Presley shaking his white ass on national television was an affront to conservative, white views and lifestyles, but it worked to liberate millions of white kids from their parents' oppressive and hypocritical legacy. Of course this liberation of white youth also meant that a select few white record company owners would make money beyond their wildest dreams, which is supported by Sun Records owner, Sam Phillips who discovered Presley because he was looking for a white man who could sing and dance like a black man. Thus, one group's cultural liberation is another person's financial gain. The black artist, if he hoped for the same financial success of his white counterparts, had to make himself palatable to white tastes. Prince's amalgamation of sounds allowed him to tap into this rebellious legacy and be perceived as one who makes rules instead of following them. His musical persona added fuel to his rebellious subject matter. This allowed Prince to be sold as a rebellious visionary, one who is refusing to be limited or controlled by arbitrary categories of what people should be. When I was in high school, I loved rock-n-roll because it represented everything that was anti-normal. On the inside of my locker I had pictures of white rock bands as well as Little Richard, Jimi Hendrix, and Prince. For the most part, my locker was decorated with white faces—Billy Squire, the Beatles, Queen, Stevie Ray Vaughn, etc. Once word about my locker and my taste in music spread to the African American students, I was deemed "white boy lover." This is where the misdirected struggle or fight begins. My high school peers had no knowledge or notion that rock-n-roll was our music. By the time we had arrived, rock-n-roll was a white medium. Therefore, any black kid who liked rock-n-roll was an "Oreo" or a "wanna be." My response was to take an elitist attitude, as much as I could in the ninth grade that "you ignorant niggas don't know your history and don't know culture. Rock-n-roll," I would assert in the halls of my high school whenever I was being teased, "is a far more cerebral art form with complex guitar solos and lyrics about more than just fucking. As for R&B and rap," I would add, "anyone can 'cry and beg,' and anyone can push the record button to steal, oops, I mean sample." This was the classic struggle of Negroes separated and fighting the wrong battle because none of us knew our history. My high school hallway battles with my peers were not as important as Du Bois versus Washington, but it was Baraka's "changing same" where African people dislocated in America choose various solutions to address the manner in which white supremacy manifests itself in their lives, which often causes conflict and petty bickering that keeps them separated instead of uniting to defeat the common evil. This is why the NAACP and the Nation of Islam are often at odds with each other rather than working together. And this is why so many African Americans remain divided over the place and importance of Prince.

This narrow view of the world caused my generation which came of age in the eighties not to be able to see the forest for the tress. Again, our fight became for individual freedom because the black church and the community were seen as oppressive forces, which did not support us in our individual endeavors but, in fact, oppressed us. Artists like Prince and Rick James unknowingly told us that it was appropriate to say "Fuck the world and its rules; I didn't ask to come here." I hated the church because it went against everything that was naturally me. Everything about me was "do, do, do," and everything about the church was "don't, don't, don't." I hated church because I had to sit still and be quite. Although there was testifying, I could not testify to what they were testifying. I had no clue. This represents a generation lost and separated from their roots in the same manner that third generation slaves were, over time, lost and separated from their roots. In fact, the present generation of black Christians who shout and testify do so more for aesthetics (emotionalism and rhythm) and for the purposes of expressing a very narrow and individualistic experience. Their shouts and testimonials are not connected to the culture or struggle of Africans in America from which those shouts and testimonials originate. Their shouts and testimonials equate to an abstracted and vague activity that is all but devoid of its roots and power.

> "In the United States, Africanisms in American Negroes are not now readily discernible, although they certainly do exist. It was in the United States only that the slaves were, after a few generations, unable to retain any of the more obvious of African traditions because of becoming Westernized and 'acculturated'" (Jones/Baraka 13).

This brings to mind the story about the Sunday ham. Every Sunday, a woman cooked ham for her family. She would purchase an eight pound ham and cook it in her ten pound pot. Before she put the ham in the pot, she would cut a pound off each side. After several years of watching her do this, her husband asked her why she cuts the ends off the ham, especially when the pot was more than large enough to hold the ham. After thinking about it, her only response was "Mother used to do it this way." The next day she told her mother that her husband had inquired about the practice of cutting the two pounds off the ham before cooking it. She said, "I told him that I do it because you used to do it." Looking irritated and amused, her mother responded, "Nut, I used to cut my ham because my pot wasn't big enough." So, the loss of history and tradition or the lack of understanding history and tradition causes us to walk blindly through life without direction and purpose, often engaging in practices that harm us rather than benefit us. Black Christians of the eighties were integrated Christians, something quite different than the Christians before the Civil Rights Movement. The power of their religion had shifted from the protection of the collective to the protection of the individual. Instead of praying for the end of slavery or Jim Crow, they are now praying for Cadillacs and the "light bill." These are not the black Christians who as James

Baldwin asserted saw themselves as very different from white Christians prior to 1975.

> "The Baptist church in which I grew up, in all but actual fact, in all but actual vocabulary, assumed that the saved were black and all the damned were white. It was a kind of fantasy revenge. And it was, very importantly, a way of getting them from one day to another, through their lives, and as it turns out through generations. But, times do change" (Baldwin, James Baldwin, 1989).

Eighties Christians were all but devoid of their Africanisms and African ideologies. And since black popular music will always be populated with the children of the black church, popular music of the eighties had lost much of its Africanisms, African ideology, power, and relation or relativity to the cultural struggle of Africans dislocated in America. In fact, most had all but accepted that exterior Africanisms would minimize their ability to take advantage of the new economic opportunities, so they became as much like white Christians as possible. Since the black church is still the largest institution of black life, this caused black folk in general to accept integration as a way of life.

Prince understood/believed that being a black man would place limitations on his ability to play rock-n-roll and also "stretch out" into some other areas.

> "'He didn't want to tour with black artists,' recalls [his mentor Pepe] Willie, very specifically. 'He wanted to tour with Mick Jagger and Foreigner, the big guys. He didn't want to be on the so-called chitlin circuit, and I can understand it. I always told him that the black artists have a double thing to do. I said, 'You can make it to number one on the R&B chart and it don't mean nothin'. Now you've gotta go Top 40'" (Hill 53).

Prince seemed to lack a real understanding of the socio-political development of African American music as well as the development of American musical categories. There is the question of whether or not Prince was purposely bending the truth early in his career because he so desperately wanted to be seen as his own man, but from 1978 – 1981 he consistently claimed not be very knowledgeable of black music. In his book <u>My Time with Prince</u>, original Prince guitarist Dez Dickerson discusses asking Prince about his influences and not believing Prince when he stated that he did not know that much about Hendrix. And according to the 1981 <u>New Musical Express</u> interview,

> "…he genuinely doesn't appear to have heard, or even heard of, a large percentage of acts with whom one might assume he would be familiar. 'When I started doing my own records I really didn't want to listen to anybody, because I figured I should just disregard what anybody else might be doing. Though I suppose subconsciously I might have been influenced just by the mood that was going on around me" (Salewicz 18).

Prince knew the power of black music, but he seemed not to know what caused it to be powerful. At the same time, I was a middle class kid who did not know anything about myself because I did not know anything about my people. Therefore, I could not testify in church. Prince represented the rebellion that I wanted and needed. So, I, like others, could testify to his songs. But I, like him, did not know against what I was rebelling in any historical sense. It is one thing to fight against racism and oppression, but that fight is often misdirected when we do not understand the root. This often causes us to alienate ourselves from those who should be our allies and align ourselves with those who are our oppressors. In most cases, our rebellions are often mute or insignificant because they are not connected to any larger, tangible, and collective socio-political struggles. Or, our lack of history makes us unable to articulate why or how our individual/personal struggles are relevant to a larger collective struggle. When Prince wrote slave on his face, the majority of African Americans assumed that it was a promotional stunt and were offended. They had never seen him make a socio-political connection with the African American collective, but now because of his own personal pain he wants to profit from their pain. Yet Prince was doing nothing more than African Americans have always done, which is to take history and recontextualize it for their own benefit, in the same manner that black Christians recontextualized the Old Testament and the Israelite struggle as a symbol for the Civil Rights Movement..

Life for my mother, my grandmothers, and their peers was a constant struggle. In the backs of their minds lay the notion that slavery and Jim Crow were just around the corner, waiting to reassert their tyrannical power over black folks. In fact, as they saw it, Jim Crow was still here; he just changed his suit and bought a computer. However, their reaction was not to retain or embrace their African or African American heritage but to become as integrated as possible. I was history-less because my mother thought that my saved soul and my middle-class education would serve me better than that "black stuff" that my father was always preaching. Hey, it was not their fault. God was stronger than Malcolm X and Martin Luther King. But because I was history-less, I did not know the struggle, history, or the prevailing Africanisms of my people. Therefore, church nor religion were important to me— not in my search for identity. And, a God in Heaven who did not deal with my earthly concerns did not make much sense to me. In truth, the only difficulties in my integrated, middle class life were metaphysical and centered around my rejection of attending church. This was the oppression from which I wanted to break. This carried over to my social life, of living in a small town where people thought that they had the right to ask you why you were not in church. What right, I thought, did they have to inquire about my being, about my personal life? I did not know that their questioning grew from the African tradition of the extended family and the fact that black folks had to know where everyone was. It was not a matter of being nosy; it was a matter of being safe. With the threat of lynching lasting into the 1970s and King's 1968 assassination validating their fear, their inquiry into my whereabouts was guided by spiritual and physical concerns. It was a matter of nurturing, protecting, and perpetuating the community. But, I did not know that, and I resented greatly that someone could feel that they had the right to probe into my life in that manner. I was an integrated kid who believed individuality to be a religion.

This notion of individuality, no matter how oft times warped or perverted, resonates in Prince's work. As he stated in 1981, "To me, the ultimate responsibility is the hardest one—the responsibility to be true to myself" (Edrei 34). He would even engage in fights when his peers challenged his individuality (Adler 57). Prince symbolized that the eighties was a time for the struggle of the black individual—a time when he would break loose and free himself from all the chains of race, class, and gender. This is why Prince's work spoke to so many of us. Yet, ironically, for people of my father's age, it was the music, the way that Prince's music signified the history of black music. Prince is the greatest musical alchemist of all times, excluding maybe Wonder. When my father's generation hears Prince, they undeniably hear every black musician who came before him. This is echoed by Miles Davis.

> "Prince is from the school of James Brown…But Prince got some Marvin Gaye and Jimi Hendrix and Sly in him, also, even Little Richard. He's a mixture of all those guys and Duke Ellington…I like Prince a little better [than Michael Jackson] as an all-around musical force…He's got that church thing up in what he does…it's the church thing that I hear in his music that makes him special…It's a black thing and not a white thing" (Davis 385).

As for my generation who did not know the history and only used it as a superficial credit card to justify our music to our parents, what we heard in Prince was his ability to rebel. He gave us the voice to rebel against race, class, gender, and, ultimately, reality. Those of us who really thought that we were embarking on a journey thought that Prince had the secret to reconstructing reality. This is what made him a metaphysical poet. Prince was a middle class kid. The most urgent and tangible issue for middle class children is finding, identifying, and asserting self as an individual. Further, a capitalistic society teaches us to make our individual mark upon the world. As scholar and founder of Kwanzaa, Maulana Karenga asserts, we think of ourselves in the context of "'me' in spite of everyone [and not] 'me' in relation to everyone" (Gates and McKay 1975). This is what the shift in the Civil Rights Movement produced. Ironically, this shift is what allows Prince to build on the work of Wonder and Sun Ra to become one of the few African American metaphysical poets of the eighties. This is more evidence of the African American's ability to make something from nothing. Even in his misguided attempts, Prince is able to refashion the medium of lyricism, specifically in his refashioning of the sex metaphor, or sex as a metaphor, or sex as a manifestation of our metaphysical concerns and anxieties.

Prince's concentration on the individual would ultimately progress to a discourse on human evolution—how does one evolve to one's highest state? Prince abandons the physical to embrace the spiritual, using sex and sexuality as the liaison or bridge between the physical and spiritual worlds. His divorce from race, gender, and class allows him more aggressively to pursue the issues of the metaphysical in secular concerns as not embraced in popular music by African American artist before him. So, with Prince there is the good and the bad, the focus and the misdirection. Embedded in Prince's lyrics and his career are all the things African Americans hate and love about themselves. He is *the* African American dichotomy. He proves that to be African American is to be a dichotomy where one is always grappling with the tension of duality. And if it is true that black music is black history, then Prince is an irrefutable part of that history, representing the post-Civil Rights era when African Americans began to struggle with their new found freedoms and with Ellison's notion of invisibility on an individual level. However, their willingness to be "as little Negro as possible" in order to gain a place in Americana caused them to be pimped by the capitalistic machine, which made the middle class feel like they were special Negroes because of their educational and economic achievements. Prince represents this dichotomy of blackness—simultaneously loving and hating yourself, affirming and denying portions of yourself at different periods for the purposes of day-to-day survival. This means being black enough to take advantage of affirmative action and white enough to join the country club. Integration created an African American who sought to be something other than African and as American as possible to survive.

Prince represents the diversity of the African American struggle and the diverse art that his struggle produces. He also represents the sometimes narrow and self-defeating practices of survival, such as the strategic need to erase one's African-ness when necessary. In doing so, his career, much as the lives and ideologies of black folks, fluctuates. African Americans have a history of claiming to be black plus something else to gain access to the power structure only to realize eventually that "they ain't gone never be shit to the power structure." Still, they are never able to completely divorce themselves from this system for various reasons. The need to find this balance between assimilation into the burning melting pot and cultural nationalism is the African American dichotomy. Prince has been all of this. He was born of Stevie Wonder's natural talent to be all things, meaning he was born into the legacy of being a griot. He created himself a mulatto to achieve the rock star icon status that he desired, which allowed him to create freely what he wanted. Like most African Americans he accepted America and Americana on its terms and rules and attempted to play by those terms and rules. He eventually realizes that he will never be treated in the same manner as Eric Clapton or Madonna. (What is interesting is that Clapton and Madonna both continue to connect and reconcile themselves and their work to black music and the culture from which it comes. They understand that black music is the backbone, the foundation, of their work, so they continuously make pilgrimages to black culture to keep up with the changing times as well as to give their work the essence it needs to survive. On the other hand, for years Prince kept himself separate from mainstream black culture because he wanted to preserve the notion of being an original individual. To commune with black culture would remove his "special" superstar status and make him just another "great" musician in the legacy of "great" black musicians. It was not until 1990 that Prince partnered with George Clinton and Mavis Staples and began to embrace and pay homage publicly the legacy of black music.) Eventually, Prince divorces himself from the mainstream system of major record labels, only to reconstruct another partnership with it. In short, most African Americans are strong Black Nationalists until a "good government" job comes along. As African Americans are more American than anyone in the country, Prince could be seen as being more African American than anyone in the race. To be a secure/confident/steadfast Black Nationalist or pan-Africanist is to be in the minority. To be a person who struggles, on a daily basis, with what one's blackness means is to be in the majority. Prince's career and lyrical content plots the journey of African Americans who bought into and later struggled with integration.

I am looking at the history of the 1980s through the work of a man who most typified the mentality of that time. Post-Civil Rights and pre-hip hop, Prince's music represents the typical integration years, 1980-87, when African Americans welcomed the possibility and potential of integration and multiculturalism and, in the end, received another bad check. The two biggest black stars of the eighties, Prince and Jackson, are the best representatives of that time. They both bought into the possibilities of integration and multiculturalism with hopes that it would allow them to become unencumbered, uninhibited artists, finally becoming all that they could be, all that they were meant to be. In the end, however, they only became disconnected from their race, unable to build institutions and relationships, which would lead to African American liberation and sovereignty. (Not that it was their intent to be activists or revolutionaries in the traditional black sense, but they both clearly believe that music has the ability to make mankind better. And Prince does wish to call our attention to the fact that if we, individuals, do not learn to love ourselves, we can never love others, and if we can never love others, we can never evolve.) This lack of addressing specific "black issues" or addressing them in a manner in which they are clearly seen as "black issues" shows that they were artists who had bought into the universality of integration, which was, at best, ineffective or lacking the power of African American music before it. So, as individuals African Americans gain money and lose their souls—not just their individual souls but their collective souls.

Prince is now a very spiritually driven artist who is quite concerned with how his work aids in the spiritual evolution of mankind, but he is perceived as being so disconnected from African Americans that his individual inner peace and revelation fail to communicate with and empower his race. Jackson and Prince allowed themselves to be walled off from their collective race in order to be "lifted up" to the mainstream of white America. As Prince would assert later in his career in "My Name Is Prince," "⚥ don't wanna be king cuz ⚥'ve seen the top, and its just a dream. Big cars and women and fancy clothes will save your face, but it won't save your soul; ⚥'m here 2 tell u that there's a better way. Would our Lord be happy if he came 2day?" By allowing themselves to become Americana figures as opposed to remaining African American icons, they lost their ability to communicate with the African American community on any level other than the cosmetic aesthetics (pleasing sounds). Even when dealing with the spirit world, it must be accessed through the physical world. This is the significance of Jesus feeding the multitudes. Jesus could not heal souls without first caring for bodies. When the work does not begin in the physical reality of the people, they cannot experience the metaphysical movements. This is the struggle of African Americans, and this is the struggle of Prince's work, balancing the physical with the metaphysical, balancing the dreams of American success with black sensibilities. It is his journey and the mirroring of his journey to the individuals within the collective that gives him significance. His stumbling, bumbling, often misdirected journey toward enlightenment and self-determination mirrors the journey of African Americans. His work is representative of the hopes and failings of integration and should be studied accordingly.

Initially, this work began when an undergraduate instructor asked us to do a presentation on any writer from any period or genre who has had the most influence on how we think about writing and the social issues about which we write. After flipping through the usual anthology list of Paul L. Dunbar, Jean Toomer, Hughes, Richard Wright, Margaret Walker, Baldwin, and Baraka, I realized that even though I admired their technical styles and accomplishments as African American writers, neither really had any direct affect on how I write or about what I write, at least not consciously. To a young black kid from the Mississippi Delta, Prince represented what I perceived as the new black ideal, the 1980s "new Negro" removed and somehow freed from the constraints of the "new Negroes" of the Harlem Renaissance and the Black Arts Movement. Prince was to become the young black individual petitioning for his own space, an artist constantly grappling with whom he was and with whom he was becoming. Together with Rick James, he represented an alternative music and manner of thinking to that of the polished, flashy commercialism of Jackson who had taken the smooth styling of Motown, removed the essence of black culture (the poetry of black life and intricate musical compositions), and replaced it with simple syncopation and purely romantic (safe) topics.

After completing the first eighty-two pages, which were basically a technical and subjective interpretation of lyrics, I realized that I had written about the lyrics in a vacuum. I had to go back and put the lyrics and the overall work into a historical and social context. Baraka's <u>Blues People</u> (1963) and Dave Hill's <u>Prince: A Pop Life</u> (1989), an essential read in the study of Prince, laid the ground work for a historical and social context. Hill's book is followed a close second by Per Nilsen's <u>Prince: A Documentary</u> (1993), re-edited and released as <u>Days of Wild</u> (2000) and <u>The Vault</u> (2004). Nilsen's book is a must read for anyone attempting to chart the career of Prince. Nilsen's publication is the most comprehensive collection and documentation of the career of Prince. <u>The ☥ Family</u>, a former biweekly newsletter edited and published by Diana E. Dawkins, has also been an excellent source of information. Dawkins has done, by far, the best job of compiling documents that testify to Prince being a monumental figure who should be studied as a significant artist in the canon of American artistry. Additionally, I was inspired by the work of Nelson George. At one time one of the most powerful music critics in America, George's tireless dedication to the critical study and appreciation of black music has provided a major foundation for studying Prince in the context of African American music. And, three phone conversations with Kevin Taylor, Senior Music Researcher for Black Entertainment Television's <u>Video Soul</u>, served as a type of spiritual influence, confirming for me that there are others who also believe that Prince is an American artist worth studying for his influence on popular American music, art in general, and culture. My work, as are the others, is just one perception of the work of Prince. What is most important is that Prince appeals to various segments of society, each with a different interpretation of his work. This is his beauty and power. He has broadened the mainstream by championing otherness.

    This book tracks and attempts to analyze the meanings and transitions of Prince's lyrical work, taking into consideration that to explore thoroughly the lyrics of Prince, one must realize that his lyrics are but a particle of the interwoven package that is Prince. The meanings of Prince's songs, his artistic theory, and his theology of life do not begin and end with his lyrics. Though the lyrics are the clearest points of reference for how Prince sees the world, there are many other aspects of his character that we must take into consideration to gain a full understanding of his lyrics. By studying Prince's lyrics, I hope to accomplish five ultimate goals. One, we must understand that popular art is a gauge or a barometer for society. When we study popular artists, we are innately studying the periods of the artists, which give us a better understanding of our history and of humanity. Though we may not like the images or the messages of popular art, it does tell us something about the times in which it is created. Two, I want to prove that Prince is a master lyricist whose work, if studied by following generations, can inspire greatness. Three, by applying a serious study to Prince as a poet I hope to bridge the gap between fine art and folk art or serious art and leisure art to provide another vehicle where African American artists who are on the fringes of respectability will be given serious attention. Unlike the Beatles or Bob Dylan, rarely are African American songwriters studied for their intellectual value. When we deny, ignore, or marginalize African American intellect, we deny, ignore, and marginalize African American humanity. Four, if art is ever going to move humanity to its highest point, we must begin to tell the truth that most academic or fine art was first folk or popular art. This act of separating fine or academic art from the masses is merely proof that artistic theory is more of a tool for cultural warfare than a tool that provides understanding. Instead of bridging gaps, artistic theory is often used to create gaps, to divide the haves from the have nots. And five, studying the lyrics of Prince is a way to gauge the full realm of black diversity, which allows us to gauge the full realm of black humanity. African Americans cannot continue to allow our fear of white supremacy to suppress our diversity for when we suppress our diversity, we suppress our humanity. The class and generation wars in the African American community are always centered on art. As long as these divisions exist, African Americans will never be able to move forward. With all of that said, one must also know that my assertions are not intended as the gospel on how to listen to or interpret the lyrics of Prince. To use Baraka's words, "Writing the book confirmed ideas that had been rolling around in my head for years and that now...there was a thrill to see my own ideas roll out, not always as 'precisely stated,' [but my ideas]...were forceful enough to convince me that I did know something about this music" (Jones/Baraka vii). If anything my work is to be viewed as a conversation that presents common and varying views to the Prince literate or as an introductory guide to those new to the idea of Prince as a popular musician making a conscious effort to produce thought-provoking songs for discussion and enlightenment. I invite you to journey with me as I explore a rainbow of creativity as long as forever and as colorful as our deepest emotions.

Minnesota as a Microcosm of America

Minnesota is place where its ideal shines more brightly than its reality. In this it is as typical as most American places.

> "If one regards race prejudice as 'an attitude with an emotional basis,' replete with preconceived attitudes that are not based upon scientific knowledge or facts, such prejudice has always existed in Minnesota. It is also true that color still retards the degree of integration in any area of the United States, including Minnesota. The struggle to overcome this prejudice and retardation has been constant there. It is to that history and struggle that we now address ourselves" (Spangler 16).

Considered the heart of liberalism, Minnesota continues to struggle with its projected persona of being a multicultural haven and the reality that its economic realities make it as much a place of racial conflict as any other place in the United States. In the introduction to The Negro in Minnesota, Carl T. Rowan asserts that Minnesota is a place full of contradictions when it comes to the race problem, and it is this contradiction that makes it all the more American. "In, fact, in September, 1852, the Minnesota Pioneer, described Negroes living in the state as 'a useful class, and here on the confines of Barbarism do as much to put a civilized aspect upon the face of society as any other class'" (Spangler 12). Rowan is then quick to show that race relations in Minnesota is about the same as anywhere else in America.

> "Yet, one hundred years after this observation, it still is a troublesome fact that only a bare handful of Minnesota school children know that the first blood spilled in the Boston Massacre was that of a black man, a runaway slave named Crispus Attucks, or that during the Spanish-American war the soldiers who rescued Teddy Roosevelt, like the one who first reached

the blockhouse on San Juan hill to hoist Old Glory, were Negroes" (Spangler 12).

We realize with Rowan's introduction that Minnesota, for better or worse, is not fundamentally different from any part of America, but its origins allow it to claim a sense of tolerance and multiculturalism not afforded to most other places in America. Somehow, Minnesota has been able to assert itself as a more tolerant state, in regards to race and gender issues. What accounts for this is not its lack of failings in these areas, for Minnesota has had more than its share of race problems, but Minnesota has not been as public about anti-race and gender laws in its legislation. Even during the height of the slavery and fugitive slave law debates a few years before the Civil War, Minnesota had no laws on the books addressing either issue. This type of lukewarm neutrality has allowed Minnesota to be painted as a more liberal state than other places. Although it has had some of the same types of social and economic contradictions, its residents have been able to say that they never legally supported slavery or the legal oppression of anyone based on race. Truthfully, the small population of African Americans caused whites in Minnesota to feel less threatened than whites in other parts of the country. A few Negroes are insignificant; more Negroes become significant. The degree of that significance and complexity is as diverse, varying, and typical as the rest of America. What makes the story of the Negro in Minneapolis so compelling is the same aspect that makes the story of the Negro in America compelling. With such small numbers in both cases, African Americans have been able to have a major, circular impact on white culture as it has had on their own culture.

> "In a great many instances, the history of the United States has been the history of minority groups of one kind or another. The contributions of these groups, their path toward recognition, acceptance, or assimilation constitute some of the elements of history. Some have been accepted without too much difficulty but all of them have undergone some form of pressure from the

majority" (Spangler 15).

Prince's work is connected to the legacy of African Americans who sought to integrate and assimilate into America, often losing more than it gained. Yet, the relative ease of assimilation in Minnesota allows the state to boast of its liberal atmosphere where African Americans could feel free to explore the totalities of themselves, allowing for a greater amalgamation of black and white cultures. This has created in a large number of Afro-Minnesotans a greater acceptance of the dominant culture's values and perspectives because they feel more accepted by the larger, white society. Even in the most horrid aspects of race in America, Minnesota has found a way to appear as being ahead of the country in race matters.

> "In 1920 three Negroes were lynched in Duluth for an alleged assault on a white girl...The lynching was condemned by virtually all the newspapers in the state, including the <u>Duluth Herald</u>. But at least two Minnesota papers defended the lynching...Further arrest of Negroes brought the total to ten, two of whom were eventually indicted for the alleged assault for which three men had already died. Eighteen members of the white mob were finally arrested and indicted on murder and riot charges. Only two were found guilty of rioting and instigating a riot and were given nominal sentences. One Negro was found guilty of assault. An attempt to get a pardon for him along with an appeal to the Minnesota Supreme Court filled the next two years, but these efforts failed. Finally, in 1925, Max Mason, the convicted Negro, was released from Stillwater prison on a conditional discharge...Thus ended the most violent outburst against Negroes that ever occurred in Minnesota...Within a year after the lynching...the legislature enacted an anti-lynching law. Unfortunately, it took a violent action to produce such a law, but it has never been invoked in the state because there have been no other lynchings" (Spangler 100-103).

Minnesota has not been free from racial incidents, but it has been able to appear as if it is less tolerant of these incidents. This false idealism, in itself, produces white and black citizens who see themselves as somehow different than the rest of the world. The psychological effect is that the whites in Minnesota can be more demanding of loyalty from their African American citizens, which often causes the majority of African American citizens to submit to this "urge toward whiteness."

The earliest African Americans or African descendants to arrive in Minnesota do so for work. This is important because it parallels the African American migration to Minnesota to that of the migrations of African Americans to other areas. It also gives us some insight of the psychological concerns or intents of the migrants. Integration for the purpose of work and survival is the dominate motivation of the African Americans who go to the area. Black Nationalism or any sense or notion of it arrives late to the Minnesota area and continues to be an almost non-factor in the lives of the majority of African Americans. The goal of these initial African Americans arriving in Minnesota was to completely assimilate into the culture like a melting pot. Because of Minnesota's location, climate, and types of employment opportunities, it gave way to and was prime for a diversity of African Americans skilled in various areas. Their diversity and skills made them, of course, an immediate asset, causing an immediate impact upon the region.

> "The exact date when the first Negroes appeared in present-day Minnesota is unknown but various sources indicate that some engaged in fur trading activities during the early nineteenth century. In fact, there is evidence that Negroes played a more varied role in the trade than some other groups, since they acted in such capacities as independent entrepreneurs, personal servants, hunters, guides, and interpreters. A few became salaried traders and voyageurs, but the most

usual and typical role was that of servant or slave" (Spangler 17).

The African American enters Minnesota history as he enters American history, as a dichotomy forced to deal with the country's schizophrenia and what would become his own schizophrenia. The African American is a commodity, and he uses this as a way to gain entrance into American society.

Because of the varied, although limited, types of jobs within the fur trade, Minnesota became a haven for a small but diverse group of African Americans. Not only did they come from places to the south of them like St. Louis, they also came from the east, including Ohio, Maryland, and New England, as well as from Canada (Spangler 18). This diverse group was small because there were few overall economic opportunities for them, and "the underground railway did not operate in Minnesota to the extent that it did elsewhere in the Northwest" (Spangler 19). Because of this small influx of African Americans into Minnesota:

> "…there were no laws or restrictions against their entering such as were enacted in Ohio, Indiana, and Illinois…Minnesota did not actually enact [constitutional provision against the immigration of free Negroes]…However, many [whites] felt that the climate in Minnesota, rather than specific laws, would act as an effective barrier to extensive Negro migration" (Spangler 19, 44).

By default, Minnesota became the liberal area of the Midwestern region because it did not have the "Negro problem" of a large migration. This, however, does not diminish the fact that Minnesota was wrestling with the slave and race issue that churned in the minds and souls of the rest of the country. This "don't ask don't tell" policy, which was informally adopted around the issue of race, seems to have cloaked and complicated the individual struggle, thereby complicating the schizophrenia of the region. James Thompson, a slave who was bought and freed by a Minnesota Methodist missionary, lived in Minnesota for sixty years from 1824 to 1884. "To him went the distinction of being the only Negro member of the Old Settlers organization. In fact, Thompson often referred to himself as 'One of the first white settlers'" (Spangler 20). Thompson's depiction of himself exhibits an identity question pondered by African Americans, especially by those in an area where they are smothered by whiteness. Thompson who rose to high social status eventually fell from social grace because of his drinking and psychological battles with identity and place. "In the end he was not well liked by either white or red and finally moved to St. Paul," which, interestingly enough, houses a much larger black population than Minneapolis (Spangler 20).

A second incident involving Dred Scott also speaks to the race problem, which lay beneath the surface idealism.

> "Scott figured in another incident at Fort Snelling [which eventually became the Minneapolis-St. Paul area] when the quartermaster refused him a heating stove until after everyone else had received one. When his owner, Dr. Emerson, heard about this, he was very angry at the officer; bitter feelings were prevalent throughout the fort over this incident, largely because a white man dared to defend a Negro, even though he was a slave" (Spangler21).

Though Thompson becomes the most typical type of African American to populate Minnesota, Scott's incident shows us that there has always been a dichotomy of African American circumstance in Minnesota and a quiet struggle to achieve the public ideal. Minnesota is a dichotomy where the ideal has managed to outshine the reality because Earth is more appealing to a person condemned to Hell. Because Minnesota was an unsettled territory until as late as 1837, it was perceived by many as more liberal on slavery as the rest of the country.

Being admitted to the union as a free state during the heavy political debates around slavery enhanced its persona of liberalism. This also meant that the state's economy was not as dependent on traditional plantation slave labor and was more dependent upon the migrant work of Native Americans and African Americans, making the Minnesota landscape more individualized. The larger communities were formed of small farms, ranches, and homesteads where families worked somewhat independent of the larger community. Therefore, there was not a vital need for social interaction in regard to economics. This would breed a strong sense of individualism found in the region. Furthermore, African Americans often acted as liaisons between whites and Native Americans in the fur trading business and in other areas. This all combined to help nurture the multicultural ideal of the territory, especially in the minds of African Americans. And one of the best examples of this pseudo-paradise is the Minnesota public schools system, which began as an integrated system and acted as a model for the rest of the territory's affairs.

> "Negro youth took their places in the classroom alongside English, French, Swiss, Chippewa, and Sioux students at an early period without any known demands for segregation. Furthermore, this school probably ranks as the first supported by public funds in the St. Paul and Minneapolis area. Further proof of this peaceful association is seen in the admonition of a resident of St. Paul that any teacher coming to the town 'should be entirely free of prejudice on account of color, for among our scholars she might find...some claiming kindred with African stock'" (Spangler 22).

Minnesota's rhetoric of Utopia fluctuated much like Prince's own Paisley Park rhetoric of Utopia fluctuated in regard to the socio-political matrix that gives rise to the man-made Utopia. As America entrenched itself in the debate over slavery, the rhetoric coming from Minnesota is also modified, though it manages to hold to its core principles of tolerance by abstaining. "Conditions changed as the territory moved into the decade preceding the Civil War and the whole country girded itself for a struggle over slavery" (Spangler 22). Though Minnesota adopted some of the anti-slavery rhetoric of the rest of the country, it did not pass the number of laws as the rest of the country, and those laws were often minor and without the teeth of enforcement as existed elsewhere. Although there were many anti-slavery groups throughout Minnesota, there were at least half as many pro-slavery voices. Feeling the pressure from the surrounding states as well as the economic pressure from having more African Americans moving to the region, there was an official separation of education by 1865 with the establishment of the School for Colored Children. However, due to a lack of funding, the state was not able to maintain both schools, and in 1867 the School for Colored Children was closed.

> "This venture into segregation ended in 1869 when the legislature passed an act which, in effect, abolished separate schools 'in corporate towns' by device of withholding funds from any public school that barred entry to pupils on grounds of 'color, social position or nationally.' From then on, Negro children in Minnesota were free to attend schools on an equal basis with others" (Spangler 34-35).

This legislation is eighty-five years prior to Brown. It allows Minnesota to boast of being ahead of and more tolerant than the rest of the country in regards to race. Not only did Minnesota not pass legislation barring the education of African Americans, it passed legislation prohibiting discrimination in education years before the nation. However, beneath this ideal was the harsh reality that if Minnesota were more liberal than the rest of America, it was only marginally so. This reality can, in fact, have a more severe psychological impact on the oppressed than Jim Crow. With Jim Crow the oppressed knew where they stood. They had a better grip on reality and their identity. The sliding scale of Minnesota policy and practice, though well intentioned, created a psychological conflict within its minority residents that continues to this day.

"This act, while legally removing the color barrier did not eliminate other deterrents to integration, such as expense and the lack of interest on the part of those affected. Thus, although Negro pupils were urged to apply for the public schools, only thirteen actually did so by the spring of 1869. All were admitted. Nor did such law remove the prejudice still existent in the minds of many, and this was probably a strong deterrent in keeping many Negroes away from schools that they were legally entitled to enter" (Spangler 35).

Even with its flaws, Minnesota was still ahead of the pace toward integration. By the time the Supreme Court rules on the Brown desegregation case, Minnesota is a model region of the nation. "In 1954 several white and Negro educators from North Carolina, Georgia, and Maryland met in Minneapolis to study integration and were impressed with what had been done" (Spangler 150). This leadership was across the board, touching many different aspects. "As early as 1949 Negroes were accorded the right to serve in the Minnesota National Guard…In 1955 Minnesota passed the Fair Employment Practices Act and established the Fair Employment Practices Commission" (Spangler 151, 153). In regard to education, economics/employment, and the military, Minnesota has been ahead of the rest of the country in moving African Americans into the mainstream of the society and allowing them access, though quite limited, to positions of power. This actuality, regardless of how well it worked or how well it was implemented, created the atmosphere of tolerance, developing an ethos in the African American citizens that life was better in Minnesota than anywhere else because they are judged by their individual accomplishments and not by their race. Even the problems of housing in the 1940s and 50s due to a growing African American population did little to damage this illusion of tolerance. This explosive housing issue was pregnant with contradictions that somehow seemed to balance the racism and the tolerance, allowing Minnesota to keep its title as most liberal state. In 1946, the Governor's Interracial

Commission conducted a survey of Minnesota's white citizens with the following findings: To the question of "Should a Negro be allowed to move into any residential neighborhood where there is a vacancy?", sixty percent asserted that Negroes "...should not be allowed to do so." When polled as to what effect would having a Negro move into one's neighborhood have on the value of the homes, sixty-four percent indicated that they believed that the value of their homes would decrease. In the question of being able to get a higher price for a home from a Negro buyer, sixty-three percent stated that they still would not sell their home to a Negro. However, when asked about the treatment a Negro would receive if they moved into a white neighborhood, the poll was more evenly split. Thirty-seven percent indicated that they would treat them as other neighbors. Twenty-six percent indicated that they would not care. Eleven percent indicated that they would try to move them out of the neighborhood. Another eleven percent indicated that their behavior would depend on the specifics of each new neighbor. Eight percent were undecided. (Spangler 132-133). This is American schizophrenia at its apex. The laws say that African Americans are equal, but the voices from the communities say otherwise. And the voices of Minnesota's white citizens are marginally better than the rest of America's white citizens. It is this atmosphere that would produce the conflicted African American, such as Prince.

Though Minnesota is not without the typical race problems of America, as early as the 1800s, African Americans in Minnesota seem to be living amongst their white counterparts and often serving in leadership roles with more frequency and ease than in the rest of the country. "It is doubtful if such an anti-Negro attitude was prevalent to any great degree against them because of economic competition, but it never became serious" (Spangler 45). We know that "serious" is a relative term. What Spangler wishes us to know is that any hardships suffered by African Americans in Minnesota between 1800 and 1961 were minimal as compared to the rest of the country. In this light, Minnesota has been able to develop and promote itself as a more tolerant region of America. An example of this is Gusa Godfrey who participated in the 1862 Sioux uprising.

> "Gusa Godfrey, a renegade Negro,...aided in the capture of white inhabitants, and boasted of killing seventeen white citizens, [still] no anti-Negro sentiment was expressed [by the majority of the white population of Minnesota]" (Spangler 45).

Godfrey is alleged to having told one white female captive "that it was great fun to kill whites because they offered no resistance" (Spangler 45). Despite this statement, Godfrey is treated as any other war criminal, and there are no reports that his deeds or words caused an uproar or a backlash of white violence or aggression against other African Americans. "In the end, Godfrey was captured with other Indians who had participated in the uprising but obtained his freedom by turning state's evidence. He died on the Santee Indian Reservation, Nebraska, in 1900, hated by Indian and white alike" (Spangler 45).

Thompson and Godfrey represent the psychological influence that a place like Minnesota can have on how one sees and identifies oneself. Because the African American population was so small and isolated, much of the African American labor worked in specialized professions that forced them to work either alone or with only white counterparts. This created a notion of individuality and a willingness to assimilate that was not as prevalent for African Americans throughout the rest of the country. Even in other areas where there was a growing black elitist class, the elitist group still saw themselves as "Negro"—just a special type of Negro, somewhere between being white and niggered. The African Americans in the Minnesota territory saw themselves on singular—individualized—terms rather than on racially collective terms. They saw themselves as special because of their craft. Their intellect, many of them thought, made them an asset to the white community. Their craft, skill, or special contribution to society somehow allowed them to transcend their race. For the black elitist class outside Minnesota, their self-worth and value was innately connected to the depravation of the rest of the race. They have worth because they are not "low-class" Negroes, which is evident in their ability to mimic white culture. Ironically, this elitist class is still psychologically connected to the "low-class" Negroes because it is the "low-class" Negroes who give them definition. For instance, middle-class blacks, such as those discussed by E. Franklin Frazier in Black Bourgeoisie (1955) and by Lawrence Otis Graham in Our Kind of People (2000), have a history of clarifying their identity and social place by illuminating the difference and gap that exist between themselves and lower economic blacks. However, in the case of individuals such as Thompson and Godfrey, their worth is not dependent upon being better than other Negroes, but upon being of value to the white community. This creates in many of the Afro-Minnesotans the "Special Negro" syndrome. Thompson and Godfrey were seemingly living the American dream that one, if given an equal opportunity, can survive and prosper on one's own work ethic and character. This existence creates an ideology or even an ethos that causes one to see oneself on singular, individual terms. Even though Minnesota, particularly Minneapolis-St. Paul, has been affected greatly by the rest of the country's struggle with the race problem, this singular-ness or notion of individuality seems to be more prevalent in Afro-Minnesotans than anywhere else because they lived more isolated and away from the collective race more than anywhere else.

Accordingly, this notion of liberalism and individuality creates a place for some of the most diverse thinking African Americans in the country. Men such as Frederick L. McGhee and John Frances Wheaton are able to make their marks on the Minnesota social, political, and economic landscape even when choosing divergent paths.

> "In 1889 Frederick L. McGhee was the first Negro to be admitted to the bar and to practice law in Minnesota

> [and]...was one of the few Negro leaders of the period to become a Democrat...Wheaton gained the distinction of being the first Negro to be elected to and serve in the Minnesota legislature. In 1889 he was elected to represent a district that included less than a hundred Negroes, and he ran ahead of his Republican ticket in a year when the Republicans lost the governorship..." (Spangler 68-69).

At a time after Reconstruction when most African Americans are being terrorized legally and physically back into second-class citizenship by the Klan and Jim Crow laws, Minnesota's African American community is engaging the professional and legal sectors of life with a great deal of success. These two men represent an African American community that was subject to hold a variety of political ideas and be more influenced by their individual politics than their racial affiliation. Moreover, regardless of their political affiliations or personal politics, they spent their lives fighting for Civil Rights in the courts and in the legislature. They are more examples of how early Minnesota presented opportunities for African Americans to be judged fairly and given the opportunity to achieve as individuals. Thus, the problem or complexity of Minnesota race politics and atmosphere is not that racism was not an issue, but that racism cannot be plotted as easily or definitively in the Minnesota region. This creates more psychological battles along the lines of identity and place for those very same African Americans. Their "accepted" places in this overwhelmingly white society was bound to create some notion of elitism in regards to how they saw other members of their own race.

> "Because many out of state Negroes evidently regarded Minnesota as an 'easy' state where law enforcement was lax, there was an influx of 'undesirables,' particularly from states in the South. As a result, 'native' Minnesota Negroes attempted to protect themselves against this influx. In many cases, local Negro leaders and organizations 'screened' the migrants and selected only those deemed 'worthy' to

enter the state" (Spangler 67).

The ability of African Americans to be directly involved in the screening of potential residents creates a sense of place, belonging, and power, no matter how delusional or limited. This sense of place, belonging, and power was not enjoyed in the same manner by African Americans in other regions of the country, living in an area dominated by whites. The notion of second-class citizens being able to decide someone else's worth and bestow citizenship on someone else creates a dichotomy in them, which resonates for generations. There becomes a large enough gap between Minnesota's ideal and its reality to measure a dichotomy in race relations and to plot that historical dichotomy in its African American citizens. This dichotomy (internal conflict) of African Americans is clearly seen in Prince as a trope of that existence and struggle.

The notion of Prince as the typical African American dichotomy will be raised a great deal in this text because it rears its head a great deal throughout his career. From the beginning Prince has been the descendent and recipient of the best and worst of segregation and integration. On the one hand he is a product of segregated America because his father is a fixture and product of the informal Minneapolis black musicians' coalition. This informal coalition existed because Minneapolis is not as liberal as it pretends to be. On the other hand, Prince represents the struggles of his father and other black musicians to integrate and have their work embraced by the larger white audience. In both cases, economics is the driving factor for segregation and integration. Money is why white folks separate from black folks, and money is why black folks are willing to turn a blind eye to this rejection and attempt to integrate into their systems—systems that are, of course, built on black labor. However, in Minnesota there was no all black business district to the same degree as in other areas of America. Self-determinism by the entire collective of black folks in the Minnesota region is a virtual aberration. There just have never been enough African Americans in the region to consider this concept realistically. Their only means of survival was to integrate and agitate for civil rights. As a means of survival, Afro-Minnesotans have been forced to play by the larger white society's rules, which has had a major influence on their psychological development, making them more willing to assimilate and embrace the white society's values and culture. Owen Husney, Prince's first manager and a local white Minneapolis businessman affirms this. "I have always resented being called just another Jewish manager ripping off black kids, but the truth is that there has been and continues to be enough racism in America and in Minneapolis to provoke such sentiments. Just a couple of days ago, I was going out to lunch with Pepe Willie [the man whom most agree taught Prince the basics about songwriting and recording] who is a black guy and another white friend. The lady at the front desk almost insisted that we eat in the basement of the 'grill' area. When we insisted that we would eat on the top floor, we could not get service. This thing continues to happen, and it continues to affect the lives of the blacks who have to endure this. What is most interesting is the varying African American reaction to this issue. You have Pepe who just says the hell with it and lives his life in the solace and solidarity of the black community. Then, you have Prince who believes that he can somehow transcend it all" (Husney 2000). Both Willie and Prince are musicians and evidence of the varying roads that African Americans have taken to deal with racism and second-class citizenship. Willie who was reared in New York interacted with a variety of races but was not force fed the "popular" and "false" notion of integration. On the other hand, Prince who was raised smothered in whiteness seemingly bought into integration. Whatever their individual choices, their lives have been pretty much dualistic as most African Americans lives are, especially the African American artist/entertainer. Willie not only came of age in a hub of New York's African American culture, but was also the nephew of Clarence Collins, who was a member of Little Anthony and the Imperials. Willie, as a young child, became the group's protégé and traveled the world learning his craft and the history of black music.

Willie learned from his days with Little Anthony and the Imperials that there is a special camaraderie between black musicians, which grows from the camaraderie of the black community. "We represented the community as artists. We thought a lot about how our work represented the community. Integration and money has changed all of that" (Willie 2000). For Willie, who relocated to Minneapolis after marrying Prince's cousin, coming to Minneapolis was culture shock. "Man, it was different. I'm from a basically multicultural background. That's what New York is. Within a few blocks, there were Puerto Ricans, Italians, Jews, Blacks, and Whites living amongst each other. Relocating to Minneapolis was like leaving a place where I had some roots to a place where I was completely foreign—overnight. And musically, there was zero black music scene. This was the toughest because I was not just proving myself as the new kid on the block. There was another dynamic, race. Just to get studio time I was constantly having to prove myself, prove that I wasn't a thug or something. There was definitely a stereotype when I hit town in '75" (Willie 2000). By the time Willie had arrived, the places for black musicians to play and record were limited. "From what I understand, there was never anywhere a black musician could record in Minneapolis. Most of what was done there was live playing. I don't think the older guys like Cornbread Harris, father of The Time's Jimmy Jam Harris, or even Prince's dad thought much about recording. So when I hit Minneapolis, not much was happening as far as getting black musicians recorded, and it was becoming pretty dismal on the stage also" (Willie 2000). Ironically, these limitations seem to have created the Minneapolis sound. "One of Prince's biggest assets is his intelligence. He has a natural ability to mix and blend anything—sounds and cultures. The combination of black records, white radio, fighting with white bands to play larger gigs, and the small but steady local black circuit all came together to create Prince" (Willie 2000). Prince did what African Americans are forced to do, make something from nothing by combining a multitude of sounds, cultures, and circumstances to construct his own reality and opportunity.

During the forties and fifties in Minneapolis, black

musicians often played for white folks to make money and played for themselves to satisfy their love of the music and their desire to perfect their craft. This created very diverse musicians who had to learn to communicate on a variety of levels and languages. One of the best examples of this is Father Nelson's contemporary of the 1940s, James Samuel "Cornbread" Harris II.

> "Mr. Harris learned to play in many different styles. Apart from blues and jazz, he could do polkas and love ballads, mambas, salsas and calypsos. He is proud of his versatility, but it was an asset he could not have done without. His most affluent audience would probably be white, and they knew what they wanted. On these occasions, most of his fellow players would probably be white too. 'The black music scene was so smothered all the time this was going on. The only way a black musician got to play was for black functions, or as the one black musician in the band, you know?'" (Hill 4)

This issue of a "black function" is as important as playing exclusively for white audiences. These black functions were mostly middle class events, so the music often represented the taste of the more affluent blacks. Again, this is another dichotomy, which is influencing the music. There was not only a class division between the races, which was influencing the music; there was also a class division within the black race, which was also influencing the music. Mr. Harris' testimony shows how race and class division influenced the psyche and the work ethic of the musicians.

> "And in some areas here, when you got off the stand, you had to go straight in the back room. A lot of people here figure that was only a Southern thing, but it goes on up here too. But there again, do you wanna play music or don't you?'" (Hill 4).

Mr. Harris' final statement speaks to a larger African American issue. Do you want a job or do you not? Do you want to survive or do you not? This survival meant molding oneself to white attitudes and sensibilities. And according to music and cultural critic Carol Cooper, the desire to survive and the uniqueness of Minnesota creates a new strain or genotype of African American, which is filtered down to Prince's generation.

> "What should be remembered about Minneapolis, Minnesota (but what is unlikely to ever show up in any 'official' demographic studies) is that the area became a magnet for ambitious young black males in the Fifties and Sixties seeking space, calm, and equal opportunity. The result was a remarkably high incidence of multi-racial families developing in an atmosphere of relative financial stability. Meaning that the 'black' population of Minneapolis is possessed of several characteristics distinct from the ghettoized norm. They haven't eradicated the dark-skinned genotype, just amplified it with yet another strain. Another genetic *mood*" (Cooper 58).

Cooper's new genetic mood or new strain of black person insinuates that the African American in Minnesota innately saw life differently than other African Americans and understood how to navigate an even thinner more complex line of racial identity to survive. But, there is, also, always the need for release, a need to have a place and time to be and do without thinking about being and doing. This is what the late-night gigs represented. These gigs were for someone other than the whites or the middle class blacks. These gigs were for the musicians and for the segment of people who represented the origins of the music. Mr. Harris concludes by showing that African Americans have been forced to live with Du Bois' "Double-Consciousness" as a means of sanity and survival.

> "Over on the north side...Cornbread and many of his peers enjoyed their music the most. 'This was fun-time. All the musicians in town would come here for jam sessions after their gigs, and play till the sun came up. Some of the best music you ever heard was played round the [north

side] before they tore it all down and put in the projects'" (Hill 5).

Mr. Harris' situation mirrors Prince's situation. With very few clubs and gigs for black musicians, Prince and his friends found themselves lobbying to play the same spots as the local white bands. First Avenue, the club made famous by <u>Purple Rain</u>, is an excellent example of how race and the umbrella of whiteness affect the development of black art. As profitable and popular as the Minneapolis black music scene was becoming, First Avenue still regulated black music to one night a week, generally sometime during the week, reserving the weekends for white bands. Prince understood that he had to contour his work to be more palatable to this crowd. At the same time, this is an example of Prince buying into the artistic and economic limitations of playing black clubs even though they have just as much if not more history and tradition as First Avenue.

Ironically, even though Prince rejects playing the local black clubs and fights to play white clubs, he is unable to completely tear or disconnect himself from the legacy of black music. His link to his local black tradition of live music is that he continues the tradition of the aftershow gig, even as he tours America and the world. To the Prince faithful, the aftershow gig is just as important as the featured concert. The aftershow exhibits the contrast between popular music (music specifically constructed to sell to a mass audience) and music as a cultural phenomenon (music that is created specifically from a cultural existence and reality to articulate that reality). At the aftershow, there are no light and sound effects, no glitz and glamour, and gone is the overly flamboyant attire. What is left is a musician and an audience. In the beginning, around 1986 and the <u>Parade</u> Tour, the gigs were often held at out-of-the-way, hole-in-the-wall joints. Since the gigs were unplanned, (Prince would have someone locate and secure a place the day of the show, and the location would not be made public until the day of or right after the concert.) Prince used them as a way to keep his musicians on their toes, as a way to stay connected to the community that may not be able to purchase a fifty dollar ticket, and as a way to satisfy his insatiable appetite for live performance. In doing all of this, Prince is connecting with his audience on a more personal level. He not only asks for and takes requests; he has more intimate or personal discussions with the audience, either about music or current events. During a 1993 San Francisco aftershow gig at the height of the Federal trial of the four officers who beat Rodney King, Prince asks "So, what do y'all think the verdict will be?" The mostly white audience responds overwhelmingly, "Guilty!" With their response, Prince lunches into "No Black Muthafuckers in the House." This is definitely not a song that Prince would be performing at a featured venue where a majority of white folks had just paid fifty dollars to hear "Purple Rain." However, at an aftershow, Prince felt freer to experiment—to do and say what he wanted to say.

    Even with an all white or majority white audience, an aftershow crowd usually includes mostly those who consider themselves true Prince fans, and not just those who are attending an event. A featured concert is going to have a large number of people who are there mainly for the event, the spectacle of something to do, and not necessarily because the music means something special to them. At a concert, there are generally people who come with a mental list of hit songs that they want to hear. At an aftershow, there are people who want the experience of Prince, an artist who is constantly challenging who they are and how they see the world. This allows Prince to have the best of both worlds like the musicians before him. But, as always, the ability to make money off this venture eventually changes it. By 1993 or 1994, these aftershows had become a part of the featured concert, becoming just another place for event seekers, causing the shows to lose much of their spontaneity and improvisation. The co-opting of the aftershow gig is just another example of the affect that American capitalism and the umbrella of white supremacy has on African American culture. In most cases, African American art yields its sensibilities to the allure and seduction of the white dollar. Prince understood or bought into the need to be diverse (to become whiter), probably more so than his friends. As local musician, activist, and icon, Morris Wilson asserts, "Prince was always attracted to the rock thing more than his peers. Look and Jimmy Jam and Terry Lewis. When they broke away form Prince, they produced more black oriented, R&B flavored work. From day one Prince wanted to be a rock star. He wanted that crossover success" (Wilson 2000). It is not the desire for mass success that Wilson cites as something negative; it is the willingness to do anything to get success that bothers Wilson, who, as a member of the Minnesota Minorities Musicians Association, participated in demonstrations to have bar and club owners include live entertainment. "Prince is to music what Richard Pryor is to comedy. Many people see them as geniuses, but all they did was sell the myth of the super-sexual Negro to white folks. It's just like with the Harlem Renaissance. White folks don't really care about our art as an intellectual form. They care about us as sexual beings. This is what Prince sold them. This is the same with hip hop. This is why black artists can't get contracts without selling some degenerate image, and this is one of the negative effects of integration." (Wilson 2000).

Jim Hamilton, Prince's music teacher in high school, provides another example of Prince being influenced by integration.

> "Hamilton had come to the area in 1965 after a spell as a piano-player in Ray Charles' band. In 1968 he picked up the threads of his teaching career, helped, he thinks, by the local school board's desire to recruit more black teachers in the wake of the social disruptions of the period. (The worst instances in Minneapolis occurred when north-side rioters burned down businesses in a four-block spread). Central High had a strong music curriculum, and a policy of setting stringent standards in order to attract pupils from outside the immediate catchment area. Prince was an enthusiastic music student, but not an *especially* outstanding one...Prince, however, came into his own in one of Hamilton's extra-curricular courses: The

Business of Music. 'When I was on the road with Ray, I used to encounter a lot of the business aspects of music. [Prince and The Time's Terry Lewis stick out in Hamilton's mind as outstanding students in the business class.] [Prince] was in it all three years that he was there. The class covered contracts and copyright, how to make and shop a demo tape around, the union situation, and more: It was letting them become aware that you can't just stroll into this world and be a star.' But Prince already had a strategy for the pop game to come. 'He was kind of a jokester in a way. We did have a few words about some of the lyrics he was coming up with. His quotation was the fact that 'Hey, I'm trying to be as controversial as possible. I have to get people to buy the records'" (Hill 15, 16).

Willie affirms that Prince's desire to achieve financial success had as much an impact on his art as his love for music and his desire to express himself. "Man, Prince was clear about one thing—he did not want to have some nine to five job. Even at fifteen, he knew what he wanted to do and was going to do anything it took to make it. Part of this meant studying and working hard; part of this meant creating what would sell. If Prince is an example of black Americans struggling in this white society, it can be seen in his creation of something like Dirty Mind. Man, when I heard that, I went the other way. It wasn't a family album...It wasn't anything that I wanted to do or felt comfortable with doing. Like most black folks, he started out with good intentions, but money seems to be able to seduce some of us. That album was partially him in the way that it blended styles and even topics, but the explicit sex was to sell records" (Willie 2000). So, it can be shown that integration, which caused the shift in emphasis from human rights to economic gains, is a major influence on Prince's psyche and his work. However, the majority of the local Minneapolis musicians do not doubt the sincerity of his work. Even his loudest and strongest critic, Wilson, says that "Prince was the product of an unstable family life. I don't want to get too personal, and I won't. But, he was forced to move a lot...a whole lot, bouncing around from place to place, never quite fitting in. If he was isolated, it was a type of psychological isolation. It wasn't so much that his friends had a problem with it, but it seemed to bother him, not quite belonging to anyone. He always seemed to have this desire to prove himself, to be the baddest and the best" (Wilson 2000). Civil Rights activist, Hollis Watkins, one of the first Mississippians to join S.N.C.C. and president of Southern Echo, a non-profit organization that provides organization, technical, and legal assistance to African Americans throughout America, believes that Minneapolis has some unique qualities that could lead to the development of someone like Prince. "Minneapolis has the two basic classes of black folks—those who attempt to integrate and those who attempt to really fight the system of oppression as best they can. Of course, they are a really small group and often conservative by the rest of the nation's standards. But there also seems to be this very interesting third group of people. They seem to create or establish another set of values and beliefs that seem almost foreign to any African American experience that I had encountered. It isn't completely devoid of African American sensibilities, but it seems more interested in creating this distant, separate, even isolated community based on utopian idealism" (Watkins 2000).

Minneapolis music critic Steve Perry also speaks to the notion that Prince's upbringing—his longing for a "place"—has played a major influence on his work, his rise to fame, and his commercial fall during the nineties.

> "Prince really conjured the whole <u>Purple Rain</u> mythology, I think, in order for him to be able to survive and to break through because, in fact, Prince grew up in a Minneapolis where there were no creative outlets for his music. There were no [local] models for the music he was drawn to make. He had to fashion it as he went along, and in the process he fashioned a whole world" (Perry 1992).

To survive and grow, art must have socio-political (human) roots. If there was going to be a new musical movement, Prince needed to fashion a world from which that music would evolve. For art to be meaningful it must be authentic. For art to be authentic it must originate or evolve from a definite and tangible cultural experience. To achieve this authenticity, Prince created a world. In his case, instead of focusing on a particular period in history or on any present movements of his time, he chose to focus on an ideal/fantasy/futuristic notion of a time when mankind had finally conquered its arbitrary walls of race, class, and gender. And to his credit, by creating his fantasy world, Prince managed to influence greatly the real, tangible world around him. Perry affirms this.

> "Prince came up at a time when the playlists on radio were as drastically segregated as the early sixties. He played a vital role, in spirit and in direct lineage, in helping to break down the barriers. Michael Jackson and Thriller get most of the credit, but I think that Prince and his whole crossover project with Dirty Mind onward had a greater impact. He simply refused to submit to any stylistic boundaries. That had a healthy impact on what was becoming a more and more segregated playlist" (Perry 1992).

Husney asserts that Prince's development as a multicultural prophet/icon was partly artistic lineage and partly planned and contrived. It seems that if Prince was thinking along the lines of economic gains, it was because that was the blueprint that he had been handed. "There was no black radio in Minneapolis when Prince was growing up. His experience was one of black records and white radio. This embracing of various styles worked to develop and propel his work. He could be seen as the new Stevie Wonder or the next Sly Stone. What he had over them was the ability to buy their records and incorporate into his work what had worked in their music. Most importantly, he was able to understand the financial value of multicultural, multi-gender appeal. Prince waged his war for individuality by separating himself from his people rather than embracing his people. The difference is that Sly and Jimi were on deeper, more culturally rooted missions of ending racism and uniting people. This difference is what ultimately destroyed Sly and Jimi and allowed Prince to continue even during his fading fame. Sly's and Jimi's success were predicated on their ability to bring people together and not on their records sales. Therefore, an event like Woodstock would mean more to them than a double-platinum album. On the other hand, a double-platinum album would mean more to Prince. Particularly for Sly—who had his one shinning moment, his Apex, at Woodstock—this would be the equivalent of Icarus flying too close to the sun. After Woodstock, Sly became disillusioned in his work's ability to change people, fundamentally, at the root of their human selves. Prince, on the other hand, was a bit more premeditated than Sly. If his mission of bringing people together failed, he could be consoled by his record sales" (Husney 2000). Poet, social critic, and music journalist, Charlie Braxton affirms both Husney's and Perry's notions. "Prince was definitely influenced by corporate rock as well as by not being intimately involved with a black collective. Corporate rock was huge in the late seventies, and its economic sensibilities pushed the 'me' generation over the edge. ELO, Peter Frampton, KISS, and Alice Cooper were examples that you could really get paid doing this. Prince was able to see them on the charts and hear them on the radio and figure out, like that rest of America, like the record companies did, that this was big business. On the other hand he was also isolated. He was not only isolated in his own city, as an African American, he was isolated from the rest of black America. Check the geography. Nothing black is near Minneapolis, but Chicago is near Detroit, D.C. is near Baltimore, and Philadelphia is near Chicago and Detroit. There was a cultural interchange and exchange between these African Americans to which Prince just was not privy. So it had to affect him on both an economic and an artistic level. All those hours of listening to black records and white radio. It affected his artistic and economic sensibilities" (Braxton 2000).

If Prince seems contrived, we must realize that what he was doing in the early years of his career is no different than what literary greats Toomer or John Edgar Wideman did. At times Prince can be either of these: Toomer who was conflicted about whom he was and Wideman who understood artistic politics and the benefits of being from mixed ancestry. As Wideman asserts:

> "'In America, especially if you're black, there is a temptation to buy a kind of upward mobility. One of the requirements is to forget.'...In college, Wideman played out what he has called a theatrical performance. As he described it later, in the autobiographical *Brothers and Keepers* (1984), 'Just two choices as far as I could tell: either/or. Rich or poor. White or black. Win or lose...To succeed in the man's world you must become like the man and the man sure didn't claim no bunch of nigger relatives in Pittsburgh'" (Gates and McKay 2326).

The question that dogs Prince most of his career is the question of sincerity. He is as sincere as a post-integrationist black kid who knew the financial ramification of a hit record and had very little adult or cultural supervision could be. And because Prince probably had at least one foot on reality as opposed to Stone and Hendrix, he is better able to deal with the ending of his purple reign and the exiling of his Paisley Park. Still, the ideologies that are housed in his music are a direct representation of an African American grappling with who he is, who he wants to be, and where he wants to go. Willie attempts to contextualize this for us. "I don't want to say that all of what Prince was doing was contrived. The man was and is a student. Just like writers read everything, he listens to everything. Even at fifteen, the only time that he wasn't listening to music was when he was playing it. He stayed in record shops, combing the isles for sounds. He put everything in his head. If there was one place he was different from his friends, he did not hesitate to put different sounds in his head and in his music. And, of course, when you are listening to all of these sounds, you are picking up all of these ideas. What do you think would happen to a kid who spent all of his waking hours listening to Hendrix, Santana, Sly, Three Dog Night, Grand Funk, Joni Mitchell, and stuff like that? He is part encyclopedia and part marketing machine" (Willie 2000).

When I asked super-producer and hit-maker, Kashif, was it a negative or detrimental thing that Prince begins his career by purposely writing songs that will sell, he answers that "It's not necessarily a bad thing. I wanted to write good songs that people liked. We have to look at it in two dimensions: the essence of being a writer and the craft of writing. The essence of being a writer is more of a spiritual thing, where you are feeling the vibe and writing what feels good on a subjective level. The craft of writing is more about the skill of writing. This is what keeps you working after the popularity of your personal style or groove has passed. Prince seems to be a bit of both. Also, he was appealing to a segment of the country that other African American writers did not write for. There was a lot of growing freedom during that time. The gay community was becoming more accepted into the mainstream. Prince was probably just feeling the atmosphere and writing for the times. In this, his music was a bit more liberating. He was writing about things that most people say in private but wish that they could say in public...I would not say that this is contrived, but more so understanding the times for which you are writing. It's funny that today Prince isn't as hot, but he has stuck to his guns about what he has wanted to do and say. This may be considered a bad business decision but seems to answer the notion as to whether Prince is in this for the money or for the craft. I consider myself and Prince to be artists, in the traditional sense of the word and not in the neo-capitalistic sense of the word. If it was all contrived, Prince would be still writing hits instead of just doing what he wants to do, which, at this time, is hurting him more than it is helping him" (Kashif 2000). Husney drives the notion home for us. "Prince's greatest asset is his intelligence. There are some people who are so intelligent that they can see past the bull of cultural walls and rise above those walls to see over into the backyards of different cultures. Prince could do this. He not only understood what made people tick on a human level, he understood what made people tick on an ethnic and cultural level. This is seen in his music. Is this contrived? Depends on how you want to use the word in this case. I think it takes some amount of genius to understand different cultures and create an art that is all encompassing of those cultures" (Husney 2000).

Like most African American movements, Prince's reign was short lived although the impact is still being felt. Part of the problem is that integration or any amount of success in America demands that African Americans accept reality and success on white terms and sensibilities, which are usually the antithesis of African American terms and sensibilities. Success in America, for African American individuals, usually means isolation from the African American collective. This is because America, whose notion of capitalism is based on the exploitation of African Americans as the permanently assigned labor class, can tolerate sporadic individual success by African Americans but not collective success. Collective success for African Americans would mean an end to the system, which continues to be the driving factor behind America's rise to and maintenance of power. This creates what comedian Damon Wayans and Wilson allude to as the special Negro syndrome, where African Americans accept individual success despite the confusion and conflict it causes within them and with their race. By Prince's second album, Willie testifies that Warner Bros was already building and treating Prince as if he was a special Negro, separating him from his band, his friends, and his community. "A lot of people think that Prince went from Owen to Cavallo and Ruffalo, but that's not true. After Owen, Don Taylor was Prince's manager for a very short period" (Willie 2000). Taylor had been the manager for Bob Marley and got his start with Little Anthony and the Imperials. "I hooked Prince up with Don, but Don didn't go for Prince's antics or a lot of what Prince was doing lyrically. Prince wanted that rock icon thing, and that wasn't Don's bag. He found it with Cavallo and Ruffalo. In all fairness, what went down was merely Warner Bros protecting their interest. You have to understand that only Prince was signed to Warner Bros, not his band members.

So, when they were giving *just him* the special treatment, it was because he was the *only person* signed to Warner Bros. This caused some problems between Prince and his band mates and stroked Prince's ego. It gave him that feeling of importance and belonging that he wanted. But this is not just Prince; he just happens to be the easiest target. I hold Jam and Lewis to the same standard. They have made millions and are considered 'black acts' and have done just as little to give back to the community as Prince. Prince takes a lot of flack for putting Paisley Park in Chanhassen, but Flyte Tyme Records is in Edina, which is also a white suburb. [And by 2007 Flyte Tyme Records was relocated to Beverly Hills, California.] The bottom line is that black folks get pimped by America's dollar because we don't have a solid identity. Prince is from Minneapolis where it is especially difficult for black people to have a notion of who they are. Most of the time, the real radical brothers are more reactionary than anything. But Prince is not the only one to fall victim to this. He just represents what happens when black folks with good intentions have those intentions exploited by the money making machine" (Willie 2000).

This special Negro status takes a person like Pryor, who is the embodiment of blackness—its pains, angers, joys, intellect, and complexities—and flattens it, making it palatable for white consumption, producing a generation that does not have the talent nor the understanding of history to be as poetic, poignant, or powerful as Pryor, who, himself, cannot sustain his sanity or his powerful art because of being swallowed whole by the establishment. The truth is that the majority of black activists and revolutionaries were either destroyed by the government or took jobs within the establishment. This is the blueprint that is left for their children. Most of Prince's local predecessors were marginalized or minimized by the establishment under the guise of integration, which means they were forced to embrace white sensibilities or die broke. A very few, such as Wilson, rage against the machine, but they remain marginal in both the white and black communities because both have embraced the fantasy of integration and have no use for Wilson's art, which reminds them of the fallacy of their worlds. Deeper still, Willie asserts that this street drives both ways. He believes that Prince's development into an isolated rock star is a product of Prince's desire and the desire of the white establishment to co-opt more black culture. Further, Willie believes that Prince's change is also related to a black community that so badly wants and needs something to validate them, their existence, and their struggle that they fall prey to the messiah complex.

> "Prince didn't really change. The people around him changed. At first, Prince was a normal person, for the most part, who would do things for himself and saw himself like he saw everybody else. Then people around him started to change. Instead of greeting him with 'Hey, Prince, man, what's happening?' it became, 'Pr...Prince, wow...how...how's it going man.' Instead of treating him like a person with a job in the music business, they treated him like a star. [His behavior changed because their behavior changed.] People would begin doing things like 'No, Prince, let me get that for you.' Once you get ten, fifteen, twenty people all wanting to do things for you, you cannot help but change and expect to be treated differently" (Willie 1992).

Prior to integration or prior to the acceptance of western ideals, Africans and African Americans seemed to look at the artist in the traditional African sense of being a griot. The griot was not valued in capitalistic terms. The griot was important in cultural terms as the keeper and teacher of the history. In understanding that one's identity is inextricably tied to one's history, the griot was most responsible for the maintenance and perpetuation of the people and their culture. It is only after the European Renaissance that the artist or the griot, in the western sense, is regarded as something strictly for leisure. Further, it is only through American capitalism that the artist or the griot becomes known in an economic sense. With the shift in direction and emphasis from humanity and sovereignty to economic gains that the Civil Rights Movement takes in the mid-seventies, the value of the American artists has become equated with his profit margin. An excellent example of this is Nikki Giovanni, who has had to fight and balance being a pop icon with being a poet/social activist. In the mid-seventies, "Giovanni [was] as close to a superstar poet as any black woman poet has been in this century" (Christian 19). The result of this new status has created a generation of post-eighties poets who want the star status without doing the work of activism. Today's spoken word artists have copied the flare and the performance skills of the poets of the Black Arts Movement, but have not copied the political activism with the same intensity. In fact, the term "spoken word" was coined to make poetry seem more hip so that it could compete with and produce the type of financial reward as popular music. Thus, spoken word becomes another example of America co-opting black art for its own purposes, which limits the art's ability to aid the people whose culture created it. To disseminate their messages to a mass audience, many of the poets associated with the Black Arts Movement began to use, with more frequency, mediums such as records, television, and radio. As they became more popular, the mainstream began to co-opt them for its own purpose. What followed their wide-spread popularity was lecturing engagements and teaching positions at prestigious white colleges. Unfortunately, the mass audience was not getting the whole message, but rather sound-bites, which made them more like pop icons than it allowed them to have the mass political affect that they wanted. Accordingly, the use of the oral tradition suffered this same fate. On one hand, the oral tradition was a familiar medium to the African American community because of the tradition of storytelling and the tradition of preaching in the black church. As ya Salaam asserts, Martin L. King and Malcolm X were great influences on the Black Arts Movement. Barbara Christian affirms that:

> "The new poetry sound, released by this revival of the word, lent itself well to emotionally involving the audience in the message that the poet was sending... [and it allowed the poet] to elicit audience response— if not action" (Christian 20).

The negative is that the use of oral presentations and the

mediums of mass communication worked to flatten or dilute the message.

> "Often, the messages were lost because of the sensationalism...the advantages of this style carry with it some disadvantages—particularly the paring away of any factor that will not elicit an immediate response. Sometimes depth, precision, and strategy are sacrificed to drama, whim, technique" (Christian 22).

By not being in control of the mediums that they were using to get their work to the public, the messages of the writers from the Black Arts Movement were easily distorted or sensationalized. The dramatic performance was the product to be sold, not the complicated thought that was supposed to be delivered by the performance. So, by the late seventies and early eighties, the poets of the Black Arts Movement and an artist like Wonder were celebrated in the black community for having "made it" as individuals. They became icons because of their economic success earned through mass media not for any social or political change that they caused. At best they could be celebrated for using their voice to give the community a vehicle to express its pain and anger, but those voices rarely resulted in any real, tangible policy change, except for Wonder using his talents to enact the Martin Luther King, Jr. Holiday. By the eighties, most art in the black community is being used primarily as a tool for economic survival and not as a tool for social change. In fact, economic survival was the primary social agenda for the black community under the Reagan administration. Wilson affirms this shift and new cultural phenomenon in the black community. "Black people embrace stars as an example of our success. We need something so badly that we'll take anything. Prince was it, not just for the local, struggling musicians but for a whole nation of black kids. His economic success signaled that they could use music in the same manner that African Americans had been using sports to ascend poverty and gain a place in this society where one's place is dictated by economics. Unfortunately, they are using his model and standards, which are driving us to hell" (Wilson 2000).

This status of "Special Negro" has its individual and collective limits. Prince's career speaks to this. Paisley Park, the studio and the ideology, is based on one's separation from society to find one's place. As a positive, it represents looking inward to find one's place, peace, and power, taking control of one's life, and using some sense of self-determination. The capitalistic perversion of this means cutting off all who pose a potential threat to your place, peace, and power. Even the physical design of Prince's studio is a manifestation of this.

> "Paisley Park has the potential to be an absolute hive of activity, but doors and passages have been arranged so that Studio B, where Prince originally recorded, and now Studio A, to which he subsequently transferred, can be completely closed off from the rest of the complex, leaving the star in perfect isolation" (Hill 16).

When my wife and I visited Paisley Park as guests of DJ Brother Jules in June of 1995, we were told, of course, of certain areas where we could not go, which we accepted as standard practice. Paisley Park is a studio, first and foremost, that just happens to be large enough to hold parties for 200 people in the waiting room, not to mention the events that can be held on the sound stage. After a few hours of being there, Jules, with a large amount of thanks in is tone, said, "Hey, man, I appreciate you not trying to wonder off or bother me about going into certain areas." Maybe it was our southern manners or maybe it was the realization that we were guests in somebody else's crib, or maybe we just wanted to party and be respectful of the man who had given us so much great music, but we were not concerned with finding any inner sanctums. And maybe I am reading too much into Jules' words, but when you walk into Paisley Park, you do feel like you are walking into Prince's inner world. The building is designed like a maze, with each room cut off from the next. It seems to represent his battle over being simultaneously public and private, a dandy and a hermit.

This conflict is more dichotomy—more African Americanism. There is a conflict in Prince to be both a man of the people and a man who defines his own world. This speaks to larger issues, which include the struggle of place and the psychological and emotional effect that this struggle has had on African Americans. Perry asserts this.

> "Nobody who has been on the scene in the past twenty years recombines musical elements as freely and as creatively as Prince has at times, but at the same time if you look at the really stellar musical careers of the Twentieth Century, you find that there are substantial collaborative relationships that happen. With Duke Ellington it's Billy Strayhorn. With James Brown it's a series of sidemen who got less creative credit in his career than they really deserve, but they were there, long term, and they contributed a lot to his sound and his sensibility. The interesting thing about Prince and, in some ways, the tragedy of Prince is that he has never been able to sustain those types of relationships. He grew up isolated. He developed his vision of where he wanted to go and who he wanted to be, and he invented himself in that mold. That attitude toward life and toward his career served him really well for a really long time. But at this juncture in his career, speaking in 1992, I wonder if he hadn't gotten to the point where he is beginning to run dry. He's beginning to lose his own self-critical faculties because he does not have stable relationships with other people who can afford to be honest with him and who can input ideas that he will respect and work with." (Perry 1992).

Willie also affirms this. "When I see a lot of interviews, there is always somebody white taking credit for Prince's talent. The bottom line is that Prince is mostly responsible for his talents. So, I taught him how to construct songs and how to record songs; he still had to learn and do the work. The truth is by the time he started working independently of me, he could work independently of anyone. Why do you think he was able to self-produce his own first album at nineteen? If anything, what people like Owen did was made him palatable to the white masses. Part of this was the marketing of mythology. This allowed Prince to become isolated and get his vision across. Prince liked this part of the deal. Prince had been in the studio since he was fifteen. He was used to working alone. Still, most of these people have taken from Prince, but given him very little in an artistic sense...You are right that the mainstream public has taken from Prince the way that Europe took from Richard Wright and other black artists who went there. Just as France was not able to give to Wright, neither has the white mainstream been able to give anything to Prince. So, after surrounding himself with a stable of white yes-men, his river is beginning to run dry. But even that statement must be brought into context. We all said that he was running dry in 1992, and in 1996 he released Emancipation, which was some of the best stuff that he has done. At best, what we can say is that art comes from the people. If the artist separates himself from the people, his art will suffer. Though Prince is a much better musician and songwriter than he was twenty years ago and still far ahead of his peers, where would he, his art, and his people be had he stayed connected to the black community?" (Willie 2000).

Prince was anointed or consecrated as the musical messiah for the black Minneapolis community. In fact, when Prince gave his first performance for the Warner Bros executives to demonstrate if he was ready to begin or headline a major tour, the announcer proclaimed, "The power and the glory, the Minneapolis story." It is interesting that Hill describes Paisley Park as having "the potential to be an absolute hive of activity," meaning that it has not reached its potential. It is a hive of activity for Prince and his selected few, but has it been a hive of activity for the local black music scene? Many in the community would say no, and many would say yes. It depends upon whom you ask and their notion of black success. Both Willie and Craig Rice assert that Prince has given back, even though there is a lot more to be done. Rice "became the first black manager to really establish himself in the Twin Cities as more and more local businessmen turned their gaze towards a very different, very big-time music scene: attorneys, marking men, entrepreneurs" (Hill 5). On the other hand, Wilson asserts that what Prince has produced is just "more of that stereotypical myth of African Americans. We make money but lose our culture and our souls" (Wilson 2000). Chazz Smith, Prince's cousin and first drummer, also affirms that there was a conscious investment made into Prince by the black community. "From day one, everybody noticed that talent and dedicated themselves to seeing that talent reach its potential" (Smith 1992). It needs to be noted that this was as much a Minneapolis phenomenon as it was a black Minneapolis phenomenon. Even Husney as a local white businessman believed that Prince was a special talent who deserved to be brought to a mass audience. "From the first day, I decided to drop everything and dedicate my life to him" (Husney 1992). Wilson, however, counters that though Husney's dedication may have possibly been sincere, it is really more representative of the way that blacks are identified, targeted, and isolated for the purposes of capitalism. "Once this individual is used for all he is worth, he is useless to both white and black America" (Wilson 2000). Husney, however, denies this notion and says that Prince, himself, is as much to blame as anyone. "I call it 'Top Ten Disease.' Something seems to happen to some black acts like a Diana Ross. They get so big that they think that they are white or are accepted as white. You have to remember that when I was with Prince we started working the black radio circuit in Detroit, Philadelphia, and Atlanta. When Prince got 'big' he basically dissed black radio. No one is bigger than their roots. When Prince's fame began to fade, he attempted to return to black radio, and they rejected him" (Husney 2000). Husney was replaced by a more "powerful and connected" entity, the Cavallo-Ruffalo Agency. Once Cavallo-Ruffalo had secured Prince to their camp, Steve Fargnoli became the one in charge of handling the day to day operations. Minneapolis insiders also assert that it was the job of Fargnoli to separate Prince from his Minneapolis roots and community, making him a special Negro, so that Cavallo-Ruffalo could better control Prince's career. Husney partially agrees that Fargnoli was able to exploit Prince's desire to be a rock icon and a "special" talent. By all accounts, Fargnoli was able to turn Prince's vision and connection away from his peers and his community and toward fame. Still, this community investment has some in the community waiting on a return. Smith brings this front and center.

> "[Prince's] career speaks for itself, really...It's been a genius career. The only thing that I could think that he could do...his next move is to come back [to the black community.] Everybody is still here. We still talk to each other. We need each other. To be out there where he is at by himself has got to be pretty scary. So, I feel for his future, in that sense. You got to come back home. It's deeper than just the music thing. You just gotta come back home, man. Then I could see him going on and doing things that David Bowie and people [like that] couldn't do" (Smith 1992).

In the 1992 interviews for the documentary Prince Unauthorized, Perry and Smith discuss Prince's need to reconnect to his roots and to the people from whom his talent comes. In 1996 Prince created probably his most complete album, Emancipation, although it was heard by less than half the people who heard Purple Rain. Since then, the notoriety of his work has lingered somewhere near obscurity until the 2004 release of Musicology. Before the later success of Musicology and 3121 (2006), by 2000 he was perceived as being out of touch with black reality both musically and lyrically. Integration has done to Prince what it has managed to do to most African Americans, their movements, and their organizations. It forced him and them to accept reality and success on its terms, rendering that success impotent in its ability to fundamentally change the socio-political condition of the people as second-class citizens. When asked in a 1998 interview on <u>BET Tonight,</u> why he was doing that interview and others like it, he responded that "Black people need something that will galvanize them." His solution is spirituality. The question for many African Americans is whether Prince has waited so long to return to the community that his return is seen, by the community, as merely a ploy to retrieve some of his lost success. Many, such as Willie, Smith, and Wilson, see Prince as another missed opportunity for African Americans to achieve some sense of first-class citizenship through their art. Prince is a product of the black community, a community which is forced to invest in itself to survive. What keeps the community alive is when those investments pay back dividends to the community. Unfortunately, many see Prince as they see most of African American culture, as having been seduced and co-opted by capitalism. On the other hand, Prince has, in his own way, integrated his search for a racial identity with his search for his metaphysical identify. Since 1991, Prince has written songs, such as "Gold Nigga," "No Black Muthafuckers in the House," "The Sacrifice of Victor," "Same December," "Right the Wrong," "Face Down," "2045 Radical Man," "When Will We Be Paid?," and "Dear Mr. Man," which tackle the issue of race in America. Only time and the keepers of the canon will decide if Prince's work has been of particular use to the struggle of African Americans. There is no doubt, however, that his work is a record of one of the many paths and directions of African Americans in their struggle, and studying his production can help us understand and create other tactics in the African American struggle for place and first-place citizenship. In this vein, Prince continues the struggle and legacy of the first African Americans to arrive in Minneapolis as well as all African Americans struggling for some sense of place and power in America.

Theory: A Method to the Madness?

"Movies interest me...painting and writing books and things like that. I think I'm into epic drama...I admire speakers more than singers. Speakers make better music...John F. Kennedy, Martin Luther King...they could move a crowd of people better than any singer could...Nixon was a good speaker...he tricked a lot of people" (Mitchell 1981).

There are two types of poetic ideals. The first type is the poet who has a definitive view of the world and uses his talents to promote that view, attempting to persuade others to accept, adopt, or adapt to that view. The second type is that of the more skeptical or conflicted poet who spends his time struggling with himself and the world. The truth is that there are no absolutes, and most poets fluctuate violently between the two poles. The latter type, no matter how much we tend to deny it, seems to be more engaging and entertaining for us. Not only is the artist struggling to find some sense of self, he often does so by questioning all that we know to be real or true. His subjective struggle often leads to our objective questioning. This is why we are enthralled with the tragic hero—i.e., the tragic mulatto struggling for place and being. Most audiences are partial to this struggle because all humans have struggled with place and being, and this familiarity, understanding, or empathy to the struggle for place and being is why so many love hip hop. Hip hop presents the inquisitive artist, struggling for place and being, presenting grand and exaggerated metaphor and imagery to reclassify and revalue society's values, thus reconstructing our lives. Of course, hip hop, as with all black art is forced to struggle against white cooperate seduction and perversion to modify or flatten its art into something that is palatable to white tastes, which often means celebrating the most one-dimensional notions of blackness so that whites can live vicariously through black art. This is also why Prince was so popular from 1980-1987. America was struggling with an identity complex, just as it is today. When the eighties roll in, blacks and whites are still psychologically cruising from the civil wars and mental scars of the sixties and early seventies. The fatigue was so heavy that most Americans were willing to accept peace or even the illusion of peace at any cost. Specifically, African Americans wanted so desperately to be accepted into the American system that they would accept a false illusion or pseudo-integration as some type of validation that their hard work, labor, and struggle was not in vain. Therefore, the eighties were about style over substance. The "me" generation was dead set on "getting theirs." There was something about the eighties that caused people to feel like leisure, luxury, and excess was a right and a privilege that Ronald Reagan was going to give them. This is articulated clearly by Gordon Gekko in the top selling movie, Wall Street (1987), in the statement, "Greed is good." This desire for leisure, luxury, and excess was most evident in the music of big hair, big clothes, and lofty ideals of a gender bending, multicultural world of Dionysian pleasure.

This exaggerated, overstated style of popular music was the society's attempt to heal its inner scars by polishing the exterior. It is also the strategy of the captains of industry to sell the myth/lie/dream that we all can be rich beyond our wildest dreams.

> "Credit card use climbed especially sharply during the Eighties and the Nineties. Between 1984 and the present, revolving credit (short-term debt, mainly credit cards) has more than tripled. Between 1973 and 1979 the ratio of total household debt to total household income rose from 58.6 percent to 64 percent...The debt-income ratio rose steadily through the Eighties and Nineties, reaching 83.4 percent of household income in 1994" (Phillips 2000).

This increased exposure to and use of credit cards, especially by the lower economic class, is not by happenstance. The captains of industry purposely targeted this sector to exploit its desire to live like the rich and famous. Additionally, by inviting the have nots into the mainstream illusion of America the Beautiful, it lessens the desire and chance of a grassroots revolution, which perpetuates the status quo for the people in power.

> "Poor people are the credit industry's growth sector; between 1977 and 1999 the proportion of households earning between $10,000 and $20,000 who have at least one credit card rose from 33 percent in 1983 to 44 percent in 1995, according to Federal Reserve economist Peter Yoo…The fact that the debt-to-income ratio has been climbing since 1973—the postwar peak for real wages—suggests that families have taken on debt in order to compensate for slow wage increases…Debt also has ideological benefits. By putting purchasing power into the hands of the vast majority without increased wages, it creates a fiction of social equality and sustains mass purchasing power even as income inequality widens" (Phillips 2000).

The rise in popularity of the music video plays a major part in selling the dream of luxury and excess to the poor, but the society, itself, was asleep at the wheel, hoping that "big brother" or "Father Reagan" would somehow steer it to safety and glory. Of course, Reaganomics did not work, and America woke to the midnight screams of hip hop and grunge. In the African American community, Prince was seen as a false prophet who had misled and sold out the community to indulge his multicultural and feminine fantasies.

> "'When he came out,' says [music author Nelson] George, 'he was the most controversial artist of the time, dealing with incest and raw sexuality and sexual ambiguity and racial ambiguity. All that worked for him. And then a new movement came in called hip-hop. Once the Rakim, Run-DMC, Big Daddy Kane era came in, the whole level of masculinity was different. There was no room for ambiguity. There was definitely a cultural backlash among men. A lot of people suddenly said,

'Prince? He's a sissy.' " (Toure 1998).

Prince represents America's ill-fated attempt to dream our way to Utopia instead of working our way to peace. The difference is with a dream, the dreamer must eventually awake. When a nation collectively awakes from a dream, we all feel embarrassed that we were even on that journey. So, the nation has attempted to dismiss summarily the eighties and anything associated with it. The reality is that there was something missing or conflicting within enough of us that allowed the dream to last for almost a decade. Prince was one of the sandmen, leading us through our reverie, covering our eyes with visions of our pseudo-Utopian selves, simultaneously appealing to our carnal and ethereal desires. With Prince, we thought that we could have it all. By the end of the eighties, we find that we are too conflicted to have anything other than the chaos of an overly industrialized world that exploits our fear and pain instead of easing or removing them. The notion that greed is good opens the doors to several types of self-indulgence. Prince taps into the nation's desire for self-indulgence, hoping to provide commentary to show that our gluttonous desire represents our lack of inner peace. And with the advent of the synthesizer, poor and minority individuals like Prince were finally given the tool/power to shape the world as he saw fit with very little resistance. In the past poor and minority individuals were forced to unite into groups or organizations to get their messages and agendas heard. Even though Rosa Parks, Martin Luther King, and Malcolm X are celebrated individually, what needs to be remembered is that they all originate from organized group movements. Even individual music icons, such as W. C. Handy, Ray Charles, Quincy Jones, Miles Davis, Little Richard, James Brown, Jimi Hendrix, and George Clinton are products of groups or long-standing collaborations with specific songwriters and producers. The synthesizer becomes a defining moment when an individual, especially a poor or black individual, would have the access to single-handedly shape cultural if not political policy.

Like Nineteenth Century French poets Charles

Baudelaire and Jean Nicolas Arthur Rimbaud, Prince envisioned listeners who no longer accept the art on traditional terms. He was competing with the technology of the day, most specifically synthesizers and video. As Walter Benjamin asserts in his essay, "The Works of Art in the Age of Mechanical Reproduction," when there is a change in how a work of art can be created or reproduced, it causes "the most profound change in [the work's] impact upon the public (Benjamin 221). The synthesizer had two direct impacts, one on economics and the other on artistic vision. The affordable home synthesizer of the 1980s allowed more individuals the freedom to make music. Because it was specifically designed to mimic a wide variety of instruments, it allows one person to articulate his vision more freely. As Kashif asserts, "The synthesizer is one device that allows you to make a myriad of sounds and orchestral textures that are a unique and whole new palate of sounds" (Kashif 2000). This allows an individual who may not be skilled in a variety of instruments or who may not have the money to pay a lot of musicians to achieve the vision in his head without the economic restrictions or limitations of the past. It must be noted that while Prince is using the synthesizer, he is also playing the guitar, the bass, and the drums on almost every single and on every album. Yet the new technology available to him allows him to do it all himself, with little assistance from anyone else. As Prince asserts, "I basically learned with two tape recorders, two cassette recorders. That taught me how to mix harmonies and run harmonies together to play along with myself" (Schwartz 1981). Through the vision of Stevie Wonder and Sun Ra, Prince uses the synthesizer to play with and accompany himself like very few have been able to do. In fact, Prince aids in making the synthesizer an instrument in its own right. Rather than just mimicking sounds, Prince used the synthesizer to create other, unique sounds, opening many doors of possibilities. Thus, the new technology reduces the struggle of one musician attempting to orchestrate, coordinate, and articulate his vision through several other musicians.

"When it was three o'clock in the morning, and I'd

try to get [Revolution drummer] Bobby Z to come out to the studio, sometimes he'd come, sometimes he wouldn't. But I've had this Roger Linn drum machine since 1981. It's one of the first drum machines ever created. It takes me five seconds to put together a beat on this thing. So from the very start, technology gave me a direct result for my efforts" (Ebiri 84-85).

This opens the door for many more young people around the country to gain access to a music career. By making the musician both producer and artist, the synthesizer also goes a long way to continuing the move of the African American musician from the collective, community experience to the individual and singular experience. Though Wonder was a master of the synthesizer, he continued to keep strong relationships with musicians to ensure that the music was able to move pass his singular, individualized notions to connect with a larger collective.

This phenomenon of moving from the collective experience to the singular experience also happens in the literary field with a more severe effect. The home computer, the Internet, and advanced software make self-publishing a very affordable and self-fulfilling endeavor. While it created opportunities for more voices to be heard, self-publishing lowered the quality of work by writers because it removed them from the writing collective. The major tools of the writer are the workshop and a competent editor, where he and his work can be worked and reworked hundreds of times before it is released to the public. With the home computer and access to a wide market through the Internet, the workshop, unfortunately, is frequented by a decreasing number of writers, while their work is being seen by an increasing number of readers. Also, since self-publishing is expensive, many writers are not able to afford competent editors, which has a negative effect on the structure and content of the work. Not only does this negatively affect the writer's quality of work, but it also lessens the work's ability to speak to and for a particular group or collective. This can be seen in Prince's work. As he became more isolated, his work stopped speaking to a mass of followers as it did when he was regularly mingling with a collective, when he was one of the people. Technology is a double-edged sword that partly propels Prince to fame and partly causes his downfall. He rises to the top as a one-man band, able to achieve his goals and fantasies, but much like the Bud Fox character in <u>Wall Street</u>, he becomes isolated, finding that he cannot have it all. In this regard, he becomes a tragic figure, where his greatest asset is also his fatal flaw. His musical ability and desire to be a one man band allow for quick access to a mass public, but his inability to build long term relationships causes his work to lose some of its tangible essence. By 1990, twelve years after he started and five years after he was the biggest commercial star on the planet, Prince is perceived as being out of touch. Yet where technology isolated Prince, Kashif had his connection to the community, which kept him from becoming too foreign to be recognized by his base listeners. Even with the diversion of their journey, initially, their careers are so mirrored that they are examples of the effect that integration and advances in technology had on African American culture.

First, both their childhoods reveal how the tradition of the extended family in African American culture is negatively affected by integration. Kashif grew up in eight foster homes, never knowing his parents. Prince, after being bounced around from the homes of relatives, eventually went to live in the home of his best friend. "I ran away from home when I was twelve...I've changed addresses in Minneapolis thirty-two times, and there was a great deal of loneliness" (Adler 57). Their two circumstances are quite foreign to the African American notion of extended family where government agencies and non-family members were often the last resort for placing a child in someone's care other than their parents. In a 2006 lecture at the Annual New York Adoption Training Conference, Dr. Ruth McRoy showed that from 1982 to 1998, the percentage of African Americans in foster care steadily increased to African Americans populating

44% of the children in foster care (McRoy 2006). And a study done in 1982 by the Council of Black Minnesotans shows that only twenty of the one hundred black children adopted in Minnesota during 1981 were adopted by African Americans, and seventy-one were adopted by white females (Belton and Harp 5). This last statistic not only shows the decreasing importance of the extended family in black culture, but it also shows the manner in which an increasing number of black children are being raised with very little connection to African American roots, especially in Minneapolis. Since integration placed the individual at the center of importance, lessening the importance of the collective, more African American families were opting not to adopt or care for children from their extended families as had been the tradition in the past. Ironically, Prince, who lived with someone who had access to his parents, seems to be more affected by his displacement; it affects the subject matter of his music more than it does Kashif's music. In fact, Kashif is able, in his music and his life, to make a stronger connection and bridge the gap to his African American community. In Prince's case, to know one's parents and to be estranged from them seems to be more detrimental than not knowing one's parents at all. Secondly, both men are child prodigies whose careers were helped by the synthesizer. Both were identified as gifted children at the age of seven, and by fifteen both were making their mark on the world as musicians—Kashif by touring with B. T. Express and Prince by honing his skills in the studio and making a local name for himself. This point, however, is where there can be shown a definite difference in their paths, which is caused by a cultural happenstance in their formative teenage years. By becoming a member of B. T. Express, Kashif was planted into a stable community of African American adults who shaped his notions about art and the art's relationship to community. Prince, on the other hand, spent his formative years in the studio, creating the fantasy world that he desired. His vision and fantasy were enhanced by Husney and Chris Moon, a local lyricist and poet—two white men who were not prone to inhibiting Prince from fashioning himself in an image and direction that would become intriguing and palatable to a larger, white audience. Thus, Prince was allowed to freely experiment with all notions of who he wanted to be, which translates into more diverse subject matters and musical styles, but less of a definite connection to the African American community.

Both men arrived at precisely the same time in history. Kashif's first solo production credit comes in 1981 with "I'm In Love," recorded by Evelyn "Champagne" King. By then, Prince had four solo albums under his belt. Prince and Kashif, born in 1958 and 1959, are both products of the sixties and seventies, with Kashif keeping his ears to the R&B tradition—remaining concerned about the positive image and psychological impact of his work on his people. Prince's ear is over the charts and radio because in the beginning of his career Prince defines his people (group) more ideologically than culturally, which is also a result of integration. Prince views "his" people as people who "think" like him, even if they do not necessarily "look" like him. Prince, unlike Wonder and Kashif, grew up psychologically isolated from his peers and traditional African American culture. Geographic population along with his drive and desire to be a musician narrowed his normal childhood experiences. "Prince played football and basketball and all those other things, but even at a young age music consumed him. By the time he was fourteen or fifteen, he was spending more time alone in the studio than he was with his peers" (Willie 2000). Moon tells an interesting story about Prince coming to his studio with a group of black kids. Moon identified Prince as the one with whom he wanted to work and gave a key to Prince to let himself in anytime he wanted as long as there were no problems, which meant that Prince had to come and work alone (Hill 30). Being identified and isolated as a child prodigy by fifteen and having a recording contract by the age of nineteen greatly changed his relationship with his peers. According to Smith, Prince became the leader.

> "Prince wanted to be the leader...We wanted to bring in another member from Flyte Tyme that was having problems...His name is David Allen; they call him

Batman. We wanted to get him because he is an incredibly talented sax player…We wanted him in the band, and we went to Prince to get him in. We said to Prince that it would be a great opportunity to get this guy in the group, and Prince said no. And we kinda then said that if Prince doesn't want him, then well we…you know…And from then on Prince kinda realized the power that he had harnessed, and we didn't really know we were actually giving it to him. But we did know that if he quits [that's then end of the band]; then its whatever he says goes…" (Smith 1992).

Even at fifteen, being the leader means becoming somewhat distant, if not isolated, from those you are leading—at least in Prince's notion of leadership. All of this allowed him to indulge his personal fantasy of creating his isolated, Utopian world.

Both Prince and Kashif are products of an age where technological advancements and the economic sensibilities of the record companies greatly influenced who they became. Adding to the isolation of Prince brought on by the synthesizer, Warner Bros also influenced his divorce from society by catering to his rock iconic status. Warner Bros is attracted to the individuality of Prince because he is their little "one-man band." They would not have to pay as many musicians, which is an ironic concern since any costs or expenditures that are required to make or sell a record are deducted directly from the profits of the primary artist. Still, with one artist, there is less overhead, creating a greater profit for the company. Because of financial considerations and the ability to have single artists produce whole and complete sounds on their own, the singular, individualized sound was becoming the trend in popular music, as evidenced by James Mtume, Kashif, Ray Parker, Jr., and Lionel Richie who all left successful bands to pursue solo careers in the early eighties. Also, the new technology opened doors for African American female songwriters like never before. Patrice Rushen was able to maneuver around the "good-ole boy's" hurdle because the synthesizer allowed her the freedom to work independently and write songs that were not hampered by male egos or interference. Just as the new economic reality of Reconstruction produced the solo bluesman who was no longer confined to a group on a plantation and could now roam, alone, from place to place, the new economic reality of the synthesizer and the advent of music companies being run by accountants produced the rise in producer-driven music, which is singular and individualized. By 1980, music was becoming more disposable because the synthesizer greatly enhanced the ability of more individuals to mimic popular trends and adhere to the beckoning call and whim of music companies. Although Disco is one result of this trend, the synthesizer accelerated this trend in the eighties. By the eighties, music had become a commodity, first, and an art, second—no longer an intricate part of a culture that created, defined, and maintained the art. In a 1981 interview Prince laments the reign of the music producer.

> "Well, a lotta records today are producer's records. To me it doesn't mean anything because I don't believe in any act, really, which has to rely on a producer. What happens if the cat dies? There you go. There goes your sound— you obviously didn't have one. The producer bakes the whole cake...and that's probably why I don't listen to music. The artist is singing songs he didn't even write..." (Schwartz 1981).

And twenty years later in the "Liner Notes" to <u>One Nite Alone... Live!</u> (2002), Prince asserts that the music companies were themselves creating culture and art rather than merely co-opting the art because creating the trends is more economically feasible since it lessens the economic risk of trying to guess which trends will sell.

> "The trouble is that the methods employed by these 'cool hunters' have become so intrusive and so connected 2 the actual world they r supposed 2 observe that the line between the observers and what's being observed has become blurred. In other words, we have reached a point where the corporate machine is so well-oiled that, through its 'market research' activities, customer surveys, and

'focus groups' of paid participants, it is actually in the process of creating the very trends that it is supposed 2 detect" (Prince, "Liner Notes," 20).

Record companies and magazines perpetuated this by elevating the producer to the role and status of artist. The producer creates the art and then plugs in artists as interchangeable, disposable parts. Thus, by 1980 the producer becomes a cultural icon like never before, further perpetuating this singularity or individuality in sound and style, which was just perfect for the video age. Once you have a sound or a product to sell, you need a face or an image to make that sound or product tangible and "real" to the public. Along with the synthesizer, Prince was making music in the video age, where image was and continues to be everything. By 1979, "Video Killed the Radio Star" by the Buggles was a number one hit in the UK and was the first video played by MTV for its 1981 debut. Thus, by the time Prince hits the scene, it is clear that audiences are just as concerned by an artist's style and image as by the music, and this is a reality that Prince and others are forced to navigate. No matter the reason for making art, one must generate some capital if being an artist is one's primary profession. One must strike a balance between making art for financial purposes and making art for aesthetic/artistic and utilitarian purposes.

We see Prince engaging in this battle throughout his career. He employs the technique of shock to both sell records and get the public's attention, which can be for two different reasons. The former represents the use of shock to make one's work a cultural phenomenon because it either surprises or rebels against something in the mainstream culture. In the case of being rebellious, the work is usually rebelling against the sense of decency or right and wrong of the older generation that the younger generation seems to have some natural inclination to disregard or separate from it. The latter, to get the public's attention, is concerned more with using shock as a Trojan horse, getting the public's attention in order to supplant a message in them once you have their attention. Dirty Mind and Controversy are excellent examples of this. Dressed in a raincoat and underwear, the video gave Prince access to millions of homes, and his image allowed him to capture the public's attention before they used the remote to change the channel. His explicit lyrics were also used to cause controversy and gain the public's attention. Yet, cloaked beneath the sensationalism and controversy was an artist who had something to say, and his message related directly to the sensationalism and controversy that he was creating. Through the use of sensationalism, Prince is questioning the society's obsession with sensationalism. "I just can't believe all the things people say. Am I black or white? Am I straight or gay?" First he gets the public's attention by projecting his sexuality in an ambiguous, androgynous manner and by lying about his race in three separate periodicals (Los Angeles Times, Rolling Stone, and the New York Daily News) from January to March, 1981. In each interview, he changes the racial mix of his parents. Then, after having established his elaborate facade, he questions why the public is drawn to look at or discuss his racial heritage. This is great marketing and an excellent way for Prince to define himself before society can, by raising and directing, if not controlling, the discourse of identity.

Realizing that television and other rapidly changing technology have greatly affected the attention spans of the public, Prince uses sensationalism and the video to compliment his lyrics. As new technology is invented, old technology becomes dull to the public's senses. The trick is to continue to create art that does not become dull to the senses. The imperative of the artist is to balance the art of sensationalism with the art of craft. The struggle is not allowing the behavior one uses to get noticed to supplant or overshadow the art. As Barbara Christian asserts, the oral poet walks a thin line. He must create an art that emotionally engages and solicits an immediate response from his audience, which, at the same time, does not sacrifice "depth, precision, [and] hard strategy" (Christian 22). This is a problem that dates back hundreds of years, even for poets Baudelaire and Rimbaud. Benjamin points to this in his essay,

"On Some Motifs in Baudelaire."

> "The question suggests itself how lyric poetry can have as its basis an experience for which the shock experience has become the norm...The problem for Baudelaire was bound to be this: to become a great poet, yet [not become what had been before him.] I do not claim that this ambition was a conscious one in Baudelaire; but it was bound to be present in him, it was his reason of state...Thus Baudelaire placed the shock experience at the very center of his artistic work...This is corroborated by evidence from several contemporaries [and]...establishes Baudelaire's alarming appearance [and] the italicizing Baudelaire indulged in when reciting poetry; [and with his] jerky gait...Baudelaire made it his business to parry the shocks, no matter where they might come from, with his spiritual and his physical self" (Benjamin 164, 165).

Baudelaire's appearance and performance are used to parallel and enhance his literary message. Thus, in his own dandyism, Prince picks up where Baudelaire stops. Through the use of shock in his dress and lyrics, Prince is able to flip the table on the taboos of sex to show that the taboo nature of sex is related directly to racism and insecurity. Prince's use of sex and sexuality is not merely to glorify the personal gratification of sex and sexuality but to show that sex and sexuality are personifications or manifestations of our psychological and spiritual selves. Prince challenges our sexual notions and identities as a way of challenging our racial and gender notions and our identities. Still, many may complain that to do all of this is to put style front and center before the art.

Style in music has become a dirty notion, but, you cannot have innovation without style, which is merely the manner in which we perform a task. Often one's style is an amalgamation of history, both collective and personal. In other cases, style can be born from a socio-political condition, such as the zoot suit or the afro, which are both reactions to white supremacy. The Black Panthers had style. Angela Davis has style. Amiri Baraka has style. Their style grew as a direct reaction against the so-called "mainstream culture," helping to produce a counter-culture. Or in many cases, black culture or style is merely the rearranging or refashioning of the dominate culture so as to give voice to the oppressed black culture. The truth is that there is always a counter-culture. There cannot be a mainstream culture without a counter-culture. Thus, the act of reacting to or rebelling against style is style. So, there are always at least two styles in any society and in most cases four. Not only are there the battling styles of the mainstream and the counter-culture, there is also the style of the young needing to differ from the old. It represents a new style, something giving the new generation its own voice. Fourth, there is the style produced by amalgamation, when either an individual or an entire culture assimilates all of the varying styles. If we understand this, then we understand that style has always been a part of music and has been as important as the music because style is what makes the music unique.

    The counter-culture is often the most powerful style because it is railing against an oppressive system and is antagonistic by nature. The group that is creating the counter-culture style must succeed or it will die. Therefore, their style is a matter of survival and not merely leisure. Often, it becomes the only voice that they have. Turning a cap backwards or sideways or wearing a hat tilted or slanted to the side may be the only voice of rebellion that the gentleman may have. Therefore, his style is not merely leisure; it is his cultural breath. A key ingredient in black music is the pain from living under oppression. This is part of what creates the "soul" in soul music. The other part, of course, is the African's ability to connect or align his physical to his emotional and spiritual because in the ancient African tradition the body is not seen as something separate and apart from the soul. Thus, the African's traditional connection of the body and soul allows him to express more freely and articulately his joy and pain, especially the pain caused by racial oppression. As Prince asserts in "The Exodus Has Begun," "And if [white oppressors] stood up and behaved like the humans they're supposed 2 as opposed 2 the way they are not, then this new power soul would not be so soulful..." Black art is powerful because of the adverse condition of the people. Everything is raised to a higher intensity because their pain is at a higher intensity than others and because they have few outlets to express their pain and fewer opportunities to address their oppression. Black people love harder and play harder because they live and work harder. This pain is most typified in gospel and blues music. No matter how cloaked it may be, the pain of gospel and blues is what resonates in Prince's work. Nelson George asserts, "Very few people handle pain with the depth and intensity as Prince" (George 1992). Miles Davis affirms this. "He's got that church thing up in what he does" (Davis 385).

Prince has managed to take his neo-message of otherness and blend it with the traditional sounds of black America. In technique, which includes his use of shock, sensationalism, and eclectic influences, Prince is certainly a postmodern artist. Postmodernism favors eclecticism in musical form and musical genre, and often combines characteristics from different genres or employs jump-cut sectionalization (such as blocks). It tends to be self-referential and ironic, and it blurs the boundaries between high art and kitsch. In <u>Modernism and Music: An Anthology of Sources</u> (2004), Daniel Albright summarizes the traits of the postmodern style as bricolage, polystylism, and randomness. The music of postmodernity is valued more as a spectacle, a good for mass consumption, and an indicator of group identity. For example, one significant role of music in postmodern society is to act as a badge by which people can signify their identity as a member of a particular subculture. In Prince's music, listeners are able to understand his particular message because they feel, sense, or perceive the semantics of the familiar sounds embedded in his work. Though the sounds are familiar, the way that he blends and juxtaposes various sounds provides a refreshing though palatable sound and feeling. The comprehensive sound of the entire song may seem different, but the ear is identifying the fragments of familiarity in each individual portion. From the bass the listener may hear Bootsy Collins or Larry Graham. From the guitar the listener may hear Jimi Hendrix, Carlos Santana, or Curtis Mayfield. From the keyboards the listener may hear Stevie Wonder or Sly Stone. From the drums the listener may hear Billy Cobham, though early in his career Prince wanted a white drummer for a rock sound. "There were a lot of local drummers that Prince could have chosen, including his cousin Chazz, who is a great drummer. But Prince wanted a white drummer" (Willie 1992). So, the force of his lyrical imagery is aided by the force of familiar sounds, which already carry their own emotional messages. When the listener is hearing the music of Wonder, Mayfield, Hendrix, Stone, and others, they are also hearing the ideologies of these artists, which are metaphysically housed in their musical styles. The same is true with lyrics. Prince's lyrical imagery evokes the memory of all of the above as well as Dylan, the Beatles, and more. Both with his lyrics and his music, Prince understands how sounds and words have their own cultural meanings/connotations. He was able to cut and paste various musical and lyrical morphemes to create an ambiance about his work, which gives his songs a figurative depth. He takes the musical and lyrical pain of others and recontextualizes it to express his own pain. Just like retail companies have been able to take the feeling of a song and attach that feeling to their product, Prince has been able to take the feelings of various sounds, rhetoric, and imagery and attach them to his messages. As Miles Davis asserts, "Prince is like the church to gay guys" (Davis 385). To Davis' statement I will add that he became the church for anyone who did not accept, internalize, or buy into the rhetoric of normality, which is what most institutionalized religions sell and perpetuate.

Rebellion, which grows from the desire of an oppressed person to articulate some sense of who he is, creates its own style. So, wearing an afro became a statement of one's social and political conscience. Carrying Miles Davis records became a social statement of one's hip-ness. In the seventies and eighties, the larger mainstream culture becomes smarter and hipper by merely assimilating or co-opting the counter-culture into itself. By the 1990s, we have Motown records selling hamburgers, the Beatles' "Revolution" and "Come Together" selling tennis shoes and computers, George Clinton becomes a spokesman for Burger King, and Prince's "Baby I'm a Star" becomes the slogan for Target Stores. This co-opting of the counter-culture works for two reasons. We all have a bit of a dandy in us. We all use style as a revolt against something or as a way to articulate our identity. Thus, we are quick to embrace someone who is using something that is familiar/similar to us, especially if we believe that the thing/artifact is being used to articulate something about the world from a similar perspective as ours. So when a retailer uses a song we like, it subconsciously connects with us on some primitive level. We associate the good feeling with the product and purchase it. Of the seven types of propaganda, this strategy is called "transfer." This can also be done with ideas and concepts. If an idea or concept is housed in a sound that his familiar to us, we are seduced into buying that idea or concept. Second, most of us want our culture (ideas, beliefs, and behavior) affirmed as valuable or meaningful. So when a major entity or institution of the dominate culture uses (co-opts) something from the counter-culture, it is affirming its value even if the thing/artifact being used is not respected by the dominate culture for any other reason than something to exploit.

With <u>Dirty Mind</u>, Prince, like Baudelaire, Rimbaud, and Benjamin before him, saw and anticipated this shift in the over importance or obsession with sex and image, especially in the blending of the audio and visual to sell records. He used this shift, took advantage of this shift, as a way to articulate his own messages and concerns and get paid while doing so. So, where beer commercials were using sex to sell their product, Prince was also using sex to sell his product. Sex just happened to be his product. Yet, part of his goal was to change the manner in which we perceive or use sex. As he was selling sex, he was also commenting on sex as a manifestation of our metaphysical selves. Much like the literary critic uses language to discuss itself, so was Prince using sex to discuss itself. And Prince anticipates that due to a lack of opportunities to liberate and express one's social and political concerns, individuals would indulge their sexual fantasies in the eighties as a tool of personal expression. Like Baudelaire and Rimbaud, Prince

> "envisaged [listeners] to whom the [hearing] of lyric poetry would present difficulties. Willpower and the ability to concentrate are not their strong points; what they prefer is sensual pleasures; they are familiar with 'spleen' which kills interest and receptiveness" (Benjamin 157).

So, Prince understood that in MTV's and Gordon Gekko's world of big hair, flashy clothes, naked bodies, and short attention spans, he would have to be as loud and as shocking as possible to be recognized. Yet, on a deeper level, Prince also understood that society's urge toward big, loud, and flashy things signified people's emptiness and misguided attempt to gain inner peace. This same notion by writers of the 1800s that sex and sexuality are socio-political expressions and reactions is also affirmed by 1930s writer Aldous Huxley, author of <u>Brave New World</u>, when he asserts that the "sexual promiscuity of <u>Brave New World</u> [does not] seem so very distant...As political and economic freedom diminishes, sexual freedom tends compensatingly to increase" (Huxley xvi). Prince would titillate and gratify his listeners physically and simultaneously stimulate them intellectually. Like Jesus going to the cafe, Prince understood that an artist must meet his audience where they are and then work to elevate them.

Along this same line, Prince was envisioning an African American class that wanted to be identified as individuals and not as a collective, and they would be willing to do anything to achieve this goal. Quite simply, black folks wanted Gekko's dream also. The prospect of more economic gain for this new middle class caused them willingly to release their African roots and embrace a new construct of themselves, even if this new construct was false. This pseudo-integrationist move toward an overly general sense of the universality of man caused a large segment of African Americans to accept an ideological history rather than one based on actual, historical fact. Instead of staying focused on particular struggles toward desegregation, which is something different than integration, African Americans began to focus on the ideology of the general goodness of mankind to which the country had been striving to achieve, no matter how limited or slow that movement had been in the past. This makes Prince's prowess on the synthesizer apropos. Just as he is able to blend sounds synthetically, he is also able synthetically to blend ideals about humanity, which caused his listeners and the mainstream to buy into his ideology of a multicultural, multi-gender Utopia. To achieve this atmosphere of Utopia, Prince takes past ideals and ideologies of sex and sexuality and blends them with past ideals of socio-political liberation and creates a gumbo effect where his ideas of sex and sexuality are given or perceived to have more weight or substance because they are paired or rooted in the sounds and imagery of sixties and seventies message music.

To blend these varying ideologies, Prince uses what Marcel Proust calls a "voluntary memory, one that is in the service of the intellect" (Benjamin 160). To evoke this "voluntary memory" Prince uses images and symbols from the past that produce a meaning and feeling of nostalgia toward the universality of mankind. In a crude or simplified form, Prince is creating a metanarrative, which is a historical, global, or totalizing narrative schema which orders and explains knowledge and experience. Prince is hoping and betting on the fact that our particular (cultural) meanings of the borrowed artifacts are "somewhere beyond the reach of the intellect, [but still] unmistakably present..." (Benjamin 160). An example of this is the reemergence of the peace symbol during the eighties. Though America was not involved in a major war, the peace symbol became a way for artists to align themselves with the ideology and the nostalgia of the sixties, which worked to give their art a greater perceived depth and sincerity. So, an artist could wear a peace symbol or flash the peace sign and become linked to the feeling of the sixties. Prince, through his use of pulling images and symbols from various cultures and time periods, is attempting to evoke a feeling, not a precise notion or thought. He is hoping that the actual, literal meaning of the image or symbol is so far beyond our dulled intellect that we only remember it as a feeling and equate that feeling with the feeling of his music. Prince draws on sixties/seventies rhetoric to create an atmosphere of rebellion. He becomes part freedom fighter, part revolutionary, and part hippie—championing something that we all love and support, sex. His borrowed rhetoric allows him to raise sex to something more meaningful than personal gratification. Sex and sexuality become their own theory and theology as a way to make the world a better place. In "Sexuality" from Controversy (1981), Prince is clearly making use of Civil Rights rhetoric and imagery when he proclaims, "Stand up everybody; this is your life...Don't need no segregation; don't need no race." He then adds biblical imagery to reinforce the importance and urgency of his message. "The second coming, I think we gotta case." The "second coming" image draws on the imagery of a messiah coming to free his people from bondage. It also refers to the second coming of the sixties, for which many are still waiting. Also in 1981, Prince and his management were brainstorming ideas and filming concert and backstage footage for a film that was tentatively titled The Second Coming, which is clearly playing with the fact that most critics were hailing Prince as the new Little Richard, James Brown, and Jimi Hendrix all rolled into one. This is all evidence that Prince clearly understands visual, phonetic, and lyrical imagery and is able to use, recontextualize the images of others to articulate his own messages.

In "The War" (1998) Prince pulls images and rhetoric from the past as well as conspiracy theories about the future to address the issue of lost or compromised freedom. His goal is to show that freedom only comes when one can define freedom for oneself by rejecting the ideology and bribes of the oppressor at all costs. In short, compromised freedom is not freedom. To reject the reality of the oppressor, the oppressed must uncover and understand the lies of the oppressor. He sets the tone for the song by invoking Gil Scott-Heron's "The Revolution Will not Be Televised." In this poem, Scott-Heron is attempting to change the thinking of black people by showing that they will never be free if they continue to wait on freedom from the mass communications system of the oppressor, which informs, orders, and structures every aspect of their lives. The oppressor creates an illusion of paradise through the use of television that numbs them into submission. Revolution will not and cannot come to them that way because television or any aspect of America's media machine is propaganda in service to the perpetuation of the American empire. If black people want revolution, they must free their minds from America's media machines, get in the streets, and start creating their own reality through revolutionary actions, which demands a reshaping of the mind.

> "<u>Green Acres</u>, <u>Beverly Hillbillies</u> and <u>Hooterville Junction</u> will no longer be so damned relevant, and women will not care if Dick finally got down with Jane on <u>Search for Tomorrow</u> because black people will be in the streets looking for A Brighter Day. The revolution will not be televised" (Gates and McKay 61-62).

Prince invokes the sixties/seventies spirit of a coming liberation with the phrase "The evolution will be colorized." Even if it makes no sense, the rhyme scheme connects with and tropes Scott-Heron's message. Prince then adds, "If u do not want to be challenged, go back to your Saturday morning cartoons." With this line he is invoking the same notion that Scott-Heron is asserting—that the masses of oppressed people are held in their stupor by the television.

Prince begins to tie together fragmented images and pieces of rhetoric until he has built his image of the neo-Babylon.

> "Do u love your country as much as u love God? We are running out of the essentials—clean air, food to eat. Underground as we speak there is a metropolis—clean air, food to eat. Will u go underground to this metropolis paradise? One condition—microchip in yo' neck. Would u stay above and await your fate? Do u

trust your God?"

After presenting the exposition, Prince submits his message that no matter what, man cannot survive or evolve without God. "Without God there is no clean air, no oxygen, no food to eat, and there is no chocolate microchip for yo' neck." The two-part message is that God is the only answer for mankind, but mankind must awake from the lies of the physical world to see the truth of the metaphysical world. This is where he truly begins to challenge his listeners' perception of the world. It must be noted that by the time "The War" is released (1998), Prince's audience is mostly white and middle-classed. Nonetheless, it is an audience that prides itself on being open-minded. For most, being a Prince fan is a sign of their openness and intelligence. Knowing this, he holds them throughout the song by repeating, "We are about the challenge what you think." On a deeper note, Prince's insistence of a multicultural fan base has often forced him to challenge America on its inhumane treatment of humans rather than along the lines of race. This is why his artifacts cannot be too literal or race specific. He must find a way to present the truth in a manner that is palatable to his white fan base. This is not to say that his evoking of God is not a sincere or effective solution. But it is more appeasing than asserting directly to white folks that they are evil. This is no different than King rejecting the term "Black Power," not because he though it was a bad idea, but because he thought those two words, combined together, would have a negative connotation for too many people. (King 323-326). Again, this is Prince's dance between art and economics. His subjective use of cultural/historical artifacts, images, icons, and symbols lends itself well to his dance. After he asserts God as the only answer, he is back to the rhetoric.

> "U teach lies not the truth. Give me candy; I take the store...Pledge allegiance to your flag, tie me 2 a truck and then u drag. U give me AIDS, your history, when it comes to mine, another day. Many died—red, black, and even Jew—claiming God was backing u. So

u say u got a cure; HIV, I'm not sure. Every seed, fruit to bear, the great Babylon I don't care. We know your name; it's the Beast; all of God's children is your feast."

Though the images are fragmented and almost incoherent, the message is clear; America is the land of hypocrisy that is killing people for its own benefit. The answer to America's deterioration, which is vintage Prince, is first realizing the deterioration and then embracing the spiritual for a solution. "The War" proposes as its solution what has become the standard Prince solution: Love or, in this case, God. "Get the righteous one's to plant the seed...the only way to get there is the truth y'all." Prince makes himself the prophet bringing the news. The sixties have been so glossed over and overly romanticized for capitalistic purposes that the veil of the sixties keeps the society looking back rather than moving forward. As long as listeners continue to look back to the sixties, Prince will be able to use its imagery to cloak himself and his messages. His use of dated but historically/culturally loaded language and symbolism allows him to equate himself with the sixties and build from its idealism. The actual meaning of the image, artifact, or symbol is not important to Prince. What becomes important in the eighties is the storyteller's ability to manipulate the artifact to produce the feeling. "It is not the object of the story to convey a happening *per se,* which is the purpose of information; rather, it embeds it in the life of the storyteller in order to pass it on as experience to those listening" (Benjamin 161). So in songs, such as "Dirty Mind," "Uptown," "Party Up," "Controversy," "Sexuality," and "Jack You Off," Prince can rail against the concept of oppression and not directly discuss white supremacy, even though this oppression of race, gender, and class evolves directly from white supremacy. By doing this, Prince is attempting to create a collective meaning and culture based on ideologies and not specific artifact. This allows his white listeners to feel a part of his struggle. As Miles Davis asserts in his autobiography, white people are more prone to support something when they can see themselves as a part of it.

> "But the record companies and white people liked [Hendrix] better when he had the white guys in his band. Just like a lot of white people like to talk about me when I was doing the nonet thing—the <u>Birth of the Cool</u> thing; or when I did those other albums with Gil Evans or Bill Evans because they always like to see white people up in black shit, so that they can say they had something to do with it" (Davis 293).

Prince creates a fantasy world that belongs to him and that he controls, but it is also inclusive of the entire society's ideologies and artifacts. Prince blends these ideologies, artifacts, symbols, and images like a survey class, but without respect to the chronological reality or an adherence to a meaning based on the specific event or moment that created these ideologies, artifacts, symbols, and images. The impressionistic blending is what allows the work to be accessed by others because they can provide their own meaning or understanding to the work. When asked about listeners' dual perception of a particular work, Prince states "Well, that's up to them. I don't want to burst anybody's bubble" (Hilburn, "Mixed Emotions," 58).

> "Where there is experience in the strict sense of the word, certain contents of the individual past combine with material of the collective past. The rituals with their ceremonies, their festivals, kept producing the amalgamation of these two elements of memory over and over again. They triggered recollection at certain times and remained handles of memory for a lifetime. In this way, voluntary and involuntary recollections lose their mutual exclusiveness" (Benjamin 161-162).

The loss or blurring of the specific meaning of an image or artifact keeps the image or artifact from being finite, rigid, and exclusive, making it inclusive or open to a variety of meanings. Prince is not trying to be historical, *per se*. He wishes, rather, to be allegorical. He and his work become tropes to represent what man has the ability to become if he can balance his physical and his metaphysical. Moreover, he becomes various personas, changing as his messages change. He becomes the allegorical griot or the fictional Homer who makes us believe that all of his images and symbols are indigenous to his personal history because the history of man is allegorical by nature. Thus, Prince is hoping that we buy into the notion that there is but one human story, and all of us are a part of that narrative. If we accept the "one story" notion, then we allow him to use various images from various cultures and amalgamate them for his own message through his metanarrative. By making himself a hybrid—race, gender, class—he has made himself a child or an artist of the world, who can appropriate any aspect of history to remind us of "our" story. And to add an appearance of authenticity, he shows himself as one who has been given, impregnated with, or possessed with the message by no choice of his own from some greater power who wants him to deliver the message to the rest of us. As in "1999," "I was dreamin' when I wrote this/ Forgive me if it goes astray." Clearly, he wants us to believe that he has no control over the visions that he receives. "I was dreamin' when I wrote this/ So sue me if I go too fast." Even when discussing the process of songwriting with Detroit disc jockey the Electrifying Mojo, Prince asserts that creating a song is akin to being overcome by some other spirit.

> "The thing is that when you're called, you're called. I hear things in my sleep; I walk around and go to the bathroom and try to brush my teeth and all of the sudden the toothbrush starts vibrating! That's a groove, you know…You gotta go with that, and that means drop the toothbrush and get down to the studio or get to a bass guitar, quick! My best things have come out like that." (Prince 1985).

To become humanity's storyteller, Prince creates himself as the mystic poet who is completely possessed or driven by his work—driven by his vision to get mankind to evolve past its arbitrary definitions and embrace the greater humanity. He is the poet type of Edgar Allen Poe, Samuel Taylor Coleridge, and Toomer, driven to bouts of insanity by the work because he is fighting against the rigid definitions of humanity by fighting against the rigid definitions of literary techniques and artifacts. It consumes him because he creates a relationship where he is subservient to the art; the art is the master, and he is merely a vessel through which it may travel to the public. He his driven by the images in his head and will not succumb or submit to anyone or anything else. Making his vision or fantasy a reality is more important than our rigid definitions of time, place, gender, and culture. Neal Karlen provides us a view of this man who lives off the spirit of his creative drive in his two articles for Rolling Stone, "Prince Talks: The Silence Is Broken" and "Prince Talks."

> "The phone rings at 4:48 in the morning. 'Hi, it's Prince,' says the wide-awake voice…Did I wake you up?' Though it is assumed that Prince does in fact sleep, no one on this [1990] summer Nude Tour can pinpoint precisely when. Prince seems to relish the aura of night stalker; his vampire hours have been apart of his mad-genius myth ever since he was waging junior-high-school band battles on Minneapolis's mostly black North Side. 'Anyone who was around back then knew what was happening,' Prince had said two days earlier, reminiscing. 'I was working. When they were sleeping, I was jamming. When they woke up, I had another groove. I'm as insane that way now as I was back then.' For proof, he'd produce a crinkled dime-store notebook that he carries with him like Linus' blanket. Empty when his tour started in May, the book is nearly full, with twenty-one new songs scripted in perfect grammar-school penmanship. He has also been laboring on the road over his movie musical Graffiti Bridge, which was supposed to be out this past summer and is now set for release in November. Overseeing the dubbing and editing of a film by way of dressing-room VCRs and hotel telephones, Prince said, has given him an idea.

> 'One of these days,' he said, 'I'm going to work on just one project, and take my time'...At four in the morning, flying into their third country in the past twenty-four hours, the band and the entire entourage of about thirty are sacked out in what looks like the sleep of the dead. Everybody's unconscious on this charter, including one of the flight attendants. There's movement, however, up in row 1. Prince's headphoned head is bopping against the back seat, his arms pounding the armrests. From the back, it looks like a prisoner is being executed in an upholstered electric chair...Now, while his band mates and support staff snooze around him, Prince keeps air-jamming beneath the glare of his seat's tiny spotlight. Listening to a tape of his own performance that day, Prince stays up all night, all the way to London" (Karlen, "Prince Talks," 104).

There are countless other stories like this one. Saxophone player, Eric Leeds, attests, "I've seen him work around the clock. When one engineer burns out, he simply brings in another one" (Leeds 1992). R&B and gospel great Mavis Staples adds to this. "He said to me, 'Mavis, sleep is a waste of time.'" (Staples 1992). He is one who is simply driven to make art. And when his listeners accept this notion that Prince is somehow possessed to create art, this mad-genius persona allows them to be more open and accepting of the sincerity of his work as well as the notion that he is driven by his work to say something important or meaningful about life.

> "The only time I feel like a prisoner is when I think too much and can't sleep from just having so many things on my mind. You know, stuff like 'I could do this, I could do that. I could work with this band. When am I gonna do this show or that show?' There's so many things. There's women. Do I have to eat? I wish I didn't have to eat...The reason I didn't use musicians a lot of the time had to

do with the hours that I worked. I swear to God it's not out of boldness when I say this, but there's not a person around who can stay awake as long as I can. Music is what keeps me awake. There will be times when I've been working in the studio for twenty hours and I'll be falling asleep in the chair, but I'll still be able to tell the engineer what cut I want to make. I use engineers in shifts a lot of the time because when I start something, I like to go all the way through. There are few musicians who will stay awake that long" (Karlen, "Prince Talks: The Silence Is Broken," 28, 85).

Through his own intriguing, mystic persona and through the use of a plethora of images and symbols, Prince creates a Utopian ideology that seems tangible and pliable to serve as an alternative to the current, one-dimensional and rigid world. These varying images and persona may have been pulled from different times and cultures, but they do come from the human experience. Prince is counting on this connection. Prince is asserting, through his use of these varying images and symbols, that our humanity gives us the right to make use of them for our own need. In fact, our connection to these past images and symbols demands that he manipulates them in this manner. "What prevents our delight in the beautiful from ever being satisfied is the image of the past, which Baudelaire regards as veiled by the tears of nostalgia" (Benjamin 189). Rather than fight this veil, Prince is using this veil of the past to cloak his work and connect it to the legacy of nostalgia. It is almost surreal the manner in which he creates new worlds by blending the old with the new. Newness in popular culture is not the original, but the illusion or the myth of the original based on one's ability to reconfigure the past—one's ability to cut and past a new world, such as through sampling. Take, for instance, The Black Album (1988), which is pregnant with symbolism. Its very name invokes the aura of the Beatles' White Album, which became a cultural phenomenon even to those who never heard it. The Black Album also represents a return to the roots of black music that Prince was seemingly eluding until Sign "☮" the Times. Then he adds mystique by refusing to release it because it supposedly goes against his "new" convictions. This plethora of meanings creates an atmosphere and an illusion where listeners from an array of backgrounds can attach their varied interpretations of the lyrics to the album and be justified. It is his fantasy world, but he has carefully crafted it in a manner that it is accessible to others who are also searching for their own fantasy to escape a physical world that has become limiting, dissatisfying, or numb to them. In piecing or quilting this new world, Prince is the master sampler as evident in his use of the synthesizer to mimic and blur older sounds, which also influences his use of lyrical images, such as his use of paisley to connect to the past. Even in "Party Up" Prince is writing an anti-war song in 1980. "You gonna have to fight your own damn war 'cause we don't wanna fight no more." This is troping and signifying at its best, even if it is being used for more personal and individualized purposes. What war is being discussed in "Party Up?" Obviously not an actual war between countries. This "war" becomes a metaphor on three levels: the internal conflict of individual identity, the individual's conflict with the society, and the war of the haves versus the have nots. "Because of their half-baked mistakes, we get ice cream and no cake. All lies no truth, is it fair to kill the youth?" The youth are not being killed in foreign wars; they are being killed by having their dreams taken and dictated to them. They are being killed by having their notions of who they are dictated to them.

Eighteen years later, he invokes this trope again in "The War." Again, we know that there is going to be a war, but both sides remain faceless. The government is the vague and impressionistic enemy, which works well since many people seem to mistrust their government. He strings together loose and fragmented notions of genocide and a secret world for the haves, to get his listeners involved in the plot. Since most of us see ourselves as the have nots, not being able to afford the secret world, we embrace his rhetoric of fighting against the powers that be. Because Prince does not want to be associated with a particular group or organization, he uses various types of rhetoric from various movements and ideologies. This allows him to connect with the masses and keep his isolated identity and individuality. Instead of the conventional manner of joining a collective movement to fight this oppression, Prince strips down to his underwear and perms his hair to liberate himself. If the group is being oppressed, the individual seeks to defy any classification. He becomes the counter-culture of the counter-culture to wage war on the society. Yet, plotting Prince's rebellion proves trying, in the least. Prince, throughout his career, has not attempted in any formal way to articulate a theory for writing lyrics. At best, he has alluded to vague, varying theories regarding both his music and his lyrics. Part of this comes from his personal, cultural isolation, which causes him to make up the rules as he goes, and part of this has to do with Prince's artistic journey. He has not put forth any specific theory because he has not decided who he is or who he wants to be, other than an artist and a man of God. Prince has been too conflicted over his own dichotomy and/or dichotomies to settle on one artistic theory. He has spent his career publicly battling with himself and with the public over the boundaries of art, popular culture, his image, and the hermeneutic circle. "I dislike anything that's pure, *per se*, and can be categorized. I like to play everything. I'd rather do a combination of things than one anything...pure. I'm not happy with anything that categorizes me…" (Mitchell 1981). Thus, his notion, discussion, and contention of the circle have changed as his position within the circle has shifted, modified, and evolved. With the soul of a poet and the mind of a philosopher, both guided by a keen economic sensibility, Prince has spent his time "poetically philosophizing" on the questions of identity and evolution and how they both are influenced by economics. In a capitalistic society one is duped into believing that one needs capital or some sort of financial resources to embark on the journey toward evolution. As Prince jokingly asserts during the One Nite Alone tour, "Money won't make u happy, but it will pay for the search." Prince is attempting to do battle with all of this at once: the purpose of art and the place of money in our lives. How does one take care of one's spiritual needs and physical needs at the same time, especially when these needs seem to be in opposition to each other? Later in his career, Prince realizes and states in his song "2045 Radical Man" that "...the whole pop scenario is just nothin' but a dream (a bad dream)/ The day you will wake is the day you get the real cream." Often, learning oneself demands doing battle with the larger society. In his rejection of prescribed, arbitrary values, he has also rejected the notion that one must prescribe to one artistic theory. Still, this is not the problem in studying Prince's work.

My research is limited for two reasons: Prince's refusal to talk about the psychological and spiritual development of his work as it relates to some artistic theory in which his work may be contextualized and the failing of past journalists to ask these questions—especially in relation to his lyrics. This does not mean that there are not excellent articles, many which are quoted in this book, that have analyzed Prince's artistry, including his lyrics, but most focus more on him as a figure of pop culture rather than delve into theoretical literary analysis. Hill does a great job in his book, Barney Hoskyns provides an interesting analysis of physical image and imagery in his article "The Second Coming Thru Purple Haze," and Carol Cooper provides insightful analysis in her article "Someday Your Prince Will Come." But no one, it seems, has been interested enough to do long term career analysis of his lyrics. Artistic criticism is not simply an assertion of whether or not something pleases our subjective tastes. As Doris Lessing asserts, "Literature is not a horse race" (Christian xiv). Literary criticism is about seeing if a writer has written well, not about whether or not you like it. At its core, literary criticism addresses the writer's goal, whether or not the writer achieves that goal, what technique and strategy does the writer use to achieve that goal, and where does that writer exist in the history or tradition of other writers. This is why the essay is so important. (Though, in the poem "Black Art" Baraka proves that one can effectively articulate an artistic manifesto in a creative work.) The creative writer needs a manifesto to alert the reader of his intentions, giving us a guide by which to measure his work. Only then are we able to judge whether or not the artist has achieved his goal. Mostly we examine the writer's voice, "more precisely the one she's gotten on the page in comparison to the one she might have in her head" (Christian xv). And we do have evidence that Prince understands that the goal of the writer is to duplicate or achieve on paper what he has in his head. "I don't like to do things that are easy. It's more of a challenge for me to write exactly what I feel at that particular time. If I think a certain thought and I put it down on paper exactly like I hear it in my head, that's a challenge to me as a writer" (Sutherland 13, reprinted in Fudger 27). Then, after the work is on paper we investigate the distance between the ideal (the theory) and the writer's final product to see how well the writer accomplished the goal. This is literary criticism. However, since Prince has produced no specific literary or lyrical manifesto, we do not know his theoretical ideal, in any thorough manner. We know that he believes that "music... was put on the Earth to enlighten and empower us, and make us feel closer to our center" (♀, VH1 to One, 1997). Although this statement tells us the effect that he wants his work to have on the receiver, we still have no notion of how he intends to achieve the effect. We are forced to go directly to the art and work backwards.

Instead of studying Prince's work deductively, beginning with a general theory and seeing if his work achieves or satisfies this theory, we must begin inductively, looking at the artifacts of his work and summarizing a theory from that. We are forced to make conclusions solely on his work, such as "Alphabet Street." "We're going down 'cause that's the only way to make this cruel, cruel world hear what we got to say. Put the right letters together and make a better day." From this line we can infer that Prince understands that to get a message across, one has to be skilled in lyrical technique. "Put the right letters together." Find the proper way to say something. So, it is not just about what you say, but how you say it. Also, the "going down" is sexual. Prince understands that sex sells. He believes that it will allow him to sell salvation. Going down represents getting down to the level of the people he wants to reach. Sex is where they are, and it is what they understand. Let us exploit their desire for and obsession with sex to show them that there is more to life, more to existence. This same inference can be made with a song like "Hello" where he ends with a dialogue about words. "Isn't life cruel enough without cruel words? U see, words are like shoes. They're just something 2 stand on. But for u, words are definitely not shoes…your time is boring unless u are putting something down…Come now, isn't life a little better with a pair of good shoes?" Even in "Billy Jack Bitch" Prince is asserting that there is a certain level of decorum and diplomacy needed if we are to have a serious and meaningful discourse about whom we are and what we expect of each other. The question to journalists in "Billy Jack Bitch" is what have they achieved by attacking his person? If language is our tool of discourse and communication, how do we plan to evolve if we are tearing each other down? "What if ♛ called u silly names, just like the one's that u called me? What if ♛ filled your eyes with tears, so many that u could not see?…What if ♛ told u that u're worth only half of what u be? Would u come forth and tell no lies? Would u come forth and talk 2 me?" Though many consider these songs to be vague, at best, they represent a writer concerned with what he wants to say and how he wants to say it. The point is how do we use words and music to make the world a better place? No matter how vague or fragmented, these songs represent some notion of an artistic theory. Prince's artistic theory has been missed because most journalists have committed three fatal flaws when interviewing Prince: concentrating on the most titillating and sensationalized tales without doing the research to verify the truth or at least attempting to see how these tales relate to or connect to the creation of the work, failing to get Prince to discuss, specifically and thoroughly, his influences and how they affect his work, and failing to get Prince to elaborate or reconcile contradictory statements made by him about himself or his work.

If we look more closely, we would find that his statements were not necessarily contradictory but merely reflective of a young African American artist grappling with who he is, where he is going, and how his work is documenting his journey. For instance, initially Prince's aesthetic is not an aesthetic that is at war with the oppressive white culture. His aesthetic is one that initially attempts to merge and assimilate into the white culture. It does not willingly relinquish its Africanism, as such, but it will couple with the foreign aesthetic, in a symbiotic relationship to produce an even more foreign symbolism. As Lisa Coleman, keyboardist in the Revolution, asserts, Prince's genius is in combining the white guitar sound with the black bass sound. We should see these sounds as artifacts or representations of particular cultures and their sensibilities that Prince combines to create or reflect a new existence. Along with the sounds, Prince uses ambiguous or impressionistic imagery, which allows the listener to attach his own, subjective meaning to the artifact. His lofty ideas of man's transcendentalism are predicated on the masses' innate belief in the goodness of mankind or their desire to create their own fantasy world. Thus, the fantasy worlds provided by <u>Around the World in a Day</u> and <u>Parade</u> sell to millions partly because of the music and partly because there are enough people who desire to have or exist in these worlds. But after a few years of this, the message and technique falls on deaf ears because his listeners need a bit more culturally specific meat (artifact). He and his work become too much of a hybrid to mean anything to a mass of people living in a tangible world. "In a sense, the middle-class spirit could not take root among most Negroes because they sensed the final fantasy involved" (Jones/Baraka 142). What is ironic is that by the year 2000 Prince seems to be most comfortable in his African

American skin in what is his lowest commercial or economic point. Thus, the major problem with Prince is attempting to place him. Every artist must be placed within or contextualized within a tradition in order to be studied. The tradition is a tradition of era, form, and theme. An artist is not just praised for what he says but how well he says it. Critics call attention to how writers do what they do by calling "attention to the form, showing how it comes out of a history, a tradition, how the writer uses it...If we and others don't understand the form, that it is a form, we can't even hear what the writer is saying or how meaningful it is" (Christian xiii). My job, as the critic in this case, is to show that there is form, direction, and a well constructed message. What we first need to understand is that Prince's form is the form of amalgamation or quilting with no regard to anything but his message, and not the actual meanings of the artifacts that he is borrowing from some other time period. He is certainly not working with any lyrical, language, artifacts that are indigenous to his time. His lyrical technique is to use images and icons from the past and to refashion them for his own meanings.

Prince's work and career have been too erratic to be considered one anything. As he has grown by exposing himself to new sounds and ideas, he has seen it has his duty to share and expose his knowledge and growth with his audience, thereby making the art more important than his ability to sell records. Still, his seeming lack of form and his socio-political sensationalism stops the academic scholars from taking him seriously, and pop critics concentrate more on the persona than the work. The truth is that for a critic to champion an artist, that artist must champion something that is near and dear to that critic's heart. No artist has ever been championed merely for form. Prince, in his deliberate attempt to make himself a metaphysical icon and to create a world that exists specifically for him, has rubbed too many important people the wrong way. Most critics do to Prince what Sainte-Beuve did to Baudelaire, merely write the artist off as being too contrived and confusing for not adhering to traditional forms. "Sainte-Beuve provided a means of escape from the problems of the poet's genius: [which he saw as] unconnected with the main tradition of French poetic literature" (Quennell 8). Like Baudelaire, when it comes to Prince's work, critics "tended to emphasize a single aspect of his protean temperament, to depict him as an amateur of esoteric vices and dark unlawful passions [concentrating more on his] streak of sensationalism" (Quennell 8, 9). There is, however, evidence of both musical and lyrical form, but both are driven by Prince's quite subjective views of the world that seem to alienate listeners and critics. Still, as Luis Hidalgo indicates, "Prince has created his own unique style...an incomparable way of making music, a style you can distinguish by the second verse" (Hidalgo 1994).

Just as there is a Motown sound, a Philadelphia sound, a Memphis sound, a Brown sound, a Wonder sound, a Hendrix sound, and a Funkadelic sound, there is a Prince sound, which also became known as the Minneapolis sound. All of these sounds carry distinct ideologies because they are connected to distinct cultural, geographic, and historical realities. What Prince learned from the past is that you must find a way to set yourself apart to be noticed. This desire to create something different manifests itself within his lyrics, as Prince becomes known as one of the most risqué or daring lyricists of his time. His goal was to make sex its own religion, and from this would flow hidden truths of human nature. To do this he becomes a master of the vivid image and the extended metaphor. His images evoke as much imagination as they provide explicit pictures. Prince's lyricism is as much a strip tease as his stage dancing. The ambiguity of his images gives, at least, the illusion that there is always something under the covers. In "I Wanna Be Your Lover," the lines are so ambiguous and blurred that Prince simultaneously appears as a sacrificial lamb and a wolf. As Miles Davis asserts, Prince can be "a pimp and a bitch all wrapped up in one image..."

(Davis 385). "I wanna be your mother...sister...brother..." He then completes his passive seduction with "I wanna be the only one you come for." The ambiguity of this line allows Prince to exist as a duality in the minds of millions. This is then troped in "If I Was Your Girlfriend" with "...would u come 2 me if somebody hurt u, even if that somebody was me. Sometimes I trip on how happy would could be." He is feminine enough to understand the female and masculine enough to please her. By becoming this duality, he is giving himself the ability to fluctuate as he sees fit. Accordingly, he used these attributes to create alternative worlds for those seeking something other than the norm. Prince recreates himself, which allows him to recreate the world, and we must see this as a part of his theoretical form or approach.

To create this alternate world, Prince's poetic form is two fold. First, he attempts to build upon the irregular, the absurd, and the exaggerated, making the familiar unfamiliar so that we can see the world anew. In a song like "Sister," the male child is molested by his older sister. By turning the traditional tables, Prince is causing us to see molestation with new eyes. Yet, by performing this song in the first person, this imagery also serves to liquefy or lessen his maleness, giving him the androgynous persona that he desires and needs to become a rock icon. Next, he crafts songs as dreams of what humanity wishes it could be. Songs become fantasies for escapism or to point listeners in the direction of their potential. Songs, such as "Uptown" and "1999," are built on fantasy and hallucination to create the world that Prince wants. The problem in studying this is not being able to show, theoretically, how Prince's fantasy world correlates with the "real" world (whatever that is in all of its subjective meanings). The problem is heightened by Prince's theoretical muteness and the manner in which he freely amalgamates both musical and poetic styles. If an artist sees himself as homeless, he often sees himself as without a definite culture. "Prince has never had a culture. A mix of races, he belongs to none.

No role to play, no goal to stalk" (Hoskyns 19).

When critics like Hoskyns believe Prince's mulatto myth, it widens Prince's possibilities and weakens his boundaries. And though Prince may not have been a physical mulatto, he certainly saw himself as an ideological mulatto. When one does not perceive oneself as having a definite culture, the artist becomes an excellent quilt maker because he is not limited or restricted by notions of what he is or what he can not be. If there are no critics who share that same view of the world, then the legacy of the artist's work will fade from our collective memories. The reason Prince's legacy is fading is because his work has not resonated or related to the worlds and concerns of the critics in power. Thus, few, if any, have been willing to show how Prince's work and career parallels with the African American struggle in this country. Because of this, few have been willing to acknowledge Prince's lyrical and musical influence on the nineties and beyond. And finally, Prince's fading presence is generational. Unlike literature, the major pop music messages cater to the tastes of young customers, ages twelve to twenty-five. Thus, most journalist who came of age with Prince and championed him twenty-five years ago have been replaced by younger journalists or are forced to cover new artists to keep the magazine for which they write current. Since people over thirty tend not to purchase pop music magazines, there is no incentive for these journals to focus on Prince's work and growth. And given the fact that he has alienated or snubbed so many writers/editors in power by following his own vision, their revenge is simply to ignore him. In a 2001 article for the Pioneer Press, Jim Walsh, who also wrote the "Liner Notes" for The Gold Experience, expressed to Prince his personal "need for [Prince] to be a big star again, to reclaim his throne and to kick all the bad music off the airwaves." To Walsh's dismay "[Prince] couldn't have cared less about my version of success, or what I thought the world needed from him. He said, 'I've been to the top of the mountain, and there was nothing there'" (Walsh 2001).

Prince's desire is to fulfill his own, personal journey of success, which is more spiritual and cultural than most critics would have bet thirty years ago. His desire to find or construct a home mirrors the Africans' "dream to return home, a psychological shadow cast by the light of the past" (Finn 6). By most accounts we know that Prince was heavily exposed to Christianity, the black church, and the strip joints where his father played. What we find is a young man trying to make sense of and amalgamate these elements. Though he initially rebelled against what he perceived as the oppressive, dogmatic version of Christianity, he understood two important factors: the body is not the natural home of the soul, but it is the vehicle through which the soul can manifest its emotions and thoughts. The soul, in Prince's music, is looking for its way back to its higher self and spends its time attempting to find this through the body. As he matures, he realizes that the body is merely a temporary and limited condition and begins to look elsewhere for his soul's home. The soul is oppressed and suppressed by the body and its physical world. Because man does not understand this struggle—is afraid of this struggle—he creates arbitrary rules to ensure social order. The soul, by its very need to evolve, rejects the limiting regulations placed on it by the physical world, just as the curve of the black body defies the regulation of the straight white line—just as black sensuality defies white hypocrisy and shame. Prince is showing how the soul's struggle with the body parallels the African American struggle of being housed in a land that is not his home, trying first to assimilate and later to build a separate nation, mostly fluctuating between these two ideals as Prince fluctuates between the body and the soul. Even in his use of European styles and structures, his quilting of those styles and structures is what makes him uniquely African American. Just as Finn asserts that "blacks wed their gods with those of Christianity," Prince was wedding his desires with the traditional imagery of popular and Christian music. His reason for doing this is two fold: to create the world that he wants and to sell records. By building on what people know and understand, it is easier for him to sell his messages. His reconfiguring of Christianity, consciously attempting to make it his own religion, parallels the African modification of Christianity. "Each of the new religions adapted itself to the particular circumstances of the country in which it had to survive. In the United States, Hoodoo, cousin of Voodoo, produced a stepchild called the blues" (Finn 6). Prince's creation of his own, unique sound, persona, and theology directly relates to his desire to survive, making him the typical African American.

    Rather than settling on one theory, Prince has settled on one belief: the purpose of art is to improve the condition of humanity, and the artist is to use whatever means that are at his disposal to achieve his goal. As for the specific techniques, he has changed the design as often as he has changed direction, which makes him postmodernist. His theory is a gumbo of styles and techniques connected only in their ability to articulate what he wants to say at any particular time. Still, he has allowed listeners to join him on his journey, hoping that his search will inspire his listeners to journey themselves. Rather than seeing his work as a definite theory, he wants his work to be more of a reference point or a catalyst, causing a catharsis in the listener, which will cause the listener to embark upon his own journey. Three examples of what Prince tries to do, theoretically, are Baudelaire, Rimbaud, and Friedrich Nietzsche. All are concerned with finding a balance between the dichotomy of the physical and metaphysical elements of life. More specifically, they all view art as the science of how we give form to the spirit world. Nietzsche asserted this by quoting Sixteenth Century poet and playwright Hans Sachs, "All poetry we ever read is but true dreams interpreted" (Adams 629). As writers and philosophers, Baudelaire, Rimbaud, and Nietzsche are mostly concerned with how language is the "thing" that connects and articulates the relationship between the physical world and the spiritual world. Our art represents man's struggle to reconcile his dual nature as a physical and spiritual being. The tension or conflict in art is man's tension within himself to balance all of his seemingly opposing forces. As an African American, Prince exemplifies this duality as African Americans continue to struggle with their innate duality of being Africans dislocated in America and being souls dislocated in the physical world, struggling to reconcile the two to the other. It is this struggle that produces the art. Nietzsche asserts "…art owes its continuous evolution to the Apollonian-Dionysiac duality" (Adams 629). In turn, Rimbaud wishes us to journey through this duality, rising or transcending above it. If need be, art for Rimbaud would be used to shock us into the reality that there exists more than our mere physical world. Once we reconcile this, we are closer to reconciling our duality.

Art, for Rimbaud and Prince, represents the ideal and our struggle to achieve the ideal. Thus, man wishes to reach perfection thereby becoming a work of art. Like Nietzsche, Prince wanted "his [listener] to undertake a quest" with him (Kreis 2000). These two theories can be plotted: the duty of the poet to shock the people into consciousness and the duty of art to uplift man, causing man to perceive and achieve his higher self and purpose for being. In both cases, there is the notion that the purpose of art is to reveal truth to man. The strategy to achieve this truth is two fold: create the most extended and exaggerated image or metaphor possible and show society its hypocrisy by juxtaposing its rhetoric with its practice. In all things, force society to face its hypocrisy so that it can evolve.

> "My goal is to excite and provoke on every level" (Hilburn, "The Renegade Prince," P1). "…radio or no radio, we're just gonna keep playing until enough people hear us, that's all. I don't' care if it sells so much as I want people to understand it, to give them a chance to see and hear it…a lotta people didn't even know the songs, you could tell 'cause they

weren't singing along, but we had their attention. They never turned away. That means more to me than them running out and buying. I just want them to listen, that's all" (Schwartz 1981).

Prince, through his rebellion against prescribed gender, race, and language rules, was attempting to make society face its hypocrisy or at least be more aware of the fact that our societal rules/rituals are, at best, arbitrary and limiting to human evolution. And it is the use of shock in Prince's work that creates the tension of love and lust, the battle between the physical and metaphysical, the carnal and the spiritual. Motown's poetry is being molested by the lustful objectification of black sensuality by white record labels. This is the tension of economics verses art and the struggle to make black art palatable to white listeners. Prince was able to raise this battle between art and economics to an art form. Thus, he must be remembered for his ability to produce creative works by walking the lines that divide the sacred from the profane or the subtle from the sensational. Like Rimbaud, Baudelaire, and Nietzsche, Prince finds a balance that allows him to put his finger on the axle of our innate human contradiction and turn or manipulate this axle as he wishes or needs.

> "Yet, when the reckoning is finally calculated, [the poet] emerges with a formidable credit-balance of brilliant observations, which reveal not only his feeling for art and his knowledge of the artist's task, but his profound understanding of the social world about him" (Quennell 11).

In Prince's music there is the constant clash of his Utopian world and the physical world as in "Tamborine" and "Around the World in a Day." "Tamborine what are u? Why are u the star of all my dreams? Are u good, are u bad? Are u just unnecessary means...2 bad we're not allowed 2 scream." In "Tamborine" Prince is both embracing the fantasy and questioning the role of fantasy.

"Guess that I'll stay at home all alone and play my tamborine." The protagonist is becoming completely separated from the outside or real world, and Prince who has constructed this fantasy world for us is also asserting that we cannot or should not lose complete connection with the real world. The protagonist is not completely satisfied by his fantasy because he is alone, and his dissatisfaction is articulated by the "awww" of dejection. Yet in contrast, "Around the World in a Day" is questioning our desire to stay in a world with no dreams—with no hopes or pathways to evolution. "Loneliness already knows u. There ain't no reason 2 stay. Take my hand; I'll show u 2 places within your mind. The former is red white and blue; the ladder is purple, climb, climb." In "Around the World in a Day" we notice that the dream is anchored with the artifacts of reality, such as the American colors. The fantasy world always has to be reconciled to the real world in order for the dream of Utopia to make sense and to be perceived by the receiver as obtainable.

> "We see the same clash between real and imaginary worlds: the propensity to dream and a hankering to escape from life...are again counterbalanced by the puritanical devotion to the task that he had set himself...but his visions were derived from his contemplation of the actual world, and his reveries centered around some concrete object" (Quennell 12-13).

For Prince, the concrete because of mankind's historical failures is the lacking physical world, which must be enhanced by dreams of a better place to be. These dreams are supposed to compel us to evolve—to seek our destiny as human beings. For those who say that Prince is too metaphysical or overly concerned with fantasy, Willie gives us another way of looking at it. Willie asserts that Prince writes songs about life; he just writes about what he wishes that life was or was not—in both cases seeking to create a Utopia. "Prince is an excellent study of popular culture and the way that all cultures manifest themselves in popular art. Popular culture represents our desires, the way that we would like for life to be. Many of us may not like the pictures that he paints, but he was reflecting society's misguided desire" (Willie 2000).

What Prince has manifested more than anything is our desire to escape our hellish reality by embracing our subjective fantasy worlds. Prince, through his lyrics, his music, his clothing, and his behavior, is saying that we can be anything that we want to be, allowing us to completely ignore, if we chose to do so, the larger society's notion of who we are or what reality is. Yet, this creation of a fantasy world runs counter to the tradition of African American art because traditionally black art is compelled to concentrate on the reality of what is. Even most African American science-fiction is compelled to begin in the bowels of oppression in some form. Prince leap frogs over what is and projects what he wants life to be. And because he does so unapologetically, using images, styles, and techniques according to his own vision and whim, Prince's work lends itself to "contradictory interpretations and appreciations... [Since] the mystery [of his work] far exceeds the actual language of the writings, no single solution and no single system explains his work...[Thus, the critic has to] reject the temptation to elucidate [the work] by means of one theory, to reduce his work to a willful unification" (Kreis 2000). I will instead show that Prince's work, like Rimbaud's, is more of an amalgamation of theories, and, like Baudelaire, Rimbaud, and Nietzsche, this works for Prince because he is attempting to reconcile our innate opposing forces. Prince's works "are the writings of the same poet but they reflect different moments and intensities and preoccupations of his character" (Fowlie 15). In understanding this, we realize two facts. First, Prince's work often holds too many contradictory assertions to be housed under one theory. Second, these contradictions are, however, the representations of a man's struggle to come to terms with the world as he understands it and to sell records while doing so. Along with getting at the truth, another primary drive, which is also influencing the art, is Prince's desire to be a pop icon, which often causes the art, in a scientific sense, to take a back seat to sensationalized symbolism—that is, symbolism for the sake of symbolism and not symbolism use to create, support, or lead the reader to a particular meaning or central issue. Thus, we find in Prince's work symbols that are meant to be nothing more than entertaining, and this causes problems when we are looking to theorize his work.

> "[Prince] explains why he started the ["Raspberry Beret" video] with a prolonged clearing of the throat. 'I just did it to be sick, to do something no one else would do.' He pauses and contemplates. 'I turned on MTV to see the premiere of 'Raspberry Beret,' and Mark Goodman [former MTV vj] was talking to the guy who discovered the backward message on 'Darling Nikki.' They were trying to figure out what the cough meant too, and it was sort of funny.' He pauses again. 'But I'm not getting down on him for trying. I like that. I've always had little hidden messages and I always will'" (Karlen, "Prince Talks: The Silence Is Broken," 28).

The driving factors behind Prince's work are the desire to be what has never been, to do what has never been done, and to get paid doing it. This is because popular art is as much about units sold as it is about theory and form. We have separated popular notoriety and critical notoriety. Prince's desire to be a pop icon often supersedes if not completely directs the art, so much so that it becomes a theory of pop iconography. To achieve this, Prince draws from the bohemian notion of symbolism—the use of unconventional and irregular styles, forms, and icons to develop an air or atmosphere, an impressionistic style of an artist struggling to provide meaning to life as well as to himself. Like Rimbaud, Prince sought to surround himself with "strange" and "isolated" artists. The goal is to be different, regardless of whether or not that difference has any purpose other than being different. In many cases, it simply means that the poet's job is to provide an alternative to the traditional or normal way of thinking or living by highlighting the Apollonian-Dionysiac forces in our lives. Prince affirms this notion:

> "Sickness is just slang for doing things somebody else wouldn't do...That's what I'm looking for all the time. We don't look for whether something's cool or not, that's not what time it is. It's not just wanting to be out. It's just if I do something that I think belongs to someone else or sounds like someone else, I do something else" (Karlen, "Prince Talks: The Silence Is Broken," 84).

Being different, which often means being extreme, is the job of the artist. It is this difference or this extremity that will shock the mainstream into the recognition of some truth. Prince further elaborates on this in a later interview. In this notion, Prince has always seen his work as an alternative to the mainstream. "Paisley Park is an alternative, not better or worse, just an alternative. That's all" (Prince, MTV Presents Prince, 1985). This alternative way of thinking is essential if humanity is going to evolve. This is one of the poet's contributions to the evolution of mankind, providing us with a different or alternative way of seeing life, even if the way is not thoroughly or completely articulated.

To create this alternative world, Prince, like Rimbaud, surrounded himself with a society of outcasts who lived by unconventional and irregular patterns, wishing to ignore and defy the arbitrary and oppressive boundaries of the physical world: race, gender, and class. These boundaries of the physical world were seen as walls stopping humanity's spiritual evolution. Prince was making himself a cult leader; Paisley Park was a trope for inner peace and a religious ideology with him as Moses. In doing this, Prince would be able to have the same affect on popular culture as Rimbaud had on the French symbolists, who admired Rimbaud more for his persona than his work. Just as the French symbolists see

Rimbaud "as a liberator of the imagination," many, such as Lenny Kravitz, Terence Trent D'Arby, Me'Shell NdegeOcello, Alisha Keys, and Andre 3000, see Prince as a liberator of the imaginative possibility in popular music, especially the possibilities open to African American pop musicians. Prince is the bridge for them to the idealism of Hendrix and Stone. Prince represents for his Paisley followers that Hendrix and Sly were not merely happenstance of fleeting Utopia or the sublime. Prince's longevity makes the idealism of Hendrix and Sly seem attainable. In Prince they see the possibility that if you are willing to face the rejection and isolation, you can construct your own world based on your ability to amalgamate history. Through his work, Prince is able to create the "seizure of his own reality." (Fowlie 18). In this, Prince achieves the role of poet-visionary, showing or pointing the way to our Utopian selves as in <u>Dirty Mind</u>, <u>Around the World in a Day</u>, <u>Parade</u>, <u>Lovesexy</u>, and <u>Emancipation</u>. To achieve this, Prince's technical goal becomes the

> "effacement of the ordinary pictures of the world. The [receiver] is immediately disorientated because the first images he sees are…all that are necessary to prove to us that we are lost in another world where we will have to revise our usual powers of sight and mind" (Fowlie 18-19).

Prince's career has been rooted in creating his new world by disorienting our current world as in "Paisley Park."

> "There is a park that is known 4 the face it attracts. Colorful people whose hair on 1 side is swept back. The smile on their faces, it speaks of profound inner peace. Ask where they're going; they'll tell U nowhere. They've taken a lifetime lease…The girl on the seesaw is laughing 4 love is the color this place imparts. Admission is easy; just say U Believe and come…"

He is able to disorient us with the fragmented images in "Play in the Sunshine."

> "We wanna play in the sunshine; We wanna be free without the help of a Margarita or Ecstasy…Turn all the lights up 2 10…We gonna love all our enemies till the gorilla falls off the wall…When the big white rabbit begin 2 talk, and the color green will make your best friends leave ya; it will make them do the walk"

And, the entire <u>The Rainbow Children</u> album is designed to disorient us, which can be seen in "Deconstruction."

> One after the other, the Banished Ones fled as they watched from the distance the destruction of the Digital Garden. With no more fruit 2 bear from its trees, the Haze was finally broken. With the rains came the awareness that NEVER AGAIN WOULD ANYONE EVER LAY CLAIM 2 THE TREASURES OF THE RAINBOW CHILDREN! As though awakened from a dream, the Muse opened her eyes…..this time as Queen.

Throughout his career Prince has used imagery to symbolize ideas as a way to reconfigure how his listeners see the world. The "Mountains" represent life's challenges. "Starfish and Coffee" and all of the images therein represent individuality and the intolerance created by miscommunication and mis-education. Thunder and electricity have become reoccurring metaphors for the power of God. And the parade represents the parade of life or people on this Earth who come and go throughout of our lives, bringing and adding different dynamics. His symbolism is his greatest asset, which is his ability to paint pictures that effectively articulate the essence and significance of our existence through his personification of ideas: "Love—nobody kno' just how it was born. Love's kiss was running all through my veins. Love say take my hand it'll be alright." Prince has been able to express many emotions through personification. Inner peace is an amusement park. Love is a color and a deity, and "Temptation reigns (like a king)." And sex has existed in Prince's lyrics as it has existed in man's life, taking many forms and filling many empty spaces. Evil and Good become dueling women. Annie Christian is Satan, and Anna Stesia is the love of God. Both are battling for the souls of man. These personifications draw the listener into the plot of the songs, making the messages more accessible. And the symbols become more accessible as Prince mixes and matches them for his need, creating an ambiguity that is, as with any poet, one of the keys to Prince's prowess. His ability to reconfigure the meaning of words, such as "cum," provides infinite meanings to lines and songs. Electricity has shifted from meaning sexual passion to the love of God flowing through the body. The song "Kiss" exists as a simplistic pleasure or a definition of love. "Little Red Corvette" is a tale glorifying sexual promiscuity and a warning of the extremes. Prince creates the imagery, dialogue, and metaphor "to hurl us into the centre of chaos, to liberate us from the ordinary patterns of thought" (Fowlie 19).

Prince knows that the bulk of his listeners are moved by the mere use of symbolism and not necessarily what the symbolism means. Thus, he turns impressionism on its head. He uses a type of symbolic impressionism where he invokes a variety of images and symbols that do not quite relate to each other in any strict adherence to meaning. For instance, the naming of the female protagonist in <u>Purple Rain</u> as Apollonia is meant to invoke ideals behind Apollo and St. Apollonia. There is no definite or precise assertion or articulation of what the female in <u>Purple Rain</u> represents, but her name lends weight to the mystery and symbolism. For those who have never heard of Apollo or St. Apollonia, the name, Apollonia, is weird, which works as another vague symbol, inspiring the question "What the hell kinda name is Apollonia? What does that mean?" Even the first couple of times she introduces herself, there are looks that suggest a questioning of her name. If nothing else, it shows that Prince is versed, even if mildly, in semiotics, knowing enough to manipulate traditional semantics for his own purposes and for the creation of his own world. Prince, then, is a dandy in his musical and lyrical attitude as well as in his dress and behavior by resisting the imposing of a definition on himself by the outside world.

> "...to this extent the artist resembles the dandy, [which is] another type of self-constituted rebel and self-ennobled aristocrat, [who is] in revolt against the pattern that vulgar commercial civilization is always seeking to impose on him, [He is] a representative of 'the best element in human pride—that need, which nowadays is too uncommon, to combat and destroy triviality'" (Quennell 16).

Prince's dandyism grows from the desire to create one's own world, to make a canvass of oneself. All artists are, in some manner, dandies because they desire "leisure" time to create something, hopefully a new world. The dandy does not want money or leisure for the sake of having money and leisure, but for the sake of creating their fantasy world through the expression of their personalities. A dandy makes himself the painting or the poem to articulate his originality or personality. He becomes the world he wishes to create. The afro, the dashiki, the black beret are accessories, manifestations, of the world that the rebel wants to create. When Baraka urges that he wants the world to be a "Black Poem," the style of dress of those involved in the Black Arts Movement represented a type of dandyism, a desire to remake the world that had been oppressing them in whiteness. Accordingly, Prince became the hybrid, the leader of the multiracial, multi-gender world that he wished to create. Dandyism is a natural part, an extension, of anyone who wishes to make a statement about the world against which they wish to rebel.

> "They have no other purpose than to cultivate the idea of the beautiful in their own persons; to satisfy their desires, and to feel and think...Dandyism is not even, as

many unthinking people seem to suppose, an immoderate interest in personal appearance and material elegance. For the true dandy theses things are only a symbol of the aristocratic superiority of his personality...It is, above all, a burning need to acquire originality, within the apparent bounds of convention" (Baudelaire 55, 56).

As dandies, Baudelaire and Rimbaud are moving the importance of art from absolute beauty to subjective beauty. A philosopher is on a journey to absolute and objective truth. A poet is on a journey to an interpretive and subjective truth. This is not, however, a complete contradiction when we realize that the philosopher's truth can only be found when we have explored, validated, and/or refuted all of the subjective, individual truths. Additionally, we must realize that philosophical truth is not the same as scientific or empirical fact. The philosopher will use the empirical process to know truth, but even the philosopher's truth, like the poet's truth, is more concerned with the meaning of the facts or what the facts reveal to or about us than just with knowing the facts. As a poet and a philosopher, Prince is attempting to know the world and make meaning of the world, which means to investigate subjective truth to know objective truth. For instance, in "Condition of the Heart," Prince is trying to show the absolute truth of a life without love, or that each life needs love to be complete. To do this, he studies and shows us three different characters and their subjective realities and truths to get us to understand a more objective or absolute truth. Though Prince presents us with three different beings with their own subjective understanding of the world, he arrives at an objective truth. We learn, if nothing else, that we all have a desire for love, and we all suffer a deep empty feeling when we do not have love.

In "Condition of the Heart" we are led to believe that Prince is focusing on the subjective realities of three different characters: "a girl in Paris," "a dame from London," and "a woman from the ghetto." As we listen to the different stories we realize that Prince's commentary is that all people suffer from a condition of heart, all people struggle to know and gain love. An objective analysis of subjective or individual circumstances reveals that we, as humans, are all the same. In this song, we find the objective by juxtaposing the varying subjective experiences until we uncover the link that binds us. In this case, it is the need for love. Yet, when we look closer, we realize that the song is not about those three characters, but about a protagonist whom we only know as "a lonely musician." It is through this musician's life and his encounters with the other three characters that we are made to realize the subjective nature of life because each relationship is unique. The only constant is the musician's search for love. In this twist, we see that the musician's life, like the dandy's life, is the poem. His encounters with the three women are how he makes meaning of his life. Each female represents a stanza in a poem. When we connect the three women, the three experiences, we have a poem because they combine like pieces to a puzzle to make meaning of life. In either interpretation of the song, we understand how important the subjective is to facilitating us to the objective. Thus, the artist must study the subjective, in himself and in his objects, so that he is able to uncover the objective and the absolute. Our struggle to find completion through love is not about us struggling with each other, but about us struggling with ourselves.

The dandy represents the height of this internal search/study. We, as a society, are not able to find this absolute notion of love because most of us do not have a very well defined notion of ourselves or of love. Prince's struggle with womankind is not built on the traditional model that men and women are innately different. He does not succumb to the belief that there will always exist these innate walls keeping them from connecting fully. In fact, his approach to the communication gap between men and women is just the opposite. Prince believes that men and women are, fundamentally, souls trapped in a body. It is the being trapped in a body that causes the conflict, not the body, itself. Thus, Prince begins with the soul as a point of reference or identification, not the body, making personalities and individual perceptions the focal point of bridging the gap between men and women. Because men and women struggle internally to define themselves, they seek to impose meaning upon others as a tool or technique to define themselves. Yet, what makes this struggle more complex is that human perception is clouded by the physicality of the body rather than being centered on the essence of human character. Although part of humanity's problem is the arbitrary manner in which we define and categorize others so that we may feel safe, this is merely a manifestation of an internal struggle. Put another way, if I am secure and comfortable with myself, I tend not to have a need to define you.

Prince's romantic struggles exist within men and women who are struggling as individuals with their own personal duality. It is this personal, individual struggle which causes struggle within the relationship. "If I Was Your Girlfriend" is forcing us to deal with the dichotomy of ourselves and how our individual dichotomy causes conflict when we attempt to couple. "If I was your girlfriend, would you remember to tell me all of the things you forgot when I was your man." In the song there is the assertion that because men and women are trained to communicate as genders (which for Prince is based on an arbitrary and flawed notion of what we are) and not as souls/personalities, then humanity can never evolve because the male-female relationship is arrested by flawed definitions. Because we do not know who or what we are as individuals, we can never build successful or effective relationships. The pain of love is the pain of struggling to love oneself while struggling to love others at the same time. At the center of this is humanity's struggle to bridge the gap of the physical and the metaphysical and equally enjoy and exist within these concepts simultaneously. Prince manipulates this conflict as a way to tantalize his listeners and simultaneously have the discussion. Prince, himself, does not have any issues with the harmonious co-existence of the sensual and the spiritual and the male and the female in one body. But, he understands that the majority of America has a problem with it, knowing that in most "there existed in [the] mind a gulf, which could be rarely bridged, between sensual and spiritual love" (Quennell

19). This desire to define ourselves and others is tied to our anxiety to survive by controlling our surroundings. Often this means creating a notion of normality that serves to limit and confine rather than to inspire creativity, individuality, and evolution. Prince is examining our desire for self-definition, which has caused us to create a world where being normal has become so narrowed and cemented that normality is more of a political or class-status concept than a human concept. His goal is to destroy this narrow and finite definition of normality by formulating or finding, it does not matter which, some liquid or elastic notion of man that will allow us to love ourselves and others—becoming more accepting of our innate individualities. In making himself a hybrid, he is hoping to connect and communicate with all of mankind in its most allegorical state—the soul. He wants to show that, at our deepest selves, we are all the same or at least have the same desires and needs. Thus, he chooses an impressionistic style which he hopes will be inclusive of souls and exclusive of the arbitrary physical definitions. "Poetry is opposed to definition because it is born in the most ineffable part of human experience. It is always just beyond language" (Fowlie 19). This is what Prince wants more than anything, to express the inexpressible, to show that we are truly spiritual beings trapped in a physical world that yields no true medium for complete expression or evolution. The true gray area and conundrum of life is that our bodies keep our souls from fully experiencing and communicating with other souls and with life, itself. This is why he asserts "Sometimes I trip on how happy we could be." For Prince it is ridiculous or ludicrous that we are unable to see each other as souls and not as bodies. For him, the fact that we are not able to bridge the gap of the body, of the physical, is a "trip," is preposterous, is a damn shame. And this is inline with the notion of there being an afterworld where souls will be free of the body to know fully life and love. So Prince becomes a dandy as a way to use every available resource to break our physical limitations, which then exposes the importance of the soul to the body.

Many critics, including Allen Leeds, cite the release of "If I Was Your Girlfriend" as a major cause in slowing the momentum of <u>Sign '☮' the Times</u>. Though Prince is being creative, many "listeners misunderstood what the record was about" (Leeds 10). In this case, Prince's very subjective imagery clashed with the mainstream's understanding of imagery, especially in regards to strict male and female definitions. Because of Prince's feminine look, many listeners took the title literally and were not willing to trust Prince's wit and artistry and assume that the title was wordplay or a metaphor with a deeper meaning. Up to that point, Prince had been able to navigate the sexual identity line, but for many he had finally crossed it. Rather than see the title in symbolic terms, many thought that Prince was coming out of the closet about homosexuality, and were turned away from the entire album. Interestingly enough, when the girl group TLC covered the song in 1994, they chose to keep the title the same, which means that they chose to concentrate on the more traditional aspects of the male-female relationship and not deal with the song's notion of breaking through to the metaphysical, probably fearing the same backlash that Prince suffered. In all art forms, the clash of objectivity and subjectivity is inevitable because the artist is always using some form to articulate his personal meaning or perception of what the world is or should be. The clash has remained because we are unable to conquer the innate subjectivity of poetry and the problem of literary criticism as cultural warfare. That is—literary criticism has not been a tool for the objective, scientific study of literature, but a tool used by the elite as a way to marginalize and oppress the lower class. Since popular art is usually an expression of the lower economic class, it tends to reject the mainstream form of the ruling class, usually by modifying it, which is seen as a perversion by the upper class. The rejection of a particular form is the rejection of a particular culture. One may reject the sonnet because the language cadence is either foreign or in opposition to one's own language cadence. The reconfiguring of a form is an attempt by the oppressed class to take the only art that is accessible to them and use it to give meaning to their particular existence. This is the essence of jazz and the tradition of African American literature. Prince builds upon this by combining forms at his own will. However, he is making meaning for himself, not the collective. He begins in the individual, in the novel, and stays there.

> "Each poet reaches in himself some private part, some extraordinary domain, by ways that are open only to him. These are not the ways opened to all other men of his period: those of culture, traditions, poetic techniques, rules and literary movements" (Fowlie 19).

This is Prince's revolt. Instead of moving toward the mainstream, his goal is to shock the mainstream from their comfort zone and move them closer to him. "I sang about what the kids were into…sex and drugs…The [ruling] community didn't want to hear about that. They wanted to hear about flowers and trees and how wonderful life would be if you were with me" (Mitchell 1981). Sometimes he succeeds in his mission to shock the mainstream into a new understanding or realization, and sometimes he fails. Yet, what is really interesting is that by 1996, nine years after it was released, "If I Was Your Girlfriend" had become a concert favorite, as evidenced by the rousing response it received throughout the Emancipation tour as well as when he performed it on The Oprah Winfrey Show. In this regard, Prince was, once again, proven to be right in his artistic sense if not in his commercial sense.

The problem with Prince is that instead of seeking to bridge the gap between intuitive subjectivity and collective objectivity, he prefers that his work, his techniques, stay in the subjective, stay in his world. He does not attempt to appease the exterior world; he merely allows the listener a pathway into his internal world by discussing subjects that a large audience can understand, usually sex. The trick is what he does with his discussion of sex and sexuality. The listener comes seeking a tale of sexual/physical gratification and gets a discourse on the politics of the body. In a pop song with the title "Sexuality," the average listener is sure that the song will be some explicit tale of sexual adventure, especially when the song is delivered by a man singing in his underwear. However, Prince tricks us and gives the listener a song that asserts sexuality as a tool for political discussion and revolt. "Stand up, everybody; this is your life...I'm talkin' 'bout a revolution; we gotta organize. We don't need no segregation; we don't need no race. New age revelation, I think we gotta case." His revolt is heightened with his attitude, which asserts that if you do not want to come, you do not have to come. Thus, the tension between Prince and the mainstream gatekeepers of the canon is that he has achieved wide-world fame even though he has paid more attention to his own desires and perceptions than to those of the accountants who run the recording companies.

> "I saw critics be so critical of Stevie Wonder when he made Journey through the Secret Life of Plants. Stevie has done so many great songs, and for people to say 'You missed, don't do that, go back'—well, I would never say 'Stevie Wonder, you missed,' Or Miles. Critics are going to say 'Ah, Miles done went off.' Why say that? Why even tell Miles he went off? You know, if you don't like it, don't talk about it. Go buy another record!" (Karlen, "Prince Talks: The Silence Is Broken," 30-31).

For Prince, especially early in his career, his notion was that the artist is on a particular journey, and if the receiver finds something that he likes or can use, then feel free to partake. But, the receiver does not have the right to demand that the artist bend his personal, subjective journey and perception to fit the need of the receiver. Years later he continues to assert, "It's our journey. If we continue working, we all continue growing, we all continue evolving. It's no one else's place to judge" (♀, VH1 to One, 1997).

These types of statements cause Prince to alienate the very critics that can explain or articulate his messages to a wider audience and help him transcend pop artistry to be canonized in a way that he is seen as significant to the evolution of humanity. Prince is seen as not wanting to strike a balance with the critics, as wanting to be worshiped as an artistic gift from God with no objective critique that may assess his work as lacking or sub par. But rather than wanting to be worshiped as an omnipotent gift from God, Prince is asserting that instead of wasting time disparaging someone's art the critic should spend that time more constructively by discussing art that he does see as well-constructed and beneficial to humanity. Of course, the critic's argument is that objective critique is what inspires the artist to improve, causing poor art to become good art and good art to become great art. However, Prince sees art or artistic taste so innately subjective that it will be impossible to come to an empirical agreement as to what constitutes good and bad art, which is, unfortunately, the central issue of most critics. For Prince, the artist's subjective form and view of the world is needed to provide the masses a varying or alternate way of seeing, conceiving, and conceptualizing the world. As Aristotle asserted, there is not one reality but several realities, and the poet does not copy life but completes reality by assigning meaning to our various realities. Prince is seeking to show that we are all innately subjective individuals who have a divine right to express and explore our subjectivity as long as our search does not inhibit another. If we are given enough meanings/perceptions/realities, we will have a better chance at truly defining our world.

In his allusiveness, Prince demonstrates Nietzsche's notion that "no one truth reveals the entire truth" (Kreis 2000). In subject-matter, form, and style, Prince, like Nietzsche, "does not belong to any well-defined movement. His mind and method of reflection defines his position as solitary, profound, and unique..." (Kreis 2000). He is allusive because, again, he is searching for his own place by combining various aspects and artifacts that must be blurred, refashioned, or molded to fit his subjective need. Thus, he alludes to things and ideas as a way to capture or borrow from them certain aspects without having to compensate for the whole of the things or ideas. And by taking only certain, often surface, aspects of things or ideas, it allows him to easily blend them into this own theories or world because his work is as much therapy for himself as it is art for the masses. In fact, the art that he produces is a blend of one third self-therapy, one third craft/skill, and one third popular marketing. He battles with this throughout his career, attempting to find a common ground or a balance for these three aspects. Like Rimbaud and Nietzsche, he is the "agonized" and "tortured" poet trying desperately to blend or balance reality and fantasy in a manner that both informs and entertains. This torture and agony can be clearly seen in <u>Dirty Mind</u>, <u>Controversy</u>, <u>1999</u>, and <u>Purple Rain</u>. In these albums Prince is writing about the difficulty of waging two battles at once: the civil battle of coming into one's own self and the complication of this battle by the impeding of the external, society that wishes to define and prescribe individuals. Prince wishes to indicate that the external battle complicates the internal battle, causing disorientation and chaos. Accordingly, until a man can define himself, he will never be able to evolve. A primary aspect of defining oneself is finding balance with all of the opposing internal forces. If a man can never balance his internal forces, he can never define himself. This battle reaches its apex in the companion pieces, <u>The Black Album</u> and <u>Lovesexy</u>. Here is where Prince invokes, at its highest, the battling principles of Nietzsche's Apollonian and Dionysian ideals as well as Horace's conflict between logic and reason.

> "Nietzsche believed that both forces were present in Greek tragedy, and that the true tragedy could only be produced by the tension between them. He used the names Apollonian and Dionysian for the two forces because Apollo, as the sun-god, represents light, clarity, and form, where as Dionysius, as the wine-god, represents drunkenness and ecstasy" (Kreis 2000).

This is the battle of man, the balancing of his opposing extremes. As Horace indicates, man is controlled by two forces, emotion and reason. Most men fluctuate violently between the two, expending oneself wildly in emotion and regretting it later in reason. <u>The Black Album</u> represents the physical struggle, and <u>Lovesexy</u> represents divine enlightenment. The secret to inner peace is to find a balance between the two. This allows humanity to evolve. This balance, however, does not come without struggle and drama. As Octavio Paz indicates in "Two Bodies," struggling for balance, order, harmony, and peace is a natural part of life, but we must recognize this struggle as natural and normal in order to conquer or live in peace with it. Further, it is this struggle that is partly responsible for what we know as the passion or excitement of life.

Prince's "philosophical reflection [is] not calm, reasoned, scientific inquiry" (Kreis 2000). Like Baudelaire, Rimbaud, and Nietzsche, Prince seeks to find himself by "wrestling with the most profound enigmas of modern life"—how does one's art make a difference in the world, what does it mean to be a successful (black) artist in America, and what does it mean to evolve to one's highest self? These are the biggest enigmas of his time: race and humanity's battle against its carnal desires. Prince's "inward path and form...can only be grossed when the reader has wrestled with his own mind" (Kreis 2000). Thus, there are three distinct types of Prince people: those who like the music, those who like the sensuousness of the work, and those who are on their own metaphysical journey in search of place, being, and transcendence to a higher form. This last group is large enough for Prince to sustain a career long after his apex of mass fame. His journey parallels their journey, and his work acts as a landscape and a soundtrack for their lives. This constant movement creates an element of urgency and frenzy in his work because there is always the element of a search. The major difference is that Prince, unlike Nietzsche, could never be a pessimist. He is an optimist because he believes that love, even in his early, angry work, can save us. Though misguided that sex would be the manifestation of love, he has been able to stay the course that somehow love will save us despite ourselves. Before love can save us, however, mankind must "revalue" its life. At the core of Prince's search is Nietzsche's "revaluation of all values" (Kreis 2000). Because Prince is, first and foremost, a pop icon, I would say that he was creating a pseudo-revaluation of all values. Prince is revaluating our values of identity, place, and power based on race, class, gender, and of his own desire to be a pop icon. If he cannot restructure these values, then he can never be the icon that he is seeking to be. His desire is to show that our reality is false or flawed because our notions of place and being, specifically race, class, and gender, are flawed as he asserts in "Uptown." "Our clothes, our hair, we don't care; it's all about being there…Set your mind free!"

Between <u>Dirty Mind</u> and <u>Controversy</u>, Prince becomes increasingly less passive and more aggressive. When performing "Uptown," instead of saying, "No, are you," to the female's question of "Are u gay?" he would, from time to time, assert, "No, is yo' mamma?" which symbolizes his more defiant tone. By the time he gets to <u>Controversy</u>, with the single "Sexuality," Prince is not just questioning, he is asserting his right to exist by asserting his notions and values as equal to if not better than the prescribed norms of society. "Sexuality is all I ever need. Sexuality I'm gonna let my body be free." There are two issues here. First is the assertion of his body being *his* body to do with as he wishes. His body is all that he has, and he is going to make his political statement with it. "I'm gonna let my body be free." Secondly, he wants to show that who we really are is rooted in our attitudes about life. "We don't need no race…Sexuality is all I ever need." His hope is to show that we are not physical beings, but spiritual beings having a physical experience. In this manner, we should relate to and communicate to each other as souls or humans and not as races, classes, or genders. And yes, part of this has to do with him not wanting to be pigeonholed as an artist because of his race, but it is still the question of wanting to be seen for the content of his character and not the color of his skin. To achieve this, Prince pulls from every source at his mind's fingertips, working and reworking various theories at his whim.

The unscientific realm of popular music allows him the leeway to move unabatedly across a spectrum of theory without having to justify or formally reconcile himself to the histories, doctrines, or dogmas of those theories. Although his images may seem erratic, his mind is contemplative, allowing him to blend what he needs and reject what he does not need.

> "His grasp of history and current events remains quirky. Prince can cite chapter and verse from biographies of Little Richard and Jerry Lee Lewis, but he seems genuinely unaware that his own life story was turned into a book a couple of years ago by an English rock critic. He knows, blow by blow, the events in the Mideast, relating the crisis to everything from the predictions of the sixteenth-century seer Nostradamus to the drug-intervention policy of George Bush. But he hasn't yet heard of 2 Live Crew" (Karlen, "Prince Talks," 59).

So, like Nietzsche, he selectively "uses his knowledge of intellectual movements and currents as dialectal elements for the formation of his own thought...[He] belongs both to his own time and at the same time he rises beyond it" (Kreis 2000). All at once he can be the multicultural idealism of Sly Stone and Jimi Hendrix, the cultural roots of James Brown, the transcendentalization of the Beatles, the angst of punk, and the well orchestrated amalgamation of Little Richard. Plotting all of these movements can be overly taxing if one is looking for a literal translation of all of Prince's influences. Again, Prince uses the artifacts of history, but for his own, subjective use. Prince pulls these images from their times and connects them to the timelessness of human history. To understand the meanings of the artifacts, as he is using them, one must look at Prince and not at the specific translation of the borrowed images and symbols. Like both Nietzsche and Rimbaud, "the only way his thought can really be studied is by going to the source" (Kreis 2000). In this, I have gone to his albums and his interviews. The rest is conjure, mine and others who have put themselves in the place of critic.

Because most critics have sought to deal with what Hill calls "The Pop Life," there is very little theoretical discussion of his music or his lyrics. This is not Prince's fault, but the fault of those who have chosen to concentrate on his popular antics rather than the work. Many will argue that there are more antics than art. A 1980 incident with music critic and writer of <u>New Jack City</u> Barry Michael Cooper seems to support the critics who say that Prince is more antics than art. Cooper asks Prince to clarify a point about the song, "Sister," and the following ensues.

> "On one of your songs, 'Sister,' are you talking about having sex with your own sister?" So [Prince] answers with a gasface/screwface on, 'maybe that voice came from the other side.' So I busted out laughing in his face. And he said, turn the tape recorder off. And he fell on the floor and rolled with laughter. Then he says, 'don't ever tell anybody I did that,' and then he said, 'cut the tape back on.' And then he went back to the gasface/screwface. So it was an act, that was his shtick, being this weird guy. But he was a normal dude man, and so nice and gracious. That's an interview that stuck out. And I gave him one of these small Bibles, it had Psalms, Proverbs, and the New Testament and he said, 'wow, thank you,' and shook my hand so tight. I'll never forget that" (Knyte 2007).

My attempt is also to show that the antics or even the "shtick" have their place—either to garner Prince a place in a world still overly concerned with race and gender or as a supplement to or a manifestation of the art. The largest hurdle is to ascertain what part is earnest and what part is hype. Even when questioned about this by Chris Rock on <u>VH1 to One</u>, Prince hints that his work is an equal balance of pop hype and a need to say something about the world.

Rock: "Early on in your career there was the androgynous thing. Was that an act or were you searching for a sexual identity?"

⚥: "That's a good question. I don't suppose I was searching really. I think I was just being who I was, being the true Gemini that I am. And there's many sides to that as well. And there was a little acting going on, too. We'd have the scene where I'd go hug the bass player; he's a man. Then I'd go kiss the keyboard player; she's a woman. You know; that's rock-n-roll."

The last phrase, "that's rock-n-roll," seems as an insignificant throw-away, but the beauty of popular music and popular culture is that it is not as concerned with formal adherence to technique, so it allows a certain amount of freedom for an artist to explore himself by manipulating various techniques. The playing with race and the playing with gender was an attempt by Prince to manipulate various forms to achieve his desired effect. Of course there is a glaring question that must be asked. How much is hype, and how much is art? What we have come to learn is that Prince felt that he needed the hype to make the kind of art that he wanted. In order not to be labeled as a male artist or a black artist, he had to break those definitions and deny those assertions before he was caged in them. Possibly, this is to what Hill is referring when he coined his book, <u>Prince: A Pop Life</u>. Any commentary on Prince must include a commentary on the art and the hype because the hype is a part of the art. The hype is, itself, art, which is a form of dandyism. This becomes the problem of constructing a scientific, theoretical study of Prince's work. Even if there is a theory, he will not "cop" to one. Instead, we are forced to analyze the manner in which he splices, cuts, and pastes together enough of his influences that our analysis of his work becomes the unraveling of the well-bandaged mummy because his work is the trope of a metaphor.

I began with Baudelaire, Rimbaud, and Nietzsche because they were neurotics, like Prince, searching for their place and meaning in the world full of hypocrisy and contradictions—neither having a problem with finding his place outside of the physical reality. I could have as easily started with Toomer or Wideman. It seems now, as I am looking back, that Wideman was more contrived, early in his career, than Toomer and could have been a better pattern for Prince. On the other hand, Wideman embraces a more tangible black aesthetic than either Toomer or Prince. That is—Wideman, by his third novel, <u>The Lynchers</u> (1973), was doing what Stephen Henderson calls writing black, where blackness becomes an ideological construct to refute white supremacy. Though Prince, by 1992, is obviously more embracing of his blackness, it cannot be said that he is writing black in the vein of Henderson or Wonder. Further, it is Prince's continued insistence of finding himself and his place outside the physical reality that makes it difficult for most to place him in the black canon. I am not asserting that Prince studied any one of these people at any depth. "Rolland de Reneville attaches Rimbaud to the mystical doctrines of India, although there is no proof that Rimbaud ever possessed a genuinely profound knowledge of Hindu philosophy" (Fowlie 20). I am asserting that what Prince is doing draws on what they were doing and must be mentioned if I plan to contextualize his work. All art must be contextualized in history and theory if it is to be assigned meaning. Baudelaire, Rimbaud, and Nietzsche leap out as obvious predecessors for Prince's championing of the intuitive subjective. The three of them seem in some manner to be working with the notion of Schopenhauer's "Subjective Idealism," which is the notion:

> "that the world is my idea, a phantasm of the mind, and, therefore, in itself, meaningless. Will, the active side of our nature, or Impulse, is the key to the one thing we know directly from the inside—the self, and therefore the key to the understanding of all things" (Kreis 2000).

This leads to Nietzsche's notion that "...the 'inquiring mind' was simply the human mind terrified by pessimism and trying to escape from it, a cleaver bulwark erected from the truth?"

(Kreis 2000). An optimistic Prince would invert this type of notion as in "Paisley Park" or in "Around the World in a Day" to show that the self is the greatest protection from the pessimistic, chaotic world because inner peace can only be found inside the individual. So then, it is acceptable and often necessary to wall oneself from the world, leaving just a window to observe the world.

The problem with this isolationist's notion of achieving inner peace is running the risk of insanity by virtue of isolation. No matter how much any of us attempt to deny it, we are social creatures who, as Prince agrees, "need to be touched in reassurance" (Hilburn, "Mixed Emotions," 58). However, one must be willing to surrender oneself to artistic insanity as a possible path to know the truth. Like Nietzsche, Schopenhauer, and Toomer, Prince goes artistically insane, losing touch with the general populous, but not before he has plotted a path back to the ideal through the individual self. The problem is that this path or theory is not sustaining without collective fellowship. Where Schopenhauer, Nietzsche, and Toomer have received help from critics, Prince has so alienated himself that few have wanted to dedicate the time and work needed to understand his career beyond that of merely a pop icon. Too many have been put off by Prince's struggle to be both a unique individual and an inextricable part of the collective: he wants to be unique to his time and innately connected to the history and legacy of popular music with all of its socio-political semantics. This is the tension in his work, the attempt to balance these dueling desires. We must remember that as a popular artist, he must sell records, so he must, at all times, balance his art with his economic sensibility, and that causes more tension and dichotomy.

Yet, no matter the hype, Prince is still attempting to construct a theory or a theology of what the world is, how to survive it, and the ability of art to make our world better. Thus, his albums are not just a collection of songs; the songs are often tied together by a running theme. Typically, he is trying to rework older ideologies to fit whatever his current concept is. Christianity is, of course, the easiest to co-opt and rework because it is so very figurative, if not ambiguous. Like Nietzsche and Rimbaud, Prince does battle with Christianity (fighting to redefine its symbolism), in order to make it be what it claims to be. The goal is to bridge the gap between the lip-service ideal of its doctrine and the reality of its practitioners. To do this, all three exercise a practice of exploiting the difference between the ideal of Christianity and the actual practice of Christians. At the core is the fight against the bigotry and narrow dogmas of the religion, which exist because man is an innately political being, who wants, often, to survive more than he wants to evolve. Prince makes the same physical and psychological flight from the tyranny of the physical world controlled by the dogma of religion as we see Rimbaud make.

> "To escape from the maternal tyranny and the house itself, so completely dominated by his mother, he fled to the garden and to the farthest point in the garden...For himself, therefore, his flight was angelic, motivated by a great thirst for purity and freedom, for a spiritual liberation" (Fowlie 125, 126).

Prince's desire is to break free of the physical world to know the metaphysical world. The dogmas and empty ritual of misused or misapplied religion and science only work to inhibit evolution. As he states, "I used to go to church until I realized that they were politicians too...mostly the ministers" (Mitchell 1981). The job of the poet is to break free from these confines and show that religion and other physical laws and principles are supposed to enhance our evolution to a higher being, not prohibit our evolution.

> "...man can't know, in the metaphysical sense, because of his human reason, which is an obstacle to knowing the infinite...The poet's role is to reveal the unity of the world...[by showing] its multiple

'correspondence'" (Fowlie 127).

For Prince, the one great corresponding element or paralleling aspect that bridges and connects the physical to the metaphysical is sex. Through sex, mankind could make its angelic flight to purity, freedom, and spiritual liberation. The revolt or revolution is in revolting against the gap placed between spirituality and physicality by the western mode of thought. This was even one of Rimbaud's greatest struggles.

> "[Rimbaud] was right in cultivating his scornful attitude toward conventions, because that was part of his escape from them. But he had forgotten one thing, one inescapable fact, his roots in the West. He was born in the Occidental marshes. The shred of reason left to him, reminded him of that. He had tried to rid himself of Western symbols: Christianity and its martyrs, inventions, art, warfare. He had secretly been trying to return to the East, to the source of eternal wisdom. But that had been a dream. A modern Westerner is the man who has harmonized Christ with the *bourgeoisie*. We cultivate the fog, and intoxication, and devotions. It is another world than the primitive wisdom of the East. What Rimbaud had dreamed of, in his revolts and his poetry, had been the purity of Eastern thought, the purity of the mind which leads one to the absolute. The experiment was doomed to failure" (Fowlie 36-37).

Rimbaud's fight with his roots in the West directly parallels the African American's attempt to kill the nigger in his mind that keeps him linked to a perception of the world that binds and marginalizes him. Frantz Fanon asserts that African Americans must kill the white man in their mind, the guiding force that causes Hughes' "urge toward whiteness." But, what is proving even more difficult is the killing of the nigger in the mind of African Americans, especially for those who know no other image of themselves. Mankind will hold fast to the dogmas and empty rituals of the physical world because these elements cause them to feel safe by giving them a tangible place. Even though these elements are harmful, man will cling to what he knows because familiarity breeds contentment, and contentment breeds the illusion of inner peace. Some slaves choose not to escape because of the uncertainty of freedom. The goal of the artist is to shock man from his contentment. Prince uses sex, the original and major sin, to shock man from a religion and a world that controls his life through arbitrary regulations. Since global power is hung on the penis, particularly the white penis, if a poet can redefine the world's notion of sexuality, he can redefine the world.

In <u>Dirty Mind</u> we are suppose to see sexuality as a normal manifestation of our spiritual selves. In <u>Lovesexy</u> we are urged to embrace sexuality as a celebration or a trope of our spiritual selves. In both cases, Prince is attempting to free us from the dogma of westernized religion so that we may embrace a notion of life that is more holistic, in regards to the physical and metaphysical aspects of our humanity. Prince's notions are more eastern than western because eastern philosophies are more accepting and embracing of sexuality and sensuality as a natural part of the human existence and as a part of man's religion (communion with God). The western or Eurocentric mode of thought divides the body from the soul. It has been the African who has liberated the European because the black blues aesthetic has asserted that "it really is okay to enjoy both the sensual and erotic sides of life" (Salaam 17). So it has been African culture that has liberated Europeans from their own limited, stoic captivity. Elvis Presley's shaking of his white ass on national television was proof that black culture liberates white folks from being caged in their own white supremacy. The problem is that:

> "the embracing of [a simultaneous celebration of the sensual and the divine] by non-african americans sometimes leads to excessiveness, even obsession, with exotica and an elevation of the other as the paragon

of sensuality or sexuality (as in the fixation on mulatto women)" (Salaam 19).

Where this confusion or contradiction is most relevant and evident is that Prince is initially striving toward the European ideal of Rimbaud and Nietzsche, and they are striving to get away from it. Just as Rimbaud's desire to return to the East was doomed to fail, Prince's desire to achieve the metaphysical world was doomed because he too did not know where to look. Early in his career, Prince knew that his philosophy was in opposition to the dogma of misused Christianity, but he had bought enough into the love rhetoric that he was willing to wage war for Christianity's symbolism. This is evident in Prince's singing of the gospel hymn, "The Second Coming," "It won't be long/ all of God's children must learn how to love," before launching into "Uptown" as the opening for the <u>Controversy</u> tour. Prince was going to make Christianity be what it claimed to be, a religion of love. What he did not understand was how deeply embedded into the minds of America were the dogmas and hypocrisy of the religion. Neither he nor Rimbaud is really able to break away from the western approach to sexuality, which is often embedded with so much lust that it is devoid of spirituality. Or, Prince is merely manipulating the European mentality for his own purposes. We find Prince in the late nineties striving for the eastern ideal through his fascination with Egyptology, allowing it to be the guiding force of <u>Emancipation</u>. Unfortunately, he is unable to convince the masses that his sexual conduct is a manifestation or a metaphor of his spiritual desire for evolution.

An additional tension in Prince's work is that he was alone in his vision and in the manner in which he crafted his vision. This would be his tragic flaw because what was initially his greatest asset becomes his greatest liability. Most artistic forms grow from some socio-political, cultural experience. Prince was not manifesting, expressing, or interpreting any particular cultural experience, or so it seemed. Prince, it seemed, was purposely divorcing himself from all existing cultures in an attempt to create a world with its own culture, taking bits and pieces of past and existing cultures—basing his world on abstract ideals, such as love, tolerance, and multiculturalism, rather than on existing cultural mores and particulars. Ironically, by doing this, Prince was becoming more African American than most. He was becoming Toomer's allegory of the new American man, which has been the hopes for the great majority of African Americans, to assimilate/amalgamate into a place where they belong. This drive toward a color-blind society means that African Americans are often forced to a universality that demands that they remove as much of their African self to be placed, measured, judged, and accepted in a Eurocentric box. Thus, the eighties, the height of integration, created a new type of African American who wanted to be a hybrid but was also forced to deal with all of the complications and hypocrisy of this desire to be a hybrid. This creates J. C. Watts, Armstrong Williams, Clarence Thomas, and Ward Connerly—men who have bought into American integration for their own individual survival. Of these four men, Connerly is the best example of how this integrationist rhetoric exploits one who hates himself to the degree that he takes the individual gains at the cost of marginalizing the rest of his race. Prince, in his search for self and survival, has also grooved along this sliding scale of self, and that makes him more typical of the larger African American struggle. Prince's singularity mirrors the lifestyle of the only black or solo Negro—the only black at a school or the only black at the job or the only black family in the suburbs. Being on this mission of singularity worked to separate Prince from his African American audience. So while Prince was able to achieve a sense of uniqueness, he became shunned by the race or community that he would need when the reality of racism eventually reared its ugly head. Yet, it must be stated that Prince is able to live in the world that he created and make peace with his isolation, partly because neither the black or the white world worked for Prince because he saw the so-called real, tangible world as more arbitrary and limiting than the world he was creating.

White patrons enjoy a carefully calculated naiveté with African American artists. This calculated naiveté allows the white patron to pour the complexity of African Americans into two very limiting boxes. On the one hand, whites want African American artists to be black enough to enjoy the richness of the African legacy, but universal enough to be palatable to white sensibilities. On the other hand, whites want African American artists to exemplify the stereotype of savagery, which allows whites to live vicariously through African American artists without the risk of the lifestyle, which is one of the reasons why so many suburban whites listen to hip hop. On a third hand, many whites have always used the African American condition as a mirror or backdrop for their condition. Tennessee Williams does this in several of his plays where the black community is seen as symbolic of the white character who is the black sheep in his family. This was also done by the white youth of the fifties and sixties when they used black music and culture as a way to vent or parallel their frustration with their parents' hypocrisy. This varying use and objectification of black culture is what drives African American schizophrenia. Adding to this complexity is that the majority of African American patrons also enjoy a carefully calculated naiveté with African American artists. Because of their socio-political existence as second-class citizens, African American patrons are willing to turn a blind eye to certain strategic attempts by African American artists to gain the white dollar. But, there is also a very thin, invisible, and definite line that the African American artist must navigate to remain black enough for his African American patrons. Unfortunately, the artist is not told where that line is until he crosses it. It may not be clearly defined, but it is certainly there; just ask Diana Ross, Tina Turner, and Johnny Mathis who, seemly, will never be considered black acts again. What we need to understand is that these socio-political conditions directly influence the artistic theory and any merit we place on the artist or the theory. From 1978-1985,

Prince, very carefully, was able to navigate this line by blurring his race and his gender. He was allowed to be this fantastical, allegorical figure because the majority of Americans, black and white, wanted this fantasy. However, once the Reagan administrations had effectively polarized the country, no one wanted fantasy, and Prince was left hanging in the wind.

> "The difficulty of classifying [a poet] as a type is the key to his character. [Prince, like Rimbaud,] was no recognizable type. No one could live with him, and he, in his quality of constant revolutionary, could abide in no one's presence for long. He is outside the law and outside the human community" (Fowlie 24).

Prince achieves this by becoming the embodiment of human contradiction. Ultimately, he is the embodiment of America's Christian rhetoric existing side by side with its hedonistic practices. And, of course, it is this contradiction that makes him uniquely African American, uniquely American, and quite the human allegorical figure. He is not just the poet; he, himself, is the poem or the character, and his work is the character's dialogue. He makes himself the fallen but liberated angel who will save us through his example of how to get and act free. In the manner of Baudelaire, Rimbaud, and Nietzsche, Prince is

> "the poet opposing his civilization, his historical moment, and yet at the same time revealing its very instability, its quirky torment. He is both against his age and of it. By writing so deeply about himself, he wrote of all men" (Fowlie 26)

Prince's journey becomes the journey of the pseudo integrated man, struggling for or toward idealism in the face of inevitable failure. Through this he becomes "metaphysician, angel, *voyou*, seer, reformer, reprobate, materialist, mystic" (Fowlie 26). His work becomes a discourse on "the drama of man, tormented by the existence of the ideal which he is unable to reach" (Fowlie 26). What holds our attention is his wonderfully crafted "images...which startle and hold us by their own intrinsic beauty, [which] were generated and formed by a single man in the solitude of his own...reality" (Fowlie 26). We experience, enjoy, are comforted by, and inspired by his fantasy while we struggle with our own reality.

      This is why Prince's work is enjoyed by such a large cross-section of the society. What defines his work is the act of doing whatever is necessary to communicate the meaning of the work, even if that radial approach somehow alienates or smothers his message. To some his work is a rainbow. To others his work is a car wreck. In either case, you are compelled to look. To understand the work of Prince is to understand that the popular and the academic do combine in his work, but neither the popular nor the academic sectors know exactly what, if anything, to do with or about Prince's work. The corporate buy-outs of publishing houses force even the academic folk to take notice of sales. Even those writing merely for tenure had to be aware of buying trends. The culture of capitalism was influencing everything, and Prince saw this coming seven or eight years prior. Thus, Prince had no problems, hang-ups, or concerns pulling from a variety of disciplines and a variety of theories within those disciplines. The goal is to shock people with the new and the absurd into some acknowledgment and realization of themselves. Even if Prince did not give people a new realization of themselves, he provided insights to alternative roads and paths. The most shocking aspect of all of this is that Prince's plan worked. There was nothing new in his shock except for the fact that he, unlike Little Richard before him, was willing to explore socio-political issues in his work. The fact that there was more than just sex in his work is what validated everything else and made Prince a cultural phenomenon. The images may have been randomly chosen, but he wove them in a manner that created the semantics that he needed to achieve or evoke certain feelings in his listeners because he painted bold strokes with a defiant attitude.

Where Baudelaire and Rimbaud have a "terrifying directness," Prince also has a terrifying directness in imagery. The goal of this "directness" is to allow the poet to capture the listener's attention and then communicate the message. At issue is the weight or primary importance of the image as entertainment or the image as socio-political artifact. In either case, what remains true is that the popular artist is unable to convey the message if he is unable to capture the public's attention.

> "For [Wendy and Lisa's] first video, Prince recommended that they try to announce themselves by making a splash, by 'doing something like jumping off a speaker with smoke pouring out everywhere. *Something.*' When he saw the video, however, Wendy was sitting in a chair, playing her guitar. 'You can't do that when you're just getting established—kids watching MTV see that and they go click,' Prince says, miming a channel being changed. 'They'd rather watch a commercial...Wendy and Lisa are going to have to do some more serious soul-searching and decide what they want to write about'" (Karlen, "Prince Talks," 60).

This indecision in Wendy and Lisa's work is the tension at the heart of any theory formed around Prince, the notion that "pop" is at the center of his work. He is attempting to balance being popular with being artistic. This is only noteworthy because the society has allowed the notion of being popular to be exclusive of being serious. He is able to exploit this because his images are well crafted and his message is, at the core, consistent: we must rise above our physical selves to be better beings. Even in some of his more dogmatic songs, such as "Erotic City," Prince attempts to make the connection between the physical and the metaphysical. What most people remember from "Erotic City" is "We can fuck until the Dawn." What most people do not remember is "All of my purple life I've been lookin' 4 a dame that would wanna be my wife. That was my intention main...All of my hang-ups are gone. How I wish U felt the same." Or even in the explicit "Sexy MF," Prince begins with "In a word or 2 its u 👁 wanna do, no not your body but your mind..." Before the sex, Prince is always stressing that the sex which is desired or about to happen is related to some emotional or psychological desire and not merely a physical desire. According to Prince's lyrics, the emotionally and psychologically oppressed or scarred have perverted and ultimately unfulfilling sex, liberated people have liberated sex, and liberated sex aids in the evolution of humanity.

Though his images, icons, symbols, and artifacts are randomly selected, the message created with his poetic technique is constant. His legacy is not a collection of love songs or erotica, though that work is carefully and calculatingly sprinkled throughout his body of work. Equally mixed with the love and lust songs are songs that attempt to comment on life's meaning: "Uptown," "Party Up," "Controversy," "Sexuality," "Annie Christian," "Ronnie Talk to Russia," "1999," "Free," "Let's Go Crazy," "When Doves Cry," "Around the World in a Day," "Paisley Park," "Dance Electric," "Christopher Tracy's Parade," "Sign '☮' the Times," "The Ballad of Dorothy Parker," "Starfish and Coffee," "Bob/George," "Lovesexy," "Anna Stesia," "Positivity," "The Future," "New Power Generation," "Graffiti Bridge," "Thunder," "Walk Don't Walk," "Live 4 Love," "The Sacrifice of Victor," "Endorphinmachine," "Gold," "Right the Wrong," "Chaos and Disorder," "The Exodus Has Begun," "My Computer," "The Love We Make," and too many others to mention. Prince developed a style of big, extended, exaggerated imagery and metaphors to get the public's attention. At the center is the sex metaphor where he reverses the role of sex. Where, in the past, other objects, events, and activities were symbols and metaphors for sex, Prince made sex and sexuality a metaphor for the manner in which man's metaphysical self manifests itself in the physical. His unique vision of the world allows him to transcribe the world in a manner that forces his listeners to see the world differently. This is his "recreation of everything that exists, a new birth of the world" (Fowlie 20). His major or primary technique was shock value. His images sought to compare what the western world assigns as the incomparable: sexuality and spirituality. He asserted that sexuality and spirituality were one and the same and, of course, interchangeable. This is why in the song "God is Alive," Prince can write that "God is coming like a dog in heat." If something is wrong with humanity's sexually, it is because something is wrong with humanity's spiritually, and if something is wrong with humanity's spiritually, it can be measured by humanity's sexually. Prince's "early tendency to lewdness, sullenness, and debauchery was a perverted form of asceticism. What is sought in excessive sexual indulgence and intoxication is far more than mere physical satisfaction and oblivion" (Fowlie 21). Prince wishes to use this reclassifying or modifying of sexuality and spirituality as a way to subvert a system based on racial and gender oppression. His goal is to be so free (uninhibited) that his sexual acts seem as sacred profanity—a profanity so philosophical that it is both satire and rebellion. To do this, Prince creates himself as the poet visionary of "Uptown," a small village that will one day take over the world and show the world how to love, unconditionally. How will he do this?—by teaching the masses that acts, such as oral sex, are signifiers of being liberated. If you have hang-ups about sex and sexuality, you have hang-ups about yourself, and these hang-ups are what the oppressors use to keep you oppressed. Thus, Prince is

> "incapable of accepting any of the familiar forms of reality [race, gender, class, because they are all based on the desire to categorize, merely for the purposes of oppression.] These he considered traps or compromises for the purity of spirit he felt in himself. He opposed [these categories] as one opposes the enemy, until they were repulsed or vanquished or forgotten" (Fowlie 22).

Prince's exaggerated style must be done to awake the sleeping masses and to motivate his peers to create art that forces the masses to see the truth. Rimbaud saw his peers as "false generators of words, hack writers and functionaries" (Fowlie 27). In the same manner, Prince became critical of his peers.

> "I'm not saying I'm better than anybody else, but I don't feel there are a lot of people out there telling the truth in their music" (Hilburn, "The Renegade Prince," 66). "All the groups in America seem to do just exactly the same as each other...They're a little too concerned with keeping up the payments on the Rolls Royce when really they should be busying themselves with doing something that's true to their own selves." (Salewicz 18, reprinted in Fudger 9, 18).

To pump some life into popular music, Prince made himself a part of the art, making himself as different as possible. (This is the type of dandy or dandyism to which Prince strives to be.) Prince, like Rimbaud, sought "to make himself stranger to his land and society and family...The *voyant* needs to become the mythic self, discoverable in the deepest recesses of earliest memory and primal fears" (Fowlie 27). As Rimbaud does in "Alchemy of the Word" Prince embraces the landscape of his reality, his memory, and his dreams to create a world foreign to the listeners, filled with his own ideals. "The literature which has fed his imagination was the forgotten once-popular book, pornography, church Latin, fairy stories, and popular songs" (Fowlie 30). Prince, too, would have his head filled with opposing and seemingly contradictory images of his mother's pornography, church hymnals, <u>Barbarella</u>, <u>Lo Dolce Vita</u>, Martin Luther King speeches, <u>The Mack</u>, Muhammad Ali, and the contradiction of his very religious father who played piano at strip joints. In opening himself to all of this at once, Prince was opening himself to a new world of possibilities, which had lain dormant in the physical world without the fire of dreams to resurrect it. Prince's "practice of poetry was a giving up of the old in order to create another world. What helped most in this strange creation were the elements in the real world which had lost this fullness and power...Poetry is the capture of the trivial and the commonplace which in the alchemy of the poetic word emerge changed and newly significant. After the derangement of senses, poetry is the creation of a new universe from sources so humble and trite that only one save the poet himself could remember them" (Fowlie 30).

To create this new world, the poet must be willing to give himself over to the hallucination—the dream of the new world that he wishes to create in an unencumbered and unapologetic manner. This is what Prince does. This is that sickness to which he refers. The hallucination is evident in the work where he seeks to create a new reality in the face of the old reality. "Uptown," "1999," "Purple Rain," "Around the World in a Day," "Christopher Tracy's Parade," "Lovesexy," "The Future," "Hallucination Rain," and "The Exodus Has Begun" are all dreams—hallucinations. In fact, "The Future" directly refers to seeing the coming new world. "I've seen the future and it will be/ I've seen the future and it works/ And if there's life after we will see...boy it's rough." The poet is the bridge between the metaphysical world and the physical world. His job is to reproduce or allow the hallucination to be produced through him so that the masses can see their destiny or potential, either negatively or positively. Just as with the Old Testament prophets, the vision is not always pleasing, as Prince asserts "I've seen the future and boy its tough." Irregardless of the pessimistic outlook, the poet has the duty and ability to "discover in beings and in objects an extraordinary possibility and transformation" (Fowlie 31). Usually, this hidden quality is something that only the poet can see. A poet, such as Prince, can point to sex and show us the underlying psychological and emotional issue of the concept and the activity. As he asserted in 1982, "Sex is something we can all understand.

It's limitless. But I try to make the songs so they can be viewed in different ways. I know some people will go right through those (messages) elements in a song, but there are some who won't" (Hilburn, "The Renegade Prince," 66). The poet may not be the first or the best. In fact it is not about being the best, but merely providing another view. Humanity's spiritual eyes and ears are so numb to the truth that it often takes many visionaries saying the same thing in different ways for it to be heard. Since we are physical beings, we are innately political beings. Our desire to survive causes us to be deaf to the wisdom of the spirit world. Marvin Gaye and Ray Charles have said it all before, so Prince is just another poet, adding another voice to the message. Where Gaye and Charles show sexuality and spirituality as being an inherent part of being human, Prince attempts to raise this discourse to a religious platform. He wants to show that sex is a way of knowing our higher selves.

> "Any attempt to experience love, no matter how irregular the form it takes, is always an attempt to reach the absolute, to free oneself from the bounds of ordinary life. The mirage of love is endless because it can never be experience solely in itself. It calls for leaving oneself, an ecstasy, just at the very time when the body is more needed" (Fowlie 32).

Sex is our attempt to reach our physical and spiritual potential. It is an attempt to get outside of oneself, to connect to something that will expand and allow us to know and understand the totality of ourselves, outside the singularity of our isolated and limited individual experiences. Thus, sex becomes Prince's metaphor for man's desire to become a complete entity. To engage in sex is the attempt to connect back to the collective and our spirituality. Prince must be noted for the creative manner in which he attempts to have the conversation.

What Prince comes to find, however, as he matures as a person and as an artist, is that sex is fatally rooted in the physical and, therefore, governed by the politics of the body more than the soul. The reason that person A is with person B can be and is often an entirely different reason why person B is with person A. Although sex can be a pathway to the sublime, it is ultimately too subjective and too impregnated with the baggage of the body to be a pathway to Utopia. As Prince asserts "When I'm recording I could have orgasm on my mind and my bass player could have pickles on his. It makes it a little rough when you listen back to a track and [the bass player's part is] not played with the same intensity" (Mitchell 15, reprinted in Fudger 15). The same holds true for all human relationships. This innate flaw of the physical causes us to cling to individualism, which becomes the only way that one can protect himself from the politics of the body. Even Prince succumbs to this. "What if everybody around me split?...Then I'd be left with only me. That's why I have to protect me" (Karlen, "Prince Talks," 59). The only truth is that we are all looking for something. This is more of the dichotomy; this internal conflict makes the individual the microcosm of the society in relation to the battle to find peace and balance with our dueling forces. Still, the sex metaphor was an excellent beginning point. If nothing else, the sex metaphor, the coming together of two people to become one entity and know completion, is a trope of man's struggle to transcend the duality of his individual self and exist as a whole, complete being. This is our desire—to become the complete, living experience as in "I Would Die 4 U," "If I Was Your Girlfriend," and "My Name is Prince," and in Prince's reconfiguring of himself as the ultimate hybrid, able to mean a variety of things to a variety of people.

Again, the essence of an effective/useful poet is the ability of the poet to redefine our reality, causing us to see the beauty of our humanity and the metaphysical truths. In this Prince is much like Sappho. In works such as "To an Army Wife, in Sardis," Sappho became a womanist/feminist by fighting the politics of the body, which is achieved by redefining our points of reference, such as love. If the poet can redefine what one can love and how one can love, the poet has effectively changed our reality. This revaluing of our values and the redefinition of our reference points leads to the creation of a new reality and a deeper understanding of our humanity. This revaluing is important for an artist such as Prince because he is working in a time where the physical, the now, the current, is valued more than the spiritual. Before he can cause the evolution of his listeners, he must first show them that the metaphysical world holds more for them than the physical. He does this by asserting that the feeling of spiritual ecstasy is twice as powerful and satisfying as physical ecstasy. In doing this he gives his audience a reference point; he is then able to take what is known as the ultimate, the physical orgasm, and then show the orgasm as being subordinate and inferior to the spiritual orgasm. Thus, the sex metaphor parallels well with the "Beaudelairian doctrine of 'correspondences' whereby a word is seen as capable of provoking sensory responses" (Fowlie 33). Sexuality and spirituality are corresponding concepts. The transformation of the sexual to spiritual titillation is expected to free man from the oppressive clutches of the physical and open him to the divine truth of the metaphysical. Sex is to be the gateway to the spiritual. Man "may reach the subconscious self which the mystics would define as the part of man open to the gratuitousness of God" (Fowlie 35). Sex and sexuality certainly open man to many possibilities about himself and the divine world.

Ultimately, Prince saw the mediums of music and language as tools to construct his personal Utopia; therefore, he had no reservations of manipulating the meanings of borrowed historical artifacts and rhetoric and making them subservient to his message. Like both Rimbaud and Nietzsche, Prince "freed himself from the constrictions of clichés [and] from the usual meanings of words…" (Fowlie 34). So, God could come like a dog in heat or could feel like race cars burning rubber in your pants. Even with a song like "Darling Nikki," where the subject matter, the imagery, and the character are all pulled from the occult and the satanic ritual, Prince sought to subvert this to show man's battle within himself. If the female can be salvation as in "Anna Stesia," then she can surely be damnation as in "Annie

Christian." Further, these notions are predications of possibilities more than they are assertions of definite realities. In both cases, the female is being accessed and used for the man's particular need, even in an ideological sense. The changing or shifting perception of the female represents the psychological battle within the male as it relates to solving the dichotomy of the physical and the spiritual. The point being that Prince is on a mission to make sense of life by creating his own world, even if the images, symbols, and metaphors are borrowed fragments, which are at times incoherent and incongruent. "These fragmenting discontinuous visions of the poems must be at best imperfect replicas of the world seen by the visionary" (Fowlie 34). None of us are sure what John saw in <u>Revelations</u> because he is not sure what he saw. What he received was a poetic hallucination of images that were foreign to him. So, Prince is well in his right to piece together fragments in an attempt to explain his Utopian world. He gives us the disclaimer. "I was dreaming when I wrote this/ Forgive me if it goes astray."

Like Baudelaire and Rimbaud, Prince has succeeded and failed to the heights and depths of few before or after him. This is because he is always reaching for the hidden secrets and ultimate joys of life. <u>Under the Cherry Moon</u>, <u>Graffiti Bridge</u>, and <u>Lovesexy</u> are all commercial flops and critical embarrassments in a popular sense of sales. But a poet can not succeed if he is not willing to take chances, especially a poet who is dedicated to finding a deeper satisfaction than mere physical gratification. Yes, Prince is obviously driven by some amount of physical gratification, such as critical acclaim and record sales, but, like the dandy that he is, all of this mystique and contradiction work to propel the message. He wants the fame just so he can then challenge our notions of fame. Thus, Prince is always challenging society by challenging himself to break from the norm, which often means to break away from some myth or persona that he has created of or for himself. He asserts this in his battle with the success of <u>Purple Rain</u>.

"In some ways, [the success of Purple Rain] was more detrimental than good. That's a very complex question. People's perception of me changed after that, and it pigeonholed me. I saw kids coming to concerts who screamed just because that's where the audience screamed in the movie. That's why I did Around the World in a Day, to totally change that. I wanted not to be pigeonholed" (Sinclair 1999).

To challenge our notions of reality and success, the artist must be ready to meet with failure. This is his challenge to society. Like Rimbaud and Baudelaire, "few men have 'warred against their fortune' with more ingenious obstinacy..." (Quennell 19).

Prince's war is realizing and remembering what is important as an artist and being able to stick with that belief even when your mission is rejected by the mainstream or the critics. "Some critics say that Lovesexy is a failure; but I go on the Internet and someone says 'Lovesexy saved my life'" (DeCurtis 61). For Prince, inspiring or comforting his listeners is more important than record sales. Every new album found Prince changing direction, especially his position within the hermeneutic circle. By constantly changing his position, he is able to repaint or remake the familiar as unfamiliar. This is the job of the poet, to make us see the world anew. Even with his failures or misses, Prince continues to strive for the artist's directive: to point the listener toward evolution. This is our destiny as creatures who are made in the image of the creator. We must create. "Because God first thought the world and then created it by his word, the creation of poetry corresponds...with the law of the cosmos" (Fowlie 35-36). As most artists who see a need to refashion the old world or create a new world, Prince is skeptical and mistrustful of the old world and its semantics. Everything, for Prince, needs to be reworked, especially our notions of race, gender, and class. Thus, the language and culture need to be reworked. This does not mean that he coined or created new words, ideals, or semantics. He just reached into history's language vault and attempted to make his own meaning of what the world should be. Thus, Prince was one who could with great ease ignore the laws of the physical. In fact, his role as a poet demands that he recreate the laws if they are not serving his evolution.

The problem for Prince and his listener is that his work is simultaneously folly and seriousness. It is folly in that he is trying to sell records. It is serious because he is trying to deal with the pain of his past. The almost indecipherable question when approaching his work is "What image, symbol, or metaphor is doing what?" Where do the folly end and the seriousness begin? Even when one cannot find the answer to the folly and seriousness question, we can acknowledge that Prince has provided amazing images, metaphors, and stories that make us laugh, cry, and think. Through his willingness to challenge himself as well as society, he has provided his generation with alternate notions of how to see and experience the world. In that, he has achieved his poetic duty. "Prince is an incredible songwriter who has remained popular because he writes what many people think but are afraid to say. His fearlessness and freedom keep his songs real and meaningful to a large segment of the society. This is one example of a good songwriter" (Kashif 2000).

Father's Son

"I wanna see my life change. I wanna be there when it changes. I don't wanna just be doing what's expected of me" (Sutherland 13, reprinted in Fudger 7). "The most important thing is to be true to yourself, but I also like danger. That's what's missing from pop music today. There's no excitement or mystery" (Hilburn, "The Renegade Prince," 66, reprinted in Fudger 9). "I only write from experience. I don't plan to shock people. I write about things I guess people are afraid to talk about" (Mitchell 15, reprinted in Fudger 9). "I look at creating new music like making a new friend. I'm often criticized for going too fast to try and say too much. I guess I like surprises, and hope that you do too..." (Prince, "Acceptance Speech for AMA," 1990)

Born Prince Rogers Nelson on June 7, 1958 to Mr. and Mrs. John and Mattie Nelson, entertainers themselves, Prince was raised in an atmosphere of diverse emotions, races, and many types of music, all of which encouraged creativity and individualism. In an interview given to Rolling Stone in 1981, Prince remembered how he and his friends would literally fight to live how they wanted to live.

> "With his taste for outlandish clothes and his 'lunatic' friends, Prince says he 'took a lot of heat all the time. People would say something about our clothes or the way we looked or who we were with, and we'd end up fighting. I was a very good fighter...I never lost..." (Adler 57)

In a 1981 Sounds interview, Prince remembered how he and his friends would often ostracize someone who was attempting to be like someone else. "I had a lot of free-minded friends who were into individuality and [in our group] you were ridiculed often for copying people and picking up trends and wearing what everybody else had on and saying what everybody else said and playing the same kind of music as everybody" (Mitchell 1981). He even recounted how he hated having to play someone else's music and sing someone else's songs because of how contrived the more popular songs seemed. "It got pretty sickening because I had to dissect these songs and teach each part to each person, so when the artist got a hit again I knew exactly what was gonna go down in the music and it was just a turn off" (Mitchell 52). He could not wait until he was performing his own material, developing his own message(s), creating his own world. Later in a 1985 interview with the Electrifying Mojo, Prince clearly states that his one and only goal has been to get his vision to the public by following his own path.

> "Well, you know, it's like...I worked a long time under a lot of different people, and most of the time I was doing it their way. I mean, that was cool, but ya know, I figured if I worked hard enough and kept my head straight, one day I'd get to do this on my own...and that's what happened. So I feel like...if I don't try to hurt nobody...and like I say...keep my head on straight...my way usually is the best way" (Prince 1985).

Probably the most noted or publicized influence on Prince as a person and a musician/songwriter is his relationship with his father. According to his former tour manager Alan Leeds, "[Prince's] mother basically walked away from him, and his father struggled to raise him and threw in the towel, and the kinds of rejection he suffered as a youngster -- it certainly doesn't add up to a very secure, well-rounded individual" (Toure 1998). As recounted by his sister, Tyka Nelson, on the syndicated series <u>A Current Affair</u> in 1990, Prince would often sneak into the bars, clubs, and strip joints where his father would be playing just to get a glimpse of what he wanted his own career to be. Prince's father, a jazz pianist and band leader, also jammed to the beat of his own drummer. In the same interview with <u>A Current Affair</u>, John Nelson recounts how he was run out of clubs because his musical style was so different. "They told me, 'Get Out! Go home and practice!' 'cause they couldn't follow this [playing the piano]" (J. Nelson 1990). Mr. Nelson's face and the notes that he is playing on the piano soften as he turns his attention to his son. "The connection between he and I is playing...music. He thinks like me, and he proves it...I can hear it...all you gotta do is listen to what he does [continuing to play] nobody else has ever listened to what I do and done anything about it." Mr. Nelson continued to elaborate, "I named him Prince [after Nelson's band The Prince Rogers' Trio] 'cause I wanted him to do all the things that I wanted to do" (J. Nelson 1990). A memorable point about the <u>A Current Affair</u> interview is the condescending tone of the interviewer. After Mr. Nelson states that he wanted his son to achieve all of the things that he was never able to do, the interviewer responds with some very sarcastic quips, "You wanted him to pose nude on an album cover?" Undaunted by the interviewer's tone or questions, Mr. Nelson replies "Yes." The interviewer continues, "Did *you* want to pose nude on album?" Without missing a beat, Mr. Nelson replies, "I don't think I'm pretty enough to do that," and continues playing the piano. After not getting the reaction from Mr. Nelson that he wanted, the interviewer turns up the heat by questioning him about his time playing for strippers.

> "Mr. Nelson: I played in trios, but most of my music was playing for strippers.
> Interviewer: And what does that require? What kind of music do you play for a stripper? [Before Mr. Nelson can respond with "I'm in the Mood for Love," the interviewer blurts "vavava voom?" Mr. Nelson becomes noticeably irritated, but remains calm.]
> Mr. Nelson: Don't get it wrong, now. Don't get the stripper and me mixed up with corn. Vavava voom, that's corn. [hits some very sharp and pronounced notes on the piano] I don't play that. You haven't

> heard nothing that I play is corny [punctuating his final comments with a flurry of notes that strike the heart of the interviewer's condemnation and sarcasm."

If nothing else, we see firsthand where Prince gets his unflappable nerve. Even on nationwide television, John Nelson was unconcerned about this interviewer's or anybody else's notion of what he or his son should be, and this attitude has certainly been inherited by his son.

Both father and son would realize their likeness and the influence it had on Prince as a person and as a musician. In a 1986 interview at the MTV <u>Under the Cherry Moon Premiere Show</u> father Nelson answers after being asked what did your son get from you, "He got everything from me. I'm Prince" (J. Nelson 1986). And in an earlier 1985 interview with <u>Rolling Stone</u> Prince had already affirmed, "My father and me, we're one and the same. My father's a little sick, just like I am" (Karlen, "Prince Talks: The Silence Is Broken," 26). Their relationship would be the lasting characteristic that Prince would inherit and hold stern to his heart throughout his career. But it was not just the music, but the varied emotions that went along with their father-son relationship that influenced the man and artist that Prince became.

> "'That's where I called my dad and begged him to take me back after he kicked me out. He said no, so I called my sister and asked her to ask him. So she did and afterward told me that all I had to do was call him back, tell him I was sorry, and he'd take me back. So I did, and he still said no. I sat crying at that phone booth for two hours. That's the last time I cried.' In the years between that phone-booth breakdown and today's pool game [between father and son on Mr. Nelson's birthday] came forgiveness. But it took many more years for the son to understand what a jazzman needs to survive. Prince figured it out when he moved into his purple house. 'I can be upstairs at the piano, and

Rande [his cook] can come in. Her footsteps will be in a different time, and it's real weird when you hear something that's a totally different rhythm than what you are playing. A lot of times that's mistaken for conceit or not having a heart. But it's not. And my dad's the same way, and that's why it was so hard for him to live with anybody. I didn't realize that until recently. When he was working or thinking, he had a private pulse going constantly inside him. I don't know, your bloodstream beats differently'" (Karlen, "Prince Talks: The Silence Is Broken," 26). "[My father] left when I was seven, so music left with him. But he did leave his piano and that's when I started learning how to play... I think music is what broke [my mother] and my father up, and I don't think that she wanted that for me...Musicians, depending on how serious they are, are really moody. Sometimes they need a lot of space; they want everything just right sometimes, you know. My father was a great deal like that, and my mother didn't give him a lot of space. She wanted a husband *per se*" (Schwartz 1981, reprinted in Fudger 10). "I think that's why he probably named me what he named me, it was like a blow to her—'He's gonna grow up the same way, so don't even worry about him.' And that's what I did" (Graustark 57).

After being kicked out by his father around the age of thirteen, Prince was left to face the world on his own, experiencing it first hand, growing from a child into a man in a matter of short years. After a short stint with an aunt, Prince spent the remainder of his high school years at the house of his best friend, Andre' Anderson who was later renamed Andre' Cymone and became Prince's first bassist. They spent hours alone in Cymone's basement, making music and plotting their dreams.—two young boys becoming men without much guidance. "Down in the basement, everything is possible and nothing is forbidden. Every impulse and feeling bypasses life and becomes sound. Down in the basement, all is soft and wet. The bass is a pelvic thrust; a single note trembling through a guitar string is a tear about to fall. Was Prince ever a teenager?..." (Hoskyns 19). Being from a "broken home" and living in poverty had varying effects on Prince's outlook on life. His early life was unsettling as Prince relates, "I have four brothers and four sisters, but we don't all have the same mother and father. It's very difficult having a stepfather—basic resentment all the way around. Nobody belongs to anybody" (Salewicz 18, reprinted in Fudger 12). Prince often chronicled his childhood as a constant state of transition and adjustment, never quite fitting in anywhere. "When I was twelve, I ran away for the first time because of problems with my stepfather. I went to live with my real father, but that didn't last too long because he's as stubborn as I am...I was constantly running from family to family" (Edrei 35). He continues. "At thirteen I went to live with my aunt. She didn't have room for a piano so my father bought me an electric guitar, and I learned how to play that" (Fudger 11). This sense of not belonging, along with the pain of poverty, began to shape the young lad's attitudes. "Poverty makes people angry, brings out their worst side. I was very bitter when I was young. I was insecure, and I'd attack anybody. I couldn't keep a girlfriend for two weeks. We'd argue about anything" (Karlen, "Prince Talks: The Silence Is Broken," 26). This constant transition and feeling of illegitimacy would become a driving force, causing Prince's physical divorce from society and the creation of a Utopian, fantasy world for his own comfort. "It used to be I'd have to be totally isolated to write things, because a lotta things I wrote concerned different visions and dreams and fantasies I had" (Schwartz 1981).

Andre' Anderson's mother, Bernadette Anderson, recounted how the boys were pretty much left to their own as long as they kept up their studies. This freedom at a young age with another male trying to find his way would greatly influence the young songwriter's experience of trying to find his voice as an artist. It would be the ambitious Prince who would go to school an hour early to earn extra credits in an attempt to graduate high school early. His first and only passion was making music, and at an early age he was willing to do what was necessary to achieve his goal. So, it is his vast experiences that echo through his music: laments of loneliness, love, and pain, gospels, calls to revolution against an overly conservative society, and the comfort of God and a better place to be. Through his songs, Prince became the illegitimate child, petitioning the society for his rightful place, advocating social justice, and continuing the quest for the true meaning of life and death. And at the center of Prince's songs is his search for place and meaning, which creates great thematic transition from album to album. Whether fact or fiction, early in his career Prince elaborated on his lyrical development a great detail. What can be gained is that the lyrics and subject matter of the songs are as equally important as the music. Even in the beginning, Prince wanted to say something about life.

> "When I got into high school, I started to write lyrics. I'd write the really vulgar stuff…I was writing things that a cat with ten albums would have out, like seven minute laments that were, y'kno, gone. I wrote like I was rich, had been everywhere, and had every woman in the world. But I liked that; I always liked fantasy and fiction" (Schwartz 1981) "I've always spent a lot of time alone, in a kind of fantasy world, and this is where I wanted to be—to be listened to and taken seriously" (Fudger 11-12,14).

Prince's early childhood disposition of otherness permeates his psychological make up and resonates throughout his art. Even if in these early interviews he was pushing the envelope of reality, he did eventually construct a world almost separate from reality, which would allow him to create and live freely with very little opposition. He created a place where he belonged. It also seems that as he matured, his approach toward writing matured, becoming more inclusive or in touch with the surrounding physical/tangible world. In doing this, Prince became a writer who had no problems dealing with and combining fantasy and reality. He combines the two in an attempt to excise his own demons as well as to paint an idealistic picture of what he believes life should be. He does all of this quite unapologetically.

> "I don't just wanna sit in the house alone and make up these nasty vulgar songs and put 'em out—I'd rather wait until I have something to write about" (Mitchell 15, reprinted in Fudger 25). "…lately, I have to be around people, I have to see different places and stuff like that…You know, it's interesting—if I try to get myself away from being a musician and just, you know, live life, I can write much better" (Schwartz 1981). "…once I told [Warner Bros] that this was the way it was, then they knew they had no choice and they'd have to try it, because they weren't going to get another record out of me otherwise…I know that I'm a lot happier than I was because I'm getting away with what I want to do" (Salewicz 18).

This becomes the dichotomy for Prince. On the one side, he is motivated by the intense, lingering pain from abandonment, loneliness, and isolation, which drives him to create a fantasy world. On the other side, he is motivated as an artist to say something about the outside, physical world that is the matrix for his own fantasy world. Much like Pecola of Toni Morrison's <u>The Bluest Eye</u>, Prince would walk the line of insanity and schizophrenia, creating a fantasy world to cope with the real world. Throughout his career we find Prince navigating this thin line between these two worlds, wearing the hat of a rebel, outsider to the "real" world, and wearing the hat of the conductor, leading his followers to find that other, inner world of peace and security.

The First Two Albums: Laying a Foundation

Prince's first album, <u>For You</u> (1978), is a pamphlet of romantic poetry. He establishes his rhyme scheme with simple couplets that echo urban sensibilities and sensitivity with commercial sexuality. With only a couple of socially conscience statements, <u>For You</u> is a combination of Smokey Robinson love poetry cut with the sharp edges of a post-disco, let it all hang out expressive style with subtle traces of Stevie Wonder coordination. Prince, at this early stage of his career, was more than content to establish himself as a musician first, but his literary talents manage to provide his listeners an indication of what was yet to come. Conservative as compared to his later albums, we get glimpses of his daringness and social awareness in the songs "Soft and Wet" and "Baby." In "Soft and Wet," co-written with Chris Moon, Prince shows that how you say something is as important as what you say. "Hey lover, I got sugar cane that I wanna lose in you…" Of course he is talking about having sex in a very aggressive manner, but it does not resonate as dogmatic. The desire to get radio play forces all artists to "tone down" their sexual statements, but Prince is toning down his sexuality with lyrical technique. Today, sexually explicit lyrics are bleeped (censored), not toned down. This bleeping says something about the times as well as about the lack of time or consideration given to lyrical craft. Prince manages to openly and carelessly speak of the enjoyment of sex between partners, escaping the bars of embarrassment without losing respect and sensitivity. Prince is establishing his notion that women are not merely objects to be used for personal gratification, but are experiences to be enjoyed, engaged, and even endured along the way to a higher completion of self.

With his strategic use of language, Prince is establishing his ability to be explicit and not dogmatic, concise and honest but not degrading. His use of words that conjure vivid and erotic images is what explodes "Soft and Wet" into the listener's mind. Words like "sugar cane" and "lion's mane" are explicit but soft, natural imagery, effectively capturing the listener's imagination without being overbearing. It is sexually playful, which is feminine as opposed to the typical, masculine assertion or dominance. He then balances this aggression on one song with an ode to responsibility on another song. In "Baby," Prince tells of an unwed expectant father, fully accepting his responsibilities. "Should we go on living together, or should we get married right away?...I barely have enough money for 2…I don't want to regret what I've done to you." By making an open reference to safe sex, something not too common in popular music in 1978, he is showing his ability to handle complex situations and emotions and still be creative. "I never would've thought that this would happen to a very careful man like me." A song like "Baby" directly refutes the notions that Prince is blindly leading a mass of young people to their moral and physical detriment. Carol Cooper asserts that, while Prince is always pushing boundaries, he has never told

> "anybody not to take precautions… You can look at it two ways. Either other aspects of the wrong way people are using their environment is making people sick, or these diseases are just what they call them—the Wrath of God. [Thus, Prince seems to be asserting] that you shouldn't repress your sexual feelings just because some official told you to. In many places in the world today you're not supposed to fuck just like you're not supposed to think. Part of thinking for yourself is avoiding people who are going to give you diseases—mental or physical" (Cooper 59).

By the end of "Baby," the female listener knows that Prince is willing to meet their every need, physical and emotional. Not only do they get the great sex of "Soft and Wet," but they also get the loving and responsible man who will be there to endure any situation. "And we'll grow stronger everyday…pretty baby, we're gonna work it out…I hope our baby has eyes just like yours." This balance or diversity of subject matter on his first album widens the artistic spectrum for Prince, helping to keep him from being boxed or limited in what he can discuss which works to widen his image. Thus, Prince's fans allow him more latitude in his artistic direction because he has been working to liberate himself from artistic chains since the beginning of his career. And, of course, it is this latitude that makes for a more rewarding experience for the listener because Prince is able to take them in a variety of directions.

Other songs, such as "My Love Is Forever," "Crazy You," and "So Blue," display the pop romantic poet. The lyrics and rhyme scheme are basic, usually a,a,b,b or a,b,a,b. Prince also uses his falsetto voice to create the feeling of sincerity and sensitivity, then changing to a deeper alto, masculine tone, playing with the persona of being a wolf in sheep's clothing, showing his ability to express the entire spectrum of emotions, becoming every aspect of a lover that a woman may need. In this manner, <u>For You</u> is a coy, submissive record that becomes more aggressive once the initial songs have won the listener's trust, almost like the act of lovemaking, itself. The entire work is a lament to womanhood and connecting with it. Songs like "Just as Long as We're Together" and "My Love is Forever" speak of completion through the romantic relationship. And even in the insecure, craziness of the male/female relationship, the romantic separation in "So Blue" is so devastating that being alone is more emotionally costly than not playing the games of love. It becomes clear that the male-female union is both a physical and emotional need, as they complete the natural union, becoming one entity. As he declares in his opening passage, "For You," "All of this and more is for you. With love, sincerity, and deepest care, my life with you I share." Every fiber of his male being is meant for connection with the female being. From the onset, Prince's union of male and female is used to achieve some sense of the human connection.

The second album, Prince (1979), produces his first top ten hit, "I Wanna Be Your Lover," and establishes Prince as a Wonder-type, musical genius and an ambiguously sensual male looking at women as equal partners in a search for Utopia within the romantic relationship. Prince establishes gender equality by having the male voice literally and figuratively expose his entire emotional self, not being afraid to express the deepest emotions, including insecurity and vulnerability. Songs, such as "I Wanna Be Your Lover," "Why You Wanna Treat Me So Bad?," "When We're Dancing Close And Slow," "With You," and "It's Gonna Be Lonely," show the male in very vulnerable and diverse lights not generally shown in popular music, which is dominated by overly masculine male images and submissive women. Statements, such as "I ain't got no money. I ain't like those other guys you hang around. And It's kind of funny 'cause they always seem to let you down...they say I'm so shy, but with you I just go wild" and "I gave you all of my love, I even gave you my body," show the male as the submissive almost conquered victim, being able to get in touch with those emotions that were so long considered exclusively feminine. Prince begins in the male R&B tradition of Smokey Robinson and the Stylistics but reverses their attempt to seduce and conquer to become the conquered. With "I Wanna Be Your Lover" Prince sets the stage for a career of gender blurring, demolishing gender walls to gain absolute gratification. He wants to be every aspect of the human condition, to feel and fill a woman's every emotional need. He wants to be her mother, brother, sister, and sexual counterpart. "His devotion will be that of a female parent, his loyalty, easy in its intimacy, like a girl sibling" (Hill 74). Prince becomes a concept record, not in its thematic subject matter, but in Prince's handling or treatment of material. It is not the subject matter that makes Prince memorable, but he manner in which he engages and presents the subject matter that wows us. "...while the song that made him a star, 1979's 'I Wanna

Be Your Lover,' snuck the line 'I wanna be the only one you come for' onto AM radio, the singer delivered it with such coy ignorance, as if feigning ignorance of what the words meant but confident they'd please his lover" (Tucker 54). With his treatment of the subjects, he was bringing a stranger form of ambisexuality to "black pop" which was allowing him to become both seducer and victim. It was the "signaling of an erotic personality which could only be assertive upon legitimization of its submissive exterior...The songs plead, quite unashamedly, for acknowledgment and understanding, or make petulant demands for attention" (Hill 74). With the lyricism and look of Prince, Prince is blurring his identity, which will allow him to create and discuss more complex notions of identity and place without the limitations of the traditional gender and race roles. This is seen in another song titled "Bambi," where Prince uses sexuality to address cultural relativity. In "Bambi," the male finds himself in love with a lesbian. He never comes to understand her choice of lover, but he never condemns her, even leaving the door open to the possibility that she may be right or at least has the right to choose, "Maybe it's cause you're so young, or maybe I'm just too naive. Who's to say, maybe you're really having fun." An offbeat perspective, but listeners come to find that Prince's openness is the key to his creativity because his liberalism makes his listeners feel comfortable and free to explore and expand who they are.

      When people discuss the early songs that make Prince a sexually rebellious icon in the world's mind, songs, such as "I Wanna Be Your Lover," "Soft and Wet," and "Why You Wanna Treat Me So Bad?," come to mind. Yet, the early song that truly created the Prince persona is "Still Waiting." Prince's whole desire is to be what he wants to be, whatever that is, unencumbered by race, gender, or class. "Still Waiting" achieves this better than any other song on the first two albums. Musically, it is awkward and quirky. It has a strong R&B piano groove, which is well regulated by a soft but steady drum beat, but the rhythmic, scanty guitar riff and high pitched synthesizer through the entirety of the song create it as a categorical irregularity. At best, it is a bluesy pop groove—a modified twelve bar approach that is concealed well by a strong falsetto, which is rare to the blues aesthetic. Not only is it a perfect pop groove, sounding like something that Joni Mitchell would write after taking downers and listening to Motown records all day, but the lyrics present a vulnerability rarely shown by male singers of the day.

> "All my friends tell me about the love they've had. Can't they see what they're doing to me? It makes me feel so bad. I'm so alone and brokenhearted. It ain't like my life has ended, but more like my life has never started. The love my friends rap about, I keep anticipating. I try so hard, but don't you know my patience is fading away."

Prince is wading the waters of jazz and blues singer Jimmy Scott, who has Kallmann's syndrome, a genetic condition that stunted his growth at five feet and prevented him reaching puberty, leaving him with a high, undeveloped soprano voice, hence his nickname "Little" Jimmy Scott. Many critics feel that Scott's vocal and physical oddity limited his success. Of course Prince does not drown in those waters because he has the life preserver of having played rock guitar on the first two albums and the anchor of "Soft and Wet" that provides evidence that he is capable of satisfying the female desire. Nonetheless, in "Still Waiting," the protagonist is completely helpless in his struggle to find love and is completely honest (vulnerable) about its emotional effect on him. "I'm still waiting, waiting for the love; still waiting, I wish on every star above. Still waiting, waiting for the love to come around." The protagonist's life is non-existent and meaningless without someone to love, and he is powerless to change or improve his condition.

The final stanza clinches and establishes the "Prince Persona." Prince reworks two stereotypes that are typical of women and not men in popular music. "People say that I'm too young, too young to fall in love." In our blue and pink gender coded society, this is what we tell young girls, often in our attempts to persuade them into abstinence. This male dominated society often celebrates a young boy's first romantic and sexual urges. We rarely tell young boys to wait on love and sex in the same manner and with the same intensity that well tell young girls. Prince then shows that this situation causes as much anguish in him as we are used to seeing in female singers and protagonists. "But they don't know, they really don't know that's all that I've been dreaming of. I spend my nights just a-crying. I spend my days just a-trying to find that love to call my own 'cause I'm sick and tired of being alone." These are not traditional male emotions. We expect a male to be seeking sexual conquest constantly, but not really looking for love. With this song, Prince builds a bridge from Jimmy Scott to the rugged but sensitive soul singer Lenny Williams, making himself the most unusual black act ever. Rock critic Bill Adler asserts "...for sheer girlish vulnerability, there's no one around to touch him: not Michael Jackson, not even fourteen-year-old soul songbird Stacy Lattisaw. At age twenty, Prince may be the unlikeliest rock star, black or white, in recent memory—but a star he definitely is" (Adler 55, 57). Prince is working in the tradition of sensitive R&B soul singers of the sixties and seventies, but there is an ambisexuality that is not found in Smokey Robinson. Being sensitive is one thing, but few, if any of these men, lose their position of power and dominance over women. Or to put it another way, few become male-less. Even in the case of Percy Sledge's "When a Man Loves a Woman," the man is not emasculated; he is merely misguided. Or as blues icon Bobby Rush asserts in his song "Hen Pecked," "I ain't henpecked. I've just been pecked by the right hen." In a backhanded way, Rush is perpetuating male dominance. Rather than admit to being dominated, he twists the situation to show that it is acceptable for the woman to have some "say" (power) if the man is getting what he wants, which is excellent loving. In their live rendition of "Stormy Monday," Bobby "Blue" Bland and B. B. King display the more traditional, macho response to pain and vulnerability. First, they express their pain and vulnerability. "Midnight finds me crying, and daylight finds me crying too." Then, their reaction is to assert their male dominance. "U better leave baby, before something happen to you." Even the seemingly sensitive R&B

classic, "In the Rain," originally recorded by the Dramatics and later covered by Keith Sweat, shows the male's need to hide his pain and vulnerability. The protagonist wants to go outside in the rain so that no one will know that he is crying. Traditionally, the male reaction to pain is to meet it with some type of aggression. As the old blues lyric asserts, "When a woman gets the blues, she hangs her head and cries. When a man gets the blues, he catches a train and rides." There is usually some reaction from the man to assert or reclaim his position of dominance. Even in the famous song by Rich Amerson, the male, in pain over losing his woman, is still assigning the female's position. Although he is crying for his woman, he misses her in all of the traditional female places. "I know you hear me cryin' oh Baby!...when I looked in my kitchen, Mamma, And I went all through my dinin' room!" (Cook and Henderson 91). Whether conscious or not, Amerson is making a clear distinction between his role and his woman's role as a way to keep some sense of his manhood during this vulnerable lyric. When Amerson uses the cow as a metaphor for his woman, this usage innately makes him the bull.

> "...even in this song there is a certain ambiguity of attitude, for example in the 'white cow' image because it repeats the imagery of a blues like "Milk Cow," where the cow...is a profound, primitive metaphor for woman. I say profound and primitive because in this context the male would obviously be the bull..." (Cook and Henderson 92-93).

In "Still Waiting," Prince achieves becoming something other than a male. There is no gender, only a longing for love, a longing for one soul to connect with another soul. This establishes his androgynous persona, creating the path and platform for songs, such as "If I Was Your Girlfriend." This also allows Prince to be explicit and not be perceived by his female audience as being dogmatic. As Miles Davis asserts in his autobiography, sexual aggression is taken differently when Prince expresses it. "…when he's singing that funky X-rated shit that he does about sex and women…If I said 'Funk you' to somebody they would be ready to call the police. But if

Prince says it in that girl-like voice that he uses, then everyone says it's cute" (Davis 385). Prince can assert physical desire and not appear demeaning, as in songs such as "I Feel for You." "I wouldn't lie to you, baby; It's mainly a physical thing...I'm physically attracted to you." His androgynous persona allows his sexuality to appear as a non-threatening, involuntary expression of honesty as in "When We're Dancing Close and Slow," rather than as an expression of machismo. "Baby, that's honestly the way I feel." There is no contradiction or sexism because there is no play for power or dominance in these early songs. He is just as weak and vulnerable as the females whom he is trying to woo. The traditional R&B "begging" song is about seduction, and one must be in control to seduce. Teddy Pendergrass is in control in "Come Go With Me," as is Marvin Gaye in both "Let's Get It On" and "Sexual Healing." Even on James Brown's "Please, Please, Please" and the Temptations "Ain't Too Proud to Beg," the rough, growling alto vocal cuts the vulnerability. Had the Temptations wanted full and complete vulnerability, falsetto-voiced Eddie Kendricks would have performed the song, but David Ruffin's grittier alto vocal is used. In contrast, Prince has relinquished all sense of control because he has relinquished all sense of maleness to connect with the deeper female being. Interestingly enough, it has been reported by many, including Alan Leeds in the "Liner Notes" to <u>Prince: The Hits/The B-Sides</u> that "I Wanna Be Your Lover" and "I Feel for You" were written as demos for Patrice Rushen. They were inspired by a serious crush on Rushen, but they failed to make her album, luckily for Prince. "Ironically, it was still another female vocalist, diva Chaka Khan, who finally placed ["I Feel for You"] on the charts in 1984" (Leeds 3). This shows Prince's lyrical range, his ability to construct personas for various messages, and his ability to connect with women as an equal and not as a distant, superior other. "I Wanna Be Your Lover," "Why You Wanna Treat Me So Bad?," and "Still Waiting" establish Prince as an impish child-god in the tradition of the androgynous Greek boys, but with enough R&B sensibility to be dangerous and satisfying. He wants an orgasm, but he wants it only as a means to a higher end. He not only wants to inform and change your sexuality, he wants to change all of your notions of the world by changing your sexuality.

<u>For You</u> and <u>Prince</u> are lyrically simple but smart records. By looking back at Prince's career, you can see that Prince was in this game for the long haul. The songs on the first two records set the table for <u>Dirty Mind</u>. In this, Prince should be viewed as a conceptual artist because he is concerned with how his songs combine and build toward a theme and how his albums weave a mosaic of a man on a journey. <u>For You</u> and <u>Prince</u> give Prince the femininity he will need to construct a career of unrestricted expression. Comfortable with his image, <u>Prince</u> marked the end of his totally romantic toned albums for the next few years. Knowing that some of the support from black listeners and the mainstream would be shaken by his next album, Prince also knew that it was time for him to step into new and deeper waters before he was defined, catalogued, controlled, and limited.

The Beginning of Controversy
with the Breaking of New Ground

<u>Dirty Mind</u> (1980) is Prince's third album and is viewed as the Prince essential by many popular music critics. The title track, "Dirty Mind," presents the understanding of sexual thoughts (and other rebellious thoughts) as being normal. In its promo for the album, Warner Bros asserts that "behind the frequently shocking lyrics is a deep belief that by removing the taboos and allowing youth to express its sexuality in all of its forms, we will achieve a more wholesome society" (Hoskyns 18). More liberating is the fact that Prince does not attempt to direct the listener in a way of dealing with these emotions, but simply provide particular events and scenarios for his listeners to ponder. He explains his process in a 1983 issue of <u>Musician</u>.

> "If I were to write a letter to a friend, and tell them about an experience, I wouldn't say how it made me feel; I would say exactly what I did, so that they could experience it, too, rather than the intellectual point of view. If you give them a situation, maybe that you've encountered, or whatever, give them the basis of it, let them take it to the next stage, they make the picture in their own mind. I know I'm happiest making records like this, making records that tell the truth and don't beat around the bush" (Graustark 63).

Prince only felt the obligation or need to express himself in a way that gave his listeners a means of looking at situations differently. What is most interesting is the manner in which he combines the theories of realism and fantasy; with some songs he presents the horror of a perverted and oppressed life and on other songs he presents the possibility of where we can go. And often he does this in the same song. His ability to paint clear and authentic pictures of the worst and best of humanity allows him to navigate the contradictions of life seamlessly.

> "With Dirty Mind Prince began to move into that domain of dreams and contradictions which is the real stuff of American stardom, a place emblematic of the agonies and ecstasies of its time. It was an album that challenged the prevailing market categorizations, and so urged listeners to place it in a category on its own." (Hill 82).

And, of course, this new direction does not sit well with many in the African American community. After Prince, Prince was a star in the black community. He was the heir apparent to Stevie Wonder. This new direction was seen by some African Americans as another example of a self-hating black person not happy with the love and respect of the black community who needed to be validated by the white power structure. "For the black media, Prince is yet another in a long line of brilliant young turks getting ready to break his back against institutionalized white indifference…[becoming just another] statement on how the black man must exaggerate and contort his image (as allegory for much of the gratuitous absurdity of being 'black' in America) just to be heard" (Cooper 58). Yet, for the people, both black and white, who charged that Dirty Mind was just a contrived record to gain crossover appeal, Cooper also asserts that

> "[Prince's black audience or anyone listening to his first two records knew] it was coming. 'I'm Yours' off the first album was a straight up rock jam…And the second album had 'Bambi,' which was also written in such a way as not to give the impression that Prince was a dilettante. So many black bands in the early Seventies diddled with the rock guitar just to prove they could. They had no real conviction, but none of Prince's rock jams are contrived that way" (Cooper 58).

<u>Dirty Mind</u> may have not been a philosophy, but it is a record that espouses a defiant attitude towards human boxes and being restricted by anyone other than oneself. "I'm not happy with anything [that tries to categorize me] but [rock/funk/soul fusion] is better than being called 'Smokey Robinson's son'" (Mitchell 1981).

In <u>Dirty Mind</u>, Prince is both reinventing and breaking traditional stereotypes held for African Americans. James Baldwin, asserts that "to be colored means that one has been caught in some utterly unbelievable cosmic joke...One's only hope of supporting, to say nothing of surviving, this joke is to flaunt in the teeth of it one's own particular and invincible style!" (Baldwin, <u>The Price of the Ticket</u>, 319-320) Hill points out, "<u>Dirty Mind</u> was nothing, if not the flaunting of a particular style in the face of suffocating expectations!" (Hill 84). Prince was becoming the sexually obsessive, black male, preying on young white girls. And yet, at the same time, dealing with social issues and building an ambisexual identity, he was stepping into the world of rock-n-roll reserved for white males. As Baldwin affirms, "to be an American Negro male is also to be a kind of walking phallic symbol: which means one pays, in one's own personality, for the sexual insecurity of others. The relationship, therefore, of a black boy to a white boy is a very complex thing" (Baldwin, <u>The Price of the Ticket,</u> 290). Throughout his career, Prince has paid for the sexual insecurities of both white and black males. Aside from Little Richard, no African American male has successfully existed as some type of ambiguous sexual identity. And even in the case of Little Richard, he was, for many years of his career, delegated to play the role of the colorful, humorous homosexual. In <u>Dirty Mind</u> Prince evolves as a totally new and unique character to black music, able to have all of the emotions and characteristics of a female, yet able to display all of the machismo attitudes of traditional rock-n-roll males, a duality that only white rockers such as Bowie and Jagger were allowed to encompass. With this new approach to black and white identities, "<u>Dirty Mind</u> created and defined its own world" (Hill 86). Throughout the album "the voice, all angelic falsetto anxiety, hovers between confession and frenzy as this alarming baby libertine makes public his most powerful private desires. It is a vision which is pure, vintage rock-n-roll; Chuck Berry would understand" (Hill 86). With the mythic, flagship capital city of Uptown given as the recording location of Dirty Mind, Prince is able to set a surreal tone of a haven for outcasts. The album's success follows suit, becoming an underground classic.

There are three other songs that stand out because of their subjects of social or political conscienceness. "Uptown," based on the arts district in southwestern Minneapolis of the same name, is about a mythological city that exercises the belief of cultural relevancy as its means of providing outcasts with a place to be themselves, "Our clothes, our hair, we don't care, it's all about being there... Uptown...set your mind free..." In the 1981 Sounds interview Prince explains, "Uptown is more or less a state of mind…it has nothing to do with financial status. It all has to do with how free you are inside and how good you feel about yourself and how strongly you feel about yourself…and what you stand for and your beliefs" (Boskamp 1981/Mitchell 1981).

> "'Uptown' is a sub-culture with a simple philosophy—to let no one categorize or explain them. In his most innocently freaky falsetto, Prince describes an encounter with a girl who steps up to him on the street to demand if he is gay. Our hero's response is indignant, and he throws a question straight back. The message is don't judge by appearances and marks the most overt statement, his desire to escape labeling by others. 'Uptown' articulated fully a preoccupation that drove Prince's work in the following years: to evade at all costs every semblance of an identity defined by roots in the real world" (Hill 88).

In the February 19, 1981 issue of Rolling Stone, Prince discusses what influenced Dirty Mind, "I grew up on the borderline…I had a bunch of white friends and a bunch of black friends. I never grew up in one particular culture…That's what 'Uptown' is about—we do whatever we want, and those who cannot deal with it have a problem within themselves" (Adler 57). He is certainly echoing Toomer's notion of there being no more Africans or Europeans in this territory, only Americans. Thus, people should be defined by their ideals and behavior as opposed to their physical being. Uptown represents the type of world Prince wished to create, "a rainbow coalition of diverse individuals whose minds had shed all shackles of class, race, and sex" (Hill 90). With <u>Dirty Mind</u> he was establishing that audience.

> "There was a lot of pressure from my ex-buddies in other bands not to have white members in the band. But I always wanted a band that was black and white. Half the musicians I knew only listened to one type of music. That wasn't good enough for me" (Fudger 11).

At the heart of this cultural transformation to a new hybrid generation is the struggle over perverted sexuality, which exists because of oppression and mis-education. "Sister" tells the story of a sexually abused male child expressing his anguish about his situation while trying to understand the situation, "My sister never made love to anyone else but me. She's the reason for my sexuality. Oh sister, don't put me on the street again. I know what you want me to do…" At the heart of Prince's liberation is his termination of psychological and physical abuse and oppression. "Sister," takes a matter-of-fact approach to the discussion of molestation. It is not psychoanalysis, but rather it is an act of realism as in the vein of <u>Native Son</u> or <u>Push</u>. "Incest is everything it's said to be." The problem with this statement is that it is ambiguous. What exactly is incest said to be? "Sister" speaks to the physical, emotional, and psychological molestation of male children by simply presenting the pain and anxiety of the child. We have the voice of the child, but there is no omnipresent voice that tells us that this act is wrong or how we should feel. Thus, it is interesting for two reasons. On the one hand, we do not generally have the same degree of concern and empathy for the molestation of boys by women as we do for girls by men. It is a double standard that works to nurture the dogmatic attitudes in males for which we later condemn them for acting out in their adulthood. This gets us to our second issue, the molestation of black males who are constantly bombarded through American culture with some notion of their super-sexuality. Prince, speaking in the first person, is showing the black male who is victimized by America's notion of his sexuality. Additionally, the male child is also attempting to navigate his abuse, as most abused children are prone to do, by constructing some boundaries or limits to the abuse, which allows for the perpetuation of this molestation. The child will comply with the abuse as long as the abuse is just by the sister and no one else. "Don't put me on the street again…I know what you want me to do. Put me on the street and make me blue."

The ambiguity of the song is what causes the listener problems. On the one hand, the bouncy, fast-pasted guitar riff and Prince's falsetto give the appearance that Prince is playing with all of this somewhat "tongue in cheek" style. However, based on the lyric, the child is not a happy camper, and Prince states that "'Sister' is serious" (Graustark 56). He is not necessarily refuting or denouncing any of this, merely putting it out there as a reality for the listener to do with as he wishes. "If people get enjoyment out of it and laugh, that's fine. All the stuff on the record is true experiences and things that have occurred around me" (Graustark 56). But, we do get the sense that he wants us to understand that the molestation has a lingering effect on the child. "She's the reason for my sexuality." Prince is asserting that sexual problems and deviancy are caused by other psychological and emotional issues. The sexual abuse is a symbol of or a manifestation of the female's need to dominate and control. "She took a whip to me until I shout…Don't put me on the street again." The traditional thought is that most abusers have been abused. So, it is inferred that the female's act of abuse is her reacting to her past abuse. This forces us to ponder the future of the male child. The song ends with the young male's pleas to his sister to stop the abuse, but they seemingly go unheard. The question that remains is why are we being given this tale? Is this a story that Prince is using as a mirror to force society to see its reflection? Are we supposed to feel pain, anger, empathy, or remorse? Possibly, Prince is asserting that if we do not heed the calls and pleas of the young male, we will continue to perpetuate social chaos. In another song, "Papa," that discusses child abuse and was released fourteen years later, Prince states "Don't abuse children, or else they turn out like me." By 1994, Prince is playing on his well-established persona of being a deviant. But even as early as 1980, Prince was viewed as not the normal R&B act. So "Sister" is effective for Prince on two levels. One, it helps shape his unusual persona by singing about a topic that was taboo for black acts and pop music in general, and it works to reinforce the general theme of the album that sexuality is a barometer of our mental and emotional health and welfare.

"Sister" is a good example of Prince being misunderstood by the masses for not specifically addressing or articulating the moral proverb in the song. Amy Lindon, music critic for VH1's <u>4 on the Floor</u>, often states that the masses of American listeners rarely get irony in popular music. I will raise her and state that they rarely get subtlety either. Songs which rely on or are open to individual interpretation on specific, controversial issues tend not to do as well as songs which announce their agenda and proceed to scream it until the end. Although "Sister" is a metaphor, it is also an exercise in metonymy, drawing the listener into the plot through the intimate and explicit point by point mapping of the details of the experience, allowing the listener's perception to lead him to the song's meaning. The protagonist is a certain way because of certain experiences, and the listener is forced to deal with how he feels about the protagonist's predicament without any moral guidance from the narrator. The twist is that there is a reversal of role assignment. The male is assigned his sexuality by the female, understands it, and is resigned to accept it. "She's the reason for my sexuality."

In "Sister" the female has the power to control ideas

about sexuality and gender roles. "Sister, don't put me on the street again. I know what you want me to do." The male is helpless against her, and is, in many respects, emasculated by the female. Further, if we go deeper and see the sister as a metaphor for America, she then controls the sexuality of all males, emasculating the black male for her own enjoyment and security. Though Prince may not have been thinking this deeply, he certainly understood how this song would work to liquefy his male imagery, allowing him to play the emasculated victim and rebel throughout his career because most listeners assume that the singer is actually the persona or protagonist of the song. So, asserting one's sexuality is also an act of war by which we determine and assert our own selves and attempt to determine the identities of others. Through "Sister" Prince shows how one is assigned a political role by having his sexual identity assigned. This is an act of war, which he then parallels in "Party Up" by showing how the young are forcefully assigned a position of submission or inferiority by the elders of the nation. This is the first example of Prince creating sexual energy and anxiety and then transferring it to a socio-political topic. What proves or authenticates that Prince is purposefully transferring the energy and emotions of "Sister" to "Party Up" is the fact that the two songs are not separated as the rest of the songs on the album, and "Sister" rages and explodes right into "Party Up." Using the angst of "Sister," "Party Up" openly criticizes war and all governmental officials who approve of war. Prince asserts that it is immoral to kill the youths of the world over the whims of a few government officials, especially when the youths, specifically poor youths, have no say in policy making and are almost powerless to escape from their assigned category. In "Party Up" the youth are assigned their roles in the same manner that the male is assigned his role in "Sister." "Because of their half-baked mistakes, we get ice cream no cake. All lies no truth, is it fair to kill the youth!?!" "Party Up" has the tone of intolerance and declaration. The revolution had started; the youths of today were not going to stand for the destruction of themselves or their world caused by a confining, arbitrary identity assignment. "You're gonna have to fight your own damn war, cuz we don't wanna fight no more!" Prince further elaborates:

"I just seem to read about a lot of politicians who're all going to die soon, and I guess they want to go out heavy because they're prepared to make a few mistakes and end up starting a war they don't have to go out and fight...I just think the people should have a little more to say in some of these foreign matters. I don't want to have to go out and die for their mistakes" (Salewicz 18, reprinted in Fudger 23, 25)

A fourth song coming from <u>Dirty Mind</u> is "Head," which along with "Party Up," summarizes the entire album and its significance: complete freedom through a sexual revolution. Let's take back our bodies; it's the only thing we have. "Head" ejaculates the sexual liberation by asserting the street theory, show me a guy who does not perform oral sex, and I will show you a guy whose girlfriend I can take. Show me a guy who is not sexually free, and I will show you a guy who is oppressed in every aspect of his life. A lot of <u>Dirty Mind</u> is street corner philosophy. The guy got the girl because of an open sexuality, allowing him to do anything for her pleasure. "...morning, noon, and night I give you head." This is another reversal of gender roles, especially for black males, where the male is catering to the whims of the female. When most listen to the song, they think that just the female is performing oral sex, but a closer listen informs us that the male is also performing the oral sex. Yet, Prince manages to subvert or manipulate this role reversal by maintaining control of the female's climax or sexual pleasure. "When I met you, you were on your way to be wed...you fool, you married me instead. Now morning, noon and night I give head." So, while the female is getting the sexual pleasure, she is still seen as the one who was seduced, mostly because of her naiveté. "I remember when I met u, baby, u were on your way to be wed... [and she said] I'm just a virgin, and I'm on my way to be wed, but you're such a hunk, so full of spunk..." "Head" knocked down all of the barriers that were being placed upon Prince and other black artists. Not only was the topic taboo for a young black artist; the music, a rock/funk fusion with a soul falsetto, captivated the urban and suburban streets of America, allowing black artists to continue their tradition of representing the totality of their musical history, letting them play what was in their hearts and not what was on a contrived playlist. "Head" also continues the modification and expansion of the myths of African American sexuality. In the early eighties, the prevailing thought was that black men did not perform oral sex. It was an affront to their "supernatural" masculinity. The myth was that brothers did not need to give head. Oral sex is an act committed by a man who is not well endowed enough to please a woman. Then here comes Prince casting off one stereotypical role to take up another, all the while keeping the stigma of the erotic, exotic black male. R&B was never like this. Teddy Pendergrass and Marvin Gaye were men's men. Prince manages to reintroduce them to Little Richard. "Tutti Frutti" combined with "Let's Get It On" and "Turn Out the Lights" to produce a freaky sexual satisfaction all for the pleasure and command of the female.

Dirty Mind is a culmination of ideas that were revolving around the edges of black music and black culture. We must understand that the original lyrics to "Tutti Frutti" are "Tutti frutti, good booty" and not "Tutti frutti, oh Rudy." Sexuality in the African American culture becomes an issue during and after Reconstruction, when the growing black middle class becomes worried that their sexual objectification by whites will hinder and impair their desires to assimilate into the white power structure. The black middle class embraced the same ideals about the body as their white masters and became very careful and selective about how they allowed themselves to be presented. The black juke joint was not a place where this new middle class would go. Prince is kicking open the doors of the juke joint for the world to see, magnifying his sexuality, hoping that it will become titillating and freeing, in the same manner that Presley's shaking of his white ass was liberating to whites. So in a very specific sense, Dirty Mind is a work which only could have been produced by an African American. When asked about being the first black artist since Hendrix to be more of a rock act than a traditional R&B act, Prince responds with insight rather than just being flattered to be a special Negro. "A lot has to do with society. There are a lot of black musicians who play other types of music, but the doors aren't open in any field like they are in R&B music. Once society changes you'd probably find a lot of great musicians...Music is pretty boring...in the States. Once society comes out of its bag, then the musicians will too" (Mitchell 1981). Prince is attempting, simultaneously, to assimilate, pacify, and assert his own sense of who he is as an individual. The plight of the African American individual is a dual journey which is as much internal as external. This is the "Double Consciousness" that Du Bois discussed. On the one hand, as a black man, Prince is attempting to force his way into the waters usually waded by white men: bashing, straight ahead, and introvertedly driven rock-n-roll. R&B confines the African American to being a member of the group. It is a quite external medium where the artist is expected to wear or at least connect to the clothing (ideals and identity) of the line of great performers. On the other hand, rock-n-roll allows white acts to root or ground themselves in the history of black music, while giving them the freedom to interpret and create at will. Thus, acts, such as the Rolling Stones, Aerosmith, and others, are able to build on the back of black music and then establish themselves as unique acts by impregnating black beats and rhythms with their European existence and ideals as in the instance of Led Zeppelin. Black acts have seldom been given this same opportunity and freedom. Although much of this has to do with white males controlling the industry of popular music, a good bit of this also has to do with African Americans' rocky search for, struggle over, and attempt to reconcile the individual identity with and to the racial identity. Dirty Mind very gets at this problem through the liberation of the body.

If Dirty Mind is overtly sexual it is so only because

the body is the only thing of value that teenagers of the eighties believe that they own. The attitude of African Americans growing up in the eighties is quite different than African Americans growing up in the fifties, sixties, and seventies. For the children of the eighties there is no S.N.C.C., no Operation Breadbasket, no Black Panthers. The Nation of Islam is still rebuilding, and the NAACP and the S.C.L.C. are seemingly, once again, aristocratic organizations. All these kids have are gangs and sex. They use both to express their dissatisfaction with the state of America. To complicate matters, the Reagan/Bush administrations would become an active catalyst in polarizing America. White America, now conscious of the new African American middle class created by the Civil Rights Movement and represented by The Cosby Show (1984), begins to ask what more do blacks want? After all of their success and achievements, about what could they be angry? The question itself is dehumanizing. Though there is an acknowledgment of racial accomplishment by African Americans, the question supposes that blacks are subhuman because whites continue to grapple with the problem of African Americans demanding an equal amount of rights in their country. The struggle for the African American individual parallels the race, which is the struggle for human rights. Traditionally, the black individual would have to take a back seat as the race attempted to gain visibility for itself first. Dirty Mind represents the black individual asserting his rights to be an individual and have his place in the world through the most subverted and taboo means, his body and his sexuality. Through sex and sexuality, Prince wishes to transform America into a new place, a primitive Utopia based on sexual and racial tolerance. And through the blending of musical styles, imagery, and stereotypes, Prince is attempting to construct a world for the individual by amalgamating history into something shared by all. Simultaneously, he is both the legitimate and illegitimate child of Smokey Robinson, Chuck Berry, Jimi Hendrix, Marvin Gaye, Stevie Wonder, and Ray Charles—in the manner that they all blended the sacred with the profane, the religious with the secular to produce a medium of popular music that is, in itself, a religion.

> "Parallels between love, sex, and a sublime state of spiritual connection had infused and dramatized the evolution of soul, a form born of the meeting of black gospel and black blues, the spirit and the body organically connected in the search for higher ground" (Hill 96).

Additionally, the seventies would bring another facet to the pot of black music, funk. Funk has three important factors. First, it allows black musicians who want to remain cool, in the black tradition, to disguise rock-n-roll guitar riffs as way-out hip music, allowing their songs to venture away from the romantic and into other aspects of the human condition. Secondly, it is edgy enough to express the black experience in America. George Clinton and Bootsy Collins are black men in America, dealing with the problems of the Negro. It is an amalgamation of black rhythm for cohesiveness, thumping base and drums to drive the lyrics home, and angry, screaming guitars to give it an edge of recklessness. Thirdly, it is about the body, "...how it looked, what it did, all the hot, nasty, lovely, smelly things about it. God would have to shake his ass or just stay home. What Prince did with funk was remind it (the music), curiously, of the sacredness it had left behind. He reintroduced the libido to the Holy Ghost" (Hill 96).

     Because of its heavy, sexual overtones, marked by music that was not thought the norm for black acts, along with Prince's indefinable sexuality, <u>Dirty Mind</u> was forced to go underground, where Prince was rapidly becoming a cult star. The general populous was not ready to buy an album with Prince staring "defiantly into the camera as if it were perfectly natural to pose in your raincoat and skivvies," especially a conservative black audience (Allen, "Prince: What U See Is What U Get," 129). The music and album covers of <u>Dirty Mind</u> and <u>Lovesexy</u> generate the ridicule of those who expect and wish for more direct and intense lyrical work from Prince without the cover of popular glam or gimmickry. Lyrically, critics would argue that, at times, Prince becomes too commercial, hiding his messages behind the music or the gimmicks, not letting his social awareness be seen for fear of losing his brash, rock and funk, street image. Yet Dirty Mind has what the records of the nineties lack, hope and possible solutions. Yes, it is general and sweeping, but the record is not vague about what it presents. It is a concise statement for tolerance and understanding to end the hate and oppression.

> "Here was free sexual individualism proposed as the solution to the warped mind-set of the authorities and masses alike. Sex was the essence of life, life was the antithesis of war, and God was the Lord of Peace. Within Prince's sexual promise, he hinted, lay the salvation of us all; he attempted to enshrine these sentiments in tablets of stone" (Hill 97).

During the midst of ridicule, turmoil, and controversy, Prince released his fourth album entitled Controversy (1981). Controversy lived up to its name, adding fuel to the fire, taking the controversy that surrounded Prince to a new high. Take a young musical genius, add "The Lord's Prayer," mixed with sexual imagery, sixties rhetoric, more religious allusions with a racial and gender strip tease, and one will have the explosive album that electrified the underworld of American music. Although Controversy is written to summarize and expand the concepts in the first three albums, his persona, his continued fusion of rock and soul, and his unique lyrical styling caused Prince to be misunderstood and snubbed by a large number of critics.

> "...Controversy was in search of an audience. In the wake of his fabulously successful, ground breaking year, I suppose a certain amount of backlash was inevitable—at least among the more fickle of critics. Some accused him of smut for smut's sake, but a curious few astoundingly argued he hadn't pushed the envelope far enough! All this senseless noise was particularly aggravating because

the single ["Controversy"] was the rare combination of an extremely accessible funk groove and a thought provoking lyric. A groove that eventually made believers of many, including this writer—old-fashioned funkateers who were stubbornly waiting for all the commotion to die down so we could see what was really behind this whirling dervish. What we skeptics soon discovered was a collection of monumental jams and a young man with remarkable resiliency. No matter the Rolling Stones gigs and the lukewarm reception to the first single, Prince was on a mission and wouldn't be denied" (Leeds 4-5).

Controversy survived the storm of criticism because it is a well crafted, musical hodgepodge with interesting lyrics and because Prince dared to be different. In a singular sense, none of the album is original, but his particular combination of the varying parts is original and refreshing. Because of the lack of musical alternatives, especially for the urban youth, from which to choose at that time, 1980-83, Prince became a cult superstar to that segment of society. I distinctly remember the image of a seventeen-eighteen year old black kid with a heavy Brooklyn street accent and attitude, wearing permed hair, eye shadow, and a leather jacket, proclaiming to a CNN television reporter that Michael Jackson was too soft for him. Prince's power lay in his ability to rebel against life itself, to say that all notions of truth and reality—race, gender, and class—were wrong as we understood them. Twenty years later that now Brooklyn man would probably only admit to that incident if he were forced to view the tape of himself as his children are now hip hop heads. But from 1980-84, Prince and Rick James were the hardest, most defiant muthafuckers on the block because their revolution did not need any validation and because their music and subjects spoke to a generation of young folks who were tired of being force fed somebody else's notions of right and wrong. Unfortunately, Prince's own isolation and his embracing of more metaphysical subject matter would be the death of Prince's commercial revolution.

<u>Controversy</u>'s diversity is its commercial weakness as much as it is its strength. "The Lord's Prayer" to a new wave beat was just a bit too much for the mainstream to follow. Because of its lyrically diverse content and unyielding philosophy of freedom without apologies or explanations, <u>Controversy</u> is usually cited when critics and listeners want to label Prince a confused weirdo. Yet, Prince has always known what he wanted to say and how he wanted to say it. Because of his liberality and not wanting to limit his thought process and the articulation of his ideas by using the rigid roles and positions of a conservative, homophobic, afro-phobic society, Prince has left the act of filling in the blanks and answering the questions to the listeners. Cooper clarifies this point after asking the rhetorical question: "what is all of this talk about a 'new breed' coming out of the <u>Controversy</u> album?"

> "The 'New Breed?'—It's no doctrine, no rhetoric. [Prince and his band are] not sloganeers the way politicians are. I always laugh when people complain that Prince's 'message' lyrics aren't specific. Where has all the 'specificity' of Mao or Marx, Franklin or Jefferson, or even Plato and Aristotle gotten us? True philosophy need be no more specific than 'live and let live.' Seemingly to Prince, the 'New Breed' are people who know how to do that" (Cooper 59).

The inquisitive style of <u>Controversy</u> is not just Prince challenging the norms of society, but also entails Prince questioning the motivation behind why we act and think as we do. This allows Prince to highlight the gap between society's ideal and its practices. When he poses the question of "Do you believe in God?" on the front cover of the <u>Controversy</u> album, he is using sensationalism to question our motives. The ideal of Christianity says that we are to love and educate the confused weirdo that he is, not attack and ridicule him. Prince's question is not only "Do you believe in God?" but "How do your actions manifest that you believe in God?"

Another factor leading to the misunderstanding of Prince is his indefinable sexuality and his being comfortable with that sexuality. It is one thing to be a misunderstood outcast; it is something else to be comfortable with that identity and the isolation that the identity creates. To be comfortable with that identity and isolation questions the society's notion of reality and social order. Permed hair, high heel boots, legwarmers, G-strings, lace, sequence, and a falsetto voice are all characteristics of Prince, which do not fit the American stereotype of maleness, especially in an industry dominated by the macho male mentality. Even in the world of rock-n-roll, boys can look like girls as long as they are dominating girls. We do not want boys who look and act like girls and are still able to gain female companionship (which is something different than sexual domination or objectification) because they deconstruct our society's order and hierarchy, which is based on definite and rigid gender roles where the man is the dominate being. In a society totally obsessed with sexuality but controlled by the guilt of its hypocrisy, Prince has managed to exploit this unhealthy situation and bring humor and enlightenment to the many aspects of the male psyche (schizophrenia). Also, along with gender bending, Prince used a great amount of racial blurring to defy characterization and limitation. Most Americans are mutts though most of us want to claim some pure breed. This racial blurring allowed Prince to access those primitive desires and anxieties which resonate at the very foundation of America. "Am I black or white, am I straight or gay" (Prince, "Controversy," 1981). Prince is even forthright in this declaration: "They say that even if you've got just one drop of black blood in you it makes you entirely black. But in fact I don't necessarily look on myself as a member of the black race—more a member of the human race" (Salewicz 18, reprinted in Fudger 23). Prince was becoming the Toomer and Nella Larsen of popular music. Instead of creating characters or epics to carry this message, he became the character—the heroic voice. The above statements about race would alienate Prince from some who wanted a more definable icon with which to identify, but it would also give him the space he needed to maneuver and control his own identity.

In his book, <u>Prince: A Pop Life</u>, Hill insists that there is too much complaining, too much wanting to have it both ways in <u>Controversy</u>. "There was no point flaunting a badge with 'Rude Boy' written on it, then complaining when people lined up to agree" (Hill 99). In this case Hill misses the point of Prince's protest. The protest in <u>Controversy</u> is not against opinion; it is against intolerance. Prince is not on the outside trying to get in. He is on the inside trying not to be smothered by intolerance. And when how one looks disqualifies him, most of us have no chance to survive and thrive. <u>Controversy</u> is the protest of the individual for the sake of individualism. Damn the tourists and fuck the government, it is the rights of individuals that we should be protecting. And before he was anything, Prince was an individual. Naive? Possibly. But it is some sort of an assertion. As Miles Davis asserts, "Then there was the music of Prince, who I was hearing for the first time. His shit was the most exciting music I was hearing in 1982...Here was someone who was doing something different, so I decided to keep an eye on him" (Davis 353). Was he the only artist at the time grappling with issues other than love and getting the girl? If not, he was certainly having his discourse with the world on his own terms and in no uncertain terms, raising it to an almost theoretical or theological discourse.

The theory/theology of <u>Controversy</u> is designed to reform people's notion of life and religion by getting people to open their minds and understand the oppression rampant in America's traditional religious and social structure. It is one young man's maturing outlook on life, a theory in development. Because of this, it is all over the place. Even Prince admits that "<u>Controversy</u> is a little erratic" (Hilburn,

"Mixed Emotions," 58). This can be a problem when one solution (sexuality) is used to take on the world and all of its problems. What we find is that the reconciliation sought will not come easily, so <u>Controversy</u> decides, in the end, to fuck itself silly and "Jack U Off." A good orgasm will ease the pain of life even if it is not able to remove or solve the pain. Possibly, Prince was finding that it will take much more than sex or sexuality to solve our problems, even if most of them are rooted there. Still, <u>Controversy</u> shows continued growth. Unlike <u>Dirty Mind</u>, <u>Controversy</u> is more self-aware, more sure of itself. It believes in itself as a statement rather than an expression. Thus, it is more external than <u>Dirty Mind</u>, concentrating on more specific aspects of society than the inward workings of the individual mind. "<u>Controversy</u> was pure justification... Side one offers a three-part education in the world according to Prince, commencing with his defense, ["Controversy,"] moving on to his diagnosis, ["Sexuality,"] and getting down to the real business at the end," the salvation of sex in "Do Me, Baby" (Hill 97).

The title track, "Controversy," questions the hypocrisy of the society in which we live. It concentrates on our prejudices and limitations in regards to how we perceive and accept people, bringing to light how fear and embarrassment are forces used by the society to control the individual or those who deviate from the norm. In an interview, Prince asserts, "Anybody that breaks out of the norm is going to get attacked. Anything different, they are going to go after it" (Mitchell 1981). In "Controversy" he is mounting the defense against the gatekeepers of normality. "I just can't believe all the things people say, 'Am I black or white, am I straight or gay?'" Prince understands that the mere questioning, itself, is a tactic to limit him by either putting him in a box in the minds of the public or as an attempt to embarrass him back into normality. Often we raise questions of a person's character, not to indict them of something but to show them the power of the society to keep the individual inline. His individual but steadfast questioning is a way to refute or denounce the power of the omnipotent "they." He is questioning the questioner to show that this meaningless hatred and fear will be the death of us all. "Some people wanna die, so they can be free." The underlying point is that society only hurts itself by limiting the individual's means of pursuing happiness and self-fulfillment because of mass fear, "Life is just a game; we're all just the same. Don't u wanna play?" Instead of allowing our fears to obstruct our evolution by limiting individuals, we should be allowing our individuals to be all that they can so that they can have a positive impact on the evolution of the society. If the individuals are limited, the society will be limited. If individual growth and expression is retarded, then social growth and expression is retarded.

      And yes, "Controversy" is commercial. It is building an image. The question is, "How far removed is the man from the image?" This is the question with which listeners and journalists alike have been grappling for years. As Edna Gundersen of <u>USA Today</u> states in her 1991 television interview with <u>Omnibus</u> concerning her visit to Paisley Park, "He's up at ten in the morning. The questions raised in "Controversy" become an issue of identity and control, as Cooper, a long-time journalist, can attest "that the media fucks with you, with your image. They're concept groupies. Interviewers are another species of tourist. Mental vampires" (Cooper 59). Let us not forget that radio, at this time, is quite segregated and restricting, especially for black artists. This is a strategic maneuver to keep his new music from being lost in the shuffle of the Warner Bros machine. Warner Bros has a black music department. In 1980 its only directive and goal is to sell R&B. If you are a black artist on Warner Bros Records, your work is handled by the black music department no matter what type of music you create. The department is only designed to market to black radio, which plays exclusively R&B. If a black artist creates anything other than R&B, his record is dead in the water before it hits the shelves, before you have an opportunity to flower and flourish. Prince needed a way around this system. Like Wideman, he recreated who he was to get air play. It was the only way for a black kid playing a neo-amalgamation of funk and rock to survive. Thus, Prince's race and gender blurring is a smoke and mirrors control tactic for economic reasons. As Little Richard has often elaborated, R&B does not mean rhythm and blues, it means "real black" (Narine 1989). R&B is a category created so that white acts, such as Boone and Presley, would not have to compete against black acts, such as Little Richard and Jackie Wilson. While giving white artists the freedom to be and create who they wanted to be, R&B served to limit African American creativity. On one level, Prince is attempting to blur or liquefy his public persona in order to keep from being controlled and limited. It is commercialization on the highest level. He is forcing both buyers and critics to be conscious of how they are listening and why they are listening, rather than just listening. Or, Prince is subverting all of that so we will pay attention to the songs. He is not only the messenger; he is the message. In one song, Prince becomes no one and every one. He is an allegory of American amalgamation, carrying the baggage of that amalgamation, simultaneously and interchangeably, as an albatross, a badge, and a shield. We are left to decide, genius or madness. Accordingly, African Americans are compelled to decide whether Prince is a Utopian social reformer or white wanna be? Many of us have remained divided along those lines because African Americans remain divided over what identity and ideology best addresses their plight in America.

"Sexuality," the second song on side one, exceeds the passive questioning of "Controversy" and is totally revolutionary in manner because it attempts to destroy a system of definitions and values by promoting another system of values. A revolutionary is one who attempts to destroy an oppressive system in order to construct a liberating system. If one only intends to destroy, he is a thug not a revolutionary. It is not the system, itself, or one's particular concept that makes one a revolutionary. One becomes a revolutionary when one is ready to destroy and build.

"Stand up, everybody, this is your life. Let me take U 2 another world; let me take U 2night. U don't need no money. U don't need no clothes. The second coming, anything goes. Sexuality is all U'll ever need. Sexuality, let your body be free.

Come on, everybody, yeah, this is your life. I'm talkin' 'bout a revolution; we gotta organize. We don't need no segregation; we don't need no race. New age revelation, I think we got a case. I'm okay as long as U are here with me. Sexuality is all we ever need.

The reproduction of the new breed, leaders, stand up, organize. We live in a world overrun by tourists—89 flowers on their back—inventors of the Accu-Jack. They look at life through a pocket camera. 'What? No flash again?' They're all a bunch of double drags who teach their kids that love is bad. Half of the staff of their brain is on vacation. Mama are U listening? We need a new breed. Leaders, stand up, organize..."

More than it is about sex, "Sexuality" is about social freedom gained through our philosophy of sex, which is also a major factor of racism. "Sexuality is all I ever need. Sexuality, I'm gonna let my body be free." Statements, such as "Stand up everybody this is your life,...don't need no segregation, don't need no race, the second coming, I think we've got a case," attack the heart of the problem: the barriers of sexism and racism. The idea of a new generation driven by a desire for freedom of thought and expression is delivered loudly, clearly, and unapologetically.

"Sexuality" marks the end to Prince's passive wait for the majority of the society to change their detrimental ways of stagnation through the limitation of expressive living. Prince calls for organization, demanding, "Reproduction of a New Breed, leaders stand up and organize. I wanna be in the New Breed, stand up and organize!" We are gonna fuck our way to a new breed of man. Reproduction will be the strategy to end oppression, and the phallus is the tool to lead us. We will just keep having sex until everyone is one color or related to someone of color. Through reproduction, the New Breed is going to construct a better race. They are going to improve and empower the babies through knowledge, tolerance, and a secure sexuality. This is vaguely Judo-Christian. If man is made in the image of God, then man is, by nature, a creator. Man's greatest accomplishment, as a God, is reproduction. It is man's nature to continue the reproduction of the race. It is our being sexual beings that allows us to achieve our God potential. Prince understands, however, that a great responsibility comes with this freedom. "Mamas don't let your children watch television before they know how to read." With this new sexuality, man must exercise responsibility. It is alright to have sex if we know why we are doing it. Thus, the play on the word "sexuality" and his concept of sex is just another attempt by Prince to demolish all the doors that hide our true selves. As he asserts, "If God wanted us to have clothes he would have had them at birth, and they would grow the same time we grow" (Mitchell 1981). Prince infers that the acceptance of our sexual essence as being natural and cultivating to more enriched lives is the first step to erasing the lies that have been shadowing American society since its birth. But, Prince does not carelessly attempt to lead listeners down a road of new found freedom. He knows that freedom without responsibility leads to destruction. Prince appeals to the very people who want to ban him, the parents of the mainstream society.

> "Mama, are u listening?...Don't let your children watch television until they know how to read, or else all they'll know how to do is cuss, fight, and breed. No child is bad from the beginning. They only imitate their atmosphere. If they're in the company of tourists, alcohol, and U.S. history, what's 2 be expected is 3 minus 3...absolutely nothing"

Prince provides a sexual education because we will need to know why and when to have sex if we plan to liberate ourselves.

And after he has covered the why and the when, he gets down to the how with "Do Me, Baby."

"Do Me, Baby" is my generation's "Let's Get It On" or "Sexual Healing." It is cruder, less sophisticated, and more explicit, but it is still a yearning for some sense of earthly salvation/completion through sex, through the union of male and female. Although it is less articulate than Gaye's pieces, it works because it indicates the lessening importance on well articulated concepts and the heightened importance on feeling or sensory impressionism throughout the work of the eighties. The children are becoming less articulate because they are living in the video age where bright images have replaced meticulous thought. So, video not only kills the radio star, but it also dilutes precise lyricism. Nonetheless, although "Do Me, Baby" may possibly lack the self awareness of "Let's Get It On" or "Sexual Healing," it seems to understand that there is something more at stake than an orgasm. The fact that it follows "Controversy" and "Sexuality" gives it the weight that the lyrical content may lack. Secondly, it follows in the line of "Sexual Healing" by having the male sense his salvation through being baptized in the female. The male not only succumbs to sexual tension but yields his position of power to achieve satisfaction. In the end, it is the male asking to be held. Through relinquishing the traditional role of power and control, the male is able to achieve a deeper satisfaction. This is true liberation because it includes the liberation of both parties: the male and the female.

We must understand that Prince is working with a slightly different notion or approach toward sex, love, and the romantic relationship. Gaye is concentrating on the concept of "love making," and Prince is concentrating on the recontextualized notion of "making love," which, by 1980, meant nothing more than "having sex." Sex, by 1980, had become depersonalized and commodified as a thing, a separate and sovereign concept, by the "Me" generation. It is no longer a metaphor for love, nor is it any longer an act of or a representation of love. Everything had been objectified, and popular music was reflecting that. Sex was now a commodity—a thing to be used for personal or individual pleasure or gratification at the will and discretion of the user. It can be for physical or metaphysical purposes, but it is viewed, in the eighties, as a more subjective and disposable activity. Though Prince has great and honest intentions, he still is existing within the culture of capitalistic individualism, using the language and concepts of this culture to articulate his own messages. Sex, like anything else, is a commodity to be used for one's own personal benefit, no matter what the purpose—sacred or profane, secular or religious. For Gaye and his generation, although sex yields physical pleasure, it is still a manifestation of emotions felt by two people for each other. The two people have some type of emotional or psychological connection and concern for each other, especially on a romantic level. "I've been really tryin' baby to hold back these feelings for so long...if you feel like I feel...let's get it on." Though sex is the act or pathway to salvation in both "Let's Get It On" and "Sexual Healing," it is by two people who clearly have an emotional or psychological connection on some romantic level. Sex, for Gaye, is not a sovereign concept or entity; it is dependent upon something else, a particle or atom of a larger molecular structure. For Prince, however, sex is sovereign. It becomes, for a time in his work, a religion all to itself that two people with no real connection other than the desire for survival or the need for escapism can use to achieve some sense of momentary completion or fulfillment. Gaye is "love making" where sex is an articulation of some "romantic" emotion or notion. Prince is "making love," hoping that the act of sex will produce love. And if not love, the act can be used for something else, such as companionship, escapism, or to rebel against and break from oppression. Additionally, during live performances of "Do Me, Baby" Prince would change the ending of the song from "Hold me" to "Somebody hold me." Even though the subject in "Hold me" is the understood but ambiguous "you," it still refers to the singular. By changing to "Somebody,"

Prince is illustrating that the "you" is interchangeable because the sex act, not the person, is what is important. This is in opposition to Gaye where the relationship is what is important. Gaye is finding salvation in the human relationship, where Prince is finding salvation through sex. It takes a few more albums before Prince realizes the importance of the human relationship. The connection that Gaye and Prince have is that in both cases, the individuals are working to save themselves and someone else. Because there are no stationary gender roles in Prince's construct, there can be no dominance, as there is no dominance is Gaye's work. This is what Prince has learned from his predecessors, such as Gaye, that good sex is sex that provides mutual salvation. Sex, for Prince, still requires a mutual investment and involvement, even if the two people involved in the act desire a different end or effect. Therefore, sex provides for the liberation of two, which reconnects Prince to the legacy of Gaye.

As <u>Controversy</u> makes sex and sexuality tools of liberation and salvation, it further opens doors for Prince to experiment with religion and religious icons. As with any other topic, Prince addresses religion in his own "New Breed" manner. He shows how greed and gluttony take our eyes off the spiritual and, in doing so, lead us to damnation. Prince illustrates this by showing the depraved actions of misguided, lost souls behaving selfishly/ destructively in search of inner peace. That perversion seems always to affect those at the bottom of society first and worse. Thus, the female archetype becomes the symbol and object that man uses to justify, ease, or addresses his fears of inadequacy. The female is at the bottom of the power ladder, suffering more than anyone else. And, she is often seen as the anti-Christ in her attempts to destroy a system based on the hierarchy of the penis. Man has a need to define, identify, and save himself in a world of chaos. One of the ways that he has done this is through the objectification of the female, especially in his literature. As Barbara Christian shows, men often swing from one end of the spectrum to the other in defining or stereotyping the female, depending on what he needs from her. Whether she is the Mammy or the Queen of the Universe, male artists often make a caricature of the female for their own benefit as indicated by Paula Giddings in When and Where I Enter (1984). The female can be man's saving grace or the cause of his fall. Regardless of the contradiction, this need to define the female shows her importance to society. Therefore, if woman is the originator of all institutions as Trudier Harris indicates in her book From Mammies to Militants (1982), then a society that oppresses and mis-educates individuals about sexuality will innately create perverse females, which will cause the creation of institutions of destruction. This echoes Malcolm X's analogy of the relation between the state of women and the state of a nation. Where there are progressive nations there are progressive women, and where there are backward nations, there are oppressed women. We understand that for Prince this is all just a trope of borrowed imagery from the Bible and from feminist theory for the sake of creating an interesting song. His lyrical mastery is shown in his understanding that we identify the female as a primary component in the construction or destruction of society. In this case, "Annie Christian" is the offspring of a sexually oppressed and perverted society who has come home to roost. The state of womankind, then, is critically important to the salvation and state of mankind—a notion that Prince will build upon throughout his career. By using the female as a metaphor for the anti-Christ, he is able to use familiar imagery to personify evil, making the song more relevant and interesting, citing Eve's offspring as the driving force behind all evil in the world, using the Atlanta child murders, the assassination of John Lennon, and the attempted assassination of former President Ronald Reagan as examples. Through this personification of Annie Christian, Prince is heightening his notion of sex and sexuality as central forces to save and damn man. As woman goes, so goes the fate of man.

> "Annie Christian wanted to be number one. The way Annie tells the story, she's his only son (maybe an allusion to Milton's Paradise Lost). Annie Christian was a whore,

always looking for some fun, being good was such a bore, so she bought a gun. She killed John Lennon, shot him down cold; tried to kill Reagan, everybody say gun control."

Annie Christian is not a whore because of her powers; she is a whore because she misuses them for physical gratification. It is not power that is wrong but how one exercises the power, especially since sexuality, for Prince, is a power. Annie Christian wanted to be number one, refusing to yield to a power higher than her. With all of these notions of gender blurring and sex for salvation, it can be difficult to see where Prince is drawing the line. Is this to be taken literally that man's inability to yield to God causes his disastrous end? Or, is this to be taken metaphorically, the battle of the sexes (God-Male and Satan-Female) will lead us to a disastrous end? The irony is that in Milton's Paradise Lost, Satan has been seen by a few critics as the victim of God's tyranny, just as characters in Prince's songs have the ability to be seen as both antagonists and protagonists, battling along the spectrum of sexuality. Most of Prince's socio-political songs speak from the voice of an oppressed other who is victimized by the heavy hand of tyranny, much like Satan sees himself in Paradise Lost. It is interesting that the male is going to spend his time fleeing Annie Christian in a taxicab. "Until u're crucified, I'll live my life in a taxicab." This is interesting because on the very next album, 1999, Prince has his male protagonist saved by a "Lady Cab Driver." Prince, no matter how much he tries to refute or deny it, is trapped into the same schizophrenic relationship with women as most men. They exist in various forms for his own purposes. Early in Prince's work, there is a battle within himself and with the female for place and power that he is not able to reconcile until he matures as a writer.

This battle for power through sexuality is then troped and paralleled in a fourth piece from Controversy, "Ronnie Talk to Russia." It is the era of the Cold War, and Prince is making a plea to President Reagan to find common ground with Russia before it is too late. America and Russia have the biggest dicks, and their politics are as irrational as men thinking with their dicks, causing their nuclear weaponry to work as a phallic symbol. For many conservative Americans, Reagan represented the replacing or dismantling of a bureaucratic government with one central figure who would no longer suffocate the rights of the states. It was a return to the Father Knows Best era, where the white male represents tyrannical control for the majority with little respect for minority rights. It is a system which thrives on the oppression of otherness. Prince is the symbolic figure of otherness, being black, rebellious, artistic, and feminine all at the same time. Yet, this all worked for him. His otherness liberated him from the confines of our narrow realities. As Baldwin asserts, to be poor, black, and gay means that America cannot do anything else to you. "I thought I hit the jackpot…it was so outrageous you could not go any further…so you had to find a way to use it" (Baldwin, James Baldwin, 1989). The late seventies and early eighties represented a time when otherness was almost the "in" thing. Prince is insinuating that there was a growing lack of patience for intolerance by the public—particularly by those who had been kept quiet in the past by their otherness. The fear of social exile and nuclear destruction that once overwhelmed us, driving the country into pandemonium, has now turned into anger, causing us to speak out for our rights. "If u're dead before I meet u, don't say I didn't worn ya!" Prince concludes "Ronnie Talk to Russia" with the feeling of disgust, focusing on how class-based ego tripping by the government can destroy the world. With "Ronnie Talk to Russia" Prince is directly petitioning political organizations in the form of their symbolic figure/ideology in a more specific manner than in "Party Up," which shows continued growth. Here, again, Prince is not on the outside looking in. He sees himself as being very American, the American youth, making American music with American sensibilities. He has a stake in the country. This comes to light when at the end of the song he states, "…before u blow up the world, don't u blow up my world. You wanna blow up my world!" Prince, regardless of his otherness, is asserting his place and standing in the world. "Don't u blow up my world!" The world belongs to all of us, not just the rich. We must all let "our" voices be heard for "our" world. Although he realizes that he is an "other," Prince is not about to allow his otherness to lock him out of the American structure or the discussion about America's structure.

<u>Controversy</u> ends with an orgasm, "Jack U Off." It is the answer to all of the world's mundane problems, especially boredom, disorder, and stress.

> "If u're lookin' 4 somewhere 2 go, I'll take u 2 the movie show; we can sit in the back, and I'll jack u off. Can't give u everything u want, but I can take u 2 the restaurant. And if u get hungry, I'll jack u off."

Even here Prince cannot resist from raising the stakes and using the orgasm as some healing agent. This is a very secular modification of the Staple Singers' "I'll Take You There," which also has a very secular, ambiguous quality due to the excessive amount of secular styled moaning and groaning by Mavis Staples. Prince plays on the history of black music and ambiguity created by mixing the sacred with the profane. "I'll only do it 4 a worthy cause, virginity or menopause. U'll have an instant heart attack 'cause I'll jack u off." Menopause is a very ambiguous transition for women. Many see it as the ending of womanhood because of the inability to have children. Others see it as the doorway to sexual freedom. Prince wants to aid in unlocking this doorway, taking the female to new heights in her life. "If u really want 2 be a star, gotta do it in yo' mamma's car; naked in a Cadillac, and I'll jack u off." The "star" image works to show the temporary high gained from sex. The orgasm can take you to new heights even if temporarily. Accordingly, for most rock stars fame is fleeting, as each star is just something to "do" until the next big craze "comes" along. Although the music business is fickle, like a new lover's attention, many of us rush toward stardom because it is a feeling, no matter how temporary, that few can match. As Barry White states in an interview with Donnie Simpson on BET's <u>Video Soul</u>, "A hit can change your life." One "hit," one good "hit," is that thing that keeps us going. Most of us live our lives in a "Pastime [or future] Paradise" living off or looking for that one "hit" of good love or fantasizing and waiting on that one "hit" of good love. Prince wants to liberate her with one good hit or stroke, which will change her life. And if Prince is leading the female to liberation through sex, a good leader creates a system where the follower is able to access leadership. Constructing his own system, Prince refuses to play by society's rules, so he bends them, allowing the female to take a turn at the wheel and become the dominate one so that she feels a sense of shared power in this new democracy. "If u're good I'll even let u steer. As a matter of fact, u can jack me off." This gender bending and blurring is inline with the other two albums and cements the foundation for <u>1999</u>. The orgasm is what's important: not how it is achieved, but that it is achieved. The orgasm represents human fulfillment. Prince was not about to be hindered by some arbitrary rules of male-female gender roles.

<u>Controversy</u> is a musical and lyrical battering ram, breaking down the walls that have divided people since the dawn of civilization: race, religion, and sexuality. "People call me rude. I wish we all were nude. I wish there were no black and white. I wish there were no rules." He is putting the question to us. Why is he considered "rude" for speaking or questioning the truth? Five years later in "Hello," Prince is still asserting this same question.

> "They called me rude often when I called their hand. They judged me and told me that we're through. 'Why can't U be like the others?...Why can't U learn 2 play by the rules?' But maybe at last it's the end because I am not like others. I'm unique in the respect [that] I'm not U."

Why do we pliantly adhere to the notions and the limitations of black and white? Are these arbitrary constructs? Can we not strip away our artificial personas and be bare (nude), be honest? And whose rules are these that we are following? Do these rules accomplish anything other than divide, limit, and control us? Through Controversy Prince explodes and expands the themes of freedom, individuality, and the sexual revolution which begin in Dirty Mind. Controversy raises the position of Dirty Mind, becoming a theory by which to live. It espouses sexuality as philosophy, if not solution. Additionally, what is important about both Dirty Mind and Controversy is that we have a young, African American male taking advantage of and reclaiming the totality of the legacy of African American music and culture. He is both rock-n-roll and R&B; he is both Little Richard and Marvin Gaye. In doing this, he is connecting the various aspects of black music as few have done before or after him.

What Prince does through instrumentation, rappers do through sampling, and they both draw on the lyrical imagery of the past to reconfigure a new present. By doing this, Prince is asserting to his growing white consumers that African Americans are not as confined and one dimensional as white folks have needed to believe in order to continue the perpetuation of African American second-class citizenship. Also, Prince is showing African American artists and patrons who have been accepting a limited understanding of African American culture that African Americans are not as limited or one-dimensional as they, themselves, have accepted. By refuting the categorizing and marginalizing of one's work along the lines of arbitrarily created racial lines, Prince is working to undo African American second-class citizenship. So the incident of Prince being booed off stage by a mostly white audience as he opened for the Rolling Stones, a group that built its career on the foundations of African American music, speaks volumes to America's race problem as it is manifested in its popular music. Why were so many white people so eager to denounce an African American artist who is simply reclaiming his legacy when they support the Rolling Stones for their interpretation of African American music and culture? The answers are fear and hypocrisy. The inability to accept Prince doing rock-n-roll music exemplifies the legacy of fear and hypocrisy by a mass of whites only being able to accept black music with a white face. This is directly related to whites only being able to understand and empathize with the struggle for civil rights when that struggle has a white face, such as American colonists being able to fight for their rights against British oppression and at the same time fight to keep Africans enslaved. This is the same as whites not acknowledging the horror of the South until two whites are killed in the midst of that struggle for civil rights, or whites not empathizing with and understanding the struggle until white, liberal intellectuals become the voices and faces of the movement. Thus, Prince being booed off the stage directly parallels H. Rap Brown being booed off the stage by an audience of so-called white liberals. In 1969 at Fillmore East, a conference was called to discuss what the "Movement" had been and where it was going. The panel included twelve speakers, only one of whom was black, H. Rap Brown. After sitting through seven or eight speakers, Brown approached the microphone. His purpose was to define "Activist," "Radical," and "Revolutionary" to show the difference between promoting self interest and promoting community interest. The majority white crowd became angry and agitated as Brown's definitions began to classify them as selfish, self-righteous, and self-promoting. Unable to deal with their fear and hypocrisy, the majority white crowd began to boo. There was a near riot. Most of the white audience members stated that they were agitated at Brown's arrogance. This statement parallels Rolling Stones' guitarist Keith Richards' attitude toward Prince by stating, "That's what you get when you give yourself a title that you have not gained or earned." It seems that Richards' real issue with Prince is Prince's innate ability to reach back, align, and reconcile himself with his black heritage, that very same black heritage which the Rolling Stones had co-opted, whitewashed, and exploited, all the while attempting to permanently divorce the music from its black roots. Those white crowds, which booed Brown and Prince, understood that they were being indicted for their fear and hypocrisy.

For a mass of whites to accept Prince and allow him and others to reclaim their African American legacy signifies the importance of African American culture and the role of Africa in the evolution of civilization. Yet, this is nothing new. Prince is merely another affirmation of African American diversity. African Americans are not a monolith. White slave owners in all of their hypocrisy understood this. In fact it was African and later African American diversity which was used to perpetuate African slavery and second-class citizenship. The only people who have not been able to understand and embrace fully African American diversity in its totality have been African Americans. Their failure in embracing their complexity makes the African American struggle to achieve first-class citizenship that much more difficult. Yet, this complexity adds to their dimensionality, adding, ironically, to their humanity. Unfortunately, African Americans have remained separated by their dimensionality instead of finding strength in it. The eventual failing for Prince would be the failing of Du Bois, his lack of inclusiveness of all African Americans. Like Toomer, Prince saw himself as some type of "new creature," separating himself from African Americans instead of embracing African Americans. Despite the country's racism, Prince saw himself as an American youngster, privy to the rights and liberties of all American youngsters. If this meant a watering down of his Africanness or African sensibilities, then so be it. Regardless of how one may feel about this ideology, one cannot refute the importance of Prince's career as a bridge for younger African American artists to follow him back to the legacy of their culture. Musically, he kept alive the spirit of rock-n-roll in the African American community. Lyrically, his message of transcendentalization added to the dimensionally and complexity of his generation, which provided more alternatives for those who followed him. And much like Du Bois, Prince, later in his career, undergoes a transformation, which changes, in many respects, his notion of his blackness, which allows him to fully embrace the totality of his African American diversity.

The Minneapolis Genius Has Come with His Message

With the combination of decent records sales and high critical praise for his first four albums, Prince was becoming recognized as a musician with something insightful to say. With his growing cult-hood in the urban community, despite little help from radio, <u>Controversy</u> put him on the edge of knocking down the walls to popular, mainstream, commercial acclaim. Prince's fifth album <u>1999</u> (1982) not only summarized his past works but set the stage for and enlightened the world on Prince, the concept. Not since Wonder's <u>Songs in the Key of Life</u> (1976) or some of the late seventies work of Parliament-Funkadelic, had an album entertained listeners as well as provoked them to thought as did <u>1999</u>. Although <u>1999</u> is not as socially relevant as <u>Songs in the Key of Life</u> because the lyricism is not as politically wide-ranging, it embodies the spirit of the experiment and showcases the diversity of African American sound and thought. Where Wonder titillated the minds of his listeners, raising pop music to a higher discourse, Prince does the same with the libido. In doing so, <u>1999</u> legitimizes the eighties shift from a collective discourse to an individualized discourse, signaling a shift from a body of politics to the politics of the body. The capitalistic "Me" generation of the seventies became the "I got mine; you get yours" generation of the eighties, absorbing and co-opting the ideals of the past for their own, personal gratification. Where the sixties and seventies were about the legitimizing of groups that had been marginalized in the past, the eighties became the era of legitimizing the individual. Prince is able to subvert this atmosphere and the social practices to communicate his own ideology of divine individualism. He uses this shift to gain mass attention because his struggle for his own identity and individuality paralleled the struggle of a great many in the society. His one reoccurring theme becomes individual liberation, and every aspect of his character and persona sells this notion. With <u>1999</u> there becomes the understanding that the hair, clothing, music, and lyrics are all interwoven to produce a single entity, espousing the notion of complete freedom from everything.

If Controversy is the structuring and conceptualizing of Dirty Mind, 1999 made it all "theology," expressing "itself as rock theatre" (Hill 111). Prince, himself, seemed to be quite pleased and aware of 1999. He seemed to understand the album's ability to communicate, in a mainstream manner, the whole of his ideals and his image, and at the same time he was concerned that people still may not be ready for the album's complexity, especially its lyrical content, imagery, and daringness. "There's a certain type of people who may dig what we're doing, but won't even listen to it because of the stereotypes or whatever...I'm real proud of the new album, and I'd hate to have things get in the way of it." (Hilburn, "Mixed Emotions," 59). It is, indeed, an album that succeeds on various levels: imagery, ideals, concepts, and music.

> "Lyrically, too, the impulse of the two genres [rock and funk] achieve a seamless blend. A generation of young white males had soused their adolescence in the apocalyptic obsessions of heavy metal: implied in the screaming pantomime oblivion of everyone from Kiss to AC/DC was some death-and-glory vision of abandonment to Armageddon, or a metaphor for it" (Hill 115).

1999 brings with it a maturity in musical and lyrical complexity, showing more growth. Each song has its own identity, which is a great accomplishment within itself with the album being a double album set—a rarity at anytime. In its complexity of music and subject matter, 1999 breaks Prince away from the pack of commercial hit seekers and R&B stereotypes. Still, what makes 1999 a well-crafted work of art is the way each song manages to maintain its own individual personality while combining to heighten the concept of the album that whatever it is that you want to do, you better do it now!

<u>1999</u> begins with the title cut, "1999," which takes on the roles of being a celebration of life and freedom and a warning of the end: "So two thousand zero zero party over oops out of time, so tonight I'm gonna party like it's 1999...mommy, why does everybody have a bomb?" "1999" asks us to face and overcome our mortality by enjoying every moment that we have. Prince sets the illusionary/surreal tone for the album by making "1999" a retelling of a dream sequence. "I was dreaming when I wrote this/ Forgive me if it goes astray...I was dreaming when I wrote this/ So sue me if I go too fast." Not only is this a recounting of a dream, but it is a dream (revelation) that is given specifically to him. The dream (vision) sequence gives weight to the message as well as keeps him from being held accountable for the details or the message. He is the poet (messenger) reporting what he saw when he was overcome with these images from his higher power. He sets himself up as the poet prophet, recounting the vision of our final doom: "...when I woke up this morning I could have sworn it was judgment day. The sky was all purple; there were people running every where. Tryin' to run from the destruction, and u know I didn't even care." The fact that the sky is purple is significant in that purple is Prince's adopted color in the same manner that Egyptian royalty adopted symbols and markings to identify themselves on monuments throughout the city. The purple sky symbolizes that the images are sent from heaven and meant to be seen only by Prince (the poet) who will have the wisdom to relay the vision to the masses. The song, itself, has dual messages in the song: the message of doom and destruction from God and the reaction/solution from Prince. Try as he might, at this state of his development Prince cannot be merely a carrier of somebody else's news. He also understands that while he is the messenger, he is included in those for whom the message is meant and reacts in his own manner. "War is all around me/ my mind says prepare to fight. So if I gotta die gonna listen to my body tonight." The picturesque lyrics and

blend of rock and soul help give Prince the American icon status he needed to walk freely across the musical and cultural spectrum. "Prince achieved a vivid fusion of HM (Heavy Metal) cosmic destruction with the redemptive blend of physicality and spirituality which lies at the core of soul" (Hill 115). On the backs of "1999" and "Little Red Corvette," 1999 becomes Prince's first album to chart higher on the pop chart than on the R&B chart. Through 1999 Prince was constructing a new mythology in popular music where multiculturalism, individualism, and sex allowed him to reign supreme.

The second song on the album is "Little Red Corvette." This image driven song is a complex but solid ground on which to land after taking the head-spinning trip of living for the moment. "Little Red Corvette" explicitly tells how a life of insouciant freedom lived to the extreme without guidance can lead to disaster. It is masterful the way Prince uses a musically and lyrically complex song as a disclaimer. Yet, Prince manages to convey the message of responsibility without taking away from the concept of living for the moment. "Little red Corvette, baby u're much 2 fast/ Little red corvette, u need 2 find a love that's gonna last/...before you run your body right to the ground..."

> "Drawing directly from the rich motivating history of rock-n-roll imagery, Prince reupholstered an established catalogue of car-girl-coital conquest metaphors to reflect his own all-concerning persona. 'Little Red Corvette' suggests the vision of Chuck Berry, focused through the false eyelashes of Little Richard; the swollen freeway of love of Bruce Springsteen, suffused with a parodic, purple braggadocio. He even smirks at his own history of sexual boasting as the music builds to a vintage teenage dream chorus, and then moves with blissful inevitability towards his triumphant score" (Hill 116).

"Little Red Corvette" has one foot on the accelerator of

sexual desire and one foot on the brake of anxiety. This male dichotomy is the driving factor of our dysfunctional relationships. Prince is showing that the need and desire for sex and physical companionship is driven as much by the psyche as it is by the penis. Furthermore, it seems to be the male who has the more difficult time navigating this area because all positions of power are hypocritically hung on the penis. The female, from what we know of her, has no hang-ups or regrets about her promiscuity. It is the male who has a problem with her sexuality. He is both awed by it and afraid of it. "I should have known by the way u parked your car sideways that it wouldn't last." He is reluctant to have relations with her, but his desire to have relations with her are too strong. She is both a succubus and a damsel in distress. The schizophrenic male psyche is conflicted by his dual desires to save or rape. Therefore, man is often unable to deal with or overcome his hypocritical, schizophrenic perception of the female. The male protagonist seemingly wants to save the female until he is overcome by his own inability to control his flesh. "A body like yours ought 2 be in jail cuz its on the verge of being obscene." Try as he might, the male, no matter how well intentioned, can not transcend his body, his penis, his need to be in control. In fact, he wishes to assert that he is saving the female because she is unable to do it herself. "Move over baby, give me the keys. I'm gonna try 2 tame your little red love machine." With all of his talk about her salvation, the male cannot stop himself from assuming the position of power. Because of this, there is no resolution in this song as in the other songs. We leave the protagonist as we find him, conflicted over his sexuality and her sexuality. In many of Prince's songs the female is able to save the male from his physical self. In "Little Red Corvette" the male is unable to save the female from her physical self. This establishes Prince's notion of the female as divine savior who has equal if not more power to redeem mankind, which he expands in <u>Purple Rain</u>, <u>Around the World in a Day</u>, and <u>Parade</u>. The female becomes the axis or the portal for the fall or salvation of man.

A few songs later, Prince is deconstructing his mystic persona by adding some simplicity. Yet, any modification to his own diverse persona continues to reflect the complexity of the constantly shifting human psyche. D.M.S.R. (dance, music, sex, romance) continues the constant evolving and redefining of the Prince persona. A sub-topic for the album, "D.M.S.R." is an undercurrent theme for the personality of Prince and a representation of his attitudes toward life. Prince brings some simplicity to the album as well as to the public's perception of him with straight forward funk cords and a straight ahead, simple declaration. Ever the painter and puppeteer, Prince defines and redefines himself on the same album, often in the same song, showing that the only constant about humanity is its complexity. All of these different facets of his personality are merely options to be explored and experienced. Prince is asserting that individuals have to right to have more than one concept or ideology of themselves and the world, and humans have the right to shift or slide along the spectrum as often and as freely as they want. Ultimately, everyone one has the right to be who or what they want to be, no matter how complex or simple.

> "Everybody, get on the floor. What the hell did u come here 4? U might as well get loose... Never mind your friends...Don't wanna be no poet, cause I don't wanna blow it. I don't care 2 win awards. All I want 2 do is dance, play music, sex, romance, try my best 2 never get bored."

Always struggling to maintain control of his "identity," Prince is dismantling his persona as quickly as he is building it, making it even more liquid than when <u>1999</u> begins. Thus, the celebration is about being: being what you want, how you want, when you want.

> "Put briefly, what deep inside Prince wants to say in the word [nude] is not flesh/hair/nipples/testicles. What he

means is *nothing*, empty of feeling, detail, indentation. He wants to take off our clothes [which is a metaphor for our expectations and fantasies that we wish to project onto him]: he's suffocating under them...we'd pinned too may hopes on Prince, and the hopes had turned into clothes [expectations], and the clothes had turned into a straitjacket" (Hoskyns 18).

With "D.M.S.R." Prince is undercutting the complex, complicated theories and personas of himself that he has been building with his first three records and even on this record. Or in the least, he seems to be constructing this linear equilibrium which gives him access to easily shift between poles of himself. Ultimately, Prince is constructing the atmosphere, medium, venue, and vehicle for the individual to find freedom and fellowship by first finding totality (completion) in one's own multidimensionality. It is an alternative thought process, not a permanent (legislated) lifestyle. For Prince, there does not seem to be Truths about human behavior other than we all being products of our environment. The only constant is God, and he forgives us for our sins. He has to; He created us. We are his children. So, just enjoy the party until He returns. Most importantly, enjoy who you are in all of the incarnations of yourself. That is the only way you get to know yourself, and knowing yourself is the only way you can evolve to your higher being.

"All the Critics Love U in New York" is the attempt at describing an ideal, liberated place where the ideal, liberated individual can exist. Every free or sovereign being needs a land, a place to call home that allows him to act accordingly. Much in the same manner of the Iliad and the Odyssey where the Odyssey represents the creation of the new individual to exist within the new government created in the Iliad, Prince must now find or create a place for his liberated followers so that their movement is tangible and has roots. This is another example of Prince taking a cultural artifact and using it for his own purposes. New York is a trope for liberalism. By connecting himself to that trope, he is able to co-opt the sentiment associated with the artifact. Even though the attempt is well meant, the use of New York being the ideal place has been marred by time showing that there is just as much prejudice and intolerance in New York as in the rest of America. But compared to many conservative American cities, New York is still considered the heart of liberalism, "U can wear what u want 2; all the critics love u in New York. U could cut off all your hair, I don't think they'd even care in New York." In "All the Critics..." Prince is asserting to the mainstream society that even though there may not be a place for him and others like him in the narrow mind of their society, everyone has a place and a right to have a place, and it may be closer to the mainstream world than the conservative members of society want. When interpreting the lyric, "Purple love and war/ That's all u're headed for/ But don't show it," journalist Carol Cooper provides an excellent assessment of the song.

> "All is fair in love and war. Royal purple, red and blue, the color of yin and yang when they become one. [As Prince would clarify years later, if there is red blood in the blue sky, you get purple rain because red and blue make purple.] People are still not serious on a mass level about the war against racism and poverty; they're also not ready for Prince's kind of love. So yes, Prince is making love and war in ways that society is not sympathetic to at the moment, so that's why it'd be unwise to show it. The war of Armageddon is coming whether people are prepared for it or not, and in 'Free' Prince talks a little more about the freedom of choice between good and evil. No government gave you that, God did. But governments don't want you to remember that—which is why they put conscientious objectors in jail. But in the war that's coming there'll be no way to abstain. Whatever you do you'll have to be behind one flag or another. Prince's flag is freedom, purple, unconditional love" (Cooper 59).

Like it or not, Prince had pushed his way through and had become a force in the music industry, and the individuals in

"D.M.S.R." were going to have a home, which meant that they would have a voice in the national debate.

With freedom being a spiritual and religious right, Prince could not miss having some religious or spiritual tone on the album. He achieves this tone through the "Free," which encourages us to be thankful for our accomplishments and the freedom we have to achieve more. Prince also realizes that we should not lose sight of the never-ending fight for freedom, "Be glad that u are free, there's many man who's not...We will fight for the right 2 be free..." "Free" is spiritual in the manner that spirituals were used by African Americans during the Civil Rights Movement of the 1960s. It is meant to stir the soul and motivate the heart in the campaign toward complete freedom. "Soldiers are a marching; they're writing brand new laws. Will we all fight together 4 the most important cause? Will we all fight 4 the right 2 be free?" Prince is pushing the fight for freedom and the notion that to fight for freedom is a never-ending battle because evil (conservatism) never sleeps and is always waiting to roll back the clock of progress. At the end of most shows during the <u>1999</u> tour, Prince would end by stating to the audience in an almost urging tone, "Don't u let nobody tell you what to do!" It seems that early in his career, the biggest sin for Prince is allowing someone else to define you. "Free" is meant to echo the importance of self-determination as a God-given right.

At this point in Prince's career, ultimate freedom manifests itself best in one's sexuality. "International Lover" shows that freedom or, in the least, escapism can be found most easily and assuredly through liberated/good sex. The appeal of "International Lover" is that it is as quirky as it is sensuous. Sex is funny because it taps into all of our primitive desires, reducing us to our basic selves. As Prince indicates, "The fact that people lose their cool behind it is [reason] enough to write about it" (Mitchell 1981). It is the one thing that causes everyone to lose their cool, no matter how cool we think that we are. We are all connected by the fact that both the urge to have sex and the sex act are uncontrollable. Very few of us control when we get to have sex and for how long the act lasts. Even in "International Lover" when Prince is in charge, playing the role of the pilot/driver, he soon loses his control and is overcome with the moment. It is this trip of unpredictable exuberance or crash landing that continues to call us to each other.

> "'International Lover' is directed as much at the funny bone as the erogenous zone. On record, it is a piece of giggly soft-porn...The all-night cocktail-bar musical setting becomes increasingly surreal, and Prince transforms into erotica's aviator and invites his chosen last dance partner to come into his cockpit. The routine safety-drill announcements of modern air travel are distorted into a kinky, murmured sweet talk, interspersed with bursts of coital turbulence" (Hill 117).

Continuing the theme of the complexity of sex and the romantic relationship, "How Cum U Don't Call Me Anymore?" presents the underside or crash landing of "International Lover." Both musically and lyrically, Prince is evoking the legacy and ancestry of African American music. This song is the perfect blend of the sacred and the profane and shows the confusion and pain that comes from mixing the two. It is this anxiety or anxious tension between the spiritual and the secular that resonates at the bottom of Gaye's and Little Richard's work as it does in Prince's work. It is what popular music is, the ability to articulate and equate the needs of the body to the needs of the soul. Prince captures the feeling of urgency and vulnerability in the same manner of his predecessors. The male is completely at the mercy and caprice of the female, longing for sexual salvation from her.

> "I still keep a picture of u by my bed. I still remember everything that u said. Tell me baby,

why did u wanna go and break my heart? I still light a candle on a rainy night. All I wanna know baby if what we had was so good, how cum u don't call me, anymore. Sometimes I feel like I'm gonna die. I'm down on my knees, begging u please, cum on home."

Prince moans, pleas, whispers, talks shit, and cries for the love of his lost savior, all the while stepping and stomping on the piano petals like the choir conductor of any black Baptist church. This is what Ray Charles means when he states that "the only difference between gospel and the blues is that they say 'Lawd, Lawd,' and we say 'Baby, Baby'" (Charles 1992). Prince has combined his feminine vulnerability with gospel urgency to further blur his image, opening more doors for himself. The lyrics are so vulnerable that a countless number of female singers have covered this song, the two most notable being Stephanie Mills and Alicia Keys. With "How Come U Don't Call Me Anymore?" Prince has come full circle, back to "Still Waiting." He begins as an impish sheep, disrobes to show the fangs of his wolf persona, and effortlessly slides back into his lamb's wool. His variety and diversity of songs keep the public guessing and allow him to further explore more aspects of his expanding personality.

What Hill means when he suggests that <u>1999</u> is filled with "Intimations of Femininity" is still uncertain for me. There is certainly a consciousness of Prince's femininity in <u>1999</u>. The question for me is the use of this "femininity." Is Prince saying something about himself, about women, about society, or about the relationships between men and women? His assuming various gender roles and positions allows him to change perspectives on all of the above questions, often all in one song. Prince causes his listeners to take notice of our gender roles, causing us to ponder about seduction and the true seducer, as well as the concept of domination and control. Who really controls the game between men and women? What really motivates the game? We are forced to look at this issue from the inside out as opposed to from the outside in because Prince is able to be all parts and every aspect of the game at once. In doing this, "Prince became a trigger word in the mass media dialogue, so attention became more closely focused on the exterior he projected" (Hill 128). His anger and provocation are coupled with his desire to seduce and convince us of all the possibilities that we as males and females may be able to achieve if we submit to each other as opposed to being confined by our arbitrary identity boxes. Unfortunately for Prince, the image and imagery were drowning the messages. His plan was working but a bit too well. He was becoming a symbol through his body, but the messages were not resonating in the same manner. This is important because this affects the reception of later works, such as <u>Lovesexy</u>.

With <u>1999</u> Prince was making himself, his body, *the* body, the *liberated* body, the banner and tool for revolution. For him our notions of male and female are an arbitrary illusion/delusion. By breaking down these walls that define maleness and femaleness, which only work to limit us, Prince is hoping that we are able to evolve in an unrestricted manner. He asserts this in a 1983 interview for <u>Musician</u> with Barbara Graustark,

> "It [feminine sensibility and sensitiveness] is attractive for me. I would like to be a more loving person and be able to deal with other people's problems a little bit better. Men are really closed and cold together, I think. They don't cry, in other words. And I think that's wrong because that's not true" (Graustark 63).

To perpetuate the lie of a rigid, unchanging maleness is to limit human evolution, is to limit humanity's ability to get at the truth, to get to our higher selves. Thus, in <u>1999</u> Prince gets down to the heart of the matter of sex, love, and soul searching through the male/female relationship. The problem seems to be our inability to understand ourselves, keeping us from understanding others. This is the pivotal point which offends or confounds many attempting to get their brains around Prince's work. Since heterosexual, homophobic white males have, of course, dominated the course of thinking in American music and in American society, any male deviating from the prescribed identities and roles risks being ostracized or banished. Yet Prince, through the sexual act, attempts to find his human completion (not his identity because he knows who he is and is secure in that) in the female, not in the male. Thus, he uses various women and various situations to complete his ideal self.

> "1999 is suffused with songs of sex and romance where women characters are conjured up as foils in strange episodes of illicit game-playing, where no one stays in any one role for long. Ambiguity is the essence of Glam. With this, Prince is able to rearrange himself into a kind of universal hybrid" (Hill 128, 130).

The most obvious example of role playing or the questioning of positions is found in "Automatic," which is the inversion of roles centering on the power struggle between men and women. The male is totally helpless to the whims of the female. "If you have any mercy, don't torture me." The computerized music and short choppy sentence structure construct a being that is mindless and reacts solely to the prompts of the female. "I'm addicted to your pleasure. I'm addicted to your pain." The male has given up the power of the penis for the exhilaration of the orgasm. And with still more constructing and deconstructing, "Lady Cab Driver" becomes the antipathy of "Automatic." Whereas in "Automatic" Prince assumes a submissive role, in "Lady Cab Driver" Prince is dominating through his victimization, which allows him to retain his femininity (which is a non-threatening vulnerability) even when being completely dogmatic. The song is divided into two parts, explication and resolution. In the explication, the male is cast as a powerless protagonist on whom the world acts. He is caught in the arms of fate, "Lady Cab Driver, roll up your window fast. Trouble winds are blowing cold, and I don't know if I can last. Don't know where I'm going 'cause I don't know where I been..." In the resolution, the male uses sex to vent and relieve his frustrations and as an act of power to achieve a sense of being. His hopelessness and urgency to gain power

> "boils up into a comprehensive blurring of the boundaries between anguish and exhilaration, almost as disturbing as it is alluring. Again, a sense of exquisite libidinal agony is communicated by the way his breathless falsetto clings on to the fine detail of the beat. In a style familiar since 'I Wanna Be Your Lover,' he ingratiates himself to his lady chauffeur with a display of pain, penury, and humility, before rolling her over on the back seat to administer a purgative, psycho-therapeutic, not to say socio-economic, bang" (Hill 131).

Combined, the two parts of "Lady Cab Driver" make Prince a Bigger Thomas type figure. He is trapped in a naturalistic fate where what saves him, his phallus, is also what dooms him because the female object is never more than a prop used to ease the pain. Because she is objectified (has no personality or identity), she is unable to save him in the manner that "Anna Stesia" or the females in "Raspberry Beret" or "Dorothy Parker" are. Therefore, the protagonist is never able to nurture the needed human relationship to cure his ailment of loneliness. It is a great emotional orgasm, but he wants more. <u>Purple Rain</u> is where he begins to look deeper to the more divine/satisfying possibilities of friendship and companionship, which eventually leads to the epiphany found in <u>Parade</u>.

By the end of <u>1999</u>, Prince has explored enough of the male/female identities and relationships that he has liquefied himself enough to be both empathetic and symbolic of the fears, insecurities, and anxieties surrounding human existence. He becomes a cult figure who is now able to become representative of or encompass a mass amount of emotions, all initiating from the condition of otherness. He becomes the reigning Prince of Otherness. And after spending over a year and a half at the top, most would think it would be easy to become satisfied with his position in the public's eye and his financial stability (especially after fighting so diligently to get to this position) and not rock the boat by changing his formula. But as we now know, sitting idle and not evolving would not be Prince. Prince now felt it was time to step into the world of cinema and take his sound and message with him.

His Purple Reign

Part of Prince's genius, as I have mentioned with the synthesizer and the use of video, is knowing in what direction music is headed, knowing how to access the music in all of its various forms, and being able to use those various forms for his own means. Thus, the next step after the video was the big screen. Since Prince had been writing his songs as concepts, building personas that represent ideals, and crafting short sketches to give his personas a vehicle to be explored, a movie was the next logical step to expand his personas and concepts. He had all of the characters. He just needed the money to make it all come to life. We find Prince using what he has, his star status, to get what he needs, a movie deal to take his vision to the next level.

> "It seemed Prince's contract with Cavallo, Ruffalo, and Fargnoli was due to expire and the managers were taking every opportunity to encourage the star to re-up. Bob Cavallo recalls receiving an update from Steve Fargnoli, who was on the road with the tour. 'He wants a movie. If we don't get him a film deal with a major studio, he won't stay with us.' The next day, Cavallo accumulated a ton of press clippings and began pitching Prince to the film community. Of course it wasn't easy convincing studio chiefs that a burgeoning rock star could be the focus of a bankable film property. Finally, after a near-deal with Richard Pryor's production company, the Warner Bros film division expressed a slight interest. But they had to know more...even see more. Desperate for start-up funding, Cavallo persuaded Warner Records Chairman Mo Ostin to loan Prince and his management team the money to begin production" (Leeds 6-7).

The songs in __Purple Rain__ (1984) created Prince as the archetype individual, struggling against a world bent on confining him to its needs. The movie planted that notion in the minds of millions and connected him to their own struggle for independence and individuality. Many critics claim that <u>Purple Rain</u> is Prince's best album because it represents a culmination of everything Prince had been working toward from his beginnings on the streets. This statement can only be true if one is speaking of "The <u>Purple Rain</u> Project," which includes the movie, album, and tour. Considered on their own, the songs represent the first time that his lyrics are used exclusively to showcase Prince's talent as a storyteller. Each song comments on an artist's attempt to fight his internal and external demons and reconcile himself to his higher power, as a person and an artist. For Prince, this becomes the purpose of art, to help man become a better being and connect to his higher power.

One of the two songs from <u>Purple Rain</u> that went to number one is "Let's Go Crazy" which continues the message of living for the moment and enjoying life before the second coming. "Dearly beloved, we are gathered here 2day 2 get through this thing called life...But if the elevator tries 2 break you down, punch a higher floor...Are we gonna let the elevator break us down? Oh no, Let's Go...Crazy!" The message stresses staying focused under the chaos of the physical world so that you are able to evolve to the spiritual world. As he asserts to Chris Rock in the <u>VH1 to One</u> interview, "'Let's Go Crazy' was about God and Satan, but I couldn't say that on the radio at that time...But if you can keep your head straight, you can beat the elevator, the devil" (⚤ 1996). The other charting songs, "When Doves Cry" and "Purple Rain," expand the themes of the effects of rejection and isolation because of otherness and the need to stay focused on the goal of evolution. The protagonist is grappling with both himself and society, attempting to come to terms with his life. Like most of us, the Kid, Prince's character in <u>Purple Rain</u>, knows and understands his flaws but still struggles to overcome them. He is just like his father: sexist and insecure. The battle is to be better than what we are, better than the dysfunctional plans that we have been given, and evolve to being a better person. All of the songs stress the central issue of transcending the flesh, the physical plane. "When Doves Cry" and "Purple Rain" display more growth for Prince as a writer because they show a writer who is not just concerned with his pain. A way to deconstruct both "When Doves Cry" and "Purple Rain" is to determine the cause and concentration of the protagonist's pain. In both songs the protagonist is affected either negatively or positively by the pain of others. But in both cases, the pain felt by the protagonist causes a catharsis in him to become a better person. Connected, both songs display positive progress of a figure working his way through his id/superego complex.

In "When Doves Cry" the unsuccessful relationship of his parents causes the protagonist pain because it is the only blueprint he has to construct a life with a female. "Maybe I'm just too demanding. Maybe I'm just like my father 2 bold. Maybe u're just like my mother. She's never satisfied." He has inherited the chauvinism and insecurity of his father, which keeps him from being able to construct a meaningful relationship. Unable to escape his genes, the protagonist feels helpless to change his future. He is unable to see past the blueprint of his father's actions. The screams that he hears is not just of his personal relationships but of his parents' relationship that continue to echo in his head. "Why do we scream at each other? This is what it sounds like when doves cry." "When Doves Cry" is an attempt to resolve dysfunction and to communicate, not as a gender, but as a human being by admitting that this gendered outlook on life impedes his ability to commune fully with a mate. The first step is to admit to the insecurity. "Touch if u will my stomach. Feel how it trembles inside. U've got the butterflies all tied up. Don't make me chase u. Even doves have pride." Being honest is the first step to transcending the physical plane. This is a step that the Kid's father, that most men, are never able to do—get in touch with what they are really feeling, which allows them to commune truly and completely with the female.

In "Purple Rain" the protagonist feels a sorrow for not being able to articulate his love for his mate. It is a concession and an apology. "I never meant 2 cause u any sorrow. I never meant 2 cause u any pain." It is the genuine sorrow felt by the protagonist toward the female that causes reconciliation and growth. Prior to this point, Prince's protagonists have been communicating in the physical because that was the only language that they knew and understood. He now wishes to communicate in another language, the language of the mind and the soul. "I never wanted 2 be your weekend lover. I only wanted 2 be some kind of friend. Baby, I could never steal u from another. It's such a shame this friendship has to end." Even with the loss of a lover, the mature Kid realizes that human relationships are the essences to life. The protagonist finally realizes that love, not sex, is the tie that binds man to inner peace, to God. These songs are significant because they display a maturity in Prince's writing when he is handling pain and relationships. The male's focus is not only on his pain, but also on the pain of others as opposed to the songs of the past albums. In the past, we never know the emotions of the lady cab driver, or the females in "I Wanna Be Your Lover," "Bambi," or "Let's Pretend We're Married." But in "When Doves Cry" and "Purple Rain" the protagonist is attempting to reconcile himself to actual human beings and not just to concepts or a faceless society as in <u>Dirty Mind</u>. It is a step toward the meaningful exploration of interpersonal relationships of the soul as opposed to the body.

<u>Purple Rain</u>, the movie, is about a struggling musician dealing with the rejection of his music while dealing with family troubles. This rejection and family turmoil are all influencing his art because the rejection of the artist's work is a rejection of the artist, making the film semi-autobiographical, semi-dramatic creation, and one hundred percent Prince. In a 1986 MTV interview, Prince claims not to have written the script (which we now know to be true), but he does admit to being given a lot of creative control. Warner Bros made a

movie based on Prince's vision, his need to explain/express his battle between his personal Utopian world and the real world, which is the matrix to his fantasy world. At the core is the Kid's need to conquer and embrace life by embracing womanhood and femininity. His father embraced death by embracing his masculinity, which is the notion/urge to dominate. As a failed musician, the Kid's father dominates the household with an iron fist, squeezing the life out of it and himself. When the movie opens, the Kid is initially embracing this same urge to dominate. We see this through his battles to dominate his romantic interest, the local music scene, his band, and the women in his band. The urge to dominate breeds death. The urge to share breeds life. The central struggle is the Kid's attempt to overcome, transcend, his male/masculine self and embrace life by constructing positive, mutually equal relationships, especially with women.

The songs written for the movie push the surface themes to strike a deeper chord and fully expose the ideologies present in the movie. "Let's Go Crazy" deals with embracing life over death. Physical death is inevitable, so one is pushed to embrace the spiritual life. In understanding Prince's definition of the word "life," "An electric word, life, it means forever, and that's a mighty long time," one realizes that life begins in the physical and carries through to the hereafter. There is a continuation, not a beginning or an ending. Thus, one is encouraged to make sure that the mind is ready to comprehend: "Instead of worrying about how much of your time is left, ask him how much of your mind." Prince is rejecting the lie and limitation of the physical world and embracing the truth and the liberation of the spiritual world. He is asserting that we stop looking for answers in the physical because those answers are limited and based on fallacy. "Dr. Everything Will Be Alright will make everything go wrong. Pills & thrills and daffodils will kill. Hang tough, children. He's [God is] coming." The only answer to our problems is a higher power, but we must stay focused and stay on course to survive the chaos and disorder of our lives. Through the other songs, the female becomes the symbol for life. The Kid struggles to break the mold of his father who is unable to fully embrace life by letting go of his chauvinism and sexism and embracing his wife. The Kid's father states, "I could make you happy if you believed in me." Obviously, Frances L. does not believe in himself and has no blueprint that shows him how to construct a relationship with his wife so that she can believe in him. At the core of their conflict is Frances' insecurity and their disagreement over what constitutes happiness. The Kid's mother states, "You never let me have any fun." Frances responds, "Don't I keep the heat on?" Where the mother (female) is finding happiness in the metaphysical of loving and laughing, the father (male) is finding happiness in the physical, symbolized by his monetary concerns. Frances L.'s inability to relinquish or move beyond the physical keeps him from constructing the relationship that he desires and needs. "I could make you happy if you believed in me." After his father attempts suicide, the Kid has a vision of his own suicide, which is inevitable if he is unable to transcend his physical, his maleness, and embrace life by connecting with his romantic interest.

"Take Me W/U" begins the embracing of the female by showing the romantic relationship as a way to escape the physical world. Unlike the previous songs, the escape is through the romantic relationship and not sex. As a maturing writer, Prince is realizing the possibilities of the male/female romantic relationship, thus realizing the possibilities of human relationships. Supporting this, "The Beautiful Ones" comments on the failure of the physical to produce love or inner peace. The notion of finding love through sex or physical beauty is being condemned and abandoned. And in "Computer Blue" Prince has come to a dead-end in finding love through sex. "Love and lust are entirely different." This seems to signal that Prince has pushed his all encompassing sex metaphor to its limit and is now ready to explore other means of expression to relate his message of freedom, liberation, and completion. This sets the table for "Darling Nikki."

"Darling Nikki" is the storyteller at his best. It is the sketch of "Lady Cab Driver" made into a tale. Unlike the male in "Lady Cab Driver" who is seeking temporary escapism, the protagonist in "Darling Nikki" is expecting Nikki to be there in the morning. According to Paulette Richards, author of <u>The Terry McMillan: A Critical Companion</u> (1999), the narrative and imagery of this song seem to be borrowed from a Satanic ritual, "Sign your name on the dotted line," and from Keats' poem, "La Belle Dame Sans Merci." This is an example of Prince's ability to co-opt images and icons from other cultures and manipulate them for his own purposes. The rendezvous with Nikki is the final descent into hell, a final embracing of the physical pleasures of life, which causes our protagonist to realize that the physical world will not yield what he needs to evolve. It is obvious that the protagonist in the <u>Purple Rain</u> songs is expecting to gain more from his sexual expeditions than those in the past. He is not just looking to escape or pass the time, he is truly searching for the higher, spiritual plane. The use of the satanic elements represents the misguided desires of the male. Instead of trying to commune with her soul to find salvation, he tries to commune with her flesh and finds only damnation and loneliness. Try as he might, the protagonist is unable to grind his sorrows away. All of this is to say nothing of the male protagonist being left behind by a bold, sexually dominating female. This song is commenting on the schizophrenia of the male, which causes him to construct an adversarial and maternal relationship with the female. The Kid performs this song when his love interest, Apollonia, enters the club with his rival, Morris Day. Apollonia is with Day because the Kid refused to help her pursue a career in the music business. Thus, by performing "Darling Nikki" when she arrives at the club, the Kid is questioning if not denouncing Apollonia's use of her physical to get what she wants. The audience should see the Kid's anger as a symbol of male schizophrenia. He demonizes her for using her physical attributes to survive, but he wishes to use her physical being as a trophy of his male conquest and prowess. The dream of "Darling Nikki" is conjured by the male psyche—his schizophrenic perception of woman as damsel and vixen, which creates a wonderful piece of storytelling. From the introduction of her masturbating in a hotel lobby, to the description of her gadgets and her sexual prowess, to her disappearance in the morning, it all makes for an excellent tale of the sexual she-devil which lurks in the minds of men obsessed with sexual conquest to prove their male worth. Prince is showing that this conquest is meaningless because real salvation can not be found in the libido. What the Kid gets are empty orgasms, which leave him still longing, "Woke up the next morning; Nikki wasn't there. I looked all over, and all I found was a phone number on the stairs."

In finally turning from the physical and embracing the spiritual, "I Would Die 4 U" gives Prince the spiritual ambiguity to which he has been alluding his entire career. "I'm not a woman. I'm not a man. I am something that u'd never understand." It is "I Wanna Be Your Lover" taken to the spirit realm. He wants to meet all the female's needs. Prince's blurring of the male/female gender lines allows him to become, in personification, a higher life form. "I'm not a woman. I'm not a man. I'm not human...I am your conscious. I am love." This is eight years before he becomes an unpronounceable symbol. Not only does the Kid realize that completion can only be found in the metaphysical, he realizes that love is not something to be found like buried treasure. He finds that love only manifests itself when we do something to manifest it. "U're just a sinner I am told. I'll be your fire when u're cold. I'll make u happy when u're sad. I'll make u good when u r bad." Through this, Prince is still breaking categories and limitations by redefining our notions of reality and truth. What is love? What does it mean to be male or female? Obviously, we do not know because everybody is singing about finding love, and few ever do. Prince seems to be asserting that if our notions about reality are wrong, then everything that is built on our notions is wrong. The way to correct this is to divorce ourselves from the physical and search for truth on another, higher plane, and this realization leads us to "God," which does not appear on the album. It is on the B-side of the "Purple Rain" single. It celebrates God's powers of creation, emphasizing that we are all created equally by the same creator. "God made a man. He made the Earth and the sea. He made us all equally." Prince is finding equality in man through the creation of every man by God. Also, he is continuing to equate creativity with God. If man is made in the likeness of God, then man is a creator not a destroyer. Thus, we should be making love not war. Though there is a contradictory dichotomy in our sexual nature, it is still the best example of our being god-like. Completion comes when we are able to transcend our physical desires and understand the divinity of our being able to procreate. Thus, we should not be engaged in the battle of the sexes, but we should be striving to remove the walls that separate male from female. Sex should not take us farther from God; it should bring us closer to him. We can only grow closer to God when we understand that God is love.

During the live shows Prince would transfer the sexual energy of "Let's Pretend We're Married" to the spiritual energy of "God." In the middle of performing "Let's Pretend We're Married," a song about using sex to ease the pains of loneliness, Prince would be interrupted by God who would scold Prince for being "bad." Prince would retort, "I know I said that I would be good, but they dig it when I'm bad." This shows the dichotomy of man in the battle between his flesh and his soul. This is the same struggle for Prince: to use sensationalism or to use pure artistic strategy. Also, this is that same dichotomy at play in African American culture because their religion has always been more than a blueprint of empty rituals, which are used merely to maintain social order. Because African Americans have existed in a situation so hellish that they believe that their salvation from earthly oppression must come from a spiritual being, the spirituality of God has seemed to resonate more in their culture. Therefore, God is not some spirit of the afterlife; He is a very real and tangible entity in their daily struggles. In addressing secular, socio-political issues, African American religion has always been submersed in and understood the concerns of physical battles. Still, this is a very thin line to walk, a balancing act that has driven many to bouts of mental and emotional anguish and schizophrenia, such as Little Richard and Al Green who both left popular music in search of a higher fulfillment, a fulfillment that they were trying to gain sexually. This is that salvation quality of Gaye's "Sexual Healing." "God" paints a picture of an artist aware of and concerned with using his art to meet people where they are and elevate them, even though he is still grappling within himself to reconcile his secular to his spiritual.

The critical acclaim and financial success of Purple Rain is one of the true peaks in Prince's commercial career. In almost every aspect of society one could find traces of the Purple Reign. However, Prince's aloofness and seeming tranquility in relation to his new found success, his honesty and commitment to his music, and never changing attitude toward his craft created criticism of his perceived arrogance and tight control of his royal court. The truth of the matter is that the machine of the mainstream media likes to tear you down as much as it enjoys elevating you. Prince is not suited to be boxed by what is considered mainstream success for any prolonged length of time. He has made a career of not belonging to anyone. Accordingly, Purple Rain is perhaps much more complex than a mass market could handle. So much of the concepts found in the past albums were glossed over in Purple Rain for public consumption. It was the image that was marketed, not the ideals behind the image. The Purple Rain and Thriller phenomena were atypical of what the eighties represented—the watering down of essence to sell sensationalized presence. From the onset of the conception of what would eventually become Purple Rain, there was a struggle between black and white ideals. The initial concept was a movie called Dreams. The question quickly became whose dream would the movie reflect? Prince and the initial writer, William Blinn, who had worked on <u>Roots</u>, <u>Fame</u>, and some other television projects, created an initial skeleton. Prince's managers and co-producers of the movie, Bob Cavallo and Steve Fargnoli, as well as the director, Al Magnoli, were not "pleased with Blinn's script; it was too interior and darkly psychological...Magnoli wanted the film to reflect the energy of rock-n-roll by employing quick, elliptical editing" (Bream 88). The emphasis of the film was changed from concentrating on some tangible, culturally rooted issue to the lavish presentation of flash. Whenever art is forced to move from the particular to the universal, it is always the black sensibilities that are most marginalized. White America enjoys black blues as long as they are not the antagonist. They can accept something that discusses the notion that life is universally difficult and that we all must suffer with some amount of pain, hardship, and injustice. But, they are not willing to validate something that makes them the cause of the pain, hardship, and injustice. This is more schizophrenic than ironic because without white supremacy there would be no blues. Like most African Americans, the Kid is celebrated for his final success, and his success is celebrated in a manner that erases the specific hurdles and struggles of race so that he may be connected to the larger white audience.

<u>Purple Rain</u> is generally seen as a commentary on Prince's struggle to make it in the business. On some level, this is true. But if you watch and listen more carefully, there is much more happening. No, it is not literally about the black community, nor does it communicate on a collective level. But we must remember that the passing narratives of the eighteenth and nineteenth centuries, which were meant to be palatable to white readers, were also meant to show the conflict of the mulatto as a trope or metaphor for the entire black race. And in business sense, the struggle of the black individual, not the entire race, is more universal and palatable to white patrons. Still, the struggle of the black individual, even in a film such as <u>Purple Rain</u>, must be contextualized by race, even when the black individual wants to ignore the influence or effects of race on his journey. Every question and

battle for place and identity is a double or dual issue for the black individual. Where do I fit in, where is my place, and where is my voice? These are individual questions for white patrons because they have never suffered institutionalized or racial segregation or oppression. Even in the case of poor whites, they are in their situation because of class and not race, which means that they (individually) can always acquiesce. As Huey P. Newton put it, a white boy can always cut his hair and join the establishment. On the other hand, when an African American is poor, his poverty is linked to the history of slavery, and that creates a completely different set of dynamics, a completely different set of obstacles to overcome, and a completely different perspective of the world. It is not stated that the Kid is a young black man struggling in a racist world that is trying to limit him by defining him, but it is inferred. It is inferred by Billy Sparks, the owner of First Avenue, and Day, as they push for more mainstream, popular music that accepts certain limitations placed on black music and black musicians. It is inferred by the Kid's black father, a broken musician, whose ideas about music and life have been rejected and beaten from him to a point where he is no longer able to control his home, especially his white wife.

Though these questions of identity and place are the traditional questions of art, they are particularly relevant to African Americans because people of African descent have been warred upon, colonized, enslaved, and repositioned more than anyone on the planet. Every ten years the collective mass of African Americans are asking, "Where am I, and who am I?" Purple Rain represents how African Americans who have been cut off from that community are forced to grapple with those questions alone, without the help of the collective history and support of the people. When you grow up in a place like Minneapolis, where your race's population is only three percent of the entire population, you have very little support mechanisms for your particular struggle. As Baldwin puts it, they are the strangers in the village who are forced to believe and accept that they have nowhere to turn but to their individual selves. This is evident in the fact that the Kid comes from mixed parents. In a literal and figurative sense, African Americans are mulattos struggling to find a place in this land. Torn from their roots, most have opted to have the discussion of identity and place on individual terms rather than on collective terms. <u>Purple Rain</u> shows this. It is about constructing and institutionalizing a notion of one's individual self. Because the image of the mulatto has become a safe image for whites, most miss the message of the mulatto as a trope for African Americans—who are a dislocated group, struggling to find roots, place, and identity. Most whites wish merely to embrace the exotic motif of the mulatto without dealing with the stigma of racism that the mulatto symbolizes. Being neither white nor black, mulattos are forced to cling to some individualized, often overly romanticized, notion of themselves as some heroic other. This notion is palatable to a larger white audience. Books such as <u>Clotel</u>, which romanticize the plight of the mulatto gain a greater acceptance than movies, such as <u>Sankofa</u>, which seek to challenge and destroy the romanticized mulatto myth.

<u>Purple Rain</u> is an important movie because it affirms the notion that artists struggle with who they are in relation to themselves, their families, their peers, and their community, and all of this goes into making the art. "When Doves Cry" is important on two levels—individual and race. On an individual level, it is a song, which affirms that artists are compelled to express the personal aspect of themselves in their art. The troubled marriage of the Kid's parents completely affects and determines who he is. In this same vein, black art must discuss life under the umbrella of white supremacy or it will be irrelevant to black people. Though there is a lot of money to be made by having the larger white population purchase one's work, the fundamental duty of art is to affirm a people's humanity by affirming the aspects of their culture, which involves affirming their particular perspective. When black artists consciously crossover to a white audience by watering down their sensibilities and struggles for a white palate, they fail to meet their requirements as artists. "When

Doves Cry" is not just about dysfunctional parents, it is about the struggle of the mulatto existence, the struggle of attempting to marry two fundamentally different perspectives of life. When the Kid calls his parents a "freak show," he is not just referring to their arguing; he is also referring to their mixed race and the problems that it causes. The watering down of the race issues causes his statement and the song to miss its cultural mark. Thus, the song is only appreciated on an aesthetic sense of pleasing sound and universal pain. More examples of this watering down is the fact that scenes of white Minneapolis police officers harassing Morris Day were cut from the movie. Initially, Purple Rain was to be seen as an American (mulatto) struggle on three levels: the Kid's civil strife, his parents' struggle, and the larger cultural clash of black and white represented by Day and the police officers. Even further, Day and the Kid's adversarial relationship should have been seen not only as musical differences but also as relating the varying differences of black ideologies of how to survive in America. Both Day and the Kid are young black men with their own notions of life and art. Their differences and similarities are what make them human, which, in turn, are what make them worth studying. The Kid represents the aesthetic ideal of human transcendentalization, and Day represents the reality check of the tangible hell where African Americans are forced to endeavor.

The poignancy of the film is that the duality represented by the Kid and Day is trumped by the duality found within the Kid. The Kid is an African American who struggles with the dichotomy of wanting artistic respect and commercial success. This is the dichotomy of African Americans. Even with the glossing over, the Purple Rain Project still would turn into a symbolic personification of a bunch of ideas about the world, which were certain to polarize opinion. "Young, Black, strong, prosperous, self-divided, unnervingly mute, and sexually programmed to subvert—this is some people's recipe for hell on Earth" (Hill 145). In the end, Prince seemed to play the Hollywood machine and the world's fascinations and hang-ups for all they were worth, taking solace in his ability to manipulate the system for his own benefit. This attitude corresponds directly with the growing African American sense of survival in the eighties. Prince, like Little Richard before him, was the precursor to a whole new generation of young, black, strong, prosperous, and sexually charged males who were intent on profiting from America's obsession with them as well as controlling their assets, thus controlling, to some degree, their identities. "The significance of <u>Purple Rain</u> lies in its ability to show a vulnerable, multifaceted Black male on the screen. It is the depth of emotion displayed by Prince that makes the film important. We've had our Shafts, our superheroes, but when it comes to Black leading men, we haven't had this kind of complexity" (Allen, "It's Raining Prince," 56). Because of his maneuvering and Middle America's fascination with the black body, Prince was thrust into superstardom, finally being accepted/embraced/molested by the mainstream music society. But through all the hype, he never seemed phased by or in awe of his new found success. The constant creator, always working on his next project, Prince felt, once again, that it was time to expand himself. So while the public was waiting to see what would be the next treat to come from the purple kingdom, Prince already had carefully finished his next album, which would be seen as the beginning of the end of the purple reign, but would also be the fulfilling of Prince, the complete creative and astute thinker. His ability to mold concepts into strong, well defined narratives would make him a popular musical philosopher.

Our Trip Around the World in a Day

Music lovers packed record shops on the release date of Around the World in a Day (1985), awaiting the sounds, lyrics, and ideas of Purple Rain II. What they received was a highly innovative and progressive re-contextualization of the legacy of popular music through the prismatic mind of Prince. This musical kaleidoscope and lyrical sermon of cultural relevancy was welcomed with open arms by the Prince faithful and music lovers but shunned by a substantial percentage of mainstream music listeners, expecting Prince to repeat himself. Nonetheless, Prince was able to ride the Purple Rain wave to another chart topping album and single before the musical mainstream gravitated to more tangible forms. Leeds provides more insight to understanding the popularity and acceptance of Around the World in a Day.

> "While revisionist history has cast the eccentric album as one of his least successful endeavors, the reality is that it sold in excess of three million units and spent three weeks as the No. 1 record in the country—no mean accomplishment, particularly since it shipped without a single to lead the way." (Leeds 8).

Leeds' assertion covers two issues. First, there is Prince's ability to be both artistic and commercial, which is viewed as an anomaly by the mid-eighties. Around the World in a Day is not as lyrically or musically accessible as Purple Rain. The pictures painted are a bit more figurative, driven more by metaphors and imagery. It shows an artist more concerned with growth than record sales, but it also shows an artist, at least at that stage, who is able to raise his artistic skills and continue to craft songs that are still palatable to a large audience. In popular art, one must entertain before he can educate or provoke thought. That is the nature of the audience. Yet, the fact that the album was shipped without a single shows that Prince is thinking more conceptually about how the songs fit together in some harmonious, cohesive form to articulate a central issue. In this, he is continuing the legacy of conceptual music rather than surrendering to the pressure to repeat his own success by crafting singles merely for mass consumption and radio programming. Thus, Around the World in a Day shows a definite graduation of Prince to the level of higher human/social conscience and creativity. But, its musical and lyrical diversity make it too eclectic and experimental to exist as a popular mainstream phenomenon. However, depth and range cause it to be considered one of the most imaginative and creative works of all time, especially in the manner that Prince combines tradition with his personal vision and talent.

The album's concept reminds us that to understand ourselves and the world is to understand the circular relationship, influence, and interdependence between society and the individual. It is akin to understanding the circular relationship between the body and the soul. The individual is an allegorical figure or a microcosm of the society. The society is the collective notion of the individual. Therefore, humanity must look inward, into the soul of the individual, viewing the individual as the soul of society. By doing this we gain a better understanding ourselves and our society. We realize that we are all the same, seeking the same physical and spiritual fulfillment. This understanding should create or lead to a domino effect of respect, tolerance, love, and evolution. And what better way to study people and human nature than to take a trip around the world. Of course, most of us do not have the time or the finances to take such a trip; thus Prince attempts to supplement our lives with his vision. My father impressed upon me that the most useful or significant artists are those who dare to take us beyond the sheets, to places where the audience is not able to go on their own. That is one of the primary jobs of the artist, to provide us with new visions and awareness. By exploring the world, we are exploring different aspects of ourselves. In this respect, Around the World in a Day is a journey narrative, much like the Odyssey, Gulliver's Travels, and Invisible Man, where the protagonist is compelled to evolve because of his experiences. And, Prince is also attempting to create a catharsis in the listener based on the experiences and travels of the protagonist. These experiences give <u>Around the World in a Day</u> a diversity, which causes it to surpass its contemporaries. Because of its diverse style, <u>Around the World in a Day</u> has been compared to everything from the paisley rock of the Beatles' <u>Sergeant Pepper's Lonely Hearts Band</u> to the experimental funk, rock, and soul of Jimi Hendrix. <u>Around the World in a Day</u> displays a passion for the aesthetics as it celebrates transcending the physical mind into the spiritual realm, rivaling the theories of poets and social critics Walt Whitman and Henry David Thoreau, while maintaining its ability to reach out and relate to the emotions, thoughts, and fears of the common man, such as in the works of Dunbar, Hughes, or Wonder. Yet, through all of the comparisons that one can draw with this album, it is definitely from the mind of the Minneapolis Genius. While the music stresses a musical genius at work, the lyrics are prime examples of Prince's ability to tell a story. The way Prince navigates the listener along the journey of different tales with a sundry of emotions is likened to Chaucer's <u>Canterbury Tales</u>, which also exhibits Prince's depth at handling characterization. Though a bit more impressionistic and broad, Prince creates characters who are personifications of the emotions and situations that he wants to explore. Each character leads us along the emotional spectrum in search of Utopia. Through these characters we are able to explore ourselves.

Prince set the tone for this inquisitive and searching album by announcing his retirement from touring at the height of his success. When asked why he wanted to retire, Prince stated he felt a calling to take a trip around the world in a day in search of the ladder. He continued to tell of a land called Paisley Park where it snows in July and tears are only for joy. Always playing with his image, Prince is consciously preparing his listeners and setting the tone for his new direction. This shows that Prince understands the struggle of growing as an artist and being able to create and sell that changing/evolving art to a public, which is compelled to remain stagnant because the industry finds it more economically feasible to sell disposable, one dimensional art. This struggle is more intense for an African American artist who exists in a society where he and his audience are deemed flat, stagnant, and one dimensional beings who are more emotional than intellectual. Again, Prince is usurping this oppression and stagnation by making himself a part of the art. He is the character; he is the message. In this, Prince is following in the legacy of merging the ideology, the persona, and the musician into one icon as in the manner of Little Richard, Screaming Jay Hawkins, Sun Ra, Bob Marley, Parliament Funkadelic, and Earth, Wind, and Fire. In the words of Bootsy Collins, Prince was making the funk legal, playable on the radio. Along with this, he was keeping alive the dramatic and the theatrical as part of the art. When most black acts were scaling back, Prince was seeing how far he could go. It was not just music, and Prince wanted to be more than just a musician. The music would be an outgrowth or offspring of a movement of sorts. In keeping this door open, Prince is a direct influence on rappers being able to put on, take off, and change identities and personas like socks. Both "The Ladder" and "Paisley Park" are songs on Around the World in a Day. A third song, "Sometimes It Snows in April," shows up on Parade. This, of course, is all commercialization and good for record sales, but it also speaks of an artist who is intelligent enough to understand that image control is essential to artistic communication and survival. Sometimes one's readership may not be ready or willing to go where the artist is trying to go. Alice Walker's Temple of My Familiar (1989) is a good example of this. After a successful run of well-crafted books that appeal to feminist ideologies, Walker published Temple of My Familiar, which is seemingly a break from her former themes and focuses more on the communal and ancestral relationship of African Americans. Also, it is one of her few books where the African American male characters are not seen as being antagonistic to the existence of women. (It must be noted that most missed the theme of Mister's redemption in The Color Purple (1982) because more people watched the movie than read the book.) It is my contention that Temple of My Familiar did not sell as well because her readership wanted more, "Black Men Ain't No Damn Good Books." But rather than abandon the themes in Temple of My Familiar, Walker had continued to explore them in Finding the Green Stone (1991) while she has also continued to champion the trials of women in Possessing the Secret of Joy (1992) and By the Light of My Father's Smile (1998). In a similar manner, Prince is not waiting on his audience to change, nor is he allowing the record company to dictate his identity to him. So although Around the World in a Day does not make as much money as Purple Rain, it garners more critical and artistic acclaim than Purple Rain ever could.

Around the World in a Day is similar to 1999 by the way each song is crafted to stand on its own but still work to complete a theme of social and spiritual self study and awareness, leading to an understanding of the interdependence of the physical and the metaphysical and a notion of how to navigate the waters between the two to find inner peace. The difference in Around...Day from 1999 is that the aesthetics of human essence are being praised with the notion that we can all have spiritual peace. 1999 is not about achieving inner peace as much as it is about having good sex until the Master comes to bring us our inner peace or rescue us from this hell. In Around...Day, the emphasis switches from physical satisfaction to spiritual satisfaction. Further, Around...Day shows a deeper construction of themes as related to Purple Rain. Where the songs on Purple Rain represent ideals, the songs on Around...Day are able to become complete allegories. Prince juxtaposes surreal situations and varied emotions to paint a course toward the Utopia promised in Purple Rain.

> "The imagery [is] derived from the hippie notion of a Utopia where people would retreat from the logic of the industrialized world [which is limiting because it only provides the pleasure of the physical] and revert to a child-like wonderment at the simpler pleasures of nature" [which allows humanity to know the fulfillment of the metaphysical] (Hill 167).

The album begins with the title track "Around the World in a Day," which invites us to join Prince on his quest for knowledge, enlightenment, and never-ending happiness. The song sets the tone for the rest of the album. "Open your heart, open your mind, a train is leaving all day. A wonderful trip through our time, and laughter is all u pay." Prince, of course, is the appointed poet/conductor to lead the listener on this journey for self, this journey for inner peace. We must escape life's meaningless toil for the physical rewards and journey inward to find Utopia. "Loneliness already knows u. There ain't no reason 2 stay. Take my hand; I'll show u. I think I know a better way." He ends by juxtaposing the physical, man made Utopia, America, to the true Utopia which is spiritual and as easily attainable. "The little 1 [Prince] will escort u, 2 places within your mind. The former [America] is red, white, and blue. The ladder is purple, climb, climb." This statement has a double meaning. First, America represents the physical, where we are, and the purple ladder symbolizes the need to transcend the physical. Secondly, Prince is asserting that even in America, the symbol of man's greatest accomplishment and wealth, there is still a need to find more, which stresses that the physical world, no matter how much of it we attain, will always be limiting.

The first stop on our journey is at "Paisley Park." Prince describes it as, "...a park that is known for the face it attracts, colorful people whose hair on one side is swept back. The smile on their faces, it speaks of profound inner peace." Paisley Park is a kingdom of peaceful paradise, a place where everyone is accepted, with love being the government and laughter the taxes. Of course, "Paisley Park" is a metaphor for inner peace. "Paisley Park is in your heart." The lesson is that one finds inner peace by embarking on a journey. Inner peace is not something that one receives as a gift. It is something that is earned through experience and soul searching. Underneath the song's whimsical attitude boils Prince's own personal journey for freedom and inner peace as represented in the naming of his record company and studio, Paisley Park. Sheila E. asserts that "Paisley Park, it's his funhouse" (E., "Prince of Paisley Park," Omnibus, 1991). Prince also affirms this after being asked by Detroit disc jockey, The Electrifying Mojo about his need to have complete creative control. "Well, I always figured that if I worked hard enough and long enough and didn't hurt anybody, I'd be able to make the music that I wanted to make." So, we find that freedom and inner peace work in a circular, almost symbiotic relationship for Prince. Accordingly, inner peace is, again, something for which one must work, and having it represents growth.

After defining inner peace, Prince takes us on the journey, which will enable us to find inner peace. The next stop on our journey is one of melancholy, sadness, and contemplation. "Condition of the Heart" tells three different stories of the effects that a love lost has on three different people. The storytelling comes through quite clearly even though Prince uses a very impressionistic style as in Crane's <u>Red Badge of Courage</u>. His characters are described as "a woman in the ghetto," "a girl from Paris," and "a real prince from Arabia." The use of the impressionistic style, providing only basic and flat detail about characters involved in specific actions or situations, allows the listener to create the scenes in his own mind, allowing him to delve into the story completely. The impressionistic style of the song connects characters from various backgrounds and classes, ultimately showing the universality of us all through our particular existences. All of these characters are driven by the desire to achieve inner peace by finding love. This affirms the humanity of us all, showing that matters of the heart are innate or organic to all of our existences. If nothing else, we all suffer from a condition of the heart. Furthermore, the protagonist is hurt by all of these characters in his quest for love, but none of them nor the pain that they inflict upon the protagonist is portrayed as malicious. Because we all suffer from a condition of the heart, all our pains and actions are relative. In fact, the protagonist is using the three characters in the very same manner that they are using him, as a stop along the way to love. "How was I 2 know that she would wear the same cologne as u and giggle the same giggle that u do?" So, in the search for love, we are all antagonists and protagonists, blindly trying to find love the best way we can,

"...whenever I would act a fool, the fool with a condition of the heart." We are all fools. Knowing this should cause us to love each other and not blame or exploit each other. Or, by knowing, as the Main Ingredient put it, "everybody plays the fool," we are better able to deal with our romantic disappointments and not allow the temporary disappointments to stop us from completing our journey toward love and completion.

The third stop takes us to a five and dime store, owned by Mr. McGee. "Raspberry Beret," one of two top ten songs to come from the album, celebrates the ability of the male-female relationship to make living worth while. We have a young boy, leading a life of boredom, whose life is turned upside down by a woman. After the spiritual high of "Paisley Park" and the emotional low in "Condition of the Heart," Prince indulges us in the physical pleasures of life. The male-female relationship is the physical manifestation of our spiritual and our emotional. It is not as fulfilling, but it is tangible, giving us something definite by which to mark our existence. The girl who enters "through the out door" gives the male protagonist something by which to measure his life, his existence. Her entering "through the out door" signifies that she has a different personality, which will add flavor to his life. The beret symbolizes the beauty of the simplicities of life and the excitement of new found wonders that can be found right under our noses if we but open our eyes and look. The girl is like a poem, where the familiar is made to seem unfamiliar, and in this we once again recognize the uniqueness and beauty. It is the minor things like the odd color of the beret and the entering "through the out door" that break the redundant pattern of his life and cause him to see life's possibilities:

> "I wuz working part-time at a five and dime, my boss wuz Mr. McGee. He told me several times that he didn't like my kind, cuz I was a bit 2 leisurely. It seems that I wuz busy doing something close to nothing but different than the day before. That's when I saw her. She walked in through the

out door. She wore a raspberry beret."

In one way Prince is reverting back to his old line of sex being an activity to pass time or make life more meaningful, yet he is also pushing forward in that it is the girl, as a person with a real personality, who is producing the salvation. She is not just another nameless, faceless body. Although she remains an impressionistically styled character, she has likes, dislikes, and concerns. "She had the nerve to ask me if I planned to do her any harm." She is human. It is her humanity that saves the boy, not merely her body.

The final song on side one is probably the most sexually charged song Prince has written, but because of the symbolism the song is rarely realized as being so. Aside from its subject matter, "Tamborine" may be Prince's most creative lyrical work because of its great metaphoric essence. Not since the works of Emily Dickinson has a subject been hidden so deeply beneath the surface. "Oh my God there I go falling in love with a face in a magazine. All alone, by myself, me and I play my tamborine." In its coyness and slyness, the song packs a compacted punch of sexual escapism. It is the Art of Masturbation, artificial and fleeting, yet powerful enough to remove us from our daily existence. We are provided sex without limitation. The mind is the poet, providing imaginary characters and settings for our plot of sex. Not only is Prince, again, showing the ability of sex to save us from our mundane lives, "Long days, lonely nights," but he is also showing that sex is as much psychological as it is physical. It is not the orgasm that is freeing and liberating. It is the ability of sex or, in this case, masturbation to create a fantasy world of escapism. Although masturbation is based on imagination and brings only temporary, fleeting salvation, sex is exactly the same. At least with masturbation one is able to completely control the fantasy, as we see the protagonist removing all that is unpleasant to his world. "I don't care 4 1 night stands with Trolley cars that juggle 17. I just want 2 settle down and play around my baby's tamborine." The act of masturbation allows him to escape entirely from the world and its pain and find a numbing peace, "Guess that I'll stay at home, all alone, and play my tambourine."

The beginning of side two brings us back to "America," the physical but contradictory Utopia: a country where the rest of the world's outsiders and untouchables want to be, and yet a country built on colonization, tyranny, and oppression of the underclass for its own profits. Still, in 1985 it was the world's symbol for freedom. This is more of that human dichotomy that Prince loves to explore. "America" casts shades of Prince's earlier records as a cry for freedom. This time, however, Prince's plea is for America to move from being symbolically free to being literally free, to live up to its creed of life, liberty, and the pursuit of happiness for all. And of course, as always, Prince is paralleling his personal issue of freedom with the collective. During the height of <u>Purple Rain</u>, a move had begun to censor lyrics. Prince answers that move with, "America, God shed his grace on thee. America, keep the children free." The movement for censorship was a major story, championed by a conservative group known as the Parent's Music Resource Center, which aimed much of their criticism at Prince and heavy metal bands. The apex of the movement was the hearings before the U.S. Senate, which featured Dee Snyder, the lead singer of Twisted Sister, and led to the advent of the parental warning sticker for explicit lyrics. So here again we find Prince at the forefront of social issues, helping to keep creative freedom alive. "America" juxtaposes this issue of censorship with issues of poverty and education. America, it seems to Prince, is too preoccupied with profanity in songs to care about starving children. "Little Sister, making minimum wage, living in a 1-room jungle monkey cage. Can't get over, she almost dead. She may not be in the black, but she happy she ain't in the red." We, Americans, sit idly, watch it all, and wonder why the music is profane. We become a country, a generation with, because of haplessness, no national or self pride. "Jimmy Nothing never went to school. Made him pledge allegiance, Jimmy said it wasn't cool. Nothing made Jimmy Proud. Now Jimmy lives on a mushroom cloud."

"America" represents our deterioration from having embraced material gain and empty ritual and having rejected love. It begs the question: How can we be so righteous that we can not bear profane language but can turn a blind eye to a child living a profane existence? At its core, "America" is not only painting an honest picture of the country; it is also asserting the need for open and honest discussion of our failings. If we do not have open and honest discussion, how can we evolve, how can we continue to be the land of the free and the home of the brave?

The next two songs clarify the purpose of our journey. They explain that this journey and many others like it are merely compulsions to fill the emotional and spiritual needs in our lives. "Pop Life," the second song on side two, is about our earthly search for space fillers to make life more exciting. Boredom is the one state that humans are constantly seeking to elude. Human beings need alternative states of being to feel like we are leading full, satisfactory lives. "Everybody needs a thrill; we all have a space to fill; everybody can't be on top, but life ain't too funky unless it's got that pop." Prince gives clear examples of "pops," million dollar checks, a new hair style, and drugs, and defines them for what they are, temporary satisfaction. The next song, "The Ladder," takes the concept of "Pop Life" and expands it to a spiritual realm. "The Ladder" showcases another of Prince's musical talents, the ability to draw from his gospel influences, echoing the sounds and emotions of the black Baptist church. In tone, Prince is able to capture the anxiety of being removed from one's higher power and the urgency to reconnect with this power. The story is about a King with wealth, power, and admiration, but no inner peace. Without inner peace, his own, personal Paisley Park, the King feels a sense of loss or incompleteness. "Now this king, he had a subject named Electra who loved him with a passion uncontested. For him each day she had a smile, but it didn't matter. The king was looking for the ladder." The sexual or romantic love of his loyal subject, Electra, is unable to satisfy the King's quest for his higher plane. So, life is meaningless without spiritual completion, and even physical love, romantic love, is unable to deliver the type of emotion that brings inner peace, the feeling of human completion, which can only be gained by obtaining oneness with a higher power. In "The Ladder" Prince is proclaiming that every human's purpose/desire is to achieve their higher being, even if we do not know by what we are being driven. "Everybody's looking for the Ladder. Everybody wants salvation of their soul. The steps you take are no easy road, but the reward is great for those who want to go." Both "Pop Life" and "The Ladder" provide a clear understanding of human behavior, the reasons why we act a certain way. We are all trying to become whole by connecting our physical to our higher spiritual selves. Some of us become misguided and need to be reminded. Art is supposed to be one tool that reminds us.

The final stop on our journey is a study in "Temptation," that thing which causes humans to stray from the path of divine revelation and completion, seeking to satisfy physical desires. "Temptation" sizzles, burns, and explodes with the battle between man and his lustful will. Musically, Prince once again pushes the limits of the mainstream by following a traditional gospel tune with a Hendrix/Santana, acid rock tune with the underlying groove of four bar, jazzy blues. As the message is being chauffeured, driven wildly, by the music, Prince attempts to show that no one is immune to the calls of the flesh. He even goes so far as to put himself in a one-to-one encounter with God, showing how people always promise to change but fall short of the expectations of God. In the end, Prince pleads for mercy, promising to be good, leaving the listener to answer the question of the character's ability to change. "I'm sorry. I'll be good. This time I promise...I have 2 go now. I don't know when I'll return." It seems more realistic that we are left with the lingering question. This album is about journeying to find one's inner self. The truth is that the journey never stops. We are always waging war with our physical in order to achieve our metaphysical selves. As Prince declares in "Temptation," "Everybody on this Earth has got a vice." The issue is not the existence of a particular vice. The issue is that we all have vices, which cause us to fall short of our goals of perfection, Utopia. But, the knowledge of this should give us strength that we are not alone. The journey/

struggle is rewarding because taking the journey is an acknowledgment of one's desire to grow and evolve. No matter how tired and worn the cliché, it is true that whatever does not kill us makes us stronger. "Temptation" forces us to look at our shortcomings and understand that this process is a constant battle. But knowing this keeps us from getting discouraged and gives us the inspiration to endure the journey.

A final piece from Around...Day is "Hello." Only available on the B-side of "Pop Life," "Hello" answers the criticism Prince was getting from not taking a more active part in the We Are the World album and Live Aid concert. "Hello" also clarifies that Prince is a man with his own mission, and he will not stray from that mission for no one, regardless of the criticism. For the most part, the allegations toward Prince were overly hyped and unfair. Prince, having an introverted personality, chose not to work collectively with other artists but to submit a song for the We Are the World album. Because of this introverted personality, Prince was labeled arrogant and unwilling to work with others. The song that Prince submitted to We Are the World is "4 the Tears in Your Eyes." The song continues Prince's theme of love as it emphasizes love as Jesus' central issue, the issue that we should remember and celebrate. Prince asserts that even with all of his special powers, Jesus' greatest act was dying for mankind. So even if we can not perform miracles, we can still be Christ-like by giving love, by giving of ourselves. "4 the Tears in Your Eyes" represents a progression to a more articulate declaration of a structured or traditional religious belief. This is seemingly not the Prince of Dirty Mind and Controversy. And even though in a 1996 VH1 interview with Chris Rock he states that he does not practice a "traditional" or "structured" religion, he is definitely invoking the imagery of Jesus and Christianity. This is important to note because it shows Prince as an artist constantly grappling with his beliefs, how to articulate them, and his being willing to do so in a public manner.

So then, Dirty Mind and Controversy articulate the

basis of Prince's spiritual evolution because they are about freedom gained through love, more specifically, love of oneself, which only comes through finding one's higher power within oneself. That is why Prince would open the concerts of the <u>Controversy</u> tour with an a cappella verse of "It won't be long before the second coming. It won't be long before all of God's children will learn how to love. You've got to love your brother if you want to save your soul." <u>Dirty Mind</u> and <u>Controversy</u> are raging against intolerance which thrives in the absence of love. Yet Prince, in those early works, is only able to deal with love in its physical manifestation of sex. Whether he is dealing with love through sex because of his own personal limitations as an artist or because sex sells is a debatable but unanswerable question by anyone except the artist. What is evident is that Prince begins with the body, which gets our attention, and moves/evolves to the spirit. This is normal. Man is first concerned with the body before dealing with the spirit. As he states in "What's My Name," released in 1998 on <u>Crystal Ball</u>, "You wouldn't have drank my coffee if I hadn't gave you cream." This is a successful method used by many, including Jesus, whose miracles all had physical concerns: making the blind see, healing illnesses of the body, and feeding the multitudes. Jesus first addresses the needs of the body so that he can heal the soul, thus showing the inextricable relationship between the body and the soul that Prince also shows in his work. Prince's work shows us that you cannot have one without the other, and to concentrate solely on one provides for a limited view or grasp of humanity.

After the rise in criticism, which had been brewing since the <u>Purple Rain</u> era, Prince releases "Hello." Along with addressing the <u>We Are the World</u> project, Prince addresses the tactics and hypocrisy of the media and Bob Geldof, the project coordinator.

> "I tried 2 tell them that I didn't want 2 sing, but I'd gladly write a song instead. They said OK and

everything was cool 'till a camera tried 2 get in my bed. I was sitting pretty with a beautiful friend when this man tries 2 get in the car. 'Hey Prince, come on, give us a smile, eh?' No introduction, 'How've U been?' just—'Up yours! Smile, that's right; u're a star!'"

There is a double or dual hypocrisy that Prince is discussing. The first is the most obvious; the press loves to create stars just so they can tear them down. Further, he is addressing the double standard for hypocrisy. The press is able to be disrespectful, but anyone who reacts unappreciatively is cast in a negative light. Also, the press is willing and able to do anything to get a story, including the invasion of privacy and not telling the full truth. The day after the recording of the "We Are the World" single, press outlets across the world reported that rather than attend the recording, Prince was somewhere bailing out bodyguards who had been attacking the press. Although Prince's bodyguards did have to be bailed from jail, that was not the cause of his missing the recording. He had never planned to attend the recording because he had already committed to submitting a song instead of participating in the mass recording. Yet, it is Geldof who seizes the opportunity to gain some headlines by blasting Prince for not attending the recording. If he was really concerned, he could have said something before the recording or when the initial agreement was made for Prince just to submit a song, instead of waiting for a media circus to criticize him. Prince uses "Hello" to question the agenda of the press and the shots of insults from Bob Geldof:

> "I know in my heart I would try 2 love U. I wouldn't try 2 hurt U despite all the ways U try 2 hurt me. U call me a fraud, an uncaring wretch, but I'm an artist, and my only aim is 2 please. Between U and yours, myself and mine, isn't life cruel enough without cruel words? U see, words are like shoes. They're just something 2 stand on. I wish U could be in my shoes, but they're probably so high U'd fall off and die. 4

U, words are definitely not shoes. They're weapons and tools of destruction, and your time is boring unless U're putting something down. What would life be if we believed what we read, and a smile is just hiding a frown? Come now, isn't life a little better with a pair of good shoes?"

Despite the wave of criticism, Prince holds to his own social consciousness by raising a question of the hypocrisy of the entire project, "We're against hungry children; our record stands tall. But there's just as much hunger here at home. We'll do what we can if y'all try 2 understand—a flower that has water will grow, and a child misunderstood will go." "Hello" ties into "4 the Tears in Your Eyes" by questioning the lack of love shown for children starving in America and Europe, especially black children. Geldof was apparently moved to start the projects after watching a television special on the poverty and famine in Africa. Though this is a worthy cause, it seems a bit hypocritical that all of these American and European stars will participate in these projects, but they have done very little for the starving and impoverished children in America or Europe. Does not charity (love) begin at home? The projects including many artists who have dedicated their entire lives to making a better world through their art, such as Stevie Wonder, Bob Dylan, Quincy Jones, Bono and others. But the majority of the group were one-timers who condemn the starvation in Africa but say little about the starvation in their own lands. How is it that these artists can attack the starvation in Africa but not attack the American and European systems, which profit from exploiting this injustice? We can give Africans fish, but we will not teach Africans or African Americans how to fish because that will destroy the exploitive relationship between blacks and whites. With "Hello" Prince is turning the mirror of hypocrisy on Geldof and others as well as continuing to challenge how we think.

<u>Around the World in A Day</u> did not have the

financial success as did <u>Purple Rain</u>, but few of Prince's or anyone else's albums have received as many positive critical reviews. <u>Around...Day</u> is the album that set Prince apart from his peers and lifted him to the level of greats, such as Hendrix, the Beatles, Dylan, Miles Davis, Quincy Jones, and Wonder. As for the record's reception, in a 1985 interview with <u>Rolling Stone</u> the man himself defends his work better than any one else:

> "I've heard some people say I'm not talking about anything on this record. And what a lot of other people get wrong about the record is that I'm not trying to be this great visionary wizard. Paisley Park is in everybody's heart. It's not just something that I have the keys to. I was trying to say something about looking inside one's self to find perfection. It's just good to know there is someone and some place else. And if we're wrong, and I'm wrong, and there is nothing, then big deal! But the whole life I just spent, I at least had some reason to spend it" (Karlen, "Prince Talks: The Silence Is Broken," 30).

A final project from this time period is "The Dance Electric," a song Prince penned for his old friend, Andre' Cymone. The song summarizes <u>Purple Rain</u> and <u>Around the World in a Day</u> and prepares his listeners for <u>Parade</u>. It is a discourse on reconciliation on two different levels. It is a song of reconciliation on a personal level for Prince because it represents atonement between him and Cymone who were best friends with the same ideals and hopes for the power of music but were separated by the physical desires and temptations of the business. Working on this song, together, allowed them to transcend their physical issues and reconnect on a spiritual level. And on a spiritual level, "The Dance Electric" discusses the need for mankind to spurn its hedonistic ways and reconcile itself to the will of God. "Good morning people, take a look out your window. Your world is falling. It's almost time to go. Dance the dance electric. The rhythm is love, and love is blind." Because man has embraced the physical, he has gone astray. His capitalistic lust and his machines have made him spiritless. His soul cannot grow in a decaying temple.

> "Look. Our world is falling—a rhythm-less house of blinded prophecy. Hear our master calling. This isn't what he wanted us to be. We've got 2 dance the dance electric. Listen to the rhythm of our souls...Look, u're living in Babylon, making but not feelin' love at all. When your youth is gone, when it comes the Dawn, a light of truth will shine, and u shall fall. See the light inside of us…Whatever u do, don't let your life go without love. It's the only life you will ever have."

The only hope for this world is a complete abandonment of the physical and a complete embracing of the spiritual. This cements the message of <u>Around the World in a Day</u> and sets the tone for <u>Parade</u> where Prince declares that man is not a physical being but a spiritual being having a physical experience. If man can stay focused on this, he can survive with his mind intact and enable the whole of society to evolve to its highest state.

The Hopeless Romantic

Just when the media and the listeners thought they had fully comprehended the complexity of Prince, he returns simply romantic. <u>Parade</u> (1986) is the music to Prince's second movie. Unlike <u>Purple Rain</u>, <u>Under the Cherry Moon</u> was not a box office smash. The <u>Under the Cherry Moon</u>/<u>Parade</u> projects were total breaks from what was happening in the mainstream of popular music or film. Rather than concentrate on the physical concerns of drugs, sex, and violence, which were saturating radio, television, and the movies, Prince chose to create a melodrama, which ponders the meaning of life and love. <u>Under the Cherry Moon</u>, directed by Prince, is a story about the different dimensions of love and love's ability to save humanity. It is set in France to black and white film to give it the feel of timeless romanticism. Unfortunately for Prince, he was trapped in a society polarized by Reaganomics, where black listeners were beginning to tire of multicultural fantasy and were turning to the very definite statements of black sensibilities in rap. He was serving salad when the people wanted meat. Furthermore, his salad did not have a flavoring that was familiar or pleasing to the aesthetic taste buds of the people.

The subject of the movie is love. The film wishes to be a discourse about love as a manifestation of God's presence, which enters into human beings and transcends us into higher beings, or at least make us realize the higher truths and pleasures of the soul over the flesh. It is the perfect plot for Prince's message. The protagonist is a man who has so embraced the physical that he neglects, manipulates, and misuses the metaphysical to satisfy his lust and greed. Yet, he finds that money is unable to give him the satisfaction that he needs, the "thing" that will complete him. He realizes that he can only find completion in the metaphysical by understanding that love is more valuable than money because it completes him. Not only does love complete him, it allows him to see the truths and gifts of the world. The movie opens with "Christopher lived for all women, but he die for one." In the film, Christopher's death is symbolized as a transcending of the physical plane. Thus, embracing the spiritual frees us and removes the blinders of the physical from the eyes of our souls so that we can truly see reality and achieve Utopia. Love forces Christopher to realize that we are not physical beings in the finite notion of physicality, but we are spiritual beings having a physical experience. Life's journey should cause us to realize this and evolve. Love is the agent that allows us to evolve because it connects us to our higher selves. As Prince's character, Christopher Tracy, puts it, "If two are in love, then the flesh is nothing. We live in a parade. Dig?"

The problem is that few got it, and even fewer dug it. The plot has two gigolos from Miami, Florida, Christopher and Tricky, played by Jerome Benton, who go to the French Rivera to marry and swindle some unsuspecting, naive, rich damsel out of her fortune. The movie attempts unsuccessfully to merge various forms of drama and comedy. The film swings from stereotypical, slapstick, shuck-n-jive comedy to philosophical musings about life to street drama, all in just a little over an hour. This produces the cinematic flaw of the film, the uneven or unbalanced genre swings the movie often makes. The film appears almost unsure of its direction. This may have been caused by the many problems which preceded and continued throughout the filming: the firing of the initial director, the replacing of the actor playing the antagonist, and Prince's battle with Warner Bros over the direction of the film. Ultimately, it comes down to the fact that critics and consumers who had taken the <u>Purple Rain</u> ride were still waiting for Prince to deliver the sequel. Prince was somewhere else now, and he pushed ahead regardless of the consequences. The music and lyrics of <u>Parade</u> represent a tapestry of African American music with traces of European influences to create the feel of an illusionary, multicultural renaissance period. Much like the jazz and literary greats from the Harlem Renaissance through the 1950s, Prince saw Europe as a place where he could expand his creative talents. His

American fans find, however, at least with this project, that while Europe may celebrate his talents, it is unable to sustain the fire and soul that ignited their love for him. Still, for his own gratification, Europe is the place that allows him to make the movie and the album that he wants to make. Throughout his career, Prince has glorified life as something not to be endured or survived but lived, experienced, and enjoyed in every realm and aspect. Through the movie and album, Prince paints a picture of life as a parade of people (their emotions and experiences) by presenting, celebrating, praising, and showcasing the aesthetics and romantics of life. As hip hop and grunge are resonating in the bowels of U.S. culture, Prince continues to divert his attention away from the issues of the body to grapple with the issues of the soul. Rather than deal with sex as a tool to address the concerns of the body, Prince concentrates on the ability of love to enable us to transform the physical. <u>Parade</u> becomes an extravaganza of Prince's ability to write romantically, exposing the many faces and facets of love. Through <u>Parade</u>, Prince pushes to the extreme by proclaiming that death is only a door leading us to an even greater parade in songs, such as "Mountains" and "Sometimes it Snows in April." This searching motif causes each song on <u>Parade</u> to be a lavish, eccentric piece of art that embodies the passion and enlightenment of discovery as in "New Position" and "Life Can Be So Nice."

Because <u>Parade</u> is written as a cohesive, singular concept, there are not many singles as in the traditional sense. Rather than trying to write hooks or jingles, Prince is attempting to construct songs that act more as particles of a whole, leading to a commentary about the human condition. It is a consensus that to fully understand the rest of the songs, one has to be somewhat familiar with the plot of the movie to relate fully the meanings of the songs with the theme of life as a parade to be enjoyed by all earthly inhabitants. Prince is viewing his songs as dialogue and discourse to be coupled with the film. There is a play, a poem, or a movement in every Prince song. He is not just writing hits; he is trying to say something about the world around us through his work. And Nikki

Giovanni asserts the difficulty of trying to say something serious while keeping the attention of the general public, "I wanted to write a poem that rhymes, but revolution doesn't lend itself to be-bopping" (Gates and McKay 1983). Prince is stepping outside the norm, the mainstream of popular music, because its rhythm does not lend itself to his message. The couple of songs which are able to exist within the programming list of radio represent Prince's ability to construct songs that maintain a balance between his personal vision to create something different and new while adhering to the tastes of his generation. "Kiss," which made it to number one on Billboard, is an excellent example of this. Working on two levels, Prince is eroding our complicated notions of love, of music, and of him. Although the simplest song, musically or lyrically, on the album, "Kiss" reaches the heights and depths of Prince's definition of love.

> "U don't need experience to turn me out…U don't have 2 be rich 2 rule my world. U don't have 2 be cool 2 be my girl. Ain't no particular sign I'm more compatible with. I just want your extra time and your…Kiss."

In "Kiss" Prince is stripping down the many façades that he, himself, has built around the romantic relationship. Instead of talking about what romantic love is, he is talking about what romantic love should be. This time love is the issue, not power, class, or race. Thus, the body is not important, even in the physical actions of love, "U don't have 2 be beautiful 2 be my girl." Where in the past the romantic relationship was a complex arrangement, "Kiss" is eroding those layers. "I just need your extra time and your kiss." As testament to the song's emotive power and its preciseness of definition, ten years later the Academy Award-winning film Happy Feet used it for over half of the film to articulate its motif and definition of love. Even more ironic is that Happy Feet is a PG rated family film that uses a song written by Prince when he was still considered the bad boy of popular music. This shows that Prince was growing and maturing and that he was surpassing or overcoming his own fears of not being mature enough to express or articulate precisely his themes or concepts to a wide audience.

The other songs convey a message of the different sides and powers of love and free thought. "Mountains" tells of love's ability to conquer all. "Life can be so Nice" looks at the joy of simply living and loving. "Under the Cherry Moon" embodies the idea that true lovers cannot be separated, even through death, for through death they become of one soul. And "Sometimes It Snows in April" defines death's place in our lives, showing it as a window to the afterlife. The lyrics are soft and simple. There is not the brash forthrightness of a revolution, but the calm and peace of understanding through revelation. <u>Parade</u> is not about the struggle to survive; it is about living—living and experiencing life as a gift from God. The parade is a metaphor for the greatness of God seen in the diversity of mankind living in harmony. Humanity reaching its potential is a manifestation of God. Love is a manifestation of God. To love is to manifest God. Thus, Prince's ambition causes <u>Parade</u> to be both eclectic and ambiguous. Much like the film, the album soars, floats, and darts between being comic and dramatic, having its tongue in its cheek and pouring out its soul. The songs move from shuckin' and jivin' and slappin' five in the funk tradition as with "Girls and Boys" and "Kiss" to lamenting over life with "Sometimes It Snows in April," to celebrating the passions of life with "Christopher Tracy's Parade" and "Life Can be So Nice." That is a wide range and assortment of topics to ask children to absorb in their leisure time, especially when the music is just as eclectic and experimental (daring) as the subject matter. The musical grooves, which seem very improvisational, stop and go and play peek-a-boo much like the subject matter. It can become quite frustrating to listeners who merely wish to dance.

The primary emotion that <u>Parade</u> is able to sustain

is urgency. Whether it is the urgency to revive the sexual passion of lovers as in "New Position," or to show that finding and giving love is not really complicated as in "Kiss," or the urgency to save a love going bad in "Anotherloverholenyohead," the urgency to live, experience, and love reigns supreme. Prince is able to show that relationships are the primary fabric that make life worth living. He is taking the same view of romantic relationships as Octavio Paz in the poem, "Two Bodies." For Paz romantic relationships create a bond where lovers "nourish and sustain each other." Thus, "human relationships are vitally important [where]...love and friendship enrich lives that are fragile and brief,...they provide the only meaning and soul satisfying values that are possible in the universe" (Rosenberg, Instructor's Manual, 181). Going back to the opening line of Under the Cherry Moon, "Christopher lived for all women, but died for one," we see that like Paz, Prince shows that love and relationships give meaning to our existential existence. Love, not sex, is the essence of life. Romance is the spirit of life. The romance of life is the play. Further, love also brings joy and laughter to the seriousness of our lives. It is a joy that sustains us in the face of sorrow and hardships. In this, Parade brings to the public's eye Prince's own brand of humor. The public begins to see a side of Prince that was buried beneath the sex, his sense of humor. If one pays attention to both the music and the lyrics, one notices a wit akin to that of Thelonious Monk and Miles Davis, especially through the use of space as a sound, and his unique take on life and sexuality. Just as love wears away our walls constructed to hide our insecurity, the veil of mystery over the royal kingdom is lifted with increased personal appearances and even a couple of interviews. Once surrounded by bodyguards and royal subjects, Prince is now appearing openly, being accompanied by a few close friends. Love frees us of our fears and gives us the security for sanity. Prince manages to show and do this while his once heightened U.S. popularity has decreased considerably during the rise of rap. This shows that what is important to Prince is not the fame but the art. Prince had a vision for <u>Under the Cherry Moon</u> and <u>Parade</u>, and he followed that vision with the same zeal and dedication as with the projects that earned more money. When the industry went right, Prince went left, and it has made, for him, all the difference in satisfying his soul.

Although <u>Under the Cherry Moon</u> and <u>Parade</u> do not have the financial success in America as Prince's other albums, Prince enjoyed a greater amount of success outside the states, especially in England and France. During the time of <u>Around the World in a Day</u>, 1985, Prince's popularity had grown enough to make him an international musical force. As many of the black artists before him, Prince continued to struggle against the limitations of the black artist in America. This, combined with the contrast in acceptance of <u>Parade</u> and <u>Under the Cherry Moon</u>, led to Prince's exodus from America to spend more time in Europe.

Genius at Work: A Poet of the Times

After the economic failure of his latest movie and his extended stay in Europe, many in America began to wonder if Prince had finally thrown in the towel or was just washed up. But just as the industry had discarded Prince, he was back. (Long time Prince followers are allowed to cringe at that statement.) This time there could be no denying the talents of the Minneapolis Genius. Prince unleashed his mind on his second double album set and created seventeen cuts of funkidness, each crafted in their own persona of consciousness, which became Sign "☮" the Times (1987). Not since Stevie Wonder's Songs in the Key of Life (1976) has an album this diverse in subject matter and music been able to exist within the mainstream of popular music. The social, street philosopher was back and better than ever. The title track, "Sign '☮' the Times," acts as a type of revelation/epigraph, illuminating the current downtrodden times, what Mojo Magazine called "20th century angst set to beatbox and Telecaster" (Davis, Vol. 4 Issue 14, 84). "Almost eerie on stage, it wasn't exactly a safe choice for a single either. But the music world seemed fascinated by the rare glimpse into the Prince politic, and it raced up the charts" (Leeds 10-11). I agree with Leeds' assertion, except with Leeds' use of "rare" glimpse. With songs, such as "Party Up," "Sexuality," "Ronnie Talk to Russia," and "America," Prince devoted a substantial amount of his lyrics to socio-political issues. Unfortunately for him, the media spent most of their time fascinated with the sexual aspects of Prince's work. "Sign '☮' the Times" is merely another step, another example of growth by an artist concerned that his work is commenting on the human condition—romantically, socially, and politically.

> "In France a skinny man died from a big disease with a little name. By chance his girlfriend came across a needle, and soon she did the same. Back home there are seventeen year old boys, and their idea of fun

is being in a gang called the disciples, high on crack, and toting a machine gun."

Although the crack and AIDS epidemics and urban violence had become a major concern by 1987, they were not yet the national topics that they would grow to become in the nineties. Here again, Prince is at the forefront and on the edge of social culture. This time Prince is not playing the role of prophet as in <u>1999</u> but the role of poet-observer.

Prince follows the pessimistic "Sign 'O' the Times" with the optimistic "Play in the Sunshine." Prince's music has always had the chord of hope running through it. Rather than just comment on or glorify the problem, Prince seeks a solution, no matter how abstract, vague, or intangible it may seem. As he states, "You can talk about symptoms all day long. But I like to talk about solutions" (Ebiri 85). "Play in the Sunshine" is the answer to the social ills presented in "Sign 'O' the Times." "Sign 'O' the Times" is filled with physical decay. In "Play in the Sunshine" Prince is once again asserting that physical decay begins with metaphysical concerns and problems, especially when one uses physical means to satisfy metaphysical needs. In order to address the physical decay presented in "Sign 'O' the Times" man must embrace his metaphysical self. "Play in the Sunshine" is Prince's unwavering answer for people seeking physical gratification without dangerous after effects. Prince's solution is consistently the same; satisfy your soul, and your body will reap the benefits. It is a whimsical but forthright interpretation of Funkadelic's "Free Your Mind and Your Ass Will Follow." "We gonna play in the sunshine. We wanna be free without the help of a margarita or an ecstasy...'Cause one day, everyday is gonna be a yellow day." "Play in the Sunshine" is a return to the escapism of <u>Around the World in a Day</u>. It is a yearning for the physical Utopia and a belief that it can be achieved without the artificial stimuli. Even in the trying times that "Sign 'O' the Times" represents, the opening of the mind and heart to love, which frees oneself from the material, is the best solution.

"The Ballad of Dorothy Parker" gets at searching for the metaphysical through the doors of the physical. Our protagonist is wiser. He understands that the physical world can provide glimpses of the ideal, but it cannot fully yield the ideal. So, sex can be an epiphany that directs us to the path of Utopia. The protagonist searches the physical partly because of habit and partly because the physical is all he knows. Though this may seem like a step back in his philosophy, Prince is merely asserting that sometimes you must use what you have to get what you need. "The Ballad of Dorothy Parker" paints a clear picture of bars, other places, and various states of mind that people use to escape from or deal with problems. As with "Lady Cab Driver," sex is used in "The Ballad of Dorothy Parker" as a means of therapy to find happiness. The females, the cab driver and the waitress, are sexual psychiatrists, leading the patient to happiness:

> "Well, earlier, I'd been talking stuff in a violent room, fighting with lovers past. I needed someone with a quicker wit than mine. Dorothy was fast...Dorothy made me laugh. I felt much better, so I went back to the violent room."

Hill effectively describes this poetic song:

> "'The Ballad of Dorothy Parker' just seems to have floated straight out of Prince's head, a muse made audible on the spot. The rhythm is elliptical and complex, and as if in some hallucinogenic daydream, he murmurs to us of bubble baths and zany cocktail-waitresses with a penchant for Joni Mitchell's 'Help Me,'...the song that marked her transition to melancholy beat-poet" (Hill 206).

What is interesting here is that the satisfaction of the sex is temporary because the protagonist returns to the violent room. So, sex is now seen as a temporary form of escapism. In his growth, Prince is no longer building sex as the ultimate or primary solution. For if sex was the solution, the protagonist would have had mind not to return to the violent room. Furthermore, the waitress' muse, which gives her creative powers to help the protagonist, is poetry. So, Prince seems to be signifying something about art's ability to heal. In fact what the protagonist wants most from the waitress is her wit, her intellect, not her body. "I needed someone with a quicker wit than mine. Dorothy was fast." And of course, Dorothy Parker is the name of a poet whose work is often quite introspective, causing one to look within to find the ability to reconcile oneself to the exterior world. The bath that the protagonist takes while listening to "Help Me" is symbolic of a baptism, a cleansing of the top soil of the daily existence, which removes the cataracts of day-to-day living so that we can see the world anew. This affirms Wordsworth's notion that poetry has the ability to make man see the truth by seeing the world anew.

"Starfish and Coffee" expands the theme of self exploration and acceptance by showing that self-esteem is essential to surviving the exterior world. The song paints a picture of isolation due to otherness that society perpetuates to keep the individual inline or under control. The plot is about an elementary school girl who is singled out by her classmates for her unusual behavior and lunch cuisine. Prince turns this scenario on its head to show the happiness that one can find inside one's own inner world. "It was 7:45, we were all in line to greet the teacher Ms. Kathleen. All of us were ordinary except for Cynthia Rose. She always stood at the back of the line, a smile beneath her nose." The song shows how social separation/segregation creates fear and intolerance between people. It is a circular event where Cynthia is alone because she is weird, and she is weird because she is alone. But, Prince's real commentary is not about Cynthia being alone or weird. The real commentary is that the class does not understand how Cynthia can be happy and content on her own. Cynthia has inner peace, which allows her to brave the world on her own while the rest of the students group together in cowardice. To make themselves feel better they highlight Cynthia's differences to other (alienate) her, but she neither submits nor conforms. She is the victor because she has inner peace.

Because Prince is telling the story from the voice of one of the students who attempt to other Cynthia, we are initially led to believe that the song will be a condemnation of Cynthia. However, he is using the student's voice to disarm the listener. We become a part of the crowd. We believe that the song is about Cynthia's differences. Then, once we are lulled into the plot, Prince quickly turns the light on us. Our narrow-mindedness is on trial, not Cynthia's uniqueness. Prince is showing how easy it is for each of us to become a part of the status quo. Our initial point of view is that there is something wrong with Cynthia. But with a quick turn of the poetic lens, we realize that there is something wrong with us for mindlessly following the crowd. This also shows that our realities are what we make of them from a combination of imagination and subjective interpretation. The other children are able to construct a fantasy about Cynthia because of her unexplained abnormality. "Cynthia wore the prettiest dress with different color socks. Sometimes I wondered if the mates were in her lunch box." The secret, ceremonial opening of Cynthia's lunch box and the finding of the unusual lunch items only act to confirm the illusions the children have about Cynthia. "Me and Lucy opened it when Cynthia wasn't around. Lucy cried. I almost died. U know what we found." What is most interesting is that the children, much like the society, feel that they have a right to pry into Cynthia's personal belongings. Merely because Cynthia is different, the children feel justified in invading her privacy as well as harassing and othering her. Through this, Prince is able to shift the view point, and, in the end, the listener is left with the feeling that Cynthia, in her detachment from the rigid regulations of normality, is able to find a sense of inner peace, a peace that the other children will never be able to obtain because of their preoccupation with prescribed normality.

"Cynthia had a happy face just like the ones she'd draw on every wall. But it's alright; it's for a worthy cause. G'on Cynthia." Cynthia survives her othering because she has inner peace, which makes her heroic.

Giving the song more credence is the fact that Prince, the champion of individuality and otherness, aligns himself with the normal children. This is important because it shows that all of us, no matter how unique or strong we see ourselves as being, have a tendency to other or isolate people because of our own fears and insecurities. It shows how easily we can fight for our own rights against oppression and at the same time oppress others. This represents the constant struggle to gain and maintain inner peace and self-esteem in a world driven to break and use individuals for its own gains. The use of fear is ingrained early into the psychological make-up of children as a force to control them. There are two fears present in "Starfish and Coffee." The first fear is the fear of alienation, represented by the children banning together to exclude Cynthia. Their clannish actions show their need to be a part of the group. The second fear is the children's fear of Cynthia's will and inner peace. If Cynthia is able to withstand the fear, embarrassment, and intimidation of the group, she will change reality as they know it. In the manner that the other children understand the world, she, the individual, should not be able to stand alone. Cynthia refutes this. At the same time, Prince does not completely vilify the other students because he wants to show that we can all endure and stand strong. By the end of the song, our narrator has come to terms with himself, which allows him to recognize Cynthia's heroic quality by encouraging her, "G'on Cynthia." With Prince, the symbol for supreme individualism, aligning himself with the students instead of with Cynthia, we see how easy it is for the individual to be swept into the mob mentality. So, we not only see Cynthia's pain and struggles, we also see her courage, which is juxtaposed against the learned cowardice of the mob. With inner strength, Cynthia is able to transcend the wall of fear.

"If I Was Your Girlfriend" builds on the notion of finding happiness and inner peace by breaking the walls of prescribed normality that regulate our romantic relationships, which are the building blocks for society. "If I Was Your Girlfriend" tells of a male lover's need to become as close to his female lover as her girlfriends or her own self. Prince is seeking to go beyond the physical limitations of society's traditional notion of the male/female relationship and the assigned gender roles. The song articulates the need to construct a higher human existence through the romantic relationship. It is "I Wanna Be Your Lover" raised to new heights with the lover having more metaphysical desires. Prince is attempting to undress as a male in order to remove the learned social barriers, which separate the male from the female. Prince is not looking for a helpmate as viewed in traditional terms. That is a distant, separate entity to provide physical compliments to his own. He sees the connection with the female as a connection to life itself. "If I was your girlfriend, would u remember 2 tell me all the things u forgot when I was your man?...Sometimes I trip on how happy we could be." If the male can connect with the female, he has changed his physical existence and plugged into eternity. It is through women that we are born and/or reborn. Prince wishes to become female, in theory/spirit, to show his willingness to commune with nature, to commune with woman, to commune with everlasting life.

"The Cross" points the way to the pure, unhindered pathway to completion and everlasting life sought in "If I Was Your Girlfriend." It is an assurance that salvation waits for all who want it. Prince shows the insignificance of the physical life's trials as they relate to the power and love of God. "Black day, stormy night, no love, no hope in sight. Don't cry. He is coming. Don't die without knowing the Cross." "The Cross" is slight affirmation of "1999" and slight deviation from "1999." It is not as extreme in the if it feels good do it because God will come to save us from the bad things that feel good, and it emphasizes the God of Love, rather than the Lawgiver or Judge. With this new image of God, Prince makes a conscious attempt to show that a union or communion with God is an individual choice. "Don't die without knowing the Cross." This one statement presents a Prince who could not have existed in Controversy, a Prince who is making a distinction between human nature and human behavior, thus acknowledging an innate sinful nature that one must overcome in order to evolve. Prior to this, for Prince, sin was a product of the society, not of the individual. With the plea, "Don't die without knowing the Cross," Prince is now acknowledging that the individual is responsible for his own, sinful actions, his reconciliation with God, and will be called to answer for both. Before, the only sin was the sin of oppression and dishonesty. Now, the individual is being called to get in touch with self and with God. Thus, inaction, the failure to connect with God and evolve into a higher being, is a sin. It is up to the individual to bear the cross to God. Freedom comes through reconciliation to one's god-self. Once the individual comes to the cross and bears his burdens to the cross, "All of our problems will be taken by the Cross." This is still the notion that there is a saving grace, which will rescue us from our imperfect selves. But now, the responsibility to initiate the process has been placed on the individual.

Also from Sign "☮" the Times is "It's Gonna Be a Beautiful Night," which is a celebration of celebration. It reemphasizes the old Prince standard that there is no better medicine than a good party. The party is the secular/physical representation of spiritual fellowship. In "Party Up" the fellowship is to protest the misuse of governmental powers. In "It's Gonna Be a Beautiful Night" the party is to celebrate life and ease the pains of the day. Music is supposed to lift the spirits of man. A common theme in Prince's work is the ability of the party to be a safe haven. It is shown as the only social gathering worth anything. "It's Gonna Be a Beautiful Night" is the antithesis of "Sign '☮' the Times." Where "SOTT" is a call to our conscience, "Beautiful Night" is a sedative. "No time for politics, this is gonna be the one." Parties, for Prince, do have a purpose. Much like "D.M.S.R."

this party's purpose is to regenerate and invigorate in order to relieve the stress of life. This does not mean mindlessness. The guy who wrote "SOTT" can not celebrate mindlessness. It means no hidden motive. It means that there is a time when souls must be able to commune and enjoy each other by sharing each other's energy. During the live version on the Sign "☮" the Times DVD, Prince chants "If your body gets tired you gotta keep moving to keep your blood circulating from your head to your feet. Brother Brooks be 'round in a minute with a bucket full of squirrel meat." The party is a fellowship. We are supposed to fellowship with each other. By doing this, we can transcend our physical.

Sign "☮" the Times received worldwide popular and critical acclaim, putting Prince back on top of the popular music world. But his third movie, Sign "☮" the Times, only received favorable critical acclaim while it flopped at the box office in the States. Even with the financial success of the album, Prince still chose to tour mainly abroad. It was as though Prince felt that he had found a home that allowed him to be as free as the messages he preached. By now, the thousands of Prince faithful in America had grown overly restless of awaiting the return of their Prince to the American stage, which allowed the alternatives of hip hop and grunge to fill the void. Additionally, American critics and listeners alike had not truly reconciled themselves to the diversity and range of Prince. One of the major criticisms of the album was that it was too eclectic. After all that he had accomplished, Prince found himself right back where he was in relation to the chains and restraints placed on artists, especially African American artists. Though many, such as Leeds, point to the choosing of "If I Was Your Girlfriend" as a single for the stalling of the album, the manner in which popular music is segmented and segregated also played a major role in the album losing steam and falling off the charts. Even after nine years of creative and quality work, the industry and the listeners wanted Prince to pick one style or one identity and be that. That is a choice that Prince has never been able to make, and his desire to dance to his own beat has cost him dearly in regards to financial success and critical study.

The Turmoil and Rebirth

The Black Album (1988) and Lovesexy (1988) are to be read as companion pieces, parts one and two of the same theme, much like Dante's Inferno, Purgatorio, and Paradiso create one, homogenous concept in The Divine Comedy. The Black Album and Lovesexy represent man's journey into the depths of his hellish bowels in order to be baptized, emerging transformed into one's higher, metaphysical self. Prince uses his own, personal journey to transcend the physical desires of wealth, fame, and respect as a metaphor for man's searching for spiritual completion. It is in these two albums where we see Prince completely turn from the physical and embrace the spiritual, but not before much turmoil and struggle. However to fully understand these companion pieces we must return briefly to Sign "☮" the Times, which was pushed under and aside by the industry and disallowed entry into the mainstream of music. The common criticism was that the album is too eclectic and experimental for its own good. As much of his earlier work, Sign "☮" the Times was never appreciated for its total worth to music and literature. It is too complex and diverse to reach the point of becoming a popular phenomenon. Prince and Warner Bros felt that they had a monster hit on their hands. When Sign "☮" the Times failed to meet their and the industry's expectations, the rumors and doubts began to resurface. Talk of Prince being outdated and the explosion of rap pushed Prince even further away from the mainstream, ever closer to that edge of genius isolation. Prince recounts his frustrations during this time in his life:

> "I'm not saying I'm better than anyone else. But you'll be sitting there at the Grammies, and U2 will beat you. And you say to yourself wait a minute. I can play that kind of music, too...I know how to do that; you dig. But [U2] will not do 'Housequake'" (Karlen, "Prince Talks," 59).

He must have felt the same frustrations attending the Soul Train Music Awards. Twice he was shunned by the industry for lesser diversified and more definable talents. This, being purely speculation, must have been the last straw in a career of playing second best because of his color and his unyielding determination to perform all types of music and take on all types of subjects and positions. Is it not strange that white entertainers, such as Michael Bolton, can perform soul music or hard core rap lyrics as Eminem and become the greatest thing since sliced bread, while black entertainers are forbidden to reclaim their own roots in rock, being forced to take the artistic and economic crumbs of the industry? The reactions to <u>Sign "☮" the Times</u> drove Prince into creating from anger and hatred as he did early in his career. This produced <u>The Black Album</u>. In the <u>Lovesexy Tour Book</u>, Prince attempts to relate or put the whole experience in perspective. Prince felt that <u>Sign "☮" the Times</u> was an album that could overshadow the success of <u>Purple Rain</u> or even match the success of a work such as <u>Thriller</u>. He wanted the perfect balance of social commentary and economic success. "Some people said they loved him, but Camille (a Prince pseudonym) said, 'Contempt'...love is no good unless felt by all." This seems to allude to the fact that, while still attempting to push his work to the limits, there is a need to produce art which is capable of being accepted by a mass market. "Camille set out to silence his critics. 'No longer daring'—his enemies laughed. 'No longer glam, his funk is half assed...one leg is much shorter than the other one is weak. His strokes are tepid, his colors are meek.'" Prince wanted to silence his critics and prove that he had not lost his street wise, hard, unpredictable, explicit edge. "So Camille found a new color. The color black: strongest hue of them all." Then he proceeds to show the erratic, angry creation of <u>The Black Album</u>:

> "He painted a picture called 'Le Grind'—hitting so tall. And then 'Cindy C' THE Vogue fantasy. Horns and vocals 2 die 4. Lollipops—in yours!—

> stroke after stroke, callin' all others a joke. Superfunkycalifragisexy. Camille rocked hard in a funky place. Stuck his long funk in competition's face" (Prince, <u>Lovesexy Tour Book</u>, 6, 8, 10).

And once completed, Prince is ready to unleash the proof of his supreme artistic prowess.

> "Tuesday came. Blue Tuesday. His canvas full and lying on the table. Camille mustered all the hate that he was able. Hate for the ones who ever doubted his game. Hate for the ones who ever doubted his name. 'Tis nobody funkier—let the Black Album fly!' Spooky Electric (another Prince pseudonym) was talking, Camille started 2 cry" (Prince, <u>Lovesexy Tour Book</u>, 10).

<u>The Black Album</u> is Prince's most emotionally charged album since <u>Controversy</u> and <u>Dirty Mind</u>. The old Prince of in your face, raunchy rock, funk, soul, and brash lyrics was back. <u>The Black Album</u> expresses an uncensored angst toward the industry and the mainstream listeners. It attacks everybody from supermodels to rappers, industry bigs and industry fakes. The lyrics are driven by Prince's fury over being labeled a soft, crossover who has been stripped of his funk card. Songs, such as "Cindy C," "Le Grind," "Dead on It," and "Bob George," express Prince's most inner anger toward life and the industry. The opening song, "Le Grind," beings with an encrypted message that serves as the albums declaration:

> "So, U found me./ Good, I'm glad./ This is Prince - the cool of cools./ Some of U may not know this, but some of U may know./ Some of U may not want 2 know./ We are here 2 give U service./ Please don't try 2 stop us 4 we come regardless./ 4 we are as strong as we are intelligent./ So come vibe with us. Funk Bible - the New Testament."

The original title of The Black Album was Funk Bible, so we understand that Prince is making a statement to all of his naysayers. To call your album a Funk Bible is to declare that it is or will be the definition and apex of all things funky, which is what he was no longer considered to be by 1988. It is clear that Prince is not only reacting to his critics but taking their challenge to regain his place as a funk master. Accordingly, the album runs the gamut of musical styles and emotions, as Prince is laying it all on the line in going to war with his peers and the industry. There is also one song that appears on some copies of The Black Album but was recorded some time before, "Old Friends 4 Sale," which laments the use, misuse, and disregard of artists as objects or chattel, especially by those closest to them. There is little doubt that Prince, with the creation of The Black Album, is trying to make a statement about his talent and his place in the legacy and history of popular music.

> "Long thought of as a workaholic, in reality Prince had seldom behaved as if recording was a job. It was simply what he did—day in and day out. Music poured out of him without any rhyme or reason, heedless of clocks, calendars or environments. But this time there was something different about his approach. Moody and hasty, for the first time he appeared truly obsessed, as if he had something to prove. The earlier material on the stillborn Black Album had been recorded as well-intentioned party music, but the project gradually took on a darker edge" (Leeds 12).

At the core of The Black Album are "Dead on It" and "Bob George." These songs articulate Prince's angst from being overpowered by rap and then discarded by the industry. From 1979 to 1985, Prince had taken on everyone and won. He was the new musical genius of popular music, wrestling that title from Stevie Wonder. He was the bad, black boy of rock-n-roll, out lasting Rick James for that title. All of his projects, songs on the radio, and his electrifying performances made him the new hardest-working man in show business, replacing James Brown. He had become the new androgynous hero, replacing

Little Richard, Mick Jagger, and David Bowie. And, he surpassed Michael Jackson for the title of weirdest pop star. Even with all of that, rap was kicking his ass in the late eighties. His response was, once again, to go to battle. His fatal mistake was trying to amalgamate something that he did not understand. He tried to rap, and it almost cost him his career.

> "Negroes from Brooklyn play the bass pretty good, but the ones from Minneapolis play it like it oughta should...See rappers' problem usually stem from being tone death. Pack the house, try to sing, there won't be no one left."

Prince was angry and in a panic. Everything that he knew about music was being questioned, challenged, and discarded as irrelevant with the advent of rap. In an article for Rap Pages Questlove, drummer for the Roots, does an excellent job of showing Prince's desire to keep his throne by any means necessary.

> "Prince was speaking for the ever-expanding, post Reaganomic attitude of non-Hip-Hoppers. There was something in the air in 1989, and let me tell you...Niggas was scared. Hip-Hop was in full swing...and Teddy Riley was weaning them into raps' new generation" (Questlove 1997).

Prince saw this movement in rap as taking listeners directly from his New Power Generation. His downfall was when he, for the first time in his career, began to have the discourse on somebody else's terms. Questlove asserts, "He tried to kill something he didn't fully understand, then after no sign of victory, he tried to take Cliff Notes in 'Rakimison' to no avail" (Questlove 1997). Prince is at his best when he is just doing his thing, when he is amalgamating sounds through a natural process of exposure and a certain respect that comes with an exposure to a certain style. In this case, he was trying to rap but did not understand the culture from which rap comes. His time spent contemplating the metaphysical issues of man had removed him from the physical issue and concerns that were being discussed in hip hop. With rap, Prince seemed determined to go to hell trying to prove that he could do it. This became a major albatross, causing his rapid downward spiral. Tony M., former rapper of Prince's New Power Generation (NPG), provided some very off hand comments that now seem insightful and prophetic. After his four-year stint with Prince, Tony M. left to pursue a solo career as a rapper. In a departing interview, he seemingly wanted to put as much distance between himself and Prince as possible, going as far as changing his name from Tony M. to Tony Tone. He adds, "The hip hop crowd don't care nothing about Prince, and Prince's fans don't care nothing about hip hop." Though general and sweeping, he is mostly accurate. Most Prince fans of the eighties and early nineties had a condescending attitude toward rap as a secondary form. They did not understand that it was not for middle class kids like them, caught up in individualistic notions of evolution. So, just like the generation that Prince's audience briefly replaced, the New Power Generation was fighting to desperately keep its place on the block. Hip Hop threatened their place. They instinctively knew—especially the self-proclaimed black rockers—that Madison Avenue would only allow one black seat at the table, and before they knew it, hip hop had snatched the seat from beneath them. Just like that, by the mid-nineties the revolution of the NPG was over. It was over for the same reasons that most revolutions end. Prince failed to connect with the generation that followed him. When they were coming of age and struggling with their situations, he was off in the heavens. Also, he became too comfortable and secure as the lone black voice of otherness and rebellion. And as I look back, his position was doomed to be temporary. His metaphysical, multicultural vision represented only a very small portion of American society. Still, he was pissed about no longer being top dog, and "Dead on It" articulates his discontent.

As songs go, "Dead on It" is pretty unmemorable except for its public challenge and criticism of rap. The song is parody, spoof, and challenge all at once. Everything is exaggerated: the slowed down, repetitious beat, as well as Prince's overly exaggerated pauses and lyrics. "I got a gold tooth that costs more than your house. I got a diamond ring on four fingers, each one the size of a mouse." Prince's major critique of rap is that it seems to be overly centered on the material, where everything is compromised for the profit. "What does that have to do with the funk? Nothing, but who's paying the bills. I'm dead on it." The fictitious rapper is dead on it because he is selling records, not because his records make any sense. Ironically, Prince is condemning a blues medium, rap, by using the blues aesthetic of exaggeration.

> "...deliberate use of exaggeration to call attention to key qualities (i.e. qualities to be upheld or dismissed, the hip or the triflin'. the ordinary is, of course, beneath contempt.) in this context, wit, sarcasm, and irony are salient expressions of exaggeration, since humor is essentially nothing but an exaggeration of reality in order to make a point" (Salaam 15).

This use of exaggeration is one of the primary aesthetics of rap music. Clearly, Prince is condemning both the style and craft of rap. This is his "blind" mistake. Here is a man, who has spent his entire career fighting for otherness, fighting for his right to exist on his own accord, and he is now marginalizing something merely because he does not understand it or because it threatens his rock star status. This contradiction is more example of human dichotomy, especially for African Americans. Prince and hip hop are more of Baraka's "changing same," just as Washington and Dubois represent that "changing same." The dichotomy is that African Americans fail to realize that we are all a part of the "changing same," struggling for the same ends even if our means are different. Our fear is that capitalism has told us that there is not much at the table, so we develop a "crab in the barrel" mentality.

Without knowledge of history, African Americans continue to engage in "misdirected" or "blind" struggles and rebellions against each other. Prince asserts in "Dead on It," "A nappy fro is better when u got a goop [process] on it." He declares this right after his insult of Brooklyn musicians. So, it is not only a musical/aesthetic issue, but an issue of how one sees and accepts the world, and Prince saw hip hop as the antithesis of how he saw the world. As he asserted two years earlier on the "Kiss" re-mix, "Never gonna cut our hair." This hair issue represents the misdirected rebellion without a cause. Prince is a supreme individualist. No one has the right to define him or tell him what to do or be. Hip hop, in his mind, was attempting to define him and his blackness. He upholds the one thing he knows that many rappers point to as a sign of a lack of blackness—processed hair. Even though processed hair represents a people who have internalized a hatred for themselves, Prince is sticking to his guns and asserting that rappers do not have the right to tell him who he is or what he can be. The question remains, "Against what is Prince rebelling?" The band of the eighties was Prince and the Revolution, was it not? What was the revolution? It certainly was not a revolution in the name of black power or cultural control because the American government had killed, imprisoned, and co-opted the Movement, leaving the black community filled with slogans, sound bites, and vampire opportunists. Prince's revolution is a self-styled, co-opted revolution for individualism, where the enemy was anybody who attempted to define him, which meant to limit him. Rap was moving music back to a place where he did not want to go—categorization based on race.

By 1980 there were no socio-political organizations manifesting themselves into the lives of individuals as they had done in the 1960s and 1970s. As activist/artist Kalamu ya Salaam asserts about his revelation of the eighties, "...I was consciously forced to recognize that not just people die. Organizations die..." (Salaam 30). First, the European Renaissance replaced God with man. Then, the eighties replaced the collective with the individual. Where the Movement stressed community interest over self-interest, the eighties media stressed self-interest over community interest. There were only traces of the civil rights spirit and remnants of its artifacts where eighties pop icons could dress themselves in the garb, articulate a few buzz words, and sell a mass of product. In the nineties we now use the Beatles "Revolution" to sell sneakers and Edwin Starr's "War" to promote the NFL. My own father had hoped that eventually Prince's revolution would turn into...something. It did, but only into a metaphysical, abstractly spiritual phenomenon as it related to most African Americans. So, Prince represented the "house nigga" to a lot of rappers. And to them, Prince responded with "Dead on It." He was fighting back, but he was waging the wrong war. For all of his struggles with musical categorization and oppression as well as human categorization and oppression, Prince's primary struggle was based in race. He could not be all that he wanted to be because he was black. Because of mis-education and mis-guidance, he waged his war initially by separating himself from African Americans to become something special, something different, a "new individual." Yet, his use of the same blues aesthetics as the people he is attempting to marginalize shows that he is very much a part of the canon and legacy of African American art. With "Dead on It" Prince is "playin' da dozens." Unfortunately, in an integrated society, the blues aesthetic of exaggeration and the "dozens" are not used to affirm and maintain culture, but to assert one's individual value over another. This represents the problems of the integrated Negro who is afraid of losing his position at the table and who only accepts or validates that which has been validated by the white power structure. This is not just Prince. Many of us, especially those of us raised in the 1980s, fall into the trap of celebrating being the only black or the special black. This goes all the way back to the first black middle class created during Reconstruction as they began to embrace European ideals and standards, which caused them to abandon African ideals and standards. So, Prince's battle with hip hop is deeply rooted in the African American's struggle for identity and place in America.

Even with this negative battle, Prince is still bold enough to challenge the unchallengeable. RUN DMC's Raising Hell (1986), which featured "Walk This Way," had legitimized the financial power of rap, and by 1988, very few black people were dissing rap publicly because very few black people want to be perceived as insignificantly black. Rap was becoming the voice of a generation and of a people. Even if you hated it, you did not publicly denounce it. And it would not be until 1995 when serious public condemnation of rap would be heard from the black community with C. Deloris Tucker. For Prince, rap did not just represent another competitor. It represented a return to strict definitions and boundaries of race and musicianship. Rap is definably black and male-oriented. He was an artist who had given up his race and his gender to be a rock icon. The rise of rap did not just mean the loss of a few record sales. The rise of rap meant the end of Paisley Park, the record company and the ideology. Rap, in his mind, threatened to take away all that he had worked so hard to gain and control. This hypocrisy makes Prince a ball of contradictions; this is what most African Americans hate about him because his contradictory nature speaks to the African American race as a walking contradiction. He fought persecution to have his own freedom and acted like a tyrant when new voices began to rise. This is more of the African American dichotomy. On the one hand, Prince certainly does have very contradictory philosophical and aesthetic notions as it relates to hip hop. Yet, those differences and contradictions are directly related to him being a middle-class African American and hip hop being a product of the African American lower economic class. So, although there are some real and definite artistic issues here, there is as much Willie Lynch Syndrome happening here, also. The question remains, "Who is being lynched?" And the song, "Bob George" as opposed to "Dead on It," is both a lynching and a resurrection. Prince is trying to kill hip hop by showing that their values are misplaced and by showing that there is nothing that they can do that he cannot do. The song replays Bigger Thomas' fate to a hip hop beat; yet, with all of his insanity and violence, we still feel empathy for George. So Prince is still denouncing hip hop, but his need to provide solutions causes him to explain George's fate so that the listener will learn from it. Even in his failure to defeat hip hop, "Bob George" becomes an example of Prince's storytelling ability.

"Bob George" is the metaphor to end all metaphors. On the surface, it is about the stereotypical black male deadbeat who inflicts abuse on his live-in lover. But if we pull back the layers, we see two other meanings. On one level, the male represents a humanity that is in a spiraling descent into hell due to its embrace of the physical world. Not only does capitalism have him in a spiral, his relationship, which is based on the physical, is descending, which is also being pulled by the gravity of capitalism. His woman is sleeping with a man who is buying her and using her for his plaything. All George can do is beat her when she returns. George is the neurotic baby boy who has yet to grow into a man, and Bob is the sleazy rock star manager who is sleeping with George's woman. Bob is the personification of capitalism's exploitive nature, and George represents those who have lost their sanity to capitalism as evident by the fact that he is as concerned with the gifts that his woman receives from Bob as he is with her sexual exploits. "New coat, huh? That's nice. Did u buy it? Yeah, right, u seeing the rich motherfucker again—that slicked backed paddy with all the gold in his mouth." The diamond ring and far coat seem to eat at George's soul. He does not own anything, can not buy his woman's love, and, therefore, feels a sense of worthlessness. Since everything is objectified in a capitalistic society, George can only regain his sense of manhood and value by beating his woman. In every aspect, George has embraced the physical and has become too blind to see his deterioration. The song ends with George going on a schizophrenic tirade, shooting at the police while having a heart-to-heart with the voice in his head.

The song's complexity is what separates Prince from

his peers. "Bob George" is not just a dramatization of domestic violence. He is not sensationalizing to sell records. What we understand most about George is that he is a man lost and in pain, using violence as his only form of therapy. Even his fantasy does not help him. George's forcing his lover to wear one of the colorful wigs that he purchased for her shows his attempt to escape the reality of his hell through fantasy. "Now put that suitcase down and go in there and put on that wig I bought you. No, no. No, no, the reddish-brown one." George's hatred for himself extends to those around him. He wishes to create a woman who submits to his every whim and need. Unlike the rest of his life, this woman is the only thing that he can control, and now he is losing that. So, in this case, Prince is equating sex and violence. They are both used to soothe psychological pain, anger, and anxiety. By forcing his woman to put on a wig and play in his fantasy, George is going to use sex as a way to escape his reality as well as a way to fuck his woman into submission. Sex and violence are equals. Sex, then, can be an act of violence or of salvation. Oddly, this is what redeems George. We know that he wants what we want. He is just misguided. Prince attempts to lead us to feel empathy or sympathy for him. George is a man in psychological turmoil as represented by his talking to himself. "Is Mr. George home? Hello, Mr. George, this is your conscience motherfucker. Why don't u leave motherfuckers alone? Why can't we just dance?" Prince is affirming what he presented with "SOTT" and "Play in the Sunshine" that physical ills begin in the metaphysical. Simply incarcerating George up will not cure him or the countless other Georges who live amongst us.

We know that George has embraced the physical both as a way of life and as a way to solve his pain, and this has driven him insane. The problem, which Prince shows us at the end of the song by having the police encounter with George, is that we, the larger society, turn to the physical instead of embracing humanity to address or save the Georges amongst us. With no love, empathy, or tolerance for George, we have no love, empathy, or tolerance for ourselves. Hence, this is the problem with America's "Zero Tolerance" toward children. Implied in "zero tolerance" is no patience for children. We tend to have little patience for those we do not love. This new zero tolerance law proves that we have little love for black children. In Pearl, Mississippi, and Littleton, Colorado, white students were given counseling to deal with the shootings and as general therapy for violence and anger management. In schools that have majority black students, there is no counseling and no in-school suspension. There is only suspension, expulsion, and juvenile detention. Zero tolerance does not save humanity. It only condemns humanity to a physical hell, making Georges out of as many children as we can. Prince shows us that when we fail to hear George, we fail to hear ourselves and doom ourselves to extermination.

Still deeper is a third possible meaning that "Bob George" expresses Prince's feelings of being discarded by the fans and the industry. In this case, he is George, the industry is Bob, and the woman represents the fans. The woman returning home all hours of the night, disrespecting George's home represents the few fans who continue to purchase Prince records merely from habit, love, and respect of his career, but they are not moved by his current work. By now, there are many Prince fans who feel that the quality of his work has deteriorated, but they continue to purchase his records merely from loyalty. (Some have even proposed that the song is a response to music critic Nelson George who had been a major Prince supporter and is now questioning Prince's latest efforts.) As such, George's questioning of his lover concerning her whereabouts could represent Prince's questioning of the fans' new musical tastes as in "Dead on It." Where his traditional fans wanted metaphysical laments, new fans want songs that are submersed in the physical world. George berates his love in the same manner that Prince is berating rappers and their fans for embracing the physical world. This reading is also given weight when Prince takes a swipe at his managers in the song, showing them as sleazy exploiters. This period saw the beginning of Prince's long battle with his managers over royalty payments and other issues that did not end for four years. He also takes a swipe at himself to show just how much distance was between him and this new generation. "U seeing that rich motherfucker again. What's he do for a living? Manage rock stars? Who? Prince? That skinny motherfucker with the high voice?!?" The ending schizophrenic battle with his conscience parallels the psychological battle that Prince has in the <u>Lovesexy Tour Book</u>. Prince is conflicted about losing his place and, through two songs and the tour book, bares this. <u>The Black Album</u> bares this.

Whatever the message, drama, pain, and conflict make for great or interesting art. "Bob George" is a memorable song if only for Prince's wit, characterization, and use of black dialect. As much as Prince is a rocker, his heavy bass and constant use of black dialect continue to connect him with the legacy of black music. Unlike "Dead on It," "Bob George" does not feel forced or fake because Prince is discussing something he knows—rejection and alienation on individual terms. In "Dead on It" Prince is trying to flow in the style of rappers. In "Bob George" Prince is simply telling a story of a dysfunctional man, overwhelmed with his socio-political condition, who seeks relief the only way he knows how, through domestic violence. In this Prince can mimic the voices and attitudes of men he has known in his life, interjecting the work with the reality of his own bouts with failure, deception, and rejection. The use of dialect allows Prince to navigate the fine line of artistic brilliance or degradation, social commentary or glorification. In this, Prince is at his best, turning the profane into the sacred by making us know the man's pain as well as his anger. The dialect and the wit show us a man who needs help. "Oh I got a gun. Think I don't? Then what's this? Oh, you quiet now, uh huh." It was not enough that he had the gun. Even that had to be validated. "Think I don't?" This is a man screaming for attention, affection, and affirmation. Still, the battle with his conscience shows that George is not just some mindless animal, but a by-product of society, which has embraced the physical and has lost its soul. This is what Questlove means when he states that "Prince was more Hip-Hop when he wasn't trying so damn hard" (Questlove 1997). Hip hop, like the blues, is the voice of a generation, grappling with who and what it is with very little direction from the older generation. In this vein, Prince was addressing the same issues with <u>Dirty Mind</u>, <u>Controversy</u>, <u>1999</u>, and <u>Purple Rain</u>. "Bob George" is a reminder of the artist who "rocks hard in a funky place" when rocking is all that he has to stay sane.

Prince also uses George to show the innate ironies and contradictions that typify black life and the witticisms that these ironies and contradictions produce. With all the things that George could say about Bob, he chooses to concentrate on his name. "B.O.B., spell that shit backwards and what u get?—the same motherfucking shit." George is asking two questions. He is asking his woman what makes one man better than another man. He is asking the universe what makes one soul better than another soul. Thus, George is another of Baraka's "changing same" who is still asking that age old African American question. "What did I do to get so black and blue" (Salaam 94). Why is this happening to me? The difference is that George is not asking this question from a collective perspective. George is asking this question from an individual perspective, because he is a child of integration. George's adversary, Bob, is just a man. George wants to know why Bob has so much more luck than he has. That is why George keeps saying, "Bob, ain't that a bitch?!?" George cannot believe the downward spiral of his life as compared to Bob's. The bad luck and hellish events of George's life are so surmounting that it is better than good fiction. This is the kind of shit that you make up, isn't it? His response is not to deny it but to affirm the exaggeration of bad luck in his life by repeating, "Ain't that a bitch?!?" It is the affirmation of the obvious, the obvious reality that others want to deny exists. It is not only a "bitch" that his problems exist. It is a "bitch" that everyone around him wants to act like there is no problem. That, for George, is the major problem, the major "bitch." He is getting the short end of the stick, or he is getting the stick put somewhere it should not be, and whoever is placing the stick there is lying that they are not placing the stick there. But even more, they are lying about the stick not being there. George's response is appropriate, "Ain't that a bitch?" Additionally, George's statement about Bob's name articulates the obvious but is also evidence of a people who are so strong willed, who are so innately creative that even their most degenerate states can produce beautiful art. George sees both the irony and hypocrisy of life. Both he and Bob are the same, just "motherfuckers" trying to make it, get over, survive, anyway they can. And that is George's dilemma. Why does he have such bad luck? George does not have that optimism that ya Salaam discusses in the traditional blues aesthetic. George has no "optimistic faith in the ultimate triumph of justice." He does not believe that "what is wrong will be righted." He does not believe that "balance will be brought back into the world" (Salaam 14). George is a fully integrated soul. So although he has an "acceptance of the contradictory nature of life," he has no "optimistic faith." It has been beaten out of him by capitalism. He is an example of the nihilism created by capitalism. George is a sign of the times and the closest that Prince comes to articulating the pains of hip hop.

Accordingly, there is no protagonist and antagonist in "Bob George," merely players of the same game. This perspective is what created the phrase, "Don't hate the player; hate the game." Integration has caused George to buy into the capitalistic notion that life is an art of war, and the winners are judged by who has the most money, not by their humanity and ability to show grace to others. That is why he continues to harp on the fact that his woman is "seeing that rich motherfucker again." George equates Bob's victory with Bob's money. The only thing that makes Bob better than him is his money. Even in his dismal economic condition, that perspective is to what George clings and uplifts to give himself value and status over his woman. "I'll slap your ass into the middle of next week. I'm Sorry baby, that's the rule. I pay the rent in this raggedy motherfucker, and all u do is suck up food and heat." He may not have as much money as Bob, but he has more money than his woman. There is no right and wrong in capitalism, only winners and losers, masters and slaves, pimps and prostitutes, exploiters and the exploited. George may lose to Bob, but he will redeem himself by oppressing his woman, who, ironically, is not his woman. She is merely on loan from Bob. In response, George uses sarcasm and wit to show that he is no fool. "For someone who can't stand no TV dinners, you sure eat enough of them motherfuckers. Who bought you that diamond ring? Yeah right, since when did u have a job?" In refuting his woman's lies, George refuses to allow life to flaunt its lies and hypocrisy in his face. He becomes as sarcastic and as exaggerated as the lies of life, as the lies of his woman who actually thinks that he will believe that she is not seeing anyone else. That is like white people actually wanting black people to believe that every thing is equal although the truth of inequality is staring everyone in the face. His woman attempts to cloak herself in a convenient and selective naiveté in the same manner that white folks do when forced to address the inequities and injustices of this society. Yet, there is something more cynical about the actions of George's woman and about the actions of white people. She does not believe that George will believe and accept her explanation, just like white people do not believe that blacks will believe and accept their explanation.

The real issue is that neither George nor black people can really do anything about the lies and injustices. George, however, is in her face, keeping her from denying that all is well, in the same manner as the blues and hip hop continue to stay in the face of America. It is not that George asks the question that gives him some heroic qualities. It is the style, the manner in which he asks the question that gives him a redeeming quality. In most cases, the only power that black people have is language. It is their only tool, their ability to critique life. George does not have the means to trump Bob, but he has the language to complain about it. Just complaining about his situation is a victory for George. He is at least able to say that I know that you are lying to me, that you are doing me wrong. George becomes a survivor through his wit and outlook on life. George's questioning of life through recontextualizing everything makes him a voice for the men in his condition. By ending with a question, Prince is addressing the pessimistic existence of George and of his society. George has no peace, and we have no peace because we have not heard him; therefore, we can not help him. Further, we can not help ourselves because capitalism has us blind to the souls of humanity. If we cannot see or hear George, we cannot see or hear ourselves.

"Bob George" represents the valley or pit of humanity. But just when all is dark and gloomy, Prince recounts of several events that lead to a refocusing of his heart. He did not want to be remembered for <u>The Black Album</u>. So, he went back into the studio and recorded another album and pulled <u>The Black Album</u> just before it hit the stores. Prince recounted that he had a vision of God, "...not some old guy with a beard, but moreso of a feeling" (Karlen, "Prince Talks," 58). That new feeling was love, <u>Lovesexy</u>. Once you hit rock bottom, which is what "Bob George" represents, there is no where to go but up. But more specifically, what we should learn from "Bob George" is that anger and hate cannot help or save us, which is why George finds himself in a shoot out with the police. Love not hate solves our problems by refocusing our emotions and goals. With his emotional reevaluation, Prince finds that for which he has been searching—love, and now he wants to give it to the world. After the explosion of angry creation, venting his rage, Prince begins to realize the error of his ways. The experience of his rage reminds him why he turned from anger in the first place. The creation of <u>The Black Album</u> is a reminder of his resolution. He remembers why he turned to the purple rain and took a permanent vacation to paisley park to experience the parade of life. In his entrance back into the midst of an unenlightened society, to provide social observation with Sign "☮" the Times, he allowed himself to be sucked back into the games of a society's searching for the earthy, for the material. But now, Prince is unable to sustain his anger. He had tasted the other side of hate, which is love, and, now, the thrill of selfish indulgence is too shallow to contain him.

> "Tricked. A fool he had been. In the lowest utmostest. He had allowed the dark side of him 2 create something evil. Spooky Electric must die. Die in the bodies of women who want babies that will grow up with a New Power Soul. Love, Life, Lovesexy...Camille figured out what to feel. Glam Slam Escape—the Sexuality Real. God is Alive! Let Him touch u and He will quench every thirst. Let Him touch u and an aura of peace will adorn u. God is Alive! Let him touch u and your own Lovesexy will be born. Let Him touch u and Heaven is yours. Welcome 2 the New Power Generation" (Prince, Lovesexy Tour Book., 10).

For the mainstream and the industry, Lovesexy is a bit much to swallow. It is composed of some of Prince's most electrifying and funky music, but the lyrics scream love and spiritual revolution not sex. To complicate matters more, the album cover features Prince posing nude among a bouquet of flowers. "Warner Bros Records swears that the cover reflects his deep spirituality and social consciousness" (Allen, "Prince: What U See Is What U Get," 71). With Lovesexy, Prince is consciously trying to transform his sexual imagery and energy into spiritual imagery and energy. Sex has always been a mainstay in Prince's music. But it is often used to achieve some type of higher emotion or mental being. The sexual metaphors have always been used to take a common, human experience and show that what we really want and are trying to find is God, and, if not to be too forward, the ultimate orgasm is being touched by God: "I wanna be your lover. I wanna be the only one you come for..." Through songs, such as "Jack U Off," "Lady Cab Driver," "Computer Blue," and "Sexuality,"

Prince shows sex as a tool used by the human race to achieve a higher form of happiness and contentment or just to bide time until that higher form comes along. He also uses songs, such as "Condition of the Heart," "Little Red Corvette," and "Temptation," to show that although we may be able to obtain delusional joy, love, and even power, eventually sex becomes just as any other drug, a temporary high. Through songs, like "Christopher Tracy's Parade," "Sometimes It Snows in April," "Pop Life," "The Ladder," and "The Cross," Prince manages to make the connection between human desires and spiritual needs. Prince's entire thematic career had been building toward <u>Lovesexy</u>. "The joy you get when you fall in love not from a boy or a girl but with the Heavens above."

Where <u>Around the World in a Day</u> raises Prince to the level of being a metaphysical poet, it is <u>Lovesexy</u> that elevates him even higher to the waters of the American transcendentalist poets, such as Whitman, Thoreau, and Emerson. Like Whitman and Emerson, Prince creates protagonists who are searching for more than what the physical world can give them. These characters seek to use traditional means, such as sex, but to refashion the sexual medium for a completely different journey than their peers by creating alternative, harmonious worlds, such as those in "Tamborine," "Paisley Park," and "Uptown." In the same manner as Whitman and Emerson, Prince's "individual stood at the center of his own universe, and he arrived at understanding not through received doctrines but through ecstatic and intuitive communion with a universe harmonious with his own soul" (Wilkie and Hurt 1073). Like Whitman's and Emerson's American scholar, Prince's protagonist "celebrates the continuous re-creation of the world in the imagination of each individual, the intuition of 'a world primal again'" (Wilkie and Hurt 1074). Furthermore, Prince, like Whitman, is able to set himself a part from his peers by successfully combining the physical and metaphysical quests for completion. Unlike many of his peers, he is able to merge these two battling forces and create a higher form of human experience. As we see in Prince, Whitman, "unlike Thoreau and

Emerson who were both nervous about the flesh, [found] no sweet fat than sticks to [his] own bones" (Wilkie and Hurt 1074). In their desire to experience the totality of human existence and, in doing so, to evolve to a higher form, Whitman and Wonder laid a foundation for Prince and others because they were "hungry to incorporate all experience: humble or exalted, male or female, minute or cosmic, spiritual or carnal. [Prince like Whitman] is, at once, the act and the observer of the act" (Wilkie and Hurt 1074). Instead of avoiding the physical, Whitman embraces it in an attempt to experience, conquer and transcend it by learning more about himself in this journey. So we find Prince, in the manner of Whitman, embracing the physical as the pathway to the spiritual. In creating this continuous pathway to the spiritual, the CD format of Lovesexy is designed as one long playing work, with the songs acting as movements, scenes, or chapters. The songs cannot be separated or experienced as singular works or tracks. Lovesexy, then, is a singular experience, meant to deliver one message: God is Love, and Love will take you higher than you have ever been. The opening song, "👑 No," is Prince's acknowledgment of there being a Heaven and a Hell. But moreso, this is Prince's clearest declaration of God as his leader and savior. There is also a declaration of a Hell, a place of judgment or punishment. More than a proclamation, this song is a revelation. Prince is admitting to having been in the dark and to having found the light, which will guide his music to make a better world. His desire is to share this love and the news that love is fulfilling, and hate will destroy you, physically and spiritually.

> "👑 know there is a heaven, 👑 know there is a hell. Listen to me people, 👑 got a story 2 tell. 👑 know there was confusion, lightin' all around me. That's when 👑 called his name; don't u know he found me…But 👑 know love is the only way…No—everybody say—if u can't find your way…Say no—if u want a drug other than God above…Say yes—if u want this thing called love…We know a better way 2 have some fun."

"Alphabet Street" follows and continues the theme of spreading the good word of Love, "Put the right letters together and make a better day." "👁 No" and "Alphabet Street" serve as the preamble to Prince's constitution of living. "Alphabet Street" exists in the physical but only so that the protagonist is able to recruit souls, using the physical to bring souls to the spiritual. "We're going down 'cause that's the only way to make this cruel world hear what we gotta say." Again, "going down," for Prince, is a sexual image, but from a literary context he has spent his career going down, meeting his listeners where they are, usually on the sexual plane, and bringing them up to a higher plane. He has been a preacher, using the icons of his listeners' lives to communicate his message. He does this in much the same manner as David uses the shepherd to relate his message to the Israelites through the Psalms. "👁'm gonna talk so sexy that she'll want me from my head to my feet...👁'll put her in the back seat and drive her 2 Tennessee." He is going to put her in the back seat of his '67 Thunderbird and drive her. This is sexual, and it is playing with the notion of using sex as a metaphor for something deeper. It is the rap by Cat at the end of "Alphabet Street" that fully articulates the mission of "👁 No." "Didn't yo' mamma tell u that Lovesexy was the Glam of 'em all. U can hang, u can trip on it, but u surely won't fall. No side effects, the feeling lasts forever." Prior to <u>Lovesexy</u>, sex had been thoroughly explored, with Prince finding that it cannot solve the ills of the soul. <u>Lovesexy</u> is about showing that spiritual orgasm is more fulfilling than physical orgasm. This spiritual metaphor only works after years of exploring the notion of sex as a substitute, an escape, or a path to freedom that provides temporary relief but is lacking when it comes to healing the pains and filling holes of the soul. This is evidence of Prince's ideological growth, of his mastery of the extended metaphor, and of his ability to signify, which in this case is to build on the past and then recontextualize that past for a new or evolved message.

"Glam Slam" is the third song on side one, and it continues the transformation from the body to the soul. It deals with the transition of physical love to spiritual love. It is also the first allusion to the combination of Love, sex, and spirituality as one entity that blends two people into one, new entity, completing their humanity and their evolution. "This thing we've got, it's alive. It seems to transcend the physical. One touch, and 👁'm satisfied. Must be a dream, it's so magical." Prince is weaving the fabrics of the physical and the spiritual, showing the interdependence of the body and the soul and love's ability to transcend man to a higher plane. Just as the male-female relationship combines and completes man, in the physical sense, man's reconciliation to and union with God completes him in a spiritual sense. The B-side of the extended, twelve inch version of "Glam Slam," titled "Escape," goes even further to promote the pleasures of the spiritual over the pleasures of the physical. "15 minutes is not enough to be out your mind in a world so tough. If U wanna escape and truly be, all the crack in Compton won't set u free." The love found in romantic relationships is one aspect to escape the physical world. Love is the vehicle. We are on a journey to find love, but one should be mindful that it cannot be found in certain areas. It cannot be found when the satisfaction of the physical is primary. Therefore, drugs will not lead to inner peace because, for Prince, drugs are physical agents. Even if they provide windows to the psychological, they are artificial, fleeting, and present only the illusion of inner peace. Music, however, will and can be one of those vehicles to finding inner peace.

Prince declares the ability of music to allow man to transcend his physical hell in the "Alphabet Street" twelve-inch version by stating "This is not music; this is trip. No it's not a drug; it's something more complex." So the purpose of art is to help man evolve. Art is a better agent than drugs because it deals directly with the metaphysical nature of man. Still, as a supreme individualist, Prince believes that we all have the ability to find peace and evolution, but we all do it in our own manner. In "Escape" he continues, "Free your mind from this rat race...Everybody's talking 'bout the party bass. How high U get is a matter of taste...." There are definitely different paths to find inner peace. His only desire is to inform us of the false methods used to find or replace God. Prince ends by showing himself as an artist who is not just mindlessly preaching love. He does not want to overly romanticize his solution. Love is not easy. Growth and evolution can be difficult processes, especially when we are surrounded or smothered by a world that caters to our physical lusts and greed. This is then compounded by the notion that only a few of us want to separate ourselves from the crowd and search for the meaning of life. Prince feels a responsibility to inform the listener that separating oneself can lead to isolation as well as attack, and this isolation and constant attack from society is what often causes most of us to rejoin the crowd and wallow in the mud of the body. "Don't get on the scale if U ain't got the weight. It's mo' harder 2 love than it is 2 hate."

Prince then flips "Glam Slam" over to show the opposite side of spiritual completion. "Anna Stesia" addresses the loneliness caused by being incomplete, not of man or woman but from being disconnected from God. This loneliness causes mankind to surrender to the body as a substitute for inner peace, which keeps humanity from reaching its potential. "Anna Stesia" is the positive equivalent of "Annie Christian." "Annie Christian" is about surrendering to one's own, physical will, which leads to self and world destruction. "Annie Christian wanted to be number one, but her kingdom never comes; Thy will be done." "Anna Stesia" celebrates submitting to God's will and connecting to love, which is to connect to life. Again, the female becomes the metaphor for reconnecting to God. The song advocates for the interpersonal relationship that man should have with God by showing the depression that one suffers when absent from God. "Anna Stesia" deals with our constant straying from God and forgetting that we are just a part of God's master play. Prince continues to show that when man strays to follow his own will, he removes himself from that protective blanket and leaves himself open to the hardships of the world:

"Have u ever been so lonely that u felt like u were the only one in this world? Have u ever wanted 2 play with someone so much u'd take anyone, boy or girl? Anna Stesia come 2 me, ravish me, talk 2 me, liberate my mind. Tell me what u think of me, praise me, craze me out this space and time. Maybe we could learn 2 love, if we was closer 2 my higher self, closer 2 Heaven, closer 2 God. Save me Jesus, we've been a fool. How could we forget u are the rule. We're just a play in your master plan. Now my Lord we understand."

The first song on side two is "Dance On." It not only provides the harsh reality of a society going down the drain, but also tells how those of society who are content to be outside spectators of the problem are just as much a part of the problem by not helping to improve the situation. Those who continue to dance mindlessly rather than to awake and face reality are the problem. This also seems to be a dig into the sides of the industry and the listeners who merely wish to perpetuate mindless dance music while the world is decaying around them. Prince infers that the struggle for individual, economic stability has us pulling in different and selfish directions without the thought that we are weakening the strings that hold the society together. "It's time 4 new education, the former rules don't apply. We need a power structure that breeds production instead of jacks who vandalize. What color is your money today?" "Dance On" is taking the Lovesexy power and bringing it back to the society. Once he has completed his individual transformation, Prince is ready to assist with the constructive completion and uplift of society. "Detroit, what's happening?" This statement has double meaning. On the one hand, Prince is addressing the crime issue of Detroit, which was supposed to become one of the black meccas. By the late eighties, many major cities had majority black populations, including Atlanta, Washington DC, New Orleans, and Detroit. These new cites were supposed to be the culmination of the Civil Rights Movement. Yet while these cites elected black leadership, the black community continued to suffer the same plights. This, for many, is an example that the values of the Civil Rights Movement had been cashed in for financial gain by the few. Thus, the turning away from morality and human rights had led the black community down a road to Sodom and Gomorrah. Thus, "Dance On" is Prince's attempt to make the masses realize that we need a spiritual agenda rather than a political agenda. On the other hand, Prince is addressing Detroit directly. Detroit was one of the first major cities to play Prince on the radio. Prince felt such a kinship with Detroit that he held his 1986 birthday concert in Detroit instead of Minneapolis as a way to thank them for their years of support. In the concert film, he proclaims, "I could have stayed in Uptown, but I wanted to come here and party with y'all." However, by 1988 Detroit as well as all of the black meccas had removed Prince from heavy rotation in their playlists. So, when Prince asks, "Detroit, what's happening?" he is reacting to the programming change. "Bass guitar in spider webs longin' 4 the funk. Uzi gun takes its place in a wagon trunk." For Prince, the new music was deficient because sampling was taking the place of instrumentation and because the lyrics were preaching nihilism over solution. Even in songs, such as "Sign '☮' the Times" and "Dance On," where he is showing the world at its worst, Prince still delivers a message of hope.

Following "Dance On" is bass driven funk pushed to the edges by blaring horns combined with Prince's declaration of love, sex, and spirituality as a divine trinity much like the word "Eloheem," entitled "Lovesexy." "Lovesexy" exists in the plural like Eloheem because it provides complete physical and spiritual emancipation, completion, and inner peace to every aspect of our life. It is the physical, emotional, and psychological experience of love, sex, and spirituality, which is the answer to the pain and disillusionment felt in "Anna Stesia" and "Dance On." "Lovesexy" depicts sex as a metaphor and a microcosm of God. In a sense, if God is love, He is also sex. "For God so loved the world that He gave His only begotten Son, that whosoever believeth on Him should not perish, but have everlasting life" (John 3:16). God manifested Himself through the womb of a woman, through a method that the human mind could only perceive as the sex act. Even Mary and Joseph had to be given divine wisdom to understand. God is perpetual creation, perpetual sex, because of his perpetual love for man. Through the Immaculate Conception, God is equated with the procreation of humanity and life. God is equated with sex. It is the sense of knowing that no feeling is like the feeling one gets from being touched by God. "Lovesexy" declares that once we have been touched by God, nothing else will do:

> "New Power, give it 2 me. It put my name upon my thigh. It makes me laugh; it makes me cry. And when ♛ touch it, race cars burn rubber in my pants. This feeling's so good in every single way. ♛ want it morning, noon, and night of everyday...with it ♛ no heaven's just a kiss away. Anyone that's ever touched it—they don't want nothing else. And ♛ got 2 tell the world, ♛ just can't keep it to myself...Come on and touch it, ♛ no u will love it...Everybody no, when love calls u got 2 to go."

As "Lovesexy" comes to a climactic end, Prince transforms the mood from the frenzied celebration of spiritual orgasm to a celebration of physical orgasm with "When 2 R in Love." It is a soulful song filled with strings, big beats, and risqué lyrics, attempting to break down the walls of conservatism and suppression that restrict and bind love and romance. He asserts that love combines and changes two individuals into one entity. They become one mind as represented by their coded and secret language. "When 2 r in love, they'll whisper secrets only they 2 can hear." He continues this transformation of the physical to the spiritual by showing that physical reaction is only a manifestation of the spiritual. "When 2 r in love, their stomachs will pound every time the other comes near." Love not only transforms us, but it causes us to see the world differently. "When 2 r in love, falling leaves will appear 2 them like slow motion rain." Within love, there are no taboos if pleasure is gained, and no physical or emotional pain or anguish takes place. Prince is again attempting to make us more understanding of ourselves and our sexualities, not viewing them as unnatural but individualized. There is no sin in the spiritual because the end result is mutual pleasure. Only liberated bodies can make the kind of liberated love that can lead us to spiritual completion and satisfaction. Good sex, the best sex, is a manifestation of love, and when two are in love, they can be free. They are free. Love is liberating. The liberated souls in "When 2 r in Love" can now use their enlightened love to strive for and lead the way to a higher existence as seen in "☝ Wish U Heaven." This whimsical song is probably the nicest thing that you can say to someone; I hope that you get to Heaven. Prince is asserting that the inner peace gained from God allows us to weather any storm, and it allows us to pass along love to our fellowman no matter how he may treat us. "Doubts of our conviction follow where we go. And when the world's compassion ceases still ☝ know…☝ wish u love, ☝ wish u Heaven." No matter what our earthly differences, our main goal is heaven, reconciling ourselves to our higher being. With hope and steadfastness, we all shall get there. "If ☝ see 11, u can say it's 7, still ☝ wish u Heaven." Prince seems to be stressing that it is incumbent upon humanity to see past our differences and release our fear, pain, and anger to achieve our potential, our evolution to our higher selves. In this, Prince is affirming Baldwin's notion that "our birthright is to love each other" and help each other evolve to our highest point of our god-selves.

Finally, bringing this album to a soothing and contemplative finale is "Positivity," which is about staying focused through positive thinking, positive living, and depending on faith to give you the strength to survive, mentally and physically. We need faith in God and in our fellow man. God manifests himself through mankind, so the song is an encouragement to treat all people equally, for we are all characters of the same play. We need each other. It is a reminder that what affects one on this Earth affects all of us. So, we must start viewing each other as brothers and sisters and defeat the common foe which is Spooky Electric, Satan, evil personified. We must understand that we all have a bit of Spooky Electric in us with which we must constantly do battle to reach our final evolution. When we realize this, we become more compassionate and understanding of our fellow man who is fighting the same internal war. This understanding should cause us to be more willing to have empathy for our brothers and assist each other, understanding that every person you help is another person who is able to help you. "Is that a good man? Why do U dog him? Tell me; if that was your father, would U dog him then?" Spooky Electric, Satan, is the greatest foe known to man. Man's salvation is the treasure in the battle between God and Satan for our souls. Being mindful of this, there is joy in knowing that the lovers of society have come a long way, but we must realize that we still have a long way to go:

> "Positivity, YES. Do we mark U absent or do we mark U late?...In every man's life there will be a hang-up, a whirlwind designed 2 slow down. Give up if U want 2, and all is lost. Spooky Electric will be your boss. Don't kiss the beast. Hold on 2 your soul. We've got a long way 2 go."

As a conceptual album, <u>Lovesexy</u> ranks with Wonder's <u>Secret Life of Plants</u> and with Gaye's <u>Here, My Dear</u>. "Every touch and kiss takes him nearer to Heaven. Every act of fornication lifts him closer to the Angel" (Hill 212). This is the work that Prince has spent his entire career trying to produce. Beneath the rebellious calls against normality and a smothering religion in those initial albums is a young man struggling to reconcile himself, his pain, and his feeling of abandonment to a religion that has been both his foundation and his damnation. He achieves the balance in

Lovesexy. However, commercially, Lovesexy is certainly Prince's most economically unappreciated album since Dirty Mind. Because of the great hype of The Black Album which managed to sell as many bootleg copies as Lovesexy's legitimate sales, people were acting as if Lovesexy was the bootleg and The Black Album was the legitimate album. Although Lovesexy is filled with tangible social and spiritual issues, the experimental music and ever present controversy drove away the mainstream press and many American music listeners. Albeit the sixties were supposedly about a new spiritual awareness, bringing peace and love, the popular music stayed away from religion. No one dare spoke of God or Lord in the traditional Judo-Christian sense. It was the rigid structure of Christianity which was supposedly responsible for the dominance over the othered/marginalized peoples in America. And where American popular music has seemed to reconcile itself to the music of the church, it still has not been able to reconcile its ideology of rebellion to that of Christianity. Lovesexy's unapologetic amalgamation of sexuality and spirituality caused too many problems, too many contradictions for American listeners. As music critic Bonnie Allen asserted in her review of the album, "Prince's latest album, Lovesexy, is as full of as many contradictions as his previous albums— and his life—have been" (Allen 70). Once Lovesexy fell off the charts, many American listeners and critics were left wondering if Sign "☮" the Times was Prince's last stop at the top. But after over two years of not touring in America, the Lovesexy tour was announced.

Dubbed by American music critics as a last ditch effort by Prince to save his quickly dying American following, the Lovesexy tour proved to be one of the greatest tours of the decade, conceptually if not commercially. This would give Prince the chance to share his new feeling and concept night in and night out with the public, and the tour was released as a VHS. The critics and music fans alike fell over themselves to get a piece of Prince. He is recognized as one of the most entertaining live performers of his generation and of all time. Nelson

George asserts that "of the four greatest performers of his generation—Prince, Madonna, Springsteen, and Jackson—Prince could take them all out" (George 1991). Unlike the shows of the past, Prince gave a passing treatment to his hits and concentrated more time to the work of Lovesexy. The first half of the show is comprised of the raunchy hits, which earned him the title, "His Royal Badness." "Bob George," from The Black Album, is the bridge between the first and second acts because the song represents the descent into the lowest depths of human hell. After "Bob George" Prince is lowered through a trap door, and is reborn, arisen and reincarnated, to perform "Anna Stesia" from Lovesexy. "1999" is added as the encore, following the "Alphabet Street" finale, to show the great passing into the next life. Once word of the nature and subject matter of the show began to circulate, the American public tended to stay away from the halls. Despite this, the collaboration of funky music, elaborate stages, and conceptual ideas acted out on stage became known as a new type of theater called Prince on tour. The live shows were a visual accompaniment to the already conceptual masterpieces that will be forever etched in the minds of all who were fortunate enough to have witnessed it. Most spiritually repressed minds, handicapped by the grips of oppressive, westernized religion, were unable to accept a spiritual revelation from the "Prince of Sex," at least not on the terms that he was presenting it. The Judo-Christian ideal of the separation of the spiritual and the secular, the body from the soul, seems to prevail. Rather than a metaphor, many saw Prince trying to fuck his way into Heaven, trying to justify his past actions, or the brother was just confused. Simply, America was not buying it.

The Commercial Storyteller: The Pop Philosopher

Shortly after the <u>Lovesexy</u> tour, Prince began working on his next project, writing and recording music for the <u>Batman</u> (1989) movie. When news of the project hit the streets, the public began to gleam with great anticipation and high expectation. <u>Batman</u> was to be directed by Tim Burton, who had established himself as an eccentric and creative figure much like Prince and was planning to make the movie a psychological and physical adventure that features the civil turmoil of the dark sides of the movie's mysterious and conflicted characters. Who else would be better suited to create the music for a movie with such three-dimensional characters, suffering from internal turmoil? This time, everyone's expectations are fulfilled. The <u>Batman</u> album was selling as fast as record shops could get them. Prince is able to transfer the on-screen story to record, telling the individual stories of each character in such a manner that the album becomes a play within a play. Although soundtracks are generally used as just another phase of promotion, Prince's poetic genius allowed him to tell the story of <u>Batman</u> through song. Therefore, Prince created something that lives somewhere between a score and a soundtrack. Prince's songs are not merely background or landscape music. His songs are part of the dialogue and script, working to push and articulate the ideas of the movie. In this he rises to the level of Curtis Mayfield or Quincy Jones. We are entertained by Prince's dynamic storytelling ability. Each song is written in the voice or persona of one of the characters of the movie, building from his history of writing songs under various pseudonyms and crediting the songs to the characters themselves. This allows the listener to experience the movement of the film's plot through the album. Not only are Batman and the Joker battling each other, they are battling themselves. In accordance to the nature of the plot, good against evil, light against dark, with each character struggling with his own civil war, Prince interjects his own themes regarding the battle over the direction of man waged between the physical and the spiritual. By doing this, Prince is able to tap into the pulse of the listeners and funnel his own issues through the already established and iconic Batman characters. Thus, the theme of man's split personality complex is portrayed through each character's internal strife, and this time the public understands it and likes it. Within a time frame of six months, Batman becomes one of Prince's top five sellers. Prince proves that he can be intense, artfully penetrating, and controversial, and still sell records while doing so. Batman is able to do what Lovesexy is not, though it is doubtful that the listening public is completely cognizant of the underlying, psychological discourse. Furthermore, it is also unlikely that those who are buying Batman are making any connection between the themes and issues articulated on the record and the themes and issues present in Prince's work throughout his career. Still, Prince is able to have his discourse about the duality and dichotomy of man and sell records.

The album opens with "The Future." It is a melancholy "1999." There is no great celebration of the end because the future is bleak and "tough." There will be no great passing into the afterlife. Batman and the Joker represent gothic-modernist, psycho-dramatic icons, acting as mirrors of human industrialization staring society in the face. Propelled by the spiritless evolution of capitalism and the reduction of history as a tool to justify oppression and exploitation, society has become a machine in the wake of modern industrialization, grinding to a spiritless groove, crushing the weak and perpetuating the strength of the strong. "I've seen the future and it works...systematic overthrow of the underclass. Hollywood captures images of the past. New world needs a spirituality that will last...I've seen the future. And boy it's rough." Both the Joker and Batman are machines of the day, products of their environment, instinctively reacting. This justifies their duality. In a sense, they need each other. They coexist much like righteousness and sin, reminding each other of their purpose in life. In their relationship, often there are times when the listener is unable to distinguish the actions of Batman from the Joker. The image of Pretty Pony, in "The Future," could be either Batman or the Joker since both are icons manufactured by society. "Pretty Pony standing on the avenue, flashin' loaded pistol—2 dumb 2 be true." Is the Joker flashing his power to control society with fear, or is Batman flashing his power to control the criminal element with fear? "Somebody told him playing cops and robbers was cool. Would our rap have been different if we only knew?" "The Future" is credited to Batman, but is Batman talking about the Joker or himself? Batman is a resentful, remorseful, reluctant hero at best, a vigilante at worst. What is interesting is that if Batman is talking about the Joker, as Pretty Pony, his feelings seem to be somewhat ambiguous, seeing the Joker as a pawn, much like himself. The "Somebody told him" seems to imply that he sees the Joker as either an existential or a naturalistic pawn in the winds of life. And neither does he seem to have much faith in the future or his ability to change its direction. It is a very existential existence in which life has been made meaningless because capitalism has stripped us of our souls and our power to create institutional change.

"Electric Chair," which follows "The Future," is credited to the Joker, but the ambiguous tone, again, allows the song to exist in the mind of Batman, also. The song struggles with the question of the innate guilt of man or the innate guilt of the intuitive individual. "If a man is considered guilty for what goes on in his mind, give me the electric chair for all my future crime." What makes this the Joker's song is that the narrator chooses crime to set himself free, much as the early Prince protagonist chooses sex to set himself free, "...make up our minds, love, 2 commit the crimes of passion that set us free." It seems that for the Joker, all crimes are crimes of passion, a reaction to the environment that created him. Accordingly, Batman often grapples with his hatred toward a society that created the need for his existence. The only fact that separates the two is that Batman continues to struggle with and manipulate his hatred for the purpose of good, whereas the Joker surrenders to his hate. Prince seems to be building from

Baldwin's notion that we are all running from the same issue, that the pimp and the preacher are made and motivated by the same fire, as much as Batman and the Joker are made and motivated by the same fire. Whom do we chose to love or hate since they are both in the same racket, the racket of survival? Accordingly, how do we feel about ourselves in relation to them since we are made and motivated by that same fire? And as the song asserts, we all contemplate and fluctuate between the choices of right and wrong. So maybe we are all potential occupants of the electric chair. However, the Joker's choice to use his hate/power for evil is what makes him an antagonist.

Both Batman and the Joker think and act on their anger, their thirst for revenge. But, their choice of how each will direct or channel his hate is what makes the Joker a villain and Batman a heroic renegade. Possibly, the Joker is speaking directly to Batman in the final line of "Electric Chair" when he states, "Our lives shocked us, making us see a trippy picture show." Possibly, Batman knows that he is fated to the same electric chair as the Joker. This is why he fights his relationship with Vicki Vale and why Bruce Wayne doubts whether his character is worthy of producing children. Yet, the Joker, in embracing his hate, can foster a relationship with Vale without reservations because by embracing the physical, he is embracing the notion of personal survival. This breeds selfishness, causing the Joker not to consider the well being of others in the pursuit for his well being. So, in many ways, the last line is also directed to Vale and to the reader. In a world where so much of what is considered good and bad is subjective and situational—based on emotional, psychological and physical survival—whom can you choose to love, whom can you choose to judge? Ultimately, "Electric Chair" is about honesty and making proper decisions. "I saw your friend first. That's who I danced with all the time I was watching you." A person being attracted to two people who are friends is a complex scenario. What is the honorable thing to do? Etiquette tells us that we should not engage a romantic relationship with either person as to avoid the pain and stress that it may cause. That is what Batman would do by putting others before himself. This is why he avoids developing a relationship with Vicki Vale. However, "Electric Chair" is credited to the Joker. He ignores the pain of others and makes a decision based on his own selfish gratification. "I've got to have you." What condemns the Joker to the electric chair is not his desire, but his actions, which is what supposedly separates him from Batman. Batman has the same desires as the Joker, but he struggles to suppress or not act on them, which saves him from the electric chair. The Joker embraces his desires for deviancy, which condemns him to the electric chair.

"The Arms of Orion," credited to Vicki Vale and Bruce Wayne, is about fated lovers whose destiny is still left to be determined. The song is taken from the myth of Orion, the great hunter, which is also a constellation. Both Vale and Wayne are secret warriors with dual personalities: Wayne's alter ego being Batman and Vale's alter ego being her work as an investigative journalist. "Orion's arms are wide enough 2 hold us together...The constellations never fail 2 light the way of love." <u>Batman</u> is quite naturalistic or has naturalistic qualities. The characters' identities and actions are formed by their environment and situation. In their prayer, "The Arms of Orion," Vale and Wayne look to fate and God for their saving grace. "When I am lost and feeling lonely, I just look 2 heaven, I find my comfort there. God only knows where U are 2night." "The Arms of Orion" flips "The Future" on its back. What sustains Vale and Wayne, as opposed to the fire of hate of Batman and Joker, is hope, a positive emotion rather than a negative, a reproductive emotion rather than a destructive emotion. "Maybe time will tell me. 'Till then I close my eyes and say a prayer for U...I'll be with U forever. This is my destiny." Realizing their powerlessness in their humanity/mortality, Vale and Wayne must rely on fate, which in this case is God's destiny for them. This is the humanity that both Batman and Joker lack. Batman and Joker have no faith in a higher power, which means neither can give life; they can only destroy life. Vale and Wayne, however, have a faith that provides hope that they can resist and overcome hate, individualism, isolationism, and capitalism with love.

In "Vicki Waiting" Wayne is contemplating the decision of embracing life in Vale or death in Batman. There is no future in Batman, which is masculinity. There is only life in letting go and loving Vale, who represents femininity and reproduction, "...when crime is your only friend, all that matters is the present, the here and now." Prince provides more calculated ambiguity. Crime is the love of both the Joker and Batman. The Joker loves to commit crime, and Batman loves fighting crime. Both are trapped in a circle with each other. Wayne is worried that he is too much consumed with Batman and his anger to be whole enough or worthy enough to become a productive partner in a romantic relationship. "Talk of children still frightens me. Is my character enough 2 be, one that deserves a copy made...until then she's held at bay by my animal-like persistence." We discover in Batman Forever that Wayne is unable to balance being Batman in a manner that will allow him to construct a relationship with Vale. Wayne is unable to overcome the physical to enjoy the fruits of the spiritual. Therefore, he leaves Vale waiting, which leaves him empty.

The ambiguous line blurring comes to a head when "Trust" is credited to the Joker. The Joker is challenging Batman for the affections of the Gotham City citizens, the affections of Vale, and the affections of the listener. It is the Joker asking the city, "Trust, who do ya? Trust, what makes U a real lover?" We know that the Joker is playing a role. However, his argument is given credence because Batman is also wearing a mask, playing a role. "Who can U trust?" They are both wearing masks. The Joker takes the role of the protagonist in "I Wanna Be Your Lover" by asserting that he can feel and fill society's every need, making himself vulnerable by presenting himself as open and honest. "I put this question 2 U cause I want U with me." The Joker proceeds to woo his prey by showing that he and Batman are no worse or different than mankind, for we all wear masks. The Joker is questioning, deconstructing, our notion of trust, showing it as an arbitrary, subjective, concept, asserting that we often only trust those whom we must or are forced to trust. Therefore, our notion that trust evolves from love is another lie that allows us to perpetuate our false civility and humanity. By deconstructing the lie of trust, the Joker is able to disarm the citizens of Gotham, lower them to his level, and capture them.

> "Love—U cannot imagine how much I wanna give 2 U…Another world awaits us, another power 2 see. Close—Don't worry 'bout nobody else, from now on U'll be here with me. Money—How much'll make U happy? U can have it all if it'll suit U rite. Sex—It's not that type of party...we're getting higher 2night."

It is the duality of Batman that allows the Joker to use his own fun, lighter persona against the dark, mysterious persona of Batman. It is here where the heroic figures of Batman become human. Usually heroes are shown as constant and one-dimensional, either good or evil; in <u>Batman</u>, the listener is forced to analyze the characteristics of both Batman and the Joker and choose a hero, based on his perception of the character's actions and the psychological motivating factors influencing the character. In some cases Batman is not sure that he is making the right decisions or is on the right path. Often, his mentor/caretaker, Alfred, must act as a guide to help Wayne balance the warring sides within him, which shows Batman as a flawed or conflicted hero, and this provides credence to the Joker's challenge.

The scene where Batman is unable to keep Jack Napier from falling into boiling hot chemicals, thus turning Napier into the Joker is a pivotal point to understanding the psyche and agenda of Batman. It is not Batman's goal to change the hearts of lost souls. Batman's agenda is revenge against the criminal element of society because he blames crime for the loss of his parents and the creation of himself. This desire for revenge causes Batman's ambivalence when trying to save the Joker. Batman has an opportunity to save Napier before he becomes the Joker. Yet, Batman shows no sense of urgency to keep him from falling into the chemicals. He only uses one hand to keep Napier from falling, not making any extra effort. Conversely, the Joker is shown as coming from humble beginnings, a mere pawn working for a rich and powerful businessman. (Let us not forget that Wayne is rich and powerful, which, in a sense, makes him a part of the establishment that has a hypocritical or schizophrenic relationship with the underclass that it both exploits and condemns.) The Joker is only a product of his environment. Batman's hatred toward the criminal element creates an ambiguous attitude in him, which ironically causes him to create the Joker. So in a manner of speaking, the Joker is valid. "Trust, who can U?" Both are consumed by anger and hatred. There are no heroes because life is relative and subjective, where perception creates both reality and truth.

"Batdance" is the culmination and climax of the album. In his attempt to articulate the personas and ideals of the movie, Prince, who is grappling with his own identity, has been overwhelmed by the energy and power of the play, which causes him to create the offspring of this experience, a character named Gemini. Gemini possesses the qualities of both Batman and the Joker in much the same manner as Batman and the Joker possess the qualities of good and evil. The song, on the surface, is a collage of the movie's characters and their abbreviated actions and ideologies. It represents the mental and emotional anguish and overload caused when attempting to deal with and reconcile our innate duality, which can evoke or provoke the Gemini in all of us. In "Batdance" the characters are battling for their opportunity to express their ideals and anxieties as they fade in and out of the interplay. Gemini, the emotional and subjective artist, is enthralled in the play. Even in his own anxiety and confusion, he pushes the madness of the play forward, "Don't stop...Don't stop dancing...No, turn the music back up...Let's do it!" In the promotional video, Gemini shoots at Prince with a sawed-off shot gun when he realizes Prince is attempting to end the experience. It is Prince, the rational and objective artist, who is able to remain in control and end this dualistic experience. "Stop." Gemini represents the power and beauty of the play, which is man's recognition of himself to a point where he becomes so enthralled that he undergoes a catharsis. In this case, we grow to understand man and his perpetual battle with good and evil, as well as the fragile thread that separates good and evil. Gemini represents the battle between good and evil that is constantly waging in all of us. Only when we are able to maintain our focus and remain an objective observer, represented by Prince, are we able to put this battle into perspective and give it meaning.

There is no closure in Batman where it concerns the civil battles of the characters. The Joker's embracing of hate seals his own fate, but the Joker's fate brings Batman no peace. Symbolically and literally, the Joker gives birth to Batman just as Batman creates the Joker. When the Joker is a very young Napier, he is the person who kills Wayne's parents, thrusting him into the life of Batman, into the role of a vigilante. Yet Batman is unable to realize, at this juncture, that hate is not the cure for hate, even though he realizes that the Joker's death brings him no consolation or solace. So, there is no closure for Batman. The listener is left to contemplate and examine the experience of the play, with the hopes that the experience will enable the listener to better analyze and reconcile his own duality. Batman allows Prince to take established American icons and use them to relate his own ideals of man and duality. The play's only purpose is that it shows us ourselves. Prince's Batman is a mirror on three levels. It mirrors the ideals, ideologies, and experiences of the movie, it mirrors the characters, and it mirrors the human experience. Like the movie, it is a play of duality. The catharsis for the listener is to recognize his own states of duality. In doing so, the listener is to realize that the states of right and wrong, left and right, positive and negative are constantly shifting and open to perception. This realization keeps us from being overly judgmental of others and more forgiving of ourselves. None of us stand without evil. The only truth is that there is a yin and yang. Batman has his Joker. If we understand this, we are better able to deal with our internal struggle and evolve.

It's All about Love

Prince's thirteenth album is the music for his fourth feature film, Graffiti Bridge (1990). The movie received very bad reviews, and the album, like Parade, suffered tremendously from the reviews. Again, the music is diverse, not like anything happening at that time. It is straight forward funk with dashes of soul and rock (much more rock than soul). The message is as unapologetic as the music; it is all about love. Lovesexy is the spiritual side of love, man, God, and a better place to be. Graffiti Bridge is the physical side of love, man, God, and a better place to be. Above all, it is a reminder that all for which one is pushing is just around the corner, but you cannot give up. Hold fast. Love is coming. "Can't Stop this Feeling I Got," "New Power Generation," "The Question of U," "Joy in Repetition," "Elephants and Flowers," "We Can Funk," "Round and Round," "Melody Cool," and "Graffiti Bridge" all represent the importance of manifesting love through our daily living. By now, the message is clear, and Prince's resolution to himself, his music, his fellowman, and God is clear. It is all about Love. Let love lead you to a better place to be.

Where Graffiti Bridge centers on finding spiritual love, the undercurrent theme is about finding a justification and a purpose to exist. In the film, the Kid, played by Prince, is looking for the greater purpose of life and his music as well as a sign or a justification to continue in the face of great resistance. This is shown when he confesses to still communicating with his deceased father. "You know, I still write imaginary letters to my dad. I'd be pretty freaked if he answered one. Maybe I'm just looking for a sign, something that says it's okay to continue." The Kid and his old nemesis, Morris Day, are now co-owners of a club, Glam Slam. The Kid wants to use the club as a forum for art that uplifts the soul and changes the hearts of men. Day's character is primarily concerned with making money, as he states to the Kid, "This music will never change anybody." Their battle represents the battle of art for the redemption of man versus art for economic prosperity. The songs articulate the thoughts and concerns of the characters, even more specifically than <u>Purple Rain</u>. The songs in <u>Graffiti Bridge</u> represent actual characters speaking to other characters, espousing their ideas.

      Prince begins with "Can't Stop this Feeling I Got." The Kid is an artist on the edge. He has taken himself as far as he can go with his own drive, love of his art, talents, and self determination. He feels his physical body and mind surrendering to the physical forces of hate and commercialism. But the spirit of love keeps him moving forward. "Dear dad, things didn't go quite like I expected. Sometimes, I feel like I'm going 2 explode...But u know what? Can't stop this feeling I got." The Kid's dad, to whom he prays, represents the spiritual/ancestral notion of music. It is the substance of things hoped for, the evidence of things unseen that keep him pushing forward. The physical embodiments of this idea are Mavis Staples and George Clinton, links to the legacy of socially conscious music and forefathers to Prince's own legacy of music. Embracing his father's memory and the mentorship of Staples and Clinton, allows the Kid to hold fast against a world that is corrupting art merely for the sake of financial gain. "Can't Stop this Feeling I Got" is Prince's declaration that no one can stop the feeling or agenda of love. Once you have love, it over-takes you, and you must share it. This is the ultimate purpose of art, to elevate man. "My body wants it down to my bones." The Kid has it, but nobody else seems to want it. Using one's art to achieve a higher self is not as popular as sex and violence. Yet despite the depths of his discouragement, he realizes that he is unable to stop this inner drive, "I can't sleep at night...I can't shake it." The final notion is that with love, the New Power Generation "can change anything...Only we [the lovers of the world] can change the world."

With "New Power Generation," we get another preamble. We, the new people of a new republic of the mind, are declaring our independence and our right to exist and pursue happiness in any manner we so choose. The New Breed revolutionaries of "Sexuality" have experienced the New Power Soul of <u>Lovesexy</u> and have become the New Power Generation (NPG). They are still as forceful as the New Breed, refusing to allow their otherness to exile or marginalize them. "Pardon us 4 breathing, but this is our world 2. We can't help what's cool 2 us might be strange 2 u." Yet, despite their differences, the New Power Generation is willing to work with anyone to create a better world, "Lay down your funky weapons. Come join us on the floor." But with or without the assistance or acceptance of the mainstream, the New Power Generation is here to make a stand and a change. "We are the New Power Generation, and we want 2 change the world. The only thing that's in our way is u. We're tired of your old fashioned music, your old ideas. We're sick and tired of u telling us what 2 do." What is different about the New Power Generation from the New Breed is that the NPG is willing to proclaim and designate a particular place of their own, which is sovereign to their way of life. "So if u didn't come 2 party, u better get up off of my block." Thus, "New Power Generation" is akin to "Uptown" but with more teeth. Prince is moving more into the collective as opposed to his individual quest and vision. In "Sexuality," although Prince is calling for organization, the emphasis is still on the individual, the atom of the molecule. Strong atoms create strong molecules. "Sexuality is all I ever need. Sexuality, I'm gonna let my body be free." In "New Power Generation," Prince is moving pass his individual notions and moving into concepts of collective nation building by replacing the singular pronoun I with the collective pronouns we and our: "our block...We are...We wanna...our way..." Again, this represents continual growth for an artist who is constantly trying to move toward his highest point of self. Prince invites the mainstream to join his movement. He is realizing that love or truth, kept in the dark, will not save the world, but die, because love and truth must be shared to survive. His notion of the collective shows his growth. We need strong and fully developed atoms to connect with each other so that the molecular structure will evolve.

"Release It," by The Time, is the third song and is the answer of the mainstream-populous to the ideals of the NPG. The Time (a Prince created R&B, funk band which I will discuss at length later in the book) represents mainstream, popular artists who create art solely to entertain and to make money. For Day, the leader of The Time, the only valuable art is art that nets a financial profit. In "Release It," Day asks the Kid to release the stage and his ownership of the club by offending him and bragging of his own musical and sexual prowess and popularity. The releasing of the stage and his ownership symbolizes Day wanting the Kid to relinquish his ideas that music can change or save mankind. The crowd reacts positively to Day, affirming his notions over the Kid's. "Release It" is what the industry and listeners have been asking Prince to do over the past three years following <u>Sign "☮" the Times</u>. Since that time, the masses do not seem to get or understand his issues or his music, not in the same manner that they understand <u>Purple Rain</u>. Further, there is the question of whether or not the general public understands Prince's underlying issues in <u>Purple Rain</u> or if they are merely attracted to the more sensational elements of sex, violence, and the opportunity to dance. In "Release It," Day is asserting that the Kid is either naive or misguided if he thinks that the general public wants more than sex and a good time from their music. "Who told u that women like men with no money?" And this is affirmed by the crowd's overwhelming reception to "Release It" as they dance out of the club, following Day to his other club, leaving the Kid broke and alone with his ideology.

In "Elephants & Flowers" and "Question of U" the Kid is still searching for the meaning of life and his art. The reaction of the crowd to Day causes the Kid to question or second-guess his direction and philosophy of art. "Boy is lonely on a long hot summer night. He's looking 4 a savior in a city full of fools. Maybe he just needs a good talker 2 give him a good talking 2?" The Kid is searching for a soul mate, someone to whom he can talk and share his pains and beliefs. He is attempting to shed the restraints and restrictions of society, "strip down" and get down to the essence of existence, "A crowd of naked bodies stripped down 2 their very souls." The existence of elephants and flowers together and in harmony represents the power of God and his ability to put into motion the harmony of all things. "There will be no more confusion....sorrow...pain." In "Question of U," the Kid is addressing his confusion and self-doubt by exploring the connection or relationship of spiritual awareness to the male/female relationship. Much of Prince's work has been about discovering higher states of being through the female. "The Question of U" continues this theme. "Which way shall I turn if I'm feeling lost? Shall I become naked, no image at all? Or shall I remain upright or get down and crawl?" The position and relation to the female determines the position and relation to God. All will be answered when he uncovers the question of the female. "All of the questions in my life will be answered when I decide which road 2 choose. What is the answer 2 the question of u?" To get to the place where elephants and flowers are in harmony, one must answer the question of woman, which is the question of life. Remember, the Kid's father is dead because he could not come to terms with his art and his wife, who is also driven insane by her husband's turmoil. Additionally, Prince is also addressing the manner in which the matrix of the artist's personal life greatly influences his art. Much like in <u>Purple Rain</u>, the Kid in <u>Graffiti Bridge</u> is in the center of a whirlwind of problems and emotions that all create havoc on his ability to remain focused on his mission of creating meaningful art. The Kid realizes that while it is acceptable to be a creative individual, everyone needs others in their life to love and motivate them. Thus, "Question of U" is asserting that one of the ways to understand and endure life is to construct positive relationships with people who care about you, something his father is unable to do.

In "Round and Round," Prince is putting the voice of

wisdom in the mouth of a child, fourteen year old Tevin Campbell. The youthful Campbell acts as a voice of wisdom, optimism, and idealism amidst the chaos of Seven Corners, which is the neighborhood that houses all of the city's clubs. Seven Corners is based on Uptown, an artistic community/business district in Minneapolis, which is somewhat of an extension of the old bohemian community/ neighborhood where Prince's father made his local mark as a musician. Although Seven Corners is an aging area, it still carries the spirit and power of art's ability to make life better. Campbell becomes the voice of that spirit. "Nothing comes from dreamers but dreams. Nothing comes from talkers but sound. We can talk all we want 2, but the world still goes around and round." The song is proclaiming the benefits of action over talk. "Can u tell me where we're going 2? What it is we're really tryin' 2 find? Is the truth really there, or is it right under our hair?" Campbell is articulating the dilemma of the Kid, searching for meaning to his work, wanting it to stand for something and inspire people into action. But the Kid is spending most of his time pondering over it. Campbell's character is a young "Kid," aspiring to get into the business. He is out on the street corners, getting dirty, trying to make it happen, which is a contrast to the perceived persona of Prince who is viewed as an artist no longer in touch with the daily concerns of the listeners and is off somewhere pondering the metaphysical problems of the universe in <u>Lovesexy</u>.

    Campbell's character is involved. Unlike the Kid, Campbell is taking his art to the people, rather than creating and musing over it in a vacuum, "sitting idle in our boats while everyone else is down the stream." Campbell, in his role as an anxious youth, represents the urgency of the movie to have art become active. "Can u tell me when we gonna get 2 it? I'm tired of fooling around; I want 2 do it." "Round and Round" serves as a wake up call, much like hip hop, for the Kid to become more involved in the physical concerns of his listeners. Also, "Round and Round" addresses the problem of the generation gap, not only for Prince's career but in general. The axis of turmoil and change on which the wheel of the sixties turned was the generation gap. The youth had grown wise and disillusioned to the hypocrisy of America and its elders. Hippies evolved from young white kids becoming disillusioned by their parents' hypocrisy of talking religion and morals but living exactly the opposite. The clash of generations is also the very issue that tugged at the fabric of African American unity during the Civil Rights Movement. Martin Luther King, Jr. was perceived as a young minister, almost too rowdy and progressive for the established, aristocratic NAACP, which wanted nothing to do with sit-ins and boycotts. In the same vein, S.N.C.C. was one of the few groups that solicited, enrolled, trained, and used young folks in the movement as opposed to the NAACP, which seemed to have an anti-youth atmosphere. However, it would not be long before King's visions would seem dated and out of touch with the next generation of youth. Through "Round and Round" and Campbell, Prince is acknowledging his distance and his need to rejoin and reconcile with the youth of the streets. It is the only way that his work will be able to move them to a higher place.

If "Round and Round" is building bridges to the future, "We Can Funk" is building bridges to the past. A duet with funk godfather George Clinton, "We Can Funk" is about achieving the highest level of creativity through human union and collaboration. Clinton represents history. The Kid represents the present, but it is a present that is withering, not connected to anything, past or future. Together, they are able to unite and produce a positive, creative future. Clinton is not just one of the musical predecessors to Prince. His music is also one of the most sampled by the new generation of hip hop. By connecting with the legacy and history of music, Prince is connecting his music to the future of music. In what would sound like a song about sexual acts, Prince, once again, is using sex as a metaphor. This time sex represents the creation of art. "Understand...there's this energy between us." There is a connection through art to come together and create. Both Clinton, who plays a musician and club owner in the movie, and the Kid are acknowledging and declaring the greatness that a creative union between them could produce. In this duet, Prince is, for the first time, acknowledging and articulating, in song, his debt to the history of the great figures of popular music, particularly African American figures. His "testing positive 4 the funk" is a testament of being in the historical line of Little Richard, Chuck Berry, James Brown, Jimi Hendrix, and George Clinton. (It must be noted that five years earlier in 1985, during an interview with MTV, Prince listed James Brown as having played a major influence on him.) Together, Prince and Clinton declare that they have the ability to create what has never been seen before, the ability to refashion the legacy of music that they both have been instrumental in creating. "I could tell u things 2 get u excited, things u never heard. U know the Kama Sutra? I could rewrite it with half as many words." During this phase of his life, Prince is definitely attempting to reaffirm the roles and connect with the history makers of African American music, having signed both Clinton and Staples to Paisley Park Records in 1987. Accordingly, they both play significant roles as community elders in <u>Graffiti Bridge</u>. Prince had also formed a relationship with jazz great Miles Davis, who spent his career as an advocate for the rights of African American musicians. "We Can funk" is a break from the personal, individualistic, creative theory of Prince. In the past, Prince has preferred to do everything himself, keeping projects under his entire control. In every aspect—music, lyrics, packaging, and promotion—Prince fought to retain complete control to insure that his personal artistic vision was achieved. Other musicians or managers were used primarily as replaceable tools in the creation of the art. In "We Can funk" Prince is using the platonic relationship to achieve a higher level of creation. The song, as an example of the creation process, speaks to the theme of man reconciling himself to man for the purpose of fellowship and evolution. We can funk. We can come together for a positive, constructive purpose, working to evolve humanity to its highest level. This demonstrates the continued growth and evolution of Prince as both an artist and a person. He is expressing his understanding that before he can grow he must find his roots and connect to his collective self.

"Joy in Repetition" takes the physical, platonic relationship and raises it to the sexual and spiritual realm. It is a dream sequence, a subconscious, surreal experience as the Kid thinks he has found his answers in Aura. Aura is an angel sent to Seven Corners to forge the reconciliation between Day and the Kid. Not understanding Aura's purpose or his own emotions toward her, the Kid begins to confuse his emotions and pursue her romantically. This represents man's inability to differentiate between needs and desires because we are too tied to the physical. The opening verses set a surrealistic scene of pimps, poets, part time singers, and a band playing a song call "Soul Psychodelicide" in a location where four letter words possess "dignity and bite." It is a worn atmosphere, where the crowd sits numbly with "an introverted this is it look." They are all going through the motions. The Kid sees Aura's ability to heal and rejuvenate and becomes attracted to her. Because of her powers, Prince, in the Kid's dream, makes Aura a symbolic creature of love's reconciling powers. The Kid believes that he can manifest love (God) if he can find someone to love. "...Love Me...These three words, just a little behind the beat. Over and over, 'till I could take no more." In finding love the Kid affirms, "Holding someone is truly believing, there's joy in repetition." Aura becomes the sign for the Kid to continue. Having love from God is not enough. It is the giving and receiving of love which is the existence of life. "Holding someone is truly believing there's joy in repetition." Love's perpetuation of itself is a repetitive, circular action, from God to man, from man to man, and from man back to God. This perpetuation of love is also a perpetuation of God, recycling himself through man. Therefore, love must be recycled if it is to exist. "There is joy in repetition."

Even though "Joy in Repetition" is a prophetic vision, the Kid is not evolved enough to understand fully Aura's purpose or meaning. After having Day and The Time steal the spotlight and Aura, the Kid answers with "Tick, Tick, Bang," an explosive, funk track, which is a return to the sexually explicit lyrics of old. It is a creation of anger. The Kid is using fire to fight fire, attempting to show that he can be just as explosive and popular as The Time. This is much in the vein of the creation of <u>The Black Album</u>. Because "Tick, Tick, Bang" is received as being contrived, it is not enjoyed or accepted by the crowd assembled on the street. This could represent Prince's own failed attempts, at this point, to recapture the street audience, the very ones who made him a cult figure. "Tick, Tick, Bang" is not where the Kid's heart is. So, no matter how funky the music or explosive the lyrics, it does not have the essence of the songs which come from his experience or emotional reality. "Tick, Tick, Bang" falls on deaf ears because it is artificial. The Kid, in a desperate act, abandons his heart for superficial fame, making the expected explosion of "Tick, Tick, Bang" a small dud. The message in the song's failure to connect with the crowd is be true to yourself no matter how isolated it may cause you to be. The rewards of being honest and true to oneself are greater than the rewards gained from going along to get along. Also, begin true to yourself is the only way that your work and life can have meaning.

"Thieves in the Temple (Twelve-inch Version)" is the Kid's moment of clarity. The thieves have entered his temple and stolen his love. Translated—commercial, money grubbing artists and businessmen (represented by Day and The Time) have entered into the Kid's private sanctuary, the arena of music, (represented by Glam Slam) and stolen his love, his right to make the music of his heart (represented by Day's seduction of Aura). The Kid's music is his lifeline, "I can hang when u're around, but I'll surely die if u're not there." The Kid is sure that Aura is his sign. He must rescue her, "I feel like I'm looking 4 my soul, like a poor man lookin' 4 gold." If the Kid does not reclaim his love, death will follow. "Voices from the sky say rely on your best friend 2 pull you through... my only friend is u [music]." With his love [music] going to artificial commercialism, the Kid's sorrow turns bitter. "...Kickin' me in my heart, tearing it all apart, 4 me and u [music] could have been a work of art." Yet he resigns himself to hold on, knowing that love can make him better than the thieves. "I'm holding on the best that I can. Love, please make me a better man, better than ones who want to count me out, better than the ones who don't know what my love's about." He then proceeds with an indictment of music going commercial, "No matter what u [music] say, u should be with me. U led me on, thinking u was Moses, herding sheep blindly through a fantasy. U done me wrong, and everybody knows it." But even in despair, the Kid refuses to admit defeat: "...the sound of my voice [music] is [still] pounding in your chest." Even though Prince is no longer considered to be the reigning figure of popular music, his 1990 American Music Award of Merit is an acknowledgement by a major organization in the industry of his influence on the current music. And his 1991 Soul Train Legend Award affirms that point. "I am the best, better than the rest, better than the thieves in the temple 2night." Why is he better than the thieves? He is better than the thieves because he sees the ultimate goal of music, which is to take man to a higher place, to aid in the evolution of humanity, and this is not happening in popular music.

"The Latest Fashion" is a comical battle between Prince and Day to decide who is the hottest, most current artist. Much of Prince's acclaim came from being associated with the cutting edge of music. By 1990, Prince was becoming old news to the latest pop craze, rap, and an onslaught of new talent whose packaging were much more marketable by MTV and BET. His inclusion of rap, musical samples, and dancers come as a reaction to the new trends in music. Also, his relationship with Miles Davis, who has always been open to new music trends and was, himself, experimenting with rap during that time, plays a role in Prince opening himself to the new sounds of the industry. Davis' fight was to keep jazz fresh and on the edge of modern music. His greatest fear was the putting of jazz into a museum, to which he speaks at length in his autobiography. Now, Prince is faced with the same battle. Day, representing the commercial, states that his words are purely artificial, only used to make money, "I know I said I loved u. But this is the latest fashion, to lie in the heat of passion." Prince represents the voice of art attempting to reconcile itself with the commercial, "People tell us what we want 2 hear. This time the tables are turned." It seems that Prince is surrendering or at least trying to find a balance between socially conscious art and economically driven art. Prince understands that he must be able to sell records to continue reaching the masses of people to which he has become accustomed. The song finishes with Prince rapping, which marks the first time Prince tries on the hat of rapper, if we do not include "Irresistible Bitch" (1982) and "Dead on It." What better way to announce and display his ability to remain fresh than with the fastest growing, most popular medium of the time. Unfortunately for Prince, it all seems contrived and too late to save a fading career. By now, word had spread of his song, "Dead on It," which appears on <u>The Black Album</u>. "Dead on It" is seen as Prince's attack on rap. Now, two years later, Prince is trying to reconcile himself to rap. It seems to be too little too late. The lingering question is, "Is he doing this to grow as an artist, or is he doing this to save his career?"

    Throughout <u>Graffiti Bridge,</u> Prince is battling and grappling with the question of how to stay fresh and current and at the same time stay true to craft. In an interview held ten years after <u>Graffiti Bridge</u>, Prince admits to still trying to walk this thin and tight rope. "It's an interesting process to remain current, remain in the now and still do those things that were good in the past." Often the tension generated by commercialism and craft gets in the way of the product, causing the art to seem unsure of itself or its direction. By writing all the songs for <u>Graffiti Bridge</u>, Prince is forced to write/speak for all of the personas of the movie. This is what gives the album its incoherent feel at times. Yet, in "Round and Round" and "Melody Cool," Prince succeeds brilliantly, writing "Round and Round" for an artist more than twenty years his junior and writing "Melody Cool" for an artist more than twenty years his senior. Although the rest of the album feels somewhat awkward at times, these two songs showcase Prince as a master of music and subject matter, creating authentic pieces for artists from two distinctly different generations. In a 1991 interview with BET's Sherry Carter on <u>Video LP</u>, Mavis Staples stated that with "Melody Cool" Prince had written her life. The song is certainly paying homage to as well as troping Staples' image as a gritty, earthy, gospel singer, who had the ability and nerve to step into secular music to touch lives. In one scene, members of The Time are attempting to seize Melody Cool's club in order to showcase new talent. This scene represents the industry's disregard for the history of music because of its greed for immediate profit. Melody quickly makes a stand for her right to remain a part of the music scene. "They call me Melody Cool. I was here long before u. If u're good I will love u. But I'm nobody's fool." Good music will stand the test of time. She gives a brief history of her legacy, in which she discusses the power of music and makes a plea for harmony and unity. "If we play in the same key, everything will be Melody Cool." There is no need to fight. There is room for all kinds of music and ideas. With "Melody Cool" Prince is completing his and the Kid's alignment with the lineage of black music and utilitarian art, constructing a case against art solely for the sake of commercialism.

"Still Would Stand All Time" encompasses the entire theme of <u>Graffiti Bridge</u>. "When a man screams, you must learn to whisper." These are the words of strength given to the Kid by Aura just before she sacrifices her life for the union of Seven Corners. In a physical world of chaos, man must learn to listen so that he can hear the voice of divine wisdom. In "☮ no" from <u>Lovesexy</u>, Prince describes the voice of the devil. "He talks so loud. He'll make u do things, hang out with the crowd. ☮ know there was confusion, lightin' all around me." In contrast to the voice of the devil, the voice of God is a whisper, filled with power. "But my Lord, He's so quiet. He calls your name. When u hear it, your heart will Thunder—U will want 2 hear it everyday." Man must be able to focus beyond the physical to recognize the essence of life, which lies in the metaphysical. We must look with the eyes of our souls and not our physical eyes. Only then will we know that love is and has been with us the entire time. We have been focusing on the wrong target. Humanity must learn to be still to find love, to find God. If falling in love is truly believing that there is joy in repetition, then it is "Love that reaffirms that we are not alone. And night and day will run together, and all things would be fine." Love, peace, and happiness is there. We just need to remain faithful, strong, and long suffering. "It's not a thousand years away...It's just around the corner. It's just around the block. If we all say yes and try, then Heaven on Earth we will find. Love can save us all." "Still Would Stand All Time" is a song for weary times and weary soldiers, as the Kid pleads, "Love, please give us a sign." For when love captures the hearts of men "then men will fight injustice instead of one another." During a 1990 aftershow in Europe, Prince elaborates on the song's meaning by stating "That means Time would stand still if you turn all that around." Perhaps Campbell, in his 1990 interview for BET's Screen Scene special on Graffiti Bridge summarizes the song and the movie best: "It's about never giving up." Because when you achieve love, time will stand still. And this is affirmed in "Graffiti Bridge," the closing song of the movie and the album. It articulates all for which the Kid and humanity are searching, which is love. "Everybody wants 2 find Graffiti Bridge, something to believe in, a reason 2 believe that there's a heaven on Earth...Everybody's looking 4 love." The tone of the song is jubilation, as the primary characters alternate verses throughout the song. The Kid finds his love and his reason to continue.

Unfortunately for Prince, with metal, rap, and pop ruling the charts, Graffiti Bridge did not fulfill its anticipated potential of sales in America. It seems that the out of sight Prince was once again out of touch with the mind of the American public. In a time of high-tech promotion of cultural personas, which Prince was instrumental in developing, his self-imposed isolation and abstract discourses seem to be his Achilles heel. By now it had been more than two years since Prince had toured the States. American fans were beginning to grow tired of hearing about Prince's overseas tours, and his abstract concepts were turning many faithful toward new means of entertainment which were more tangibly rooted in the reality of every day, i.e. rap and grunge. Even with the early positive reviews, Prince felt the critics were, once again, missing the point of <u>Graffiti Bridge</u>. "No one's mentioning the lyrics. Maybe I should have put in a lyric sheet" (Karlen, "Prince Talks," 57). The mass public, critics, and music buyers were unable to receive the message in the madness.

One Gem of a Talent

After having his last two albums connected to and somewhat limited by movies, Prince is ready to return to unlimited creativity. His fourteenth album, <u>Diamonds and Pearls</u> (1991) reflects this attitude. Even as late as 1991, it was still accepted that nothing in the music industry generates as much excitement as a new Prince album. This was the case with <u>Diamonds and Pearls</u>. With a new set of youngsters to capture and a faithful following to reclaim, Prince is determined to capture and express the feeling of freshness that an industry leader possesses. This time a new generation of listeners opened their arms to Prince while the old faithful enjoyed another ride with His Royal Badness. <u>Diamonds and Pearls</u> represents the diversity of Prince. He is an encyclopedia and a prism of music. He has the ability to take all that has come before him and create his own, unique brand of music-literature and, in doing so, expand the world of popular music. In his article, "The Musical Alchemist," for <u>El Pais</u>, Luis Hidalgo asserts that "The difference is [Prince's] influences, his musical inspirations, the ease with which he assimilates them and then reinvents them with his own personal imprint. Prince has created his own unique style...an incomparable way of making music, style you can distinguish by the second verse" (Hidalgo 1994). <u>Diamonds and Pearls</u> acts as a small prism to reflect the history and variety of music-literature. It includes everything from gospel to straight forward jazz, from the big band sound to hard core funk, rock, and soul. The lyrics cover issues from salvation to economics, from comments on social independence and politics to love and romance. With <u>Diamonds and Pearls</u>, Prince is once again championing his philosophy of obtaining and being at peace by asserting, unapologetically, that God is the answer for a world struggling with its flesh and looking in the wrong places for direction and identity. "Thunder" is a forthright fusion of funk and gospel, proclaiming and echoing the presence and power of God. "Thunder all through the night, promise to see Jesus in the morning light, Take my hand, it'll be alright. C'mon save your soul tonight." In songs such as "Walk Don't Walk," "Cream," and "Push," Prince is persistent in his messages regarding the importance of a positive self-esteem and living by one's own terms. These songs stress the importance of thinking for oneself and not being controlled by peer groups or the society:

> "Don't walk on their side of the street. Don't walk where it feels the best. Don't talk 2 people u meet unless they walk the way u want them 2. Walk like u need the ride. Don't walk with a confident stride...and people will walk all over u." "U will hit cuz u got the burning desire. It's your time. Everything u do is success. Cream, get on top. Cream, don't u ever stop." "Every time u get some, people try and get it back. They'd rather see u on the run, than see u have it like that. Every time they stop u, u gotta tick more than they tock. Push, don't stop until u go."

Songs, such as "Money Don't Matter 2night," "Live 4 Love," and "Jughead" address balancing the priorities of life, love, and money. Through these songs, Prince confronts the injustices that common people face due to the extremism of capitalism, which produces greed rather than love. Prince portrays the poor as pawns in the game of capitalism controlled by big business and the government. More specifically, he addresses the use of the poor in the military and the economic struggle of the common man to ascend from poverty. He also discusses his own money matters and directly attacks the music industry in "Jughead":

> "Look here's a cool investment, they're telling him he just can't lose. So he goes out 2 try and find a partner, but all he finds are users. Money doesn't matter 2night. It sure didn't matter yesterday. Just when u think u've got more than enough, that's when it up and flies away. Guess u are better off making sure

that your soul is alright." "They told him flying planes was supposed 2 be cool. Maybe 👁 was better off staying in school. How can 👁 live 4 love 👁'm calling? Live 4 Love, without Love u don't live." "Man, 👁'd go broke and hit the skids before 👁 work 4 a rich suckers kids. Man, a contract ain't no pension plan. And years after this, u're still gonna make the grands. Like Little Richard, that man's records are still selling, and that man could die broke. So fellow artists push 4 yours and watch the money minders as we settle the score."

All of these songs discuss the exploitation of the poor and undereducated. Prince's response is to promote the importance of education and to reject the physical. Those who are properly educated are less likely to be exploited. The protagonist in "Live 4 Love" is in his predicament because he was educated to be a laborer. In "Money Don't Matter 2night," Prince is stressing that mostly the poor and undereducated are on the frontlines of war. And in "Jughead" Prince, through Tony M., laments how black artists, such as Little Richard, have been exploited by record companies because they were kept in the dark about the business of art. Education liberates all of these people. Further, those who do not desire the physical are less likely to be exploited. Prince is preaching that we turn from the physical, from the dangling carrot of capitalism; then, we will not be pimped or exploited. This is not the pie in the sky theology of not wanting anything of the Earth. In "Jughead," he asserts that we should fight for what is rightfully ours. But, if you do not deal with a snake, you will not be bitten. This is what makes "Walk Don't Walk" so significant. It interjects the need and importance of self-esteem. Positive self-esteem will give one the courage to chart one's own course. The economic leaders of society do not want individuals; they want a mindless mass. By becoming the individual of "Walk Don't Walk," one can not be exploited or fall into the traps of "Live 4 Love" and "Money Don't Matter 2night."

Moving from the collective to the individual, "Daddy

Pop" is a direct declaration to the critics that Prince is still a force with which to be reckoned. Prince's general issue with the popular music industry is that being able to play every form or style of music is a liability rather than an asset. With <u>Diamonds and Pearls</u> Prince is attempting to show that talent, not gimmickry, is what the people want. "Daddy Pop" forthrightly proclaims that if talent is what people want, they need to look no further than him. One might be able to dismiss Prince's pop, icon image and style, but no one can dismiss his talent. And the fact that he has accomplished so much on his own terms truly makes him a "Daddy Pop" of the business.

> "See my brother talkin' plenty head, Steady wishin' he could sleep in your bed, Steady wishing he was in your car, Just a steady wishin' that he was who u are...Pop Daddy—Daddy Pop, Punchin' in the rock and roll clock. See all the people wonder why, U set your goals high—high as the sky!...Daddy Pop is the writer and love is the book, u better look it over before u overlook. See all my critics wastin' time, Worryin' about the Daddy while he beat u blind. Get your life 2gether—stop your crying. Whenever u say that u can't—That's when u need 2 be tryin'. What kind of fool is this, that thinks Daddy will miss. What kind of boy would dis a list as long as history itself. ♛ got grooves and grooves up on the shelf. Deep purple concord jams. This party ♛ will slam. ♛ don't think u understand, Whatever u can't do—Daddy can...Oh my brother, there ain't no stopin'. Check the record. Poppa Daddy's comin', (Ring di di ding) somebody's calling...'The Jester's on the phone!' He just one in a long line that wanna see me!"

Of course, there is also romantic poetry. "Diamonds and Pearls" and "Insatiable" are classic Prince ballads. "Diamonds and Pearls" is the declaration of commitment with a musical pop orientation, while "Insatiable" is a brash but smooth Prince poem of intimate confession and longing, echoing the soulful sounds of "Do Me, Baby," "International Lover," and any number of Motown's beautiful poetry. The tunes' contrasting moods and range of subject matter display Prince's diversity and universal appeal through his depth of craft. Very few artists have the talent to release two songs during the same week to two culturally different outlets (BET and MTV) with both songs then having the ability to crossover to the other medium. In the case of "Diamonds and Pearls," the song crossed back over to the BET, <u>Video Soul</u> market and became a number one song on the <u>Video Soul</u> countdown. Additionally, "Diamonds and Pearls" is more wearing away at the material, physical facade to achieve love, which is the essence of life. "If ☮ gave u diamonds and pearls, would u be a happy boy or a girl? If ☮ could, ☮'d give u the world, but all ☮ can do is offer u my love." Love is more valuable because it gives humanity its meaning and value by connecting us to each other, connecting us to inner peace, thus bringing us closer to completion. "This will be the day that u will hear me say that ☮ will never run away. ☮ am hear 4 u. Love is meant 4 2, now tell me what u gonna do." Love is not only valuable, but it is meant to be shared. And, it increases in value, in power, the more often that it is shared. The day that we realize the power of love is the day we move closer to God. Love is more valuable than any physical ornament or monetary object because it allows us to transcend to our god-selves.

"Insatiable" is at the other end of the spectrum from "Diamonds and Pearls." It successfully walks the tight rope between erotica and pornography, showing that the line separating the two is craft, one's mastery of language. "Insatiable" displays the mature, well-crafted writer who is able to be sexy and sensual without being demeaning or dogmatic. Prince is able to be passively aggressive by proclaiming his most intense and insatiable desires and then relinquishing control by pleading with the female to "do" him instead of demanding that she allows him to "do" her. He puts the female squarely in control, allowing her to be an acting agent and not merely an object upon which he is acting. "No one ♛'ve ever, knows how 2 handle my body the way u truly do." Where it is traditionally the male who attempts to bait and lure the female into liberating herself or freeing herself from the constraints of society's prescribed notion of her gender, Prince assigns himself as the one needing to be liberated. "Like a wildcat in a celibate rage, ♛ want u alone in my dirty little cage." Even in heat, Prince is able to resign his position of power and put the female in the driver's seat. This is what makes his work so compelling and liberating to women. They feel empowered by and through his lyrics. In fact, according to music critic Nelson George, even at the lowest points of his popularity, Prince managed to maintain his female audience intact. "…not all Prince fans changed with the times: 'Of all the artists I knew, I don't know anyone who's had so many unabashed women fans who love him to death'" (Toure 1998). By ingratiating himself to them, Prince is able to get from them what he wants, again walking that fine line between Little Richard and Ike Turner. He is able to gain the ultimate in satisfaction: sex, orgasm, completion, and salvation.

<u>Diamonds and Pearls</u> showcases Prince's range as a musical and lyrical genius. Whether it is sex, salvation, or social issues, Prince proves that he has the knowledge and the skill to be creative when exploring any issue. Thus, his work resonates on a deeper level because he is addressing and presenting the totality of the human experience. It is also more proof that Prince can be commercially as well as artistically creative, producing songs that have the backbone of the past and the flavoring of the present. Not only would this album temporarily silence his critics, but it would put Prince back at the nucleus of the music field and back atop the music charts.

⚥ (1992) or <u>The Rock Soap Opera</u>, as Prince deems it in the segue to "The Sacrifice of Victor," is another explosion of Prince's lyrical talents in search of his deeper self. The central issue of the album is the journey to find identity and the reward gained from soul searching. The plot is about a musical prince (heir to the King of Pop's throne) who travels to Egypt to meet a Princess, heir to a billion dollar throne, whose father has been murdered by seven men who are a part of a plot to seize the throne. The seven men are personifications of the seven deadly sins, which Prince must conquer to achieve his new spirituality/ identity. The seven men also represent, through their blind lust for power, the battle that man must wage with the flesh to achieve a higher self. Once victorious, Prince emerges as ⚥, which becomes his new name and the title for the album.

The album opens with "My Name Is Prince." It is a declaration of his musical identity. It continues the theme of "Daddy Pop" from <u>Diamonds and Pearls</u> as it elucidates his talents and achievements in the music industry. But it goes further to indicate that Prince is looking for more than being the prince of the music world. He is searching for more than mere fame or fortune. An example of this is his releasing such an eclectic mix of music as ⚥ after <u>Diamonds and Pearls</u>, which had Prince back at the top of the charts and back on the radio. The releasing of ⚥ continued a unique pattern by Prince since 1985—the releasing of a chart toping album one year and the releasing of an economic flop the next. <u>Around the World in a Day</u> sold in high volume, but not as much as <u>Purple Rain</u> because Prince was making a conscious effort not to duplicate <u>Purple Rain</u>. <u>Parade</u>, which followed <u>Around the World in a Day</u>, was also a conscious effort by Prince not to duplicate himself, and it sold less because it was so different. <u>Sign '☮' the Times</u> sold in high volume; <u>Lovesexy</u> did not. <u>Diamonds and Pearls</u> sold in high volume; ☥ did not. This pattern can be traced even further back to his earliest albums. After moderate success with <u>For You</u>, <u>Prince</u> sold well; <u>Dirty Mind</u>, which is a conscious attempt by Prince not to be labeled merely as a Stevie Wonder type, did not sell well. However, it received much critical acclaim and is still cited as the Prince essential. <u>Controversy</u> was moderately more successful than <u>Dirty Mind</u>, and <u>1999</u> became multi-platinum. This represents an artist not concerned with the formula of success or duplicating himself for hits.

> "I had put myself in the hole with the first record because I spent a lot of money to make it. I wanted to remedy that with the second album. I wanted a 'hit' album. It was for radio rather than for me, and it got a lot of people interested in my music. But it wasn't the kind of audience you really want. They only come around to check you out when you have another hit. They won't come to see you when you change directions and try something new. *That's the kind of audience I wanted*" (Hilburn, "The Renegade Prince," 66).

Prince has been an artist constantly grappling with the need to balance being artistic with being a popular icon. He knows that to remain a self-contained, self-determined artist, he must generate capital. Therefore, the production of hit songs is important because hit songs allow him the freedom and space to explore other avenues of his art. This is not to say that his hits have not been artistic successes, but these albums which tend not to sell as well are used to define, redefine, liquefy, and establish Prince's iconic stature. Artistic freedom seems to be as important as economic success. For Prince the fear is that to follow up a mega hit with another mega hit is to firmly implant oneself into a rigid identity.

It is difficult enough not being labeled or pigeonholed by one's major success. To follow that success with similar work only serves to entrench the artist further into that mold. Once an artist becomes a statue in the public's mind, he is dead because he is not allowed to grow. Prince asserts this.

> "A lot of people think that fame affects my work, but it doesn't at all. I think that the smartest thing I did was record <u>Around the World in a Day</u> right after I finished <u>Purple Rain</u>. I didn't wait to see what would happen with <u>Purple Rain</u>. That's why the two albums sound so completely different...You know how easy it would have been to open <u>Around the World in a Day</u> with the guitar solo that's on the end of 'Let's Go Crazy?' You know how easy it would have been to just put it in a different key? That would have shut everybody up who said that <u>Around the World in a Day</u> wasn't half as powerful as <u>Purple Rain</u> or <u>1999</u>. I don't *want* to make an album like the earlier ones. Wouldn't it be cool to be able to put your albums back to back and not get bored, you dig? I don't know how many people can play all their albums back to back..." (Karlen, "Prince Talks," 30).

Hits are only valuable because they give Prince the ability to follow his own muse and vision with the next project. The flip side of this approach is to become so unpredictable and indefinable that enough people are not able to identify with you or get their brains around your work. This also has been the case with Prince. But the journey is often so imaginative and filled with well-crafted music and lyrics that one takes the ride with Prince just out of curiosity of what he will do next. He has been allowed to fail more than most because the pay-off is usually greater. "My Name Is Prince" builds upon this pattern of asserting that he is not overly concerned with hits or the rock star's lifestyle. Prince has been more concerned with what impact his music makes and his growth as an artist.

"My Name is Prince. ☬ don't wanna be king. ☬'ve seen the top, and it's just a dream. Big cars and women and fancy clothes may save your face, but they won't save your soul. ☬'m here to tell u that there's a better way. Would our Lord be happy if He came 2day?"

The song ends with what seems to be a simple, catchy dig at Michael Jackson, regarded as "The King of Pop." But in the context of this album, Prince seems to be alluding to a deeper process one must undergo to achieve a deeper sense of fulfillment. "U must become a Prince before u're a King." There is a process that we all must endure or undergo to be remade or reborn. True identity is the identity that comes through experience. No one can appoint themselves anything. Prince gets his name from his father's band, The Prince Rogers Trio. So, in many ways, Prince's journey has been the journey of his father. At this point, Prince wants to embark on his own journey, turning away from the expectations of his father and the expectations of the music industry. In a 1996 interview with Bryant Gumbel, ☥ stated that he saw himself not only a slave to Warner Bros, but a slave to the prescribed notion of being a recording artist. He wants to escape from the slavery of the system, which, up to this point, he has been a part of that perpetuation.

"Sexy MF" follows and is, on the surface, a raunchy, sexy, funk jam about physical attraction. However, it is, underneath, the initial physical attraction that the protagonist has toward the Princess. The song shows physical beauty as a manifestation of one's innate, inner characteristics. Although Prince is declaring the Princess to be a "Sexy Muthafucker" in his most dogmatic tone, he is clearly trying to find a deeper connection with his new found mate. "In a word or 2, it's u ☬ wanna do, no, not your body, but your mind..." The song is about the endeavor to find true sexuality, which is sexual attraction from the interior, not the exterior, which allows humanity to cultivate a deeper relationship. "We need 2 talk about things. Tell me what u eat. ☮ might cook for u." The mate for which Prince is searching must be complete on the inside as well as on the outside, "When it comes 2 life 2 be this man's wife—U got 2 be well educated on the subject of fights; ☮ mean the prevention of. In other words—the R.E.A.L. meaning of this thing called love. Are u up on this?"

"Love 2 the 9's" continues this theme as a proposal to take the relationship to the limits of the body and soul. He wants more than the physical. He wants the complete union of male and female, which makes them something more than what they are as individuals. He wants to be loved "2 the 9's." He begins by questioning the female's emotional depth. He wants to know the depth of her emotional waters and how in touch with them is she. "U say that u love me like a river. A river u say that'll never run dry. ☮'d rather hear u say 4ever. Instead of smilin' ☮'d rather see u cry." He is questioning her ability to be touched by emotion and feel the same if not greater stimulation of the soul as found in the body. In order to achieve this, the emotions must be communicated openly and honestly. There is no positive end to the poker face game of love or in the deception of emotions to gain love. "...u should have played an Ace. Instead u played the queen. u'd be better cheatin' than tryin' 2 read my mind." Love takes us to our highest point, but we cannot get there if we are dishonest or vague. Dishonesty keeps us from knowing ourselves and our mates, prohibiting our evolution. And an ambiguous communication of our emotions always leads to confusion. Once we know ourselves, the security of this allows us to be honest. Only then can we love fully, only then can we "love 2 the 9's."

"The Morning Papers" is the story of the Egyptian Princess and her American love. Prince details the problem of the age difference, the Princess being only sixteen, and the scandals of the press. It is a beautifully written song, which uses age (youth) as a metaphor for revitalization. In today's society, we frown on relationships where one party is over eighteen and the other party is under eighteen. However, prior to the 1950s, it was not uncommon for a young girl of fifteen or sixteen to be married to a much older man, often in his twenties. Because women were expected to bare several children, it was thought that they should begin young so that their strong bodies could endure the strain of birthing. Because of this, the young, female body has become the western symbol or icon for womanhood, sensuality, and sexuality. Though this notion of womanhood can be demeaning and objectifying to women, Prince is taking this image and refashioning it for his own metaphor of finding salvation through the freshness/purity of woman as well as troping and subverting this refashioned image. It is only the reporter in the "Segue" to "The Sacrifice to Victor," who gives the Princess' age. Because the reporter, played by Kirstie Alley of <u>Cheers</u>, is portrayed as a tabloid journalist willing to do or say anything for a story, we are never sure how old the Princess really is. The song only states that "He realized that she was new to love, naive in every way. Every school boy's fantasy she was, that's why he had to wait." Possibly in youth, the Princess represents the freshness of love, which allows the protagonist to find more than the physical. It allows him to find his own rebirth through woman, which has been a reoccurring theme in Prince's work.

Further, "The Morning Papers" also may be an allusion to the press' reception to the concept of this entire album. Would, as in the past, the majority of critics and reviewers fail to search for the deeper meaning of the album and simply bash it because of their own lack of knowledge or insight? Prince is commenting on the notion that seeking the complexities of a work of art is secondary to the sound-bites and catchy phrases which sell papers and magazines. "Should we ask the ones who speculate when they don't know what it's made of? Or should we ask the moonlight on your face or the raindrops in your hair? Or should we ask the man who wrote it there in the morning papers?" From his comments about the early reviews of <u>Graffiti Bridge</u>, Prince still seems to be concerned that no one is taking the time to analyze and understand the subject matter of his work. "The Morning Papers" may be another expression of that concern. It is his expression of sadness and anger that critics have not done their jobs when it comes to his work. Therefore, they will fail to comprehend the messages behind ☥, failing to recognize the declaration of love and the theme of its journey narrative.

"7" is the climax of the story. It discusses the chaotic journey to find oneself, which, in many cases, never ends. What we do know is that this journey is as much internal as it is external, becoming another <u>Odyssey</u>-like tale. The murderers who represent the seven deadly sins must be killed so that mankind may evolve. All individuals must pull back their external layers, their external lives, to find the essence of who they are. This whole journey has the same feel of Jean Toomer traveling to the South to get in touch with his black heritage. Prince is, in some sense, coming to terms with himself and his evolution; yet, he is also very willing to leave open as many doors as are closed. There, then, is a notion that the search for self never ends because the evolution of self never ends. The best for which we can hope is that we are able to remove those people and things in our lives that hinder our growth.

> "All 7 and we'll watch them fall. They stand in the way of love, and we will smoke them all with an intellect and a savoir-faire. No one in the whole universe will ever compare. ☙ am yours and u are mine. And 2gether we will stand through all space and time—one day all 7 will die."

In conquering the seven deadly sins, Prince, his female companion, and the New Power Generation will be reborn as new creatures. "And we will see a plague and a river of blood. And every evil soul will surely die in spite of their 7 tears—but do not fear. 4 in a distance 12 souls from now, u and me will still be here." The lyric is biblical as he alludes to a new spirit world, which sounds very much like new Jerusalem in its description, "There will be a new city with streets of Gold. And there will be no death 4 with every breath, the voice of many colors sings a song that's so bold. Sing it while we watch them fall." "7" is an allegory of man's need to find his true self by shedding the physical. In the promotional video for the song, Prince kills seven of his former personas as a way of shedding the old to take on the new.

"And God Created Woman" continues the theme of evolution, showing the male-female relationship as the nucleus or primary particle of evolution. Woman represents the yin to the male's yang, which is the completion of the higher self. Prince recounts God's creation of Eve through Adam. "In a deep sleep ♕ fell. And the music starts to swell. And one of my ribs he took, and he made flesh of my flesh, bone of my bone. And God created woman." By beginning with the creation, he is showing that the union of man and woman is natural, ordained by God, and essential in the search for higher existence. "And we were naked and did not care. There's a time 2 take and a time 2 share. 2 in love, all around and all aware..." From there, Prince moves to assert that the battle of the sexes or the separation of man from woman is a plan of evil: "Temptation sweet and so much...Many serpents who have lied." But we are affirmed that we have the power over the serpents. "Temptations...surely die if neither one of us shall ye touch." Still, he warns that yielding to the temptation that separates man from woman is death: "Then again we could die from the rush." In the end, Prince proclaims that nothing on Earth can break the bond of male and female. "And if ♕ never see u again, it's alright. ♕ am guilty of no sin. They can have u but ♕'ll have your soul in the end, Soul of my soul." Relationships are the saving grace of the physical world because it is through relationships that we can shape, strengthen, and recycle ourselves.

"Three Chains of Gold" represents the climax of the evolution to a higher being. The Princess' father is murdered by the seven men to capture the three chains of gold, which when placed together form ⚜. The Chains symbolize an inner strength gained from the knowledge of identity, which is derived from a meticulous search. Whoever holds the chains becomes ruler of the throne because he possesses the secrets to transcending the physical plane. The murders symbolize a society that has equated evolution with material gain and has strayed from the path of metaphysical enlightenment. This story is coupled with the plot of two lovers attempting to make their connection to find their higher place. "We both do nothing and call it love. Is this love?" By the end, the lovers have different paths. So the suffering of the heart is coupled with the suffering of the soul. ⚜ begins this tale by showing that one can overcome suffering and pain by not focusing on the physical and keeping one's focus on a higher meaning. "If 👁 don't see the pearls fall from the sky, If 👁 don't hear the accusations of blasphemy...This is the best day of my life." Often our physical knowledge of life is what limits our evolution. As he states on the <u>Rave Un2 the Year 2000</u> DVD, "Time is a trick" because man's time and reality do not correspond to God's time and reality. Thus, the seeing and hearing of physical negativity symbolize how we are limited or tricked into believing in the limits of our physical abilities. It is not the falling or the "accusations of blasphemy" that are damaging, but it is the knowing of them or acknowledging of them that is damaging. It is the equivalent of an artist who spends too much time listening to negative or even positive criticism. He must learn to close his ears and eyes to the physical voices and follow the metaphysical voices. Often, we are required to take a leap of blind faith, relying on the metaphysical voice to guide us to our destiny. The three chains of gold are symbolic of a person's essence or ideal self, which evolves, develops, or is somehow made to manifest itself through the wearing away of an outer, physical shell. Once one is made to realize or come into touch with one's "symbol" of self, which is the symbol of our innate divinity and connection with God, one is able to withstand the world and evolve to a higher life form. "👁 got three chains of gold, and they will shine 4ever...If one of us has to die, u will go before me." This evolving principle in ☥'s work seems to be based on his study of Egyptology and alchemy.

> "Alchemy was the study of purifying base metals to the point where they became gold. The alchemists believed that base metals were merely gold filled with impurities, which could be purified into pure gold forms through a process. There can be no doubt that Prince adapted the alchemists' symbol for soapstone and combined it with his older male/female symbol, creating his new name" (Dawkins, Vol. 4 Issue 22, 129).

Except for the circle at the top, the soapstone symbol is the exact same symbol for Prince's new name. ☥ assimilates the alchemists' beliefs into his own notions of how humans evolve into higher life forms. His basic belief is that "God is inside all of us," waiting on us to do something to manifest his presence in our lives. Our physical journey is the purification process through which we evolve back to our pure form, reconnecting with God.

"The Sacrifice of Victor" is the declaration of the new creature of the Dawn, ☥. It represents the spiritual notion of "My Name Is Prince." ☥ has come full circle through his adventure with the Egyptian Princess to find his own three chains of gold. It is interesting that Prince sets the rebirth of his character in Egypt (Africa), the mother of civilization. In "The Sacrifice of Victor," ☥ discusses the struggle and search for identity and victory of an individual and a race. Through the use of an extended metaphor, he is able to deal with the dual struggle for identity by the African American race and by African American individuals. This notion of the dichotomy and the struggle between the collective (community) and the individual is at the core of African and African American literature as evidenced by writers, such as Chinua Achebe, Adelaide Casely-Hayford, Toomer, and Ellison. ♀ builds on this tradition while interjecting his personal story, which is signifying at one of its highest levels. By doing this he creates a call and response technique: the ancestral call and his individual response. This expands and shifts his persona from the separated, isolated individual to being seen more as an amalgamated entity. Ironically, this shift reconnects him to his refashioned, fictionalized mutt (mulatto) persona created for <u>Dirty Mind</u>. In "The Sacrifice of Victor," ♀ shows that the key to evolution is coming to terms with one's identity, which means to come to terms with one's ancient and antecedent lives and understand that an individual is a collective singular. This is what ya Salaam means when he asserts, in his poem, "My Name Is Kalamu," "I am African-Diaspora, I am ancient and new" (Salaam 21). In this, ♀ pulls the universal from the particular by showing that the world is populated with mutts who are all looking for a home. Before these mutts can find a home, they need to find an identity. Identity is the key to survival and evolution because it provides roots to withstand the winds of life and a history, which provides a blueprint for evolution. In returning to his past and his history, ♀ can now evolve.

Along with returning to Egypt, ♀ returns to the church, the root of the Civil Rights Movement and the root of popular music. Coming home to Africa, coming home to the church, ♀ is ready to announce his new identity and proclaim his victory in his reincarnation. "Church, if u will, please turn 2 the book of Victor." The first verse is written in the first person "I" but is obviously a metaphor for the historical oppression of the individual and the African American race. "☕ was born on a blood stained table, cord wrapped around my neck. Epileptic 'til the age of seven. ☯ was sure Heaven marked the deck." An epileptic seizure is when one loses control of one's mind and bodily functions. The epilepsy of the child represents the state of African slaves, who had no control over their minds or their bodies until they were able to mature as citizens and be recognized as humans. The cord around the neck symbolizes the oppression and arrested development of African beings in America; it is literally a lynching metaphor. From there, he begins to build metaphors on top of metaphors until the allegory is completed. The most prominent image is a mother protecting her child from child abuse, which alludes to his own troubled childhood as well as the arrested development of African American children. The second major image is school bussing, which brought false integration and did very little to develop the African American community. Then after firmly blending the individual and collective images, he is back to the objective but more journalistic observer "I" with "Never understood my old friends laughing, they got high when everything got wrong. Dr. King was killed, and the streets started burning. When the smoke cleared, their high was gone." After the social and historical commentary from the objective observer, ☥ moves into the realm of the personal "I", acknowledging a Bernadette (who is possibly Bernadette Anderson, the woman with whom he lived through his high school years and the mother of his first bassist, Andre' Cymone). "Bernadette, the lady, she told me, 'Whatever u do son, a little discipline is all u need.'" By mentioning the role of Bernadette, Prince is paying homage to the tradition of the extended family, which is also a trait of African American survival against slavery and urbanization. Finally, ☥, after having acknowledged his history, turns to his future. "My feet might get tired, but ☯'m gonna keep on walkin' down this road, and when ☯ reach my destination...That's when my name will be Victor, Amen." Even in acknowledging his future, he uses the language and tone of the past—of the Negro spirituals. Again, this shows that our futures are guided by our past.

Thus, our identity, knowing who we are by knowing from where we come, is the rock and compass that sustains and guides us.

"The Sacrifice of Victor" weaves in and out of personas so that the lives of ☥, the individual, and the African American race seem to merge into one persona, troping the tribe metaphor of traditional African culture. The message is clear, one who suffers unjustly for righteousness or in search of identity will be victorious, but only when he comes to understand the significance of the historical collective and individual struggle for inner peace and identity. At the end of the entire saga, Prince has become ☥, who now knows who he is, where he is going, and, above all, how he got there. This is a Prince that did not exist in the first albums. This is a Prince rooted in history and tradition, specifically the African American musical tradition. Prince, as ☥, embraces and develops new sensibilities. Along with his spiritual awareness, ☥ becomes more racially conscious. Where Prince had been prophesying about the Dawn, ☥ has found his Dawn. In this analogy, ☥ serves as Prince, a coming out record by ☥. Where we had Prince by Prince, we now have ☥ by ☥, which represents the journey of Prince to ☥.

The Gold Experience

It is difficult to discuss The Gold Experience (1994) since I know that there are some who will be using a different text or set of songs than I will be using. The Gold Experience that was released to the public on September 26, 1995 includes only twelve songs. It is my contention that The Gold Experience originally included nineteen, possibly twenty or more songs. Due to the long, drawn out fight/process to get it released in a manner that would please the various parties involved, by the time it was released for public sale, it had been negotiated and edited to twelve songs. We know by Allen Light's August 1994 article for Vibe that the album was finished and "in the hands of mangers and lawyers and Warner Bros Records as they negotiate how or if *all* this music will be released" (Light 46). To understand, we must go back in order to come forward. So let us begin with what we know. We know that in the fall of 1991 Prince released Diamonds and Pearls.

There is a notion that Diamonds and Pearls has much the same intent as Prince, Prince's second album. It is an album made by Prince with a conscious attempt to prove that he still had the ability to produce hits and that he can funk, roll, and soul with the best of them. In fact, in an appearance on the Arsenio Hall Show a few weeks before the release date of Diamonds and Pearls, Prince mouths the words, "What ever you want!" after the final performance, "Daddy Pop," which is a funk workout that combines and culminates with a rap. The song proclaims Prince to be the Daddy Pop of popular music, citing that he has a musical "list as long as history itself." And even though the album did well, producing top ten singles, Prince did not prove anything that the industry or listeners did not already know. He was already credited with being one of the greatest entertainers and songwriters of all time. No one, critic or otherwise, has ever questioned his song writing ability or musical talents. Diamonds and Pearls is perceived as a very polished album by a talented musician doing everything that he does best. Even though the maturity and depth of his artistry are clearly illustrated, the album fails to push, challenge, or break new ground in the manner of his past albums. It is not that Prince was attempting to reproduce that past music, but it was and is his goal to push himself and his listeners by staying on the edge of what is new, exciting, and innovating in the field, both musically and lyrically.

Accepting this notion of having to remain on the cutting edge can be a trap. When one gains acclaim for being an innovator, it is also easy for one to become lost in the shuffle when the rest of the pack catches up or pulls even with you. One is often fighting a constant battle where just producing well-crafted work is not enough. <u>Diamonds and Pearls</u> is well crafted, and it is innovative, but only in Prince's already, well established ability to blend sounds like few before him. It does not prove, establish, define, or redefine anything, so Prince is viewed as not living up to his ability or past. This is often the central flaw in popular culture. The newness of something is just as important as the quality of it. Often, the newness of something can overshadow the quality of it. Prince is still creating well-crafted work, but now he and his ideas are no longer considered new, hip, or cutting edge. This is the largest obstacle to overcome, especially when it is perceived by the new, younger buying public that you have thumbed your nose at and distanced yourself from the new generation. Popular music is based on popularity, which is equated with the amount of one's record sales. Record sales are determined by one's ability to speak to and echo the sounds and concerns of the current buying public. Though there are many socio-political factors, aspects, and elements which contribute to one's record sales, the bottom line is still the amount of sales. There are very few articles in <u>Vibe</u> or <u>Rolling Stone</u> about visionary artists who do not sell records. <u>Vibe</u> and <u>Rolling Stone</u> must sell issues to survive, just as record companies must sell units to survive.

Though Prince moved units with <u>Diamonds and Pearls</u>, it was not the amount of <u>Purple Rain</u>, so he had become old news, playing second fiddle to the artists at the top of the charts.

After <u>Diamonds and Pearls</u> Prince began to dig deeper and explore who he is becoming. However, it is a bit difficult to grapple with whom you are as a well established, financially secure, critically acclaimed songwriter. According to Richard Wright in <u>Black Boy</u>, physical hunger is what drives the artistic hunger. In most cases, once an artist has satisfied his physical hunger, it becomes difficult to maintain that level of intensity toward his art. As Prince stated in a 1981 interview, "Poverty taught me that I had to work" (Mitchell 1981). Often, as with the case of Prince, after a certain amount of success one becomes more absorbed with the aesthetics of the work in contrast with how the art represents a particular group of society. Individual success increases the risk of creating art that may be soulful but fails to connect to a larger audience. The result of Prince's searching after <u>Diamonds and Pearls</u> is ⚥ (1992). The ⚥ album represents the soul searching of an artist grappling with what it means to have "made it" as an artist. We must understand that no one actually remembers becoming thirty or remembers becoming top dog. We all somewhat wake up one morning and say, "Damn, I'm thirty." From top to bottom, ⚥ is some of Prince's most complex and challenging music to that point. It is all over the musical and lyrical spectrum. It is everywhere but the center. And that remains the problem. The truth is that to make kids think, you must capture their attention. That usually means making them dance. ⚥ is a very engaging, inquisitive, and challenging record on an aesthetic/artistic level. But, it remains too complex, abstract, and above tangible issues. It is too ambitious and becomes ambiguous to kids who want to dance. The record succeeds in being a thesis by a legend on how to amalgamate musical history, personal history, and the current musical trends into one sound. It is a school lesson and not a funk jam. It is a formal discourse and not a voice petitioning. It may be too conscious of itself. Thus, there becomes a sense that Prince has gone as far as he can with the public. Truthfully, Prince's conversation/dialogue has never been directly with his listeners. It is with himself and his higher power. The audience is just eavesdropping on the work in progress. By 1992, Prince had reconciled himself to sex and its uses, to himself, to society, to God as he understood it all, and ascended to the heavens of artistic aesthetics and critical theory. As he, himself, indicates, "Prince did retire. He stopped making records because he didn't need to anymore. It's fun to draw a line in the sand and say, 'Things change here'" (Light 47). The 1993 release of <u>The Hits 1 and 2: The B-Sides</u> is evidence of this line drawn in the sand. Here is a greatest hits package from an artist who has created a career by never looking back and always driving forward. Even the four new songs included on <u>The Hits</u> are, for all practical purposes, the last of Prince songs that do not deserve to be confined to the vault, but they do nothing to expand or evolve his artistic career. The searching was over; Prince had become what he had so long been grappling toward, a person at peace with himself, his life, his art, and his surroundings.

June 7, 1993, the word comes that Prince has changed his name to an unpronounceable symbol, ⚤. The official explanation appears at the end of the video collection <u>Three Chains of Gold</u> and reads:

> "Epilogue. Upon the seventh day of the sixth month, Nineteen hundred and ninety-three, Marking the beginning and ending of cycles of creation, Prince, reaching the balance of thirty-five years, put into practice the precepts of perfection: Voicing bliss through the freedom of being one's self, Incarnating the New Power Generation into six periods of evolution, giving Birth upon himself to regenerate his name as ⚤. For in the dawn, all will require no speakable name to differentiate the

ineffable one that shall remain."

He further elaborates to Light in the August, 1994, interview for <u>Vibe</u> magazine:

> "'I followed the advice of my spirit.'...it is the age-old questions of naming and identity...born Prince Rogers Nelson [he] goes on to explain, 'I'm not the son of Nell. I don't know who that is, 'Nell's son,' and that's my last name. I asked Gilbert Davidson [His manager at the time and former president of NPG Records] if he knew who David was, and he didn't even know what I was talking about. I started thinking about that, and I would wake up nights thinking, Who am I? What am I?' But it essentially came down to the music" (47).

Prince/♀ finds a way to continue. He finds something deep within him that drives him to continue. And that is all the explanation most of us need. He found a way to continue to push himself and his listeners. Maybe he decided that he is not "there" yet. Maybe he has decided to engage the questions of the next generation. Whatever the reason, he has found a way to make songs that take risks. Yet, from this point things begin to run together and get blurred. Most popular music critics, such as Kurt Loder, suggest that the name change is just another gimmick to boost a failing career. Some speculate that the name change is a tactical move to give himself leverage to release music during his dispute with Warner Bros. And some choose to take him at his word that the name change comes from a continuous search for identity, spirituality, and artistic creativity. Whatever the reason, six or seven months after the name change, ♀ begins to appear at impromptu gigs with new music representing his new self. The 1993 European tour for the ♀ album would mark the end of ♀ relying on his past songs as safe havens in concerts or simply resting on the success of those songs.

Since the name change we have received nine albums: Come, 1-800NEWFUNK, The Gold Experience, Chaos and Disorder, Emancipation, Crystal Ball, New Power Soul, The Vault, and Rave Un2 the Joy Fantastic. We know, however, that at least ninety-five percent of the music which appears on Come and Gold can be accounted for by August/September 1993. And we know that ⚥ was in a rush to get his new music to the public. What we do not know is if all twenty plus songs were to be on one album, or if there should have been two albums that were to be released as companion pieces. We do know, by Light's article, that two songs, "Days 'O' Wild" and "Ripopgodazippa," were on The Gold Experience in May of 1994, over a year before its release, but are not on the version released in September of 1995. We also know that ⚥ appeared on Soul Train in the spring of 1994 and performed what was deemed "four new experiences," which included "Acknowledge Me" and "Love Sign," neither of which appears on the publicly released version of The Gold Experience. There is a vague indication by ⚥, himself, that the album would not reach the public in its original, unedited state as he says to Light, "'We have a new album finished,' he says conspiratorially, 'but Warner Bros doesn't know it yet...'" (Light 47). Also, a film short, The Beautiful Experience, which has the same concept of experiencing human emotion and thought through interaction with a computer as The Gold Experience, gives us some sense of what was meant to be on The Gold Experience. The other songs, which do not deal necessarily or directly with the interactive concept, may have been meant to be included on an EP which could possibly be a footnote or introduction to The Gold Experience entitled Come. If we follow this analogy, we have the following collections:

The Come EP, which should have included only "Come," "Space," "Pheromone," "Race," "Dark," "Solo" and "Letitgo," and the double CD of The Gold Experience should have included (Please note that order is equally important): "Interactive," "Endorphinmachine," "P Control," "Acknowledge Me," "Shhh," "We March," "Love Sign," "Hide the Bone," "The Most Beautiful Girl in the World," "319," "Days 'O' Wild," "Now," "Loose/Papa," "Ripopgodazippa," "Shy," "Billy Jack Bitch," "☮ Hate U," "Dolphin," and "Gold."

The <u>Come</u> EP is dark, stoic and serves to end Prince's career and introduce ☥'s career. The album credit is given to "Prince 1958-1993." The essential songs to the EP's concept are "Come," "Solo," and "Letitgo." The "Come" that appears on the EP is a more jazz/funk arrangement that receives a looser, more ambiguous, sexual treatment than the "Come" that appears on the film short, <u>The Beautiful Experience</u>. The "Come" single of <u>The Beautiful Experience</u> is more literal and direct about the "dawning of a new spiritual revolution." Yet, those who are familiar with the latter can still hear the tracings of spirituality, the cross the line to a better life, in the former, especially when coupled with "Space," which follows "Come" on the EP. Conversely, there are two songs for "Space": "Space," the single which focuses more on physical relationships, and "Space," the "Universal Love" mix that focuses more on the spiritual connection of the male-female relationship. Unfortunately, the ambiguity of the lyrics obscures the message of the songs. However, "Come" and "Space" are able to act as exposition pieces to clarify his new direction. "Come" is an invitation on two levels. First, ☥ is inviting the listener to cross the line separating the physical from the metaphysical. Remember, Prince is dead as indicated by the cover of the <u>Come</u> CD. So, he has crossed the line to ☥, and he is inviting his audience to join him. He is building upon Funkadelic's notion that if you free your mind, your ass will follow. Secondly, once you come to the spirit world, you will "cum"—meaning you will experience a spiritual orgasmic epiphany/revelation, which will lead to a revolution, liberating your mind from physical limitation. "Space," then, comments on what physically happens when we cross the line. It begins in the physical with the romantic relationship and shows that love, romantic or platonic, is the catalysis that propels us toward evolution. We are put on this Earth to love; it is the thing that helps us transcend the space between the physical and the spiritual.

"Solo," which finds a home as a bridge between "Come/Space" and "Letitgo," is a song articulating sorrow, disillusionment, melancholy, and despair. It seems that Prince has reached a point of emotional dead-ends: no way up and no way out. He states that he is "Solo my name is no mo'." In "Solo" there is a concession to death, waiting for the angels that sing overhead. The human being can no longer continue as Prince. He has transcended that identity, which encases him and prohibits his growth. He feels trapped by the <u>Purple Rain</u> phenomenon that everyone, listeners and Warner Bros, is stuck on hearing and remembering. Prince has become a shell that ☥ must remove if he is to survive and evolve. And if "Solo" is death, "Letitgo" is the rebirth. As a confident soul, Prince/☥ declares a new attitude on life. Accordingly, "Letitgo" was promoted as the song which answers the questions concerning the name change and future plans. The song does not address either specifically, but it does allude to the ongoing problems with Warner Bros and his new attitude toward life. "Letitgo" addresses how he has been a closed shell, especially in relation to his frustrations with the business aspect of the music industry, and now the time has come to let it all go.

> "Ready or not, here I come. All my life I've kept my feelings deep inside; never was a reason 2 let somebody know...Until now all I wanted 2 do is do what I do, and bang on the drummer and love so-and-so. But now I've got 2 letitgo. Lay back and let the vibe just flow. I wanna just letitgo. Lay back and let my feelings show. I'm ready 4 the real. Give me something I can feel. 4teen years and tears I've longed 2 sing my song, but a horse

couldn't drag your ass 2 put me on. But now I've got an army, and we're three million strong. This song will ring in your ears when we are gone"

When he is asserting that he is going to let it go, does he mean his emotions, his image, or Warner Bros? It would seem that he would mean Warner Bros because he has always been open and honest in his lyrics. Yet he could be possibly indicating another direction lyrically. In 1987 with the signing of Clinton and Staples to Paisley Park and the 1990 edition of three African American male dancers, Prince becomes a more tangibly issue oriented writer. His songs become more conscious of his situation of being an African American.

The first New Power Generation album in 1992, entitled <u>Gold Nigga</u>, has some very powerful messages of race in America, including "Black M. F. in the House," which comically treats racial tension in the daily American existence, and "Gold Nigga," which discusses the individual gaining success, legally, and then aiding others to ascend poverty. Songs written for Tevin Campbell's second album, <u>I'm Ready</u> (1993), have some very forthright statements about being black in America, including "Paris 1798430," which discusses African Americans going to Paris to escape American oppression and to find equality, and "Uncle Sam," which addresses African Americans being treated as second class citizens even after having served in the military during times of war. The songs, "Undertaker" and "U Will Be Moved" on Mavis Staples' second Paisley Park album, <u>The Voice</u> (1993), discuss urban drug decay and racial injustice. And finally, the second New Power Generation album of 1995, entitled <u>Exodus</u>, has more candid messages about being black in America and the unfair treatment of African American artists, including "Count the Days" and "The Exodus Has Begun." Could this possibly be the new direction? For so long Prince fought for his rights as an individual. Now, possibly, he is fighting for his rights as an

African American, or at least, becoming more conscious of it. Whatever the direction, the Come EP lays the foundation for The Gold Experience.

I must admit that I am not completely comfortable about taking liberties (modifying/changing) a work of art that an artist has released for public consumption. But, I do not believe that the version of The Gold Experience that was released in September of 1995 is the complete work. We must look at the whole work on its own terms to correctly assess it, especially considering that this was to be ☥'s coming out work, marking his new direction much like Dirty Mind was for Prince. As evidence, "His album covers used to include the phrase 'May U live 2 see the dawn.' The Gold Experience opens with the words 'Welcome to the dawn'" (Light 50). To remove four songs, "Interactive," "Acknowledge Me," "Days 'O' Wild," and "Love Sign," destroys the cohesiveness of the work. It also keeps the listener from knowing primary experiences that speak directly to the core of The Gold Experience. For those without the additional seven songs, I will attempt to compensate their experience.

"Interactive" is the introduction piece. We live in a time of the Internet and a shrinking world because of the immediate access of data and communications. "Interactive" is posing that we go one step further, even further than virtual reality. We should go online with ourselves, our identities, our emotions, and our thoughts; then we will be able to interact in a manner of creating a homogeneous, universal space of experience. "Interactive" recontextualizes the older premise of Dirty Mind and Controversy. In these two albums Prince is using sex and sexuality to break through the arbitrary, physical walls of oppression based on gender, race, and class. Now, ☥ is doing the same with the Internet. The walls of the physical world will be dissolved by the technology of the Internet, making us all hybrid souls. We will be able to experience each other in and through the purity of our souls.

"Endorphinmachine" follows as it gives the description of the vehicle that will be used to go online and access the experiences, and it explains all of the experiences available to the user. It embodies the philosophy of the album as ☥ states, "☥'m looking for logic in a think tank." The endorphinmachine is for those looking for more than the physical from life. The endorphinmachine is designed to take you higher, as the man asserts, "Every now and then, there comes a time when you have to defend your right to live and die again." Each new experience is a new life. So by seeking a vast array of experiences, we are seeking new lives to live, which cause us to evolve.

Once we are introduced to the concept as well as to the vehicle that will allow us to experience the concept, we begin our experience. "P Control" is a suitable opening experience if we consider the legacy of Prince's work. Throughout his career Prince is very concerned about the attempt to gain power through sex in many of his early songs, such as "Automatic," "Lady Cab Driver," "Sexuality," "Little Red Corvette," and others. "P Control" celebrates the power of women through their sexuality. No, it is not a song that feminists will like, but it does address the very real issue of sex as power. In his own way, ☥ is giving props to women who know how to use their "P control" and use a male's own sexism and lust against him. The song presents three females who take advantage of men whose actions are controlled by their sexual desires. But more specifically, it celebrates females are able to be disciplined and not fall into the stereotypical trap of being mere objects and pawns for male pleasure.

> "Pussy got bank in her pockets before she got dick in her drawers. If brother didn't have good and plenty of his own in love Pussy never did fall. And this fool named Trick wanna stick her, talkin' more Schick than a Bic 'bout how he gonna make Pussy a star if she come and sing a lick on his hit. Pussy said 'Nigga, U crazy if U don't know every woman

in the world ain't a freak. U can go platinum 4 times [and] still couldn't make what ♕ make in a week. So push up on somebody wanna hear that cuz this somebody here don't wanna know.'"

He even admonishes the females who fall into the trap and then try to pressure other females to lower themselves to being merely objects of male pleasure. But he has his female protagonist stand firm and overcome their pressure. "And step she did 2 the straight A's, then college, the master degree. She hired the heifers that jumped her and made everyone of them work 4 free? 'So what if my sisters are triflin'? They just don't know.' She said 'Mama didn't tell 'em what she told me, 'Girl, U need Pussy Control.'" He ends by sending a message to males who are unable to handle this type of woman, "Don't u even think about calling her no ho', u juvenile delinquent." By doing this, ⚥ is making a statement about the gender double standard as well as showing how this standard ultimately hurts or limits men from obtaining or achieving their full potential as humans by not viewing women as equals. <u>The Gold Experience</u> is about the journey to evolve. Sexuality is still a door through which we need to walk, a hurdle that we need to climb. It is our most immediate and tangible issue, which must be continuously addressed, to demolish the walls keeping us from our spiritual selves. "P Control" is forcing us to address our sexual hypocrisy, which keeps us from evolving. The album then proceeds to explore various other emotions and experiences.

Most of the songs are companion pieces that are either opposites or supplementary. These are "Interactive" and "Endorphinmachine," "We March" and "Love Sign," "The Most Beautiful Girl in the World" and "319," and "Days of Wild" and "Now." Where "We March" is political, "Love Sign" is social. Where "The Most Beautiful Girl in the World" is about inner beauty, love, and commitment, "319" is about physical beauty, lust, and illicit sex. They are both centered on the question of commitment. In "319" we are given great sex that leaves us empty, and "The Most Beautiful Girl in the World" fills our void by asserting that beauty begins with a person's soul/character, which is why love is more fulfilling than sex. And, where "Days 'O' Wild" is the social, "Now" is the individual. In both cases, the individual is fighting not to be smothered by society's arbitrary rules. "Now" might be a rap, but it expresses the same rebellious spirit of <u>Dirty Mind</u>.

> "Tennis shoes and caps, now that's phat up until the day another wanna laugh behind your back, sayin' we all look the same. God bless America, home of the brave. ☮'d rather dress 2 make a woman stare. ☮'m puttin' on somethin' that another won't dare. It's a freezer burn compared 2 cool. If U still got loot, then who's the fool? Everybody wanna take the stand. Mind your own motherfucker; let a man be a man. ☮'ma tear shit up y'all; that's my style. These are the days of wild."

The juxtaposition of each companion piece causes the meaning of each song to be more clearly illuminated to the listener.

"We March" enters into a new realm, political organizing and action. About one week or so before the Million Man March on Washington, D.C., organized by Nation of Islam leader, Louis Farrakhan, former NAACP leader, Benjamin Chavis, and educator/philosopher, Cornell West, and held on October 16, 1995, ☥ sent to them "We March" to be used for the March. "...the Artist Formerly Known As Prince sent to us a tape of a song on his latest album, and it is about marching" (Farrakhan 1995). "We March" goes further than the abstract individual/social themes of the past. Now, ☥ is urging the individual to get involved in tangible social and political activities and organizing to affect specific political change. "If we want a change, then come on get in line the next time we march."

He is stepping outside his own Paisley, New Breed world and advocating involvement with and in other social and political organizations. ☥ is dealing with specific issues, such as opportunities for financial and community development as well as assuming personal responsibility for the betterment of the race and advocating for change in the attitudes and actions toward women. "We March" is drawn along different lines than "Uptown," "Party Up," "Sexuality," or even "New Power Generation." Where they voice anger at intolerance, they are still structured on Prince's utopian, Uptown ideology of a multiracial, androgynous existence, and stop short of attacking, in any real sense, white supremacy or the marginalization of African Americans. "We March" is speaking specifically to the needs, angers, and pains of African Americans. "If this is the block my people fought so hard 2 liberate, how come 👑 can't buy a piece of it even when my credit's straight?" Unlike the Prince of <u>Dirty Mind</u> and <u>Controversy</u>, ☥ is calling for both political action and retaliation, which moves beyond love or sex as the answer. "Now we clarify 4ever, in other words, as long as it takes. We got no use 4 ice cream without the cake, and we got no time 4 excuses. The promised land belongs 2 all. We can March in peace, but u best watch your back if another leader falls."

After addressing the collective, ☥ moves to the individual. "Loose/Papa," I have grouped as one experience. Both songs create a commentary on how the childhood affects the adult. In "Loose," we are given an individual who is condemned for being wild, loose, and non-conforming. "Everybody wants 2 know what's wrong with u. They say u acting like a crazy fool." In "Papa," we are given the events that may have led to the individual's behavior in "Loose." The child of "Papa" is abused by being beaten and placed in a dark closet by his father. Eventually, the father goes into a tirade and shoots himself. The child is left scarred for life as he adds, "Don't abuse children, or they'll end up like me." The child in "Papa" is the adult in "Loose." It is the ID/SUPEREGO experience. The individual in this experience has not developed an EGO to balance the ID/SUPEREGO. He floats from one extreme to the other because of his dysfunctional upbringing. Here, ⚥ is expanding what he began in "Sexuality." "Mamas don't let your babies watch television before they know how to read, or all they'll know how to do is cus, fight and breed...They only imitate their atmosphere." For years, ⚥ has been a consistent supporter of funding the educational needs of children, donating on a regular basis to the famed Marvin Collins School in Chicago. Through "Loose/Papa," he is asserting that a society gets what it deserves when it poorly invests in, poorly educates, or poorly protects its children. The real fear is that the child in "Papa" has become a man in "Loose," and he seems bent on releasing his anger on society. This is his warning when he asserts, "Don't abuse children, or they'll end up like me." If society does not solve the problem in "Loose/Papa," it will be unable to develop the individuals that it needs to complete the revolution in "We March."

Continuing to address the issues of the dysfunctional individual, "👁 Hate U" is "The Beautiful Experience" turned inside out. In this experience hate is not in opposition to love. Hate is love—mutated and changed through the experience of rejection/deception. It is a new interpretation of there being a thin line between love and hate. This hate is not to be seen as a separate and opposite emotion. This hate is to be seen as an organic characteristic of love that, because of something gone wrong, will grow from love: "👁 hate u so much, 👁 wanna make love until u see..." The hate generated is dependent upon the perversion of love. Or, hate is seen as the mold that grows from decaying love. "👁 hate u like a day without sunshine. 👁 hate u, 'cause u're all that's on my mind." It has a mutated or perverted courtly love attitude or tone because pleasure and pain seem to be amalgamated into a new type of surreal experience. It has a bitterness that is dulled by its agony as in Dante's "Because You Know You're Young in Beauty Yet" where the male protagonist continuously swings the emotional pendulum throughout the piece. If sex can be used as a tool for domination and control, then hate can surely be seen as a perversion of love. What is most interesting is that "The Hate Experience" is the only experience that the user of the endorphinmachine has to affirm that this is the experience that he is attempting to gain. After the user selects "The Hate Experience," he is asked if he is sure that this is where he wants to be and is prompted to reenter his choice. Are we being made to ask if there are some experiences better left alone, or are we merely being forced to ponder or analyze the logic and earnestness of our emotions? Can you truly hate someone whom you love, or is this merely more of the manifestation of ill will from a society not in touch with its emotions because it is unable to properly articulate what its emotions are?

"Billy Jack Bitch" regains a balance between emotion and reason that "👁 Hate U" does not have. Where "👁 Hate U" throws reason to the wind and submerges itself in blind passion, "Billy Jack Bitch" attempts to examine and defuse negative emotionalism through inquisitive discourse. Reportedly, this song is directed toward Cheryl Johnson, a.k.a. CJ, a columnist in Minneapolis who has not only written several negative reviews about ☥'s work but has continuously engaged in personal attacks, calling him names such as "Symbelena." In his response to her, the artist we find here is more mature, mellow, and level-headed than the Prince of old, which accounts for the keen poetics. Rather than returning negative with negative, he involves himself in a civil discourse, attempting to show or question how anyone expects to get positive from someone if they treat them in a negative manner.

"What if 👁 called u silly names, just like the ones that u called me? What if 👁 filled your 👁s with tears, so many that u could not see? What if 👁 told u that u were only half of what u feel. Would u come forth and tell no lies? Would u come and talk 2 me?"

"Billy Jack Bitch" is not cued as a single or prompted experience like the other songs, but it continues to speak to subjects common throughout the overall experience of the album. If it is the experience of anger or frustration, the lyrics are so thoughtful and eloquent that the tone becomes non-confrontational. Instead of fighting fire with fire by attacking CJ, the song is as a yearning to communicate. It is "Dirty Mind" and "Controversy" without the edge of anger. That youthful anger is now replaced by the tone of inner peace, which provides the ability to live life on one's own terms and deal with the ramifications. And since he is at peace, he can have peaceful discourse, even with those who engage him with negativity.

"Dolphin" is the experience of soul captivity and transformation. It is certainly directed at Warner Bros. "How beautiful do the words have 2 be before they conquer every heart? How will u know if ☝'m even in the right key, if u make me stop before ☝ start?" Like dolphins, the spirit of the artist can not flourish in captivity. ☥ sees himself as a slave to Warner Bros. Like many slaves, ☥ looks to death to end his slavery. He is refashioning the notion of the old Negro spiritual, "Before I'll be a slave, I'll be buried in my grave and go home." "U can cut off all my fins, but 2 your ways ☝ will not bend. ☝'ll die before ☝ let u tell me how to swim." He acknowledges the financial gains that he stands to lose, but inverts the discussion to show that humanity is losing much more by exploiting people for financial profit. "Why must my brother have 2 go hungry when u told him there was food 4 all? This is the man that stands next 2 the man that stands 2 catch u when u fall." Man, because of capitalism, has lost sight of humanity and the process of evolution. For ☥ the only answer is death, which will be the death into life. The death of his relationship with Warner Bros will bring life to his art. "If 👁 came back as a dolphin, would u listen 2 me then? Would u let me be your friend...👁'll come back again, as a dolphin." After the transformation process of "Dolphin," we are ready to seek and understand the gold, the essence of life.

"Gold" is the pinnacle. It is the realization, the epiphany, for which we have been looking throughout this experience. "Gold" represents the fruits of the search, or at least the understanding of the search. It is an acknowledgment of the struggle that must come with the victory. In fact, the experience of the search or the struggle is in many ways rewarding in itself. The mere act of moving, of trying to grow, is a success because it is, in the least, an attempt to refute or change the status quo. The song has a definite undercurrent that is very anti-contentment. It opens with a direct statement against being satisfied with mediocrity:

> "There's a Mountain, and it's mighty high. U cannot see the top unless u fly. There's a molehill of proven ground; there ain't nowhere 2 go if u hang around. Everybody wants 2 sell what's already been sold. Everybody wants 2 tell what's already been told. What's the use of money if u ain't gonna break the mold...and all that glitters ain't gold."

"Gold" ends in declaration and assertion. No, everything that glitters "ain't" gold. The shine of life is often the internal; the gold is at the center of life for which one must dig to find. Those who wish to continue to search for the true gold should be given every opportunity and not ostracized. This coincides with Prince's issues with Warner Bros. As an artist Prince wants more than the fame that comes from selling a lot of records. He has never been content with just releasing hit records that do not attempt to elevate the listener. If a record company is having philosophical issues with one of its artists, why not merely release that artist rather than hindering the artistic growth, especially when the company treats the artist as if he is a washed-up has been? "There's a lady, 99 years old. If she led a good life, heaven takes her soul. That's a theory, and if u don't want 2 know, step aside and make a way 4 those who want 2 go."

Whether or not we believe in someone else's notion of reality or not, none of us have the right to hinder another from pursuing happiness, as long as that pursuit does not infringe upon the rights of others. What needs to be made clear is that this hindering and oppression comes in many forms. Often, we can see the most obvious, such as Jim Crow laws or exploitive business practices and relationships. But, the true war for freedom is fought on a daily basis against the prevailing attitudes of the larger community. Black children are enslaved from infancy because this society limits or arrests their dreams. Black children are not taught hobbies because capitalism has perverted their perspective of life. The only dream that they have is survival, which is based or rooted in the physical or the material. They grow up attending to only one aspect of themselves, the physical, and end up with half lived, unfulfilled lives. For most black children, their notion of themselves and their blackness is defined in what they cannot do and what they cannot be. Prince is refusing to accept and submit to this lowered expectation. As he asserts to Anthony DeCurtis in a 1996 interview with Rolling Stone, "People say I'm crazy for putting slave on my face. If I can't do what I want to do, then I'm a slave. When you stop a man from dreaming, you make him a slave" (DeCurtis 61). The gold of life is the dream, is the ability to search and have hope. Black children used to be taught to shoot for the moon, for even if they missed they would be among the stars. Today, black children are taught overwhelmingly to expect the worse so as not to be disappointed. They are given a glass ceiling mentality, which keeps them from striving for their dreams. It keeps them from having dreams at all other than physical survival, which is often perverted into a lust for material things. ⚥'s fight has been to eradicate this type of mentality or thinking. He does this by challenging himself and society and by willingly taking the ramifications of going against the grain.

With The Gold Experience we begin a new chapter in the life of ⚥. And no, very few will ever be able to totally separate his new work from his past work. He should take that fact as a compliment. But we should also admire the manner in which ⚥ is attempting to challenge himself. He, publicly, is refusing to rely on his past. So he has drawn a line in the sand. I hope we can respect him for that and critique his work for where he is going, not for where he has been. He is asking a lot. He is asking that we take our art (even our so-called "popular" art) seriously, that we challenge ourselves and the artists. The Gold Experience does that. It leaves behind his past as ⚥ begins a new journey, developing and re-developing his sense of his art and who he is. The evidence is that the music is brilliant and the lyrics moving. But Warner Bros was unwilling to allow ⚥ to be all that he can be. A man succeeds most when he chooses to fail on his own terms. The editing of The Gold Experience is unfair to both ⚥ and the listener. By 1995, it was obvious that Warner Bros felt that ⚥ is not the asset that he once was. But how cruel and evil is it to send this message and, in turn, disallow him to stand or fall on his own accord. Even worse was their keeping him captive like a dog or a slave when it became obvious that they had no intention of promoting him in a manner that is constructive to his art. Yet, even in an edited form, The Gold Experience is still a solid work with excellent grooves and powerful lyrics. The songs are coherent and fully developed. The twelve songs that are left manage to maintain a cohesive feel and articulate the concept.

The Personas

At length, I discussed Prince's ability to blur gender and class roles to take on various personas, points-of-view, or even streams of consciousness in order to deliver a multitude of messages. I am convinced that this speaks directly to Prince being an African American constantly at war with a society wishing to control his identity. Every inch and second of perception is an ongoing battle between Prince, music critics and listeners, and the industry all attempting to define his identity. This also speaks to a prolific artist who deeply understands the relationship and problem of identity and success in America. As Terence Trent D'Arby related about his conversation with "symbol man" in a fall, 1995, appearance on VH1's 4 on the Floor, unlike an artist who had their first album become a major success, Prince took refuge in that by having to construct a career over several years, he was able to play with and reinvent who he was as often as he wanted. Questions of identity and mass marketability only begin to cloud Prince's career after the mega success of Purple Rain. Before Purple Rain, Prince is able to freely move in and out of various musical styles and genres at his own will. This elusive image and progressive evolution through an amalgamation of identities is not something that took place by happenstance. Prince is able to liquefy his identity by creating multiple personas and surrounding himself with a cultural rainbow of artists. The best examples of Prince creating other personas to liquefy his own image are Jamie Starr, The Time, and his use of female artists.

Of the three personas, Jamie Starr represents the most stable, definable, and identifiable persona that Prince assumes (the role of producer). Because of his vast musical talents, Prince is able to evolve into a musical machine, a one man recording company with ideas and subject matter that touch every human experience and cross every contrived category. Initially, it is Jamie Starr in whom the role of producer and manager manifests itself. Through

Jamie Starr, Prince is able to address all of the ideas in his head. Being a producer of other acts serves as a vehicle to experiment and create a diversity of sounds and concepts without the fear of over-saturating the market or being limited by public perception/prejudice. Also, this is a way for Prince to manipulate the public's need to identify with a specific icon of their cultural origin. Through Jamie Starr, Prince has hit records on both black and white charts and avoids labels which would restrict his movement. To achieve this, Prince uses real people through which to funnel his visions. The actual name "Jamie Starr" appears and reappears throughout his career but is more prevalent early with The Time and Vanity Six. In most recent times, the name of the producer is Paisley Park. In the lapses of Jamie Starr as producer, many other pseudonyms arise, generally as songwriters, such as Christopher Tracy, Joey Coco, Alexander Nevermind, Spooky Electric, and Camille. But they all serve the same goal, to allow Prince to express his eclectic styles and messages without being handicapped by his own image. Thus, Prince's ability to blend race, class, and gender roles is achieved by being able to manipulate his speaker's voice, tone, and perception.

Moving from the first person passive, sensitive male voice of his early records, which portray Prince as the victim or the seduced as in "I Wanna Be Your Lover" and "Why You Wanna Treat Me So Bad?," Prince progressed to a more active, assertive voice in "Head" and "International Lover," the rebel in "Controversy," "Sexuality," "Let's Go Crazy," and "New Power Generation," the philosopher in "Sign 'ꙮ' the Times," "Pop Life," and "Mountains," and the storyteller with moral advice in "Paisley Park," "Condition of the Heart," and "The Sacrifice of Victor." Prince's various personas and voices have allowed him to breathe life into a spectrum of ideas and emotions, forcing his listener to entertain varying perspectives on life. In the beginning, Prince is certainly thinking about as well as playing with his identity as a songwriter, an artist, and a person. However, he realizes in the end, as Dr. Frankenstein realizes, that to create a character/idea is one thing. To sustain and nurture it, while controlling it, is something altogether different. Time after time, with groups, such as The Time, Vanity Six, The Family, and even his own bands, Prince has found that it is impossible to implant his own ideas and characters in real people and use these people as his own personal vehicles of alternative expression. Yet, Jamie Starr does allow Prince the opportunity to stretch and grow as a songwriter and producer without having to reconcile his diversity to a myopic public. But in the end, even though the messages are his, someone else is the messenger. It is that messenger who has to deliver and be accountable for the message. While he is able to write about topics which the public might not have associated with his Prince image, very few are willing to be accountable for or carry someone else's message for any prolonged period of time.

The Time is a definitive example that we have of Prince exploring and grappling with who he is as an artist. On his early records, Prince deals with introverted subjects in which he muses to himself aloud. With The Time, Prince is externally musing about who he is by recreating himself as an entire band. Even though many believe, as retold in Hill's book, that The Time may have been primarily founded to pay a musical debt to Morris Day, it is obvious that The Time is an alter-ego of Prince, created to hold Prince's R&B audience while he explores other musical genres. Morris Day, the leader of The Time, admits that he believes "the whole thing was never meant to be more than a side act" (Goldberg 50). Where Prince is introverted, abstract, and whimsical, singing about social revolution through sexuality and individuality while waiting on the Armageddon to deliver us all, The Time is extroverted, realistic, and straight forward, singing about being hip and cool and identifying with a particular race of people. Where Prince is indefinable in clothing and music styles, The Time is black. In a period when Prince is attempting to explore all of his possibilities of being a rock star, The Time allows him to stay in touch with his R&B roots, write songs about partying, chasing girls, being cool, and being in love without being trapped in the genre. Unlike the coy, elusive Prince albums which need time and thought to be fully understood, The Time's first album, <u>The Time</u>, "stomped, posed, and purred...[It] became an immediate R&B smash" because it purposely spoke to the sensibilities of African American music listeners (Hill 103). The creation of The Time represents more of Baraka's "changing same"—the recontextualization of culture for the sake of survival. Yet, The Time is not the average, ordinary R&B band of the 1980s. They, like Parliament-Funkadelic, Earth, Wind, and Fire, War, Maze, and the Ohio Players before them, find a way to move beyond their slapstick, stereotypical exterior of being the coolest brothers on the corner and touch other non-physical concerns of their listeners. Their music and songs are able to expand an identity, which subverts the stereotypical images they are playing. Yes, hell yes, this is us at the pool hall, and on the corner, and at the clubs. The Time represents the cool ass hoodlum nigga that white girls fantasize about, black girls are drawn to despite their concerns, and white boys hate over their admiration. And yet these are men who are conscious of the world around them. America is forced to take The Time humorously, or it would have been forced to face the misconceptions about the dimensionally of the black race, especially if it were to accept that Prince is the driving force behind the band.

    The cool that the Time represents is a mutation of the attitude of cool, which grew from the fear of white oppression: don't talk too loudly, don't make white people angry, don't get too excited, don't make a scene, just be cool and everything will be alright. This attitude about being cool (remaining calm in adverse situations for survival) evolves from an imposed condition to a statement about being able to handle stress constructively, which is the ability to remain focused and unnerved in the face of adversity. Being cool has nothing to do with the exterior or the material. It is the interior sense of cool that Prince uses to create both his own ideology and the essence of The Time. "Cool means being able to hang with yourself. All you have to ask yourself is 'Is there anybody I'm afraid of? Is there anybody who, if I walked into a room and saw, I'd get nervous?' If not, then you're cool'" (Karlen, "Prince Talks," 58). To create this notion of cool in The Time, Prince had them watch old tapes of Muhammad Ali as a part of their training and preparation. Ali remains the embodiment of cool as the notion of self-actualization and self- determination. Moreover, Ali is the embodiment of cool in the vein of representing or being stylishly hip, *avant-garde*, or setting the pace or trends in the culture. Unfortunately, to make art safe for mass marketability, popular culture tends to make a caricature of the political culture, which is the matrix for the popular culture. In short, Morris Day is another rebel without a cause. His coolness does not have or is not rooted in some socio-political defiance. It does not have the socio-political statement or meaning of Miles Davis or Ali and is merely an empty (although entertaining) display of aesthetics. So then, this cool is open to being overly saturated with the negative connotation of cool as represented in the Gwendolyn Brooks poem, "We Real Cool." "The Pool Players. Seven at the Golden Shovel/We real cool. We/Left school. We/Lurk late. We/Strike straight. We/Sing sin. We/Thin gin. We/Jazz June. We/Die soon."

The grooves and songs about urban black life become smothered by vanity, permed hair, and the female conquest. The Time is created to sell records to black people who have been forced/seduced into a tradition of being conservative and safe, purchasing party and love songs rather than message music. This also caters to the sensibilities of whites who are the larger market. Yet, the band strikes a chord because the songs are well-constructed and because they, no matter how watered down, resonate the black tradition of style and flare, in language and in music. More than anything, it is the lyrical witticisms of Day along with the music that captures the hearts of African Americans. Signature phrases by Day allow The Time to penetrate deeply into the souls of America and present something to which black America could relate. The statement, "What time is it?" became the first signature of Day and The Time. This works on two levels. On the first level, the history of black people is to be on somebody else's time. Therefore, what little time blacks have for leisure cannot be wasted. African Americans constantly need to know "What time is it?" This is why African Americans tend to be a bit more crude and harsh when criticizing art and culture. Booing is something that does not bother African Americans because they have little time and even less money, so "this shit better be good or y'all gone hear 'bout it." Day's constant concern with time puts the band at the center of African American culture. Furthermore, in the American society of "time is money," people who want to appear important are always asking "what time is it?" or are constantly checking their watch as if they have somewhere else to be. Day's phrase satirizes this American obsession with time as well as black America's adoption of this aspect of capitalism, even when African Americans have no capital with which to be concerned. This is more of the blues aesthetic, exaggeration, which is also parody. The slaves mimicking of the masters evolves into the general habits of the race and is most evident in the black politician always arriving late and leaving early. Along with social satire, this concern with time also acts as comic relief because the audience's response to Day always checking the time is "You know he ain't got nothing to do," but he is admired because he thinks enough of himself to demand that you respect him and his time. On the B-side of "What Time Is It?" there is a mock interview between Day and some overly professional, female journalist. Of course, the plot is that Mr. Cool is going to melt her exterior and use her as another conquest. After every question, Day asks, "What time is it?" Becoming irritated after the third or fourth question, the interviewer snaps, "Why are *you* so worried about the time." Day responds, "Cause I got somewhere to go." "Where?" she replies, and Day ends, "To the top." Even if the interviewer does not think much of Day, he values himself and his time, which is an affirmation of black people and their culture. African Americans appreciate and gravitate to The Time because Day is asserting that they, their culture, is cool, is of value and merit.

Prince is working in the tradition of black dialect and style. During the interview, Day is signifying through a modified version of the dozens and the use of exaggeration to promote his music as what is new by showing how other styles are old and obsolete. Even sometimes to our detriment, African Americans have no problem adapting and changing for the sake of survival. This is one reason why African American dialect and style change so quickly. The other reason is because the powers that be need to continuously sell something. As quickly as African Americans create culture, Madison Avenue co-opts it and sells it back to them and the rest of the world, causing African Americans to create something new for themselves, which is again co-opted. But that is why black music has a perfect partnership with cooperate America. It is always changing because black people are always grappling with who they are. Day exemplifies this when he is insulted by the interviewer saying that his music has a funky beat. "I know you didn't say funk. Funk is something you can learn in school, and ain't nothing funky about being cool." The truth is that The Time was and is a funk band, recontextualized funk, but funk nonetheless. This is black music, always recontextualizing the past so that the next generation can hang its identity on it. Prince even uses The Time to take a swipe at himself, putting more distance between himself and The Time. After being asked about his style, Day replies, "See, most people were born in a birthday suit; I was born in a zoot suit." Here, Day is reaching back to stay ahead. He is sampling history to make something new. He continues. "Wait. Let me say something to all the fellas out there. Take off them blue jeans and them new wave clothes and get you some baggies (baggy dress pants with exaggerated pleats, which closely resemble the pants of a zoot suit). It's about freedom, right? Well, stay at the motel with the biggest ballroom. Cause ain't nothing like a fresh pair of baggies." And as typical of call and response, one of the members responds, "I know that's right." The comment about the "new wave clothes" is a direct statement about Prince. <u>Controversy</u> and bits of <u>1999</u> are heavily influenced by new wave, which grew from punk. Music and culture share a circular relationship. For Day to say take off new wave clothes is to say take off new wave ideals and attitudes. The Time is being cast as the Prince nemesis, from which a battle of styles and ideologies would allow both to rise to the top. In this they are the perfect embodiment of Baraka's "changing same."

Finally, The Time is important because Day uses the braggadocios attitudes of Muddy Waters and Bo Diddley to refashion the blues attitude for his persona. It is this same braggadocio attitude, which is inherited by the hip hop generation. The song, "Cool," is a brag or a toast. It is Muddy Waters' "Mannish Boy" and Bo Diddley's "Go Bo Diddley" combined with the swagger, attitude, self-confidence, and poetics of Ali. This attitude has been, of course, mutated and slightly perverted by capitalism because Day spends most of the song talking about the material things that he has and the places that he has been. But, the song manages some saving grace by shifting the emphasis from the material to Day's essence. [Remember, all of the songs on The Time's first album are written by Prince. Even in cloaked form, Prince will not allow himself to write something that emphasizes the physical or material over the metaphysical.] "If you wonder how I do it. It's just one simple rule. I'm just cool." This is important because it implies that cool is not about what you have, own, or possess but about who you are. So, anybody...well, almost anybody, can be cool. Day is not cool because he has a lot of things. He has a lot of things as a manifestation of his coolness. The Time, then, has the perfect name because the most valuable asset that one can have is time, not money. Furthermore, "Cool," for all of its materialism, ends with a call and response between Day and the band, which shows that the material things are merely a manifestation of their spirit.

"Day: Band.
Band: Yo'!
Day: Is anybody hot?
Band: No!
Day: You kno' why?
Band: Why?
Day: Cause we're so cool.
Band: Oh."

The Time could not miss. They represent the hip-ness and style that embodies black culture, especially those aspects that white folks perceive as authentic. They coined phrases, invented daces, "The Walk" and "The Bird," chased and conquered women, and funked the night away. They are as raw as the blues, as tight as Miles Davis' bands, as loose/improvisational as Charlie Parker, and contained enough rock to echo Ernie Isley and Hendrix.

The first Time album puts black street attitude, no matter how watered down and mutated, in the face of America. "Cool," "Get It Up," and "The Stick" epitomize this attitude with "Cool" being The Time's Declaration of Independence. Even songs, such as "Get It Up" and "The Stick," which speak of sexual urgency and frustration, manage to escape from being what is considered the standard R&B "begging" song. With The Time, these songs are handled in a manner that show the male keeping sexual urgency and frustration in a minor perspective as opposed to the many Prince songs on the same topic. The only thing at stake, for The Time, in these songs is an orgasm, not the state of the human condition as in a Prince song. For The Time there is the notion that if an orgasm is not achieved, then, oh well, there is another girl around the corner. Further, <u>The Time</u> is a smart album with songs, such as "Girl" and "After Hi School." These songs balance the bravado, thus balancing the image of the band. "Girl" reassures the female listeners that Day, the lead singer, is secure, mature, and honest enough to admit that life is about more than sex. "I'm having trouble baby ever since you went away...I guess I need a little time 2 get my head 2gether." And even if quirky and whimsical, "After Hi School" makes an honest attempt to show that the guys have issues on their mind other than image, parties, and sex. "Hey you, what cha gonna do after hi school?" The Time is a bit more than just the pool playing hustlers in Brooks' poem, though we are never sure how much more. This is a part of their mystique. They are black, but an infinite blackness where the bottom gets deeper the more you dig.

The second Time album, <u>What Time Is It?</u>, is as smart and powerful as the first. The album cover once again presents us with street corner hustlers with something to hide, as bassist Terry Lewis is photographed reaching into his suit coat to locate a concealed weapon. In this case, the something to hide is intimacy and sincerity. <u>What Time Is It?</u> combines the cool-ass hustler facade with songs of confession and security. Songs, since his own second album, Prince has been unable to write for himself. What the smooth, soulful sound of R&B provides over the thrash and funk of rock-n-roll is the space for elaborated emotion without ulterior motive: love and sex for the purpose of physical satisfaction and not to change the world. "OneDayI'mGonnaBeSomebody," "I Don't Wanna Leave You," and even "Gigolos Get Lonely Too" contain a certain face-value sincerity through the confessional tone that the songs involving the male/female relationship lack on <u>Dirty Mind</u> through <u>1999</u>. "OneDayI'mGonnaBeSomebody" begins where "I Wanna Be Your Lover" ends or is unable to go. To claim that "one day I'm gonna be somebody" is to admit to an inferior value/status position. This is not the Prince of those third, fourth, and fifth albums. It is a song about self improvement to make people proud. "One day I'm gonna be somebody, gonna make my mamma proud." The Prince of <u>Dirty Mind</u> through <u>1999</u> is not concerned with making people proud or pleasing any agenda but his own. Through The Time, Prince is able to address romantic and platonic relationships as key elements needed for human completion without having to be mystical or surreal. "I Don't Wanna Leave You" also expounds on some of the more intimate statements of <u>Prince</u>. There is no power play for love, only the need for partnership. And if nothing else, "Gigolos Get Lonely Too" is honest. It is the confessional of the stereotypical black male stud. (Yes, he has been involved with a lot of women. And yes, he will continue to be involved with a lot of women. But that does not mean that he does not want to know what love is.) "Guess you've heard of my reputation. I've had my share of foolin' around...Just once I wanna make love without taking off my clothes. Just once I wanna make love with somebody who really and truly knows...that money don't mean happiness." This song does want to go further than the sheets but not into the realm of some divine, spiritual completion as on those Prince albums of this period. This song is about physical love and companionship, not some spiritual completion as in the Prince songs. Accordingly, the sensitivity is balanced with the persona of the band remaining cool, street corner, club brothers, wanting a "Wild and Loose" female, someone whom they can call at "777-9311" to get into when they are feeling "right." And "The Walk" synthesizes the album, capturing, as "Cool" does on the first album, the entire street wise persona of the band. When everyone else is on the dance floor losing their cool over their sexual desires expressed through dance, The Time simply walks to the groove.

The Time, in two albums, carves a place in African

American music by echoing their underground lives, showing a resemblance of the African American self both in drama and humor. The Time, unlike Prince, does not take itself overly serious, allowing their songs to remain very matter-of-fact as opposed to the ambiguity of Prince records. The project rides the grooves and expresses itself in the language of black folk from the street. And even though the third Time Album, <u>Ice Cream Castles</u>, comes in the midst of The Time break up and is not as smart, it still manages to salvage enough of the past persona to put itself on the map with mainstream, white America. In relation to <u>Purple Rain</u>, <u>Ice Cream Castles</u> manages to achieve the sense of being in opposition to the direction of the Prince persona. Songs like "Ice Cream Castles" and "Jungle Love" remain more straight forward and direct about topics such as interracial relationships than the later penned "U Got the Look," managing to bring humor to this complex subject. "The Bird," "My Draws," and "Chili Sauce" remain Time classics for their dialect use, party atmosphere, and slapstick humor, while remaining the standards for projecting what is stylishly cool in African American culture. On many levels, the relationship between Prince and The Time is quite complimentary. Prince is drama. The Time is feel good humor. With The Time by his side, Prince has the best of both worlds, being able to create surreal, illusionary records as <u>1999</u> while still producing funk and chill records such as <u>The Time</u>. The problem? The Time (the real band members) was maturing. The monster overtakes Dr. Frankenstein. As he admits in his 1985 radio interview in Detroit, Michigan, with DJ personality, the Electrifying Mojo, "They were, to be perfectly honest, the only band I was afraid of. Nobody could wreck a house like they could" (Prince 1985). At this early stage of his career, Prince is unable to pull Jamie Starr back and allow the creation to live on its own. He seems to be unable to make the distinction between artist/creator and producer/manager. For Prince, there seems to be no distinction. The Time is created for his purposes, as an avenue for his creative ideas. There could have also been (this being purely speculation) the fear of The Time stealing Prince's grassroots, black following, such as the black kids from Detroit who where Prince's first major audience.

Unlike Prince, there is no ambiguity in the dress or the lyrics of The Time. They are, for the most part (excluding the one white guy and the hair styles) traditional black men, playing traditional black music, with traditional black subjects. Prince's audiences of the early and mid-eighties is as ambiguous as he is: young, punk, funk-n-roll black and white kids who are, quite possibly, still looking for their own identities. Who was to say that these kids would not grow up and become black nationalists or conservative republicans, both of whom are quite unreceptive to the music and message of Prince? The middle eighties under the Reagan/Bush administrations saw America polarize against itself. Religion, race, and gender walls are re-drawn, and there is no place for ambiguity. You are either with us or against us. In this type of atmosphere a group like The Time could flourish, and Prince would find it difficult to keep his head above water with the rise of rap, which forces even the most mainstream black pop groups to assert a certain amount of blackness as their membership card into the culture. Before rap, it was quite common to see a white leading lady in a video for a black act. In the majority of black videos prior to 1986-87, black acts are merely mimicking their white counter-parts. Rap causes a shift in the racial imagery, where black acts are found in their more authentic surroundings as opposed to the more integrated scenery of the early black videos. In this type of climate where artists are asked, demanded, to be or show a definite connection to the black community, Prince seems like a fish out of water. Still, in the years following the disbanding of The Time, Prince continues to plow ahead with his refusal to draw or accept a definable identity. He stays alienated and opinionated in his "life according to Prince," and it affects his record sales, while The Time is all but forced to reunite and are about as popular now as one can be without a new album or hit record. Whatever the specifics, The Time project threatens to overtake the master and ultimately ends in an ongoing dispute over the direction and creative input between the creator and the creation, but not before Prince is able to add a greater dimensionality to his image and his work than most African American artists had been allowed throughout the history of popular music.

With the girl acts, Prince is able to explore and manipulate notions of his own femininity as well as the male domination fantasy. Vanity, Wendy and Lisa, Cat, Sheila E., and Jill Jones allow Prince to move freely and easily from Chuck Berry's machismo, to Little Richard's non-threatening femininity, to James Brown's puppeteering of dancing girls, to the roles of big brother and lover.

> "The very absence of clear statements of identity [especially in the use of females to enhance his feminine persona] correctly suggests that there are no firm definitions in the sexual realm—and, as Prince's ideology patently insists, for outside forces to impose arbitrary standards of 'normality' upon them is an abomination" (Hill 135).

Prince is determined to have it all by being all of it. The girl groups not only balance the male imagery of The Time, but they make Prince a supreme, androgynous hybrid. He is Cupid, Oedipus, Narcissus, Pan, Don Juan, and Mandingo all at once. The creation of these female personas exemplify the manner in which Christian male writers created stereotyped, female caricatures for their various needs be it Mary Magdalene or Mary the Virgin. Prince will be able to commune with, save, and ravage women, simultaneously. Accordingly, Vanity Six is clearly created as the fantasy girl group, the sexually aggressive female, looking to be taken to the heights of sexual gratification by the capable male who exists in The Time's "Get It Up." "Get it Up. Tonight I can no longer hold it. I need seven inches or more." With this line, Vanity Six is able to turn the tables on the most macho persona of Prince, The Time, by reversing their song, which is a plea for the woman to be more sexually driven. By demanding the male to be more sexually potent, Vanity Six is usurping the position of power with the male's own words. The group becomes a symbol of the ideal vixen to be both saved and dominated all for the glory of manhood.

Vanity Six, both literally and figuratively, represents a competition with Rick James. As rumor has it, Vanity was dating James when Prince seduces her away from him to join his camp. Both James and Prince then create girl groups as sexual and artistic competition. The artistic competition is to see who can sell the most records with the creation of a new band. The sexual competition is to see who is going to be the new bad boy of rock-n-roll. They both are raunchy. They both are musical, and they both are androgynous, though James clearly is the most masculine of the two. Still, a successful girl group gives both of them an air of sexual prowess as well as taps into feminine sisterhood that both need to become the rock icons that they desire. Through this battle, they aid in a redefinition of African American music, creating a new black pop icon by impregnating black music with the angst and style of punk and new wave. They are taking the definition of the blues musician as "outlaw" and reconfiguring it. White artists can take the blues outlaw persona and have commercial success because they are not as threatening as black men. Black popular music never had a bad boy, not in the manner of Presley, Jagger, Bowie, or Jim Morrison. Before James and Prince, black music could not afford a bad boy, someone who would drive white girls crazy and inspire white boys to mimic and worship them in the same manner as they would worship guitar gods like Eric Clapton. Even Clapton admits that Hendrix's explosion onto the scene caused as much fear as it did motivation in white rockers.

Hendrix was taking what Clapton and others had been doing and returning it to black music, with the full force of social anxiety and sexuality. Clapton admits in VH1's History of Rock 'n' Roll that "[Hendrix] was taking what all of us had been doing and putting it through the roof." Clapton forms a mutual admiration society with fellow guitarist, Pete Townshend, because Hendrix threatened to replace them. In VH1's History of Rock 'n' Roll, Townshend admits that he asserted to Clapton that "He's [Hendrix] going to put us out of business." When Hendrix leaves Europe, Clapton and Townshend find that they no longer need their friendship and drift apart. In their beginnings, James and Prince are knocking hard on this very closed-door society. They are reinventing what it means to be a rock star, which is something very different than what Michael Jackson is doing. (Jackson is reinventing what it means to be a pop star.) Even further, their battle also refashions the sixties' notion of girl groups, which had already been deconstructed by LaBelle and Millie Jackson during the seventies. Vanity Six and James' Mary Jane Girls bring an attitude and style that influences artists like Salt-n-Pepa, Klymaxx, Adina Howard, TLC, Foxy Brown, Li'l Kim, and Destiny's Child. Even En Vogue would have to be sexy and sassy, bringing more sexual force than the Supremes.

The songs on the Vanity Six album are simple and speak to the sexual fantasies and frustrations of aggressive, liberated women. "Nasty Girl," as Vanity fills the role, is every adolescent male's fantasy. "Don't you believe in mystery? Don't you wanna play my game? If you ain't scared take it out. I'll do it like a real live Nasty Girl Should. I'm looking for a man to love me, like I've never been loved before...Tonight I'm living in Fantasy, my own little Nasty World." The whole song is built on fantasy, which is a major part of the adolescent male psyche. This time the sex is for sexual gratification, but it is a relief from sexual frustration, which is caused by rigid gender roles. Vanity might be too much woman for the typical male who has the typical hypocritical and perverse relationship with women: wanting to conquer every woman he meets but also wanting to marry a virgin. Only a liberated male, like the Prince persona, is able to deal with a woman the likes of Vanity. So, Vanity is also a trope and a literary technique, balancing Prince's femininity by "rehabilitating the cave man stereotype of masculine potency which in other ways their mentor, Prince, appeared to be undermining" (Hill 132). Vanity Six, much like The Time, gives Prince the best of both worlds.

In "Drive Me Wild," the youngest member of the band, Susan, assumes the role of a submissive female, willing to be anything asked. "I'm a radio, call me up and make a request...I'm a Cadillac, wherever you want just drive. I've never been driven. Baby, you're the first. Come on baby drive me wild." Here, Prince is playing to the hypocrisy of the male ego. In two songs, we move from the powerful female to the submissive female, both for the male's pleasure. The male's fear and intrigue of the female in "Nasty Girl" is the excitement of the untamed mare. The only things worth conquering are those that no one else has been man enough to conquer. The feeling in "Nasty Girl" is exhilaration through the challenge of conquest. The feeling in "Drive Me Wild" is one of power and dominion over womankind, giving both his male and female listeners the best of both worlds.

Even with all of the aforementioned sexual imagery, the song that most ingratiates itself to the male ego is "If a Girl Answers, Don't Hang Up." The song stages a telephone conversation in which Vanity calls a boyfriend to take her on a date, and another female answers the phone. There is the usual "cat fight" as expected. And even though the girls conclude that the man is not worth the trouble, "There're two things we can't stand. One's a jive talk man. The other's a jive talk man with no money," the argument alone is enough to stroke the male ego. At the same time, Prince allows Vanity to keep her persona as a strong, liberated woman. In three songs, Prince is able to explore the spectrum of the identities, fantasies, and insecurities of male/female sexuality and relationship. He constructs his discourse with graphic and illicit sexual overtones, which camouflages the psychodrama, allowing him to achieve this reconfiguration of gender roles. Prince's use of women to both subvert and stroke the male ego displays his ability to further manipulate ideals about sex and sexuality, allowing him to liquefy his own identity. As Miles Davis asserts, He is "almost like a pimp and a bitch all wrapped up in one image." (Davis 385). This seems to insinuate to the women who listen to or work with Prince that he is incapable of being a sexist in a true sense of the word. Sexism is not merely oppression based on gender, but the designation of roles for women by men who find those roles wholly incomprehensible for themselves. In the case of Prince, if he asks a woman to wear a bikini and high heels and prance around, begging for attention and affection, it is not something that he, himself, has not already done. Through his behavior he is kept from being a true sexist. With Prince, sexual positions and identities are all one ride with each partner taking a turn at the wheel. His carefully constructed androgyny causes his machismo and his femininity to balance each other, allowing him to enter a greater range of psychological and emotional doors than his predecessors or his peers.

Hill insists and makes a strong argument for Jill Jones being the strongest and most complete female to be used by Prince as a feminine persona. He asserts that Jones, through her performance of Prince penned songs, moves from persona to individual, adding, "She might even go on to sustain her artistic life independently from him" (Hill 137). It might be noted that Hill's book was finished in 1989, and we have not since heard from Ms. Jones. But, unlike Jones, Sheila E. has managed to continue her career independent of Prince, mostly because her career did not begin with Prince. Hill's assessment of Jones is her ability to interject much of herself or her 1990s feminine sensibilities into the songs written by Prince. "Her own delivery of 'G-Spot' trades on a parodic sense of puzzled wonderment. It is just one aspect of her several feminine personae which, between them, comprise a kind of mirrored image of those assumed by Prince himself" (Hill 135-136). In Hill's assessment, Jones remains unique because in her delivery of Prince songs she is able to "elude identification" (Hill 136). Jones' ability to liquefy her own identity is what seemly impresses Hill most. "Her tone slips from the declamatory to private, shifting from poetic-romantic dilemma of 'Violet Blue' to 'All Day, All Night's dizzily overstated symbolism" (Hill 137). Jones, unlike other Prince females, is not static. Not only do her emotions and tones fluctuate, but also her point of view. What may account for this is Prince's maturity as a producer and his new found ability to allow a project to have its own life. Unlike his relationship with The Time or many of the other female personas, Prince is, to some degree, allowing his original idea to be married with the other artist's idea. Dominion and the need for power are being replaced with security, artistic development, and an understanding of artistic cooperation. Thus, Jones is given more freedom and leeway to interject much of herself into the project. Jones, then, becomes an example of Prince's growth and understanding that an independent woman provides more of an opportunity for the male's personal growth and evolution.

Wendy and Lisa, the female duo of the Revolution, have the opposite affect on Prince's persona as it relates to the mission of the other female associates. Where the other women were used to promote Prince's black exotica, having their pale whiteness juxtaposed to Prince's exotic blackness, i.e. his duo with Sheena Easton, Wendy and Lisa are used to whiten-up Prince, allowing him access into the mainstream society and into the sisterhood of femininity. In fact, Wendy and Lisa work for Prince in the same manner that Little Richard's persona worked to balance the masculinity of his band. Little Richard's band was composed of very masculine black men who were as physically imposing as they were talented. Having Little Richard lead the way into the clubs would disarm the white males who were already leery of having their women titillated by and dancing to the beats of black men. Little Richard's persona made his band palatable. Wendy and Lisa do the same for Prince. "Wendy makes me seem all right in the eyes of people watching. She keeps a smile on her face. When I sneer, she smiles. It's a good contrast" (Karlen, "Prince Talks: The Silence Is Broken," 86). The question is to whom does Wendy make Prince seem all right? The obvious answer is too women, in general, and to white America. Wendy and Lisa cause Prince to appear safer and more palatable, like a rapist using a female attorney, because they also liquefy him, making him whiter and more feminine. Prior to Purple Rain, Prince was a black act with a black band, even despite the success of 1999. The three most noticeable faces, which are seen in the front of all the videos and at all the concerts, are Brownmark, a black male bassist, Prince, front and center, and Dez Dickerson, a black male guitarist. It is not only a black act, but a black male act. "It was not till the departure of Dez Dickerson and his replacement by a white woman guitarist, Wendy Melvoin, that the sexual/semiological focus of the group changed its balance from masculine to feminine" and from black to white (Hill 134). Here, Prince is purposely emasculating himself as well as whitening himself to gain access to the American mainstream. Wendy and Lisa are effective on several levels for him.

> "Wendy and Lisa represent a moral counter point to Prince's 'masculine hang-ups,' [their] special closeness...invited speculation that the girls might be something more than just friends...The very absence of clear statements of identity correctly suggest that there are no firm definitions in the sexual realm" (Hill 135).

By blurring the gender lines, Prince is effectively blurring the race and class lines. This is how his revolution works. It is a revolution that attacks all forms of oppression through the dialogue of sexuality because sex is the driving factor in this society. In a July 21, 1986, cover article on Prince in <u>People</u>, the cover caption reads, "Would you trust this man with your daughter?" The article is referring to a contest sponsored by MTV where the 10,000th caller wins a date with Prince and has him preview his new movie, <u>Under the Cherry Moon</u>, in her home town. The winner is Lisa Barber, a twenty year old white female from Sheridan Wyoming, one of the whitest towns in America, true farm and fish country. So <u>People</u>'s caption fits because the magazine's core audience is mainstream white America. Even after his mega <u>Purple Rain</u> success, Prince may not have been viewed as a traditional black artist, but he is still battling his black exotic presence in the mind of white listeners. His use of sex and sexuality has not worked like he had hoped. Instead of being viewed as a unique soul having a physical experience, he is viewed as another freaky black artist. One Sheridan citizen added, "We cheered for anyone who dressed weird or was black" (Durkee 61). It is Lisa who comes to his aid, hoping to assist Prince in his transition into a rock star icon. "He is very conscious of his reputation, and I think he's making an effort to turn it around. Basically, he's an easy-going guy" (Durkee 53).

All of this speaks to the ongoing issue that race and sexuality still prevail in our notions of who and what people are. Wendy and Lisa work to subvert these issues for Prince, but it is not just with their physical image. Their formal, classical training synthesized with Prince's brash funk and new wave style to create a perfectly amalgamated music. This eventually allows Prince to pen songs, such as "I Wonder U," for Wendy to take the lead, giving his albums and his live shows a more eclectic, multidimensional feel and presence. With Wendy and Lisa, as with Shelia E., Prince is at the top of his game in manipulating the public's perception of him. This makes Prince the ultimate pimp on two levels. He is a pimp who makes women feel so safe and secure around him that they freely give of themselves to him. He is also a pimp who is able to seduce the public through the manipulation of their fantasy of the black mulatto, the black-white sexual relationship, and their fascination with black sensuality. As rapper/actor Ice T asserts, "pimpin' ain't easy, but somebody gots to do it." Prince did not create himself; America created Prince. As Don King, America's other greatest pimp, asserts, "If there was no Mike Tyson, America would invent one." Prince is the mental figment of the exotic black, which has been fermenting and rolling around in the minds of Americans since the first European contact with Africa. Prince simply uses all of this as a way to gain access to mainstream Americana.

If Vanity is the physical mirror image of Prince, and Wendy and Lisa are the spiritual mirror image of Prince, then Sheila E. is the complete synthesis of the two. Since both Prince and E. are musicians who want their work to have a significant impact on society, each will explore any avenue their muse takes them. With Sheila E., we find Jamie Starr more open and mature. Sheila E. begins as a Jamie Starr Project, as Sheila E., herself, retells in her 1991 interview for <u>Omnibus</u>. "When I came in I didn't see any drums. I asked where were the drums. He said 'I want you to sing.' I said, 'Sing? I can't sing'...He changed my name from Sheila Escovedo to Sheila E." The rest is history. It is obvious that Sheila E. starts as a project much like The Time. But this time, as evident in her career, Prince is willing and able to allow the creation to grow, mature, and flourish without him. It should be noted that unlike the other aforementioned artists, Sheila E. already had an established career as a musician, having worked with prominent artists such as Marvin Gaye and Lionel Richie. Also, her father is a well established musician, having played with the likes of Carlos Santana. Their relationship is more of an equal marriage of skills. Sheila E. supplies her talent, and Prince supplies the imagery and direction. In Sheila E., Prince remolds and sculpts the female image that begins in Vanity to better mirror his own image. This time, it goes deeper than the physical exterior. While all Vanity is allowed to or can offer are looks and sexuality, Sheila E.'s talent allows Prince to mirror himself musically and ideologically. Because of her musical talents, Sheila E. can carry the imagery and the ideology without the need of having Prince at her side. To the public, Sheila E. becomes the female Prince, composed of all the same ideals and imagery. It is his best attempt at creating the woman that he, himself, would be, the mate which he desires in "If I Was Your Girlfriend."

While Hill proclaims Jill Jones as the perfect female manifestation of Prince, he spends more time showing how Sheila E.'s persona works to illuminate and broaden Prince's persona. Sheila E.'s clothing, music, and lyrical themes are identical to Prince. There becomes the notion through songs, such as "The Glamorous Life," "A Love Bizarre," "Koo Koo," and "Sister Fate," that E. is on the same journey to transcend the physical for metaphysical utopia. More importantly, E. has the same amount of range as Prince. She can be coy in "Sister Fate," transcendental in "Oliver's House" and "The Belle of St. Mark," sexually aggressive in "The Glamorous Life" and "A Love Bizarre," and political in "Koo Koo." Thus, she is a woman who can meet all of Prince's needs because she can understand him, enlighten him, sex him, and save him simultaneously. The climax happens when the video for "Sister Fate," which is a song about E.'s secret lover, flashes an image of Prince from the "Raspberry Beret" video. And while conducting a television interview, E. answers quite submissively that Prince is indeed the person to whom she is referring in "Sister Fate." With this public appearance and seemingly reluctant confession from Sheila E., as if she was ordered to keep the relationship secret, the whole facade becomes complete. Prince is able to complete his ideal construction of himself as the ultimate mate: feminine enough to understand, comfort, conform, and submit when necessary and masculine enough to fulfill a woman's every sexual need and desire. This "secret" confession by Sheila E. gives the illusion of letting the general public into the private world of Prince, that one is being given information or being allowed to see Prince on an interpersonal level. This all works in adding the element of sincerity, which is a driving voice behind confession and liberation, which also works to get the public to believe or buy into the persona and the hype.

> "From the moment of Prince's retreat from the publicity machine, the women associated with him became his connecting point with the information media. Once constructed for grand-scale consumption, his girls become his emissaries to the outside world. Through them, Prince planted himself firmly at the confluence of contemporary squabbles about how men are, and what women want them to be. The different characteristics of those around him all found an echo in some compartment of his own composite persona: He could simmer like Sheila E., be innocent like Jill Jones, nasty like Vanity, or introverted and a bit spacey like Wendy and Lisa. And this feminization opens doors. The flair with which he managed to reprogram his sexual enigma to fascinate as much as shock was vital to his long-coveted deliverance to a mass audience. From Little Richard to David Bowie to Boy George, straight, white record buyers had fallen hopelessly in love with distant, fragile pop icons who broke the gender rules. It was his irresistible variation on this tradition that clinched Prince's grand metamorphosis from a star into a phenomenon" (Hill 140-141).

By 1990 we no longer see Prince using actual artists as characters to project his various identities. He also has begun to work with mostly established artists, such as Clinton, Staples, Patti LaBelle, and Bonnie Patti, rather than the new talent with which he had worked in the past. Prince seems to have become satisfied with the blurring and liquefying of his own identity to a degree that he feels free to work with other, established artists to push and expand himself further. By 1991 the song writing pseudonyms of the eighties are replaced with Prince or Paisley Park. By this point, Prince, the individual, is accepted as being all things to the music industry. He has written songs for such diverse acts as Nona Hendryx, The Bangles, Sheena Easton, Howard Hewitt, Nona Gaye, Kenny Rogers, and a duet with Madonna. Additionally, his work has been covered by such diverse acts as La Toya Jackson, Chaka Khan, Cyndi Lauper, Stephanie Mills, the Pointer Sisters, Tina Turner, Tom Jones, Sinead O'Conner, Ginuwine, TLC, and D'Angelo. Prince also has been sampled by a ton of rappers, including 2pac, Public Enemy, and M. C. Hammer. He no longer needs to create personas to expand his identity for artistic growth. Prince is now able to explore the avenues he has created for himself. And by fighting to expand his own style, personality, and persona, Prince also works to expand the doors and creativity for all African American artists who must continue to fight against the limitations of a racist industry.

Sex

> "More than my songs have to do with sex, they have to do with one human's love for another which goes deeper than anything political that anybody could possibly write about. The need for love, the need for sexuality, basic freedom, equality...I'm afraid these things don't come out" (Sutherland 13, reprinted in Fudger 28).

Of all the books and articles that I have read concerning Prince, Dave Hill's <u>Prince: A Pop Life</u> achieves best the goal of analyzing and communicating information while remaining objective. Yet even he falls short of analyzing fully or accepting a genuine belief toward the message(s) of Prince's work and his reconciliation to himself, his music, society, and his spirituality. Hill, as others, becomes entrapped into the story of Prince and sex for sex's sake or sex for the sake of becoming a rock god, which has more to do with capitalistic connotations than artistic or spiritual connotations. For Prince, sex is not just for physical gratification. Sex is primarily used as a tool to achieve some other, higher state of satisfaction and self-completion, if only for a moment. Thus, Prince's discourse about sex is related to his desire to say something about life. "I think my problem is that my attitude's so sexual that it overshadows anything else that I might want to say. I'm not mature enough as a writer to bring it all out yet" (Sutherland 13, reprinted in Fudger 7). Despite his youth, Prince realized early that sexuality is a driving force behind the behavior of mankind and is the particular element that links man to the universality of humanity. An image, such as "God is coming like a dog in heat; he's looking for soldiers with strong feet," shows Prince's ability to amalgamate all of our separate worlds into one continuum. This image is sexually explicit and righteously indignant. It contains the three prerequisites for a Prince image: shock, picturesque, and precision. The image is shocking because it breaks the Eurocentric mold of separating the concerns of the body from the concerns of the soul by applying sensual/sexual attributes to God as well as comparing him to something lower than man, a dog. It is picturesque because it takes the urgency of a dog in heat and vividly parallels it with the urgency of God's mission to save mankind. It is precise because the image is not vague. A dog in heat is the symbol of urgency and determination. As a dog in heat stops for nothing until it fulfills its mission, so will God stop for nothing until He fulfills his mission. Again, Prince's goal is to say something about humanity's sexual nature and show how this sexual nature parallels our metaphysical nature. Thus, God can have an orgasm, which gives deeper meaning to our orgasms. His messages are electrifying and penetrating because he starts with what we know and builds from there. Prince is troping the sexual metaphor by equating the sex drive to the essence of life. Spring is the ultimate metaphor for God, for reincarnation, for life. A dog in heat, though dogmatic, gives God's return to Earth an urgency that the image of bees pollinating flowers does not have. Like Wordsworth's notion, Prince is painting the tree in such a manner that it becomes unfamiliar to us so that we can recognize it in its infinite beauty once it has been re-presented to us.

From For You through 1999, sex, sexuality, and sexual liberation are the primary tools to achieve the fulfillment of life. For Prince, sex is the key ingredient to season or embellish the meals he serves. It is in the way he writes and sings words such as "cum" as in, "cum over here," the way he dresses and dances, and the androgynous image he constructs to deliver certain feelings of femininity or vulnerability. But underneath and between the sexual imagery is a poet with much to say about life. Sex is the Trojan Horse through which Prince has gained access to the public through the canal of radio and television, penetrating the holes of our eyes and our ears, impregnating our brains and our hearts. Most importantly, what has kept so many of us returning to him is his willingness to explore our various notions regarding sex and the manner in which these varying notions manifest themselves in every aspect of our lives. His audience believes him when during the Purple Rain tour, while dressed in a blouse, purple see-through pants, and a g-string and singing about God, he asserts, "I know you better than you think I do." His audience trusts him because he has been unafraid to battle publicly his own contradictions of the physical and the spiritual, love and lust, God and Satan, which eventually overflowed into other socio-political areas of their lives. And his audience is not offended or bothered by his sensationalism because effective or successful writers seek to create ambiguity through imagery and symbolism in order to convey deeper messages beneath their surface topics. Prince uses sexual intercourse and sexuality as a trope or a metaphor for man's metaphysical self. His concentration in sex has been rooted in his belief of the duality of man, meaning that man exists as a dual being, flesh and soul, physical and metaphysical, psychological and emotional. Man is by nature a dichotomy, and sex/sexuality is the axis on which this dichotomy revolves. Sex may be the ultimate metaphor for the dualism of man and the act to connect man's two dueling sides. The act of sex allows mankind to transform its state from creation to creator and allows two people to become united as one. Sex also has the ability to provide, even if an illusion, the states of love, shelter, belonging, and companionship, which all work to comfort the natural anxieties of fear, loneliness, and insecurity, providing the illusion or false sense of completion. Prince even admitted that early in his life he was guilty of using sex to compensate for emptiness in his life. "I had moods when I couldn't figure something out, and so I ran to vice to sort myself out, like women or too much drink, or working in order to avoid dealing with the problem" (Simonart 1998). Through the use of sex and sexuality, Prince is able to discuss these issues and concerns of humanity's struggle to understand and reconcile itself to its dichotomy and evolve to a higher life form.

In the beginning, Prince is able to use the Christian dichotomy of sex and guilt to his advantage. Since the Puritans came to America under the guise of religious freedom, but proved themselves to be one of the most oppressive and hypocritical forces known to man, America has been a country obsessed with sex and controlled by guilt, living under the umbrella of hypocrisy as a natural by-product of their existence. The Puritan religion establishes the blueprint and the standard for social behavior, which sees sex as an act of procreation and not for pleasure. In stark contrast, however, it is the slaveholder offspring of the Puritans who creates and fashions a double standard toward sin and sexuality through their perverse relationships with slaves. By refashioning this conflict, Prince is commenting on American hypocrisy and remains inline with the blues aesthetic in the

> "celebration of the sensual and erotic elements of life...the blues aesthetic emphasizes and enjoys the sensual and erotic elements of life. while this is apparent in all our dance, in all our music, in all the delight we take in physical beauty, it has taken us quite a number of centuries to get repressed puritanical peoples to accept that it really is okay to enjoy both the sensual and erotic sides of life. we are not arguing that any of these characteristics are exclusive to blues people, even though, within the context of the u.s.a., it may seem that way. on the other hand, the embracing of this concept by non-african americans sometimes leads to excessiveness, even obsession, with exotica and an elevation of the other as the paragon of sensuality or sexuality as in the fixation on mulatto women [which Prince refashioned and worked to his artistic and commercial benefit]. this objectification of people is really a corruption of this basic concept that is essentially about an informed view of one's own sensual and erotic self, rather than an obsession

with someone else's sensual and erotic self...a true blues aesthetic locates sensuality and sexuality not in the other but in the self" (Salaam 14, 17-18).

Understanding this "objectification of people" through their race and gender, Prince combines his own sense of self and sexuality with the mythology of black sexuality to forge a revolution that he hopes will free himself and others from the constraints of this arbitrarily designed system. He may not achieve his ultimate, ideal goal, but he is able to build upon the work of Gaye and others to create a "sex metaphor," which yields some of the most interesting lyrics and images of popular music by navigating the borders of pleasure/pain, righteousness/sin, normality/perversion, passion/obsession, and ecstasy/despair. If he can not have one without the other because of humanity's innate dichotomy, Prince finds a way to embrace and exploit them all for his own purpose and pleasure. His goal is to remove the negative connotation of sex and sexuality placed there by a history of hypocrisy. Even when American leaders such as Thomas Jefferson forthrightly asserted that America must have a separation of church and state in order to protect the rights of all men, America has never been able to break from this rigid, oppressive social structure which is derived mainly from the Puritan religion. This is mainly because leaders such as Jefferson were leading morally double lives and were consumed by their hypocrisy to oppress Africans in order to justify their immoral treatment of them. It is very appropriate that Jefferson is considered one of the founding fathers of America who embodies the very persona of Americanism since both his personal and professional lives helped to cement this blueprint for American perversion and hypocrisy.

Jefferson was able to fight unyieldingly for his own rights while at the same time denounce the rights of Africans in order to perpetuate his own first class citizenship through the social and economic exploitation of

Africans. Publicly he is able to denounce African intellect and humanity by denouncing the poetry of Phyllis Wheatley as "below the dignity of criticism" (Gates and McKay xxxi). However, privately he is able to participate in a lengthy sexual relationship with his slave mistress, Sally Hemings, who is the embodiment of that which he denounces. How does one lie or wallow in the mud and not get muddy? Furthermore, this American hypocrisy still perpetuates itself in the minds of white Americans as seen in the whitewashing of this relationship between Jefferson and Hemings in an attempt to show that their relationship was one of love and mutual respect. This could not have been the case considering Jefferson's public loathing of the Negro. Furthermore, a slave can not have a mutual relationship with a master because she has no power to terminate the affair. This hypocrisy and perversion becomes the blueprint for American relationships, not only black and white, but also male and female. Men, specifically white men, continue to enjoy a perverse and hypocritical relationship with women. Black men become a symbolic pawn for everyone, including themselves, and are subverted to the most heinous and perverted status, being objects of lust and loathing simultaneously. This struggle to justify or reconcile oneself to this hypocrisy and perversion saturates American art, especially American literature. Hawthorne's <u>Scarlet Letter</u> and "Young Goodman Brown" are social commentary showing how the American social structure is established under the oppressive umbrella of the American religious structure, which holds everyone accept white males to certain standards of morality and ethics, thus constructing a hypocritical way of life for white males, allowing them to sexually exploit the rest of the country for their perverse pleasure. The misogyny of hip hop, then, represents the black male's need to assert his will and dominion over black women to gain some sense of humanity through manhood. During slavery, black men did not beat their women because they were not allowed to beat them. You can only beat what you own. Since the end of slavery, black men have fallen into the trap of practicing sexism to gain some sense of humanity and manhood. The other tactic to gain manhood and first-class citizenship is to date and marry white women. Prince does both. He is able to puppeteer women and flaunt his legion/stable of white and light-skinned black women, which allows him to be perceived as a "Man" of power.

> "Even though there are numerous rumors about [Prince's] alleged (bi)sexuality/androgyny, still he is seen as dominating the pop music scene in terms of the popularity of his product. As long as he dominates (sells), his alleged deviance is tolerable" (Salaam 134).

Prince, following in the line of Little Richard, plays on his mulatto persona, his complex gender status, and America's fascination with the exotic black, using all of this to entice America's interest. Moreover, his androgyny makes his overt sexuality less threatening. Once he has America's interest, he impregnates his songs with the seeds of socio-political commentary. The problem for Prince is America's inability to take an African American seriously, especially when they are enthralled by his sexuality. He becomes a caricature of what Baldwin is able to create in his persona and in works such as <u>Giovanni's Room</u>.

Still, Prince is able to become both a trigger and a symbol for sexual liberation, leading to some larger socio-political liberation by eroding the conservative constraints placed on African American artists. Although the 1920s is viewed as an era when America loses its innocence and idealism due to the First World War, it is in the 1960s when large moves and gains are made in removing the American social structure from underneath the control of the American religious structure. Viewed as the era of the sexual revolution, the 1960s was a decade of restlessness and revolution from the Civil Rights Movement to the Women's Rights Movement. Both these movements are viewed by the conservative majority of American whites as attacks on white men and the system of American hierarchy based on a dominance by white males. So, the revolutions of the sixties were centered very much on sexual revolution, since America has been dominated by white males who have assigned women to second-class citizenship and have emasculated all non-white males from power. Accordingly, the white male penis continues to be the symbol for power, and elements are kept in place to disenfranchise the vagina and the non-white penis. This has created schizophrenia in American culture where the white male's fascination and fear of the black penis and black sexuality creates a perverse relationship where black males are constantly created as flat, one-dimensional caricatures to pacify white anxiety while simultaneously satisfying white curiosity. Rarely are black males celebrated or praised for being intelligent or being able to balance their physical prowess with their emotional and intellectual prowess. Thus, black males are either emasculated or raised to a supernatural sex stud stereotype. In doing this, black males are assigned a subservient role to white males and black and white females because of their perceived inability to be cerebral or metaphysical beings. This forced assignment or position creates heightened tension between black males and the rest of America as Baldwin affirms in The Price of the Ticket that the relationship between a black boy and a white boy is a strange and curious thing.

This forced role assignment also creates a perverse relationship between the black male and the black female as shown in Wright's Native Son, Walker's Color Purple, Terry McMillan's Waiting to Exhale, or Hurston's Their Eyes Were Watching God. In each novel, the black male who is sympathetic to the struggle and hardship of the black female is a rarity. And more specifically, it is obvious that the pain inflicted by the black male onto the black female is a result of the pain inflicted by the white male onto the black male. Still, the most damaging relationship to the black male psyche and quest for humanity is the relationship between the black male and the white female, especially when they both are flattened to their symbolic, ideological rebellions against the oppression of white males. As Baldwin asserts in <u>A Rap on Race</u> with Margaret Mead, the black male-white female relationship perpetuates the black male's objectification because he becomes merely a symbol of rebellion for the white female.

> "[White women] come to you for the most part as though you're some exotic—well, they really come to you as though you're some *extraordinary* phallic symbol...As if you're nothing but a walking phallus...no head, no arms, no nothing, just a phallus...the act of love becomes an act of murder in which you are also committing suicide" (46).

The white male dominated society creates a sexual system that so objectifies the black male that he becomes utterly powerless. In an attempt to rebel against this powerlessness, black males often attempt to co-opt, modify, or reinvent their stereotypes, especially in popular culture so that they become larger than life. They attempt to subvert and sell back to both black and white America the thing that America hates and loves. This action is an example of a rebellious flaunting of style in the teeth of American oppression that Baldwin discusses in <u>The Price of the Ticket</u> (320). Thus, sex as the ability to control or liberate has been one of the primary tools of power of American history. So this whole issue of human sexuality is linked to the human being's need to obtain and have dominion over oneself and over others. Sex not only allows us to create, but a person perceived as possessing a certain sexual prowess is almost perceived as a human deity. This person is perceived by the mass of the American society as being able to satisfy physically, which means having the power to move or transcend a mate to a type of utopian state of being. Sex is not only powerful;

sex is power. And the myths and lies about sex are major factors for the mental perversion, racism, and violence that keep this society at odds with itself. Prince, with his heavy sexual and bisexual over tones, is establishing himself as the walking stereotype, contradiction, and controversy of a nation and the world. Because of the myths surrounding his sexual prowess, the black male continues to be feared, envied, and hated. To counter these emotions, the black male has often been forced to emasculate his gender to gain entry into the white world, especially corporate America. Prince, in his visual and lyrical imagery, becomes the representation of the sexual misfit, longing for liberation, willing to take part in, if not leading, the revolution to sexual freedom and satisfaction, which he hopes leads to total freedom and satisfaction. Lying underneath the sexual revolution is the hidden agenda of gaining humanity and place. To achieve humanity and place, Prince uses the visual imagery of Little Richard, Johnny Mathis, and Jimi Hendrix to produce the desired effect of a non-threatening, sexual nymph, and rarely allows the public to see the full brunt of the machismo of Chuck Berry, Bo Diddley, or James Brown that he also possesses and slyly expresses from <u>1999</u> onward. His machismo can only be whipped out once he has firmly established his femininity.

In Prince's early work, there is a depersonalization of the sex act because of the lack of intimacy and sharing that is expressed. The protagonist in the early songs has ulterior motives and emotions than merely constructing a romantic relationship. The protagonist is attempting to use sex and the romantic relationship to fill other human voids, desires, and struggles to obtain a sense of completion. As a result the protagonist creates images that objectify the female, making her something other than human: sometimes a mere tool, sometimes a pathway to salvation. In the so called "love songs" of <u>For You</u> through <u>1999</u>, something else is happening besides the idea of love making, and the female is as inanimate as the physical setting or environment. This is quite evident in the fact that over the course of the eighties, the term "love song" is replace with "slow jam." Love is no longer the prime objective; sex is. Prince's counterparts and the generation that follows him are unable to construct the characters or scenarios that keep their songs from being merely dogmatic because sex, not love, is the essence of their work. Because Prince is clearly looking for something other than romantic love through sex, these early songs are void of the sentimentality of love. And because the public is not searching for a deeper meaning, it merely embraces the dogmatism of the songs. This produces a generation of writers whose emphasis is mostly on sex and not on love, who are mostly concerned with satisfying a selfish lust and not the sharing of amour. Yet, beneath Prince's dogmatism, is an artist looking to say more about the necessity and importance of human relationships. Prince's wit (the fusion of his unencumbered outlook on life, his ability to find new ways to express old ideas, and his keen insight of sexuality as man's socio-political barometer) is what keeps him always one step ahead of his listeners, other song writers, and the critics.

The first two albums discuss the irresistible pull of women and the inevitability of losing one's will and self-control to the desires of the heart and the flesh. From the first album, <u>For You</u>, songs such as "I'm Yours," "Falling In Love," "Just as Long as We're Together," and "Soft and Wet" denote relationships where the male falls uncontrollably in love with the female because of some natural power that the female exhibits over his psyche. He is lured to her like a mosquito to light and suffers a pain, which is, innately, a part of the pleasure experience of love. The songs are driven by a sense of urgency and anguish caused by a male struggling to overcome his gender concerns and limitations. Prince begins his lyrical cat and mouse game of blending machismo and femininity that both excites and disarms his female counterpart through the use of role reversals. With "In Love," "Crazy You," "Just as Long as We're Together," and "I'm Yours," Prince constructs, deconstructs, and reconstructs his male-female image, becoming both seducer and victim all at the same time. In "Soft and Wet" he is the seducer/liberator, openly and honestly declaring all of his nasty and explicit desires, hoping to liberate the female from her conservative notion of sexuality. He then presents his own need to be liberated in "In Love." "Ever since I met you there's something inside of me that keeps me wondering won't you set me free. Take off these chains, and I'll take off yours." The reversal is that he is not asking that he be allowed to remove her chains. He is asking that she remove his chains, that she liberates him. From there he moves to an even more vulnerable position in "Crazy You" where he is overwhelmed by the essence and personality of the woman.

> "You got a strange way about you, kinda of crazy, but I love you just the same. You make me wanna do everything. I'm just a crazy fool, lost in a world of love I get from crazy you. I'm so strung out thinking 'bout the crazy things that you do."

Prince's take me as seriously as you want to attitude allows him to open the doors of liberal and free thinking to a conservative group of African American listeners and fuse their sounds and way of life with the white rock youth of America. The declaration of his lover being "Soft and Wet," breathlessly over an up-tempo beat of fused rock and soul is a refreshing image of a sensitive male with the ability to explore sexuality without getting trapped into needing to espouse the machismo male superiority complex. "Soft and Wet" sets the tone for a career of males and females exploring and enjoying the rewards of sex and sexuality on equal terms and not the superior-inferior relationship that was and still is common to popular music. A lyric, such as "Hey, lover, I've got sugar cane that I wanna lose in u 'cause I can't stand the pain," is sexual without being dogmatic because of soft, natural imagery. Also, the ambiguous use of the word "lose" is erotic but not demeaning because it, in an inverted sense, puts the woman in control or in the very least makes her equal to the male because she is not being dominated or driven into submission. The ability to lose oneself or gender in a woman is a double-edged compliment. On the one hand, to become lost physically in a woman is to make an allusion about her vagina size, is to make an allusion about her promiscuity. Yet, she is never denounced nor demonized for her promiscuity. In fact it is her sexual liberation that makes her more appealing because Prince finds in her a doorway to his own liberation. Further, "lose" is an ambiguous image on which Prince builds to discuss finding salvation in women or womanhood. If a man can lose himself, metaphysically, in a woman, he can be reborn a new creature.

This playful ambiguity of "Soft and Wet" echoes Motown and Stevie Wonder. It represents the dedication to craft, to master language in such a way that there are several hidden messages, which must be decoded. Once they are decoded, one gains a revelation of human nature and not mere dogmatism. Lyrics, such as "I really wanna play in your river," are sexual and sensual but not demeaning, making his songs more engaging and tantalizing. Then, his ability to take a metaphor and rework it amplifies the listener's attraction to his work. Whereas in "In Love," a "river" represents the sexual image of a woman's vagina, in "My Love Is Forever" a "river" becomes an emotional and spiritual image. "You're the wind and the rain. You can cry a river that can take away my pain. Your sky is so blue." To "cry a river that can take away pain" is ambiguous and suggestive. Knowing that this is the same guy who wrote "Soft and Wet" we wonder if this is meant to be taken as physical pleasure or emotional pleasure. The point with Prince is that there is no real line separating the two. The image as well as the intent is double voiced; it is both physical and emotional for love and passion are based in the physical and the emotional. Here, as in "Soft and Wet," the male is being baptized and reborn in the woman. Whether that baptism is taking place in the vagina or in the heart is left for the reader to decide. As early as the first album, Prince is making an allusion, a reference, to the ambiguity and duality of the physical and the spiritual. He is laying the foundation for finding completion through woman. This early but raw lyrical prowess entices the listener to delve continuously beneath the cover of Prince's lyrics to find deeper meanings. The listener appreciates the search, the riddle, as a constructive exercise of one's mind, which signifies the ability of art to elevate the public. "Baby" then adds another dimension to the Prince persona by dealing with a topic which had been rarely discussed in popular music, unwanted pregnancy. With all of the sexual explicitness of "Soft and Wet," "Baby" reminds us that there is a price for everything, much in the same manner as "Little Red Corvette" does. Additionally, Prince's use of the first person adds to the impact of the song by allowing the listener to experience first hand the discussion between the involved parties much like the discussion about abortion in the short story "Hills like White Elephants" by Ernest Hemingway. Much like Hemingway's story, it is the discussion and the subject matter that capture the reader's attention. The discussion of an unplanned pregnancy in a 1978 pop song is as rare as Hemingway's discussion of abortion in 1927. The subject matter lends credibility and balance to the album and the artist as a serious writer. "Baby what are we going to do? I barely make enough money for two. Should we go on living together? Should we get married right away?" The uncertainty makes the protagonist a real person, grappling with the responsibilities that come with this new found sexual freedom. Through these songs, Prince presents us with a protagonist who is thinking about sexual liberation and its responsibilities.

In six songs, Prince moves from liberator to hostage, from seducer to prey, from active stud to passive, he-damsel in distress. Yet, he does not stop there. Prince has more gender blurring to do. In "Just as Long as We're

Together," Prince is helping to redefine the notion of romantic relationships through redefining gender roles and commitment by assigning the female the role of stud, while he plays the part of the concubine. "You can live your own life, and I'll live mine because I would never try to bring you down. Even if I only get to see you some of the time, I'm just happy when you come around." Here, he is reworking the "Me and Mrs. Jones" notion, giving the female all the power in deciding the terms of the relationship. The female, not the male, is free to come and go as she pleases. By giving her the power and the freedom, he is able to get what he wants, sex. Sex validates the relationship because the body is all that they have. By empowering the female, Prince is also improving his chances for better sex and a better relationship. And in "I'm Yours" he continues to liquefy his persona by positioning himself completely at the call, mercy, and whim of the female. "Never have I made love before. Never have I wanted to 'till now." Are we to believe that the very same guy who wrote "Soft and Wet" is a virgin? This is more ambiguity. The guy who wrote "Soft and Wet" is not a virgin, but he has never made love, as opposed to merely having sex. Prince is implying that there is much more to this "sex thing" than we acknowledge or more than we understand. The notion is that two people can achieve something more, something higher than a mere orgasm, but only if they are willing to remove the chains of the physical. "I'll do anything you want. You're the teacher. Show me how." Again, Prince is ingratiating himself to the female power, believing that by relinquishing his power he will achieve a greater satisfaction.

The second album, Prince, discusses the emotions of insecurity and loneliness. In "Bambi," the protagonist is driven by an anguish of not being man enough to conquer a lesbian lover. What keeps this from being completely dogmatic is that the protagonist is able to reconcile himself to her way of life. "Maybe it's cause u're so young, or maybe I'm just too naive. Who's to say; maybe you're really having fun." This acceptance of her choice of lover allows him to overcome the insecurities of his penis, making him a more alluring mate for a female. Also, Prince is expanding the exploration of personal fulfillment and gratification through questions of sexual preference. "...maybe you're really having fun." This is a bit different approach to Issac Hayes' discussion of the male enjoyment or intrigue with lesbian lovers. The female in "Bambi" is celebrated for her ability to exist outside the traditional male-female relationship. Yet, Prince is able to strengthen and expand his own persona of being a complete, secure, and open male lover by accepting the female's choice as merely another ride to sexual ecstasy, which is merely a venue or medium to spiritual completion. "With U" and "It's Gonna Be Lonely" are odes to insecurity, which is confronted and safeguarded by sex. Being with his mate or being in a relationship is only an actuality for the male if he is physically inside her. Again, sex not only consummates the relationship, it validates it. The two being physically apart or away from each other's presence evokes a paranoia and anxiety for the male. "It's Gonna Be Lonely" tells of a lover's fear of being alone. The lover is not just concerned with the mate leaving but is also concerned about being left alone in the world, which he is no longer able to escape through sex. In both songs sex affirms and defines the relationship because sex provides the illusion of companionship and inner peace.

Further, "I Wanna Be Your Lover" combines and culminates gender roles for Prince, allowing him to gain power over the female, gaining a sense of completion. He first presents himself as powerless, not being as the traditional male, "without machismo, without cash" (Hill 74). Prince manipulates his ability to deconstruct or remove himself from the traditional male position of power, which allows him to gain more power. He is relinquishing power over the physical to gain power over the emotional, which, in later works, becomes the spiritual.

He wants to represent every emotional safeguard in her life: her mother, her sister, her lover. Behind his gender blurring is his "impulse to possess, control, even dominate. It is the beginning of his inverting traditional sex roles in order to effect entry into the feminine world" (Hill 77). "I Wanna Be Your Lover" is Prince's Trojan Horse, allowing him to penetrate the sorority of womanhood and become an honorary member without giving up his penis. This is a great contrast to someone like actor Alan Alda who has been one of the most notable male feminist supporters. Most men have been quite cynical of Alda because he seems to be against maleness and not just against sexism. On the other hand, Prince, like Smokey Robinson before him, is celebrated because young men believe that Prince, as would Robinson, will eventually "get the panties." Even the symbol of hip hop, thug life masculinity, Tupac, asserts "I love women like Prince loves women." So for all of his femininity, Prince is seen as a wolf in sheep's clothing. Still, on a less cynical note, "I Wanna Be Your Lover" is an interesting song because it moves away from the physical, sex and money, and places emphasis on the soul. Being a "lover" is not just being a sex mate, it is also showing love in every aspect of one's life. It means to make love or to show love in every aspect of the mate's life, tending to the whole/complete romantic needs of a mate, making for a more complete relationship, which makes for a more complete life.

Continuing to redefine himself, Prince moves from the passivity of the first two albums and becomes the aggressor in <u>Dirty Mind</u>. With his androgynous persona well established, he is able to assert his machismo without being perceived as overbearing, sexist, or dogmatic. <u>Dirty Mind</u> is the beginning of the liberation. It presents the sexual liberation which can liberate any oppressed person from all walls, cages, and limitations—sexual, religious, or racial. For so long, the revolution and liberation of oppressed people usually started with social oppression, working toward individual oppression. But with Prince, there is no need to wait. Let's just declare ourselves (individuals) free and act accordingly. First and foremost, there has to be liberation from the most exterior symbols that control or align us with a certain group: clothing and hair. Stripped down to a bikini and a raincoat and wearing processed hair, Prince strips himself of any sign-signifying garb that aligns him with anyone except freedom. The hair also enhances his redefining of blackness or his lack of affirmation of what traditional blackness is considered to be. Prince, in effect, is redefining the perception of blacks in America and speaking for those blacks, mainly middle class, who do not mind being called American and claiming America as theirs with all of the rights and freedoms thereof, and the sexual motif of <u>Dirty Mind</u> is the battering ram for the entire liberation. The title cut, "Dirty Mind," is a song about horny youth (also read restless and irritated youth) who accept sexual and other rebellious thoughts as normal without the need for justification or validation by a group. Thus, Prince is posing the question, "Is the liberation of youth from the mindless existence of conservative parents a dirty idea?" More importantly, what is a dirty mind, and who has the authority to define it as such? The right to choose and not be chosen for, which is emphasized in "Party Up," is now on the table. <u>Dirty Mind</u> is the beginning of a general, impressionistic, and sweeping utopian ideology based on sex and sexuality. Hey man, fuck war and hate, let's have sex and party up! Still, in <u>Dirty Mind</u> there seems to be a definite division between love and sex. In fact, <u>Dirty Mind</u> has nothing to do with love, other than the lack of love. The poetry is too angry and dissatisfied to love anything. Even when attempting to deal with romantic love, the album's edge seems to deal more with loneliness and pain, which are by-products of a society smothered by the oppression of otherness.

"When U Were Mine" and "Gotta Broken Heart Again" exist on opposite ends of the romance spectrum trying desperately to meet. "When U Were Mine" follows in the early tradition of Prince's songs about sex. It is not sex for physical gratification or love, but for companionship and control; when you were mine, you belonged to me, sexually. The protagonist identifies with his lost mate through the sharing of clothes and sex. "When u were mine, I used 2 let u wear all my clothes." (Possibly there is also a sense of self-identification through the female.) Sex is the signifying element that the lovers are still together, even if there is a third, fourth, or fifth partner. "I never cared. I never was the kind to make a fuss when you were there, sleeping in between the two of us." Even though there is no exclusive, monogamous commitment, the sex creates a feeling of closeness and belonging, which manages to remove the fears of insecurity and loneliness. Once the sexual relationship ceases to exist, then there is nothing that connects the protagonist to his mate. He no longer owns her, no longer controls her. And in contrast, "Gotta Broken Heart Again" is a more emotional song of heartbreak and heartache. There is sadness expressed in the loss of a lover, but she is still more objectified as something that has been stolen, "...stole my ole lady away from me, now I'm just as blue as I could be." The protagonist then equates the loss of the female to the money spent trying to retrieve her, "...ain't got no money to spend. I spent it all on a long distance phone call, begging honey please come home." In both songs sex is more tangible than love. Thus, when there is no sex, there is no relationship. The eighties generation objectifies and commodifies everything, and sex is a tangible good that can be bought, sold, and manipulated for personal gain. In this manner, sex becomes more important, more valued, than love or compassion. This is not to say that it is the intent of Prince or his peers to promote sex as something more valuable than love, but this mentality toward sex is certainly seeping its way into the consciousness of popular music. In this instant gratification age, sex is seen as more tangible, more substantive, than romance.

In <u>Controversy</u>, sex becomes the flag of revolution, growing from the sexual liberation of <u>Dirty Mind</u>. The sexual look, tone, and lyric are an attempt to drive forward a new generation called the "New Breed." Being straight or gay, black or white is not the issue. Being comfortable with oneself and guilt free is most important. One is oppressed through fear, ignorance, and guilt. <u>Dirty Mind</u> proclaims that a clear understanding of our sexual selves will save us from this trinity of oppression. <u>Controversy</u> attempts to prove and reassure that sex and sexuality will save us from the trinity of oppression. To do this, Prince has to educate. This education removes the fear and relieves the guilt by showing that sex and sexuality are merely natural extensions of who we are. "Stand up everybody, this is your life," from "Sexuality," is a call for young people to take control of their lives, which begins with their sexuality. The notion of what is meant by "Sexuality is all I ever need. Sexuality, I'm gonna let my body be free," remains a lingering, ambiguous, all encompassing trope. In his use of sexuality, does Prince mean the quality or state of being sexual or the expression of sexual receptivity or interest? It seems that Prince is combining the two notions of sexuality to assert that all humans are by nature sexual. It is the one quality that is universal to us. Accordingly, to suppress one's sexuality is to suppress one's personality. Gaining an understanding of one's sexuality is one of the primary steps to knowing oneself and liberating oneself. The themes of <u>Controversy</u> are built around free, uninhibited self-expression of one's personal ideas and emotions and the open receptiveness of the ideas and emotions of others. When we come to terms with our sexuality, we come to terms with our humanity, which allows the individual to live a more healthy and unencumbered life.

<u>Controversy</u>'s sexual revolution begins with a role reversal of intolerance, where Prince asserts his intolerance of intolerance. "I just can't believe all the things people say. Am I black or white, am I straight or gay? Some people want to die so they can be free. Life is just a game. We're all just the same." For Prince, it is time for

stereotyping and limiting to stop. To him, how one looks will no longer matter. All that matters is what is in your heart. The quiet liberation movement of <u>Dirty Mind</u> is over. Prince declares his rightful place in society. "I think we gotta case." In <u>Controversy</u>, sex and sexuality are the tools, shields, and flags for revolution with songs, such as "Controversy" and "Sexuality." But as a growing artist, he also begins to rework and evolve his sex metaphor. As Prince begins to stretch his sex metaphor in many different directions, he learns how to take that same sexual tension, energy, and imagery and transfer it onto other subjects. Once the body is liberated, one becomes empowered to liberate oneself from other, external issues or, at least, learn how not to be confined by them. So not only is there sex for revolution, <u>Controversy</u> continues the theme of sex for security and power in "Private Joy." The female in "Private Joy" is not just a girl; she is his private joy/toy/tool. No one else can play with or even know about his private joy. This is maximum controlling power. The flaunting of power and superiority may also be seen in the line, "Only I know baby what turns you on." The male ego is on a rampage with its sexual power. Turning one on can be read either sexually or as a control maneuver. The clinching of this subtle monopoly is, "...U've been mine ever since. If anybody asks u, u belong 2 Prince," followed by a "Cum on baby, get up." This is a command not a request to participate in the fun. "Private Joy" represents man's need to obtain companionship by control and isolation. It is a private affair that one can control. Further, one can not allow the ambiguity, which Prince is one of the best at achieving, to bypass unnoticed. This "private" joy may be his own penis, which may be all the male protagonist is able to control. And he even seems to have trouble controlling it, "Cum on baby get up." It is still a command.

"Do Me, Baby" explores the emotional anguish of suppressing personal desires for social norms. The couple stands on the edge or at the crossroads of satisfaction.

However, the female's reluctance to liberate herself is keeping them from acting upon and satisfying their desires. Here, Prince is making use of the traditional understanding and concerns that his audience is bringing to the song. Females are taught one set of sensibilities, and men are given another, and it is the male who is often the one trying to persuade the female to relinquish her sensibilities in regards to sex. Yet Prince's image and history give this persuasion a heightened sense of meaning. There seems to be a notion that the protagonist is not merely trying to the get the female to have sex with him. He seems to be attempting to get her to relinquish her sexual sensibilities, which are symbolic of her notions about life—her notions of right and wrong. The male, of course, is experiencing an extreme amount of pressure and agony from unsatisfied wants. The song expresses well the urgency of the moment where the lyrics are complimented by screams of passion/frustration and light chit-chat, all designed to woo a potential lover into sex. This time the anguish of the romance/sex song has been switched from some exterior motive to an interior motive. This is an example of Prince's ability to express different types of emotions and viewpoints while discussing the same topic. "Controversy" and "Sexuality" inform the listener that sex is going to be the medium to achieve total liberation. "Do Me, Baby" gets down to the liberation.

    The concept of liberation, like any new phase in a person's life, causes fear: fear of the unknown and fear of what people will think for taking this step toward freeing oneself when so many are content to be held captive and oppressed. The end of "Do Me, Baby" culminates with Prince attempting to calm, reassure, and guide his mate through this act of liberation. Sexual liberation falls directly inline with socio-political liberation because our socio-political identities are tied to our sexual identities, our gender, and our prescribed roles and behavior patterns. Again, Prince is using sex as a tool for liberation, realizing that this sexual liberation is often a major and scary step for most. "What are u gonna do? U just gonna sit there and watch?" Prince is imploring his mate and the listener to participate in his sexual liberation. He does not want passive spectators; he wants active participants. Then, in a very impressionistic manner through the use of carefully placed synthesizer notes, moans, and sporadic mumbling, Prince begins to question the whole act of sex and our perceptions of it. "Isn't it suppose to take a long time? I'm not going to stop until the war is over." He is redefining his partner's notion of sex as something with definite purpose and meaning. And as quickly as he redefines this act, with himself being the conductor on this journey, Prince shifts gears to show that this is a two person activity with mutual satisfaction/liberation gained only through the full cooperation of both of the involved parties. He invokes this by demanding, "Help Me!" in a contrastingly more feminine falsetto tone than the more masculine alto toned spoken lines prior to this. He ends this ride by completely relinquishing his position of power and strength, pleading to be consoled and safeguarded by his partner. "Just hold me." This shifting of roles reconfirms that sexual liberation is about mutual involvement, something that the master-slave, Jefferson-Hemings, relationship cannot be. With Prince, sexual liberation is not about dominance; it is about companionship, two people aiding each other to achieve something that only the union of two can bring, something higher than a physical orgasm. For Prince, sex is about two people liberating each other, no matter the oppression, fear, or anxiety. Even in songs where sex is used for dominance or to gain power, he first shows the hole of emptiness. In some of the songs, sex is used to temporarily ease pains and ills. In some songs, sex is used as a door to greater truths and heights. "Do Me, Baby" is about going higher, using sex as a medium to achieve the sublime. This feeling/revelation is then used to address other aspects of one's life. Sex is medicine. How one uses that medicine is up to them. Sex is power. How one uses that power is up to them.

Songs like "Ronnie Talk to Russia" and "Annie Christian" follow in the same mood as "Uptown" and "Party Up" but do not use the same type of sexual overtones to articulate their messages. With his sexual liberation metaphor and imagery firmly rooted in the minds of the American public, Prince is now able to freely pursue other avenues of creating and expressing thoughts and ideas with a variety of music and imagery. In "Ronnie Talk to Russia," Prince takes the sexual anxiety and urgency which begins in "Private Joy" and transfers it to socio-political concerns. The two songs include the same screams, yells, and grinding guitar as the songs which use the sexual metaphor, but "Ronnie Talk to Russia" takes that landscape of the songs rooted in sexual tension and urgency and embeds a specific socio-political concern at the forefront without the use of the sexual metaphor. Prince is able to address these socio-political issues with the same intensity because they exist in a circular relationship with sexual liberation because all oppression begins with the body, be it gender, class, or race. The liberation sought in "Sexuality," "Do, Me Baby," "Private Joy," and "Jack U Off" is parallel to the liberation sought in "Controversy" and "Ronnie Talk to Russia." Furthermore, the battle for socio-political liberation is also personal for Prince. The use of sexual, biracial, and bisexual illusions allows Prince to demolish the walls of limitations before the industry and the public are able to place them firmly around him, limiting his growth and expression. By beginning at the cutting edge of style, music, racial identity, and sexual identity, there is no where to go but off the deep end. The confusion and chaos allows Prince, not the media, to set the tone for his career. And, as the protagonists in his songs, Prince uses sex as a tool, grabbing America's and the world's attention and manipulating our emotions and ideals. Then, under the cover of the sexual metaphor, Prince slips or inserts his social agenda or gripe. So, it is no coincidence that "Ronnie Talk to Russia" falls between "Private Joy" and "Let's Work." Musically, the screeching and grinding guitar that ends "Private Joy" segues to "Ronnie Talk to

Russia," and there is an undertone of mumbles that bridge the two songs. The listener is able to transfer the sexual energy from "Private Joy" to "Ronnie Talk to Russia." And this energy is heightened by the fact that both songs are in the mode of pleading for relief, one for sexual relief and one for political relief. Accordingly, "Ronnie Talk to Russia" then explodes, orgasm style, into "Let's Work," which is an ambiguous title that contains more pleading and demanding for sexual liberation. The genius is in the transferring of energy, which gives each song on the album an added sense of urgency. We find that the desire for sexual liberation is the same as the desire for political liberation.

1999 is an illusionary, surreal album that uses sexual images to convey its messages. It is a credit to Prince's ability to dictate to the public images of himself and his music. 1999 is not about the sexual revolution, nor does it try to be sexy. Nevertheless sex is all over the album, acting in various roles. Unlike the past albums, Prince uses sex more as a spice in a recipe, rather than the driving force of the song. The songs, "D.M.S.R. (Dance, Music, Sex, Romance)," "Let's Pretend We're Married," "Automatic," "Delirious," and "Little Red Corvette" deal more with the neurotic problems of the character than with sexual desire or even the use of sex to solve the problem. Now a more mature writer, Prince is expanding or diversifying his concentration on the problems of being human, which makes sexual dissatisfaction a particle of the human condition and not the entire human condition. Only "International Lover" actually deals in-depth with sexual gratification, and this is only after the state of loneliness has been conveyed to the listener. 1999 is definitely about what is going on under the covers, not the covers of the bed, but under the covers of man's outward appearance and actions.

Besides the use of sex, what should be noted is Prince's elaborate and masterful use of the extended metaphor, the traditional comparing of the human body to a car and airplane, which displays his lyrical mastery and links him to the lyrical legacy of rock-n-roll. The car and airplane metaphor are probably the most machismo illusions in American popular culture. Americans have always had a love affair with their cars. So, why not have a love affair with one of the most desired of all American cars, a corvette. Then add the code word "little" to equate small or feminine (American males often refer to their cars as she.), make it red to symbolize hot and hard to handle, and you have invented one of the most desirable cars/women in American history. Even further, the color red can be seen as symbolizing the light-skinned black woman who is the most desired by all American males, who, through her skin tone, represents the perverse sexuality of white males. What are light-skinned African Americans, but walking symbols and offspring of the rage of white male lust and sexuality? This schizophrenia is also seen in the long history of white women who endure great risks and dangers to achieve a tan the hue of light-skinned blacks. Thus, "Little Red Corvette" is another example of Prince's lyrical mastery of compacting and encoding a song with several messages. The song shows that sex and sexuality are complex and complicated, based as much on the psyche as the body. Yet although seductive in sound, "Little Red Corvette" is meant to warn not praise. Sexual liberation does not mean sexual irresponsibility. The little red Corvette is living on the edge of irresponsibility, hopping from bed to bed, showing all the signs of going off the deep end. "I could tell by the way she parked her car sideways, it wouldn't last...love 'em and leave 'em fast...a pocket full of Trojans (condoms), some of them used...[room full of] pictures of all the jockeys that were there before me." "Little Red Corvette" is not only stating that love is more satisfying than sex, but that sex on the edge can be disastrous. "U need 2 find a love before u run your body 2 the ground." Yet for all its warning, it is still filled with machismo. The protagonist is in no way attempting to get the car to stop. He only wants her to slow down long enough for him to become the exclusive and permanent driver. This song is, as the American male psyche is, schizophrenic in its desire to be both pimp and savior. The motives of possession and control are still there, even if buried beneath supposed sincerity. "A body like yours ought to be in jail/ Give me the keys/ I'm gonna try to tame your/ Little red love machine." So in the end, the protagonist is still only attempting to win the prize of a fine ass freak to show off. The warnings of life on the edge are lost to the mass public because of the heavy-handed machismo of sexual fantasy.

As we think we are about to drive off into the sunset with our newly gained Corvette, Prince decides to take us on an excursion down the many roads of sexuality. One trip, "Automatic," is popular, tongue and cheek masochism. The pleasure and the pain of love are not opposites, but the same. They exist as a continuum rather than as two sides of a coin, "Cause when u cry, me cry, boo hoo. It's automatic 2." The attempt to gain power is as enjoyable as exercising the power. The looking "4 a needle in a haystack" is not a duty but a pleasure of submission. The tension of reconciling male to female and pleasure to pain is the essence of the relationship. Prince is constructing the male/female relationship into an ambiguous, androgynous creature to understand and experience the totality of the union. He is able to do this by deconstructing gender roles.

> "A basic element in the chemistry of 'Automatic' was that its characters seemed to have inverted the conventional relations of sexual power; Prince played the faceless servant to a dominant (and equally faceless) mistress—or mistresses, for Heavens sake. And this was pretty much consistent with the way his whole look, not to mention his inventory of mannerisms, had taken on more of what were usually defined as feminine characteristics" (Hill 129).

The closer Prince moves toward abstract and spiritual concepts, i.e. <u>Purple Rain</u>, <u>Around the World in a Day</u>, <u>Lovesexy</u>, and <u>Graffiti Bridge</u>, his general appearance and mannerisms become more feminine as it is defined by American culture. Yet, this is not the homosexual feminine. This is the feminine in breaking free of the traditional male gender roles, opening himself to multi-pathways toward completion through the male/female relationship. It seems that Prince is attempting to find a way to become the complete living experience. The most prevailing pattern is that his physical persona becomes more feminine for the albums that primarily discuss transcending the physical plane. The hair becomes longer and more flowing, the eyelashes are longer and fuller, there is more make-up, and his lips express a more exaggerated pout. This change in appearance represents his notion that man must take off (remove) the learned personas of the physical world in order to achieve the spiritual. Both women and men must strip and take on (embrace) the other's personality if humanity is ever going to bridge the gender gap and evolve. This symbolism does not merely exist in his personality. In fact his exterior is only a manifestation or supporting setting for the symbolism present in his work. Prince wants us to see nudity and femininity metaphorically not literally. Thus, the <u>Dirty Mind</u> and <u>Lovesexy</u> covers of Prince's nude feminine poses should be seen as his physical transformation that is meant to parallel his metaphysical transformation which is being discussed by the lyrics. So, his femininity in "Automatic" allows him to be both victim and seducer. For the majority of the song, the male is being controlled. "U ask me if I love U; it's automatic 'cuz every time U leave me, I die; that's automatic 2. U ask me 2 forgive U when U know I'm just an addict. So stop the music baby, U know U're all I wanna do…I'll rub your back forever; it's automatic…I'll go down on U all night long, it's automatic. And even when I'm right, I'll be wrong." Yet, by the end of the song, the male protagonist is back in the driver's seat. In one song, the tone switches from helpless pawn to purple pimp, showing that role reversal is an innate part of the searching process in the romantic/sexual relationship.

> "Don't say no man has ever tasted your ice cream. Baby U're the purple star in the night supreme. U'll always be a virgin for no man deserves your love. I only pray that when U dream, I'm the 1 U dream of...There's no 1 else like me. I'm the best U'll ever find. No 1 else could understand U, U're 2 complex."

The experience of dominance/submission in "Automatic" becomes aggression and anger in "Lady Cab Driver." In a 1983 <u>Musician</u> interview, Prince elaborates on the use of sex in general and in "Lady Cab Driver."

> "Musician: Is the word "sex" almost interchangeable sometimes?
> Prince: Yes. I think everything basically is. Like in 'Lady Cab Driver,' for example, 'sex' is used in two different contexts. One is anger.
> Musician: Does that imply an S&M kind of thing? A lot of people might perceive that from the record.
> Prince: Well, that's up to them. I don't want to burst anybody's bubble, but the whole idea was that a lot of people make love out of loneliness sometimes.
> Musician: And they want to be touched in reassurance?
> Prince: Yes, exactly. It just went from anger and you start saying, 'well, how long can this go on? This is a person here. I have to be human.' The right spot was hit so..." (Hilburn, "Mixed Emotions" 58).

Sex, then, is a tool to achieve power. Our sexuality is the philosophy and manner in which we exert power and dominance in our lives. The American system of hierarchy has been founded and hung on the penis. The penis is the metaphor and tool of dominance in society as Dr. Frances Cress Welsing shows so effectively in her book <u>The Isis Papers</u>. In "Lady Cab Driver," the male is using his tool to drive home his dominance, hoping to gain a sense of being. Because of his insecurity and lack of power from being captured in the clutches of life, the sexual aggression he inflicts on the lady cab driver is used to convince himself more than the female or the listener. He is not preaching or proclaiming his dominance, but merely thinking aloud as in self-affirmation. The listener is simply a passer-by who is stealing a look/listen at the two people getting it on for the hell and salvation of it. As Hill asserts, there is much more going on than an orgasm.

> "Prince dedicates his every pelvic propulsion either to some particular object of his love, or else some target of his revulsion. God, predictably enough, comes out on the credit side of this rapid coital appraisal. The real-life jealousy he has said he once felt toward his brother—very possibly Duane, the tall half-brother on his father's side—gets a [poke]. The extremely affluent, meanwhile, enjoy a carefully qualified damnation; the exemptions are selected with considerable strategic wisdom, given the rate at which Prince's own bank account would have been swelling at this time. (It's only the greedy one's he hates!) As Prince pumps out this litany of moral ticks and crosses, a glut of ideological reinforcement and self-reference, the lady cab driver herself squeals and groans and probably makes a mess of the upholstery. Flipping over the coin of 'Automatic', it is plain that she is at his mercy. Is this submission fantasy or a rape? Or are they just doing it right?" (Hill 131).

Trading a cab for an airplane, "International Lover" is the other extended, sexual metaphor. Even though sexual gratification seems to be glorified, loneliness and the search for companionship are actually being discussed.

The lines, "Baby, it appears to me, that u could use a date tonight...I know it's been a long time since u've been satisfied. I can tell by the look in your eyes," seem to be implying that the sex, which is about to happen, is more inspired by loneliness than passion or lust. Hey, we are both here alone, being lonely; let's have sex. Then begins the jet airplane metaphor:

> "My plane's parked right outside. Don't u wanna go for a ride?...U are flying aboard the Seduction 747...for any reason there's a loss in cabin pressure, I will automatically drop down to apply more...We are making our final approach to satisfaction. Please remain seated 'til the aircraft has come to a complete stop. Thank u for flying Prince International. Next time u fly, fly Prince International."

In both "Little Red Corvette" and "International Lover" the rides, of course, are representations of the sexual acts. They are trips to escape the chaotic world, journeys to paradise. So if the female is a corvette, the male has to be symbolized as something much stronger, harder, faster, and essentially more powerful—a jet airplane. This type of symbolism is ripped right from the pages of Chuck Berry's macho dominated world. Underneath Prince's feminine persona lies a male conqueror, longing to attract, win, own, and control his women. Yet at the same time, there is a need to achieve a spiritual connection through sharing either emotions or bodies. Even his most feminine traits are aspects of his persona used to tap into the psyche and comfort zone of the female's femininity in order to achieve completion and evolve to a higher being.

"Delirious" simplifies the complex discussions about neurosis and addresses the physical reaction to the opposite sex. For the most part, it deserves mention as one of the few songs that concerns itself purely with sexual attraction and desire. It has nothing to do with any of the human anxieties. And unlike the other songs mentioned, "Delirious" is a short lyrical piece. This could indicate that, as a primary topic, sex and sexual attraction are less profound and interesting when it is sex for sexual gratification only. Yet, after the great sex of "Delirious" is finished, we are left with and forced to address the time after sex as "Delirious" is followed by "Let's Pretend We're Married," which is more inline with the early Prince sexual lyric. It is both melancholy and abrogating in emotion. It carries the tone of the album into the pseudo or even anti-romantic line. There is not one love song on 1999. All of the songs about the male-female relationship are more about the search for something else and the use of sex as a tool to find it or as way to pass the time while waiting for it. Life and the pain that comes with life are going to end soon, and, since nothing lasts forever, let's just pretend we are married all night long. Loneliness, again, is the driving force. "My girl's gone, and she don't care at all...since u are alone like me, come on baby let's ball." The word ball is meant to be read by the listener as sex, but with Prince ambiguity is ever present. This is not to give excessive credit to Prince's talents, but he has made a career on existing in a state of ambiguity and duality. "Ball" is a term that was used widely by songwriters of the fifties, such as Little Richard and Jerry Lee Lewis. These two used the term so interchangeably that it carries with it the baggage of heavy ambiguity that makes it so appealing to Prince. And since Prince's usage of the term, rappers have again redefined the word for their own use. With that in mind, "ball" can encompass all of the meanings associated with pleasure, meaning that intimacy and escapism do not only mean sexing our brains out. However, the point of the song has to do with the pretense of marriage, the pretense of love in order to make it through the night, the "pretense"—facade—needed to make it through life. Let's have a ball and escape this hell. It is the sexual act not the orgasm that allows us to escape. We continue to get sexual fix after sexual fix to relieve the pain in our lives. Why get married? That causes pain. Let's just pretend we're married, skip the emotional, and shortcut to the physical. And tomorrow night, we will do it all over again.

"Let's Pretend We're Married" is addressing and representing the changing times and values of American culture. America is a culture based on euphemisms, lies, and hypocrisy. The Civil Rights Movement caused America (young, white America) to awake to these lies and hypocrisies. Institutions such as Christianity and marriage were seen as the bastions of America's hypocrisy and oppression and were either abandoned or so modified that they lost their absolute power. Not only were people leaving traditional religions, the institution of marriage was being severely modified, if not abandoned all together. When Prince asks, "If you ain't busy for the next seven years," he is commenting on the rising divorce rate in America. Between 1960 and 1980 the divorce rate increased two hundred and fifty percent. Because of historical institutionalized oppression and hypocrisy, individuals were rejecting the collective for their own personal, individualized satisfaction. There is no more community interest over self interest. Even with this, we must understand that it is the oppression and hypocrisy of the mainstream culture that creates the counter-culture. Marriage is failing America because the principles on which it is built are in shambles. In the eighties, marriage is equated with the antiquated, insufficient, and oppressive values of the past or is viewed as a hindrance to professional careers and self-fulfillment, especially for women. Yet, we still want the personal gratification of marriage, which includes sex and companionship. Even more, we want those personal gratifications right now! The push button age of easy access is saturating every aspect of our lives. We are willing to sacrifice essence and value for speed immediacy. We are answering the question of "Do you want it right, or do you want if fast?" with a resounding "Fast, dammit!" We no longer want to dedicate the time and effort of building something with the chance that it will not last or it will not be what we wanted or thought it would be.

In the sixties and seventies people created or built organizations and constructed alliances with the hopes of making the world a better place, and many see those dreams or institutions has having failed. So, rather than continuing to buy into another failed institution, let's pretend we are married; let's play house. Let's see if we can get personal satisfaction without the drawbacks or side-effects or commitment or marriage. This attitude is justified by the fact that all of the established institutions were playing with our lives and getting rich doing so; Watergate and Wall Street become the tropes for this. The government is pretending. The public school system is pretending. The political organizations are pretending. They all are merely perpetuating the status quo on the backs of individuals who believe in the system. Once the individuals recognize this hypocrisy, it becomes a natural progression for individuals to put their interests before the interest of the community. Unfortunately, this plays right into the hands of the powers that be, which retains power and even prospers through the fragmenting of communities into individuals. "Let's Pretend We're Married" mirrors eighties ideology. It is the difference between motivation and organization. The sex metaphor can, like a good Jesse Jackson speech, motivate people to act or react, but it fails to organize people to construct permanent systems of solutions. Though Prince is preaching that strong individuals make for a strong society, the masses merely embrace the selfishness of individuality. Sex remains, even for his listeners, a selfish act of personal gratification and escapism. In the rejection of one system or set of values, the oppressed fail to establish a completely different system with a completely different set of values and goals. Most either attempt to integrate into the oppressive system and change it from the inside, and others divorce themselves from the system and live isolated. In either case they become fragmented, isolated, and ineffective, gaining only minimal individual success or gratification.

"D.M.S.R.," which follows "Let's Pretend We're Married," is an attempt to lighten the melancholy mood of inevitable destruction or at least put it all into perspective. It is, for the most part, a celebration of the liberation that has always taken place in Prince's music, even if only in his own world. It is a call for the members of the society or the club to get off the wall and liberate themselves through dance and music, which have long been mediums and metaphors for sex and the romance of life. To bide time until the destruction of the world, "D.M.S.R." adopts a party attitude rather than a melancholy mood. In this manner it is much akin to "1999." Might as well live your life the way that you want to live it before it is all too late. Though "D.M.S.R." seems to be a contradiction, it is not. Sex is serious, but it is not to be prescribed or regulated for procreation only under the umbrella of marriage. Furthermore, the reality is that men behave in the manner that they do to capture mates, to have sex. As Paul Stanley of the rock group KISS affirms in an interview with MTV for its <u>Real Sex</u> series, "Every kid who straps on a guitar does so to get a girl. All of your social and political statements come later. Girls come first." In "D.M.S.R.," Prince affirms, "I don't wanna be no poet 'cause I don't wanna blow it. I don't care to win awards. All I wanna do is dance, play music, sex, romance. Try my best to never get bored." Yes, there are more important concerns than having sex, but they are driven by our desire to have sex. One wants/needs a revolution when he is not given the right to life, liberty, and the pursuit to happiness.

The foundation of civilization is male-female relationship. If one is not able to nurture a constructive male-female relationship, one will be unable to nurture a constructive society. "All I want to do is dance, play music, sex, romance," but the socio-political matrix causes me to pay more attention to other areas of my life. This echoes Baraka's poem "Black Art" when he asserts "Let there be no love poems written until love can exist freely and cleanly." Many black poets misinterpret this statement by Baraka as meaning that black poets should not write love poems. On the contrary, what is meant is that love poems cannot be written if black people do not exist in conditions that are conducive to love. Therefore, modern-day black love songs are often dogmatic because the black existence is often dogmatic. It is the socio-political landscape or matrix which causes a song like "D.M.S.R." to mutate into songs like "Automatic," "Something in the Water (Does not Compute)," and "Lady Cab Driver," where the protagonist is acting against this socio-political matrix as he is acting upon his sex partner. So, Prince's answer to the complexity raised on <u>1999</u> is that dance (individual expression), music (effective art), sex (personal expression and a gateway to utopia), and romance (the metaphysical combining of male and female for a higher purpose) are what is needed to take us to a higher place.

On the heels of <u>1999</u>, <u>Purple Rain</u> attempts to personify all of the evolving ideals and notions of Prince's past into the characters of the movie. Thus, the characters created for the movie and album represent many of the emotions that Prince has been expressing through his music: the paranoid control freak, tyrant father; the neurotic, nagging mother; the power hungry, egotistical nemesis; the self-concerned, lonely brat; and the unconcerned non-understanding, emotionless public. Sexually speaking, <u>Purple Rain</u> tends to express these emotions by isolating individuals into one-dimensional beings. Physical and emotional characteristics are allowed only to come together and reconcile in "Purple Rain" and "I would Die 4 U" when the transformation from body to soul is complete. The sexual imagery of the quest and liberation is contained in "Computer Blue," "Darling Nikki," and "The Beautiful Ones." These songs tell of the sex act's inability to yield complete emotional and spiritual satisfaction. They follow each other on the album and in the movie as the mapping of the search by the protagonist:

the search for love and the search for completion.

"The Beautiful Ones" begins our journey for love through sex. It is the initial sexual attraction, leading to lust. The protagonist is looking for love in the wrong place, in physical beauty. He is building a relationship on sexual attraction. The result is a confrontation about a rival lover, which is also based on physical attraction. If a relationship is rooted in physical attraction or beauty, it has no base on which to stand and will eventually fall or be abandoned for a more beautiful thing/person. "The Beautiful ones u always seem 2 lose." The relationships fail because they are constructed on false foundations. We are living in a society that attributes inner qualities to physical appearance. We are falling in love with bodies and not souls. As long as we continue to do this, we will suffer the repercussions of building our lives as straw hut houses. "Paint a perfect picture, bring 2 life a vision in one's mind. The beautiful ones always smash the picture, every time."

"Computer Blue" continues the realization that love and lust are at different ends of the human emotion spectrum. In "Computer Blue" the body acts as a machine, mindlessly going through relationships and sex partners looking for completion. For all of its trouble, all it gets are broken parts. "There must be something wrong with the machinery" or something wrong with the search for love. There is nothing wrong with the machinery but something wrong with the programming. Humans must be reprogrammed about their notions of love. "Poor lonely computer. It's time someone programmed u. It's time u learned; love and lust, they both have 4 letters, but they are entirely different words. Poor lonely computer, do u really know what love is?" There are two interesting notions about this passage. One, this passage is not included in the song but on the lyric sheet. This points to the notion that Prince is very serious about his lyrics and wants his listeners to read the lyric sheets for the entire message.

Secondly, this passage is credited to "The Righteous 1" and would be read by a female voice during the live performance of "Computer Blue" during the <u>Purple Rain</u> tour. This passage indicates that humans cannot program themselves to reach completion, but must be programmed by a higher power. Lust is of the body. Love is of the spirit. Therefore, the body must yield/submit to the spirit, yield/submit to the higher power to know love, to know completion. The fact that the voice of "The Righteous 1" is female affirms that Prince believes that man must find salvation and completion through woman. This is what Wendy, Lisa, Jill, and Apollonia all represent to the Kid. In battling with Day and his father to prove his masculinity, the Kid is embracing death—death of himself as symbolized by the deaths of all of his relationships. He is following in the pattern of his father who is never able to embrace femininity. The ultimate challenge is to transcend maleness, his natural inclination to dominate and to control, and allow the women in his life to play fertilizing roles, which will allow him to evolve. This is seen most clearly when he forbids Apollonia's request to work with Day to further her career and when he rejects songs from Wendy and Lisa. His desire to dominate hinders him from evolving. It is only when he realizes through his father's attempted suicide that the only thing waiting at the end of the road of dominance is death. As Prince is maturing as a writer, he is showing that completion is a spiritual (emotional) act and not a physical act. This is found in seeking the metaphysical benefits of human relationships.

"Darling Nikki" continues this theme as it is one last attempt to find completion through sex. "Darling Nikki" is about one neurotic attempting to find happiness with another neurotic whose lair is filled with sexual devices that are suppose to enhance our ability to experience or find utopia. Not only do these sexual devices signify the female's promiscuity, they also symbolize humanity's embracing of artificial stimuli to achieve emotional and spiritual pleasure and satisfaction. Many in society, like the male protagonist, find temporary, momentary, satisfaction. In the morning, however, everything is still the same, and the protagonist is left alone. "Woke up the next morning, Nikki wasn't there. Looked all over, and all I found was a phone number on the stairs." "Darling Nikki" is asserting sex's inability to bestow completion. To follow this road is a hopeless journey, leading one down the road to destruction. Through his experience with Nikki, the protagonist is beginning to see that sex does not yield love as affirmed in the afterword, which is played backwards amidst a storm of swirling winds. "Hello, I'm fine 'cause I know the Lord is coming soon." To paraphrase, sex ain't saving me, so I might as well wait on the Lord, thus reaffirming the message of "Computer Blue."

If <u>Purple Rain</u> is the promise of the journey toward utopia, then <u>Around the World in a Day</u> is the representation of that journey to and the finding of utopia. <u>Around the World in a Day</u> deals with the individual's ability to discover self and others while discovering inner peace. It is an expedition of the mind, heart, body, soul, and world. It attempts to cover every human emotion in an attempt to experience, reconcile, and move to higher truths and living. Sex is not left untouched. Through sex, Prince explores fantasy in "Tamborine," boredom in "Raspberry Beret," and the inner journey and struggle to find love and the higher spiritual state in "Temptation."

Probably the most elaborate and extended metaphor Prince has crafted is "Tamborine." It is a song about fulfillment, loneliness, and guilt all found in the act of masturbation. The tamborine represents the sex organ. The chaotic sound of tamborines behind Prince's moaning and screaming creates a sense of urgency to be loved. The combination of dynamic sound imagery and the slight attempt to conceal the topic heightens the anxious tone of the song. "Oh my God, here I go, falling in love with the face from a magazine...Long days, lonely nights, too bad we're not allowed to scream. All alone, by myself, me and I play my tambourine." Why is the protagonist not allowed to scream? Is he afraid of being discovered, or is he attempting to keep some grasp on reality, which keeps him from becoming lost in the fantasy? The sound imagery is reminiscent of Poe's "Bells," while the hidden sexual theme screams Emily Dickinson or Zora Neale Hurston's pear tree metaphor in <u>Their Eyes Were Watching God</u>. And the fantasy of achieving inner peace through masturbation is raised by the wit and imagery in "If I Was Your Girlfriend." Merging the sentiments of romantic and social urgency, "If I Was Your Girlfriend" deals with the most common and fragile thread of connection and nation building for the society, the male-female romantic relationship. It concentrates on the inability of males and females to fully connect because of their inability to communicate with each other. It is this inability to connect or control that leads to the masturbation in "Tamborine."

The masturbation in "Tamborine" represents one's exploration of self and mind for the emotional satisfaction not found in the real world. The protagonist has an empty room, a magazine, and his mind to create a complete world of fantasy with "trolley cars that juggle 17." The protagonist has completely retreated from society or the outside world. He would rather, "stay inside and play around [his] baby's tamborine." By the end of the song, the female actually appears to be there through the voices of Wendy and Lisa. Interestingly enough, Wendy and Lisa are not credited for their work on the song though their voices are distinctly heard or mimicked. In fact, the only credit is given to Prince. This lends more power to the song. Masturbation is an individual activity where one fantasizes/creates a whole world for his pleasure. Sex, or masturbation in this case, takes on the idea of escapism as in "Let's Pretend We're Married." But here, it attempts to build an entire world. Through the masturbation scene, the protagonist is able to gain security and love in a world created especially for him. Fantasy replaces reality so that one is able to manipulate the world for his pleasure. The female's voice shows just how virtual or real the imagination can be. She is there, but she is not there. And a far greater number of us than will admit have opted for fantasy over reality, for the illusion of inner peace over the reality of living in hell. As comedian Damon Wayans asserts in his HBO special, masturbation is not just about sex, nor is it just about fantasy, but some hybrid of the two. In this context, masturbation serves the same purpose as sex, proving once again that sex is as much a psychological endeavor as it is a physical endeavor.

Next we find boredom being satisfied with sex. We have a young male in a dead end job, in a small town, going nowhere, doing nothing. "Raspberry Beret" is a comment on the human spirit's desire not just to exist but to experience life and achieve some sense of satisfaction and fulfillment. Our protagonist is "busy doing something close to nothing, but different than the day before." He is living a life of constant nothingness. The female represents a new day, time, or occurrence in the life of the protagonist. Again, the female is representing life. Though the most important fact about her is that "she walked in through the out door" and that "she wore a raspberry beret," she still represents the medium through which the protagonist finds something. Though still objectified to some degree, the female in this song manages to rise to a higher level of humanity than the female characters prior to "Darling Nikki." This construction of a two dimensional, female character represents more growth for Prince as a writer. Sex is still being celebrated, but the female character moves from being merely an object, to being a woman, to being human. She is given very distinguishing characteristics, both physical and psychological. And even though she "isn't too bright," she attempts to express her concerns about this event. "She had the nerve 2 ask me if I planned 2 do her any harm." It is not just her being female, but it is her uniqueness which relieves our protagonist from his boredom. The shift removes the emphasis from sex and places the emphasis on the partner. The protagonist is reminiscing. However, he is not just remembering the sex; he is remembering the female as well. This represents more growth for Prince as a writer.

This evolving theme of sex is expanded in "Pop Life." After "Raspberry Beret" shifts the emphasis of completion and evolution from sex to relationships, "Pop Life" reduces sex to a passing thrill, used mindlessly as many other quick fixes by people to achieve a temporary high or emotional gratification. The celebration of romance or the mere communing with another being in "Raspberry Beret" allows Prince to mature in his writing about sex. "Raspberry Beret" does not abandon sex; it simply lessens its importance by celebrating the woman as much as celebrating the act of sex. "They say the first time ain't the greatest, but I tell ya if I had the chance 2 do it all again, I wouldn't change a stroke 'cause baby I'm the most with a girl as fine as she was then." Although it is an enjoyable experience, sex, alone, is not enough to build a relationship, which will be a path to completion. The protagonist is not just remembering the good sex, he is remembering the woman with whom he had the sex. It is not sex in a vacuum, but something about the woman that makes the sex so enjoyable. Her beret symbolizes that it is human uniqueness that is special and not the sex act, itself. This shift allows Prince to concentrate more on the metaphysical aspects of relationships. In order to do this, Prince begins to show that sex is lacking when it is just for physical gratification. As with the other quick fixes, sex also falls short in satisfying our need to find a constant high to survive. In the extended twelve inch version of "Pop Life," Prince adds, "What's the matter with your sex? Is fifteen minutes your best? Guess you gotta get it off your chest." Mindless sex is artificial and spiritually unfulfilling. Even the act of sex becomes short-lived, providing temporary satisfaction. Until the female in "Pop Life" is able to understand and find true love, her sexual gratification will continue to be lacking, forcing her to continue her search. "Why you need another love when you know my love's the best, but I guess that's pop life." This also speaks to the fickle nature of record buyers and the fleeting fame of pop stardom. Pop stars are just something to do until the next craze comes. In parallel to this, humanity is perpetuating the pop life, searching for something to fill the empty spaces. Fads come and go as man is constantly seeking the new experience to camouflage or dull the pain of boredom and restlessness from having no inner peace. Prince is asserting that until humanity realizes its need for inner peace and turns to the spiritual world, our joy will be fleeting and our search will never end.

Bringing <u>Around the World in a Day</u> to a sizzling and contemplative end, "Temptation" explores the differences between lust and love. It is concerned with sexual obsession and the confusion of this emotion with love. The protagonist has associated the emotion of lust with the emotion of love, having lost the way to love on the road of lust and sexual gratification. At the end of the journey, the protagonist is left to confront God about his ideas of sex and love. It is important to realize that the protagonist is sentenced to death and not hell, for the wages of sin are death. This may be taken to mean that the constant misuse of sex is irresponsible and leads to physical punishments, such as STDs and death. By the end of the song, the protagonist finds a new meaning of love and lust, as any altercation with the almighty will cause. "Love is more important than sex. Now I understand." The protagonist will need this understanding if he is to complete his journey to inner peace. This is a never-ending journey as the protagonist continues his quest even though the album ends. "I must go now. I don't know when I'll return." At this juncture, Prince has taken us through the <u>Purple Rain</u>, and we have enjoyed "Paisley Park" with our new found psychedelic peace. With our new understanding, we will be able to enjoy and participate in the <u>Parade</u> of life.

Sexually, <u>Parade</u> represents the exploration of the male-female romantic relationship. In the romantic songs of <u>Parade</u> there is an urgency to construct relationships that will lead to our evolution. For Prince, monogamy has yet to be explored in the same depth as the sexual relationships. Prince is pondering and paralleling the possibilities and similarities of monogamy to man's devotion to a higher being. In <u>Parade</u> Prince is celebrating life and all of its relationships: God and the individual, the individual and society, and the individual to the individual. "New Position" sets the tone with a plea to save a dying relationship. It is the standard sexual seduction, but this time the reason is not only for sexual gratification but to hold a love together. "We've been together 4 2 long. U've got 2 try my new funk." With the use of the word funk, Prince is lending ambiguity to the song. Funk has long been used to mean anything from music, to sex, to freedom. And here, it is attempting to liberate a couple from the mundane routine of their lives by giving their relationship a freshness or newness. It may be an attempt to get love through great sex, but it is not an attempt for control or escapism as in the past. Now, to goal is to achieve love. The honesty and courage of "New Position" gives it an intensity. Rather than trying to deny that there is nothing wrong with the relationship, the protagonist faces the problem with the hopes of saving the relationship. This discussion of honesty is explored in greater detail in "Do U Lie?" which also helps to shape the album's atmosphere set by "New Position." "Do U Lie?" is an ode to honesty. "When I lie awake in my boudoir, I think of u dear. Do u think of me, or do u lie? When I'm in a sad and lonely mood dear, I cry 4 u dear. Do u cry 4 me, or do u lie?" There can be no love without honesty. Two people cannot connect if they are unable to embrace their real feelings. "I say that I'm in love mama...Tell me do u feel it 2, or do u lie? Do u cry from the inside out dear? Are they only artificial tears? Do u really mean it when u cry?" Prince is reaching back and refashioning his own history or ideology as in a song such as "When U Were Mine." Remember, in the early songs monogamy is not a prerequisite for a meaningful relationship. In "Do U Lie," although the protagonist suffers pain because of the extra affairs of his mate, what really seems to hurt him most is her dishonesty as he keeps asking the question, "Do u lie?" The importance of balance between the physical and the metaphysical is highlighted in "Do U Lie" because the physical seems meaningless to the protagonist without the commitment of the heart. Unlike the early songs, sex is not as important as gaining an emotional commitment.

"Under the Cherry Moon" and "Girls and Boys" continue this discussion of balancing the physical with the spiritual, dealing with physical attraction and the social restraints of love. <u>Under the Cherry Moon</u> is about a black, street hustling gigolo who falls in love with a rich, white girl—the nightmare of the American hierarchy. And of course, her daddy is having none of that. In both songs the protagonist is lamenting of a love that he can never have because she is promised to another whom she does not love. This is courtly love poetry, the denial of love because of social or political restraints as in Dante's "Because You Know You're Young in Beauty Yet" or as in <u>Sir Gawain and the Green Knight</u>. Although Prince attempts to use sex as a concession, it is unable to relieve the anguish of the lovers' desire to engage in a full, complete romantic relationship. "How can I stand 2 stay where I am? Poor butterfly who don't understand. Why can't I fly away in a special sky? If I don't find my destiny soon. I'll die in your arms under the cherry moon." The protagonist finds that his multicultural, transcendental world is very much so connected to the physical, black and white world, and he is realizing that wishing it away or ignoring the real world is not a solution. The physical world seemingly cannot be completely defeated by the metaphysical alone. At some point we must return to the physical world and get our hands dirty. The saddest notion for the protagonist is the inability of sex or even romantic love to overcome the restraints of the physical. Their love has to wait until the afterlife. "Lovers like us are born to die." "Maybe we could keep in touch. Meet me in another place, space and time." The title "Girls and Boys" indicates that sex and love is natural between girls and boys. "*Vous etes tres bell, mama, girls and boys.*" This is another one of those double, ambiguous affirmations. "You are so beautiful, mama, girls and boys." Literally, the female is beautiful. Figuratively, the existence of love between girls and boys is beautiful. But, in this case, the social restraints are making it impossible for the two to connect. Maybe love is not enough? Sex is certainly not. Prince's courtly love commentary is not militant or radical like Marcus Garvey or Malcolm X; it is more in the line of Du Bois or Toomer. These arbitrary walls are not wrong just because they are racist; they are wrong because they keep him from living how he wants to live—integrated and multicultural. Ultimately, these walls are wrong for Prince because they keep humanity from evolving to its highest form. If we can never see past the walls of race, we can never get to the essence of our souls, which allows us to evolve. The tone of "Under the Cherry Moon" and "Girls and Boys" is one of dejection, sorrow, and bitterness. It is almost as if Prince is conceding to the physical restraints and the members of society who enforce these physical restraints. We are left wondering if he is surrendering to the restraints and choosing to place his faith in the afterlife and wait for happiness there. "Lovers like us were born 2 die." "Meet me in another place, space, and time."

Yet, in the darkest moments of doubt, the romantic in Prince will not allow him to accept social restraints on love. Love, for him, is bigger than society's arbitrary borders. "Kiss," as sexy and seductive as it is, finally achieves a total break from the socio-political restraints on sexuality in the romantic relationship. It manages to draw a dividing line between love and sex. Literally translated, the only thing that matters for a relationship to work is extra time and intimacy, sex comes later. And in fact, the sex is enhanced only through a strong emotional relationship. Accordingly, by simplifying the prerequisites for love, he is removing the socio-political restraints. Prince is refuting the fact that the physical is the most important aspect of love. "U don't have 2 be beautiful 2 turn me on...Ain't no particular sign I'm more compatible with." All of these, for Prince, are arbitrary assignments. Love is not about any of these. Love is about attraction, but it grows from time and effort. "I just need your extra time and your...kiss." And if kissing is a physical act, it is only a manifestation of the soul, the need of the soul to articulate and consummate its being. This is more growth from the songs on <u>Dirty Mind</u> and <u>Controversy</u>.

In "Anotherloverholenyohead" Prince goes one step beyond "Kiss" to show that only love can complete life. It expresses a commitment to oneness as "I Wanna Be Your Lover" but stops short of the control and power play. The "We were brother, sister, united all for love" speaks of the mutual commitment needed from both parties for a relationship to flourish. The song celebrates a relationship based on equal admiration and respect. The sexual plea, "U know there ain't no other that can do the duty in your bed," is only a part of the relationship. In the early songs, sex is the essence of the relationship; it is now reduced to an equal aspect with love, caring, and sharing. The protagonist is still declaring himself the best man for the job, but he understands that the female must freely choose him because of love and nothing else. And staying inline with the movie, the protagonist is asserting that the love he can give is more fulfilling and valuable than the riches of his rival. This song is played in the movie after the protagonist rejects a monetary offer from the female's father to terminate the relationship. Prince is expressing the need to reject the physical and embrace the spiritual. "Anotherloverholenyohead" asserts that love offers more rewards and satisfaction than can be found in the physical. Further, one has to be crazy, blinded by the lies of the physical, not to understand this. Therefore, "U need another lover like u need a hole in yo' head."

Parade continues the transition from the physical to the spiritual, from sex to love, started in Purple Rain and elevated in Around the World in a Day. Now, sex is no longer needed to discuss other issues about mankind and life. Prince has come into his own as a mature songwriter, able to deal with the emotions of fear, loneliness, and spirituality without the all encompassing imagery of sex. He has finally reached the point in his career where his sexual images no longer overshadow his work, at least not purposely. With maturity, confidence, and a desire to express himself in new and innovative ways, Prince is ready to unleash a collection of works where sex is for sexual gratification, and social and political issues are expressed without the limits of the sexual metaphor. This happens in Sign "☮" the Times. The Romantic songs such as "Slow Love," "Hot Thing," "Forever in My Life," "Adore," and "It" do not have the ambiguity of past songs and concentrate solely on the emotions of love, romance, and sex. Only two songs continue the past theme that there is something more happening under the covers than the desire for orgasm. "The Ballad of Dorothy Parker" shows how sex can be used as psychological therapy, and "Strange Relationship" examines dysfunctional relationships as byproducts of dysfunctional individuals existing in a dysfunctional society.

In "Strange Relationship" Prince shows that individuals within a romantic relationship exist within a circular or interdependent relationship with society. The behavior of the institution influences the individuals, and the individuals' behavior, in turn, reflects and influences the institution. Thus, the romantic relationship becomes the axis upon which all relationships and society, itself, rotates. Prince asserts this by showing how individuals in romantic relationships have their actions influenced by exterior forces as much as their actions are influenced by the interior forces of romantic desire. This exterior force is, again, the socio-political matrix, which creates the identities and ideologies of males and females. Therefore, males and females are not reacting to each other but to their lingering romantic histories and to society's prescribed notions of what it means to be male and female. The problem is that the romantic histories of the two mates are marred, scarred, and perverse, and the roles are based on the game of dominance, which perpetuates competition between the individuals. "I guess u know me well; I don't like winter, but I seem to get a kick out of treating u cold. Oh, what the hell, u always surrender. What's this strange relationship we hold on to?" Prince is showing how males and females bring into a relationship a set of perceptions, which are often misguided or incorrect, especially when they, without reason, attempt to place these perceptions on new partners. Our reactions are not to our current mates but to past lovers who are still shaping how we perceive and interact with new partners. The surrendering, to which Prince alludes, is not one individual surrendering to another, but the manner in which we all surrender to the game. The question Prince asks is why do we do this? "What's this strange relationship we hold on to?"

In "Strange Relationship" the competition causes the distinction between love and hate to become so blurred that no lines of the relationship are distinguishable, even pleasure and pain. "Baby, I can't stand 2 see u happy. More than that, I hate 2 see u mad. Baby, if you left me, I might do something rash. What's this strange relationship?" Even sex is powerless to resolve the tensions or give dominion to someone. "I took your body. I took all the self respect u ever had." Yet, the male finds no happiness or completion after his conquest. What, now, is the use of having sex? It has lost all ability to resolve, reconcile, or allow us to escape from our strange relationship, from our strange world. This is because these dysfunctional relationships occur because of dysfunctional people. "I guess u know me well. I don't like winter. But I seem to get a kick out of doing u cold. Oh what the hell?

You always surrender. What's this strange relationship that we hold on 2?" Prince is indicating that our dysfunctional romantic relationships are merely manifestations of our dysfunctional souls. We cannot fix our romantic relationships until we fix our souls, or at least fix the sociopolitical matrix that envelopes the romantic relationship. "Isn't this a shame this ain't a movie. Then u could rewrite my every line." The only thing that is going to save humanity will be humanity's ability to rewrite the gender roles, which will then cause us to treat people as humans and not as genders. And of course, to reconstruct the gender roles is to reconstruct society.

Moving from the issues of gender, Prince moves to the issues of race with "U Got the Look," which is the primal attraction of peach and black. Prince is the black, and Sheena Easton, a white woman from Europe, is peach. Prince's use of African American dialect heightens this metaphor of interracial dating, which continues to be a controversial issue for America. In this song, sex is social. "U Got the Look" is physical, the desire of the outer. The black boy wants to hump the white girl. The sexual attraction is based on color, which also indicates that this once all saving sexuality is nothing more than a learned trait and not a natural evolution. "Color u peach and black. Color me takin' aback. Crucial, I think I wantcha." Interestingly enough, it is an African American woman (played by Cat, the African American female dancer of Prince's band) who plays the role of Shockadelica, from the song of the same name ("Shockadelica" b/w of "Sign '☮' the Times," which is about a controlling, sexual she-devil), who retrieves Prince away from Sheena Easton in the video. This certainly speaks to the frustration and anger felt by many African American women seeing their successful males take white women as symbols of success. Sheena Easton is dainty and prissy. Cat is strong and aggressive. Successful African American men often turn to subservient white woman to the anger and dismay of African American women who have been what Zora Neale

Hurston called the "mule of America," from having to carry everyone else's weight. In the video for "U Got the Look" Prince is dragged off by Cat, disallowing him to indulge himself in his desires for Sheena Easton. "U Got the Look" examines the desire for the stereotypical notion of beauty, which is also the American prize. "U must have took a whole hour just 2 make up your face. Closin' time, ugly lights, everybody's inspected." Prince is also raising the sexual tension by juxtaposing the primal issues of race. He is taking the Eurocentric, pristine image of Easton and pumping her full of black female attributes. "I've never seen a pretty girl look so tough...Color u peach and black." In the video Easton is doing her best hip "sista" imitation. This plays beautifully to Cat's persona of a being a strong aggressive black woman, as Easton is still "pale" in comparison to Cat. This interplay creates sexual tension, vague and impressionistic, but powerful nonetheless. Prince is raising the dress of the sexual attraction to reveal that something is happening underneath the covers of humanity's exterior facade as evident in its unusual sexual behavior and tendencies. Prince is questioning what beauty is and what influences our notions of beauty. "Ugly lights, everybody's inspected." Because it is the video age, the song does not have to be well articulated, merely suggested. It works, raising the eyebrows of quite of few critics and music buyers. This also works to keep Prince's persona of "His Royal Badness" squarely intact.

"U Got the Look" is an interesting work to ponder. Sign "☮" the Times is Prince's first so called "Black" record since 1999. Purple Rain, Around the World in a Day, and Parade are viewed by many African American critics and consumers as cross-over records, aimed at white audiences. Jet and Ebony magazines became major critics of Prince's lack of African American imagery, citing the lack of African American employees and his continuous barrage of white women. Then with Sign "☮" the Times his band becomes primarily African American with an African America female dancer who is always on his arm.

Cat serves the very same role and purpose as Wendy and Lisa did, but only in reverse. Where Wendy and Lisa gave Prince access to mainstream America, Cat works to reaffirm that some of Prince's heart is still with black America by reaffirming his attraction to black women. Cat becomes Prince's Trojan Horse back into the hearts of black women and black America as she plays his on-stage love interest and female reflection during the 1987 and 1988 tours. Yet in the middle of all this, there is "U Got the Look," a duet with a white woman. This is conflicting if not confusing to say the least. But, the life of black folks is confusing and oft times contradictory—like the black nationalist and his white woman or the permed-hair revolutionary. Furthermore, the song becomes a major hit in the black clubs. Go figure. Black people are use to this type of dichotomy—taking what they want and discarding what they do not want. Prince is capitalizing on all of these anxieties and complexities of race in American culture. We are intrigued by race and sex. This is why the O. J. Simpson trial had America and the world glued to the television. Prince both ponders and perpetuates this intrigue years before O.J.

Then as quickly as he constructs complex metaphors, he strips them with "It," which is a different type of sexual liberation. "It" is the liberation of being able to say, I think about fucking when I think about you and not have this statement perceived as being negative or dogmatic. "I think about it all the time. It feels so good it must be a crime. I wanna do it baby everyday. When we do it girl, it's so divine. I could be guilty 4 my honesty, but I've got 2 tell u what u mean 2 me." This is a part of the Prince banner. There is nothing wrong with good sex between two willing, loving partners. "It ain't no joke; it's natural fact." Sex is no joke. It is nothing to treat lightly even when being playful: literally or figuratively. However, if sex is natural, what is wrong with admitting one's desire for or enjoyment of it? This is the question and tension of "It." The protagonist is being completely honest even though he fears the repercussions of his honesty. "I might be guilty 4 my honesty." This gets us back to the original Prince sex songs, fighting to break free of the guilt associated with sexual desire. In the <u>Sign "☮"</u> <u>the Times</u> movie concert, Prince combines "Forever in My Life" with "It." "Forever in My Life" is the ultimate love song about commitment and completion through love. The sex in "It" becomes the language through which that love is voiced. The first part of the performance is the declaration of love and commitment in "Forever in My Life," and the second part of the performance is the consummation of the love with "It." We learn that the best sex is not being experienced by two people with perfect bodies and supernatural sex drives. The best sex is being experienced by two people who love each other. Love enables them to break free of the social constraints on sex.

The one song that stays to the formula of sex for therapy is "The Ballad of Dorothy Parker." It is a sexually surreal song in the form of "1999" and an escapism throw back to "Automatic" and "Darling Nikki." This time, the sex is not for liberation or revolution; it is for mental and emotional healing as in "Let's Pretend We're Married" and "Tamborine." Prince's maturity makes the song more contemplative, removing the dogmatism or masochism of "Lady Cab Driver." The song deals with the emotions experienced from a society overrun with theft, violence, and hurt caused by a lack of intimacy and self-exploration. The society is represented as the "violent room" from which the protagonist wishes to escape. Actually, it is the sharing of intimacies, not sex, which serves the purpose. What the protagonist wants is someone with whom he can talk. "I needed someone with a quicker wit than mine; Dorothy was fast." And even though they share a symbolic bath, it is clear that the protagonist is only looking for emotional comfort. "Bath? I said cool, but I'm leaving my pants on 'cause I'm kinda going with someone." He is eventually helped and is able to return to the daily activities of society, receiving a symbolic baptism: being taken away from the world, submerged, and coming back whole and refreshed. "Dorothy made me laugh. I felt much better, so I went back 2 the violent room." Through the interaction with the waitress, he is able to put life into perspective and gain a peace with it and himself. For Prince, women hold the healing powers of humanity, and men must submerge themselves within women to find the essence, the beauty of life.

The love songs of <u>Sign "☮" the Times</u> exhibit Prince's ability to display the various emotions and viewpoints centered on the same topic. He is continuing the theme of the importance of relationships by showing the complexity and complications of establishing and maintaining relationships, especially the issue of balancing physical and emotional concerns. "Slow Love" is the sex that grows from love. At the other end, "Hot Thing" is sex for sexual gratification. It concerns itself with the mutual satisfaction of both partners, especially the need to satisfy the female counterpart. When there is no psychological power play, the female is viewed with a certain reverence, providing a spiritual connection. In "Hot Thing" the beginning is very physical, but by the end of the song there is a transcending to a higher plane of satisfaction. The motive is to satisfy the soul sexually, "I could read u poetry, and we could make a story of our own." The reading of poetry represents the attempt to connect on an emotional or metaphysical level, which will enhance the physical pleasure. "Adore," then, is the collaborative efforts of the physical attraction of sex and the emotions of love, thus becoming the culmination of "Slow Love" and "Hot Thing." The emphasis is as much on sex as it is on love, but neither overshadow the other; they compliment each other. The new element is the commitment to love. "Until the end of time, I'll be there 4 u. U own my heart and mind. I truly adore u...Heavenly angels know u are my fix...This ain't just 4 kicks." In the past, sex was separate from love, or a tool used to create love, or a vehicle used to escape the hardships of life. Now, love and sex have become equal and at times the same. Sex is, finally, a communication of love. "4 all time I am with u; U are with me." And with the reconciliation of sex to love, Prince is now able to deal with the pure emotions of love, companionship, and friendship. "Forever in My Life" is Prince's first romantic song since "So Blue" from his first album that has no reference to sex. However, instead of lamenting lost love as in "So Blue," "Forever in My Life" is celebrating the building of new lives through the power of love. Prince is finally able to create a love song without sex, a song about commitment to another lover, forever: a relationship where the sorrows and bad times are solved with love and not through sex. "Forever in My Life" is about maturity. Prince alludes to coming to a crossroad of decisions and not making the same mistakes twice. This time he is not blinded by the physical. "Forever in My Life" represents a mature writer not handcuffed by sex and unconcerned with it.

> "There comes a time in every man's life when he gets tired of fooling around. Juggling hearts in a three ring circus some day will drive a body down 2 the ground. I never imagined that love would rain on me and make me want 2 settle down. Baby, it's true. I think I do. And I wanna with u. Baby I want u forever. I wanna keep u 4 the rest of my life. All that is wrong in my world u can make right. U are my savior. U r my light. Forever I want u in my life."

Now having reconciled himself to himself, to man, to woman, and to God, it is time to take the revolution to a higher plane. Spirituality has been cloaked under the longing to get off for his entire career. Now it is finally time to remove the veil of sex and allow the spiritual message to "cum" flowing from his soul. Prince dives headlong and in his own princely manner. The music world, the industry, the critics, and the general population of music listeners, as a whole, are not ready for <u>Lovesexy</u>.

Yet, what is most puzzling is that everyone who was familiar with Prince should have seen <u>Lovesexy</u> coming. The essence of his work has been love of mankind, love of life, love of self, and love of your higher self, God. <u>Lovesexy</u> represents the highest of all loves, "the love you get when you fall in love, not with a girl or a boy, but the heavens above." <u>Lovesexy</u> is an attempt to describe the greatest feeling the human body can experience, being touched by God. In the first ten albums, sex is a road leading to inner peace and love, a drug creating the illusion of inner peace and love, or a drug that simply dulls the pain caused by a lack of inner peace and love. In the physical world, the sexual orgasm has no superior. Therefore, the spiritual orgasm, being touched by God and experiencing His love, has no superior. <u>Lovesexy</u> is the transferring and transcendentalization of physical sex and love to the spiritual realm. This type of symbolism, the use of familiar objects, experiences, or emotions to describe unknown objects, experiences, or emotions is akin to typology, the style used by John in his descriptions in <u>Revelations</u>, which is further affirmation of Prince's lyrical talents.

"Lovesexy" and "Glam Slam" are the primary songs, which show the connection between physical and spiritual orgasm. Statements, such as "Heaven's just a kiss away," "When I touch it, race cars burn rubber in my pants," and "It wrote my name upon my thigh. It makes me dance. It makes me cry," create images of physical stimulation and gratification and attribute them to spiritual fulfillment. "Glam Slam," which is also about romantic love, shows the achievement of spiritual happiness through romantic love. "This thing we got it's alive; it seems to transcend the physical. One touch and I'm satisfied. Must be a dream, it's so magical." "Glam Slam" also works on the same level as the intense, highly sexual poetry found in <u>Song of Solomon</u> from the <u>Bible</u>, or as the feet washing scene between Jesus and Mary. These passages from the <u>Bible</u> connect or parallel sexual passion and intensity to the feeling of being loved and touched by God in the same manner as "Lovesexy" and "Glam Slam."

Lovesexy is not the stuff of which pop hits are made. It is too experimental, musically or lyrically. And who is going to take Prince seriously about saving your soul? But Lovesexy is not about religious conversion. Lovesexy is about the experience of love, peace, and tranquility through a new found spirituality. Lovesexy is about being so overrun with spiritual exhilaration that one just has to give this stuff away. As Prince states to Veronica Webb during a 1995 interview for the London television show, The White Room, "Kisses are like tears. The only ones that are real are the ones that you can't hold back." Prince's music and lyrics have been fueled by this notion that there is something in him always trying to break free from the confines of the physical. He begins with sexual desire and then transfers or equates this sexual desire for the search for something deeper. An empty soul is constantly propelled to search in a restless and relentless manner to find some completion and some peace. What he finds is that once you have that peace, it swells in you, as if you are always on the verge of orgasm. As one minister once said to me about the gospel, "When it's in you, it's got to come out like a raging fire." This is Lovesexy, and Prince has to get it to the public, no matter the record sales or the ramifications. It is like an orgasm. Love causes you to ejaculate it all over the world. Furthermore, Prince is not trying to convert anyone. He is just expressing a new feeling, the love of God. Lovesexy is meant to be seen as a sharing, not as a sermon. Unfortunately, the past messages have been missed, so it is inevitable that this message is missed. Very few understand that the core of his early songs are not rooted in sex for physical satisfaction. Rather, there is a void in the human soul, and sex is an attempt to fill it. Sex is a step, building toward higher grounds. Lovesexy is that higher ground. Lovesexy is also the ultimate artistic orgasm for Prince. It is the apex of his sex metaphor. With this ejaculation, Prince has released and completed the ultimate sexual image, God as the supreme Phallic symbol. Prince is now able to evolve even more and explore new territory.

<u>Batman</u> is a different type of neurotic experience for Prince, the writer. The study not only deals with the dual personalities of man but also their isolation from self and society. Both Batman and the Joker represent the duality of evil and good in man. Within each character wages the civil war of dualism. This project allows Prince to explore the complex psyche of man without having to code or season it with sex. <u>Batman</u> represents a total break for Prince from the use of sexual imagery and subjects to convey his messages. The characters of <u>Batman</u> are driven not only by emptiness and hatred, but also by an obsessive preoccupation with those emotions. The Prince sex/romance lyric, no matter how explicit or dogmatic, is about replacing negative emotions with sex to bring about positive emotions, even if temporary. The characters of <u>Batman</u> are so absorbed in negative emotions that they attempt to heal their wounds by inflicting pain, fear, and anger upon others. Prince's sexual solution will not work because it tends to bring people together, providing an opportunity to find love. Keep in mind that Prince's understanding of sex is not the same as the pornographic or dogmatic understanding where one person is completely objectified for the pleasure of another. Thus, at the core of Prince's sex metaphor is mutual gratification. The <u>Batman</u> characters are isolationists and seem to gain some sort of primeval gratification from their pain. They are not searching for solutions to heal their pain; rather they want to hold on to it like a badge or a monument to their struggle. Sex would lower their shields and allow other emotions to enter as evident in Bruce Wayne's inability to construct a long-term relationship with Vicki Vale.

<u>Graffiti Bridge</u> is the physical side of <u>Lovesexy</u>. It deals more directly with man and his relationship to man as well as his relationship to God, so it vaguely uses the sex metaphor in "Question of U" and "Joy in Repetition,"

where Prince draws the parallel between romantic and spiritual love. All the other songs are references to achieving the higher power of life by keeping the faith and leaving oneself open for the experience. The one sexual reference, "Tick, Tick, Bang," to stay inline with the movie, is made only to compete for the attention of an angel, posing as a lady, and the club crowd, which represents music buyers. In a desperate attempt to draw attention to his messages, the Kid resorts to sexual images much like Prince's use of sexual images to capture the attention of listeners. However, the Kid's attempt falls on deaf ears. This failed use of sex represents sex's inability to solve society's problems or its lack of depth at handling the complexity of our humanity. Whatever the reason, sex now lacks the power to reach the spiritual realm. Sex can be a metaphor for spiritual ecstasy, but it can not deliver us to the promise land. Graffiti Bridge is the next stop in evolution, and sex is now merely a step on the ladder to evolution. Regardless of Prince's ongoing evolution, Graffiti Bridge made as much noise commercially as Lovesexy. The public still is not ready to buy ideas of spirituality from Prince, especially when his music is no longer connecting to the heartbeat of the buyers.

1991 marked a new beginning for Prince and his career. Although his name change does not take place until well into 1993, Diamonds and Pearls marks a new era for Prince. Taking his last twelve albums into consideration, Prince has achieved more lyrically than any other artist before him, except Wonder or Dylan. As a songwriter, he has managed to chart topics that other artists fear to discuss. By Graffiti Bridge, Prince has become the mature and masterful poet and storyteller. He has managed to push himself in all directions, growing from a young, angry soul into a polished poet-philosopher. His use of sex is lessened by his maturity in songwriting. In his twelfth and thirteenth albums, Diamonds and Pearls and ⚥, he does not use nor need the sexual imagery to express his views about life and mankind. By now, sex as a topic is no longer ambiguous.

Love songs are love songs. Sex songs are sex songs. And his statements of the social, political, and human condition concentrate on the specific issues and are no longer hidden under a longing to get off.

Emancipation

Emancipation has been a continuous theme in the lyrics of Prince, which is taken to new heights during his name change to ☤; however, his emancipation has to do with individual emancipation rather than group emancipation. This is because he views society's strength to be its individuals. An oppressor is only able to control groups if the individuals of that group submit or accept the bondage, internalize that bondage, and perpetuate it themselves through their individual lives because bondage is as much psychological as it is physical. As Carter G. Woodson asserts, controlling the mind allows the oppressor to control the body. So in order to gain freedom, the individuals of the oppressed group must have an active role in defining their liberation, emancipation, and freedom. Thus, ☤'s emancipation has been about each individual defining his own terms of freedom, which is in opposition to the major flaw with Lincoln's "Emancipation Proclamation." Five years after the release of Emancipation, Prince would assert more forthrightly in "Avalanche" from One Night Alone Live! that Lincoln's "Proclamation" is flawed because Lincoln was a racist who never sought to provide equality to people of African descent. "He was not or never had been in favor of setting our people free... Abraham Lincoln was a racist who said 'U cannot escape from history'" With the "Emancipation Proclamation," the larger white society is defining freedom for the black population. In fact, African Americans are not allowed to develop any policy or have any discussions about their own freedom and liberty until 1964, one hundred years after the "Emancipation Proclamation." Even the Thirteenth, Fourteenth, and Fifteenth Amendments are merely white rhetoric about black freedom, with white people interpreting and developing the documents of freedom and liberty for African Americans. ☤'s whole career and ideology flies in the face of this. From day one, he has been asserting his right to define who he is, constantly pushing to erase the limits and boundaries of his freedom. In Prince, Dirty Mind, and Controversy, he is defining his own sexuality, race, and gender in order to free himself from those physical confines. ⚥'s emancipation exists on two levels: liberating humanity from the physical confines of race, gender, and class oppression and liberating the soul from the bondage of physical confines. In both cases, he has continued his discourse of walking away from the confines of the body and embracing the freedom of the spirit. At the core of his journey has been his battle for artistic freedom, which is smothered in the physical oppression of record sales as the defining factor of an artist's worth.

Ultimately, ⚥'s career has been about rejecting the larger society's notion of reality and success. If you cannot define a man's reality, you cannot define his success. If you cannot define his success, you cannot control him. Therefore, when Warner Bros and the industry in general (including the magazines) want to define his success, ⚥ sees no other recourse than to abandon it all. We must understand that this act of divorce is not an easy act, especially when your whole notion of identity and self-worth has been predicated on this system. When half of who you are is based on a system, to leave or walk away from that system, no matter how oppressive it is, is to walk away from half of yourself—to destroy that system is to destroy half of yourself, especially if you helped to design the system. This is the battle for African Americans. African Americans have been unable or unwilling to pull the trigger, which destroys the system based on racism and their connection to it. It is not that African Americans do not want to be free. But, to break away from the American system of capitalism is almost like separating Siamese twins. You know that part of you will die, and you do not know if you will be able to survive without your other half. Or, in many cases, divorcing themselves from the American system of capitalism, for many African Americans, is like the removal of a breast to remove the cancer from the body. Although one wants to be free of the cancer, one is hesitant to remove a part of oneself that is so vitally important in defining oneself. One is left wondering if she will be the same without the breast. Accordingly, if I kill the nigger in me, what will I be? Sometimes complacency in oppression and poverty seems safer than the risk of liberation. I may not have much, but at least I know what I have. If I journey into the wilderness of freedom, I do not know what is waiting for me. ⚥, like most African Americans, is left almost immobile, straddling the fence of freedom/liberation—one foot in the quicksand of integration and one foot on the uncertain, sliding scale of black nationalism. His fluctuation does not make him a hypocrite, only a human—merely another African American battling with what it means to be free and, moreover, what it means to accept the responsibilities and economic uncertainties of self-determination.

With all of that said, however, ⚥ does take the leap into self-determination. He is releasing his records on his own label and on his own accord. He tours when he wants, and, in the summer of 2000, he opened Paisley Park to the public for his seven day birth-day festival, allowing tens of thousands to travel from around the world and commune with him at fifty dollars a pop. Most importantly, he has proven to himself and to his critics that he can make the ideology of Paisley Park as an alternative lifestyle a reality and be financially secure at the same time. The difference is that he has done it with his eyes and his talents always focused more on the art of the work and not the economic gains of the work. This is the difference between him and the ocean of other artists. While others are trying to record hits, ⚥ has always been more interested in creating a body of work that has some social, if not political, impact. Thus, his records have always been about varying themes and concepts of the human soul and its existence in this physical world. This is not to say that he is not a business man and that he has not made records based on what is selling. Nevertheless, he has made many more records that cut against the grain (mainstream) of popular music. Even <u>Purple Rain</u> is not a mainstream record. It is a record that forces the mainstream to expand its borders and include him. And after time, because of his dedication to his vision and not their charts, the mainstream closes its boarders, rejecting his work like the body rejecting an incompatible organ. The marginalization of his popularity represents an artist more concerned with the human value of his music—how it engages and challenges the public's musical and lyrical notions and beliefs—than with the economic value of his catalogue. ⚥'s ability to earn a living with this attitude should be a point well taken by young artists. The truth is that his work and his attitude influences more in hip hop and the following generations than will openly admit. And by 1992, ⚥ believes that he has freed himself from the obvious confines of gender and racial oppression, allowing him to make the music of his heart. He was then feeling another type of oppression, artistic oppression due to slumping sales. Because of his decreased sales, Warner Bros assumed that it was in a more powerful position to limit and dictate his creative output and process. By 1993, ⚥ has lost his control and dominance over the pop charts. Warner Bros is telling him what he can and can not have on his records and how many albums he can release. It is the unthinkable for ⚥ who has done nothing but meet his artistic and professional obligations, as he asserts:

> "There are a lot of great things in this business of music that we are in, but there are some things that are not so great, like the rights of an artist to do with his art what he wants, when and how he wants, even when he delivered the music he agreed to fifteen albums ago" (⚥, "Acceptance Speech," <u>Celebrate the Soul Awards,</u> 1994).

With the above statement, ⚥ is echoing the sentiments of sharecroppers who meet their half of the agreement but are refused fair pay and respect by the plantation owners. In fact, the record industry works similarly to sharecropping. Artists, like the farmers, are loaned a certain amount of money to produce records in the same manner that farmers are given a line of credit to produce crops. If the records do not yield enough to pay the loan, the artists become indebted to the record company in the same manner as farmers become indebted to plantation owners. This debt allows record companies to exploit artists. This system creates artists who are constantly working to pay debts instead of producing the music of their hearts. Also, because of these debts, these artists, like the sharecroppers, can never focus on ownership and control of their work. They can never gain sovereignty because they are always in debt.

⚥ feels that he is being refused fair compensation and respect by not being allowed to produce the music of his heart in the quality and quantity that he wants. This all speaks to a deeper notion of the innate exploitative nature of American capitalism. On the one hand, Warner Bros treats ⚥ like a washed-up has-been. On the other hand, Warner Bros refuses to release him so that he is free to market his art to and through other avenues. The slavery/oppression becomes manifest in Warner Bros actions. Although the company does not think that the artist is capable of producing art that can gain them a profit, they disallow him the opportunity of following the pursuits of his artistic love by denying other companies the opportunity to invest in and distribute his work. In addition to Warner Bros specific actions to limit or control is production, ⚥ realizes that artists are enslaved by the system which defines reality and success and then binds them to the limited definitions. ⚥'s issue is not merely with Warner Bros but with the entire recording industry. Thus, signing with another label will not free him from the oppressive system. He realizes that he must either work to change the system at its core or completely divorce himself from the system and create his own system. His dilemma is akin to the decision of African Americans, choosing between integration and black nationalism. Does one attempt to integrate into a system, hoping to change it at its core by gaining some influence over the policy decisions? Or, does one completely separate from the system, believing that separation is the only way that one can gain sovereignty. ⚥ has chosen to blend the two concepts. In doing so, he has walked the same path as most African Americans, which is a blending of the concepts of black nationalism and integration. Even with the combining of the two concepts, one notion is clear. It is virtually impossible to gain success (sovereignty) by integrating into a system where others maintain their success (sovereignty) through perpetuating your second-class citizenship. Even by having his own record company, ☥ finds that his struggle is never ending because he is still forced to use the industry's record shops, radio stations, magazines, and video programs. Personal emancipation comes at a heavy price. By challenging a system where everyone gets paid from your work before you do, you risk being alienated by everyone. You are risking becoming an island with very limited means and vehicles of getting your work to the public. This becomes the real struggle and test. How badly does one want to be emancipated? What is one willing to lose? ☥ proves that he is willing to lose it all for his sanity, serenity, and sovereignty.

Aside from his battle with Warner Bros, the ultimate emancipation for ☥ has been the emancipation from the illusion of the physical, believing that life is about mind over matter and that we can reach our higher selves if we are able to see past the lie/illusion of the body and the physical plane. "Time is a trick. You have one birthday, one day of birth. But you keep counting birthdays; your mind gives up, and your body deteriorates" (☥, Rave Un2 the Year 2000, 1999). True bondage begins when we submit to the limits of the physical world. This is, in a sense, what his work has always discussed. This is, in a sense, what Emancipation is articulating. Who defines reality and truth? Who defines success? Why do we accept other people's notion of truth, reality, and success? Once the artist understands that the notions of truth, reality, and success are subjective, then the artist has already freed himself from the psychological bondage, which is the most powerful bondage. Therefore, Emancipation is a success because it happens in exactly the manner that ☥ wanted it to happen. Record sales alone do not make works of art successful. Their mere existence makes them successful, the ability of the artist to take the idea, the metaphysical thing, and transform it, making it physical. That is success. ☥ is again redefining our prescribed notions of success by putting the emphasis on our artistic and spiritual desires. An album on a major record label that sells only 100,000 copies is deemed a flop because the record company does not make the amount of money that it intended. Yet, when an artist can independently sell that album and get what ☥ calls "the lion's share" of the profits, then it becomes a success because ten dollars multiplied by 100,000 units sold is still one million dollars. In this case, the artist, not the company, is reaping the benefits. This is also a success because the artist who succeeds or fails on his own terms is defining his own notions of success and reality. Furthermore, how can selling 100,000 copies of anything be deemed a failure? 100,000 people were moved enough to purchase an album. That is an artistic success, developing a fan base which allows the artist to sell enough of his art to sustain his well-being, allowing him to continue to create and distribute art on his own terms. At some point, when an artist has amassed enough financial gain, he should become secure enough to create the art of his heart, where the purpose is to elevate people rather than earn a profit. This is the direction in which ☥ has been headed since day one. This is the ultimate reward of his years of labor, to make the music of his heart without concern for records sales. Moreover, the economic reality is that most artists gain about ten percent of the total profits. So, if an independent or self-published author sells 2,500 books, that is the equivalent of selling 25,000 books for Random House. What sense does it make to work twice as hard only to relinquish the rights to one's work, make less money, and have less artistic control? The real success is awaking to the illusion of exploitation, the illusion of capitalism.

☥'s first break from Warner Bros comes with "The Most Beautiful Girl in the World" in 1994. Due to the ongoing haggling between ☥ and Warner Bros, he is able to strike a side deal with Mo Austin, a former record executive for Warner Bros. One must understand that many of these record executives who act as talent scouts, marketing men, and in the capacity of artist development coordinators are merely handlers, plantation overseers, scouring the lands to colonize and enslave artists for the companies. Austin, however, is different in that he is willing to create common ground between ☥ and

Warner Bros, which allows Warner Bros to continue to profit from the art of ⚥ and allows ⚥ to be as artistic and productive has his soul desires. Through this arrangement, ⚥ is able to get a distribution deal with Bellmark Records for "The Most Beautiful Girl in the World," which is owned by Al Bell who formerly owned Stax Records. The problem is that this arrangement is not the standard practice that the record industry has established or follows. For the record company, all art by its artists should be owned by the company, as well as generate a profit only for the company. The deal that ⚥ secures for "The Most Beautiful Girl in the World" is the antithesis of the record industry's notion of the artist-company relationship. With the deal brokered between Austin and ⚥, he is free to have some of his music marketed and distributed by outlets other than Warner Bros. This allows ⚥ the ability to retain the rights to some of his work while producing and distributing as much product as he wants. When "The Most Beautiful Girl in the World" becomes number two on the charts and Warner Bros realizes that it does not own or distribute it, the company quickly puts a stop to the deal brokered between Austin and ⚥. When ⚥ realizes that Warner Bros has the legal right to deny him the ability to record music for another company or have his music distributed by another company, even if Warner Bros refuses to market it, he realizes that he is no longer in control of his career or himself. Furthermore, when he realizes that Warner Bros owns his name, Prince, and his likeness, and that neither his name nor his likeness can be used by him or anyone else unless Warner Bros gives permission, he begins writing slave on his face to symbolize how he understands his reality. Once Warner Bros takes legal action to terminate ⚥'s relationship with Bellmark Records, ⚥ understands that he can only achieve freedom by leaving Warner Bros and the traditional system of making and selling music.

Along with the legal issues, what also clouds <u>Emancipation</u> is the high volume of music that ⚥ is releasing and the unorthodox behavior he uses to express his anger and pain. The large quantity of music seems to obstruct itself.

So much music with so many different musical styles and issues seem to be too much for the average, radio-video music patron. From 1994-1996 ☥ releases five albums, with the last two coming less than six months apart: The Gold Experience (its lead single is released more than a year before the album), 1800NEWFUNK, Exodus, Chaos and Disorder, and Emancipation. Again, ☥ is attempting to break the mold, the blueprint, the reference point in our brains for how an artist should produce art and what the patrons can handle.

> "Perhaps, one day, all the powers that are will realize that it is better to let a man be all that he can be than to try to limit his output to just what they can handle. 'Our [Warner Bros] sources tell us that there's just too much music.' Well, my sources, all of you, tell me to be all I can be. For this, I am eternally grateful. Peace and be wild" (☥, "Acceptance Speech," Celebrate the Soul Awards, 1994).

As he had related earlier in 1993 in the Three Chains of Gold video, ☥ comes to a crossroad in his life where the established system of defining what artists can be and how they create and sell music no longer allows his soul to flourish. It is obvious that by saturating the market all of his music will not sell, just for economic reasons. But what is important to ☥ is that the music is released and available. The question is often asked, "How much money does a man need to feel secure enough to dedicate his life to spiritual enrichment and evolution?" Whatever the amount is, ☥ is at that point and wants the opportunity to evolve, free from economic restraints. Exodus, then, is the new flag of liberation. ☥ is not merely demanding his freedom; he is behaving as a free man. He is free because he has declared himself to be free, not because the industry acknowledges his freedom, not because the media acknowledges his freedom, and not because the listeners acknowledge his freedom. In fact, all of these entities do not acknowledge his freedom or his cause, and this is what makes his work significant. It is easy to be a revolutionary when someone is paying attention to and validating your cause. In ☥'s case, very few are paying attention to or validating his fight against the industry, including the millions who have consistently supported his work. He and his movement are the butt of everyone's joke. Regardless of this apathy for his cause, he does not change his direction to sell more records. He becomes a great representative for Du Bois' notion that one must fight for what one believes to be right and for one's freedom even when it is not popular. The way to gain respect and achieve one's goals is to "insist continually, in season and out of season" (Gates and McKay 640). By doing this, ☥ is showing himself as an artist first, one who champions causes first and panders for records sales last.

    That is the mantra of <u>Exodus</u>. "The Exodus has begun," regardless if anyone is listening or not. But is that not the way that an exodus begins, under the cover of the night? Most slaves do not wait for the master or the other, scared slaves to give them permission to escape. These run-away slaves are the most dangerous to the system. They, through their actions, can become a lighthouse to the other slaves and must be punished and used as an example. Above all, the master cannot allow the other slaves to perceive that the run-away slaves have gained any amount of victory or sovereignty. That is when the exodus becomes a problem, and laws and codes are passed to make it more difficult for slaves to gain freedom. A great example of this is the success of the <u>Musicology</u> album. Record companies and some artists complained that <u>Musicology</u> should not be listed atop the Billboard charts because they considered the sales to be illegitimate due to the fact that the album was sold with the concert tickets. However, if America is a free enterprise system, how can one private business tell another private business how it can sell its product and for how much? If the artist is willing to sell his product for less because he is more concerned about the art than the finance, who should be allowed to stop him? Many magazines and record company executives asserted that with the new policy, he would never have another top selling album. Then the follow-up to <u>Musicology</u>, <u>3121</u> becomes number one without the help of a tour. ⚥'s initial exodus is only a problem when "The Most Beautiful Girl in the World" becomes a top ten song. Before then nobody cares whether or not ⚥ leaves Warner Bros. The minute the slave begins making money for himself, the masters need to put a stop to the exodus. This also leads to the firing of Bennie Medina and Mo Austin who, as the overseers, were held responsible for brokering a deal which gave ⚥ the freedom to record independently. The tactics of Warner Bros to tighten the reins on ⚥ cause Exodus to become a very angry album that manages to achieve a poetic sense through its effective articulation of the pain and bitterness felt by many artists toward the music industry.

"Get Wild," the first song on Exodus, means to get free. The often used phrase by Prince, "Peace and be wild," means to find your inner peace by living your life to the fullest by breaking the chains that bind your body and your spirit. "Get Wild" is the album's proclamation. The song's introduction is a phone call by an artist to the newly established NPG Records, which has been established in the aftermath of the dissolution of Paisley Park Records.

"'Hello, is this Paisley Park?' 'No, this is not that record company. This is NPG Records.' 'Are you conducting a talent search?' 'Yes, that's true. We are conducting a world wide talent search.' 'What are you looking for?' 'First and Foremost, you have to get free. When it becomes time to download your work into your friends [fans] computers, you can't have any other contractual obligations. Second, you have to get smart: the more substantial your education, the more substantial your income in the new city. And thirdly, above all else, you have to GET WILD!'"

"Get Wild" articulates the ability of music to liberate people and the need for people to liberate themselves from the routine of mindlessness. ⚥'s emphasis is always on the individual's responsibility to free himself. This is why the receptionist emphasizes that the artist must be educated.

"When u're sick of that nine 2 five, and u're ready 2 cum alive. And u've looked both high and low, but u can't find a trumpet to blow....Polyvinylacetate will keep your monkey high...When u wanna get in the groove, but the music don't make u move. Hip the DJ 2 a new CD—anything by the NPG. When u can't find the g to your gold, and the charge to your battery's low, and the smoke's too thick to blow, there's a brand new high we kno'."

"Get Wild" is urging the individual to get free of normality before he becomes a permanent slave to routine. Even fashion is seen as an exterior manifestation of the soul's need to get free. The emphasis is not so much on what you wear but that you wear something different to break the monotony of life. "Pick a funky outfit, short and see through...And u kno' what shoes to wear—the ones with heels so high they'll scare ya." Every fiber of our being, every aspect of our lives should be dedicated to getting free from society's prison of normality, especially when this society is merely using us as food for its machine. The individual must be able to free himself from the mental shackles and live life on his own terms. Only then can the individual evolve to his highest form. An elevated form of music, "Polyvinylacetate," can aid in this transformation, but we must find a way to distribute this form of music to the masses.

With "Count the Days" ☥ is lamenting his time left with Warner Bros, which is also a metaphor for the individual's desire to escape the bondage of society's oppressive and arbitrary rules. The song expresses sorrow in being bound to a contract, but there is hope that this too will pass. With the guitar, falsetto, and spirit of Curtis Mayfield, "Count the Days" is angry and bitter. It is an example of ☥ being able to refashion style and form and encode it with his messages that speak to his personal issues and the issues of his time. Mayfield created modern day spirituals by infusing civil rights freedom songs with urban sounds, sensibilities, and attitudes. ⚥ then takes Mayfield's formula and refashions it to fit his personal struggle, moving from Mayfield's collective to his individual. Still, this layering connects ⚥ to Mayfield, thus connecting him to that legacy, even if artificially. ⚥ begins with the notion that he is willing to commit commercial suicide through his retaliation not to promote any music that Warner Bros releases under his name. If he has to suffer the frustration of not being able to create as he wishes, then Warner Bros will suffer the loss of profits. "Here's a church, and here's a steeple. Here's a muthafucker that 👁 got 2 blow away. Here's my chance 2 cure the ills of the people, but not until 👁 make this muthafucker pay. Oh, baby, 👁 count the Days."

⚥ then addresses the media, retaliating for the manner in which it, as a tool of the industry, makes a spectacle of his name change and belittles his issues with Warner Bros. In many cases this is often the plight of an African American who gains some sense of commercial success but still wants to fight against personal and racial injustices. Often, the press will ask, "What's a million-dollar Negro so upset about?" The reality is that individuals like ⚥, Oprah Winfrey, Michael Jackson, Denzel Washington, Michael Jordan, and others represent less than one percent of the African American socio-economic reality, yet people like Rush Limbaugh and Bill O'Reilly always evoke their names when they want to discuss the successes of the Civil Rights Movement. Further, when an African American has achieved a certain amount of success, it is usually in the face of twice the obstacles of their white colleagues. Carlos Santana affirms this when he asserts that "Prince is a genius. He is one of the greatest talents that this country has produced, but he has to do a strip tease to get noticed." Not only is there a double standard, but African Americans are ridiculed in the press for being ungrateful if they speak against racism. Comic, Damon Wayans jokes in his 1996 HBO special that often African Americans who have amassed some financial success are put on the spot by white reporters when they are asked about racial issues. "You be sittin' there thinkin' 'bout that check, and you say, 'Naw sir, ain't no racism.'" Even Sammy Davis, Jr., who was beloved by white audiences because he was both hip and non-threatening, often asserted that America wants African Americans to just smile, dance, and shut up. ⚥ confronts the media for its treatment of him and the fact that it seems more interested in tabloid journalism than issues of socio-political interest. "Here's the interview. Here's the time. If ꙮ keep your secrets will u keep mine? If we hurry we could catch the train. If it was up 2 u, ꙮ would die in vain. That's why ꙮ count the days." The dying "in vain" represents a man who is ready to surrender his commercial success if it means bringing truth to the light. "We could catch the train." We could evolve, but the media is only concerned about sound bites that sell papers by perpetuating the spectacle of popular culture rather than analyzing it as a microcosm of American life. Yet, even with the anger at having his talents wasted in the machine, ⚥ finds joy in the fact that he will be free from this game, free to play his own game on his own terms. "Great day in the morning, the choir sings a pretty song. Everyday ꙮ'm with yo' ass is another day wasted, swear it's another day 2 long. ꙮ'm counting. Muthafucker, ꙮ count the days." Until he gains his freedom, ⚥ laments that he will be incomplete "like Frankie Beverly without Maze." Therefore, he counts the days to his freedom, waiting for the day when his art will no longer be limited or controlled by someone other than him.

"The Good Life" is a trip down memory lane. This song is co-written with childhood friend and bassist, Sonny T. To escape the pain of his predicament, ⚥ looks to his childhood in Minneapolis and finds joy in the reasons why he wanted to make music. He was touched and inspired by everything around him, and he grew up wanting to imitate his heroes and share the inspiration that he received as a child.

"Every day after school, u knew where 2 find this brotha. Uptown at every movie show, out of my life 2 another. That was the only thing that 👑 wanted 2 do. That was my drug of choice. 👑 left all those funny smelling cigarettes 2 the American boys."

"The Good Life" refutes the notion that one cannot make a living by one's own terms. It is attacking the notion that the best lawyers go into private practice, and the mediocre lawyers work for the government or do community service. ☯ is asserting that you can have the "good life" even if you play by your own rules. In fact, playing by your own rules makes whatever reward you gain even sweeter. Much like the undercurrent storyline of <u>Purple Rain</u>, ☯ is asserting that hard work is its own reward because no one can take away anything that you have earned. Over half of the scenes in <u>Purple Rain</u> are centered on rehearsal or people discussing craft. People are working. Even the notoriously sarcastic Kurt Loder of <u>Rolling Stone</u> and MTV agrees in his 1984 article "Prince Reigns" that the movie makes practice and hard work look cool. In "The Good Life" the protagonist thanks his mother for providing a blueprint to success, which is hard work. This is why ☯ feels that he does not owe Warner Bros anything else. He has delivered the music that "he promised fifteen albums ago." "Mama worked all night, went to school by day. Wanted 2 get her Masters degree, so she could make a better way. Set an example for her babies that we'll never 4get. Guess that's where my spirit comes from, eternally..."

Focus and hard work lead to freedom because hard work makes you knowledgeable and strong. A tree with strong roots can withstand a violent storm. ☯ will withstand this storm because of his strong roots. As he does in "Sexuality," ☯ advises the parents to give their children strong roots to survive life's storms. "Mama...don't let your children watch television before they know how to read." These strong roots will make the children independent and will allow them to make better decisions.

"Peace 2 the mothers that know the key 2 future. The battles of the future will be won by those who teach those baby boys and girls. This is our plea to the brothas who are tired of the barely getting by. Instead u should try 2 see your future, map out your stops and make sure that no one dies."

Slaves who get free need a plan. ⚥ is proposing one possible solution for artists and for humanity. His advice is not to follow his plan, but for each individual to begin mapping or plotting a plan of action. Become an active agent in your future and not a passive pawn. This will lead to the good life, a peaceful life, a fulfilled life.

"Cherry, Cherry" moves the album into the romantic realm but is also a metaphor for the album's theme of the necessity and exigency of freedom. It parallels the innocence of lost youth to the loss of idealism in the music industry. In the beginning, Cherry is a bright-eyed, idealistic, young girl with "👀s like a pool of twenty-four carrot diamonds." She is initially determined to live her life on her own terms. "Everyone said she'd soon be dead, but Cherry replied 'At least 👀 had some fun.'" The narrator sounds like a fan lamenting a fallen pop star whose idealism has been crushed under the heel of the industry. Figuratively, Cherry is the artist who is defined and assigned roles by everyone else for the pleasure of everyone else but herself. Literally, "Cherry, Cherry" examines the complexities and complications of the female persona, male hypocrisy, and the tragic fate of the female who is unable to break free from the arbitrary and sexist restraints of her gender. Cherry is the ultimate female contradiction, invented in the male psyche. She is a sexually liberated vixen in school girl's clothing. She is a cheerleader who also wears a raincoat with nothing underneath but underwear. She plays her role well by having two male partners who fulfill two roles or needs for her. She finds comfort in the younger, passive protagonist, and she gains adventure through her older, more worldly but abusive boyfriend. Cherry is the female who needs to be both protected and conquered by men, much like artists who are both loved and hated by the industry. They are loved for the manner in which they make money for the company. They are hated when the company can no longer control them. In the same vein of the artist, it is Cherry who suffers and not the males. She suffers because she is unable to reconcile herself to or overcome her roles; therefore, she surrenders to suicide in much the same way that young girls surrender to pregnancy and mediocrity, in the same way that most artists surrender to the industry. On the surface, Cherry's suicide seems to represents the fate of many young girls who commit social suicide by submitting to the stereotypes about them. However, in this case, ⚥ is asserting something else. Cherry's boyfriend becomes abusive when he realizes that she is engaging in an affair, in the same manner that Warner Bros became abusive when ⚥ used Bellmark Records to distribute his song that went to number two on the charts. Instead of surrendering, Cherry fights back, using the only means that she has, suicide. Many believed that the tactics used by ⚥ would result in the end of his career. Even here, ⚥ is again challenging our narrow notions of truth, reality, success, and career. Is one a musician because he has a record deal, or is one a musician because he makes music? Using martyrdom, ⚥ makes himself, through Cherry, a Christ-like figure by showing that sometimes one must chose death to gain life. Though romantic, the theme here is still about the soul's need for liberation and freedom. Cherry dies because she is not able to escape her prescribed role in society. If the soul cannot have liberty, it will choose death.

"Return of the Bump Squad" is the resurrection after Cherry's death and returns the aggressive tone to the album. This time it is directed at the radio DJs and artists who have surrendered to the industry, making and promoting mindless and unimaginative music. For ⚥, making music is not about hits; it is about using art to elevate. This is missing in the industry. This lack of elevation causes his anger. As he did with "1999," ⚥ is raising, elevating, the status of the artist to that of savior/prophet to save the music from the exploitation of the industry.

> "From out of nowhere, so they came, smelling like they wearing Magic Shave. 'What's that funky Smell!?!' Some fool with a red mask, totin' a one-ᴡd base, pulled it out, stuck it up in the police officer's face and said, 'Bow down muthafucker, surrender your rod. Nothing can save u unless His name is God. Better get yo' house in order; it's getting late. It's the return of the bump squad coming your way.'"

♀ draws a line in the sand between artistic achievement and commercial success. The material gains, such as awards, money, and women, are hollow and, at best, temporary. They will not help you withstand the storms that test your character. They will not help you evolve to your higher self. "U don't understand where ᴡ'm comin' from; ᴡ don't want your woman if she's acting dumb. She ain't got no money, so how she gonna pay. The girl can't handle it when they grab a hold of me and say 'Bow down muthafucker...'" After showing that those who are too tied to the physical or too overly concerned with the physical are unable to help him, ♀ reinforces the savior/prophet motif of the poet by using biblical imagery, paralleling the artist with Moses.

> "Ya'll hold that groove 4 a while, while ᴡ take out the good book. As they journeyed from the Mount by the way of the Red Sea 2 encompass the land of Eden. And the soul of the people was much discouraged because of the way. And the people spoke against God and against Moses. Wherefore have u brought us up from Egypt 2 die in the wilderness. So we sing. U can bump, but u best get your house in order and get back in those music books u know changed your juvenile delinquent asses...and turn that loop box down...Hey shorty. Ain't y'all got any mo' records? Well, why in the hell don't y'all use 'em. ᴡ'm tired

of hearing the same ole songs all the time."

♀ is using the biblical reference to denounce fear and ignorance. The fear is being afraid to walk away from the system that oppresses you because you are afraid of what is in the wilderness. Many artists want to escape the large record companies, but where else would they go? ♀ is fighting this fear with education. "Getting back in the music books" represents a returning to craft over fame, substance over mere presence. If an artist is well crafted, skilled, and knowledgeable in his talent and the business, he does not have to wait on a company to give him a record deal. As Booker T. Washington asserted in <u>Up from Slavery</u>, if a man can make or fix something, he will always be able to employ or feed himself. A skilled artist will always have a job because the industry needs him more than he needs the industry. If individual artists would hear and comprehend this fact, the balance of power would change instantaneously. However, the individual is always fighting against the anonymous voices of the society that are used to scare and embarrass the individual back into his place. At the beginning of the reading of the Bible passage, there is a voice that yells at the reader in order to silence the reader. "Chill out nigga. We don't need that shit. Broke ass muthafucker." This voice represents the voice of society attempting to scare or embarrass the individual into submission. The protagonist continues with his message, and, by the end of the passage, he is the only voice heard. One must be steadfast, but one can only be steadfast if one has knowledge because knowledge is the greatest weapon to fight fear.

♀ ends the song with a final dig at the current music scene. Since 1995, the radio seems to be flooded with songs using the same samples. It is difficult to tell one song for the next. This is because the companies make money from sampling. Generally, when an artist wants to sample a song, he is encouraged by the company to choose one that is in its catalogue. Not only is the company profiting from the artist, but it is earning money before one record is sold because the artist must pay the company for the use of the sample. This practice is stifling to the creativity of the industry. This also shows the importance of education. Because there now exists a generation that has been educated without any type of training in the arts, they do not have the same respect and standards toward creativity. Today, music is popular because of its ability to conform, not for what new aspect the artist is bringing to the form. "Return of the Bump Squad" is the anthem and assertion that the New Power Generation is coming to return craft to the table. When asked by Veronica Webb in a 1995 interview for the London television show, <u>The Sunday Show</u>, if they are trying to elevate or transform the kids' musical experience, Michael B., drummer for the NPG, asserts, "We want them to have a musical experience."

"The Exodus Has Begun," like "Return of the Bump Squad," is pulled from the bowels, the fertilizer, of Parliament-Funkadelic. It is psychedelically funky and mystic, troping the images of "Sir Nose," the fictional character and alter-ego of Dr. Funkenstein. Sir Nose's job is to stop the Funk, which is a metaphor for keeping knowledge from the people. ⚥ is raising the notions of capitalist pigs to that of alien invaders from whom the world and the arts must be protected because the arts represent the soul of humanity. "The Exodus Has Begun" is serving notice that ⚥ and other artists are not waiting to be free; they are taking their freedom. "The exodus *has* begun." The New Power Generation is going to save the world with funky music and meaningful lyrics that cause a revolution, causing the slaves to leave Babylon. "Now these are the days of the New Power Generation. The funkiest suckers of the new gold nation—Polyvinylacetate, new power soul—guaranteed 2 stick 2 the roof of your Oldsmobile." Though acrimonious, the New Power Generation is led by love, for vengeance belongs to God. What the NPG does, they do in love, even if it means running the thieves out of the temple.

"These are the names of the children of the sun—

pumpin' the love sign in the days of wild, tearin' shit up with a vengeance, and still they smile though their lives were made bitter with hard labor and no pay. These are the children who will come 2 say the day."

Turning his message directly to the industry, ⚥ sounds an alarm of the inevitable demise of the industry. Much like in India and South Africa, the oppressed have numbers on their side. All they have to do is stand up, be counted, and use their numbers.

"Behold, the children of the New Power Generation are more and mightier than u—u that have scorned and held back the inevitable must now come 2 grips with the truth. All that is good in the ☽s of Heaven will rebuke your powder monkey ways. And let that same Heaven have mercy when the wrath of the Sun knocks upon your gate."

⚥ then moves to reveal the practice of deception used by the industry to keep the artists in the dark. "Spatch cocks in black face offer us pennies when its millions upon millions they reap. How in the world can we call ourselves equal when their wages out weight the time that they keep." It is this illusion, the evil ways of the oppressor, that justifies the wrath of righteousness that will be needed to return order to life.

"And if they stood up and behaved like the humans they're supposed 2 as opposed 2 the way they are not, then this new power soul would not be so soulful, and the water they're in would not be so hot. The exodus has begun..."

⚥ leaves us with a notion that this rebellion, as are all rebellions, is a direct reaction to oppression. This has always been the primary voice of African American art, to rebel against oppression. It is the trials and tribulations of the people that make their art so "soulful." So by leading this charge against the industry, ⚥ is merely taking his place in the legacy of

African American artists who have created art as a tool used by the oppressed to gain a sense of humanity, first-class citizenship, freedom, liberation, and sovereignty.

Following the release of Exodus and an interview on London television, ⚥ released a statement from Paisley Park on December 22, 1995, which "wasn't very detailed, but outlined his feelings." Following this initial release, ⚥ released another document entitled "Message from the Artist" on one of his many websites, The Dawn.Com at http://www.thedawn.com/action/message/html. It was later reprinted by The ⚥ Family. "Message from the Artist" is a personal note from ⚥ to summarize and clarify the confusion around his name change and his battle with Warner Bros. During the London television interview, ⚥ appears with his face completely covered, refusing to talk, choosing to talk through his band members. His covered face represents and is protesting the fact that Warner Bros owns his image and any likeness of his image. His refusing to speak represents and is protesting the fact that Warner Bros owns his voice, his art, his tool to speak and express himself. Communicating through his band members represents the filtering, editing, and censorship process which is common and organic in the traditional artist-company relationship. Obviously, the masses did not understand his tactics or simply do not care because of his perceived bizarre behavior. Many African Americans were offended when he wrote "slave" on his face, believing that he was merely attempting to exploit the legacy of slavery. Others just did not understand his methods. I was often asked by those who saw the London interview, "Why was he on television with a scarf wrapped 'round his face?" Others would ask, "Why would that fool give an interview and refuse to talk?" To clarify the interview and his general issues with Warner Bros and the music industry, he delivered the following posting to clarify his issues.

"Welcome to the Dawn...these words from Paisley Park are from me. My ultimate message is a cry for solidarity amongst artists and a reprieve from the greed of entertainment executives.

My message stems from a lifetime of development as an artist and as a businessman, and my increasing awareness of a greedy structure within the music industry that unjustly rewards large, slow corporate management teams, while overlooking and not protecting its bread and butter—the artists.

As difficult as it is to admit now, when I began my career with Warner in 1978, I had a lot to learn. The transition into the artist I am now hasn't been a smooth one. I don't want other young artists to be mislead in the same way. I'm expressing my feelings so that others will learn from my mistakes. I also want all established artists to understand the issues and know that there should be a better way to join with me to create that new path.

A little history...

At 37 years old, I have been a recording artist for Warner Music for what will be seventeen years this April. I was only 19 years old when I recorded my first album as Prince. Recording for a large label was new and exciting. I had an opportunity to reach millions of people around the world, not just my faithful following here in Minneapolis around the club scene. As time passed, the realities of the music industry and its current hierarchical pecking system sunk in. Artists are last on the totem pole in terms of recoupment.

My path has been a long and arduous one. In the beginning, both youth and excitement towards the opportunity to have an album produced made me, as Prince, naive. Savvy lawyers claiming to have my interest at heart, long in bed with the record companies they pimp, offered me what seemed to be a lucrative contract, without fully explaining the ramifications of its terms. I wrote an album a year for many years until I realized a trap had been laid. I would never be able to leave the legacy of my music to my family, my future children or anyone, because "Prince" did not own the Masters—I did not, and still do not, own my Art.

For most of all of my adult life, I have labored under one construct. I compose music, write lyrics, and produce songs for myself and others. My creativity is my life; it is what guides my everyday, my sleepless nights. My songs are my children. I feel them. I watch them grow, and I nurture them to maturity. I deliver them to my record company, and suddenly, they are no longer mine. The process is painful. I have been long ready for a new program. The time is now.

As an artist, I want to share my music with others. I

crave the experience of writing and sharing with others. It is what I do as an artist, as a human being. I take pleasure in the fact that others are able to share in my joy once the process is complete. My fans are my children's friends; I respect them and want to communicate with them.

As a businessman and the owner of NPG Records—the label that released "The Most Beautiful Girl in the World"—the 1994 Number One release by an independent, I realize that the record companies are a natural part of the food chain. It is the record label that allows a musical artist to reach out to his or her audience, but that does not mean that whichever organization markets and distributes the music should own the final product, i.e. the Masters.

What I have learned as both an artist and a businessman is that a middle ground must be developed. All artists, whether new or established, must have a substantial ownership interest in the music they create. Conversely, all record labels need an incentive to market music and push it through their distribution systems; still, that incentive should not be ultimate control. Record labels have no right to enslave the creators.

The first step I have taken towards the ultimate goal of emancipation from the chains that bind me to Warner Bros was to change my name from Prince to ☮. Prince is the name that my Mother gave me at birth. Warner Bros took the name, trademarked it, and used it as the main marketing tool to promote all of the music that I wrote. The company owns the name Prince and all related music marketed under Prince. I became merely a pawn used to produce money for Warner Bros.

By my 35th birthday, June 7, 1993, I was beyond frustrated with my lack of control over my career and music. It seemed reminiscent of much that had been experienced by other African Americans over the last couple hundred years. They had turned me into a slave, and I wanted no more of it. The dilemma had only one clear solution. I was born Prince and did not want to adopt another conventional name. The only acceptable replacement for my name and my identity was ☮, a symbol with no pronunciation, that is a representation of me and what my music is about. This symbol is present in my work over the years; it is a concept that has evolved from my frustration; it is who I am. It is my name.

I look forward to the release of <u>Emancipation</u> in the near future. It will be The Dawn of the next phase of my life as a musician. It will represent my freedom from the past, and it will be a continuum of what I have started here today.—written by ☮ for

The Dawn Website."

The "Message from the Artist" comes eleven months before the release of Emancipation. There is one additional album released between the posting of the "Message" and prior to the release of Emancipation. This demonstrates Prince's own savvy and grasp of image control. The "Message" works in many of the same ways as those early 1980 interviews do before the release of Dirty Mind and the 1985 interviews before Around the World in a Day. ⚤ is consciously preparing his listeners for his next phase, fighting against the knee-jerk reactions to his past behavior and the general dumbing down of the music listeners. Once again, ⚤ is challenging his listeners, forcing them to analyze why they listen to what they listen. He, also, is using his personal struggles as a metaphor for a larger struggle for freedom and liberation. Many state that it is difficult to feel sorry for a millionaire slave. However, ⚤ is not talking about the money, but the general oppressive relationship that exists between artists and companies, which is signified by the disproportionate sharing of the profits. In a capitalistic society, art is a commodity on two levels.

On one level, it is a commodity for socio-political change. It is the only capital/resource that some people have to participate in the discourse and policy making activities in the society. Secondly, art is a commodity because it allows artists the opportunity to earn capital and turn their ideas and hopes into realities. If my art represents my hopes and dreams, then the capital that it generates will allow me to make those dreams and hopes a reality. When an artist is not fairly compensated, he is physically and psychologically enslaved because he is not getting a fair return on his investment or labor. ⚤ is certainly echoing thoughts about the exploitative nature of capitalism and its dehumanizing characteristics that reduce people to objects by objectifying, commodifying, and co-opting their labor and their ideas. Capitalism is not just exploitive because one person is forced to work for another person. It is exploitive because individuals are not allowed to work for themselves through a system designed to marginalize a certain group of people by limiting their education and their resources. "The company owns the name Prince and all related music marketed under Prince. I became merely a pawn used to produce more money for Warner Bros." He became a pawn because he did not understand nor was he thoroughly educated in the terms of his contract. ☥ is fighting the objectifying and dehumanizing of people for profit, which inhibits humanity's evolution to a higher life form. This becomes even clearer with his next album, Chaos and Disorder.

Chaos and Disorder has two hurdles, the diversity of music and the name change issue. Even as late as June, 1996, critics are still discussing the name change rather than the music, a full three years after the name change. For instance, the June 21, 1996, review of Chaos and Disorder in the Philadelphia Inquirer dedicates the first three-fourths of its review to a discussion of the name change. Very few reviews of Chaos and Disorder get right to reviewing the album without a cloud of off-handed comments and digs about the name change. Even with these hurdles, Chaos and Disorder works on two levels. Lyrically, it provides the problem to be solved by Emancipation in the same manner that The Black Album provides the problem to be solved by Lovesexy. As part one, Chaos and Disorder represents the turmoil in our lives that is caused by our existentialistic existence in this cruel and illogical world. It is the storm, the heavy rain, that on the surface seems counterproductive because we are looking with our physical eyes. Yet, if we look deeper, we realize that April showers really do bring May flowers. The storms of our lives are just the rains fertilizing us, making us stronger. That is why each issue discussed in Chaos and Disorder has a solution, which prepares the listener for Emancipation. The combination of the two albums reiterate 1999 and Purple Rain's message for us to remain steadfast and weather the storm because enlightenment and salvation are coming, as Prince asserts at the end of "Let's Go Crazy," "He's [God is] coming." In fact, the storm is needed so that we are able to recognize and appreciate enlightenment. Musically, Chaos and Disorder works because ✦ is able to strap on and plug into his guitar icon status without fear of alienating Emancipation. Rock-n-Roll by African Americans is seldom or rarely heard. Lenny Kravitz is not the only African American rocker; he is just the only one that the industry will tolerate, mostly because of his unyielding commitment and his evolving talent. However, Kravitz would not have had his opportunity had it not been for the unyielding commitment of ✦ as Kravitz admits, "When I saw Prince, everything changed. I thought 'here's somebody doing it, getting it right.'" D'Arby also affirms the effect that ✦ had on careers like his. "He made it possible for me to do what that voice in my head tells me to do." So Chaos and Disorder allows ✦ to reaffirm his title as one of the most crafted guitar players of his generation, while stretching even further on Emancipation, further stretching the spectrum of African American diversity in popular music.

"Chaos and Disorder" opens the album with ✦ ranting about a society that is evolving industrially but decaying spiritually. In turning to man, to industrialization, mankind seems to be turning away from Nature, away from God, away from their own souls. Money, not God, is the prize, and it causes us to adopt a Machiavellian attitude toward life. "Carjack used 2 fix flat tires. Cadillac used 2 be a Benz." These are two examples of how man's greed has perverted his ideals about civilization and evolution. The automobile is the symbol of American prosperity and industrialization. Because of man's declining morality, the automobile is now a symbol of greed, status, and man's willingness to do anything to have prosperity. Black kids now carjack for prosperity in the same manner that the ruling class perpetuates the underclass' second-class citizenship for its own greed, in the same manner that Europe carjacked (raped, pillaged, and plundered Africa and America) for its own greed. Furthermore, there seems to be no end to this greed, when symbols such as the Cadillac are no longer valid symbols of American prosperity. Man's insatiable appetite for power causes him to set arbitrary values of self-worth based on one's economic worth. Thus, the value of an automobile is no longer equated to its performance but to its cost/class status, in the same manner that a person's self-worth is not based on his character but his economic worth. "Cadillac used 2 be a Benz." The Cadillac used to be the top of the line car, but now it has been replaced in the minds of society mostly because the Benz costs more or simply because the ruling class has decided to anoint the Benz has top car because the lower class has been able to gain access to the Cadillac. Thus, we become a society with no moral or spiritual grounding, setting arbitrary rules and standards to satisfy our physical day-to-day concerns and desires. Thus, Paris Hilton is famous not because of her talent or moral character but because she is rich and the society lusts or fetishsizes her wealth. This lack of inner peace, this lack of spiritual grounding, causes man to continuously seek the next big high, the next big "pop" to dull the pain or to create the illusion of peace. "Big joint never got u higher. Freebase costs u in the end." This lack of peace makes mankind restless, looking for anything to make it feel at ease, even if it is a lie or an illusion. We become a generation that is roaming aimlessly in the wilderness because it has lost its history, its past. "U're played used 2 mean top forty. Now forty days of being played ain't proud." Things seem to lose value merely because they are considered old and irrelevant. Tradition and heritage no longer have value because we now live in a disposable culture created by our myopic vision for instant physical gratification. Our spiritual investment in capitalism and industrialization has us in a chaotic spiral, moving us farther away from our center, "i'm getting' hit by mortar everywhere i'm loitering. Chaos and Disorder ruling my world 2day."

"Chaos and Disorder" is quite different from "1999" in that there is no celebration of a passing into the great beyond. It echoes the more pessimistic vision of "The Future" from <u>Batman</u>. It is clear that ⚧ sees this world as a world built on entropy for the sake of entropy, which is a misguided notion of freedom. He is asserting that freedom without responsibility leads to disaster. This is a direct assertion of

Maulana Karenga's notion of freedom from his essay, "Black Art: Mute Matter Given Force and Function,"

> "...freedom does not exist in the abstract. It is not an independent living thing; it lives through us and through the meaning and message we give it. And [a person] may have any freedom to do what he wishes as long as it does not take the freedom from the people to be protected from those images, words, and sounds that are negative to their life and development" (Gates and McKay 1976).

One would think that this is a major development or growth for ☥, but it is not. As early as his first album, ☥ is singing about the responsibilities and consequences of all of our actions, including sex. "Baby," from his first album, <u>For You</u>, discusses the emotions and problems of an unplanned pregnancy. So well before he has established his sex metaphor, he is discussing the risks and issues of sex and sexuality. "Chaos and Disorder" is merely a continuation of a man who is concerned with human direction and the journey to a better place. This includes commenting on the question of doing something just because one is able, capable, or free to do it, rather than doing something because it leads to evolution. Clearly he sees a world that embraces the former and is missing the latter. The poet's job is to absorb all of this and ejaculate it onto the canvass and onto the people in a way that the stench of the subject causes mankind to realize its detrimental ways. "i'm just a no-named reporter. i wish i had nothing 2 say, looking thru my new camcorder, tryin' 2 find a crime that pays." This is the job of the poet, to turn the camera on the society so that it is forced to see its detrimental ways. As Baldwin asserts, writing is about getting at the truth, even when that truth is not popular.

Often the job of the poet is a thankless job as evident in "Dinner with Delores," which is the kiss-off within the kiss-off. <u>Chaos and Disorder</u> fulfills ☥'s contractual obligation to Warner Bros. Assembling the album with songs that are not radio friendly is the final kiss-off to Warner Bros. "Dinner with Delores" articulates the literal kiss-off. Delores is an all encompassing trope for the music industry and listeners, with whom ♀ has grown bored of entertaining. The song laments a date with a girl who has nothing more to offer than sex, which is what she is expected to offer. This is also all that she wants from him. Delores represents fans and record companies that want to hold ♀ to his old title of "His Royal Badness." Delores is stuck in a mold, trying also to hold him there, and the protagonist is having no more of it. "Her bell's just-a-broken since 1984...Damn Delores, pick another subject please. Introduce the carpet 2 something other than your knees." The bell that has been broken since 1984 symbolizes the manner in which Warner Bros and listeners have hounded ♀ to repeat the sounds and success of <u>Purple Rain</u>. Thus, the thought of having sex (or sharing an intimate moment) with Delores is not stimulating; it is the same old thing with the same type of girl. The thought of making music is no longer stimulating; it is the same old thing with the same type of audience. "Dinner with Delores" sets the tone for the album and the next phase of his career. He ends by declaring "i've run out of cheeks to turn." This is not the album that either Warner Bros or the general public wants from Prince, but ♀ is no longer Prince; so ♀ does not care, which is why he can end the song "Dinner with Delores, no more, that's the end."

"Same December" begins where "Dinner with Delores" ends and continues to reject the old notions of success. The song is another indictment of the capitalist atmosphere that pits humanity against itself for a few worthless trinkets. "Same December" encourages humanity to see beyond the trees of temporary financial gain to perceive the forest of inner peace.

> "Once was a golden idol that went 2 all the winners. Needless 2 say, it didn't make 'em feel any less a sinner 'cause the very next morning the whole damn world was the same. The idol's still shinin' but the voice inside, it said 'there ain't no winners in the game.'"

At the heart of America's capitalism is race, and the ten percent who control the money exploit the race issue so that poor whites and poor blacks continue to fight for reasons that they do not fully understand.

> "Once was this ball with a line straight down the middle. One side was black and the other one white, and they both understood so little. And they spent their whole lives tryin' 2 tell each other what time it was. And all along it did not matter what either said, because u only know what u know; u only see what your heart will show. U only love when your soul remembers [that] we all come from the same December, and in the end that's where we'll go."

"Same December" builds upon the issue raised in "Color" from the 1800NEWFUNK compilation. ☧ is discussing race as a political and economic construct, which is used to assign individuals a certain place because of their race. Baldwin addresses this in both The Fire Next Time and Evidence of Things Not Seen. Black is as much a social-political and economic construct as it is a cultural construct because people of African descent have been assigned the role as the permanent labor class. Black represents any non-white group who starts at the bottom of the class system: Africans, Native Americans, Italians, Asians, Jews, Hispanics, Indians, and Irish. The trick or the fallacy of capitalism is President Reagan's assertion that "hard work and the magic of the market place" will allow anyone to prosper in America. This is not true. If hard work was the only prerequisite, then African descendants would be at the top of the class system. The small print of Regan's idea is the "magic of the market place."

For American capitalism to work, there has to be a permanent labor class. America has assigned African Americans, Native Americans, and the Latino and Hispanic populations as its permanent labor classes. America creates this permanent labor sector by denying them equal access to education. This unequal access to education keeps them from acquiring wealth. By not acquiring wealth, they are not able to influence the political system. Accordingly, the lack of proper education keeps African Americans encased in their prescribed places. This is the conflict for the individuals in "Same December" who do not understand the game that they are playing, "...they both understand so little." Educator and political activist, Asa Hilliard asserts, "Black folks are playing softball, and the rest of the country is playing baseball." Black people believe that hard work is the only prerequisite to the American Dream, and this is their destruction. They do not understand that white flight keeps them othered and in high risk areas. So even though a group of African Americans are able to leave the ghetto, the larger, white society simply identifies and assigns those middle-class African American neighborhoods as high risks. Though they gain capital, they are still forced to pay more and live unequally, as they continue to invest in an unjust society and blindly pay more to do so, as in paying more to be mis-educated or trained to be labor only. By not understanding this, African Americans continue to integrate and invest into a system designed to oppress them, instead of separating themselves from the system like the Asians, Indians, Jews, Italians, Irish, and the whites who keep their traditions and cultures, thereby keeping a bond with themselves as a collective unit. Without this bond, African Americans are fragmented (divided and conquered) by integration and kept in their place of the permanent labor class.

The final aspect of monopoly capitalism is the game of keeping poor whites afraid of blacks, thus keeping the two groups from constructing a new collective, a poor people's collective. As long as blacks are the laborers and poor whites are middle management (slaves and overseers), they will continue to clash over the golden carrot. "Color" addresses this issue of African Americans being painted a certain class (color) in order to hold them in their places.

> "Color me black if u color me like u. Color me angry if u color me less than ꤰ do. Color me happy

if u teach me what 👁 need 2 know. Color me gone if u don't 'cause every child has a right 2 grow. Love is my color when 👁'm shown love n return. But if 👁 am not, u can guess what 👁 have learned. Color me green if 👁 can not have what u got. Color me blue until 👁 do 'cause the fire will shout from being hot."

☥ is indicating that class and race are inextricably tied because the assignments are used to designate blacks as labor and protect white supremacy. This is cultural and psychological warfare that is ingrained early into the minds of African American children. Millions of African American children are told to "sit yo' li'l black self down," with black being a synonym for ugly or bad. So the color "black" is encoded with a negative connotation. Both "Color" and "Same December" show how this construct works and how it is implemented. From an individual standpoint, Prince is accessing his own situation with Warner Bros. Yet, he is also using his personal situation as an example for understanding the historical mistreatment of people of color.

"Right the Wrong" seeks to make the oppression and exploitation in "Color" and "Same December" a universal issue by expanding the discourse to include Native Americans. By aligning themselves with other people of color, African Americans increase their chances of gaining power and sovereignty in America. African Americans represent fourteen percent of the American population. However, people of color represent thirty-five percent of the American population. Across the globe, people of color represent the majority of the human population. Unfortunately, diversity or ethnic differences is keeping people of color apart rather than bringing them together to fight the evils of human oppression and white supremacy. Europeans have colonized most of the world and continue to benefit from exploiting the labor of people of color. Over sixty million Africans were lost to the middle passage and the global slave trade. Sixty-eight million Native Americans were wiped out when the Europeans began colonizing South and Central America. Through "Right the Wrong" ☧ is paralleling his struggle against oppression and the African American struggle against oppression to the Native American struggle. "Did u hear the one about the boy just seventeen? Three years hard time 4 stealin' ice cream. First offense, and all his dreams are gone. How long, oh, 'fore we right the wrong?" This passage could be about any child. However, the statistics tell us that white children more often than not get counseling for their juvenile offenses, and children of color often get some type of jail time. ☧ seems to be writing to the empire or the oppressor, urging it to right the wrong or suffer the consequences. "Nor shall the guilty be forgiven, until they can find it in their hearts 2 right the wrong." ☧ is building on his notions in the song "U Will Be Moved," which was penned for Mavis Staples and appears on both <u>The Voice</u> and <u>1800NEWFUNK</u>. Again, ☧ is asserting that those who gain from the oppression and exploitation of others will suffer the wrath of God.

> "U will be move when the baby let's out his very first cry, moved when u think of how hard he'll have 2 try. He'll grow up on an empty stomach and try his best 2 listen 2 a teacher readin' from a school book with half the pages missing. Surely when the rain comes, u will be moved."

☧ is using rain as a symbol of power and as a punishment by God, which is then troped in "Right the Wrong." "Before long u won't hear nothing but the crackle of flames...It seem like we could stop the flow of snow in the sky today. i guess the weatherman, he likes the rain, ain't that insane?" "U Will Be Moved" is the gateway or foundation for "Right the Wrong" through which ☧ directly denounces America's system of oppression as unrighteous and ungodly. "U will be moved when the baby makes all the grades; moved u will be when they don't hire him anyway." Even with his anger, ☥ proposes a solution "to a system that offers no guarantee...that education is the answer and love is the only key." It is this hope that resonates in all of his music and explodes in "Right the Wrong." "And even though injustice took them hills away, one day we'll get 'em back. The Sun's gonna shine that day when we say 'Right the wrong.'" This is what sets ☥'s work apart. He finds a way to grapple with issues but also raise that grappling to a discourse of finding solutions, not glorifying the problems. Even in the bleak "Same December" there is a solution to the game of capitalism. Save your soul by walking away from the game and learning to love.

> "Until the demons fall as far as anyone can fall, when they reap what they done sowed, i'll be standin' tall. We spend our whole lives tryin' 2 dog the other man, when what we need 2 do is try 2 give him all we can."

The tone in "Right the Wrong," "Color," and "U Will Be Moved" is anger and reprehension. These are not pleas; these are warnings to the oppressor that he will reap what he sows, and as Booker T. Washington asserts in his "Atlanta Compromise," from his autobiography, <u>Up From Slavery</u>. "Nearly sixteen millions of hands will aid you in pulling the load upward, or they will pull against you the load downward." Although Washington is being passive, his message is clear. How whites treat African Americans will result in what they reap. Ironically, white Americans have yet to realize how the crime and violence in America's streets is directly tied to slavery, Jim Crow, and the continued perpetuation of the second-class citizenship of African Americans. To accomplish the tone of reprehension, ☥ is finding his heroic voice through biblical imagery in much the same manner as Margaret Walker Alexander. Just as R. Baxter Miller asserts in his essay, "The 'Etched Flame' of Margaret Walker: Biblical and Literary Re-Creation in Southern History," that Alexander is signifying through biblical imagery to parallel and magnify the struggle and heroic essence of African

American people, ♀ can be seen using the same technique in "U Will Be Moved," "Same December," "Color," and "Right the Wrong." Like Alexander, ♀

"deepens the portraits by using biblical typology...Through biblical balance [♀, like Alexander,] sets the white oppressor against the black narrator. [♀, like Alexander, speaks as] the prophet-narrator... 'Ages ago the Lord put His rainbow in the clouds. To the descendants of Noah it signified His promise'...[♀ has replaced the rainbow with rain, fire, and snow, which are all biblical images and used in natural disasters to punish those not submitting to the will of God. Just as Alexander draws on biblical imagery to assure her African American readers of certain victory against their white oppressors by aligning them with the Israelites, ♀ uses the same types of natural disasters to connect his listeners to this religious, historical, and cultural legacy, which gives them hope by asserting that their oppressors will be punished by God. And like Alexander, ♀] frequently blends the secular and religious 'folk' who share a communal quest. [Like Alexander, ♀ blends] historical sense with biblical implication [thus] interpreting the meaning of the earth to bridge the distance between past decay and present maturity when the narrator celebrates the promise that injustice will not go unpunished. [Like Alexander, ♀ uses the harsh tone of the Old Testament, invoking a sense of authority because of some inferred covenant with God.] The symbolical level dominates the literal one, and the poem portrays more deeply the human condition [of the oppressed. This allows] the narrator to profit from the gothicism. [Through the combination of current events and biblical imagery] the reader associates myth and history, [which gives ♀ and the oppressed a heroic persona or, in the least, aligns the current-day oppressed with the lineage and heroic struggle of the Israelites. Further still, ⚘ is inline with Alexander because of his embracing what Salaam calls the innate or ultimate goodness of the universe. Unlike the generation that follows him, ⚘ does not embrace Richard Wright's rage. He, instead, embraces Alexander's humanism. His portrait, like Alexander's] images not only the myth of fragmentation and dissolution, but the courage necessary to confront and transcend them" (Killens 591-601).

⚘ is not merely preaching that God is going to punish the evil. His ultimate message becomes the righteous will be rewarded because only love can conquer hate. With this use of typology, ⚘ falls inline with the legacy of African American literature, which is to recreate, reconstruct, and refashion myth, history, and legend to celebrate and give African Americans a sense of place, purpose, and self-worth. ⚘ is destroying the lie of white supremacy by equating the current-day white oppressors with the oppressors of the Bible who are destroyed by God because of their sins. Thus, people of color become the chosen people. This is the largest step of growth for ⚘. In these four songs he is pushing directly against white supremacy. In the past, he railed abstractly against oppression. Now, oppression has a face, a history, and a legacy. Through his use of biblical imagery, ⚘ is asserting that there will be a retribution. The child in "U Will Be Moved" grows up and leads the revolution in "Right the Wrong." ⚘ is asserting that we should not punish the child but the system that creates the child because this system will eventually contaminate all of the children. In The Fire Next Time, Baldwin warns that the black boy and the white boy are brothers in the same house. If something inflicts one, the whole house is contaminated. Further, ⚘ is asserting the same notion that Malcolm X is asserting when he states that chickens do come home to roost. The mass shootings and killings in suburban schools involving disturbed and disgruntled white teens in Pearl, Mississippi, Littleton, Colorado, Jonesboro,

Arkansas, and other places represent the turning inward of the violence and anger of whites that for so long has been aimed at and internalized by African Americans. As ☥ is asserting in "U Will Be Moved" and "Right the Wrong," white people are spending so much time perpetuating white supremacy that they are not noticing how that violence is being internalized by their children. This teenage angst and violence, which had been linked to African American children, is now seeping into white neighborhoods. Much like his commentary on AIDS in 1987, ☥ is right on target as a social poet.

Moving from the collective back to the individual, "i Rock Therefore i Am" asserts that the mindless urge toward normality and pseudo-culture amalgamation is the axle upon which the wheel of confusion and oppression turns. For years now, the greatest criticism of ☥'s work is the diversity and unique flavor of the music. There is no exception on Chaos and Disorder. Because of the hard rock edge and introspective lyrics of the album, many reviewers found "i Rock, Therefore i Am" out of place and overly eclectic. Rather than being an asset, ☥'s ability to play a variety of music and amalgamate cultures has been more of a liability because it makes it difficult to cage/categorize him and difficult for narrow minds to get their feeble and constipated brains around his work. With all of the mixed reviews of Chaos and Disorder, "i Rock, Therefore i Am" is the lightening rod of musical complexity and confusion that is a perfect representation of his career. Jon Beam of the Minneapolis Star Tribune states that "This declaration of self-confidence is funky, slinky, freaky and the only hip-hop thang Prince has ever done that seems natural." Charles Waring of Blues & Soul states "Just as I was beginning to despair of finding something to really get my teeth into, the dubiously titled 'I Rock, Therefore I Am' kicked in with its infectious funky groove and some excellent vocals by Rosie Gaines." The song is in the vein of "Daddy Pop," in that he is proclaiming that his talent and creativity lies in his willingness to be different. Throughout the song, ♀ proclaims "i don't need u 2 tell me i'm in..." I am because I am, not because you [the industry] made me, so I do not need you to validate me. Liberation begins with oneself. Once you stop looking for answers in others, you will find the truth that you need in yourself. Poet Jolivette Anderson affirms this in her book, <u>Past Lives, Still Living</u>, when she asserts, "I never knew the color blue until I started looking for the me in you." ♀ is refusing to be blue because of anyone else's picture, perception, or expectation of him. Even on a rock album, ♀ refuses to be boxed.

"Into the Light" takes the funk and self-determination of "i Rock, Therefore i Am" and sows it into metaphysical soil. The song is about man reconciling his physical self to his metaphysical self, understanding that complete peace and happiness can only be found when man taps into the light within himself that connects him to the light of the creator. The courageous person in "i Rock, Therefore i Am" gets his strength from his inner peace. It is his metaphysical fortitude that allows him to withstand the forces of the physical. "Into the Light" affirms Ntozake Shange's assertion in <u>For Colored Girls</u> that in order to survive humanity must find God in ourselves.

> "From out of the darkness, before there was time, there came a sound that enters the mind through a door that's deep in your soul. Through every pore of your body it goes...And as sure as this candle burns, every soul must return into the light."

♀ is attempting to make us see the fruitless journey of searching for peace in the physical, asserting that man is missing the metaphysical gifts and truths of the universe from toiling too much in the physical. Man must find a way to get back in touch with his innocence, that part of himself that has not been spoiled or jaded. "4 every flower that grows even a baby knows that as sure as the candle burns, every soul must return into the light." However, ♀

is not overly romantic or simplistic in his solution, which is why "Into the Light" is followed by the melancholy "i Will."

The journey into the light is not an easy one. It is often a lonely expedition as ☥ has found throughout his career. To go where no one has gone or to travel the road less traveled is not a popular course. "i Will" laments this feeling of isolation, but ☥ asserts that whoever goes this route will not be alone, although it might seem as such. "i will walk this road. i will. It's gonna be hard, but i know i will. People come, and they'll go, but i'll still face up 2 the truth and just grow." The dedication to enlightenment and righteousness is a long and often lonely road, but there is a peace that comes from this journey that makes it all worth experiencing and enduring. "i will fight this fight. i will. i will sleep 2night." To gain this peace, one must learn from one's past journeys such as <u>Around the World in a Day</u> and stay focused. "i've been down before, but i'll still remember what i came 4." The journey is to change the world by changing oneself, to find peace with the world by finding peace within oneself. This often means fighting to change those who do not understand the journey nor the struggle and those who could care less about making the world a better place. "i will get 2 u, and then i'll help u get through. U've preyed on many a fool until no one cared about u, but i will." Again, ☥ is stressing Baldwin's theory that our birthright is to love each other, not oppress each other. This often means having to save people who do not love you.

> "You must accept them with love because they are trapped by a history they do not understand... integration means that we, with love, shall force our brothers to see themselves as they are, to cease fleeing from reality and begin to change it...for this is your home" (Baldwin, <u>Fire Next Time</u>, 22, 24).

☥ is still attacking hate and mis-education with love and

education. People hate and go astray because they lack the truth. ⚥ is attempting to provide the truth that the physical world is a temporary illusion which blinds us from the metaphysical reality.

"Dig U Better Dead" returns the confrontational tone of the album. The literal translation is that people like ⚥, Jimi Hendrix, and Kurt Cobain are worshipped once they die some horrific death, leaving them as martyrs for their times. ⚥ has defied this, not allowing himself to be placed in a museum or marginalized for somebody else's fantasy of him. The figurative meaning is that people tend to "dig u," like u, better when you are "dead," asleep, to the truth so that they can exploit and use you. A dead artist is an artist who is no longer stimulating and influential. And in an economic sense, the legacy of a deceased artist can be exploited for economic gain. Influential (living) artists are dangerous to the status quo. The more ⚥ rejects the status quo, the less he is courted by the press who are controlled by the industry. The same was initially true for John Lennon, who was blasted by a press that wanted him to stay a teen-aged mop-top who wrote catchy pop tunes that are devoid of social commentary. Now, after his death, Lennon's legacy has been co-opted by the ruling class, which did not receive him warmly during his artistic evolution. "A long time ago u took six months of walkin', talkin' on the other side. What started out as an experiment turned into a heaven-sent message that saved your ass from dyin'." The experiment is "The Most Beautiful Girl in the World." Warner Bros did not think that ⚥ would be able to market a record on his own and hoped that a flop would force him to become more traditional and conventional in his approach to making and selling music. The problem for Warner Bros is that the song went to number two on the charts. The "ass" that is saved is both ⚥'s ass as well as the general ass of the artists.

⚥ is challenging artists to look at his independent

success and use it as a guide for their own emancipation. "Somebody said...in life there's always peaks and valleys, and if you're lost they won't show u the way. That same somebody said 'i dig u better dead,' But, i'd much rather see if your God is what u say." ☥ is challenging artists to confront the vague but omnipotent "somebody" who is always casting doubts on artistic independence, like the Warner Bros record executive warning of the problems of releasing too much music. This is the same somebody who will look back at the artist's career and lament how he was ahead of his time, while he is selling the artist's unreleased catalogue of music, which is owned by the company. That is why he "dig[s] u better dead." The capitalists continue to use both fear and the golden carrot to control the artist's vision. "And with an awesome power they stuck. First, they offered up the buck. Right in the middle they stuck a toke or 2, what the fuck?" Eighty-five years after Hughes published "The Negro Artist and the Racial Mountain," African Americans are still being seduced by the white dollar to lessen their humanity, making themselves and their art more palatable to white tastes and desires. "The Negro artist works against...bribes from whites...'Be stereotyped, don't go too far, don't shatter our illusions about you, don't amuse us too seriously. We will pay you'" (Gates and McKay 1270). Companies want disposable art that they can control and manipulate at will, until the artist has been milked and drained dry. "One minute u're hot. Tell the truth, and u're not. That's the noose that they hang on a goose like u." Above all, the industry hates self-contained, sovereign individuals. Super producer and Time member Jimmy Jam asserts in an interview with BET's <u>Video Soul</u> that, "Record companies tend not to deal with artists like Prince because he gets three or four checks before anyone else gets paid, including them." Along with getting fairly compensated, ☥ is challenging the general notion of what constitutes a pop star by asserting that striving to be unique and creative innately hinders the system, which is established to produce cookie cutouts of what is popular. "Whatever u do, don't make somebody happy. Don't dress 2 freaky and make their daughters stare. Then u'll find out how deep the valley truly be. If u plan on catchin' the bus, u better have plenty fare." Artists must be business people if they plan to control their own future. Any man who is not at least part owner of his craft or art is all fool. So, if you are going to be different, you need security, which is both financial and spiritual.

"Had U" is the second and final kiss-off of this album, which is, in totality, a kiss-off to Warner Bros. ☧ is not expecting Chaos and Disorder to reach multi-platinum sales. In fact, he knows that it is not. Nobody is buying rock-n-roll from African American artists, and this is what Chaos and Disorder is. Yet, it is not exclusively rock-n-roll, although it is mostly rock-n-roll. That is the kiss-off. Even in his defeat of having to give Warner Bros three more albums to honor his contract, he is still shaping and reshaping his career. The frustrated rock-n-roller is back from the past of Dirty Mind and Purple Rain. "Had U" is ☧ smirking defiantly into the faces of those who want to proclaim him a has been. "Missed u. Called u. Found u. Begged u. Convinced u. Saw u. Held u. Kissed u. Fondled u. Tempted u. Undressed u. Smelled u. Wanted u. Asked u. Thanked u. Minded u. Hurt u. Disappointed u. Fuck u. Had u." ☧ has lived and is continuing to live his life on his terms. That is the ultimate emancipation. That is the ultimate kiss-off that even in defeat he is accepting that defeat on his own terms, which makes his career a success.

Emancipation is released while reporters and critics are still reviewing Chaos and Disorder. In a 1996 Forbes interview reprinted by The ☧ Family, there is a clear notion that ☧ is not worried about overly saturating the market. Having people buy every album is not what is important. Making money is not his ultimate goal. His goal is to get the music recorded and released so that it may impact society.

"He wants to flood the market with his work. That's something Warner would never let him do, and it was the issue that helped trigger the split...a Warner executive states, 'Despite his brilliance, one record after another causes burnout.' If so, then it's burn, baby, burn, the singer retorts. 'My music wants to do what it wants to do, and I just want to get out of its way. I want the biggest shelf in the record store—the most titles. I know they're not all going to sell, but I know somebody's going to buy at least one of each.' With the marketing shackles off, his fans can expect what the poet Shelley called 'profuse strains of unpremeditated art'" (Dawkins, Vol. 4, Issue # 20, 116).

The period from 1994 to 1996 may have been the most productive and prolific time of any artist's career, and Emancipation is the crowing jewel in that productivity. Bell affirms this by declaring, "At a full three hours, there's a heaping helping of music. I don't recall seeing anything like this before, but I would not bet against it" (Dawkins, Vol. 4, Issue # 20, 116). Still, there is a reality that ultimate freedom, independence, and sovereignty are driven by one's ability to gain capital. For the first time since 1999, ☥ seemed to be concerned about the success of a record because Emancipation is not just about him. It is about the emancipation of art and artists. There is some amount of pressure to sell records in order to prove that an artist can be independent and take care of his physical needs. ☥ aggressively markets Emancipation because he knows that the industry is watching, and other artists are watching to see the results of this experiment. In an October 1996 interview with Star Tribune music critic Jon Bream, ☥ affirms "'This is my most important record... I'm free, and my music is free'...Emancipation [Bream asserts] may be his most adult, mature and musically richest record yet" (Bream, "☥ Says He's Free at Last," 1996). Though concerned about sales, the work is still front and center, reflecting his life. ☥'s music is transforming because he is transforming. On <u>Emancipation</u>, he is freely expressing his metaphysical concerns like never before, attempting to amalgamate his studies and theories of ancient history and spirituality and show how all of that is affecting his work. An October 17, 1996, <u>Rolling Stone</u> article notes that

> "In its meticulous structure, <u>Emancipation</u> is based on ☥'s studies of the Egyptians, the building of the pyramids and how the pyramids were related to the constellations. They were a message from the Egyptians about how civilization really started" (Dawkins, Vol. 4 Issue # 22, 127).

☥'s work on <u>Emancipation</u> reflects his never-ending and always evolving search for the meaning of life. His search has taken him back to the original civilization, Egypt, to examine how they studied metaphysics, which consists of both cosmology, the physical study of the universe, and ontology, the philosophical study of the universe. The Egyptians' study of metaphysics is important because it represents, for ☥, man's attempts to gain a holistic understanding of life and its meaning and not just part of it by concentrating on either the physical or the metaphysical. The Egyptians' notions of metaphysics represents, for ☥, man's ability to transcend his physical self and gain true enlightenment. Diana Dawkins, editor/publisher of <u>The ☥ Family</u>, provides insight to all of this by providing excepts from the book <u>The Orion Mystery</u> by Robert Bauval and Adrian Gilbert.

> "The pyramids were based on solar calculations and served as tombs for the pharaohs. These tombs were based on the belief of Osiris. Osiris was a man/god considered to be the first mythological king of Egypt. His sister, Isis, was also his wife. Osiris was the oldest son of the goddess of the sky, Nut. Osiris established the rule of law over the people, he taught the religion and civilization, and

the country prospered. Osiris' and Isis' brother, Seth, was jealous and murdered Osiris, cutting up his body into pieces and scattering them all over the land of Egypt. Isis secretly gathered up the pieces of Osiris and magically put him together again, creating the first mummy, long enough for the two of them to conceive a child. Then Osiris transformed into a star, Orion, and became ruler of the Kingdom of the Dead, called the Duat—a place of afterlife...that was thought to exist within the Orion star system. The child of Osiris and Isis was named Horus, who challenged his uncle Seth and won rule over the land by proclamation of the sun god. Horus thus became the first Pharaoh of Egypt. The story of Osiris' transformation into a star is key to the star religion theory. The authors believe that the pharaoh's building of the pyramids and mummification rituals were all necessary to their own eventual transformation into and rebirth as stars in Orion after their death" (Dawkins, Vol. 4, Issue # 22, p. 128).

⚥'s creation of <u>Emancipation</u> on the structure of the Egyptian pyramids represents his search for transformation and rebirth as a higher metaphysical being. The character of Isis also affirms his lifelong work that man must save himself by connecting with woman, which is life. Along with Dawkins' information, we must also understand the importance of the Pyramid Texts, which are carved on the inside walls of the tombs and were meant to be seen by the gods on the other side. The Pyramid Texts are part obituary and part resume, documents that prove to the Gods that the ruler has lived the type of life that allows for his transformation into the afterlife. Also, along with the Pyramid Texts, the rulers are made to take an oral examination to prove that they are knowledgeable enough to enter into the afterlife. This proves that the Egyptians valued personal and individual enlightenment. The lyrics on <u>Emancipation</u> stand as the equivalent to the Pyramid

Texts and the oral examination. So, ☥ achieves both the structural aspect and the theme/subject matter aspect for the Pyramids.

> "Here's how the pyramids relate to the structure of <u>Emancipation</u>. A pyramid is made up of three sides and four triangles (3 x 4 = 12). The dimensions and positioning of the Fourth Dynasty pyramids, particularly the Great Pyramid of Giza, were extremely precise. Three: <u>Emancipation</u> is made up of three discs and totals three hours of music. Four: There are four covers on <u>Emancipation</u>— 'Betcha By Golly, Wow,' 'La-La Means ♛ love U,' '♛ Can't Make U Love Me" and "One of Us." Twelve: Each disc has exactly twelve tracks on it. Precision: Each disc is exactly one hour in length" (Dawkins, Vol. 4, Issue #23, 34).

The covers or remakes also represent the importance of history, record keeping, and ancestry to the Egyptians. A remake or a cover, in its pure and non-economic sense, is a way to connect to one's legacy or tradition by paying homage to the legacy. It shows a reverence and respect for those who made it possible for you to exist. This is important because these songs are ☥'s first covers. This is another step in his growth by continuing to acknowledge his history and connecting to his peers. He achieves the goal of precision with the manner in which he crafts each song to lyrically and structurally embody the theme of the album. As he states in a 1997 interview with <u>Musician</u>, "The body of a human (when healthy) runs like a sequencer. It was obviously programmed a long time ago by an absolute genius. This was the notion behind the groove 'Human Body' on <u>Emancipation</u>. Every track of the song is its own 'cell,' so to speak, running in harmony with its 'cellmates.'" As for the theme of transformation, the songs all echo the theme of searching for a higher plane of well being, pleasure, and understanding. Specifically in relation to Osiris finding his transformation through the love of Isis, ⚥ indicates that his transformation is found through his love for his wife, Mayte, which is a doorway to a higher transformation. As ⚥ affirms, "She [Mayte] makes it easier to talk to God," as Isis is Osiris' doorway to the heavens and to immortality. Thus, disc two is almost entirely dedicated to his search for the perfect female through whom he can transform.

The time, effort, and craft put into Emancipation did not go completely unnoticed. Emancipation received the type of critical acclaim to rival that of 1999, Around the World in a Day, and Sign "☮" the times. Bream of the Minneapolis Star Tribune asserts:

> "Prince's Emancipation Proclamation is a bedazzling three-hour assertion that he is the most prolific, expansive, visionary and musical pop music maker since the Beatles. This three-disc collection is the Minneapolis superstar's most adult, mature and jazziest record" (Bream, "New Prince Triple Play," 1996).

Jim Farber of the New York Daily News raves:

> "He releases thirty-six songs with no terrible ones and at least twenty-five good ones. To make this monolith more digestible, each of its three albums boasts a distinct character. The first CD takes on the deep easy grooves of modern R&B...The second album stresses adult-pop ballads...the third album swings experimental. By reviving a flair for songwriting long gone in modern R&B, while rendering vocals more sober and his lyrics more thoughtful, one of pop's most maddening figures rewards our patience at last" (Faber 1996).

And Edna Gundersen of USA Today affirms:

allow him to produce himself. In a 1980 interview on American Bandstand, Dick Clark asks ☙ why he held out so long for a record deal, and he states, "They wouldn't let me produce myself." Even early in his career, ☙ has an uncompromising vision. In "White Mansion" he discusses the industry's attempts to get him to compromise that vision for the golden carrot.

> "Hey there, what's your name? Can u tell me how 2 play the game? So ♛ really have 2 cut my hair. Now, that's a cross ♛ could never bear. Sell my publishing—what a laugh! ♛ don't know Bo, but ♛ do know math. Back 2 Minneapolis, there u go. U can't find your house underneath the snow."

In 1996, Oprah Winfrey asked ☙ why he stayed in Minneapolis after all of his success. He stated "it's so cold it keeps all the bad people out." In 1978, Warner Bros wanted him to assemble a touring band using musicians from Los Angeles, but he fought to use the musicians from his home town. These two incidents are examples of ☙'s desire to make music based on his own notions and his willingness to take less for being true to himself. They also echo John Cougar Mellencamp's notion of the benefits gained from staying true to certain values by remaining rooted in a "Small Town." ☙ now has his big white mansion on the top of a hill, and he has it on his own terms, which makes it more rewarding.

"Emale" is the alter ego of "White Manson" and discusses the problems of industrialization—man moving away from nature and toward urbanization. Where ☙ is celebrating the individual who has the fortitude to withstand the forces of physical temptation in "White Manson," "Emale" is lamenting the majority of society that has submitted to the physical. In this computer, gotta-have-it-now age, man is living unnaturally. Capitalism causes us to prey on each other like predators. ☙ personifies industrialization and capitalism into a singular impressionistic persona, which preys on a female's pain and desperation. First, ☥ shows how humans are reduced to being less than human to become fuel for the machine. "Wanted—any woman whose first name begins with A-Z." People are just pawns, nameless, soulless objects in the game of capitalism. The "Wanted" represents the want ads of our daily newspapers and the attitudes of an overly industrialized society. These ads rarely seek personality, creativity, or individuality. They only seek degrees, certification, and experience. These three qualities mark a potential employee as a stoic, flat, and often one-dimensional carbon copy. These companies only want persons who can be used as interchangeable pegs in their machine. Because fear has caused the majority of us to accept the notion that we cannot survive on our own terms, the majority of us mold ourselves to become interchangeable pieces, never realizing that we are molding ourselves to be exploited. "The King takes a pawn." Those who control the system feed off the desperate. They feed off the desperation of the poor to construct or piece together lives for themselves from the fragmented and discarded pieces from the upper class.

Capitalism preys on the disadvantaged who commit certain acts that they think will help them, but actually these actions disenfranchise them even more. This is where the exploitation begins. "He couldn't wait 2 tell her till after he got the Nella, her love would only even the score. It seemed her darling fella stole a hellalotta bucks from the corner store. The declaration of war that followed she never believed." The desperate or the disenfranchised become the system's concubines because they are trapped into perpetuating their own servitude or second class citizenship. The relationship between the male and female is an example of the devolution of individuals who have accepted or internalized the system. The term "Nella" is an ambiguous one, which is both sexual and violent because it can mean either "nail her," which is slang for rough sex, or "vanilla," which is a slag for money and the female's sexual anatomy. The fact that this woman's body is being used to even the score is a trope for the manner in which human beings and our relationships have mutated into nothing more than capital or commodity. Sex is no longer a communication of love but an act of violence, power, and currency exchange.

> "In the darkest corners of where widows mourn, that's were he whispered her name. He said: 'We can do it here, my dear, but 👁 fear your tears will fall like rain. Because 👁 must tell u while 👁'm deep in your smell, u got the man 👁 want 2 inflict with pain 4 running a game with my paper. 👁'm turning the boy 2 vapor. Now 👁 wanna do the same 2 u if u don't tattoo my name upon your train.'"

By working within the system, the female perpetuates her own exploitation because the system is designed to feed off her weakness and desperate situation. As Salaam asserts, most of us become cynical "because we realize that the better we do our jobs, the more difficult it will become to overthrow the system" (Salaam 143). Just like capitalism preys on and exploits the weak, the persona in "Emale" exploits the female because of her desperate situation. Therefore, a capitalistic system is not only run by pimps, the system, itself, is a pimp—a perpetual pimp. The only way not to fall prey to the system is not to believe its promises and hopes. ⚥'s personification of the entire system into one figure makes this painfully clear. The female in "Emale" comes to a negative end because she looks to the physical to save her, thinking that she can actually beat the system. In the end, she is just more fuel for the machine.

"Slave" and "New World" are companion pieces which continue the rail against the exploitation of the lower class. Both center on the deception of the underclass by the power structure to keep the underclass running like a hamster on a wheel, chasing the fictitious food of success. Ironically, the underclass knows that something is wrong, but the ruling class has a way of manipulating reality to keep the underclass in the dark and running. "Like candle slowing burning, ⚓ can feel my world unravel. Hemisphere upon hemisphere lie beneath my soul." The ruling class will use a combination of unreachable rewards and lies to keep the underclass engaged and working. "My enemies keep it turning, but now they pound the gavel and judging me accordingly...like fashion statements they lie 'U be lookin' so good 2night, Kid.'" Everything is done to maintain the illusion of success or the illusion that eventual success is just around the corner, which allows the ruling class to maintain control of the underclass. "Where they learn hypnosis? How'd they keep me under 4 so long? Break the bread ⚓ earn, just keep me far from closest; ⚓ need their kind 2 illustrate what's wrong." As the protagonist is being crushed by the all encompassing "They," he realizes that he must look to himself, not to the world to save him. God/inner peace exists within the individual. The protagonist cannot look to the world, he must go inside and depend on himself. "Everybody keeps trying 2 break my heart. Everybody except for me." A strong sense of self is what will be needed to break free. If we look at global colonization, the only groups that have survived are groups who are able to keep a knowledge of self by continuing to maintain a knowledge of their culture. The Jews and the Asians have prospered because of their strong ties to their culture. In contrast to this, African Americans are still struggling to remove the umbrella of white supremacy because they are still struggling with their identity. "Slave" emphasizes that the oppressor cannot save the oppressed; the oppressed has to find a way to save themselves.

"New World" continues this theme of deception and illusion. "When the lines blur every boy and girl, how we gone make it in the new world?" "New Word" shows that the ruling class has total and absolute control because the underclass is playing a game designed by the ruling class. "When u try 2 find some isolation, but the tracker u got from vaccination keeps playin'—'U'll Never Walk Alone...' There're always listening—especially on the phone!" Even when you go for help you are going to the enemy. This is how many African Americans feel about appeals to congress or the courts. The job of congress and the courts is to maintain and perpetuate the good of the society by perpetuating the status quo. If this is the job of congress and the courts, why would it make any radical changes that would stop its own perpetuation? This is what the "tracker" received from "vaccination" symbolizes. And ⚥ is also invoking the history of Tuskegee, which still causes African Americans to be distrustful of doctors and the entire medical profession. The underclass is controlled because it blindly accepts relief or so called relief from the very system that oppresses them. Individuals are always controlled and constantly monitored for the good of the societal machine. That is why ⚥ is asking his listeners to be skeptical and critical of all new discoveries that make life better. The question is "better for whom?"

> "Did u hear about the new pill?—It feels like sex!, guaranteed 2 thrill with no ill side-effect: a pill that will stop the wrinkles, a pill that will stop the pain, a pill that will make a baby never seek political gain. What's it all 4? When u can alter biology—who or what, then my friend, will u and 👁 be?"

It seems that the cure is worse than the illness. Humanity so desperately wants the quick and easy fix that it mindlessly accepts whatever the so-called leaders give them without engaging in critical thinking to analyze the prescribed solutions. Humanity is in so much pain that it confuses being numb or being in an intellectual coma as being cured. This is the same tactic or affliction that is used in Aldous Huxley's <u>Brave New World</u> where the masses are given drugs and sex to pacify them and make them better workers. ⚥ is warning his listeners not to surrender to the Borg mentality of assimilation. All hope is lost when people lose their individual identities, becoming just another part in the societal machine. "When the melting pot stirs, how we gonna take it? When u can't tell him for her, how u gonna fake it?" The vision is bleak, but it is not without hope. ⚥ cannot write songs without hope. That defeats his purpose for writing. The hope for the "New World" is our "Love 4 1 Another." Right after he asks the question, "How we gonna make in this brave new world?" he answers with "Love 4 1 Another." Love is an action verb. If we do unto others as we would have them to do unto us, we will not have to worry about the Borg mentality or oppression. And along with love, ⚥ is still promoting individuality. "When the melting pot stirs, how we gonna take it? When u can't tell him from her, how u gonna fake it?" He is asserting that we must fight to retain our individuality, which is the basis for our personality and creativity. If we lose ourselves, we lose our creativity. If we lose our creativity, we lose our ability to evolve because we are merely living to perpetuate the status quo, and the status quo does not desire individuality or creativity. The status quo is only concerned with one mission, and it is not evolution. The status quo is concerned with staying the same so that the people in power can remain in power. This is why bureaucracy begets bureaucracy. Those in power create enough paper work, enough checks and balances, to make sure nothing changes. Creativity breeds effectiveness [doing it better by working smarter and not harder], and effectiveness breeds evolution.

"Face Down" is the other answer to "Slave" and "New World" and returns some of the earlier angst. More than angst, however, ⚥ is forcefully asserting his right to be who he wants to be as well as answer the critics by asserting his own notion of success. In an interview with Gundersen he affirms that <u>Emancipation</u> has "an overall tone of exhilaration. In the angry songs, I found a sense of closure. I don't mind going into that dark corner [for] answers, but you got to get out before the spider webs grow on you" (Gundersen, "The Artist Is Free," 1996). More than anything, "Face Down" asserts that if you play by your own rules and terms, then you cannot be a failure based on anybody else's rules and terms.

> "Somebody once told him that he wouldn't take Prince 2 the ringer, let him go down as a washed up singer. Ain't that a bitch, thinkin' all along that he wanted 2 be rich. [Prince] never respected the root of all evil, and he still don't 2 this day. Bury him face down; let a mf kiss a ass—ok?"

Specifically, ☥ is addressing the assertions of many in the media that the name change is a gimmick to save a dying career. The issue for ☥ is how can this be a gimmick when he has never cared about sales in the same manner as the rest of the industry? He then moves to show that the real issue that Warner Bros and the media has with him is not playing by their rules.

> "Told 'em that he wanted 2 sing a song about a black child goin' buck wild, and they just laughed in his face. 'Talk 2 your lawyer, but u got no case. What u need 2 do is keep your place. Next time u pull a card it better be an ace.'"

☥ is making a direct reference about his battle with Warner Bros to release the <u>Gold Experience</u> in the manner that he wanted. The "song about a black child goin' buck wild" is "Days 'O' Wild," which is on the original version of the <u>Gold Experience</u> but is not on the version released for sell. ☥ is addressing the fact that any artist with a standard contract has no control over what is released under his name. He is asserting that the best way to deal with oppression is to flee the plantation. Thus, the final stanza shows ☥'s determination to do whatever to free himself, including committing what some would call artistic suicide. ☥ is ready, willing, and able to accept the ramifications of his actions for his freedom. This, then, becomes the message of the song: Do what you feel is right and never allow yourself to be pimped for money. Those who care about you and love you will always support your efforts to grow and evolve. Never mind the rest. "It's in his will—👁—read it. He shot 2 kill—He said it. 4 those who know the number and don't call...Fuck all y'all." The number is the 1-800-NEWFUNK line through which ☥ is now selling his material. ☥'s stance has always been that you are either with him or against him. The liberation comes when one is able to accept the ramifications of that ideology. When one has inner peace, one can live with that ideology. In fact, one needs inner peace to follow that ideology.

Accordingly, the inner peace discussed in "Face Down" also provides us with "Style." For ☥, style has always been a metaphysical thing, an attitude that manifests itself in one's physical appearance and behavior. Style cannot be bought or even co-opted because the kernel of style is one's own personality. One cannot have style when lying or faking the funk. "Style is not a lie...Style is not something that comes in a bottle...Style is not a logo that sticks 2 the roof of one's ass. Style is like a second cousin 2 class...Style ain't the jeep u just bought when u know yo' broke ass got bills." Style only comes when you are able to accept yourself, your positives and your negatives. "Style is not biting style when u can't find the funk…Style is not lusting after someone because they're cool. Style is loving yourself 'til everyone else does 2." Style is not just being unique; it is being able to accept one's own uniqueness until others evolve to see the truth of its beauty or at least are overcome by your security with yourself. "Style is a gold-tooth smile with an attitude. Style is peaceful wild postin' the rude. Style is growing your own food. Style is a non-violent march." Along with self-confidence and being comfortable in one's own skin, style is having a vision that grows from self-love. When one is comfortable with oneself, one can spend more time painting one's future instead of following someone else's blueprint, which is often a dead-end for the follower because the game plan is not designed to highlight the followers' skills. "Style ain't sitting courtside with the owner of the team. Style is owning the team and charging them all a fee." For ☧ style is not about what you have but about what you do, and those who find peace with themselves tend to have a flair for living that makes life easier and more enjoyable.

One's style also manifests itself in how one approaches and handles problems. "DADADA" presents two ways to address problems. The song is divided into two parts: the rant and the resolution. ☧ is clearly showing that rap is the medium for disgruntled African American youth who have been given a bad check for their parents' legacy of work. At the same time ☧ is also constructing a discourse between how he approaches a problem and how many rappers approach a problem. In hip hop there seems to be more of an emphasis on the problem. In ☧'s work there seems to be more of an emphasis on the resolution. (We must note that we should not generalize all of hip hop with what is played on television and radio.) In the liner notes ☧ asks, "Get it all out…alright, cool. Now what?!" He seems to be asserting that just presenting the problem does not solve it, nor should discussing it make us feel like we are making things better by merely raising the issue. This is a major progression for the writer who wrote "Sister" in 1980. That writer just wanted to raise some issues. The evolved writer now wants to answer some questions and solve some problems. The rapper, Scrap D, vents about the problems faced by many African Americans: stereotyping, crime, unemployment, the generation gap. The rapper's lyrics are not included in the <u>Emancipation</u> lyric booklet, which has to be purchased separately from the album. The first lyrics of the song are performed by the Scrap D. Instead of including his lyrics, there is a note attached: "Is venting worth the ink?" There, for ☧, is the notion that we know what the problem is. Let us, then, start dealing with some solutions. It is not about having the right or proper solution. It is about moving along the discourse. ♔'s response is titled "Solution." From there he begins. The crux of his solution is that we need to stay focused on our real purpose, which is not to make money. Our real purpose is to evolve to a higher being. Render unto Caesar because we do live in a physical world, but do not let the physical world blind you from the truth. Now many will say that this sounds more like the pie-in-the-sky theology where black folks are looking to some ghost of a God to solve their problems. This is not the case. Here, the notion is that if you have your eyes on the goal of evolving to your higher self, you cannot be pimped by capitalism. If your goal is not to master capitalism, then you tend not to work for slave wages. You tend to follow your heart rather than your pocket book. As long as you want what the master has, the master will be able to pimp you to work for him.

> "Ask yourself your destination, what the source of your inspiration be, and u will find a spirit tryin' 2 get u back 2 your mind like it was in your mamma's belly. Live and let live was the order of the day. What u say? Loving 1 another is the only way."

Following his initial response to Scrap D, ♔ presents three separate issues of how chasing the physical has taken our eyes off the spiritual. What is more interesting is that these next set of lyrics are on the lyric sheet but not in the song. (In the recorded version of the song, Scrap D has more lines/lyrics than ♔, but in the lyric booklet ♔ has more lines/lyrics than Scrap D.) This points to a songwriter who is concerned about his listeners reading and understanding the lyrics. Thus, the lyric sheet is as important as the song, itself. The next stanza discusses how man needs to stop listening to the physical and start searching the spiritual for our answers.

> "Time and time again, ☬ was getting' the feelin' that ☬ couldn't distinguish my friends from my

enemies. Then ☤ got on my knees and asked my Saviour please show me how 2 tell the pimps and the liars from the chosen 1s, the quick deniers who live by the gun. Just tell me what ☤ need to do, and ☤'ll do it. Show me what hill 2 climb—☤'ll go through it."

☥ is showing that the problem is two fold: putting faith in mammon over God and not understanding that African Americans play a game that is designed to cheat them. The oppressed should not be asking the oppressor for relief. That is as illogical as venting. ☥ moves to show that by not understanding the historical context of our lives as it relates to slavery and miscegenation, African Americans will continue to toil in servitude and not know why. So, the real problem is playing the game at all.

"And what's the story behind your name? Trace it back far enough and don't be ashamed when at the root of your family tree somebody be quite different than u be stands up and says repeat after me—We're the only race that will succeed in the land of opportunity—MF please!"

In the final stanza of his response/solution, ☥ is stressing that we must learn to move beyond the symptom and deal with the virus—stop missing the forest for the trees.

"U could see a man who beats a child as a good father, or u could see this man as a father beating on himself. Either way, if your heart fills up with sorrow, then u probably know that the seeds he plants 2day will feed this man 2morrow. Tell me now. What u say? 'DADADA.'"

The response to any problem should not be a rush to vent, blame, or single out individuals. The proper response to any problem is to find a solution that will keep the problem from reoccurring. Once we realize this, we are on our way toward enlightenment.

"My Computer" builds on "DADADA" to articulate that the search for a better life, the journey to evolution, is difficult and most times lonely because most have surrendered to the falsity of the physical. Again, like Margaret Walker Alexander, ☥'s "portrait images not only the myth of fragmentation and dissolution, but the courage necessary to confront and transcend them" (Killens 596). The song deals primarily with the isolation of walking the road less traveled. "It was Sunday night. Instead of doing what ☥ usually do, ☥ scan my computer, looking for a site." The protagonist is unsuccessful in finding someone with whom he can bond and find companionship because most have surrendered to the physical world. "Nothing on TV ☥ ain't seen before. Another murder on the news, ☥ can't take no more. Evil incorporated, blowing up bombs and thangs." The realization is that when you are struggling against the status quo for a better life, friends will reject you because they do not want you rocking the boat or the system into which they have invested time and faith. This is the greatest fear, being isolated from community, even when you are working for the good of the community, working for people who do not know that they need help and who do no want your help. One of the best examples of this is how the black teachers in Jackson, Mississippi, all but unanimously shunned and rejected Medgar Evers when he was trying to fight for, protect, and empower them. The teachers' fear of the white power structure allowed Evers to be identified, alienated, and attacked. The people whom you are trying to assist are often the people who attempt to use the forces of fear, embarrassment, and guilt to force you back into the fold of the status quo. "☥ called an old friend of mine just the other day. No congratulations, no respect paid. All she did was wonder if the rumors were true. ☥ said: 'No, ☥ ain't dead yet, but what about u?" In an attempt to create a sobering reality about staying the course of building a better world, "My Computer" moves pass presenting the glory of a strong, independent rebel and expresses the truth about being an independent thinker. Independent people often spend a lot of nights alone. For most, the struggle and journey is too difficult. Humanity has this basic need for love and emotional shelter, which causes most of us to surrender our souls for the illusion of peace and security through physical companionship. The Civil Rights Organization, Southern Echo, deals with this isolation during its training sessions. They discuss and get new members to understand how to deal with this fear and isolation that comes with fighting against the powers that be, against the status quo to make wrongs right. "My Computer" does not ignore or romanticize the issue of loneliness, nor does it give the impression that one will always be able to deal with loneliness. In fact, we leave the protagonist as we met him, scanning his "computer, looking 4 a site, somebody 2 talk 2, funny and bright...make believe it's a better world, a better life."

Once ☥ has constructed the issues and problems as he sees them, he presents the answer that it is still love that can and will save us. The socio-political songs are paralleled with the love songs to keep the cohesive tone and theme of liberation and freedom. The album promotes the notion that investing in romantic relationships is the antithesis of and more fruitful than investing in capitalism. Love is the greatest value worth obtaining, the only value that fulfills humanity. Thus, all of the love songs on <u>Emancipation</u> resonate the feeling you experience when you listen to the love songs on <u>Sign "☮" the Times</u> and <u>Lovesexy</u>, the feeling of an artist who has, once again, evolved. None of these songs could have been written by the guy who existed before <u>Purple Rain</u>. That guy is trying to evolve, but he is not there yet. By the time he gets to <u>Emancipation</u>, love and sex are for salvation. Sex is an act of love, which takes us to a higher plane. At the center of this is the romantic relationship and its symbolic quality of God's love for his children. Human beings need healthy and whole romantic relationships so that they are able to evolve into whole spiritual beings. That is to what each of these songs speak. In a November 12, 1996, interview with Edna Gundersen for USA Today, ⚥ affirms this search in his work and that he has finally achieved some sense of peace as represented in the Emancipation songs.

> "There's always been a dichotomy in my music; I'm searching for a higher plane, but I want the most out of being on earth. When I met Mayte, I looked at my situation and wondered what I was running from. Am I lonely? Is that why I surround myself with so many friends? I don't think I knew the answer until I got married and made the commitment: 'I will take care of you forever.' When she walked down the aisle, and I looked into the eyes of this woman-child, I could see our future and the eyes of our child. At moments like that, you are floating. There is no ego" (Gundersen, "The Artist Is Free," 1996).

The male-female relationship represents completion of self and an evolution to a higher form. That is what the love songs on Emancipation echo.

"Somebody's Somebody" begins our journey through the discourse of the romantic relationship to find peace and completion. "Somebody's Somebody" raises the stakes of "Let's Pretend We're Married," which uses sex as a way to gain momentary peace. "Let's Pretend We're Married" understands that sex only provides a fleeting, temporary peace. "Somebody's Somebody" wants more. It presents a writer who is now willing to make the commitment to the relationships that the writer of "Let's Pretend We're Married" is not willing to do. In "Somebody's Somebody" ⚥ is longing for peace through companionship. First, he builds an atmosphere of loneliness, not sexual desire.

"It's two o'clock in the morning, and 👁 just can't

sleep. Outside the rain is pourin', and 👁'm lonely as can be...This big ol' world can be so empty, livin' in it all alone...It's two o'five in the morning, and 👁 got no one 2 call. 👁 long 2 hear another voice inside these lonely walls...👁 need 2 feel someone beside me. 👁 can't be alone no more."

This song presents a songwriter who has matured and understands that the physical does not hold the keys to inner peace and completion, so sex is not the answer to his loneliness, "👁 realize in its best disguise, a pretty house don't make a home." "House" represents the physical, and "home" represents the metaphysical, what the "house" can be transformed into by love. This is the same notion as expressed in Luther Vandross' "A House Is not a Home," "...a house is not a home when the two of us are far apart, and one of us has a broken heart." ☥ is not hungering for sex; he is hungering for companionship, someone to whom he can talk and hold. "There's a hunger deep inside me, oh how the fire burns. 👁 wanna give good love 2 someone and get good love in return...Some 2 hold me, in that hour midnight, someone 2 console me, when things ain't going 2 right." This song understands that loving someone and being loved gives you a sense of place and being, and that gives you peace. To love is why we are here. Love makes us "somebody," gives our lives meaning; we become "Somebody's Somebody," which gives meaning to our lives.

"Damned If 👁 Do" is a more mature writer's discussion of the issues raised in "Strange Relationship" from Sign "☮" the Times. In "Damned If 👁 Do" the protagonist is struggling to build a relationship with a woman who is acting on him, but reacting to her past lovers. This is a major problem in romantic relationships. People who have been hurt or disappointed in the past tend to build walls to keep other lovers at a distance. The new lover spends his time trying to demolish those walls but usually surrenders from emotional fatigue, "👁'll fill your cup. 👁 won't do it like Kevin. Damned if 👁 do, damned if u don't. U say u want me 2 love u, but when I try u won't. Maybe we should say good-bye." The person who has constructed the walls is always trying to make the new lover jump through endless hoops to prove his love, to prove that he will always be there, no matter what. "Tell me what's up with the teenage indecision. I'm mad in love, but u won't give me permission. U said: 'Be here at 9.' Then screamed at me 4 not givin' u more time." The stakes are often elevated and continue to rise, with the antagonist always pushing the limits of what the new lover will endure to prove his love. "Tell me the truth. How many u do it 2? I smell the vermouth every time I don't get 2 kiss u." Often, the new lover stops trying to prove his love. "Enough's enough. If u don't want my lovin', then I'll give up." Yet for ⚦ quitting is not always the answer. He fights anger and hate with love. "Damned if I don't try 2 make u see yourself the way I do."

The purpose of relationships is to give and not just receive. "Damned If I Do" shows us an evolved writer, more concerned with what he is giving than with what he is receiving. Many people go on dates or become involved in relationships for what they can receive. How many go on dates or become involved in relationships for what they can give? Again, love is an action verb. Even in a fleeting, fading relationship, ⚦ creates a protagonist who is as much concerned about how he leaves an ex-mate as with what he receives from her. Therefore, ⚦, the consummate optimist, ends "Damned If I Do" on a positive by leaving the door open to the possibility of the infinite, instead of finite negativity. He takes an innately pessimistic phrase/concept, such as "Damned if I do, and damned if I don't," and turns it on its head, showing that there are always options, always possibilities. "Maybe we should say goodbye; maybe we should say I do." The "I do" is not just to the relationship; it is to love. To say "I do" to love is to say "I do" to life, for love presents the opportunity for new life and new opportunities. Rather than close the door and accept death—death to love, which is death to life—he is saying that even in our broken relationships we have the power to make them better by being better people. We are not acted upon by life; we act upon life. Rather than accepting the traditional notion of being damned if he does or not, the protagonist realizes that he is only damned if he surrenders to negativity. ⚥ is asserting that we always have a choice no matter how grim our circumstances appear. We can say goodbye to love and die, or we can say hello to love and evolve. Although the mate has quit on love because she has been hurt in the past, ⚥ is asserting that she/we have the power to remove the pain and make love. This is what he means later in the album when he asserts that "the only love there is is the love we make." Humanity is damned if human beings surrender to the existentialistic or naturalistic illusion that we are fated not to find love. The truth is that we do not find love; we make love, and we are damned if we never realize this.

"In this Bed 👁 Scream" is simply poetic, driven by vivid and precise images of the person who did not fight for love and now regrets it. "2 these walls 👁 talk, tellin' 'em what 👁 wasn't strong enough 2 say. 2 these walls 👁 talk, tellin' 'em how 👁 cried the day u went away...How did we lose each other's sound?...Maybe we can stop the rain from coming down." He paints a clear picture of lovers who complete each other and the emptiness and incompletion felt when that relationship goes astray.

> "In this bed 👁 scream, lonely nights 👁 lay awake thinking of u. If 👁'm cursed with a dream, a thousand times 👁 feel whatever 👁 put u through. How we gonna put this back 2gether? How we gonna think with the same mind, knowing all along that life is so much better, living and loving 2gether all the time?"

⚥ is raising the stakes of the ordinary love song. He is clearly articulating that without love there is no completion, no evolution to a higher form. "In this car 👁 drive; 👁'm looking 4 the road that leads back 2 the soul we shared. With my very life, ☮'d gladly be the body upon the cross we bare." Giving this song even more intensity concerning the importance of relationships is the fact that this song was either started by Wendy and Lisa or was inspired by Wendy and Lisa. In either case, it is ☥ doing what Prince was never able to do, examine past artistic decisions and relationships and wonder if he could have handled, constructed, or maintained them better. This is a far cry from the man who once said about his revolving door of musicians, "I don't miss anybody or anything." Both Wendy and Lisa stated that when they were fired, they never saw it coming. They were at their peak, cranking out some of their most creative work. Yet, Prince, wanting to go in a different direction, called them, seemingly out of the blue, and informed them that he was "going through a new phase." Sometimes in our desire to evolve, we often divorce ourselves from the past too hastily. "In this Bed ☮ Scream" seems to be a work acknowledging what happens when we end or quit on relationships too soon. What followed the departure or the disbanding of the Revolution, which is responsible for Purple Rain, Around the World in a Day, and Parade, are Sign "☮" the Times, The Black Album, and Lovesexy. He moved from the metaphysical to the funkidly tangible, attempting to balance it all on Lovesexy. Where the Revolution albums are seen as crossover albums, Sign "☮" the Times and The Black Album are seen as a return to his funk roots. Possibly, Prince did not think that the Revolution could give him all that he needed to be. Even so, "In this Bed ☮ Scream" seems to be a concession of regret of not being able to balance it all, having to surrender something to gain something. And maybe that is the struggle. Again, as ☥ states, "It's difficult to stay current and still do the things that worked in the past." That is the challenge of evolving. This challenge has been a major issue for African Americans. In the rush to integrate, we have relinquished too much of our Africanism or our African Americanism. When you relinquish the culture that enabled you to survive and evolve, you relinquish your road map. "In this car ☮ drive; ☮'m looking 4 the road that leads back 2 the soul we shared." With no clear road map from our past, we have a difficult time plotting our future. Recently, a good number of African Americans have realized this, and there continues to be a resurgence of interest in African and African American history, even if just on a surface, artificial, level. More and more African Americans are beginning to realize that their past may hold a key to their future, even if they merely end up overly romanticizing it. This is what ☥ is doing in "In this Bed ☯ Scream"—looking back and questioning, for the first time in his career, if he could have made some wiser choices. Often our romantic relationships are a barometer of our lives. When we analyze or question our romantic history and the decisions that we make regarding our romantic relationships, we are ultimately trying to find the meaning of our lives.

After we analyze our past, we can then move forward to celebrate the romantic relationship. "Sex in the Summer," which was initially titled "Conception," shows the attraction of males to females and the conception of children to be as natural as the changing seasons by paralleling the actions of humans to the change of the seasons. Summer is when mankind, like all other animals, strips down, revealing their bodies and their desires.

> "Sex in the summer, getting' it on...checkin' 4 bikinis, layin' in the sand...The Mamas in the short dress, blowing in the breeze. The Papas just a-prayin' 4 the gust that will bust that butt out, please...Everybody's got a black book, in case of emergency, in case the sun is shinin' at the beach."

However, just when you think you have a simple little ditty, with no undercurrent message, ☥ slips it into the last stanza. Actually, the message begins in the previous stanza by troping the name of the popular sixties group The Mamas and The Papas who sang about love, nature, and man returning to nature to evolve. ☥ raises this trope by indicating that all males are Papas, and all females are Mamas; therefore, we should understand both our natural desires as well as our responsibilities, which go along with these desires. Here, ⚥ is evoking the blues aesthetic of the "celebration of the sensual and erotic" as a natural extension of our metaphysical selves. "the blues aesthetic emphasizes and engages the sensual and erotic elements of life...this is apparent in our dance, in our music, in all the delight we take in physical beauty" (Salaam 14, 17). Even at his most spiritual and metaphysical, ⚥ cannot separate the joys of the soul from the joys of the body. For him, they compliment each other because the body is the pathway to the soul. One cannot exist without the other, and to talk about one without the other is absurd. "Can't u feel a new day dawning? All believers will see an end 2 suffering and every disease. Every waking hour will soon be spent kissin' each other. Angelic sisters and brothers, clap your hands 4 1 another." As always, there is much more going on than an orgasm. As with "Sexuality" and "New Power Generation," ⚥ is proposing that the New Breed will make the Earth better by populating it with new hearts. The message is that humanity should not stifle sexuality, but use it as a way to make the world a better place. Prior to this last stanza, ⚥ establishes sex as a metaphor by equating it to creating music, "...we can jam on a brand new tune, improvise all through the night. It'll be just like having sex in the summer..." Sex is for procreation, but this is a double fulfillment. Sex allows individuals to complete their purpose for being on Earth, and it is a primary medium for humanity to evolve back to its god-state. The perk is that it is quite pleasurable. Although we should thoroughly enjoy the pleasure of sex, we should never lose sight of its significance. On <u>Emancipation</u>, ⚥ is still declaring sex as a tool to make the world a better place, but he is also presenting the notion that this must not be taken lightly or irresponsibly. The best, most fulfilling sex exists within strong, committed relationships.

"One Kiss at a Time" and "Sleep Around" are instructions to the psychologically/sexually challenged. Love is about what you will do for someone else. Both songs emphasize the importance of being a liberated lover in order to satisfy your mate as well as being conscious enough to ensure that one is attending to the mate's needs. If we remember "Head," the protagonist got the girl because he was freer, more liberated, than her mate. The same holds true in these two songs. "Oh, 👁 see this is want u wanted, one kiss at a time, 👁've got 2 be up on it if 👁 want 2 make u mine." His first lesson is for women, stressing to them to allow the man to go as far as needed to bring ultimate pleasure.

> "This is something every girl should know. Every part of u comes alive when u take it slow. Every nervous twitch that happens when my tongue is there, my lips up and down your back and every single hair, all makes up the beauty of your grand design. Every man has got a duty, and 2night 👁've got 2 do mine."

Then he moves to the male, suggesting that the male lower his walls of masculinity and explore his mate. Do not be afraid to ask or be led. One might find what he wants quickly by letting go and letting the moment drive the car. "This is something every man should see. Give your woman what she wants and give her want she needs. Ask her in a whisper that only 2 can hear, 'What can 👁 do? What can 👁 say, baby?' Forget your single fear." ☥ is addressing and undressing the fears of both males and females. He is telling males to forget their masculine anxieties and fears. By doing this they will be able to get their mates to release their anxieties and fears. He is promoting communication in the bedroom, where there seems to be a lack of it. A countless number of women are afraid to tell their mates what they want for fear of being labeled overly sexual or a tramp or a freak. Also, men, who are threatened by the thought of a woman who may be more sexual than them, use the female's fear and insecurity to hide their insecurity by perpetuating their mate's fear and insecurity. ☥ is asserting that all of the problems of the world begin and end with our male-female romantic relationships. If humanity improves this aspect, it becomes closer to evolving and reconciling with God. "If every man could love their woman the way that 👁 love u, time would stop and the sky would fall, and all would see the glory of what true love could bring." It gets no clearer; ☥ is finding salvation in the male-female relationship.

"Sleep Around" is more direct and sexual than "One Kiss at a Time" but has the same message. "Sleep Around" also represents more growth for ☥ because it is a more intellectual discourse of the subject than "Head." "Head" is straight forward and does not attempt to be a discourse. If a guy will not perform oral sex on his woman, then he will lose her to someone who will. "Sleep Around" is attempting to elaborate on this notion. If one does not take care of a mate's sexual desires, the mate will find someone else who will. Thus, males need to stop living this hypocritical life and accept the fact that, as Ray Parker, Jr. states, "A woman needs love just like you do. Don't kid yourself into thinking that she don't...Don't mess around, come home and get your feelings hurt." In the past, ☥'s work has been about liberating himself through women. Now he has turned his attention to males, reacting to the surge of testosterone and hypocritical masculine dominance, which is once again ruling the charts in the late nineties. Being able to control and objectify a woman may be pleasurable for a man, but it will never allow him to construct a relationship that fulfills and elevates him to metaphysical heights.

> "Do it like she like it, so your baby don't wanna sleep around. Give her what she wants when she wants [so] when it comes 2 u she's down. Baby, let me read her journal, or should 👁 say: she turned around and it was gone. The innuendo reads eternal, or should 👁 say: every other page 👁'm on. When she comes to cook your dinner, u can ask her if what 👁 say is true. The secret will remain within her, but her shade of red will turn yours blue."

♀ is attacking the hypocrisy of men wanting to have sex with every woman they meet but then marry a virgin. This hypocrisy drives the assigned "good girl" to descend secretly the pedestal to satisfy the desires that she cannot with her chosen mate. Just as Hurston's Janie is forced to flee from the insecure oppressive arms of Logan and Jody into the arms of Tea Cake in <u>Their Eyes Were Watching God</u>, ♀ is asserting that men are still losing their women because they are too insecure to allow their women to experiment in all of their humanity. This hypocrisy becomes the wall separating men and women, keeping them for communicating and connecting on any level, keeping them both from reaching their full evolution. They cannot evolve because they have their eyes on each other instead of on and toward God.

> "Maybe u recall last summer when u saw her riding in my car. A kiss or 2 later she was back in your bed, smellin' like a fallen star. Just because she's fine u think she don't wine & dine with everyone u know. As long as u're fooled, 👁'm cool. She says she gonna put me in her video."

The difference between "Sleep Around" and a song such as "I'm That Type of Guy" by L. L. Cool J is the central figure. In L. L. Cool J's song the emphasis is on the male's pleasure. It alludes to the female's frustration, but it focuses on the male's sexual prowess and his ability or any man's ability to steal another man's woman. The woman remains a passive and objectified trophy waiting in the vault to be stolen or rescued. The man still holds the power. L. L. Cool J's song is about one male being more adventurous and more sexually pleasing than the other male to win the girl, but it stops short of a song, such as "Treat them Like they Want to Be Treated" by Father M. C., which was denounced by several rappers for not being masculine enough. "Sleep Around" emphasizes the woman's issues, the woman's concern. In fact, the female becomes the aggressor. The male protagonist is acted upon by the female. This speaks to ♀ being able to empathize, communicate, and connect with the opposite sex because he has erased all boarders separating the two. This is because, more than an orgasm, he is seeking a spiritual connection by letting the female be all that she can. The commentary is that males fail to achieve spiritual connection and ecstasy because they cling too forthrightly to their rigid and arbitrary gender roles. For ♀, the emphasis is on liberating women so that men need not feel threatened by a sexually aggressive female, especially when they are searching for maximum pleasure.

"Soul Sanctuary" continues our theme of salvation through eros. "Loving u in silence, knowing that it's right. Under your gaze ꙮ ponder this love 2night. Unbothered by the chaos swirling round outside. In your arms is where ꙮ want 2 live and die." ♀ is again troping his own work buy building and layering on the notion presented in <u>Chaos and Disorder</u> that we are living in an existential world. He is now submitting that love is what refutes existentialism in much the same manner as Gabriela Mistral does In "Serene Words" or in the manner that Octavio Paz does in "Two Bodies." For Mistral the beauty, power, and order of nature is the example of God's love and power, which refutes the notion that we live in an existentialistic world. For Paz, human relationships give meaning to our world and refute existentialism. ♀ is combining these two approaches by paralleling the sanctuary that Mistral finds in nature to that of the sanctuary that Paz finds in human relationships. It is within the sanctuary of love where we are the most protected and the most fulfilled.

"Under your gaze ꙮ peacefully exist. Sanctuary, baby, nothing compares 2 this. In my darkest hour u can be my bliss. All of me ꙮ give 2 thee down at your feet. The reassurance in your rhythm speaks 2 me...Your screams are like a prayer. In the dark u r there, my soul sanctuary."

Eros is where man can get back to his most natural place, experiencing all of the pleasures that God originally intended. "Loving u in passion, unmolested in this garden. Mango and nectarine, sweet honey dew, ꙮ beg your pardon; my mouth runneth over from ecstasy. It's true, baby; ❤ love the taste of u." Love removes all shackles and creates a space just for two, so that lovers can find their Garden of Eden even in the midst of the physical world.

"Dreaming about U" continues the poetic layering, where ♛ weaves images that expand the surreal and transcendental atmosphere of being baptized and rescued by love. In all of these songs, ♛ is practicing Wordsworth's notion of painting the tree in a manner that removes the cataracts from our eyes so that we are able to see, once again, the beauty of the tree. The songs discuss the same theme, but present different variations. This is what makes ♛ a poet. Ahmos Zu-Bolton, author of <u>Ain't No Spring Chicken</u> and <u>A Niggered Amen</u>, states that the great thing about being a poet is that "you get to rewrite and restate your feelings and thoughts on many of the same subjects throughout your life. As I have grown, I can better articulate my thoughts." Adding to this, Dr. Jerry W. Ward, author of <u>Black Southern Voices</u> and <u>Trouble the Water</u>, often asserts that it is the well-crafted poet who can make the familiar unfamiliar so that we can see it in a new, better, and clearer light. This is what ♛ is doing in all of these songs. There is no more hiding his agenda. Love will save us, and we must start with romantic love. We must deal with all of its aspects: its pleasures, complications, complexities, and anxieties, examining it from all sides and variations to fully comprehend it. "Dreaming About U" continues our look at the complexity of love and the human relationship by concentrating on honesty's ability to cut through or dissolve the complexity. "If the wind blew every petal from your precious red rose, would u be afraid of what u'd find?" He wants her to be honest with herself so that she can be honest with him. Then, their relationship can be unencumbered like the fantasy relationship in "Tamborine." How do we make the fantasy, the ideal, come to life? "Dreaming of U" begins in the same manner as "Tamborine," with the protagonist alone. "When ❤'m alone in my room, and every time ❤

do what ☮ need 2 do, ☮ can't stop dreamin' about u."

With "Dreaming of U" ☥ is expanding his notion in "Tamborine," trying to fulfill his fantasy in the physical, trying to make his fantasy a reality. However, there is a continuous conflict between the flesh and the soul, both battling to define what the romantic relationship will be. The protagonist is acknowledging this conflict, but even more, he is confessing this conflict to the mate, hoping that his confessional brings them closer together. "When my sane twin reigns, claiming your aims r 2 maim my subconscious in2 being with u...betting on the notion that if my lustier twin prevails, like the ruins of Rome, ☮ will lie helpless at your feet." The protagonist is conflicted. He wants to make love to her, and he wants to fuck her. He has both sacred and profane feelings for her. Somehow he must find a way to reconcile these emotions; further, the female must help the male reconcile his emotions. Only then will they be able to evolve.

> "Here we stand amidst your core; the petals on this rose ☮ adore. If the inside is kind...kind in a sense that one will come from all, and the wish that u wish will come true if u call. But if not, u will fall, and ☮'ll still be alone just dreaming about u with this ball in my stomach just dreaming about u."

"Dreaming about U" is layered with confliction. At the beginning of the song, the protagonist is masturbating as in "Tamborine." Masturbation is a conflicting action where the person is using the body as a route to the mind because masturbation is about the psyche, about the world that the person is trying to create. And yet, masturbation is also primal and, in a sense, represents failure. If the person were successful in securing a mate for the evening, then he would not need to masturbate. ☥ uses the conflict of masturbation to discuss the protagonist's conflict of constructing a relationship that will be satisfying on all levels: body, mind, and soul. The problem is that the male is worried that the female will be offended by his desires even though his sexual desires are apart of his desire to commit to her. Thus, ☦ is once again making a statement about how our sexual insecurities and misconceptions keep us from having fulfilled lives, which underscores his notion that sexuality is a barometer to gauge humanity.

The issues raised in "Dreaming about U" are addressed and resolved in "Joint 2 Joint" and "The Holy River." "Joint 2 Joint" and "The Holy River" are companion pieces, much like "Pop Life" and "The Ladder." "Joint 2 Joint" is the physical, and "The Holy River" is the spiritual. "Joint 2 Joint" is funky, electrifying, and raunchy with three different musical and lyrical movements that culminate at the point where the physical, no matter how exciting and exhilarating, is still seen as lacking. The three movements represent the search for love through the body. "Before 👁 melt the wax 2 quizzical, let me just say that u r physically the most toned one 👁've ever seen...there is not another one in the universe so supreme. Yeah, u got the rock 2 give a brotha cream." Sex is the best that the physical has to offer, and she seems to be the best that the female race has to offer for sex. However, this moment, this feeling is fleeting and meaningless. Not only is it temporary, but it costs much more than what the participants are often willing to pay or understand how much they must pay. "Joint 2 Joint, nothing comes 4 free. If u show your love, u can get wit me." In the physical everything is about an ulterior motive, a manipulation based on something that the body needs; therefore, the orgasm should not be confused with the satisfaction and completion that comes with love. So, in the third movement, ☦ shows the often crushing reality of those who have given their hearts, their souls, in the game of sex (physical).

> "Oh great, now u think that u're my soul mate. U don't even know what kind of cereal 👁 like. Wrong, Captain Crunch, with soy milk 'cuz cow's r 4 calves. U'd probably take me 4 half. U don't love me; u're

just a faker. U only want me 4 my acres."

The physical has so many primitive desires and needs, which are difficult to recognize and understand when one is looking for love. ☥ is addressing the notion that too many relationships are based on the physical aspects of life rather than love. He is not contradicting himself, but he is clarifying himself. Sex with no regard for love is a dead-end. "Joint 2 Joint" is the last straw. It represents what "Darling Nikki" is to Purple Rain, a final attempt to find peace in the physical. After the emptiness of the physical in "Joint 2 Joint," ☥ turns us to the completion of the spiritual in "The Holy River," speaking as one who has tired of "Joint 2 Joint" and is now ready for more.

In "The Holy River" ☥ has found clarity by understanding the journey of his past and realizing that he has been searching for love (completion), while he has been running from the absence of love (loneliness). Instead of running toward love, he has been running away from pain. Thus, pain has been the acting agent and not love, which is why he has not found love. Many never find clarity because they do not know for what they are looking. "The Holy River" proclaims that one has to search one's soul for the answers of the soul. In the past, ☥ was searching the physical because he thought that was the source of his pain. "The Holy River" recognizes the importance of moving beyond the physical and affirms, as does "Lovesexy," that no orgasm is better than the completion found in the metaphysical.

> "Let's go down 2 the Holy River. If we drowned, then we'll be delivered. 👁 can still see the picture upon the wall: one 👁 staring at nothin' at all; the other one trying 2 focus through all the tears. U can try and try, but there's nothing 2 hide. U can run from yourself and what's inside. U got 2 find the answers 2 the questions that u most fear."

The "one 👁 staring" refers to the 1999 double album set.

At the center of both albums is an eye. The eyes appear to stare blankly into space. These eyes represent Prince looking for something. "The Holy River" represents a final focusing on what needs to be seen. It is not the world that needs to be repaired. Individuals need to look within and repair what is wrong with themselves; then we can repair the world. Out of frustration, we turn to the physical and artificial stimuli to numb ourselves and escape our pain. "Surrounded yourself with all the wrong faces, spending your time in all the wrong places, putting yourself in things that only make u cry." These "things" or "people" do not help because before one can give, show, or accept love, one must know what love is and be able to love oneself. "People say they love u, and they want 2 help; but how can they when u can't help yourself. The more they say they love u, the more u just wanna die." Even music has lost its ability to heal and elevate. "The band's playing at the club tonight, and they're bound 2 groove. There u are, think u're high. U can't ask yourself 'cuz u'd only lie." The importance here is that music, which ☥ has always presented as a divine entity, is now recontextualized as merely a physical expression or road to a higher place. And by doing this, he has come to the end of all of the physical pleasures of life, including sex, music, and friendship. "U can't call nobody cuz they'll tell u straight up, come and make love when u really hate 'em. Relationships based on the physical over and done, they're over and done."

With the entire physical world losing its power to save him, it is then that the protagonist realizes that God is that for which he has been searching. God is more satisfying and constant than sex, music, or human relationships.

> "And then it hit 'cha like a fist on a wall. Who gave u life when there was nothing at all? Who gave u some permission 2 rise up everyday? If u ask God 2 love u longer, every breath u take will make u

> stronger, keepin' u happy and proud 2 call his name—Jesus."

It is the recognition of a higher power that gives you peace with the rest of your life, with the rest of the world. Now everything else is satisfying and fulfilling because you have inner peace. Too may of us think that mastering our chosen fields/professions will make us better human beings. This is a capitalistic mentality where one is valued because of his economic achievement or class status and not because of his soul. ♀ realizes his flawed direction and reverses his search. As he asserts in his 2004 Rock-n-Roll Hall of Fame speech, freedom without direction will lead to moral decay. Instead of using the physical to achieve the spiritual, he is now seeking God first so that God may manifest Himself in every aspect of his life.

> "Let's go down 2 a Holy River. If we drown then we'll be delivered. If we don't then we'll never see the light. If u die before u try, u'll have 2 come back and face the light 'cause when u believe it u got a good reason 2 cry."

The inner peace from God can now manifest itself in our relationships. This is evidence of more growth because in the past, ♀ was looking for God through sex and then the romantic relationship. Now, he has realized that God must be found first. Then He will manifest Himself in our daily lives. "👁 called my girl...👁 asked her 2 marry me. She said yes. 👁 cried. That night 👁 drowned in her tears and mine, instead of a glass of sorrow and wine." Now with clarity, he can look back on his life by looking back on those searching eyes on the <u>1999</u> album and reflect. He can now find joy in his search, in his coming to terms with his life and the world, and in finding clarity. "Lookin' back y'all 👁 don't miss nothing except the time. And when 👁 see that picture on the wall, the one 👁 staring at nothing at all, my 👁s trying 2 focus, but these are much different tears." The "different tears" signify that ♀ has finally found inner peace. His journey is complete. This is his Dawn as he asserts to Rock in the <u>VH1 to One</u> interview, "This is my personal Dawn."

Having now found the Dawn, our protagonist is ready to assume a deeper respect and responsibility for the male-female relationship. He shows this in "Friend, Lover, Sister, Mother/Wife" and "Let's Have a Baby." "Friend, Lover, Sister, Mother/Wife" discusses the journey and the search that is required to find a good mate and develop a positive relationship. Through our past relationships we have learned more about ourselves and the variations of ourselves found within the opposite sex. These experiences allow us to evolve into better beings and better mates.

> "If ☬ ever held a hand, it was only because ☬ had never held your hand. That was part of the plan. ☬ had 2 get it right if ☬ was 2 b your man. If ☬ ever kissed your lips, ☬ needed time 2 cross the others off my list. A higher high 2 the trip ☬ wanted u 2 go, that was my wish."

This search is necessary to make ourselves ready to know and recognize our perfect mate. It is because of that search that one knows when he has found the right one. We make mistakes, but we grow and evolve when we are able to learn from those mistakes and become better people.

> "If ☬ ever shared a bed, it was only cuz ☬ wanted 2 live up 2 what the people said...Now ☬'m living instead everyday just 2 say u're the only one who's ever in my head...The ☬s of my child ☬ see every time u look at me, and sweet baby would smile like a light that shines 4 all 2 see."

Once we have found our mate, it is now time to consummate that relationship, not with sex but through procreation. When two people become a couple, they become one. As an entity, their evolution is the same, to be god-like. "Let's Have a Baby" takes "Forever in My Life" one step higher. If we are to commit to each other, we must also be ready to commit to parenthood. Sex now has a deeper responsibility than just healing our wounds and ceasing our fears and anxieties. Sex is how we become god-like and populate the Earth. This is our duty as lovers: lovers of mankind, lovers of the Earth, and lovers of God. "u can't wait no more. Let's have a baby. What are we living 4? Let's make love...'Isn't it a miracle that life comes from inside.'...Isn't it funny, that when u are truly in love, how just the thought of such things can bring u so much joy." Life now seems incomplete without fulfilling the duty of procreation. "u can't even go 4 a ride—believe me, honey, u've tired—without thinking about a little baby right here by my side." ♀ has come full circle from "Sexuality." "Reproduction of a New Breed, leaders stand up and organize." The declaration is the same. The New Breed must repopulate the Earth with properly educated children who will lead the revolution of the New Power Generation. However, the anger and angst of "Sexuality" has been replaced with love and understanding. We will not fuck our way to utopia; we can only love our way to utopia. And this point is echoed and affirmed by the "The Love We Make" and "Emancipation."

"The Love We Make" and "Emancipation" close the album by declaring and cementing love as the answer to all our problems. "The Love We Make" is a plea for mankind to stop looking for love and to start making love. "The only love there is is the love we make." As long as humanity is waiting on something or someone to make the world better, the world will never evolve into what it should be. This is more affirmation that love is an action verb that only exists if mankind brings it into being. There can be no love without humanity making love. "Desperate is the day that is 2morrow 4 those who do not know the time has come 2 whip the dogs that beg, steal or borrow from the table God set 4 his son." It is time to be counted. As Martin Luther King, Jr. asserted, "a man who stands for nothing will fall for anything." Accordingly, a man who stands for nothing is worth nothing. ☥ is asserting that it is time to stand for love. "Wicked is the witch that stands 4 nothing all the while watching 2 see u fall. Deeper than the ditch that bred your suffering is the one being dug right by them all." Love is a metaphysical element that will manifest itself in the physical world only when people act as a catalyst or a medium for it. "Happy is the way 2 meet your burdens no matter how heavy or dark the day. Pity on those with no hope 4 2morrow. It's never as bad as it seems until we say." Humanity has the power to set their lives in order to commune with God. "Precious is the baby with a mother that tells him that his Saviour is coming soon. All that believe will cleanse and purify themselves. Put down the needle. Put down the spoon." ☥ ends by defining love as something that works for the collective and not for the individual. Yet, it is the individual who must journey to access this power to change the world, with the understanding that making the world a better place improves the condition of the individual. "Sacred is the prayer that asks 4 nothing while seeking 2 give thanks 4 every breath we take. Blessed are we inside this prayer 4 in the new world we will be there. The only love there is is the love we make." The only way to know this love is to get free from the physical, emotional, and psychological shackles.

  Both songs seem to infer that this society is no longer capable of nurturing individuals who wish to evolve to their totality because society has overly embraced the physical and all of its nihilistic aspects. When individuals begin to reach or strive toward their totality, the society is threatened by the loss of a piston to the engine. So, the job of the society is to smother the individual. All of the society's institutions work toward this aim of keeping the individual enslaved for its own benefit. Yes, individuals do have an innate responsibility to work collectively to nurture a constructive society, but the society must also allow the individuals the ability to evolve into their higher being. The goal of the society should not be to perpetuate wealth or its physical survival, but to perpetuate the evolution of man back to his god-self. The problem is that the ten percent of the people who control society do not want individuals evolving back to their god-self because they are not able to control and exploit those who do evolve back to their god-selves. The music business mirrors this process; it is designed to handle a limited output by its artists in order to perpetuate the status quo. Since ⚥'s early years, his goal has been to share as much of himself with the public as possible. The double album, which is a rarity, is the norm for him. The industry's boundaries and limitations of artistic productivity are too confining for his soul. The individual must free himself from this bondage or his soul will die. This is his declaration in "Emancipation." "Every since 👁 was a little baby, 👁 had 2 have double everything. When they tell me that's enough, that's when 👁 wanna fill my cup 2 the top, Johnny—hear me sing."

  This filling of one's cup does not represent a selfish individualism. On the contrary, it represents what happens when one person becomes enlightened to the limitations of the physical and the fulfillment of the spiritual. Individuals whose minds are submersed in and limited by the physical accept what they see in the physical as total reality, not being able to conceive of any other reality, such as spiritual possibilities, realities, or truths. In only striving to see and understand the physical, they only have half of their knowledge; their cups are half full. This is symbolized by Plato's cave. The people in the cave have their backs to the cave's opening and are watching the shadows of the outside world as they appear on the wall of the cave. Since they are ignorant to the outside world, they think that the shadows on the wall are reality. Thus, they have a false or misconceived understanding of reality. In order to achieve perfection, humanity must first understand and master reality. The people in the cave can never achieve perfection because they have a flawed notion of reality. ⚥ wants knowledge of both the physical and the spiritual so that he can have a whole vision and have a whole and complete understanding of life. He wants his cup to be full. Most people go through life with half filled cups, with half led, incomplete lives because they accept the realities and truths of others who, themselves, have only limited knowledge. Further, the ten percent of the population that controls the other ninety percent of the population exploits the ninety percent because of their lack of vision and knowledge. ☥ is declaring that only through full and complete knowledge of the physical and spiritual will a person be able to break free and fill his cup and achieve his potential. In fact, the knowledge that you gain demands that you break free and evolve. As Frederick Douglass asserted, the more he came to know and understand of his predicament, the more he came to hate and resent the system that enslaved him.

> "The reading of these documents...brought on another [pain] even more painful than the one of which I was relieved. The more I read, the more I was led to abhor and detest my enslavers. I could regard them in no other light than a band of successful robbers, who had left their homes, and gone to Africa, and stolen us from our homes, and in a strange land reduced us to slavery. I loathed them as being the meanest as well as the most wicked of men. As I read and contemplated the subject...discontentment...had already come, to torment and sting my soul to unutterable anguish. As I writhed under it, I would at times feel that learning to read had been a curse rather than a blessing. It had given me a view of my wretched condition, without the remedy...but for the hope of being free, I have no doubt but that I should have killed myself, or done something for which I should have been killed" (Gates and McKay 328).

☥ is asserting that it is only natural for one to seek the truth and then, after knowing the truth, be driven to evolve in fulfillment of the truth, crushing anything that stops or hinders that evolution. Anyone who limits your physical, emotional, or psychological growth and fulfillment enslaves you. Correspondingly, anyone who enslaves you has to bear some amount of contempt for you. This is what ☥ means when he states, "It's pretty difficult to work for someone who hates your guts. Now they [Warner Bros] will say other wise, but I know that they did" (☥, VH1 to One, 1996). Not only is his animosity justified, it is validated. To vent this animosity and fight for his freedom, he turns to his only tool, his art. "Ever since Eve did unto Adam what somebody been sho' nuff doin' 2 me. ♛ been tryin' 2 break the chain, get my little ass out the game. ♛'d rather sing with a bit more harmony." "Emancipation" carries in its soul the anger and bitterness of "The Exodus Has Begun." He is unable to sing in harmony because Warner Bros has kept him on his knees with a broken back and an ill at ease spirit. As he indicates in "The Exodus Has Begun," his life has "been made bitter with hard labor and no pay." He tries to keep a jovial tone in "Emancipation" but his anger creeps out to show itself. During the time leading to Emancipation, his songs mirrored blues and slave songs. "Every tone was a testimony against slavery, and a prayer to God for deliverance from chains" (Gates and McKay 316). Try as he might to gain individual liberation and freedom, by 1993, ☥ had come to realize that he could not escape the collective bondage of African Americans through his own individualized fight. Therefore, his songs between 1994 and 1996 regained the fire and anger of Dirty Mind and Controversy. This time, however, he is singing for another type of freedom, which includes a deeper notion of racial injustice. ☥'s answer is for complete emancipation (separation) from the illusions that maintain the individual as a half evolved atom in the monstrous molecule of society. Only then will the individual be able to completely evolve. We are all atoms in the molecular structure of society. Though we are interdependent upon the molecular structure, some of the atoms are profiting more by regulating the evolution of other atoms. This, in turn, hurts and inhibits the evolution of the entire structure. Only when each atom is allowed to evolve in a manner that nurtures and causes all of their talents to flourish will the entire molecule reach its potential.

The songs leading to <u>Emancipation</u> clearly show that ☧ had become cognizant that racism is what most inhibited his growth. Unless we are able to defeat this force, some particular atoms will never be able to evolve. If this is true, then the entire molecular structure will not be able to evolve. "Emancipation—free 2 do what ☮ want. Emancipation—see u in the Purple Rain" only if we are all allowed to flourish. One may not agree with ☧'s methods, strategy, or tactics, but he is clearly asserting that racism is the force that must be conquered; it is the force that drives and leads to all other types of oppression. If the individual is to get free, he has to find some way to overcome racism. In the past Prince attempted to liquefy himself to the point where racism's mores and dogmas would not apply to him. Now he has realized that racism is not about the hatred of color, but is about assigning a specific group as the permanent labor class. Therefore, the only way to defeat racism is to acknowledge it and then abandon all systems based on it. The record industry and all of its components—distribution, record shops, and magazines—are designed to limit and exploit black artists in a much more dogmatic manner than white artists. The only way to defeat this oppression is to abandon the system. The artist cannot evolve if he is limited by the amount of work he is allowed to produce and the type of topics he is allowed to discuss.

Censorship is not the job of the artist; it is the job of society. An artist should never stop to edit or censor himself. That stifles the output, the productivity. It is society's job to decide what it can and cannot use, taking what it needs and discarding the rest. In this manner, the society loses control over the artist and the ability to make the artist, like all other individuals, a slave for the greater good of certain members of the society. Often, the greater good is not about evolution; it is often about perpetuating the status quo. When the individual breaks free, the society loses its laborer for the status quo in much the same way that plantations lose their labor base when slaves are emancipated, the same way that record companies lose their capital base when artists are emancipated. "Johnny please, when ☮ was on my knees, my back was broken and my spirit ill at ease. Now it seems just like the autumn leaves, yo' money's turned from green 2 brown, and now u best believe." Why is there such poor public education? The society needs its permanent labor base. Are artist kept in the dark to enable companies to control their labor base, their cash cows. ☮'s liberation from Warner Bros has turned the money that they earn off him "from green to brown." Enlightenment brings emancipation. Only when you evolve can you see the Purple Rain. Only when you get free can you love and produce without limits.

With <u>Emancipation</u> ☮ is again ahead of the pack by working to change or redefine the notion of success in popular culture. Independent record companies had been around for years. Yet, ☮ becomes one of the few "major" or "established" artist to walk away from the major labels and start his own at a time when he could have still shopped a deal with any of the other major labels. Even his distribution deal with EMI kept him in complete control. Instead of allowing them to own or control his work by allowing them to invest in the creation of the art, he brokered a distribution deal where he paid them upfront for their services. In short, EMI was working from him and not vice versa. His move is the equivalent of self-publishing or the equivalent of writers who sign with smaller publishers, such as Gwendolyn Brooks' dedication to African American publishers such as Third World Press or Walter Mosley giving one of his books to Paul Coates to aid in the development of Black Classic Press or even John Grisham walking away from the big signing bonus of the major publishers to form a partnership with a smaller publisher, giving him more control over the art as well as a larger sum of the profits. The notion of success is changed because one does not have to sell a million units to be seen as successful because of the lower overhead and the absence of a company hoarding all of the profits. The notion of success changes because individuals are defining success and not the major corporations or the media, which is the propaganda arm of the major corporations. With <u>Emancipation</u>, ⚥ is defining success for himself. And most of that success is rooted in finding inner peace. Despite the anger, there is still a strong notion of ⚥'s inner peace with the fact that <u>Emancipation</u> is probably his greatest work even if it will not be heard by half the amount of people who heard <u>Purple Rain</u>. That is acceptable to ⚥ because his journey is about using his art to take himself and his listeners to a higher, spiritual place: a place where money and fame cannot take you, a place where the masses listening to music in the nineties do not want to go. When asked by Bryant Gumbel during a December 19, 1996 interview for the <u>Today Show</u> about the lacking sells of <u>Emancipation</u>, ⚥ is at peace with his project and himself.

> "Gumbel: 'The album debuted at number eleven on the charts. Second week it went to thirty-eight, then it went to fifty-eight. It's still at fifty-eight. Are you disappointed?'
> ⚥: 'No, not at all...I've made my money off of it already.'"

He further elaborates to Anthony DeCurtis in a November 28, 1996 interview for <u>Rolling Stone</u>.

> "At one point when [⚥ and Anthony DeCurtis] stroll through Paisley Park, ⚥ gestures toward a wall of gold and platinum records. 'Everything you see here is not why I created music. Every human being wants to achieve clarity so that people will understand you. But when the media tells somebody what success is—No. 1 records, awards—there's no room for intuition. You've [the media] put words in their heads. For me, the album is already a success when I have a copy. <u>Lovesexy</u> is supposed to be a failure, but I go on the Internet and someone says, '<u>Lovesexy</u> saved my life'" (DeCurtis 61).

It seems that for ⚥'s whole life, his whole career has been about and working toward Emancipation. Much like with Lovesexy, he is driven to be his own person, driven to be who he has to be regardless of the ramifications. Sheila E. affirms this in a MTV interview when she answered questions about the music on Lovesexy. "People say 'Why is he doing this music?' He is doing this music because he has to do this music" (Sheila E. 1988). ⚥ also affirms that he is driven by his spirit, something that is more powerful to him than anything that the physical world holds.

> "...people say I'm a crazy fool for writing on my face. But if I can't do what I want to do, what am I? When you stop a man from dreaming, he becomes a slave. That's where I was. I don't own Prince's music. If you don't own your masters, your masters own you" (DeCurtis 61).

He has outgrown the traditional or conventional structure of the music industry in his quest to evolve as a human being through his art.

> "⚥'s identification with Coltrane—a driven musical genius and spiritual quester who seemed intent on playing himself out of his skin—is plain...'John Coltrane's wife said that he played twelve hours a day. I could never do that, play one instrument for that long. Can you imagine a spirit that would drive a body that hard? The music business is not set up to nurture that sort of spirit'" (DeCurtis 61).

And in a February, 1997, interview with Chris Rock for VH1 to One, ⚥ clarifies his notion of past accomplishments, present journeys, and reconciling the two.

Rock: "Is this The Dawn?"

☮ : "My own personal dawn, it is, yes. It's a time period where you figure out where you're going, you've completely judged where you've come from and laid out all the pieces, and you know exactly what it all means at that point."

Rock: "I watched an interview with Mike Tyson recently where he was watching an old tape of himself, and he said, 'I can't beat that guy.' When you see old tapes of yourself, do you find them intimidating?"

☮ : "Oh, not at all."

Rock: "Can you beat the guy? Do you wanna beat the guy?"

☮ : "No, I don't want to beat the guy. You know I pick up some reviews of my work from time to time. You'll hear a lot about, 'Will he ever match the success of such-and-such and such-and-such.' See, I'm not on that road. I've been in the business twenty years now, and that's a long time. Purple Rain and that whole situation, Thriller and that whole situation, Like A Virgin and that whole situation, I mean, that was a time period. The Beatles are never gonna capture what they did in the beginning if they continue working. If we all continue working, then we all continue growing, I think. And it's our journey. It think that we've lost sight of the fact that music, I believe, was put on the earth to enlighten and empower us, and make us feel closer to our center."

Emancipation reached double platinum in just thirteen weeks, making it one of the best-selling multiple CDs of all time. It peaked at number eleven on the Billboard chart and spent twenty-one weeks on the chart. That is not bad for a flop. And while ☮ is exploring his new self, the Prince legacy is not forgotten. During 1997, there are two multi-platinum albums with covers of Prince songs. Mariah Carey's Butterfly includes a cover of "The Beautiful Ones," and TLC's Crazy Sexy Cool includes a cover of "If I Was Your Girlfriend." Ginuwine's multi-platinum album The Bachelor, which peaked at number twenty-six, includes a cover of "When Doves Cry." Two other soundtracks that include covers of Prince songs peaked in the Billboard's Top 100. Romeo + Juliet includes a cover of "When Doves Cry," and Scream 2 includes a cover of "She's Always in My Hair" by D'Angelo. Also, ⚤'s 1997 tour reached the eighteen spot, earning $24.6 million in concert ticket sells. (Data provided by The ⚤ Family.) All of this should make us reevaluate how the media dictates to the public its value system and its notion of failure and success because by 1998, ⚤ is out of sight and out of mind, after one of his best years. In fact, there are millions of artists who would kill for a year like ⚤'s 1997. Still, the Emancipation project is viewed as not achieving its potential because the people who own the record companies, who also control the magazines, do not want young artists to see ⚤'s Emancipation as a victory for him or for other artists. The man earned more than fifty million dollars in 1997, and, still, it is considered a bust because he is being judged by capitalistic standards, which have us all chasing the golden carrot instead of living to fulfill our souls. This is the same type of attitude that perpetuates the false urgency and necessity for African Americans to gain a crossover market in order to survive. Somehow, if African Americans are not making the "white dollar" or are not validated by "white folks," they are a flop. This is, again, tied to capitalism and what Langston Hughes called an "urge toward 'whiteness'" by the black middle class to feel validated and fulfilled. This is an urge to which even ⚤, himself, had become a slave and would find it difficult from which to break free. This also relates to the mental/psychological bondage about which ⚤ has been singing since his third album. In striving to achieve a certain amount of success, one is often asked to change or surrender something of himself that may not be palatable to the ruling class' sensibilities. Through Emancipation, ⚤ has come full circle: first by integrating into and subverting the system with Dirty Mind and now dismantling it or, in the least, abandoning it. In much the same way of Antigone and Hamlet, ⚤ becomes a Christ-like figure by sacrificing his body for his metaphysical, artistic, freedom and the freedom of the masses. And much like the tradition of African American survival, ⚤ has worn a multitude of hats and walked a multitude of roads to find inner peace, freedom, and sovereignty. He may not have the popularity, hype, or glitter of when he first started, but he continues to survive on his own terms.

Since <u>Emancipation</u>, ☥ has seemed to all but turn his back on the industry, still only playing by his rules and terms. The best example of this is that he continues to release an album a year. His themes are still focusing on man's evolution to a higher being, and he is releasing albums on his own label, marketing them mostly through the Internet. Even though the 1999 <u>Rave Un2 the Joy Fantastic</u> was a collaborative effort between NPG and Arista Records, ☥ was only willing to sign a distribution deal with Arista, which allowed him to retain the rights to all of his work as well as market it through his Love4oneanohter, NPG.com, and 1800NEWFUNK.com websites. The work released since <u>Emancipation</u> has been a combination of old and new material. Still, all of the songs find ☥ singing about clarity, rather than singing about trying to find clarity. The best example of this is "Welcome 2 the Dawn," which is from the <u>Truth</u> and is a part of the <u>Crystal Ball</u> collection. No longer waiting for the masses to understand or catch up, ☥ is writing for those who want it, who want to know what clarity is. "When the things u know r right r far from what they seem, when the past becomes future, and time becomes a dream, when the light of God is the only thing life will redeem, welcome 2 the dawn." ☥ is still preaching that to the achieve this clarity one must get completely free of the lies and illusion of the physical world by listening to and reconciling to the spiritual world. "When the voice u hear commands u 2 entertain the absurd, and when u do, the action unlocks the apocalypse of that u've heard. When the day that lies before u seems the darkest, in a word...welcome 2 the dawn." Yet, to achieve clarity and the Dawn, individuals must take responsibility for their actions and for their growth. "Every piece of a puzzle and every name a clue, every charge u make is karma, so be careful what u do." What is most clear is that ☥ has found an inner peace by releasing his desire for fame and embracing his desire for completion, as articulated in "The Truth" and "Don't Play Me," both from <u>The Truth</u>. Jim Walsh in his July 18, 1997, "<u>The Truth</u> Review" for the <u>St. Paul Pioneer Press</u> hits the nail on the head in showing the relevance of these two songs.

> "On the opening title track of the mostly acoustic album, <u>The Truth</u>, the musician growls over a stark, bluesy guitar riff worthy of Lightning Hopkins: 'Everybody's got a right to love. Everybody's got a right to lie. The choice you make, it ain't no piece of cake. It ain't no muthafuckin' piece of pie.' <u>The Truth</u>, then, is about facing up to, and making choices. Big ones, little ones. Tough ones, easy ones. And over the course of his 39 years, the prolific Chanhassen artist has obviously been through changes that came from making such choices. As a result, his 18th album—an even more overly spiritual (and personal) work than the highly spiritual <u>Emancipation</u> of last year—is a road map to the lessons he has learned and the person he has become" (Walsh 1997).

By showing us his journey, ⚥ is challenging us to look at how we conceptualize the truth. What is the truth? Who defines the truth? What makes truth, truth?

> "What if half the things ever said turned out to be a lie, how would u know the truth? If u were given all the answers, would u stop 2 wonder why? What if time's only reason was 2 give us something 2 fear? And, if so y'all, the end of the journey's so clear."

Once we realize what Aristotle attempted to show Plato that there is not merely one formula for Utopia or happiness, we become closer to clarity. This is because we begin to comprehend that understanding and tolerance, not power and oppression, are the best examples of our spiritual evolution. The truth is that our power is in our diversity and our willingness to relinquish the physical and love the various souls of humanity. If we are not allowed to fulfill the destiny of our diversity, we will decay before reaching our potential. However, if we are ever able to fulfill this destiny and tell the truth, we would begin our transformation to becoming higher beings. "We would all trade bank accounts and move to Neptune."

"Don't Play Me" is a double assertion, a double signifier. The obvious is don't play me on the radio because I will not perpetuate your lies. The undercurrent is don't play me for a fool because I am hip to your game. In both cases, ☥ is asserting that the choices to market and sell an artist are as much political as they are cultural. He is not vilifying this. He is, however, asserting that the real crime is when we lie that politics has nothing to do with the decision to market or promote an artist. Yet, Prince had realized this as early as 1981. "...you can look at the charts and you know for a fact that your record is better than some of the things that are over you. But I could look at it objectively and realize why those records were ahead of mine, that it's all basically business politics." (Schwartz 1981). The choice/struggle for the artist is not acquiescing to be accepted and not remaining as slave labor, not remaining the stereotype that the system needs you to be for its own survival. Most typically, African American artists are not allowed to evolve and grow in the manner as white artists. White acts are allowed to be artists in the full meaning of the term and celebrated for their artistry. African Americans are celebrated for their hit making ability. The difference is that the system is constructed a bit differently when it comes to nurturing the artistic visions of white artists as opposed to African American artists so that album sales weigh more heavily on the careers of African American artists than they do on the careers of white artists. Karlen affirms this.

> "When Prince invested ten million dollars into building Paisley Park he was blasted by the press which was saying that 'he was crazy; that thing's never gonna work. It's only going to be his little play pen, but it won't make any money.' However, had he bought ten million dollars worth of cocaine, everybody would

have said, 'well, that's okay'" (Karlen, "The Prince of Paisley Park," <u>Omnibus</u>, 1991).

⚥'s career has been about defying the critics and surviving in the face of their criticism. "⚥'m in the news again 4 payin' dues my friend. ⚥'m not the ganda u prop in my way." The dues that he is paying is payment for his freedom and punitive damages for abandoning the traditional methods of living and being, but these are dues that will pave the road for others who want to follow their own visions, especially African American artists. "Don't play me. ⚥'m the wrong color, and ⚥ play guitar." Finally, this is a clear assertion from ⚥ that his whole career has been a battle against the limits that the industry puts on African American artists. He continues by indicting the industry for its racist and hypocritical practices. "Don't be mad at me, the curtain puller in this game. Maybe how u call us all niggas ain't the same." However, in the wink of an eye, the evolved writer shows that his peace and his reward comes from a higher place, a more honorable place, and a more valuable place. "It's all good when u know the only fame is the light that comes from the God and the joy you get from calling his name." Walsh further indicates that ⚥ is clear in his understanding that his banishment from television and radio has more to do with politics than it has to do with craft.

> "On the spooky 'Don't Play Me,' the former Prince fires a barb at the music industry, Ebonics and those who would still see him as the precocious imp who flashed his butt on the <u>MTV Music Awards</u> a couple hundred songs ago. He offers this declaration of independence: 'Don't play me. ⚥'m over 30, and ⚥ don't smoke weed. ⚥ put my ass away in the music ⚥ play. ⚥ ain't the type of stereo u're trying 2 feed. ⚥ use proper English, and ⚥'m straight. ⚥'ve been 2 the mountaintop, and it ain't what u say'" (Walsh 1997).

⚥ is able to resign himself to the notion that although he, as every artist, wants his work heard by as many people as possible, it is not worth selling his soul or having his messages so diluted that getting a record deal and releasing the work defeats the purpose of being an artist. Walsh affirms this:

> "In the end, however, The Truth, attempts not to ask questions but to answer them. As the artist sings on the title track: 'The question is, what did you stand for? The question is, who did you save? When it gets right down to the nitty and the gritty, did you take more than you gave?'" (Walsh 1997).

⚥ finds peace in knowing that art is suppose to uplift and that our purpose on this Earth is to make life better. He does not want to be a part of the culture whose main goal is to rape society for all its worth, never giving back to balance the scale and cycle of life. However, there is also a deeper truth that this defiance is still a heavy and difficult road to travel. Dawkins raises some issues along these lines in her review of The Truth and assessment of ⚥'s general behavior since his break with Warner Bros.

> "I have to admit to more than a little confusion. We've all heard ⚥ say 'I'm a free man. I'm a happy man.' in several recent interviews. This album does not sound like the work of a free, happy man. There are many tracks here of bitterness and discontent, including a continuation of ⚥'s disaffection with the recording industry, sentiments we thought had finally been left behind. Almost every track on this album looks backward; the ones that aren't bitter are wistful and melancholy. We are also confused as to why this album is not available for purchase, even though it's been complete for many months. Wasn't this one of the reasons ⚥ left Warner Bros, to get his music out faster?" (Dawkins, Vol. 5 Issue 18, 104)

Though many of Dawkins assertions are correct, she fails to realize that ⚥ probably had to deal with a transition period that he did not expect. Being on a major label has its perks: your album is in every store, your record is on the radio, and your touring expenses are covered, even if all of the cost are later deducted from your earnings. It costs money to press CDs, mail complimentary and promotional copies of those CDs, and book engagements. These were things that ⚥ was used to Warner Bros doing for him, or, at least, they would provide him a budget to do it. Now he does not have the luxury of the machine backing him. This does not mean that he regrets his choices, but we all have a tendency, because of our physical nature, to become addicted and dependent upon the machine. The sadness or melancholy nature of The Truth is not one of regret, but is one that acknowledges that individuality and independence are always a struggle, even if the rewards are great.

A final, noteworthy song released during the Emancipation period is "She Gave Her Angles." This song not only continues ⚥'s discourse on the power of womanhood to save mankind, but it also exhibits his storytelling ability. This song is about sacrifice, the notion that love is about what you can do for someone else, which gives you the greatest joy. Through this sacrifice, the two lovers are lifted to a higher plane of existence. Their evolution, the evolution of man and woman as united romantic partners, aids in the evolution of humanity.

> "Fate, as she designed it, took her from her man. Destiny and love don't always go hand in hand. As the world lay waiting, like an embryo in a womb, she gave her angels that night in June. She gave her angels 2 a man because her man had none 2 watch over him 'til she returned. Her man, her lover, her son, her father—all these things he meant 2 her. She felt it right. She gave her angels that summer night."

Clearly for ⚥, love is an action verb which manifests all that mankind needs. These four songs, as well as others released after Emancipation, speak to the issue that our notions of "great" and "best" are warped and absurd.

Good (pleasing and beneficial) art does not always find you; you must be willing to search for it. The most interesting art is not being sold by major companies; therefore, one should be willing and open to explore the realms of the unknown for it. In that same manner, we should be willing to search for enlightenment, looking in places where we may not normally look. ☥'s quest is not merely about his music; it is about fighting arbitrary definitions and fighting the people who desire to define our world for us. Art and truth are subjective, and the public's notions of each are as widely fickle as there are opinions. As Aristotle asserts, individuals desire happiness, but they all desire it differently. ☥'s discourse has been to make us face our subjective realities and not be hypocritical about them. This is our first step toward freedom and evolution. Our second step is accepting who we are and then working to evolve to a higher form. His work proves that freedom, no matter how difficult the struggle, no matter how lonely the road, is worth whatever one has to endure to gain it. One can only evolve when one breaks free of the lies and the illusion of the physical. Further still, true emancipation means being able to break free of the lies that cause fear and selfishness so that we are able to love. Loving others is an emancipation that comes when we believe that love, not money, will save us. As the man asserts at the close of the Emancipation liner notes:

> "Emancipation 'see u in the purple rain...' True freedom takes place in the spirit. Many will try 2 shackle that spirit, 4 many have none of their own. Step 2 the right and uppercut them all. Never stop believing that if nothing else—things change. Evolve in2 the light and all disorder will cease. Live4loveandlovewilllive4u. ♛ wish u heaven— "

The Dawn of the Rainbow Children

Since 1998 Prince has made public statements which confirm that he is a Jehovah's Witness.

> "Yes, my current single, 'The One.' That went from a love song to a song about respect for the Creator -- God. The lyrics' meaning changed for me after reading the New World translation of the Bible [the Jehovah's Witness translation]. It has to be the New World translation because that's the original one; later translations have been tampered with in order to protect the guilty" (Simonart 1998)

My discussions with him confirm that bassist and funk pioneer Larry Graham played a significant role in his conversion as most people who have followed Prince's career know. My brief time spent with Prince came as a result of an article that I wrote, "Prince and Michael Jackson: Two Sides of a Different Coin," in which I assert that Prince's situation with Warner Bros was a different matter than Jackson's situation with Sony. The article was passed along to Prince, he liked it, and flew me to Paisley Park. He had also read the first and second editions of this book, and liked my approach and some of my insights. I was flown there partly because Prince was interviewing potential co-authors for a book project. Needless to say, I did not get the job. But, the few months spent in correspondence allowed us to construct a very rough draft of an introductory chapter. Because I signed a confidentiality contract and partly because I hope that some of what we crafted finds its way into his book, I will not be discussing in detail what we discussed. But, I will say that I met a man who is truly committed to his religious beliefs, especially the manner in which he uses his art to inspire and teach others. In fact, the theme of his book will center on the notion that an artist's relationship with God must be the roadmap that guides and governs his productivity. I say all of that to say that meeting Prince was an affirmation that from the beginning of his career he has been an artist grappling with how his work contributes to society, and that is what my work in this book attempts to reveal.

From 1999 to 2007, Prince has been unwavering in his desire to produce art that reflects his personal relationship with God and that also makes commentary on how humanity should parallel its behavior to the will of God. Yet, Prince's commitment to his relationship with God does not lead him to chase a "pie-in-the-sky" theology, which has no impact on man's physical life. In fact, as Prince has evolved spiritually, he has also evolved socially and politically. His theology is parallel to that of the Civil Rights Movement in that man's relationship with God should guide his relationship with his fellow man, which also means that God wants man to struggle for political liberation as well as spiritual liberation as evident in "Dear Mr. Man" when he asserts, "Matthew 5:5 say: The meek shall inherit the earth. We wanna b down that way, but U been trippin since the day of Ur birth." The fact that he quotes scripture in the middle of a political treaty shows that Prince is on a journey seeking something more than just the election of officials. For Prince, political activism must be subservient if not secondary to spiritual activism. And if we are talking man's hierarchy of need, since <u>Lovesexy</u> Prince has asserted that seeking first the Kingdom of Heaven is the answer to man's troubles. This chapter will focus on the notion that since his becoming a Jehovah's Witness, Prince is mostly concerned with using his work as a way to teach and manifest the love of God, especially in regards to social change.

In 2000, Prince released a cover of the Staple Singers' "When Will We Be Paid" as a B-side to an independent single on his own NPG Records. For some this might not be an appropriate song to discuss in this chapter, but it identifies the heart of Prince's theology. For Prince, a religion that does not seek to liberate man from his political and economic oppression is useless. To echo the words of Malcolm X when he was asked why he taught hate, Malcolm replied that he was providing love teaching, not hate teaching. It was Malcolm's goal to teach African people to love themselves. Unfortunately for their white oppressors, once African people learn to love themselves, they can no longer abide in a situation where they are abused. God said that we are to love and forgive our enemies; He did not say anything about hanging out with them, especially if they refuse to change their ways once they have been shown the light or the "Truth" as Prince asserts. Thus, Prince is aligning himself with the Staple Singers who sought to use the power of God to manifest social and political change. Also, he is echoing their work in that he employs the haunting qualities of the gospel organ combined with the dominate bass and beats of secular music. The music drags like a funeral procession but the beat makes it more akin to a military march, echoing the Civil Rights era. And his phonetic shouts, hollers, and amens give the song a bluesy mood, which affirms the Staple Singers. As the speaker, Prince assumes the role of preacher, which is amplified by the call and response of an amen corner. The song begins with a logical plea for reparations. "We fought in your wars in every land to keep this country free y'all for women, children, and men, but every time we ask for pay or loan that's when everything seems to turn out wrong." Next, logic is supplemented with emotion by showing the injustice and horror that have been inflicted on African people. "We been beat up, called names, shot down and stoned." The song is certainly evoking the notion that those who suffer for righteousness will one day be greatly rewarded.

In the final stanza, the song combines logic and emotion, echoing the sentiments of Frederick Douglass' famous Fourth of July Speech when he asks "Will we ever be proud of our country, 'tis of thee? Will we ever sing out loud 'sweet land of liberty?'" The lyrics ascend like a sermon, building point on point until he reaches his King and X climax. "We've given up all of our sweat and all of our tears, scuffled through this life for more than three hundred years. When will we be paid?" The song is demanding a justice that restores African humanity. There is as much pain as there is anger in his voice and lyric. The phonetic troping in his voice and the music articulates that the speaker is seeking a moral justice and not merely a legal justice, especially since he tropes "My Country, 'tis of Thee," also known as "America," which claims in its fourth stanza that God is the author of America's liberty, in much the same way that "America, the Beautiful" claims that America is great because "God shed his grace on thee." Thus, the song raises a moral question and not a legal question of how can America claim the blessings of God if it refuses or withholds those blessings from its own citizens, who have shed just as much if not more blood and sweat as anyone one else so that America could become great. Prince then combines or bookends this political and economic discussion with a social discussion of America's greed and perversion. On the A-side is a song which articulates that America's lust and greed have permeated into every aspect of American life and created chaos by poisoning all of America's institutions, especially the male-female relationship.

The A-side to "When Will We Be Paid" is "U Make My Sun Shine," which is a duet with Angie Stone that takes Prince's political angst and uses it to discuss the treatment and state of women, especially women of African descent.

> "Come on over here baby. Put your ass right down here on this throne. Don't U say nary a little word until U learn how 2 leave, leave that devil alone. Let me run it down. I'd keep your paper coming in real steady. I could tell U what the "I" in the pimp stands 4 if U're ready. Your eyes are wide shut. U cannot even see that behind your back, he calls U names, but U're still a queen 2 me"

In the poem, "Dry Your Tears, Africa!" Bernard Dadie

calls Africa a "pitiful princess." On the one hand Dadie is lamenting the fallen state of Africa, but he is also acknowledging Africa's glorious past, which works to encourage her people to struggle to return Africa to her glory. Prince is doing the same in "U Make My Sun Shine." Despite the current plight of the black woman, Prince states that she is still a "queen" to him. Stone then adds,

> "I gotta stop lettin' them devils (Define what it takes 2 be a woman) Stop lettin' 'em tell me what it takes 2 be a woman. Gotta never stop believing in me, myself, and I (Me).
>
> Pretty little lies that the rich keep using, I opened up my eyes. The only reason they're winning is 'cuz I keep losing. Gotta get back 2 my rightful place. This is the subject of my song. The queen of the human race, this is where I belong"

Prince is asserting that what is killing African people, especially African women, is a low self-esteem, which is caused by a lack of knowledge. This is why Stone asserts that she has to "stop lettin' 'em tell me what it takes 2 be a woman." All women are bombarded with false, perverted notions of what perverted males want them to be, and women of color suffer this plight at a greater level because the African woman has remained the symbol for sexual desire since slavery. Prince's solution is to provide these women with a truth that tells them who they are. And by now, the truth, for Prince, is the word and law of God.

> "Heaven sent angel so divine (Heaven sent), U're my complement (So divine). U make my sun shine at night…Come here now pretty baby let me take U somewhere and put your real clothes back on. We've both been in the dark much 2 long, but now that we got the knowledge of the truth we can both be strong, kings and queens getting' it on!"

This notion of being in the dark or being misled is a religious image of mankind being in darkness since the fall from grace, which began with the separation of Adam from Eve. Prince covers this notion at length on <u>The Rainbow Children</u>. The act of putting the clothes back on the female is a symbol that addresses the nakedness that Adam and Eve felt once they were exiled from the Garden of Eden and also refers to the exploitation of the female body, especially the body of color. Added to this is the fact that he calls her a "pretty baby," even in her fallen state, which asserts that there is more to the beauty of a woman than her body, thus calling her his "perfect complement." From album one Prince has seen the female has his "perfect complement," using sex and sexuality to tap into a deeper more fulfilling connection to womanhood, to life. By now, Prince understands that the metaphysical connection must be found through the soul and not the body. This is why he must put her clothes back on so that he can explore and connect to her soul, which allows him to connect to the universe or God.

True to his form, Prince begins in the physical with "When Will We Be Paid?" and ends in the metaphysical with "U Make My Sun Shine." It is no coincidence that songs such as "Beautiful Strange" and "One Song" also begin to appear around 1999/2000 as they continue to comment on Prince's desire to find oneness with his higher power but also seek oneness with mankind and the universe that surrounds us. In "Beautiful Strange," which appears on the remix version of <u>Rave n2 the Joy Fantastic</u>, Prince is asserting that God is there but our minds are so focused on the physical that we cannot see Him. "Strangely beautiful beautiful strange, that's what we said instead of the name. If U count the times He took all the blame, U would find the reason behind the game. In the darkness we must look 4 the way. Words so strange that only the mind can say. If it makes no mind what color or holy day, why is this game the only one that we play?" If a person has done something incorrectly all of his life, when he sees that act being done correctly it will appear strange or wrong to him. This is Prince's point. We have lived in evil or without the truth for so long that it is difficult for us to embrace it because we do not recognize truth or goodness for what it is. Therefore, to live a life of love or a life based on love rather than on how much money one can make is strange to this capitalistic society. Prince is asserting that the ways of the West have so clouded our minds that those of us who live in the midst of it have been sick for so long that we do not know that we are sick, especially if we were born into sickness. This is something he affirms in a 1999 interview for <u>MTV 1515</u>.

> "We played in Tokyo once, and we gave tambourines away and put them on the seats, the first hundred seats, in the venue. After we finished playing, these kids put the tambourines back on the seats and walked single-file out of there, no problems. They left the tambourines because nobody told them that the tambourines belonged to them. Now, there's something in them that's not in our children that we really need to address, because we're looking at the future when we see the burnings, you know, when we see brothers getting dragged in trucks down streets to their death. We're looking at the future, and either we can get in here now and fix that and do the best we can to help God fix it, or we can…[Shrugs]…you know, punch the clock in" (Loder, "The Artist: A Conversation," 1999).

This sickness into which we are born keeps us from connecting with God, the universe, and our fellowman. Yet, in "One Song" Prince writes to assure us that connection to the "Beautiful Strange" is possible.

> "I am the universe, the sun, the moon and sea. I am the energy 4 that is what I believe. I can be

contradiction 'cuz that is all I see, but I am the universe, and the universe is me.

I am the one song (Ah yes), and that one song is free. All things come from this one song (Yes they do, uh), the garden and the tree. If everything, everything is present, what is will always be. This here is the first and the last song and all that come between."

For Prince, how we treat each other as human beings is as important as to which church we belong. As he asserts in "The Love We Make" from <u>Emancipation,</u> "The only love there is is the love we make." He affirms this in "One Song" when he states "When language falls like a wounded soldier, and it's covered by the sea, all the sadness, all these unanswered questions keep me company (Company, company, company come 2 me, come 2 me please!). Here at the center of it all (I know) I know that U can only come from me." We must connect with God because it is only through that connection that we can manifest His will and goodness. To put it another way, the only reason that the antagonists of "When Will We Be Paid?" exist is because man refuses to connect and submit to the will of God. For Prince, to be disconnected from God is to be disconnected from life and is to be open to evil.

Sadly for Prince, our current system causes anyone who wants to do the will of God or simply live a life based on love and not money to be a "Radical Man." In "2045 Radical Man" Prince is on the offensive. He is not lamenting as he does in the above mentioned songs. He is looking for, calling on, demanding that we become radical beings, which means to stand against this system of cash. With the opening of the song, Prince is doing his best Louis Farrakhan impersonation against a backdrop of cheers, shouts, and amens. "How can a non-musician discuss the future of music from anything other than a consumer point of view? These few people make decisions for the bulk of us, without consulting any of us. Sales and distributions of our futures, uh! If this world were fair and right, they'd give up the car keys this very night." Of course Prince is directly addressing his personal conflict with Warner Bros, but as I have discussed at length in this book, one of Prince's strength is taking the individual or the personal and connecting it to the collective. "2045 Radical Man" appears on the <u>Bamboozled</u> soundtrack, which is a Spike Lee film that discusses the continuing exploitive images of African people in television and film. <u>Bamboozled</u> is a perfect bookend for another film titled <u>Dancing in September</u>. At their core, both films raise the question of the responsibility that African people have in creating or taking roles that merely affirm or perpetuate their negative stereotype. So, throughout the song, Prince demands the listener to "take a stand," echoing and evoking James Brown the entire time.

> "Flash forward, 2045, what did you stand for in the life of your pride? When faced with the final judgment of today, who profited from the game that you and your niggas play? Radical man/Save the life. Come on take a stand. Give that money back. Let's make a plan. The brand new currency, taking care of one another—You and me (Radical man).

The most interesting aspect is that in a world that is so corrupt, being radical is as simple as not remaining a fool or labor for the machine. Prince is not asking that his listeners take up weapons and storm the capitol. He is simply asking that we no longer take part in the perpetuation of our second-class citizenship by being pimped for the money. "Give that money back. Let's make a plan." But of course, in a world where the oppressed have been designed to be nothing more than labor by the faulty education system, for them to even consider making a plan to leave the system is a rebellious act. As Prince said to me, "We're not trying to fix or tear down anything. We just want to, need to walk away from this system because it is rooted in evil." (Prince 2002). Yet, when we analyze Prince's sentiment closely, we can see that it is a radical notion. As a mentor of mine, Dr. Jerry W. Ward, editor of <u>Trouble the Water: 250 Years of Black Poetry</u>, stated to me, "Do you really think that the oppressor is just going to let you walk away?" Ward is right. No master just allows his slaves to leave. That is why America had a Civil War. But that is also Prince's dual point. On the one hand, he is preaching education and love by asserting that the oppressed just leave. But he does open this song mimicking Farrakhan. Let us not forget his words in "We March," when he states "We can march in peace, but you best watch your back if another leader falls." Prince is prepared to go to war, just like David went to war with the Giant. But his war is not to take over or colonize. His war is to gain the ability to become sovereign beings. "Flash backwards, 1999 (backwards, 1999). In a world shot full of viruses, see (Tell me) how'd y'all stay alive? (Everyone of y'all) depending on this so called man for everything you got comes from his hand: food, water, the clothes you wear. How many of y'all niggas really care? To care (to care)" So to be a free thinking, critically thinking being is to be radical.

George Clinton was right when he warned "Think. It ain't illegal yet." For Clinton could see a time when even in America it would be almost if not illegal to think for oneself and question the powers that be. Thinking and questioning is what killed King, X, Medgar Evers, John Kennedy, Bobby Kennedy, Fred Hampton, and so many others—their audacity to question the power structure. Even Lincoln, who had no desire to see African people become equal to their white brethren, is killed for the mere suggestion of freeing blacks, and this is important if we understand that the "Emancipation Proclamation" did not free African people from slavery. So, to be a radical man is to be a thinking man who not only question the powers that be but is also willing to create his own value system as

Prince asserts "We claim Miles Davis, not Michelangelo. We playin' D-flat in the funk. You better act like you know. We don't care, what Albert Einstein did. I'd rather know, rather know (what?) how to build a pyramid. James Brown, Chuck D., and Jimi, turn me up louder now. I don't think y'all hear me." Prince is challenging this society by challenging what it holds dear. In the West, man is valued if he has money, status, or power. And though we know that the Egyptians were as vain and as petty and as power hungry as any other people, the pyramids represent for Prince their ability to transcend their physical inequities to construct something that attempts to combine and elevate the physical with the metaphysical. The pyramids are not just secular temples to man's vanity. They are also, for the Egyptians, temples that hold the secrets of the universe that are stored until man is ready to reclaim and properly use these secrets for the evolution of mankind. And this is also inline with the history or tradition of black music, which is why Prince evokes the names of legendary artists who spent their lives trying to use their art to benefit, move, or elevate mankind. In doing this, Prince is also questioning what it means to be civilized. Is the civilized man one who creates the technology that causes mass destruction, or is the civilized man one who heals the people with art and love? And which of these men will lead us to destruction or evolution? Prince is trying to do his part by using his art as a vehicle of teaching and inspiration: to teach the African being who he is, which should inspire him to reclaim his greatness. For it is the "Radical Man" who will manifest the "Rainbow Children."

Released in 2001, _The Rainbow Children_ reaches for a higher musical mantle. First, if you are looking for a CD filled with nicely cut and packaged hit singles that are radio and _Billboard_ friendly, _The Rainbow Children_ ain't for you. However, if you are looking for a diversified musical experience with lyrics that take you further than the sheets, then _The Rainbow Children_ is up your alley. The biggest knock on Prince's latest efforts is that his albums sound incoherent because the songs stop and go with no specified direction. The truth, however, is that his albums are coherent, and they do have direction; it is just that the direction is not toward <u>Billboard</u>, nor is he attempting to craft songs that are easily packaged for radio. Prince's direction has been to become the best musician and lyricist that he can, which often means to stretch pass the charts, to juxtapose notes, sounds, chords, and other musical and lyrical ideas that produce—God forbid!!!—something...different!?! Many see Prince as one who has ceased to fulfill his potential. On the contrary, <u>The Rainbow Children</u> is proof that Prince continues to fulfill his potential. It is just that he never saw hit records as the "be all—end all" of his potential.

    Most of the songs on the album have at least three musical movements. These multiple movements become a motif, as Prince continues to be one of the best in the pop field to use sound as a metaphor. For instance, in "The Work, Pt. 1" he is noticeably using a James Brown inspired riff that echoes soulful, black power semantics, which he laces with lyrics about the "hard" but necessary "work" that needs to be done for "revelation to come to pass." The music sets a mood of the black power struggle, then Prince infuses his notions of a metaphysical struggle, which exists along side the physical struggle. "Every time I watch the other people news/ I c a false picture of myself, another one of u/ They try 2 tell us what we want, what 2 believe/ Didn't that happen in the Garden/ When somebody spoke 2 Eve?" This connecting the black struggle to the metaphysical is quite essential to Prince's own theory, as evidenced by how he uses the term "Devil" throughout the CD to refer to the physical devils who exploit people for their wages. He then uses those physical devils as a trope for the metaphysical "Devil" in "Rainbow Children" and "Muse 2 the Pharaoh" because in Prince's theory the ultimate battle is in the metaphysical realm and not the physical realm, as also evidenced by "Digital Garden" and "The Everlasting Now." On one level, the multiple movements create a trope for Prince and his inability to be confined to arbitrary categories. On another level, the multiple movements represent his need to continue to grow, searching for the sound or idea to take him to the next level. As he states in "Last December," which has the most drastic musical changes and movements, "Did u ever find a reason Y u had 2 die?/ Or did u just plan on leaving/ Without wondering y?...In ur life did u just give a little/ Or did u give all that u had?/ Were u just somewhere in the middle/ Not 2 good, not 2 bad?" The musical movements combine with inquisitive lyrics to echo the desire of jazz musicians, such as Sun Ra, who wanted to show that within the soul of music is a desire to go somewhere and become something that transforms us. Thus, the lyrics of <u>The Rainbow Children</u> are pointing the listener in a direction, and the music is acting as a guide.

For the first two-thirds of the CD, Prince is challenging our notions of what a "pop" song can be by challenging the conventions of what sounds can be combined. While the first few songs are held on our musical radar by well measured/regulated beats and a soul-like mesh of hypnotic keyboards, Prince takes from that line and constructs grooves in various directions, attempting to expand himself and what we know as "popular music." Again, this expansion serves as a trope that works as a backdrop for what the lyrics want to do, which is to destroy our archaic understanding of what it means to be man and woman, what it means to be human, what it means to be living in truth, which also reflects in what it means to make art. He begins with a creation song, as all good myths do, and his creation covers the fall and redemption of mankind in "Rainbow Children." "With the accurate understanding of God and His Law they went about the work of building a new nation: The Rainbow Children." Playing on the myth of Osiris and Iris and Adam and Eve, Prince asserts that the new nation will only be created if we are able to build constructive relationships between man and woman. "As prophesied, the Wise One and his woman were tempted by the Resistor. He, knowing full well the Wise One's love 4 God, assimilated the woman first and only. Quite naturally, chaos ensued and she and 5 others were banished from the Rainbow...4ever." This ideology is nothing new for Prince, for man's fall from grace and his salvation have always been linked directly to man's relation to woman, most notably in "And God Created Woman" and in a more secular sense in "Raspberry Beret" and "Forever in my Life," where it is the female who has the power to fertilize man's life. In fact, he affirms this by invoking a line from a much older tune, "Sexuality," with "Reproduction of the new breed leaders Stand up and organize!" This line affirms that Prince is using sex as a metaphor for metaphysical union and that sexuality is a trope of human identity. The following songs continue to pontificate over the fall and redemption of mankind. The music acts as a guide, continually changing the mood as the lyrics take us down a sundry of issues and solutions. The songs are an amalgamation of funk and jazz, with an avant-garde sensibility, where Prince pushes the instruments to their limits of sound, hoping his moving in various musical directions will push the listener to free his mind and become open to the messages.

The Rainbow Children is avant-garde in that it is pushing and questioning what we know as truth and beauty in the sense of pleasing music and gratifying ideology. It is not avant-garde in the sense of "wanting to be art for the sake of art." Prince is too influenced by black musicians to think of art outside the context of man's daily existence, even if his inclusion of the metaphysics has put him at odds with what has been on the charts for the past ten years. Working with the definitions provided by Walter Davis in his essay, "So You Wanna Be an Avant-Garde Fan?," The Rainbow Children is avant-garde in the sense that the "Freebop" of Ornate Coleman, the "Expressionism" of Coltrane, "Restructualism," and the "Post-Modernism" of Wynton Marsalis all come together to serve as aspects and foundations of what the term "avant-garde" meant to the artists who were working within that certain framework. In accordance, the music of <u>The Rainbow Children</u> seeks to open alternative musical pathways and ideas that are then articulated through the lyrics. In "1+1+1 is 3" he asserts, "As she fell in2 the Sensual Everafter, out of body/out of mind, he stroked her hair a hundred times. And as she fell deeper in2 the hypnotic unwind, he counted his way in2 the suggestive mind. Planting a seed that bears fruit on the tree, he said, 'repeat after me...1+1+1 is 3.'" Falling in love is not an ending to a journey; it is the seed to our higher, metaphysical journey. Thus, love is about possibilities as jazz and funk are about possibilities as evolution is about meeting and fulfilling all of life's possibilities. Throughout the CD, the songs interact in a circular, call and response, manner, where the emotion of urgency and the notion of a quest are amplified by the experimental fusion of varying sounds. On top of the silhouetted jazz grooves, Prince coordinates funk, soul, and gospel in a manner that shows both the brilliance of black music as well as the innate and organic link that black music has to spirituality in all of its forms.

Then, just when you have slipped into the experimental form of this album, he hits you with "Family Name," which is classic Prince: classic in that Prince is able to take what he has done in the past and evolve it into where he is now...classic in that it is Prince's electrified, thumping bass line beneath his piercing falsetto...classic in that it is Sly and the Family Stone meets Curtis Mayfield, and at the end of this meeting, the song explodes into Prince making his case that he is the best guitarist of his time, which he proves later in the final movement of "Last December." Lyrically, "Family Name" is about the fallacy of the oppressor's story, the fallacy of white supremacy, and how this fallacy is used to oppress the Children of the Rainbow.

"First of all, the term 'black and white' is a fallacy. It simply is another way of saying 'this or that'...'this' means the truth, or 'that' which is resistant 2 it. When a minority realizes its similarities on a higher level--not just 'black'--but PEOPLE OF COLOR, and higher still 'INDIGENOUS,' and even higher still, 'FROM THE TRIBE OF --' and yet higher -- the 'RAINBOW CHILDREN'...When this understanding comes, the so-called minority becomes a majority in the wink of an eye. This action will cause a Reaction or Resistance. The source of this Resistance must b banished as it is in direct conflict with the initial action. It cannot b assimilated, 4 its very nature is resistance. In other words, ONE CANNOT SERVE 2 MASTERS. U r either 'this' or 'that' which is not 'this.'"

"Family Name" climaxes into "The Everlasting Now," where the album shifts into overdrive, leaving the listener with the question, "What the hell happened to the direction of the first part of this album?" Where jazzy soul was the dominate form of the first two-thirds, funk dominates the last third. As with the other songs on this album, "The Everlasting Now" has at least two musical movements—three, depending on how you are counting. Again, it is the funk chords and the refrain of "Don't let nobody bring you down!" that drive this groove, which is seconded by the horns that come late into the jam, which, in one final movement, shifts into James Brown cookin' with Jimi Hendrix at 2:30 a.m. With the lyrics, Prince is once again employing the metaphoric "I" as a way to connect the individual to the collective. Many of the verses seem quite true to his personal story, but he uses the impressionistic style best seen in <u>Around the World in a Day</u> or in "The Sacrifice of Victor" from 1992's ☥ CD, which allows his novel to assert the universal. Prince is continuing his theme of freedom and liberation and his ability to link that theme with the collective, moving from a focus on the individual to a focus on the masses. He is definitely talking about his liberation from Warner Bros and from a world that he sees as based on entropy, but he is also using his personal as a metaphor for liberating the masses with truth.

> "Mirror, mirror what u c?/ Have I still got those dark clouds over me?/ Or am I really feeling what I feel?/ The last days of the Devil's deal/ Mirror what u c?/ Devil, devil what u know?/ U been here since 1914, but now u got 2 go/ U been hidin' behind corporate eyes/ U wanna war, but u can't fight/ Devil u got 2 go...Teacher, teacher what u say?/ Did we really come over in a boat?/ Did it really go down that way?/ Or did I arrive b4 u and ruin Thanksgiving Day?/ Teacher, what u say."

Driving <u>The Rainbow Children</u> is the notion that the songs are meant to please and enlighten—to move both our bodies and our souls in a positive direction. Prince bookends the CD with love, because in his theory, only love can save us. The first song, "Rainbow Children," concentrates on the love between man and woman. The last song, "Last December," concentrates on the love between God and mankind. "Did u love somebody/ But got no love in return?/ Did u understand the real meaning of love/ That it just is and never yearns? When the truth arrives/ Will u b lost on the other side?/ Will u still b alive?/ In the name of the Father/ in the name of the Son/ We need 2 come 2gether/ Come 2gether as one." The motif is still liberation—the liberation that has been there since day one—but now Prince has successfully merged his desire for individual liberation with the necessity of collective liberation. And this liberation must take place in the metaphysical before we can achieve physical liberation. With the insight of Stevie Wonder, <u>The Rainbow Children</u> is able to construct a theology of Funkadelic's "Free your mind and your ass will follow," and the music is another lesson in just how spacious the spectrum of music can be if we allow it to be all that it has the potential to become.

Following <u>The Rainbow Children</u> are a couple of

collections that were released primarily on the internet through NPG Records, <u>Chocolate Invasion</u> and <u>The Slaughterhouse</u>. They are noteworthy because they document Prince's continued output/productivity without mainstream major record label backing, but only a few songs continue the theme of using art to educate and uplift humanity, and most of them are found on <u>The Slaughterhouse</u>. But it must be said that all of the songs that are included on either collection could be downloaded independently of the entire collection and were also found on other collections. The three most notable songs are "Silicon," "Y Should I Do That?" and "Golden Parachute." In their more impressionistic manner, Prince continues to comment on what he sees as the flaws and dangers of this society. "Silicon" is, of course, in reference to silicon breasts and Silicon Valley, both of which are symbols for man's need to escape reality and create a plastic/false reality. Even though Silicon Valley represents the fulfillment of the American dream as well as the apex of American ingenuity, Prince is able to show the myth of this dream by showing that this dream is not actually available to all American citizens, which makes the notion of American democracy and its value or merit void. Prince begins, again, with the importance of thinking critically. "One day U'll get outside the doo-rag when U really want 2 contemplate this, jacked up (Jacked up) paranormal situation that your people got into. Can I hip U? Long ago who considered the outcome? Now I'm thinking that a cat like U would be troublesome and sock U in the mind tangling curriculum guaranteed 2 leave U in a state of delirium." Prince is raising the issue that while African Americans are existing in their myopic world of narrow and dead-end dreams, someone is thinking about the best way to keep them there. Thus, there continues to be two educational systems in America: one that produces the leaders who move to Silicon Valley, and one that produces the labor class that remains in the hood. "On a magical rope of silicon U can bet that they'll be chillin' in Babylon, thinking about a way that they can split the proton while U eating all the bloody chicken and dead prawn, Mickey D. shake and a filet mignon, swearing up and down U the picture of health, now come on!"

Ignorance is killing the oppressed, which is why Prince points to the poor diet, which is a leading cause of death for most impoverished people due to a lack of knowledge and economics. "Leave that blood alone. Don't U know that dead blood kills interferons, making the immune system victim 2 whereupon any known virus can boot up and log on to www.U.com." The African American diet, as well as the diet of most impoverished people, can be directly related to their economic condition. Even the slaves understood this as evidenced by a passed along slave rhyme, "We Raise de Wheat:" "We peel de meat/ Dey gib us de skin;/ And dat's de way/ Dey take us in; We skim de pot,/ Dey gib us de liquor,/ And say dat's good enough for nigger." Yet, Prince knows that he is on shaky ground with this topic because the traditional African America diet, fast food not withstanding, is a source of heritage and joy despite the fact that it leads to early death. I always found the movie <u>Soul Food</u> interesting because the very thing that they glorify in the movie is also the thing that kills the family matriarch. Additionally, despite the fact that Prince has always engaged his listeners critical thinking, the majority of record buyers still do not want anything but sex from him. Thus, he feels prompted to acknowledge the fact that many may not be willing to hear this message from him. "Now U've found me, now that U're here. Let's talk about the U in this con. If U're getting bored don't front, just yawn. This is the kind of stuff that requires patience. Never mind the rhyme just relax and wax the song...Break it down, later on, come break down, y'all." So while Prince understands that his current subjects are not the songs of which pop hits are made, he is more concerned with the production of utilitarian art than merely continuing the assembly line of hits.

"Y Should I Do That When I Can Do This" is a direct response to his fans and detractors. There are several online fansites that are dedicated to Prince, with the most noted being Uptown.com, Housequake.com, and Prince.org. These sites, which do an excellent job, for the most part, of commenting on Prince's career as well as keeping fans abreast of the new and upcoming events or records, also have a good number of subscribers who lament for the Prince of the eighties. And this is true of journalists and music critics who often begin their reviews of Prince's latest efforts with the assertion that Prince is not making the music that he use to produce, which some feel they must do in order to contextualize the current work. Yet, often, their comments seem more like arbitrary hate/angst rather than objective commentary, but I must admit that I would be at the other end of the subjective spectrum. Prince, however, has often said,

> "I think that I'm constantly changing. One thing I notice is that some people want me to play like I used to play, and what they forget sometimes is that I was there, I did it, so for me to do it again is not gonna be so exciting. If I'm going to play "Let's Go Crazy," then I don't want another song that sounds like that, because I've got that slot filled. I'm always trying to look for something new" (Prince, The Art of Musicology, 2004)

"Y Should I Do That When I Can Do This?" is Prince wondering why he should cease growing, exploring, and experimenting. As he stated to me, "How much money do we need to earn before that is no longer our main objective?" (Prince 2002). The song begins with his declaration that he has already done what most want him to redo, so for him to keep doing that would be meaningless to him.

> "U were just conceived on a Friday night; I was on stage wasting brothers in a real fight. Every time

they copped my space down I worked it harder, stripped down 2 my underwear and spanked them like they father. Never before had people seen a vision so bizarre. Play a hand that's equal 2 mine. Look at my cards. I heard your little groove, and I raised U another. On a Sunday morning would U play that smack 4 your mother? Huh, I believe U would think otherwise. A few CDs from now when the software that U're banging's not alive, in a real battle those loops y'all got [will] suffer TKO's. Until U're playing in front of 70,000 U'll never know… This a grown folks job. All the young dogs need 2 recognize."

Though he understands the well wishes of his followers who want him to reclaim his old glory by repeating his old work, Prince asserts that would be the antithesis of what art is. Also, Prince has never been concerned with pleasing an audience. As quoted earlier in this book, he states that he is not looking for the fan who only wants to check him out when he has a hit on the charts. He appreciates the love and support, but to be a Prince fan is to understand that Prince is making music for himself and for his journey. "My brothers in Manhattan say, 'Got 2 shut these haters down G.' He say, 'Dog I got yo' back but U gotta, U gotta make a sound' (Make a sound). Like we used 2? Well, U might be pissed 'cuz y would I do that when I can do this?" Of course, the counter-argument is that Prince has become too self-indulgent or too full of himself to be objective and/or critical. His answer to this is that "Prince was an excellent editor," which infers that he no longer edits himself for radio or hits, that his interest is to make the music that he wants to make, buyer be damned.

Yet, Prince also finds hypocrisy in the fact that the leading figures of the industry constantly refer to him as dated and unmarketable but still want to profit from his work. And he voices his frustration about this hypocrisy in "Golden Parachute." Prince is once again combining the personal with the collective by paralleling his dispute with Warner Bros to the struggles of all people who are exploited by the greed of capitalists. Wikipedia provides a very basic definition of "golden parachute":

> "A golden parachute is a clause (or several) in an executive's employment contract specifying that they will receive certain large benefits if their employment is terminated. Sometimes it is only in the case that the company is acquired and the executive's employment is terminated as a result, but not always. These benefits can be severance pay, cash bonuses, stock options, or a combination of the items. The benefits are designed to reduce perverse incentives.
>
> The use of golden parachute has caused some investors concern since they don't specify that the executive has to perform successfully to any degree. Their concern is understandable since many golden parachute clauses can promise benefits well into the millions. In some high-profile instances, some executives cashed in their golden parachute while under their stewardship their companies lost millions and thousands of workers were laid off as a result." (http://en.wikipedia.org/wiki/Golden_ parachute)

I provide this definition of golden parachute to make it clear that Prince is a poet of his times who continues to make meaningful commentaries about his society. In 2001 and 2002 ENRON and WorldCom were the major stories of the evening and nightly news. These companies became the symbols for corporate evil and capitalistic greed, especially when it became known that their high level management made hundreds of millions while raping their middle-class investors and employees. And when you consider that companies, such as Sallie Mae and Fannie Mae, which were created to aid low income citizens in gaining equal access to education and home ownership, have recently been forced to make restitution for their predatory lending practices, it seems that every aspect and institution of America has been poisoned with greed. And having long ago equated record company owners to slave merchants, Prince is lamenting the colonization of black art for the gains of a few who do not produce the art and are not interested in using the art for the good of the people who produced it.

> "Here's 50 million dollars—go'n leave us alone—in appreciation 4 all the creations we now own. U brought us jazz, rhythm & blues, hip-hop even soul. 2 own every piece of intellectual property—this is our goal.
>
> Here's 50 million dollars 2 go along with this boot! Just keep your mouth shut and never tell of the plan 2 conquer and control the very soul of man."

For Prince, art is the soul of man. Thus, to colonize and pervert man's art is to colonized and pervert his soul. And if we agree with Baraka that art, especially music, is the barometer of mankind, especially African Americans, then the violence and misogyny of the music reflects a people who are immersed in a violent and misogynistic matrix. So where pimp culture and strip club culture were just aspects of a larger culture, they are sovereign cultures themselves that dictate the way of life for mainstream society. Now everything, including education and art, are merely hustles that one uses to gain capital, which forces us all to see ourselves as either a pimp or a whore.

> "17 years old, misled by so-called parachute down this cold road into this web of deception (spiders and snakes and bears); money made but never spent, never mentioned (golden parachute). Ah let's make a toast, 2 the host, 2 the man with the most. They worship U, all up under U, applauding

(golden parachute). One who in truth created nothing, nothing—In essence, a fraud"

Rumor has it that Prince is referring to Clive Davis. While interviewing a couple of musicians (none of whom were ever employed by Prince) for the second edition of this book, Prince was engaged in a difference of opinion with Clive Davis as how best to market <u>Rave Un2 the Joy Fantastic</u>, which was signed to a distribution deal with Arista. In fairness to Davis, one of the musicians stated that "Clive seems to feel that Prince doesn't live up to his contractual obligations." So there was definitely a strong rumor that Prince did not think highly of Davis. Davis is one of the most powerful men in the business, yet he has never played or sung one note. To someone like Prince, this is ludicrous as well as a perfect example of how colonization works. The whites come to Africa, take what does not belong to them either by force, trickery, or seduction, and use it for their own benefit and profit, leaving the blacks to suffer in ignorance and poverty. This is why Prince has been able to live with the successes and failures of living on his own terms. As he often states, "If you don't own your masters, your masters own you." So, self-determination is just as important to Prince as hit records, and with <u>Musicology</u> and <u>3121</u>, Prince shows that he can have both.

By 2004 Prince had not been in <u>Billboard</u>'s Top Twenty since 1996 with <u>Emancipation</u>. But <u>Musicology</u> changed that trend, and <u>3121</u> kept the new trend going, giving Prince his first album to debut at number one. Now to be fair, many in the industry, especially the leading record companies, asserted that it was dirty pool when Prince included <u>Musicology</u> as a part of the ticket package for the <u>Musicology</u> tour, which, of course, increased sales. As announced in the article by Joe D'Angelo, "<u>Billboard</u> Sours on Prince's <u>Musicology</u> Sales Experiment," "Both SoundScan, the company that tracks record sales, and music industry trade <u>Billboard</u> are putting their foot down and revising their policy of allowing album sales to be piggybacked with concert tickets" (D'Angelo 2004). However, as indicated by the June 18, 2004, article, "That's the Ticket: Prince Schemes to Top Billboard's Charts" by Raymond Fiore of Entertainment Weekly, Billboard decided to reverse their policy only after complaints were raised by major record companies:

> "…record labels cried foul, complaining that the CD-concert combo sets an unfair precedent in tallying sales. Now Billboard announced an amended policy that stipulates, 'the consumer must be given the option to purchase a CD with a concert ticket for [the sale] to count toward the chart,' says Billboard chart director Geoff Mayfield" (Fiore 20).

This complaining by the major record companies is just the usual frustration of a slave master when a slave has a successful emancipation. The last thing that record companies want known is that artists do not necessarily need them. At 100,000 units at $10 per unit for himself, Prince makes as much as he did when he was selling one million units for Warner Bros. So, the question remains, why work for a slave master when you can be free, happy, and profitable working for yourself? This modifying of how CDs can be "counted" is just another attempt of the slave master to control the slaves or limit the number of runaway slaves. This is no different than McDonald's complaining that a local soul food restaurant has decided to give their customers more food for their dollar. No one complained when record companies started giving away enhanced CDs instead of just plain ole' regular CDs. The real issue here is that the gatekeepers of commercial art want to ensure their monopoly on the "product" by limiting the rewards for a free artist, thus ensuring that no one can exist or be successful without them.

Additionally, why is it a "scheme" if a businessman decides that he wants to give his customers more bang for their buck? Why is it a scheme not to be greedy? If two men have the same type of cars for sale, is it a scheme if one man sells his car for less? If so, then "capitalism" is a scheme, is it not? As an African writer, I try to keep my books at a price where people who do not or can not ordinarily purchase books have the ability to do so, and I have been able to do this for all but one of my books. Is that a scheme? Is it a scheme to say, at some point, how much money must I make to feel like a success? Why is it a scheme for a man to say, "In reward for having supported me for over twenty years, my goal is to make sure that my CDs are offered at the best price?" In reality, fans can still purchase the CD in the record store or directly online if they want. However, many fans, in support of Prince's decision to break away from the slave masters, have chosen to purchase the CD online or wait until the concert. The "purchasing venue choice" is the biggest problem for the record companies. Since 1996, the majority of Prince's sales have not been through the traditional venue. When a "big name" act has a successful CD, it has a far-reaching effect because people go to the store for one CD and purchase two or three CDs by different artists, allowing minor or unknown acts to profit from the success of another, which means more money for the record companies. Thus, a major act's success is not just good for his sales but for the industry as a whole, which is why <u>Thriller</u> is hailed as saving the industry from years of slumping sales. Sales through unconventional mediums (especially mediums not controlled by the slave masters) keep the consumer from the traditional watering holes that are controlled by the slave masters. It is not the record companies who have the right to be enraged because Prince is out-selling their slaves. The music lovers should be enraged because record companies continue to create policy and an atmosphere that gives them the right to limit our exposure to a variety of music, which allows them to make billions off poorly constructed art. If more high profile artists followed Prince's "underground railroad," we would get back to "that feelin' music gave [us] back in the day."

For more than two million fans, <u>Musicology</u> and <u>3121</u> evoked memories and feelings of yesteryear. Even long time nemesis Rick James declared that Prince was one of the few artists carrying and keeping the legacy of the funk. "Musicology" as a title track and a lead single serves as yet another declaration of intent, as he stated during the <u>Tonight Show</u> performance of the song, "School's in...bring yo' whole family." And during the tour, he would assert, "I'm proud to be of the old school." So with "Musicology" Prince is, once again, throwing down the gauntlet to his peers as the funkiest man alive because he has come to "keep the party movin'/ just like ☞ told U/ Kick the old school joint/ 4 the true funk soldiers." The bass and horns clearly are paying homage to James Brown, while the guitar licks and flicks like a sizzling fire. Prince is stating quite literally that today's music pales in comparison to the past. "Wish ☞ had a dollar/ 4 every time they say/ Don't U miss the feeling/ music gave ya/ back in the day." But Prince is not pointing to himself. He is serious when he states that "school is in." This jam is didactic for he is pointing his listeners toward the holy grail of funk masters. "'Let's Groove,' 'September'/ Earth, Wind, and Fire/ 'Hot Pants' by James/ Sly's gonna 'take U Higher'/ Minor Keys and drugs/ don't make a rollerskate jam/ Take Ur pick—turntable or a band." So the title of the song, "Musicology," is appropriate because Prince is teaching. By embracing the term "musicology," Prince is embracing what it means to be an elder or a griot. This is an important step in the evolution of a man/artist who is all about evolving, showing that he can embrace aging as a sign of wisdom and not just as getting old or dated. Accordingly, Prince even shows that part of being a master is to always be a student. So, he shows that even at the top of his game, he can learn, grow, and evolve, which is what music/art is supposed to generate. Once a man who tried to marginalize rap in 1988, with the song "Dead on It," in

2004 he pays homage to a couple of hip hop artists whom he sees as having perpetuated the legacy of excellence in black music. "If it ain't Chuck D./ or Jam Master Jay/ Know what?/ They're losin'/ 'Cause we got a Ph.D. in/ Advanced body movin'." The use of the term "Ph.D." cements the mood of learning the legacy, of learning the craft, something that he feels has long disappeared in popular music. And with his new treaty, Prince is ready, once again, to mount a war on radio, a war on what a hit song can be, a war on what an artist is supposed to be. Yet, unlike the rebel of <u>Dirty Mind</u> and <u>Controversy</u>, this Prince is a man who sees and accepts himself as an elder, as someone who has the responsibility to point the next generation toward a higher purpose.

Though neither <u>Musicology</u> nor <u>3121</u> qualifies as a concept album *per se,* the majority of the songs continue to perpetuate the notion that Prince is an artist who has matured in how he wants his art to impact society. As he states in a 2004 BET interview for <u>The Art of Musicology</u> when asked about not performing some of his raunchier material, he replies "I would like to think that I am older and wiser." Some see Prince as trying to erase or rewrite his past by not performing some of his older work and by writing new love songs or slow jams that seem to have one foot in the bedroom and one foot in the pulpit. I take it that Prince is more concerned about how his work impacts his audience where in the past he did not think as much about how the sex and sensationalism may be having a negative effect on his audience. Dez Dickerson, original Prince guitarist, states in his book, <u>My Time with Prince</u>, that there came a time for him where he could no longer reconcile the notion that they would be performing a song like "Head" with teenagers in the front row. "Call My Name," "What Do U Want Me 2 Do?" "The Marrying Kind," "On the Couch," "Te Amo Corazon," "Incense and Candles," and "Satisfied" affirm that Prince is still a sensual, sexual being, but that his sexuality is merely an aspect of his humanity or that his sexuality is guided by his desire to be a better person. Where early in his career sex and sexuality were the battle grounds for liberation, now they are vehicles for communicating love and the connection to a higher being. And yet, if people had been really listening to what he was saying on those early records, the Prince that we have today would not be so surprising or unfamiliar.

> "We've all used shock value to sell things…I used shock to get attention. But back when I was doing the freaky songs in the freaky outfits, we were exploring ideas. I wanted my band to be multiracial, male and female, to reflect society. The song 'Sexuality' is about education and literacy. 'P Control' and 'Sexy MF' are about respect for women. Go and listen to the verses. All people focus on is the hooks" (Jensen 31-32).

What is different is an artist who is more mature at articulating what he wants to say, an artist who has played with and refashioned his image enough that he no longer feels a need to have to play hide and seek, and a man who is no longer interested in trying to sweeten or sensationalize the mood so that we will accept the message. Truly, most were not getting the message because the message was being lost to many in the glow and glitter of the shock and sensationalism. So with his new songs, the imagery and word play are still there, but they lack the purposeful ambiguity or dual meaning, especially where a political or spiritual meaning used to be cloaked or symbolized by or with a sexual metaphor. On <u>Musicology</u>, "Call My Name" expresses the same passion as "Slow Love," from <u>Sign 'O' the Time</u>, but there is not one reference to sex. Of course, the inference of sex is given with the statement, "calling out my name," but the call is one of emotional connection, not physical. Prince is asserting that this call for an emotional connection is more fulfilling that the sexual encounter or act: "I heard Ur voice this morning/ Calling out my name/…But it let me know that my name/ Had never really been spoken b4/ B4 the day ☮ carried U/ Thru the bridal path door." "Call My Name" is an ode to love and commitment, not sexual satisfaction.

    Marriage is asserted early in the song so as to state that passion and sex are at their best when they are guided by love and commitment. Yet, Prince cannot help but raise his solution to the theology of love can save the world. "☮ heard a voice on the news sayin',/ People wanna stop the war/ But if they had a love as sweet as U,/ They'd 4get what they were fighting 4/ What's the matter with the world 2day?/ Land of the free? Somebody lied!/ They can bug my phone/ Peep around my home/ They'd only c U and me/ Makin' love inside." "What Do U Want Me 2 Do?" continues this theme of the importance of commitment and honesty. "☮ got a woman, U got a man/ So we got 2 do what's right/ U'd get beheaded in other lands/ If ☮ were in Ur arms 2nite." Clearly for Prince, the world's chaos begins with the deterioration of family, and strong families are based on solid relationships between men and women, especially men and women who are faithful to marriage. "The Marrying Kind," in much the same way as "Sleep Around" from <u>Emancipation</u>, warns that when a man has a good woman, he must do all he can to keep her because there is nothing better than a good woman. "'Honey, ☮ tried 2 tell him/ That U were the marrying kind/ A faithful one-man woman/ Best he would every find." The speaker is asserting that if the male continues to mistreat his woman, someone who appreciates her will come along and take her. "If U leave her now/ U ain't never gonna see her again/ She's gonna need a shoulder 2 cry on/ She's gonna need a friend/...☮ tried 2 tell him that if U run 2 me/ ☮ won't run away." And "On the Couch" is simply sultry. As national disc jockey Tom Joyner often asserts, very few write a slow jam like Prince. In this case the tension is not just the desire to have sex. The tension is the struggle to suppress one's physical desires and live by a higher code. "☮ know we agreed 2 b married/ But it's hard, girl/ So hard girl/ ☮ can feel the blood racin' with the thought of U tastin' me/ 4 that ♛ beg Ur pardon." Prince has never been one to ignore the struggles of the flesh. This song is clearly stating that we do not just have religious conversions and live happily ever after. "On the Couch" is a nod to all of the fans who want Prince to perform "Head." He still loves "Head" as much as he ever did, but he is striving for higher ground. The last thing he wants to do is have folk think that he has become some angel or some hypocrite. More importantly, by acknowledging the struggle, we do not set ourselves up for failure, and we allow ourselves the opportunity to be wiser and not put ourselves in compromising situations, "U shouldn't of let me unzip Ur dress." The most powerful aspect of the song is that it ends without final resolution, which seems to assert that the struggles of the flesh will forever be with us, and the moment we realize this is the moment that we are better prepared to live for a higher purpose. The most dangerous thing we can do is lie to ourselves. The embracing of God does not make us perfect; it simply strengthens us for our never-ending journey toward perfection.

<u>Musicology</u> also has three forthright social and political pieces: "Illusion, Coma, Pimp & Circumstance," "Cinnamon Girl," and "Dear Mr. Man." "Illusion" is classic Prince in that it highlights his wit, his ability to turn things inside out and force us to see them in a new manner. In this society where using or taking advantage of people has become the norm, Prince raises the question of who is really being pimped. Richard Pryor asserted that black men have sex with white women as an act of rebellion and vengeance. Although this is true in some cases, these black men should understand that in many cases they are being used as Mandingo, Bigger Thomas studs by the white female as a way to assault her parents' hypocritical family value structure. As John Allen Stevenson asserts in his article "A Vampire in the Mirror: The Sexuality of Dracula," for white people social adultery is the greatest crime committed against whiteness/humanity. "She knew

which fork to use/ But she couldn't dance/ So he hipped her 2 the funk/ in exchange 4 the finance/ who's pimping who when/ nobody gets a second chance?/ This is the story of illusion/ coma, pimp and circumstance." The song never proclaims either character, the rich "lily white" old lady or the young "dirty dog," as the protagonist or the antagonist. In some ways, "Illusion" evokes Bill Withers' line of "use me 'til you use me up" or even in "Ain't no Sunshine," when he states "I know I outta leave the young thang alone/ but ain't no sunshine when she's gone." In "Illusion" everybody's cards are on the table. Even when the young buck spends her money and she catches him with another woman, the older female seems to have had no illusions about the relationship or what she is getting. "He spent her money oh so well/ Takin' baths in cold Cristal/ He took a trip 2 burn an old flame in 'Frisco/…When Doris caught him in her arms/ she shrugged her shoulders and said, 'no/ harm…/Just put Ur name on this pre-nup/ and we can all hit the disco.'" The statement about the "pre-nup" raises the question of who is getting played. The young man will have materials lavished on him for providing sex, but there is no opportunity for him to change his stars or his class. With that "pre-nup" more than likely he will be rode hard and put up wet. We leave the song with the notion that both are shallow and deserve each other, but there also seems to be the notion that the male is being played as much as the female. Though men are conditioned not to care about being objectified, we get a sense that this dude is empty, if not perpetually lonely. Maybe "Illusion" is affirmation that "Gigolos Get Lonely Too." Also, we see that the money is not enough to fulfill him because he continues to run back to an old flame. Thus, "Illusion" is a cautionary tale about the inability of money and sex to make us happy.

"Cinnamon Girl" and "Dear Mr. Man" are directly political. They exist as a linear continuum, where "Cinnamon Girl" begins in sadness and grows to angst, and "Dear Mr. Man" is "sick and tired of being tired" to paraphrase and echo Civil Rights icon, Fannie Lou Hamer. Both songs are an indictment of America's greed and lust for power, with the notion that America has created or caused all of its own ills.

> "As war drums beat in Babylon/ Cinnamon Girl starts 2 pray/ ☮ never heard a prayer like this one/ Never b4 that day/ Tearful words of love 4 people/ She had never met b4/ Asking God 2 grant them mercy/ in this face of holy war/
>
> Cinnamon Girl of mixed heritage/ Never knew the meaning of color lines/ 9/11 turned that all around/ When she got accused of this crime/ So began the mass illusion/ War on terror alibi/ What's the use when the god of confusion/ Keeps on telling the same lie?"

Prince is clearly asserting that the war against terrorism is a sham and that the Bush administration has used 9/11 and religion as a cloak to colonize the Middle East's oil. And with Bush being elected twice, it seems that the "god of confusion" is winning. However, Prince is determined to provide strength and encouragement for those willing to fight for what he sees as right.

> "Don't cry, don't shed no tears/ One lie won't make us fear/ 'Cause we know how/ This movie's ending/ As war drums beat in Babylon/ And torched the blood red sky/ Militants bomb with 4eign guns/ Both sides—children die/ Cinnamon Girl opens the book/ She knows will settle all the scores/ Then she prays alter the war--/ That there will not be anymore."

The "Cinnamon Girl" video shows an Arab child, living in America, torn between two worlds. Her American friends see her as a symbol of evil, and her parents fear that she is becoming too westernized. At the apex of her frustration, after her parents' store has been vandalized, she decides to blow up an airport terminal. The video shows the girl walking into the terminal and committing the act, but after the explosion, we see her standing in the terminal, having changed her mind. The outrage of conservative radio missed the song's and the video's message. The child's rage is ultimately defeated by love and empathy. When the child arrives at the terminal, she begins to see the people there not as evil Americans but as human beings. This is what Prince means in the last lines of the song, when instead of trying to settle the "score," "she prays…that there will not be anymore" wars. Even in his outrage, Prince is guided by love.

The discourse of "Cinnamon Girl" is continued in "Dear Mr. Man." Even though there is angst, rather than call for violence, Prince initially calls for dialogue. "What's wrong with the world 2day?/ Things just got 2 get better/ Sho' ain't what the leaders say/ Maybe we should write a letter" Prince is not just calling for rhetoric, but for active discourse where the people unite and present their concerns to the elected officials. He is not saying that he is writing a letter, but that "we should write a letter," that people with likeminded concerns unify and petition the government. He then provides a list of what's wrong, concentrating on the hypocrisy of the government and the wealthy.

> "Dear Mr. Man/ We don't understand/ Y poor people keep on struggling/ And U don't lend a helping hand/
>
> Who said that 2 kill is a sin/ And started every single war/ That ur people been in?/ Who said that water/ Is a precious commodity/ Then dropped a big, ol' black oil slick/ in the deep blue sea?/
>
> Who told me Mr. Man/ That working around the clock/ will buy me a big house in the 'hood/ with

cigarette ads on every block?"

By the time Prince finishes his list, he has moved from sorrow to frustration to anger. In the middle of his listing, Prince attempts to be led by scripture, but his frustration overwhelms him. "Matthew 5:5 say:/ The meek shall inherit the earth/ We wanna be down that way/ But U been trippin' since the day of Ur birth." His frustration causes him to realize that it is useless to work within the current system because an evil tree cannot bear good fruit, much the way W. E. B. Du Bois, a major voice for integration, denounces this agenda and moves to Africa once he realizes that it will be impossible for African people to gain first-class citizenship in America. "Ain't no sense in voting/ Same song with a different name/ Might not be in the back of the bus/ But it sho' feel just the same/ Ain't nothing fair about welfare/ Ain't no assistance in AIDS/ Ain't nothin' affirmative about ur actions/ 'Til the people get paid." So Prince ends with the notion that it is time for the righteous to take back the land. "Ur thousand years r up, Mr. Man/ Now U got 2 share the land." The "thousand years" is a loose reference to the Thousand Years Reign or Millennialism where some Christians, including Jehovah's Witnesses, believe that man will be given one thousand years to get right with God while the earth has been returned to Jesus. Because the phrase is not quite in context with the faith of Jehovah's Witnesses, this phrase is simply an allusion to the notion that the time that the evil doers have left is short, as Prince is warning the evil doers that there will be a price to pay, as he does in "U Will Be Moved" and "Right the Wrong" several years earlier.

3121 has more spiritual overtones than Musicology and just as much funk. The title track, "3121," is akin to "Uptown" and "Paisley Park" in that it is a declaration of the place to be. However, by now, Prince's liberation is spiritual liberation. He still wants the freaks to come, but now he is seeking Jesus Freaks who want to come spiritually. Though not as specific or articulate as "Uptown" and "Paisley Park," "3121" continues the theme of a space where the liberated lovers of music and the critical thinkers can come together and fellowship. More specifically, it pays homage to the home he was renting in Los Angeles where he hosted after-hour parties, which he has been doing since 1987 at Paisley Park.

> "Through the gates Knock on the door/ Put Ur Clothes in the pile on the floor/ Take Ur pick from the Japanese robes and sandals/ Drink champagne from a glass with chocolate handles/ Don't U wanna come? 3121/ Gonna b so much fun 3121/ That's where the party b 3121/ U can come if U want 2/ But U can never leave/
>
> Look over there There's another turn-on/ Butterflies scared that they're going 2 b awake all nite long/ Dancin' in Ur belly Like a ballerina/ In spite of Ur efforts 2 calm them down"

Prince paints a scene that is impressionistic but has enough detail that our memory of the Prince who used Caligula's orgies as inspiration causes our minds to fill in the gaps with our own imagination. And it helps our fantasy that he moans and growls almost every syllable over a thumping bass and an eventually grinding guitar. Notions of clothes piled on the floor and chocolate dripping everywhere inspire us to flights of fantasy. Yet, though he may not want the sex, he does want our imagination. These parties, both at the LA house and Paisley Park, are famous for their guest lists and legendary jam sessions. One night may showcase Stevie Wonder, Lenny Kravitz, Carlos Santana, George Clinton, and even Miles Davis going back to the 1987 New Year's Eve jam. These parties are not about hanging out with famous people. These parties are Prince's attempt to bring all the music that he loves to him. This is what his spirit needs, and he is inviting us to partake, enjoy, and grow as he grows. "Futuristic fantasy/ This is where the purple party people b." Everybody needs a home or a center where they can fellowship with others who support, nurture, and push them, a place where they can feel comfortable to be themselves, which allows them to experiment and evolve. Every major art movement from the European Renaissance, to the Harlem Renaissance, to the Black Arts Movement, to the Motown explosion all had one thing in common, a center or place where the artists could conjugate and share.

Though <u>3121</u> debuted at number one, some have referred to the album as being "Prince light" with a "third less funkativity of "regular Prince." The CD showcases Prince's musical and lyrical range. "Lolita, "Te Amo Corazon," and "Love" are bouncy pop standards. "Black Sweat" is stripped down funk that rivals "Kiss" or "It." "Incense and Candles" and "Satisfied" are classic Prince slow jams. "Fury" is more proof that Prince is a guitar legend. "Beautiful, Loved and Blessed" is part Staple Singers' "Respect Yourself" (though not as funky) and part Harold Melvin and the Blue Notes' "Wake Up Everybody." And "Get on the Boat" shows Prince as a prism if not a kaleidoscope of music and words, combining funk and salsa with a Mayfield narrative.

The love songs continue to be guided by Prince's desire to show love as a spiritual thing or experience. "Lolita," which upon hearing the title we hope to be the next "Darling Nikki," is a more mature man trying to address if not change his relationship with young women from seducer to elder. "U're a VIP at least to me/ Come here and show me some ID/ ♛ Know U're fine from head 2 pumps/ If U were mine we'd bump/ U're much 2 young 2 peep my stash/ U're tryin' 2 write checks Ur body can't cash/ U can't hang with this, girl/ Lolita U're sweeter but U'll never make a cheater out of me" And in transition to a more mature love, "Te Amo Corazon," a Spanish inspired groove, continues the theme of man finding salvation through the female. "At 42 thousand feet above the sea/

That's where U and 👑 first came 2 b/ From the dust of the earth and knowledge tree/…At once when 👑 first laid eyes on U/ 👑 saw heaven and earth anew/ Everyone else saw my brown eyes no longer blue/ Te amo corazon." In "Incense and Candles" Prince is navigating the line between sexuality and spirituality.

> "👑've been waiting 4 U baby all night long/ So 👑 could get somebody 2 play this song/ The jam that's got a beat like it's making love/ 'Cause u're the only one 👑've been thinking of/ Come in2 my room of incense and candles/ 👑've got something that U won't know how 2 handle/…👑 want 2 look 4 the milky way and when 👑 find it/ 👑'm gonna make U scream my name as if it was divine."

This more mature Prince is cognizant of not sounding hypocritical, so he adds, "But we both know that we gotta praise the one who made ya/ Give props 2 Ur mama 4 the healthy food she must have gave ya/ 4 the meek at heart these words they might sound like a sinner/ But the truth is that U're sitting on every one of Ur dinners." The body is not evil, just man's intentions. However, if our intentions are properly guided, then they will manifest themselves in a fruitful manner.

"Love" is simple and poetic as Prince presents us with a couple conflicted by their definition of love. Faulty communication is at the root of most of our romantic conflicts. Even dishonesty is an aspect of poor or flawed articulation. But more specific to "Love," Prince is discussing the problem of two people not being equally yoked and not taking the time or effort to communicate properly.

> "Stop telling me what U want me 2 hear/ Stop telling me what 2 fear/ Stop trippin' on something U overheard/ Love is winning without a word/ Stop giving me Ur 'wish list'/ Love is free from all this/

> Love is not a game U can play on the floor/ U gotta stop keepin' score/…U can skate around the issue if U like/ but who's gonna get U high in the middle of the nite?/
>
> What's the point of giving me ultimatums? Smiling at my friends when U really hate 'em/ Tryin' 2 convince me that ☺ should 2…what's the point?/ Stop worryin' about what people say/ When it ain't gonna stop them anyway/ Love can do anything if U try/ Come on…Spread Ur wings…Let's fly. so high
>
> Like a bird flyin' over the sky/ U know it never stops/ From the abundance of the heart the mouth speaks/ Love is whatever U want it 2 b"

Love is not the thing that exists in the happily ever after; it is a product of work. The listing or addressing of common issues suffered by most romantic relationships takes the notion of love from the fantasy to the real, and shows it as something at which we must work to achieve. However, the underlying message is that we must be honest in our intentions and in our articulation of our intentions if we ever hope to manifest or achieve love.

And finally, "Satisfied" is the reward of the labor. Prince is moaning, growling, and cajoling his lover that it is time for her to allow him to satisfy her. Yet, even with all of this heat created by vocal and musical passion, Prince does not relinquish his theme that love is more powerful and pleasing than sex. The song opens with the notion that it is baby making time. "B4 we get started/ R we all alone?/ 'Cause ☺'m about 2 get open-hearted/ It's time 2 send Ur company home and turn off Ur cellphone/ Baby, can't U c/ ☺ just wanna get U satisfied." We are being bombarded with the brash Prince of "Do Me, Baby," "International Lover," and "Adore." "This is gonna be a long nite/ A little bit longer afternoon/ Girl, if we get this thing right/ Oh, U gonna get satisfied real soon/ Can't U see ♕'m just tryin' 2 get U satisfied." We are presented with a man on a mission. "♕'m gonna seek this thing like a buried treasure/ Like Columbus sailing over the sea/ Until ♕ discover the land beyond expertise and chastity/ ♕'m just tryin' 2 get U satisfied." However, the bridge of the song exposes Prince's new mission, "♕' ain't talkin' 'bout nothing physical/ 'Cause 4play starts in the mind/ ♕'m just tryin' 2 get U 2 think about doing things That U've always wanted but could never find." As any effective writer, Prince is playing with what we know and how what we know affects what we perceive or understand. Rather than running away from his history or past themes, Prince uses them to lure us into his cave, but once we are there he presents us with emotional and spiritual delight and not physical. Again, Prince is not saying that sex is bad. He still likes it "soft and wet." But his message is that sex is better when guided by love.

From the romantic to the religious and social, Prince is determined to convince us that we can have life more abundantly if we go to God. This theme echoes in "The Word." "No matter how shiny Ur lips/ They'll never b streets of gold/...There's no reason 2 feel uneasy/ There's no reason 2 feel such pain...Don't U wanna go get saved?" "The Word" would fit comfortably on <u>The Rainbow Children</u> as it explains how much better life is with God while addressing the notion that there is a war being waged for the soul of man, and we must prepared to do battle.

> "The night is calling U 2 act/ Act upon every urge/ U can't get no satisfaction/ if U ain't got the courage/ ♕ don't know what U're afraid of.../ Who's gonna saves us when them spiders get next 2 U?/ Spinning their sticky webs around what U do/ We've gotta safeguard against the 4ked tongue and the treachery of the wicked one/ Get up, come on. let's do something/ Don't matter how far U have 2/

The Truth has 2 b told."

And the power of God's word is its ability to manifest a new reality in us, which is seen in "Beautiful, Loved and Blessed." For Prince, what will protect us from the evil doers are inner peace and a positive sense of self, which comes from being filled with and shaped by God's word. "When U found me 👁 was just a piece of clay/ 👁 was 4mless/ U gave me a new name/ With the breath of life 👁 now live abundantly/ All 👁 needed was the potter's hand/ And the blood on Calvary." Prince is also careful to remind us that once we are blessed we must stay focused on God so as not to go astray.

> "But 2 much power can sometimes turn 2 shame/ 2 much desire/ Sometimes makes U feel the same/ But 4giveness is how U win the game/ 👁 begged 4 truth, now 👁 know the truth/ And that is when U came and said 👁 was/ Beautiful, loved, and blessed/ 👁'm better than the day b4 cause U made me confess that 👁'm beautiful, loved, and blessed."

Again, arriving at conscienceness or salvation is not the end but the beginning. To be beautiful, loved, and blessed is to know that one has a power inside them that supersedes whatever this life can throw at him.

> "A constant battle 2 stay ahead of the game/... Always trying 2 break U down thinkin' that'll raise 'em up/ 👁 just wanna b happy/ Come take this bitter cup from me/ If 👁 were 2 ever write down my life story/ 👁 could truly say through all the pain and glory/ 👁 was just a piece of clay in need of the potter's hand/ When U whispered in my ear the words 👁 so clearly understand/...When U're free U're really free indeed/ All U gotta do is plant the seed/ Wake up it's a new day"

From "A Change Is Gonna Come," to "People Get

Ready" to "I'll Take U There," to "Someday We'll All Be Free," Prince is a student of music, especially its tradition of social commentary and inspiration. In 1980 Prince's "Party Up" is an anti-war song, which seems odd to some since there is no war to protest. However, America was immersed in a power struggle with Russia, the Middle-East was a bed of killer bees and fire ants, and the Iran Hostage Crisis was nearing the one year mark. Many young people were feeling the political angst of the time. So even though there was no singular military action, such as Vietnam, there was enough happening to raise the concern of young people. In this same vein, "Get on the Boat" is a nod to the past as well as inspiration for the present. "Get on the boat/ We got room 4 a hundred more/ Look outside Ur window/ Tell me what U c/ Coming up the mountain 4 a new philosophy/ Every single color/ Every race and every creed/ Lookin' 4 the truth U'll that's gonna set somebody free." Unlike "1999," which is a more objective or journalistic reporting of the end of the world, "Get on the Boat" is hopeful for humanity by preaching that although some will be left behind, everybody has the opportunity to be saved. "All across the nation/ People doing what they can/ 2 avoid the tribulation/ That will be great throughout the land/ Everything in darkness must come out 2 the light/ When we love each other/ that's the only way that's gonna b right/ Get on the boat/ We got room 4 a hundred more." Ushered by horns, congas, and bouncing bass, <u>3121</u> ends as it begins, a celebration of and an invitation to the journey to become more and better than we are.

Two final works to mention are "The United States of Division" and "SST." Although written close to a year apart, these songs work as bookends if not call and response. The companion essence is interesting because "The United States of Division" was released through NPG Records in 2004 just after <u>Musicology</u>, and "SST" was inspired by the events of Katrina. Prince is asserting that what leads to the moment where poor people are left to die as public spectacle even though we have the resources to save them is caused by the fact that we live in a fragmented land divided by greed. Close to forty years after the 1968 Kerner Commission Report, we still live in two Americas, separate and unequal. Yet a year before "SST," Prince is lamenting this in "The United States of Division."

> "2004, still at war and everybody hates Americans/ Flyin' in an aero-plane with pen in hand/ Over miles and miles of deep blue/ Wonderin' if it was all part of a master plan/ Forget the 1 and become 2/
>
> How could Ur brother hear the same music/ Yet somehow dance 2 a different tune/ 👁 guess that once U go divide this precious land/ This precious land will divide U"

America's chickens are coming home to roost. The evil that whites have inflicted on people of color that has divided this land is now infecting the entire globe. But what is the worst for Prince is that African Americans, himself included, are now as much a part of the problem because they have bought into and internalized the mythical dream.

> "Drivin' a brand new Cadillac through my neighborhood/ Everything still look the same, uh/ Everything except the fact 👁 wish 👁 could/ Take away the pain
>
> We let <u>Superfly</u> straighten up our curly hair/ He took the Afro out the game/ It's kinda cool but the guns and drugs 2 much 2 bear/ 10 years later <u>Scarface</u> came"

Prince is being as self-critical as he is as being critical about the race. It is obvious that much of Prince's style comes from the Blaxploitation era. In fact, there are two specific aspects from the film <u>The Mack</u> (1973) that are directly found in Prince's work. First, when the Goldie is trying to turn out his first female, he states, "I wanna be your mother, your father, your brother, and your sister." Prince uses the exact line in his first top ten hit, "I Wanna Be Your Lover" (1979). And taking into consideration Prince's long flowing permed hair, we can now understand that where he was trying to craft an effeminate persona he was also directly paralleling the pimp culture of the time. Secondly, the scene in Purple Rain where Morris Day has Jerome dump a young lady into a dumpster is frame for frame identical to a scene in The Mack. So as an elder, Prince is not just telling others to check themselves, he is admitting to his own flaws that need to be addressed. And as he has lost himself, so has much of the African American community lost themselves from integrating and assimilating into a system that breeds evil perpetuated on the subjugation of the black body. The ironic twist of The Mack is that Goldie thinks or embraces pimping as a revolutionary act, as an alternative to joining his brother's more organized, militant organization, but as a way to rebel against white oppression and construct a sovereign life for himself. However, Goldie finds that eating of evil fruit will eventually lead to death. To this, Prince's solution remains the same; go to God. "A united state of mind will never be divided/ The real definition of unity is 1/ People can slam their door, disagree and fight it/ But how you gonna love the Father but not love the Son?" For most people, it is easy to love God because there is no daily physical contact with God. But to love the Son, which is a metaphor to love man, the physical being, for Jesus was deemed the Son of Man, is to transcend our physical and love despite our flaws. Katrina shows that we have yet learned to love our fellow man as we love ourselves.

Needless to say, Prince's pleas go unheard in the same way that Wright's pleas in Black Boy, Native Son, The Outsider, and White Man, Listen! go unheard. And this is how we arrive at this moment in time where black anger rages like a forest fire while poor people are stranded on rooftops awaiting their death because a glutinous government refuses to serve them. Yet, Prince, like both Wright and Alexander before him refuses to stop preaching his message. And more like Alexander, Prince refuses to relinquish his belief that love can save us if we open ourselves to it. But part of opening ourselves to it is actually teaching love in the same manner that we teach algebra, shop, or gym. So, in "SST" Prince appeals to humanity's humanity, asking them to consider the moral consequences of their actions.

> "Who will be a guest in Ur tent?/ Certainly not the ones who don't repent/ And keep givin' guns 2 the poorest of our nation's sons/…Who will be the 1 in His bed?/ Certainly not the 1's who put thorns on his head/ And wish him dead while they took his daily bread/ Which 1 is of value 2 u?/ The 1 depleting the oil supply/ Or the One that renews it/ And keeps the peace/…
>
> Who will be a guest in Ur tent?/ R U gonna be happy with how Ur life has been spent?/ Did U have open arms 4 each and everybody U met?/ Or did U let them die in the rain?/ Endless war, poverty, or hurricane/ Then it's time 4 another groove."

From 1978's <u>For You</u> to 2005's "SST," Prince has been constant in his belief that love will save us. His definition of love may have changed over the years, but whose definition of love and success does not change during the transition from childhood to adulthood? And this continues to be the beauty and power of his work. He is an artist who continues to challenge himself to grow and evolve, which causes an evolution in all that he contacts.

Poets' Praises for Prince

This following chapter represents two years of conversations, dialogues, and interviews that I have had with various poets who have an admiration for Prince as a poet. I decided to add this chapter because it is important to note that so many African American poets, from so many backgrounds and generations, testify to some amount of influence that Prince has had on their life or on their work. All but one of these writers are African American, and it can be easily seen through all of their testimonies that Prince has been a major force in putting the diversity of African American identity at the forefront of American popular culture. Additionally, he is also a master lyricist whose work runs the spectrum in its ability to inspire other poets. In these very edited forms, I tried to capture their deep respect for Prince as well as the passion that each of these writers have for his work. I must admit that it continues to be a joy, traveling the country, finding other African Americans who are as moved by Prince's work as I am. It is clearly evident that Prince is an artist whose work belongs to the great canon of African American art. Further, his work has played a significant role in helping to define African American art and its aesthetic. What is central in this chapter is not just that these are published writers, but that they are writers with diverse backgrounds who can still be linked or connected by the work of Prince. That, for me, is the greatest testament that I can give a writer. That is the testament that I want to make of Prince's work.

Tony Medina

Medina is the author of <u>Emerge and See</u>, <u>No Noose Is Good Noose</u>, <u>Sermons from the Smell of a Carcass Condemned to Begging</u>, <u>Memories of Eating</u>, and co-editor of <u>Catch a Fire</u> and <u>In Defense of Mumia</u>. Born in the South Bronx, he now lives in Harlem. You can find him there or traipsing the globe in search of common sense and compassion as he lectures, reads poetry, and engages audiences with dialogue. He also teaches English at Long Island University in downtown Brooklyn.

The year was 1984 and Prince's "When Doves Cry," as well as the rest of the <u>Purple Rain</u> album, grabbed me. My uncle, Reynard (R.I.P.) had the album, and I played it constantly and saw the film a thousand times. Although his music was my initial love, songs like "Erotic City" and "Irresistible Bitch" made me notice his lyrical prowess. I just liked his unique approach to issues that others were handling so mundanely. I would place him along side Stevie Wonder—on top of the list—for being the most prolific and having the most range. I admire any artist who is continuously searching. Prince represents a sort of all encompassing college aesthetic. Like a sponge, he is absorbing all that has come before him as well as what his contemporaries are creating and spewing it out through his multifaceted range. His constant search and need to grow cause people with limited knowledge and short attention spans to complain about his current work, wanting him to duplicate <u>Purple Rain</u> or <u>Sign "☮" the Times</u>, but they do not understand that he is constantly in movement—forward. Still his influence is undeniable. Just listen to people like Lenny Kravitz and D'Angelo to name a few.

His unique and metaphoric approach to sex is one of his most appealing traits. With Prince, or with Dolt Lawrence, sex is spiritual, a way to connect to one's higher being. It is clear that he loves and worships women. He is also lustful and loves to be nasty. But we must not allow that to overshadow the importance of love and spirituality in his work. Sex cannot be divorced from either. In fact, it is a natural extension of both, of our search for a higher place.

    Because of his lyrical approach, Prince leaves the door open for some interesting possibilities in popular culture. Imagine if Prince were to infuse his musical lyrics with a more revolutionary message, one that alludes to the sentiment he expressed about his former record company when he carved "slave" into the shadow of his beard, branding himself and other artists as nothing more than mere chattel to the record companies. Imagine him extending what he did lyrically on <u>Sign "☮" the Times</u>, expanding into the twenty-first century of mergers, downsizing, and disease. He is definitely a poet of his times, marking the beat of direction and pointing those who come after him to a higher creation of art.

Dr. Preselfannie Whitfield McDaniels

McDaniels is a professor of English at Jackson State University where her area is American Literature with an emphasis in African American Literature. She has also published several articles and given many lectures on the issue of "mothering" in African American literature.

My first realization of the power of Prince's lyrics to move people was when my mom slapped me in the mouth as I unwittingly sang the lyrics to "Darling Nikki," including the words "masturbate" and "grind" with perfect pronunciation. What amazed me was Prince's ability to talk about sex in a perfectly normal manner, as if it were not taboo subject matter, and get a rise out of people. Since then, "When Doves Cry" and "Sometimes it Snows in April" have always stayed with me. Not for their literal meaning, but for their symbolic richness. Not many are able to paint pictures as vividly as Prince.

His new theme of the religious is a non-threatening mode of expression, but it grows out of his career long struggle and search for the higher meaning of his life and his art. It is good that he is able to stick to his artistic guns, showing younger artists that what is most important is not how much money you make but the artistic legacy that you leave. In doing this his work becomes timeless. His timelessness and time spent as an artist make him one of the great ones, definitely. Also, his hard work allows many other African Americans to stretch out and evolve in different areas. He added so many facets to the entertainment business—music, movies, poetry, fashion, art. Unfortunately, when an African American fights against being limited or controlled, they are often viewed as giving up black sensibilities or selling out. In Prince's case, I do not look at it as an orchestrated attempt. Hey, he grew up in Minneapolis/St. Paul. Having lived there for two summers, I realized that his racial environment was quite different from any place else in the country.

I also feel that because of the hype, the imagery, and the sex metaphor, people are missing what is really great about Prince, which is his artistic mastery of several genres. Sure, sex is definitely a metaphor in that body of work, but not to a great, great extent. There is so much more that needs to be explored. Most importantly, Prince has continued to keep growing. His range of topics have broadened, and his spiritual message is permeating most of his work.

Dr. David Cornberg

Cornberg is a writer, painter, actor, and teacher. His latest work is a collaborative translation from Chinese to English of a book of contemporary Taiwan fiction, <u>Four Fables</u>, with the author, the Taiwan writer and artist, Do She-Sun. Cornberg also supplies the introduction to the book. It is available in paperback from amazon.com.

I remember seeing his picture and being struck by his boyish sensuality. Then I read a short bio of him and learned that he played six or eight instruments before he was ten years old. I was very impressed that he had such talent and that he had chosen to express it in pop music. As a semiotician, I was more interested in the signs and signals he made with his body, his clothing, his guitar, and the settings of his videos than I was in his words. I remember one time I was the poet in residence for the Anchorage School District in Anchorage, Alaska. I was sharing house-sitting duties with a teacher from a high school in which I was doing many poetry workshops in English classrooms. The teacher was female, and she and I happened to be watching TV together when a brief clip of Prince came on. This was around 1985. She made some disgusted sounds, shook her head several times, and then more or less growled. The content of her growl was that she knew many girls at the high school thought Prince was very sexy, but she could not see why. I looked at Prince who was flashing big bright dark eyes, a slender, smooth chest exposed by an unbuttoned shirt, and a smile of gorgeous white teeth all in rhythm with a very good beat and a seductive voice. I thought to myself that I could not see why girls would not find him sexy.

Lyrically, the most significant message, theme, or issue of Prince's work is you be who you are, who you wanna be, or who you just put on, and then take the consequences. What is interesting is that he used his body, literally, as a way to aid in the articulation of that message. This relates directly to his generation, the eighties generation. In the past African Americans had this type of collective feel. Prince was demanding that we view them individually and on their own individualistic terms. This is me. This is who I am and what I do. If you do not like it, vote with your fingers and turn it off or change the channel.

I think that McInnis is right in asserting that Prince is doing something unique by using sex as a metaphor if only because the meaning of any poet/singer/writer's work is a negotiation between that person and an audience. There is no way that anything even close to sex as content would have only one meaning. He was driven to the top, and sex was one of the cars.

I think that his adoption of a symbol is a brilliant move in a world increasingly accustomed to scanning surfaces and making rapid decisions about acceptance or rejection.

Mark Rockeymoore

Rockeymoore is a poet/fiction writer and a member of the online workshop group de Griot Space.

In 1982, in a record store in Spokane, Washington the song, "Controversy," was playing, and I wondered who he was. The song was a revelation. I had to find out who he was, although I did not purchase the album at that time. As I got more into his work, I began to perceive Prince as a songwriter with interesting and thought provoking lyrics. "The Ladder," "Thieves in the Temple," "The Arms of Orion," and too many others to name all have a poetic quality about them. You can hear the poet in the work. His most significant message became sex is not a sin, love is not a sin, and God and sex can exist comfortably within the same mindset. In doing this, he was removing some of the dogmatism and sexism from sex, which popular music often has because of its male dominated playlist. This was very liberating. Because of his unique approach and liberating work, he ranks a ten. Prince is top of the line because he refused to give into the repression of the 80s: the concentration on greed. Prince's message was the opposite of all of that. He spoke to the heart, trying to move his listeners past the physical and into a deeper or higher realm. However, his vision and his ability to stick to that vision, regardless of economic gains, became a double edged sword for him in the African American community. There is respect for his resolve but a lack of understanding of his spiritual side. He is seen as a brotha, but not the average brotha.

Most importantly, Prince's work and songs about sex were more than physical gratification. It was an expression of the love that he feels for women as a whole and the soul mate concept in particular. I also believe that he was and is dealing with his own issues with regard to sex. The manner in which he amalgamates sex and spirituality was a synthesis that he was in the process of making real in his own life. With his marriage to Mayte, perhaps he has come to some resolution. His work has moved, evolved from the salvation in the physical to salvation through human connection. In doing this he has evolved as an artist. He can make hits whenever he wants, but he does what he wants and follows his artistic muse. In that sense he has continued his tradition of autonomy from record labels and public opinion, practicing artistic self-determination as championed by the writers of the Black Arts Movement.

Dr. Chezia Thompson-Cager

Thompson-Cager is director of Spectrum of Poetic Fire: A Reading Series at Maryland Institute College of Art, where she teaches. A 1999 recipient of the Maryland State Arts Council Individual Artists Award in Poetry and the 1996 winner of the Artscape Poetry competition for Power Objects, she has published three poetry books: Power Objects, Jumpin' Rope on the Axis, and The Presence of Things Unseen: Giant Talk. Her work also appears in the anthologies, Catch a Fire, Dark Eros, Moving Beyond Boundaries, and Thy Mother's Glass. Her journal publications include The Maryland Poetry Review, The Black Arts Quarterly, KOLA (Canada), New Writers (Trinidad and Tobago), Obsidian, LINK, and the BMa: The Sonya Sanchez Literary Review. She is currently editing the new Diva Squad Poetry Collective anthology When Divas Laugh to be released with their tour in 2001.

I spent a lot of time with Prince's first album when it came out. I was amazed by his range of talent, as well as his lyrical imagery. He was clearly working in a poetic tradition. Even in the beginning, I could see that he was playing with androgynous imagery. His lyrics are very intellectual, beyond the norm of bump and grind rock lyrics or sing me up and down blues lyrics—both of which I like. His work has a way of making you think. His work changed my life as a young teacher and gave me a deeper understanding of my whole humanity. That is—if Prince had in fact effectively harnessed his feminine side, then I could and should acknowledge and harness my male side to enhance myself and my work. The predominant idea being it would make me a stronger woman without making me less feminine in any way. It was a novel idea thirty years ago.

Unlike many others before him, Prince makes a conscious attempt to ignore contextual reality. He does not allow contemporary context to define his capabilities...For Africans in the American part of the Diaspora, color still defines who we are, what we can say and where we can go socially and economically. Acculturation into mainstream society is still the measurement for access to privilege, status, and visibility. Prince appears to make a conscious effort to transcend that bondage, taking a more global approach to his aesthetic, than the limited national one that is prescribed by American mainstream puppeteers.

Prince's greatest strength is that he is willing to deal with both collective and individual issues. He politicizes the personal in a way that sets up a dialogue about racism, sexism, incest, millennium madness, love and happiness, family etc. He is a genius when it comes to dealing with topics that no one wants to touch in commercial song.

I believe this willingness to challenge status quo ontology through musical innovation is connected to a concept of claiming both parts of his sensuality. You have some people out there talking about getting in touch with their feminine or masculine selves but not in the manner that he is doing. Prince has crossed arbitrary boundaries between male and female costuming and performance. In doing this, he has freed himself to merge aesthetic elements in new ways to make bold statements on a range of subjects.

Some African Americans may have a problem with this, which goes back to their being uncomfortable with the incredible Little Richard and the whole *gender bender thang*. It speaks somehow to the vulnerability of African American men, at risk for being systemically emasculated over and over again because the driving element of the disenfranchisement strategy is sexual dominance and the need to escape by getting high off a variety of things. What they seem to miss is that Prince is not talking about celebrating homo-erotica. Rather, he is talking about becoming more in touch with our humanity, breaking down and moving past those arbitrary walls and rules which confine our individual genius and make us act like non-humans.

In American history, recent and past, the black body has been the symbol of oppression. Through an artful engagement with sexual cliché and sexual acts, Prince forces the American mainstream to face its own hypocrisy about sex, the Atlantic Slave Trade, and the true nature of Democracy. He keeps my attention with his growth and evolution. Over time, his work has become less angry, especially after his marriage. He deals with black issues in a more direct manner, instead of being cloaked...Most importantly, his work refutes the notion that black men and black women have some sort of innate conflict with each other and cannot successfully form families and extended communities. This is because his work has for years seemed to empower African American women, through a discussion about all kinds of women. He connects with us: how we function in the world. We are endowed with a sense of personal power from his work.

I would love to do an *original opera* with Prince...something that would move into the area of literature and music in a different way than X or Treemonisha, T. S. Eliot, or Langston Hughes. Prince is the ultimate balance of music and lyrics through the development of a narrative voice and a consistent source of "high drama..." Almost every song he writes is a perfect dance between the music and lyrics. It would be great to do a poetry reading with just him so that you could hear the lyricism outside the sheer power of the music. (This would also work with Tracy Chapman, Dylan Thomas, Nina Simone but not many other musicians. The writing would not be strong enough.) He is a blessing and a bard for a new age that rocks...axe.

Saul Williams

Williams is cited as one of the leading figures in the rise of spoken word/performance poetry during the nineties. He co-wrote and starred in the Cannes and Sundance award-winning film, <u>Slam</u>. He has also been featured in the documentaries <u>Slam Nation</u>, <u>Underground Voices</u>, and <u>I'll Make Me a World</u>. He is the author of <u>The Seventh Octave</u> and <u>She</u>.

I have always seen Prince as an artist with important and thought provoking lyrics. My favorite album is <u>Parade</u> from the <u>Under the Cherry Moon</u> film. "Sometimes It Snows in April" is just beautiful on several levels, lyrically, metaphorically, and just the pure beauty of the imagery. There is also a lot of good stuff on <u>Around the World in a Day</u>. That album is also multilayered. "Condition of the Heart," again, speaks to so many issues of romantic love. Prince is an amazing writer, an amazing poet. One of my favorite Prince lyrics is "No one plays the clarinet the way you play my heart." That's a very simple and yet complex notion about the ironic nature of romantic relationships. Of course Prince is a poet. There is just a natural connection between song writing and writing poetry. There is a natural evolution that occurs. Most songwriters, if they write long enough, will eventually begin to write poetry, and most poets will eventually write songs. I know that has been the process for me. And even the acoustic stuff that he has recently done on <u>Crystal Ball</u> shows his evolution as a poet/writer, stripping down the music and giving more detail and emphasis to the lyrics.

Prince's use of the sex metaphor is dynamic. He shows how sex has always been used to tap into something deeper in our lives, moving beyond the mere physical gratification that it supplies. Prince shows us how people use sex to fill holes and voids in their lives. Also, his work gives insight to the emotional skills that it really takes to navigate the complications of our sexualities and other love making issues. His ability to express this and make others feel connected to this is amazing.

The greatest thing that is happening with Prince now is how he is allowing African Americans to feel a real kinship with him, not necessarily through his new work, but just by getting out more and mingling more. It is important that African Americans get to see him referring to himself as black. For him to be at a Q-Tip release party is important. He is making both racial, artistic, and generational links that are important to the legacy of African American art. It was important for him to establish himself and not be controlled so that he could do the work that he wanted, but it is also important that African Americans are now able to lay claim to that body of work as ours. That is important to our artistic spectrum. That diversity is important for young people coming along and looking at the blueprint of black art and having his work as one of the choices from which to choose. His work/career says something meaningful and wonderful about African American diversity, and that is important on a socio-cultural level.

Askhari

Askhari's work has been published in Essence, In the Tradition, Testimony, Sex and the Single Girl (forthcoming), Black Issues Book Review, Catalyst, Rap Pages, and Urban Profile. She is currently editing Convictions, an anthology of black prison writings (www.Askhari.com), and is the moderator of de Griot Space, an online writing workshop (www.deGriotSpace.com).

Sure, i dig Marvin Gaye and Donny Hathaway, but Prince was my first. Even though my mother told me he was nasty, i let him in my bedroom. i put a big poster of Prince on my ceiling so that i could lay under him, look up at him, admire him.

They say, and i believe that image is everything. Well, not everything, but...well...Prince has image. What he writes, wears and does—what goes into making him "Prince" seduced the child, the teenager, and then the woman in me into feeling liberated. Who else can put on a g-string and sing about God?

Prince challenged us (his audience), challenged himself, and set himself up as an entity away and apart from the mainstream. When he transformed his name into an unpronounceable symbol, i shouted "right on" and "hell yeah!" The artist was not going to be the industry's slave. He was going to be true to himself, not us, the fans, not the people who buy his CDs, not the record company, but himself. Was it slightly selfish?—yes. So what? We have to learn to respect those of us who struggle against oppression, whether we understand that particular brand of oppression or not.

It wasn't just image. His music made something still unnamable in me move. i could see, via his work, the movements of a man, an artist, struggling with life and with the inevitable challenges of growth. He rarely, if ever, sings a song the same way twice. But, it never bothered me that i could spend hours memorizing all the words to his songs and then go to an concert and not even recognize the songs because he had morphed the music into something different. This excited me, inflated me into a lover: not of Prince, but of music.

Many artists are either very lyrical or very musical. To say Prince is both is not to do him justice. Prince plays approximately twenty-seven instruments, writes most of his own music, and seeks out his own musicians. He is a musician, not a singer, or just a performer, but a musician. He cares about the auditory experience of his audience. But, he didn't just try and touch us with music—he also used words.

He was my first favorite poet. i would read his album inserts like books, inspiration to write rising by the word. i mean if "Adore" is not a poem, if "The Ballad of Dorothy Parker" and "Sometimes it Snows in April" are not poems, if "When 2 R in Love," "Nothing Compares 2 U," and "Old Friends 4 Sale" are not poems, then somebody please tell me—what qualifies as poetry?

And you know what? The first time i had sex—a Prince song was playing. For years, when i wanted to get it on, i would have to listen to Prince songs with brief intermittent performances by Marvin Gaye. Prince's music made me feel righteously freaky. Prince made me feel free to search for sexual satisfaction with songs like "Head," "Soft and Wet," "Hot Thing," "Slow Love," "International Lover," and the indomitable "Do Me Baby." i started wearing really expensive lingerie because Prince surrounded himself with sexy and potently poised women who could make lace sing. He had female musicians and writers before it was fashionable, which for me, as a young person, was new. i can honestly say his musical manhood helped me shape my sexual and gender identity.

Prince makes me think. Each piece of music is always a metaphor for something larger. See, there is this thing going on now that, for me, is the dumbing down of music. People don't want to think. They don't want poetry. They are looking for something that rhymes and has a good beat. They give it a ten just because they can dance to it.

Prince is not just my first, but my only. Sure, i dig D'Angelo, but there will never be another artist who enters the collection of my spirits in the way that Prince did—rowdily, righteously, and with rhythm. i will not allow the others who call themselves artists to influence me in the way that he did. Nothing compares to him. The majority of the artists today do not have the range, the desire, or the courage. Sign "☮" the Times, [i guess]...

Umar Bin Hassan
of The Last Poets

The Last Poets are rappers of the Civil Rights era. They took their name from a poem by South African poet, Willie Kgositsile, who posited the necessity of putting aside poetry in the face of looming revolution. The Last Poets are modern day griots expressing the nation-building fervor of the Black Panthers in poems written for black people. Amiri Baraka proclaims, "The Last Poets are the prototype Rappers..." They teach what America does to its black men, what black men do to themselves, and WHY! Their classic poems "Niggers are scared of Revolution," "This is Madness," "When the Revolution Comes," and "Gashman" were released on their two record albums, Last Poets (1970) and This Is Madness (1971). Hassan continues to write, publish, and lecture all across the globe. (This bio can be found at The Last Poets Website, http://www.math.buffalo.edu/~sww/LAST-POETS/last_poets0.html, which is coordinated by Snally Gibson.)

    I love Prince both as a musician and a lyricist. He is probably the greatest musician who has ever lived. And because he understands the intricate and delicate balance between music and lyrics, I would love to work with that brother. I would go somewhere in the woods for a month, close myself off from any disturbance, just to write for his music. I really don't want to go back into the studio because of the way that the Last Poets have been treated by the industry, but Prince is one of the few people who could make me reconsider. One thing about Prince is that his lyrics are often about real life. No matter how you feel about it, it's honest but yet artistic. By doing this he makes people face a lot of things about themselves, especially their sexuality, and that makes people uncomfortable. Also, I love how he has made his battle with Warner Bros public. This is another tragic event in African American culture and art. But usually, big name stars are reluctant to take on the industry for fear of losing the crumbs supplied by the industry. So Prince is not only important artistically, he is also important in a socio-economic context. He has taken that energy and spirit of liberation and freedom in his art and made it a real and tangible thing.

The same thing that they did to Prince is what was done to the Last Poets and so many others. Prince is using himself as a red light to other young, black artists. When one of the greatest artists of our times gets dogged by his record label, it speaks volumes to our continuing struggle for first-class citizenship and artistic freedom and growth. I love his statement when he talks about how difficult it is to work for someone who doesn't like you. He said that I know that they don't like me, and that they didn't like me. That's a feeling that most African American artists have. We all have worked under that umbrella at some point of our lives, and it is stifling to your art and to your growth. How would you like to go to work everyday and work for someone who doesn't like you and is still going to exploit you because of your talent, and exploit you more than he would his white employees? It is not the same thing as suffered by white artists. When a white owned record company does not like its black artists, it is a deeply rooted cultural thing, not some artistic differences bullshit. You know that they don't like you because you are black and something that you are doing is offensive to their white sensibilities, which is deeper than their artistic sensibilities, so the treatment is different. Hell, black people in general go through this, not just black artists. You have to get out from under that or you will go crazy. Unfortunately, too many of our artists are not able to get from under that umbrella until it is too late, until they have internalized that inferiority or fear that stifles them forever.

Conclusion

Prince can truly be described as a renaissance man: a man with a song for all occasions and emotions, whose primary vision is to create work that makes us better. Though not mainstream, Prince has managed to touch people from all walks of life, providing us with a different way of looking at people, times, cultures, and situations, bringing generations closer together through music and literature. The fact that there were over ten different fanzines and fan websites in five different languages dedicated to him is evidence of his ability to transcend cultures and identities to touch lives. His name change to an unpronounceable symbol, ☥, only symbolizes his continuing attempt to grow as a person and an artist. So, where do we go from here with ☥, especially since he has now re-taken his name of Prince? What shall we expect next of him? These are questions that those who have listened to Prince over the years have grown not to feel a need to ask. The experience of something new is all they await. Prince has taken those who want to go on an emotional and thought-provoking trip that somehow never seems to end and is constantly expanding itself. Creative creativity probably best describes Prince's work. He truly believes that it is his obligation to create and broaden our realms of thought and experiences. And, Prince has done this without losing the ability to make us dance and feel romantic.

The question is often asked, "Why write of the lyrics and subject matter of Prince?" The formal academies of the twentieth century are still looking beyond the realm of popular culture for greatness and motivation. Too often, those who exist in the realm of popular culture, who truly have their fingers on the pulse of the society, are ignored or pushed aside by the academic scholars. There is a notion by academic scholars of the form being more valuable than the subject matter or the effect of the work on the buying public. And since those artists who create in the realm of popular culture are not primarily concerned with the rigid accountability to form or scholarly documentation, popular artists are considered as secondary to artists concerned with form and academic/scholarly criticism. Thus, the area of literature has continued to be controlled by middle-class whites and aristocratic blacks of the academy, spurting conservatism and Eurocentric dominance. We are still writing back to a Eurocentric center. Even our Afrocentrism is reactionary in that too many of these scholars have a problem celebrating the accomplishments of African Americans who are not cloaked in their narrow banner of Afrocentrism. Gone are the thoughts, emotions, diversity, and lives of the common man, i.e. the community folk found in McKay's <u>Home to Harlem</u> or Shakespeare's groundlings. It has been the medium of popular music that has produced our modern day writers and poets of the people. Artists such as Dylan, Hendrix, War, Smokey Robinson, Prince, Parliament-Funkadelic, The Last Poets, Stevie Wonder, Public Enemy, 2Pac, and Arrested Development stepped forward and filled the voids. The noted critic and poet Larry Neal asserts "James Brown is the best poet we got baby" (Cook and Henderson 80). Even the legendary Bob Dylan called Smokey Robinson "America's greatest poet." In his paper, "Tight Rhymes, Phat Beats, and Loose Canons: Rap Music's Inclusion in African American Literature," Will Crawford asserts that a key ingredient which led to raps dramatic rise in the eighties was the silencing of the African American male voice by the large publishing houses. Popular music became one of the few mediums where one would be able to hear the almost uncensored concerns of young, African American men. Yet, as Baraka asserts, popular music has always been a medium which gives voice to African Americans. With this decline in mainstream publishing of creative and edgy literature from African American male writers, popular music began to fill the void. Further, very few in any medium were having the discussions that Prince was having about African American individuality, the struggle to reconcile one's individual identity to one's racial identity, and the need to prioritize this struggle in the context of evolving into a higher life form. And in the popular music of the early and mid-eighties, Prince's voice was one of the few grappling with what it means to be a post-Civil Rights Negro, living under the illusion of successful integration. As such, popular culture becomes the only medium that would allow an artist such as Prince the freedom to grow and evolve without the rigid constraints of race, gender, and class that are commonly found in the formal areas.

Since the early twenties, popular music has been one of the major mediums, connecting the mass populous of America. Wonder affirms that "Music is a world within itself; it's a language we all understand" (Wonder, "Sir Duke," Songs in the Key of Life, 1976). Though this language is universal in that it deals with the emotions common to all of humanity, its true power lies in its particularity—the beats, the rhythms, and the topics originate in distinct cultures. The beauty is the ability of an artist to take his particular language/existence and provide us with a way to identify with and express ourselves to others who are outside our particular reality or existence. Prince's work became the voice of the othered: in its particular and universal connotation, and it inspired me and others to search for our place in this universe. Initially, his work (his lyrics) is speaking for a very small segment of society—middle-class African Americans who see themselves stuck between a racial identity and an individual identity, trying desperately to reconcile the two and achieve self-fulfillment and self-actualization. Yet, it is his music, his perfect blending of a history and legacy of sounds, which bridges the cultural and generational gaps and connects this small segment of society to the entire society. Along with the music, he borrows lyrical imagery from the past to make his message seem more palatable and familiar. This bridge, however, is a double-edged sword. It is positive in that it shows our innate humanity of needing to be and belong. It is a negative because mass acceptance tends to dilute the message to make it more palatable to the masses. A phrase, such as "All you need is love," becomes so bland that it loses its power to move the masses to become better by embracing human diversity. Thus, when Prince asserts, "We're all just the same; don't you wanna play?" it loses its power and becomes merely a cliché. Additionally, the beauty and power of art is corrupted when the language is co-opted and commodified merely for economic gain. Art, by its very nature, will make or break a society. When an artist creates, he is making one of two statements: I like my culture, and I want to celebrate it; or, there are some problems within my culture that we need to discuss. If black art is an innate, organic production of the black condition in America, it must, then, comment on the black socio-political condition. This commentary, this art, is designed, by its very nature, to destroy or, in the least, wail against whatever is oppressing the artist. Unfortunately, white record owners have created a way to take the emotional power of black music and strip it of its social commentary through economic bribes. The popular music artist labors under the same struggles and temptations as other black artists. As Hughes asserts, "'Be stereotyped, don't go too far, don't shatter our illusions about you, don't amuse us too seriously. We will pay you,' say the whites'" (Gates and McKay 1270). For the exchange of money, black artists working in the popular realm are often forced to pay attention to sales first and craft later.

Ironically, Wonder's <u>Songs in the Key of Life</u> opened the door to these bribes. Never before had an African American artist dominated artistically, economically, and culturally like Wonder did. Indeed, white artist winning awards such as Grammies began thanking Wonder for not releasing an album so that others would have an opportunity to win (to gain financial accomplishments). Yet, for all of his success, Wonder continued to see himself as a black artist, firmly rooted in the traditional sense of being a griot, providing voice and identity for his people. However, his success opens the eyes of both the recording industry and black artists to the potential for economic gain by black artists. Wonder's economic success parallels the new economic opportunities for a new generation of African Americans attending white universities on the heels of the Black Student Movement. Because of these new economic opportunities, by 1975 success in the Civil Rights Movement was being equated with material and economic gain because of the growing black middle class. African American artists coming after Wonder's triumph are merely trying to duplicate his economic success and not duplicate the nature in which his work is a talking book for his people. Interestingly enough, this same cycle or phenomenon happens just ten years later with N.W.A.'s <u>Straight out of Compton</u>. On the one hand, <u>Straight out of Compton</u> is a lighthouse for a new mode of self and collective expression for the African American community. It resonates the pain and anger of the African American community. It is a record written by black people, for black people, and to black people. Unfortunately, its success makes it another material/artifact to be co-opted by white America, refashioned and resold, removing the intellectual power so that it becomes more palatable to white America. Now, the success of a black artist is not that his work gives voice to his particular segment of society but how many units he sells.

    The first artist to test the waters of the Stevie Wonder's success is Michael Jackson. Jackson's brother, Jackie, recounts a story when he catches M. Jackson in the mirror just before the release of <u>Thriller</u>. M. Jackson is before a mirror with twenty-five million written on the mirror. As J. Jackson passes his brother in the mirror, he hears his younger sibling say, "I'm going to sell twenty-five million records." Fearing for his brother's disappointment, the older brother attempts to bring his younger brother back to reality. "No Michael, no one sells twenty-five million records. You *might* sell ten, fifteen maybe, but not twenty-five." J. Jackson then adds to this story, still in disbelief, "He sold forty million records!" So although the influence of African American music on American mainstream popular music had been recognized, the artists themselves do not realize their economic power until Thriller. Thriller changes the game. Jackson takes what Little Richard's career merely hints and transforms the African American artist into a type of star phoneme never before imagined or realized, to rival that of the Beatles, the Rolling Stones, and Presley. As the old Sun Records owner, Sam Phillips, once stated, "If I could find me a white man who can sing and dance like a black man, I'd be a millionaire." Presley walks into Sun Records, and the rest is history. The rest is history because Phillips was verbalizing the unspoken rule of Jim Crow that saturates the mentality of America: white people will never support a black artist in such a manner that allows him to become one of, if not the most, influential forces of the business unless that black artist is willing to surrender the black sensibilities that are threatening to white America in order to gain economic rewards.

In the primal depths of their souls, the mass of the white society understands that to validate black music is to validate black intellect and the struggles of black people, which acknowledges white culture as the antagonist of this struggle. Because of this, black music has to be whitewashed so that the rhythms are made palatable to a larger white audience. Therefore, rigid categories are created so that white acts can interpret black music in a manner that a white audience can enjoy the music without the burden of the innate, socio-political commentary. Jackson and Prince represent the fulfillment of Phillips' prophecy. Here are two black men who are well versed in the legacy and history of black music but are also looking for a way to transcend their perceived restrictions of race. However, Jackson and Prince are merely the apex, not the beginning. This racial liquefying begins when popular music begins, because music categories are drawn as much along the lines of race as musical style. That is why all black music, gospel or secular, is initially called "race records." Wonder's success is merely the proof that white record owners need to affirm that the time is now right to exploit black music for all that it is worth. A white act doing black music is merely that—a white act doing black music. And as with all languages, something is lost in transition. Pat Boone is cool, but he ain't Little Richard. At some point the white record owner needs a black artist who can carry the power of black music to a larger white audience. The commercial and cultural success of <u>Songs in the Key of Life</u> hints that the time is possibly near. The companies just need someone a little less black. Michael Jackson is perfect. He was a child prodigy of black music who understands and accepts the notion that a black artist must "crossover" to be considered an American success. With the success of <u>Thriller</u>, every major company wants their own Michael Jackson phenomenon. Warner Bros thought that it had its clone in Prince.

Ironically, Prince is in many ways a blessing and a headache for everyone: Warner Bros, the music industry, and the white and black patrons. He is a blessing in that he is a musician, which Jackson is not. He is a blessing in that he sees himself as heir to the entire legacy of American music and thought. These aspects allow him to create a more diverse and creative form than Jackson. Prince sees music as a form that can both capitalize on and influence social thought and progress. However, he is a headache because he addresses his personal artistic and cultural goals before he addresses the artistic and cultural goals of the company or any particular race or segment of society. Ironically, this is initially an asset for Warner Bros, which is able to pimp and exploit this ideology by selling Prince as a special Negro who is palatable to a white audience. Yet later it becomes a headache for them because Prince refuses to play by their rules. Wanting to be more than just a commodifiable form, Prince wants to do the music of his spirit, regardless of the commercial ramifications. This also means releasing more music than the Warner Machine has allotted for its assembly line system. Although his goals greatly influence the music, his ideology is also a double-edged sword for African Americans. On the one hand he is refuting the limitations placed on black artists by expanding or, in the least, articulating the diversity of African Americans. In this case, he does embody the ideology of Sly Stone and Jimi Hendrix. On the other hand, his isolationist attitude causes him, initially, to separate himself from African Americans, causing them to perceive him as another brother who sells out for the economic gains. With all of this, Prince is a form/category buster, sacrificing much to do what he wants to do. As journalist Steve Perry asserts, Prince should be given the most credit for keeping the doors of possibilities open to all musicians.

Just after the end of the 60s, music becomes pigeonholed and stagnated, which allows companies to create music for high volume consumption. Corporate rock and disco help redraw the musical lines along race that Motown, Hendrix, and Stone had worked to destroy. Form was driving and killing the quality and integrity of popular music in much the same manner as with the white teen idols of the late 50s. There was not much thought nor creativity being put into much of the music or lyrics. There were mostly syncopated and synthesized sounds to emulate what was selling. Thus, there were not many strong, statement making or individualized albums like Wonder's or a few others being produced during the seventies. Musically, the seventies become a party going nowhere with white record owners reaping high rewards by legalizing black beats and rhythms for white listeners. At the same time, there is a growing counter-culture of white acts who are taking, refashioning, and recontextualizing rock-n-roll so that it speaks exclusively to their concerns and is almost devoid of its black roots by the time the eighties roll around. By the time we get to the eighties, rock-n-roll has been firmly established as white music. At the same time, there are acts like Madonna who sell first to radio as a black act, and then video allows her to sell her white face. By 1980, black artists in popular music had been boxed, narrowed, and limited like never before. Michael Bolton and George Michael become the leading R&B acts of the late eighties. This co-opting and commodifying of black music continues to go in cycles with everyone benefiting from this amalgamation of cultures except black artists. The same happens again in almost an identical fashion with Mariah Carey ten years after Madonna. Yet before Madonna and Carey can gain their success, Jackson and Prince have to become the final pieces in the puzzle in the periodical trend of the whitening of black music, which occurs every ten years or so. Ten years after Carey, we have 'Nsync, the Backstreet Boys, and Brittany Spears. Black people invent it, and white people commodify it because race still disallows large numbers of whites to accept black music on a cultural and intellectual level, except when that music is devoid of any socio-political commentary that truly challenges the white power structure.

Prior to this latest whitewashing trend of the late nineties, Prince steps into the picture in 1978, bringing his different and indefinable sound, demolishing the walls of limitations on music and ideas. His daringness throughout the eighties brings immeasurable changes and opens doorways for greater discoveries of individuality in music, making him a leader and catalyst of the eighties. Prince's attempts are to reverse the trend of boxing black artists. Instead of having white acts doing black music, Prince is a black act fighting to play the spectrum of music. Even when whitewashing his physical imagery, he hopes that the listeners will hear the resonating black bottom and sounds in his music. He asserts this about <u>Around the World in a Day</u> and <u>Parade</u>, which are seen as crossover records, when he says, "They are very funky records." Then, realizing the power of music, Prince uses this powerful medium to express a plethora of views affecting society. His initial message is that we should view people as souls instead of bodies. Although idealistic, it is also a part of his own plan to be all that he can be. As he evolves, his primary message becomes God is Love, and Love is the only valuable worth obtaining. Yet even with his spiritual message, he never stops fighting for his right to define himself. Secondly, Prince has single-handedly given African Americans the right and opportunity to perform their own music on both a commercial and artistic level. Since the success of Presley, the music industry has divided the music into contrived and controlled playlists, allowing only white artists to succeed in doing several types of music, while black artists have been forced to play in the shadows and fight over the crumbs from the industry. Thus, the African American artist is limited in subject matter as well as musical genre. Prince's entire career has been a showcase of the various dimensions of African American culture, degrees of black, and variations of the blues and jazz. And, he has managed to do this while at the same time telling the stories of his society and creating and establishing his own identity as a person and as a musician/songwriter/entertainer. Prince's career serves to show that African Americans are as diverse as the music they have created through the years. Although both whites and African Americans have been unwilling or hesitant to accept this belief, Prince kept pushing the walls until he freed a mass by first freeing himself. In this sense, he is a griot, even if not in the strictest African connotation. He is a griot in that he is a bard, a teller of stories, and a voice for his times, attempting to plot that voice along the line of culture, change, and history. Fighting for his artistic rights and freedoms as an individual, Prince worked to keep open the doors of diversity and opportunity for his race, ensuring that African Americans are seen as the beautiful bouquet that they are. Prince's actions should be seen as an attempt to fight against the monolithic perception of African Americans, stemming from the equating of Africa, which is a continent, to England, which is a country. When this narrowing and marginalization of Africa occurs, it works to narrow and marginalize the diversity of Africa and her descents. Thus, Prince's chief contribution, along with his music and his lyrics, is his fight to exist within, benefit from, and celebrate the amazing kaleidoscope of African American diversity. His career is as much about identity control and racism as it is about the art that he produces. His fight helps to liquefy and expand the notion of what it means to be black in America and what it means to define oneself. "Peace and be Wild" (⚲ 1995).

Bibliography

Adams, Hazard, ed. Critical Theory Since Plato. Fort Worth: Harcourt Brace Jovanovich College Publishers, 1992.

Adler, Bill. "Will the Little Girls Understand?" Rolling Stone. February 19, 1981: p. 55, 57. (archived at Prince in Print. http://princetext.tripod.com/i_stone81.html.)

Akhenaton. "The Hymn to the Aton." World Literature: An Anthology of Great Short Stories, Drama and Poetry. Lincolnwood: NTC Publishing, 1992.

Albright, Daniel. Modernism and Music: An Anthology of Sources. Chicago: University of Chicago Press, 2004.

Allen, Bonnie. "It's Raining Prince." Essence. Vol. 15, Issue 7. November, 1984.

Allen, Bonnie. "Prince: What U See Is What U Get." Essence. Vol. 19, Issue 7. November, 1988.

Anderson, Jolivette. Past Lives, Still Living: Traveling the Pathways to Freedom. Introduction by Haki Madhubuti. Jackson: SheProphecy Press, 2000.

Ansen, David. "The New Prince of Hollywood." Newsweek. July 23, 1984.

Asante, Molefi Kete and Abu S. Abarry, eds. African Intellectual Heritage: A Book of Sources. Philadelphia: Temple University Press, 1996.

Baldwin, James. The Fire Next Time. New York: Vintage Books, 1962.

Baldwin, James and Margaret Mead. A Rap on Race. New York: Dell, 1971.

Baldwin, James. The Evidence of Things Not Seen. New York: Holt, Rinehart, and Winston, 1985.

Baldwin, James. The Price of the Ticket: Collected Non-Fiction 1948-1985. New York: St. Martin's Press, 1985.

Baldwin, James. James Baldwin: The Price of the Ticket DVD. California Newsreel, 1989.

Bangles, The. "Manic Monday." Different Light. Sony, 1986.

Baraka, Amiri. Blues People. New York: William Morrow & Co, 1983.

Barnet, Sylvan. The Complete Signet Classic Shakespeare. San Diego: Harcourt Brace Jovanovich, 1972.

Baudelaire, Charles. My Heart Laid Bare: Edited with Introduction by Peter Quennell. New York: The Vanguard Press, Inc., 1951.

Bauval, Robert and Adrian Gilbert. The Orion Mystery. New York: Crown Publishers, 1994.

Baumgold, Julie. "Glitter Slave." Esquire Gentleman. Vol. 3, No. 2. Fall, 1995.

Beatles. Sgt. Pepper's Lonely Hearts Club Band. EMD/Capitol, 1967.

Beatles. Yellow Submarine. EMD/Capitol, 1999.

Beatles. The Beatles: 1967-70. EMD/Capitol, 1973.

Belton, Steven L. and Katherine S. Harp. <u>Adoption and Foster Care Placement of Black Children in Minnesota: A Report</u>. St. Paul: The Council of Black Minnesotans, 1982. (Archived at http://archive.leg.state.mn.us/docs/pre2003/other/830094.pdf.)

Benjamin, Walter. <u>Illuminations</u>. New York: Harcourt, Brace, and World, Inc., 1968.

Berry, Chuck. <u>Chess Box: Anthology</u>. UNI/Chess Records, 1988.

Bloom, Steve. "Paint It Black." <u>Soho Weekly News</u>. February, 1980.

Bland, Bobby "Blue" and B. B. King. "Stormy Monday." <u>Live on Beale Street</u>. Malaco, 1998.

Boskamp, Mick. "Interview." May 9, 1981. [Part of this interview was published in <u>Sounds</u> in the article "Posin' 'til Closin'" by Tony Mitchell.]

Braxton, Charlie. "Personal Interview." November, 2000.

Bream, Jon. <u>Prince: Inside the Purple Rain</u>. New York: Collier Books (Macmillan Publishing Company), 1984.

Bream, Jon. "<u>Chaos and Disorder</u> Review." <u>Star Tribune</u>. October 16, 1996. (archived at <u>Star Tribune.com</u>)

Bream, Jon. "♀ Says He's Free at Last." <u>Star Tribune</u>. October 26, 1996. (archived at <u>Star Tribune.com</u>)

Bream, Jon. "New Prince Triple Play: Dance, Maturity, Romance." <u>Star Tribune</u>. November 19, 1996. (archived at <u>Star Tribune.com</u>)

Breitman, George. Malcolm X Speaks. New York: Grove Press, 1965.

Brooks, Gwendolyn. "We Real Cool." Selected Poems. New York: Harper Perennial, 1944, 1963.

Brown, James. Solid Gold: Thirty Golden Hits. Polydor, 1977.

Brown, James with Dave Marsh and Bruce Tucker. James Brown: The Godfather of Soul. New York: Avalon, 1996.

Campbell, Tevin. "Graffiti Bridge Opening Show." Screen Scene. Black Entertainment Television. Fall 1990.

Campbell, Tevin. I'm Ready. Quest Records, 1993.

Car, Roy. "Man of Many Colours'." New Musical Express. September 20, 1986.

Carey, Mariah. "The Beautiful Ones." Butterfly. Sony Music, 1997.

Cesair, Aime. Discourse on Colonialism. New York: Monthly Review Press, 1972.

Charles, Ray. Ray Charles: Genius of Soul. PBS, 1991.

Charles, Ray. The Best of Ray Charles: The Atlantic Years. Rhino, 1994.

Christian, Barbara. Black Feminist Criticism: Perspectives on Black Women Writers. New York: Pergamon Press, 1985.

Clapton, Eric. History of Rock-n-Roll: The Guitar. VH1. 1999.

Clapton, Eric. Behind the Music. VH1. 1999.

Cocks, Jay. "His Highness of Haze." Time. August 6, 1984.

Collins, Bootsy. Back in the Day. WEA/Warner, 1994.

Constantine, Alex. The Covert War Against Rock: What You Don't Know about the Deaths of Jim Morrison, Tupac Shakur, Michael Hutchence, Brian Jones, and Jimi Hendrix. New York: Feral House, 2000.

Cooper, Carol. "Prince: Someday your Prince Will Come." The Face. June 1983. (archived at Rock's Backpages Library. http://www.rocksbackpages.com/article.html?ArticleID=8294)

Cortez, Jayne. "How Long Has Trane Been Gone." The Norton Anthology of African American Literature. New York: W. W. Norton & Company, 1997.

Crawford, Will. "Tight Rhymes, Phat Beats, and Loose Cannons: Rap Music's Inclusion in African American Literature." Presented at the 1999 Jackson State University Black Writers Conference. October 22, 1999.

Cymone, Andre'. "The Dance Electric." A.C. Columbia, 1985.

D'Angelo. "She's Always in My Hair." Scream 2. Capitol Records, 1977.

D'Angelo, Joe. "Billboard Sours on Prince's Musicology Sales Experiment: Magazine changes policy on tallying albums sold with tickets." MTV.com. June, 2004. May 8, 2007. http://www.mtv.com/news/articles/1488027/20040528/story.jhtml.

Dante. "Because You Know You're Young in Beauty Yet." World Literature: An Anthology of Great Short Stories, Drama and Poetry. Lincolnwood: NTC Publishing, 1992.

Dante. The Divine Comedy: The Inferno, Purgatorio, and Paradiso. New York: Alfred A. Knopf, 1994.

D'Arby, Terence Trent. "Interview." 4 on the Floor. VH1. Fall 1995.

Davis, Miles. Miles: The Autobiography. New York: Simon & Simon, 1990.

Davis, Walter. "So You Wanna Be An Avant-Garde Fan?"

Dawkins, Diana. The ☥ Family. Vol. 2, Issue 25. December 10, 1994.

Dawkins, Diana, ed. The ☥ Family. Vol. 4, Issue 5. March 2, 1996.

Dawkins, Diana, ed. The ☥ Family. Vol. 4, Issue 14. July 6, 1996.

Dawkins, Diana, ed. The ☥ Family. Vol. 4, Issue 16. August 3, 1996.

Dawkins, Diana, ed. The ☥ Family. Vol. 4, Issue 17. August 17, 1996

Dawkins, Diana, ed. The ☥ Family. Vol. 4, Issue 22. October 26, 1996.

Dawkins, Diana, ed. The ☥ Family. Vol. 4, Issue 24. November 23, 1996.

Dawkins, Diana, ed. The ☥ Family. Vol. 4, Issue 25.

December 7, 1996.

Dawkins, Diana, ed. The ♀ Family. Vol. 5, Issue 2. January 18, 1997.

Dawkins, Diana, ed. The ♀ Family. Vol. 5, Issue 4. February 15, 1997.

Dawkins, Diana, ed. The ♀ Family. Vol. 5, Issue 16. August 2, 1997.

Dawkins, Diana, ed. The ♀ Family. Vol. 5, Issue 18. August 30, 1997.

Dawkins, Diana, ed. The ♀ Family. Vol. 6, Issue 2. January 17, 1998.

DeCurtis, Anthony. "Free at Last." Rolling Stone. Issue 748. November, 28, 1996: p 61-64. (reprinted by The ♀ Family. Vol. 4, Issue 25 p. 149, and archived at Prince Lyrics.co.uk. http://www.princelyrics.co.uk/viewarticle.asp?article=13)

Diddley, Bo. Chess Box Set. UNI/Chess Records, 1990.

Dickerson, Dez. My Time with Prince: Confessions of a Former Revolutionary. Nashville: Dez Dickerson/ Pavilion Press, 2003.

Douglass, Frederick. Douglass Autobiographies: Narrative of the Life, My Bondage and My Freedom, and the Life and Times. New York: Library of America, 1994.

Duffy, John. Prince: The First Illustrated Biography. London: Omnibus Press, 1992.

Du Bois, W. E. B. Souls of Black Folk. New York: Gramercy Books, 1994.

Durkee, Cutler. "Prince Charming: His Movie's a Smash—in Wyoming." People. Vol. 26, No. 3. July 21, 1986.

E., Sheila. The Glamorous Life. Warner Bros Records, 1984.

E., Sheila. Sheila E in Romance 1600. Paisley Park/Warner Bros Records, 1986.

E., Sheila. "Interview." MTV News. MTV. 1988

E., Sheila. "Prince of Paisley Park." Omnibus. London: BBC Television. 1991.

Easton, Sheena. "Sugar Walls." A Private Heaven. One Way Records, 1984.

Easton, Sheena. "Eternity." No Sound But a Heart. One Way Records, 1987.

Ebiri, Bilge. "Prince: The Y-Live Interview." Yahoo Internet Life. Vol. 7, Issue 6. June, 2001: p 80-85. (archived on Prince in Print. May 10, 2007. http://princetext.tripod.com/ i_yil01.htm.)

"Ebony Gives Insight into Prince and His Love for Privacy and Purple." Jet. October 29, 1984.

Edrei, Mary J, ed. The Year of the Prince. Cresskill: Sharon's Starbook, 1984.

Faber, Jim. "Emancipation." New York Daily News. November 19, 1996.

Fairchild, Michael J. Rock Prophecy: Sex and Jimi Hendrix in World Religions. New York: First Century Press, 1999.

Fanon, Frantz. Black Skin, White Masks. New York: Grove Press, 1991.

Fanon, Frantz. The Wretched of the Earth. New York: Grove Press, 1986.

Farrakhan, Louis. "Press Conference on the Million Man March." BET News. Black Entertainment Television. October, 1995.

Father M. C. "Treat Them Like They Want to Be Treated." Uptown's Block Party: Vol. 1. UNI/Universal Records, 1996.

Finn, Julio. The Bluesman: The Musical Heritage of Black Men and Women in the Americas. New York: Interlink Books, 1992.

Fiore, Raymond. "That's the Ticket: Prince Schemes to Top Billboard Charts." Entertainment Weekly. Issue #770. June 18, 2004. (archived at http://www.ew.com/ew/article/0,,649922,00.html.

Fowlie, Wallace. Rimbaud's Illuminations: A Study in Angelism. New York: Greenwood Press, 1953.

Fudger, David, ed. Prince In His Own Words. New York: Omnibus Press, 1984.

Fuller, Hoyt. "Towards a Black Aesthetic." The Norton Anthology of African American Literature. New York: W. W. Norton & Company, 1997.

Funkadelic. Free Your Mind…And Your Ass Will Follow. Detroit: Westbound, 1971.

Gates, Henry Louis and Nellie Y. McKay, eds. The Norton Anthology of African American Literature. New

York: W. W. Norton & Company, 1997.

Gaye, Marvin. The Master: 1961-1984. PGD/ Motown, 1995.

Gayle, Addison. "Reclaiming the Southern Experience: The Black Aesthetic 10 Years Later." Black Southern Voices. New York: Meridian, 1992.

George, Nelson. "Prince of Paisley Park." Omnibus. London: BBC Television. 1991.

Goldberg, Michael. "Purple Rain Star Morris Day Goes It Alone." Rolling Stone. September 13, 1984.

"Golden Parachute." Wikipedia.com. 2007. May 5, 2007. http://en.wikipedia.org/wiki/Golden_ parachute.

Giddings, Paula. When and Where I Enter. New York: HarperCollins, 2001.

Ginuwine. "When Doves Cry." Ginuwine The Bachelor. Sony/550, 1996.

Graham, Larry. The Best of Larry Graham: Vol. 1. WEA/ Warner Bros, 1996.

Graustark, Barbara. "Prince Talks! Stranger than Fiction." Musician. No. 59. September, 1983.

Green, M. "Prince." People Weekly. August 20, 1984.

Gundersen, Edna. "Prince of Paisley Park." Omnibus. London: BBC Television. 1991.

Gundersen, Edna. "The Artist Is Free...A New Day Dawns." USA Today. Life: D1. November 12, 1996. (archived at USA Today.com)

Gundersen, Edna. "Emancipation Proclamation: Outstanding." USA Today. Life: D1. November 21, 1996. (archived at USA Today.com)

Harris, Trudier. From Mammies to Militants: Domestics in Black American Literature. Philadelphia: Temple University Press, 1982.

Hawthorne, Nathaniel. Scarlet Letter. New York: Penguin, 1983.

Hawthorne, Nathaniel. Selected Tales and Sketches. New York: Penguin, 1987.

Helfer, Andrew. Three Chains of Gold. Paisley Park/Piranha Music/D.C. Comics, 1994.

Hemingway, Ernest. "Hills Like White Elephants." Men Without Women. New York: Scribner, 1997.

Henderson, David. 'Scuse Me While I Kiss the Sky: The Life of Jimi Hendrix. New York: Bantam Doubleday Dell Publishing, 1982.

Henderson, Stephen and Mercer Cook. The Militant Black Writer in Africa and the United States. Madison: University of Wisconsin Press, 1969.

Hendrix, Jimi and Charles S. Murray. Crosstown Traffic: Jimi Hendrix and the Post-War Rock 'n' Roll Revolution. New York: St. Martins Press, 1991.

Hendrix, Jimi. The Ultimate Experience. MCA, 1993.

Hendrix, Jimi and Tony Brown. Jimi Hendrix in His Own Words. New York: Omnibus Press, 2000.

Hendryx, Nona. "Baby Go-Go." Female Trouble. 1987.

Hendryx, Nona. "Baby Go-Go." <u>Transformation: The Best of Nona Hendryx</u>. Razor & Tie Records, 1999.

Hidalgo, Luis. "The Musical Alchemist." <u>El Pais</u>. October 23, 1994. (reprinted in <u>The ⚥ Family</u>, Vol. 2 Issue 25, 149).

Hilburn, Robert. "The Renegade Prince." <u>Los Angeles Times</u>. Calendar Section. November 21, 1982.

Hilburn, Robert. "Mixed Emotions: Prince on the Music." <u>Musician</u>. No. 59. September, 1983.

Hill, Dave. <u>Prince: A Pop Life</u>. London: Faber and Faber. 1989. (New York: Harmony, 1989.)

Hill, Lauryn. "Superstar." <u>The Mis-Education of Lauryn Hill</u>. Sony, 1999.

Hill, Michael. "Prince: Born to Come." <u>New York Rocker</u>. June, 1981.

Hilliard, Asa. "Lecture." Presented at the 1998 Jackson State University International Conference. March, 1998.

<u>Holy Bible (King James Version: Amplified Version)</u>. Grand Rapids: Zondervan Publishing House, 1995.

Hoskyns, Barney. "Prince: A Second Coming Thru Purple Haze." <u>New Musical Express</u>. April 2, 1983. (archived at Rock's Backpages Library. http://www.rocksbackpages.com/article.html?ArticleID=1167.)

Homer. <u>The Iliad and The Odyssey</u>. New York: Barnes and Noble Books, 1999.

Hughes, Langston. "The Negro Artist and the Racial Mountain." The Norton Anthology of African American Literature. New York: W. W. Norton & Company, 1997.

Hunt, Dennis. "A Strange Man Who's Too Hot for Radio." Los Angeles Times, 21 December 1980. (Hunt's article was reprinted in shorter and longer versions in The Tuscaloosa News, December 26, 1980, and the San Francisco Examiner-Chronicle, January 25, 1981. So, technically the time frame is from December 80 to March 81.)

Hurston, Zora Neale. Their Eyes Were Watching God. New York: HarperCollins, 1998.

Husney, Owen. "Personal Interview." November, 2000.

Huxley, Aldous. Brave New World. New York: HarperCollins, 1998.

Jackson, LaToya. "Private Joy." Heart Don't Lie. Epic, 1984.

Jackson, Michael. Thriller. Epic/Sony Music, 1982.

Jackson, Millie. "I Wanna Be Your Lover." An Imitation of Love. Jive, 1997.

James, Rick. Bustin' Out: The Very Best of Rick James. PGD/PolyGram, 1994.

Jensen, Jeff. "Don't Call It a Comeback: The Weird, Wonderful Return of Prince." Entertainment Weekly. Issue #761. April 23, 2004. http://www.ew.com/ew/article/0,,610723_1,00.html

Jones, Jill. Jill Jones. Paisley Park/Warner Bros Records, 1986.

Jones, LeRoi. *Blues People*. New York: William Morrow & Co, 1983.

Jones, Liz. *Purple Reign: The Artist Formerly Know as Prince*. Secaucus: Carol Publishing Group, 1998.

Jones, Tom. "Kiss." *Best of Tom Jones*. PGD/PolyGram TV, 1998.

Kael, Pauline. "The Charismatic Half-And-Halfs." *New Yorker*. September 20, 1984.

Karenga, Maulana. "Black Art: Mute Matter Given Force and Function." *The Norton Anthology of African American Literature*. New York: W. W. Norton & Company, 1997.

Karlen, Neal. "Prince Talks: The Silence Is Broken." *Rolling Stone*. Issue 456. September 12, 1985. pp. 24-30, 84-86.

Karlen, Neal. "Heroes of the Revolution." *Rolling Stone*. Issue 472. April 24, 1986.

Karlen, Neal. "Ladies in Waiting." *Rolling Stone*. Issue 472. April 24, 1986.

Karlen, Neal. "Prince Talks." *Rolling Stone*. Issue 589. October 18, 1990. pp. 56-60, 104.

Karlen, Neal. "Prince of Paisley Park." *Omnibus*. London: BBC Television. 1991.

"Kashif Biography." *Brooklyn Boy Books and Entertainment*. (Online Posting). November, 2000. http://www. brooklynboy.com/bios/kashif.htm.

Kashif. "Personal Interview." November, 2000.

Katz, Larry. "Prince: Vice Is Nice." Boston Real Paper, April 2, 1981. https://sites.google.com/site/prninterviews/home/boston-real-paper-2-april-1981.

Khan, Chaka. "I Feel for You." I Feel for You. Warner Bros, 1984.

Killens, John Oliver and Jerry W. Ward, Jr., eds. Black Southern Voices. New York: Meridian, 1992.

King, Martin L. The Autobiography of Martin Luther King, Jr. Clayborne Carson, ed. New York: Warner Books. 1998.

Knyte, Andrew. "Profiles: Barry Michael Cooper." NJS4E.com. April, 2006. http://www.njs4e.com/bmc-b.html.

Kravitz, Lenny. Behind the Music. VH1. 1999.

Kravitz, Lenny. Rave U2 the Year 2000. NPG/In Demand Pay Per View Network. 1999.

Kreis, Steven. "The Revolt Against the Western Intellectual Tradition: Friedrich Nietzsche and the Birth of Modernism." Pagesz.net. (Online posting). August 8, 2000. September 20, 2000. http://www.pagesz.net/ ~stevek/intellect/lecture25a.htm/. (History Guide.org. http://www.historyguide.org/intellect/lecture27a.html. February 28, 2006. July 1, 2006.)

L. L. Cool J. "I'm That Type of Guy." Walking With a Panther. PGD/Polygram/Def Jam, 1989.

Lamont, Paul. "Is Prince Getting too Big for His Lace Britches?" Right On! June, 1985.

Lauper, Cyndi. "When You Were Mine." She's So Unusual. Sony, 1983.

Leeds, Alan. "Liner Notes." Prince: The Hits/The B-Sides. Paisley Park/Warner Bros, 1993.

Light, Allen. "☥ Breaks the Silence." Vibe. Vol. 4, No. 6. August, 1994. pp. 44-49.

Lindon, Amy. "The 1995 Grammy Show." 4 on the Floor. VH1. Fall, 1995.

Little Richard. The Georgia Peach. Specialty, 1991.

Loder, Kurt. "Prince Reigns." Rolling Stone. August 30, 1984.

Loder, Kurt. "The Artist: A Conversation with Kurt Loder." MTV 1515. November 5, 1999. http://www.mtv.com/bands/archive/p/prince/princefeature99.jhtml. (also posted at http://www.princelyrics.co.uk/viewarticle.asp?article=9)

Love, Robert. "Furor Over Rock Lyrics Intensifies." Rolling Stone. Issue No. 456. September 12, 1985.

McMillan, Terry. Waiting to Exhale. New York: Simon & Schuster, 1995.

McNamara, R. J. "Prince Dominates Sales." Rolling Stone. October 11, 1984.

Madonna. Like a Virgin. WEA/Warner Bros, 1987.

Madonna and Prince. "Love Song." Like A Prayer. WEA/Warner Bros, 1989.

Marsh, Dave. "Why Prince and Bruce Springsteen Now Seem Hotter than Michael Jackson." TV Guide.

February 23, 1985.

Marsh, Dave, ed. George Clinton and P-Funk: An Oral History. New York: Avon, 1998.

Mary Jane Girls. Best of In My House. PGD/PolyGram, 1994.

M.C. Hammer. "Pray." Please Hammer Don't Hurt Them. EMD/Capital, 1990.

Mayfield, Curtis and the Impressions. Anthology: 1961-1977. UNI/MCA, 1992.

McRoy, Ruth G. "The Color of Child Welfare Policy: Addressing Disproportionality." Presented at the NYS Citizens' Coalition for Children, Inc. 17th Annual Statewide Adoption Training Conference. (Albany New York) May 12-13, 2006. (Posted at NYSCCC.org. http://www.nysccc.org/Conferences/2006Conf/2006ConfHandout/Color.htm.)

Mellencamp, John Cougar. "Small Town." Scarecrow. PGD/PolyGram, 1985.

Milton, John. Paradise Lost and Paradise Regained. New York: Penguin Group, 1976.

Miller, Jim. "Naughty Prince of Rock." Newsweek. December 21, 1981. 98:75.

Miller, R. Baxter. "The 'Etched Flame' of Margaret Walker: Biblical and Literary Re-Creation in Southern History." Black Southern Voices. New York: Meridian, 1992.

Mills, Stephanie. "How Come You Don't Call Me Anymore?" Merciless. Casablanca, 1983.

Mills, Stephanie. "How Come You Don't Call Me Anymore?" The Ultimate Collection. HIP-O Records, 1999.

Mistral, Gabriela. Selected Poems of Gabriela Mistral (with translation and introduction by Langston Hughes.) Bloomington: Indiana University, 1957. (Berkeley: Serendipity Books)

Mistral, Gabriela. "Serene Words." World Literature: An Anthology of Great Short Stories, Drama, and Poetry. Lincolnwood: NTC Publishing Group, 1992.

Mitchell, Joni. "Help Me." Hits. Warner Bros, 1996.

Mitchell, Tony. "Posin' 'til Closin'." Sounds. June 6, 1981. (Part of this interview was published in the magazine, but a great deal more of this interview was not published in the magazine, and exists in its entirety as a well-bootlegged audio CD, mostly known as the Amsterdam, Holland interview with Mick Boskamp on May 9, 1981.)

Morrison, Theodore, ed. The Portable Chaucer. New York: Penguin, 1975.

Nadell, James. Bob Marley, Jimi Hendrix and Black Music: Profiles in Fanonist National Culture. New York: Winston-Derek, 1995.

Narine, Dalton. "'Blue-eyed soul': Are Whites Taking over Rhythm & Blues?" Ebony. July, 1989. (archived at Find Articles.com. http://findarticles.com/p/articles/mi_m1077/is_n9_v44/ai_7698861)

Neal, Larry. "The Black Arts Movement." The Norton Anthology of African American Literature. New York: W. W. Norton & Company, 1997.

Nelson, John. "Interview." <u>MTV Presents: Purple Rain Premiere Party</u>. MTV. 1984

Nelson, John. "Interview." <u>A Current Affair</u>. NBC . 1990.

Nelson, Tyka. "Interview." <u>A Current Affair</u>. NBC. 1990.

New Power Generation. <u>Gold Nigga</u>. Paisley Park/Warner Bros Records, 1992.

New Power Generation. <u>Exodus</u>. NPG Records, 1995.

New Power Generation. <u>New Power Soul</u>. NPG Records, 1998.

Newton, Huey P. <u>To Die for the People: Selected Writings and Speeches</u>. New York: Writers and Readers Publishers, Inc., 1995.

Nilsen, Per. <u>Prince: A Documentary</u>. London: Omnibus Press, 1993.

94 East. <u>Minneapolis Genius—The Historic 1977 Recordings</u>. Hot Pint II, 1977.

O'Connor, Sinead. "Nothing Compares 2 U." <u>I Do Not Want What I Haven't Got</u>. EMD/Chrysalis, 1990.

"100 Greatest Guitarists of all Time." <u>Mojo, The Music Magazine</u>. June 1996.

<u>Only in America</u>. HBO. 1999.

Palmer, Robert. "Is Prince Leading Music to a True Biracism?" <u>New York Times</u>. December 2, 1981.

Parker, Dorothy. <u>The Poetry and Short Stories of Dorothy</u>

Parker: Modern Library Series. New York: Random House, 1994.

Parker, Ray Jr. and Raydio. "Woman Needs Love (Just Like You Do.)" Woman Needs Love. Arista, 1981.

Parliament. Tear the Roof Off: 1974-1980. Chronicles/Casablanca, 1993.

Pastis, Steve. "The Man Who Invented Rock 'n Roll." Pop Art Times. (Online Journal). Zads Entertainment, Ltd. 1996. http://poparttimes.com/archives/9809note.html.

Paul, Billy. Me & Mrs. Jones: The Best of Billy Paul. Sony Music, 1999.

Paz, Octavio. "Two Bodies." World Literature: An Anthology of Great Short Stories, Drama, and Poetry. Lincolnwood: NTC Publishing Group, 1992.

Paz, Octavio. Octavio Paz and His Completed Works. Mexico: Fondo de Cultura Economics, 1994.

Pendergrass. "Come Go With Me." Greatest Hits. EMD/Capitol, 1998.

Perry, Steve. "Interview." Prince: Unauthorized. Simitar Entertainment, Inc., 1992.

Phillips, Karen. "Chapters of Eleven." Alternative Press Review. Vol. 5 No. 1. Spring, 2000. http://www.altpr.org/modules.php?op=modload&name=Sections&file=index&req=printpage&artid=154. Reprinted from The Baffler, Issue 11, 1999.

Pointer Sisters. "I Feel for You." So Excited. Planet, 1982.

"Postmodernism." <u>Wikipedia.org</u>. http://en.wikipedia.org/wiki/Post_modernism.

Potosh, Chris. <u>The Jimi Hendrix Companion: Three Decades of Commentary</u>. New York: Music Sales Corporation, 2000.

Prince. <u>For You</u>. Warner Bros Records, 1978.

Prince. <u>Prince</u>. Warner Bros Records, 1979.

Prince. "Interview." <u>American Bandstand</u>. ABC. 1980.

Prince. <u>Dirty Mind</u>. Warner Bros Records, 1980.

Prince. <u>Controversy</u>. Warner Bros Records, 1981.

Prince. <u>1999</u>. Warner Bros Records, 1982.

Prince and the Revolution. <u>Purple Rain</u>. Warner Bros Records, 1984.

Prince and the Revolution. "God" b/w of "Purple Rain." Warner Bros Records, 1984.

Prince and the Revolution. "4 the Tears in your Eyes." <u>We Are the World</u>. Columbia/CBS Records, 1985.

Prince and the Revolution. <u>Around the World in a Day</u>. Paisley Park/Warner Bros Records, 1985.

Prince and the Revolution. "Pop Life." Twelve Inch/Extended Version. Warner Bros Records,1985.

Prince and the Revolution. "Hello" b/w of "Pop Life." Warner Bros Records, 1985.

Prince. "Radio Interview with the Electrifying Mojo."

WHYT: Detroit, Michigan, 1985. (Posted at <u>Prince in Print</u>. http://princetext.tripod.com/i_mojo85.html.)

Prince. "Interview." <u>MTV Presents Prince</u>. MTV. 1985.

Prince and the Revolution. <u>Parade</u>. Paisley Park/Warner Bros Records, 1986.

Prince. <u>Sign "☮" the Times</u>. Paisley Park/Warner Bros Records, 1987.

Prince. <u>Lovesexy</u>. Paisley Park/Warner Bros Records, 1988.

Prince. <u>Lovesexy Tour Book</u>. New York: Brockhum, Inc., 1988.

Prince. <u>Batman</u>. Warner Bros Records, 1989.

Prince. <u>Graffiti Bridge</u>. Paisley Park/Warner Bros Records, 1990.

Prince. "Still Would Stand All Time." Performance during an Aftershow in Germany from an Unauthorized Video Recording, 1990.

Prince. "Acceptance Speech for the AMA Award of Merit." <u>1990 American Music Awards</u>. ABC. 1990.

Prince and the New Power Generation. <u>Diamonds & Pearls</u>. Paisley Park/Warner Bros Records, 1991.

Prince and the New Power Generation. <u>⚥</u>. Paisley Park/Warner Bros Records, 1992.

Prince and the New Power Generation. <u>Three Chains of Gold</u>. Paisley Park/Warner Bros Reprise Video,

1993.

Prince. <u>The Hits/The B sides</u>. Paisley Park/Warner Bros Records, 1993.

Prince. "Black Muthafuckers in the House." <u>This Is my Night</u>. (Unauthorized Recording of San Francisco Aftershow—DNA Lounge, December 4, 1993. KTS, 1993.

Prince. <u>The Black Album</u>. Paisley Park/Warner Bros Records, 1988, 1994.

⚥. <u>The Beautiful Experience</u>. Paisley Park/Point of View Films, 1994.

Prince. <u>Come</u>. Warner Bros Records, 1994.

⚥. "Acceptance Speech for Lifetime Achievement Award." <u>Celebrate the Soul Awards</u>. FOX. 1994.

⚥. "Interview." <u>The Sunday Show</u>. BBC. 1995.

⚥. <u>The Gold Experience</u>. NPG Records/Warner Bros Records, 1995.

⚥. "Acceptance Speech for the 1995 AMA of Merit." <u>1995 American Music Awards</u>. ABC. 1995.

Prince. <u>Chaos and Disorder</u>. Warner Bros Records, 1996.

⚥. <u>Emancipation</u>. NPG Records, 1996

⚥. "Performance and Interview." <u>The Oprah Winfrey Show</u>. Harpo Productions. November 1996.

⚥. "Interview with Bryant Gumbel." <u>Today Show</u>. NBC. December 19, 1996.

☥. <u>VH1 to One</u>. VH1. 1997.

☥. <u>Crystal Ball</u>. NPG Records, 1997.

☥. "Interview." <u>Musician</u>. April, 1997.

Prince. <u>The Vault</u>. Warner Bros Records, 1998.

☥. "Interview with Tavis Smiley." <u>BET Tonight</u>. BET, 1998.

☥. <u>Rave U2 the Joy Fantastic</u>. NPG/Arista Records, 1999.

☥. <u>Rave U2 the Joy Fantastic (Remix)</u>. NPG/Arista Records, 1999.

☥. "The Artist: A Conversation with Kurt Loder." <u>MTV 1515</u>. November 5, 1999. May 10, 2007. http://www.mtv.com/bands/archive/p/prince/princefeature99.jhtml. (also posted at http://www.princelyrics.co.uk/viewarticle.asp?article=9)

☥. <u>Rave U2 the Year 2000</u>. NPG/In Demand Pay Per View Network, 1999.

Prince. "U Make my Sun Shine."/"When Will We Be Paid?" NPG Records, 2000.

Prince. "2045 Radical Man." <u>Bamboozled Soundtrack</u>. Forty Acers and a Mule/Motown, 2000.

Prince. <u>The Rainbow Children</u>. NPG Records, Inc., 2001.

Prince. "Personal Conversation." August 30, 2002.

Prince. "Liner Notes." <u>One Nite Alone…Live!</u> NPG Records, 2002.

Prince. The Chocolate Invasion. NPG Records, 2003.

Prince. The Slaughterhouse. NPG Records, 2003.

Prince. Musicology. NPG Records, 2004.

Prince. "Acceptance Speech." 2004 Rock-n-Roll Hall of Fame Induction Ceremony. VH1. 2004

Prince. The Art of Musicology. BET/MTV. April, 2004.

Prince. "Interview with Tavis Smiley." The Tavis Smiley Show. PBS, 2004.

Prince. 3121. NPG Records, 2006.

Public Enemy. "Brothers Gonna Work It Out." Fear of a Black Planet. Def Jam, 1994.

Quennell, Peter. "Introduction." My Heat Laid Bare and Other Prose Writings by Charles Baudelaire. New York: The Vanguard Press Inc., 1951.

Questlove. "Someday Our ⚥ Will Come?!!?" Rap Pages. April, 1997. (reprinted by The ⚥ Family. Vol. 5 Issue 18, 106

Redding, Noel and Carol Appleby. Are You Experience? Inside the Story of Jimi Hendrix Experience. New York: Da Capo Press, 1996.

Richards, Paulette. "Personal Interview." August, 2000.

Robinson, Smokey and the Miracles. 35 Year Anniversary. PGD/Motown, 1994.

Robinson, Smokey. Ultimate Collection. UNI/Motown, 1997.

Rogers, Kenny. "You're My Love." They Don't Make Them Like They Used To. RCA, 1986.

Rosenberg, Donna, ed. World Literature: An Anthology of Great Short Stories, Drama, and Poetry. Lincolnwood: NTC Publishing Group, 1992.

Rosenberg, Donna, ed. World Literature: An Anthology of Great Short Stories, Drama, and Poetry (Instructor's Manual). Lincolnwood: NTC Publishing Group, 1992.

Roswell, Clint. "Prince Is Partying Up to the Gold and Platinum." New York Daily News, 29 March 1981: B14.

Rowan, Carl T. "Introduction." The Negro in Minnesota. Minneapolis: T. S. Denison, 1961.

Rush, Bobby. "Hen Pecked." Hen Pecked. 601 Records, 2005.

Russell, Lisa. "Prince Got the Girl in Purple Rain, but Movie Rival Morris Day Is Stealing some of His Thunder." People. Summer, 1984.

Salaam, Kalamu. "The Psychology of the Pimp: Interview with Iceberg Slim." Black Collegian. 5.3. 1975.

Salaam, Kalamu. What Is Life? Chicago: Third World Press, 1994.

Salaam, Kalamu. "Black Arts Movement." The Oxford Companion to African American Literature. New York: Oxford University Press, 1997.

Salaam, Kalamu. "Personal Interview." August, 2000.

Salewicz, Chris. "Prince: Strutting with the new Soul Monarch." New Musical Express. June 6, 1981. (archived at Rock's Backpages Library. http://www.rocksbackpages.com/article.html?ArticleID=6813.)

Salholz, E. "Getting the Princely Look." Newsweek. October 1, 1984. 104:84.

Santana, Carlos. Best of Santana. Sony/Columbia, 1998.

Sayer, Mike. "Interview about H. Rap Brown." June 8, 2000.

Schwartz, Andy. "Prince: A Dirty Mind Comes Clean." New York Rocker. June, 1981. (archived at Rock's Backpages Library. http://www.rocksbackpages.com/article.html?ArticleID=6116.)

Selvin, Joel and Dave Marsh. Sly and the Family Stone: An Oral History. New York: Morrow, William and Co., 1998.

Shange, Ntozake. For Colored Girls Who Have Considered Suicide When the Rainbow Is Enuf. New York: Scribner, 1997.

Shelley, Mary. Frankenstein. New York: Pocket Books, 1994.

Simonart, Serge. "The Artist." Guitar World. October, 1998.

Sinclair, Tom. "The Artist: The Online Interview." Entertainment Weekly. May 28, 1999. May 10, 2007. (archived on Prince in Print. http://princetext.tripod.com/i_various99.html.)

Slim, Iceberg. The Pimp. Oakland: Holloway House

Publishing Co., 1997.

Slim, Iceberg. The Naked Soul of Iceberg Slim. Oakland: Holloway House Publishing Co., 1998.

Sly & the Family Stone. Anthology. Sony Music, 1981.

Smith, Chazz. "Interview." Prince: Unauthorized. Simitar Entertainment, Inc., 1992.

Spangler, Earl. The Negro in Minnesota. Minneapolis: T. S. Denison, 1961.

Springsteen, Bruce. Born in the USA. Sony/Columbia, 1984.

Staples, Mavis. "Prince of Paisley Park." Omnibus. London: BBC Television. 1991.

Staples, Mavis. "Interview." Video LP. Black Entertainment Television. 1991.

Staples, Mavis. The Voice. Paisley Park/Warner Bros Records, 1993.

Staple Singers. The Greatest Hits. Fantasy, 1999.

Stevenson, John Allen. "A Vampire in the Mirror: The Sexuality of Dracula." PMLA Vol. 103, No. 2 (Mar. 1988): pp. 139-149. JSTOR. May 5, 2007. http://links.jstor.org/sici?sici=0030-8129(198803)103%3A2%3C139%3 AAVITMT%3E2.0.CO%3B2-0.

Sutherland, Steve. "Someday your Prince Will Come." Melody Maker, June 6, 1981. (archived at Rock's Back Pages.com but not yet posted on their site.)

Sweat, Keith. "In the Rain." Make It Last Forever. WEA/Electra, 1988.

T., Ice. VH1: Behind the Music. VH1, 2000.

Tate, Greg. "Painted Black." Village Voice. April 14, 1987.

Taylor, Kevin. "Phone Conversations/Interviews." September, 1995. November, 1995.

The Time. The Time. Warner Bros Records, 1981.

The Time. What Time Is It? Warner Bros Records, 1982.

The Time. Ice Cream Castles. Warner Bros Records, 1984.

Thoreau, Henry David. Walden, or Life in the Woods and Other Writings. New York: Barnes and Noble Books, 1992.

TLC. "If I Was Your Girlfriend." Crazy Sexy Cool. BMG/Arista/LaFace, 1994.

Toure. "The Artist." Icon. October, 1998.

Townshend, Pete. History of Rock-n-Roll: The Guitar. VH1. 1999.

Tucker, Ken. "Someday My Prince Will Come: Love and Lust in Minneapolis, A Review of Dirty Mind" Rolling Stone. February 19, 1981: 54-55. (archived at Prince in Print. http://princetext.tripod.com/r_dirty_mind.html

Turner, Tina. "Let's Pretend We're Married." B-side of "I Can't Stand the Rain." Capital, 1983.

Vanity Six. Vanity Six. Warner Bros Records, 1981.

Various Artists. 1-800NEWFUNK. NPG Records, 1994.

Virgil. The Aeneid. New York: Vintage Books, 1990.

Walker, Alice. Color Purple. New York: Simon & Schuster, 1982.

Walker, Alice. The Temple of My Familiar. Simon & Schuster, 1989.

Walsh, Jim. "Liner Notes." The Gold Experience. NPG/Warner Bros Records, 1995.

Walsh, Jim. "The Truth Review." St. Paul Pioneer Press. July 18, 1997. (Reprinted and archived by The ⚥ Family. Dawkins, Vol. 5 Issue 16, 94.)

Walsh, Jim. "For Prince, it's all about Sex, God, and Rock 'n' roll." Pioneer Press. June 14, 2001. (Posted at http://www.princelyrics.co.uk/viewarticle.asp?article=37.)

Ward, Jerry W. "Interview/Conversation." June/August, 2000.

Waring, Charles. "Chaos and Disorder Review." Blues & Soul. July 23-August 5, 1996.

Washington, Booker T. Up from Slavery. New York: Dover Publications, 1995.

Waters, Muddy. Greatest Hits. Golden Stars, 2000.

Watkins, Hollis. "Interview." November, 2000.

Wayans, Damon. HBO Comedy Special. HBO. 1997.

Welsing, Frances Cress. Isis Papers. Chicago: Third World Press, 1991.

White, Charles. <u>The Life and Times of Little Richard: The Quasar of Rock</u>. New York: Da Capo Press, Inc., 1994.

Whitman, Walt. <u>Leaves of Grass</u>. New York: Barnes and Noble Books, 1994.

Wilen, Dennis. "Prince Explains His Royal Secrets." <u>LA Herald-Examiner</u>. March 27, 1981.

Wilkie, Brian and James Hurt, eds. <u>Literature of the Western World</u>. Vol. II. New York: Macmillan Publishing Co., 1992.

Willie, Pepe. "Interview." <u>Prince: Unauthorized</u>. Simitar Entertainment, Inc., 1992.

Willie, Pepe. "Personal Interview." October, 2000.

Wilson, Morris. "Personal Interview." November, 2000.

Withers, Bill. <u>Bill Withers' Greatest Hits</u>. Columbia, 1981.

Witter, Simon. "Prince is an Asshole: Interview with Jesse Johnson." <u>New Musical Express</u>. November 29, 1986.

Wonder, Stevie. "Sir Duke." <u>Songs in the Key</u>. Taurus/Motown Records, 1976.

Wonder, Stevie. <u>Journey Through the Secret Life of Plants</u>. PolyGram International, 1979.

Woodson, Carter G. <u>The Mis-Education of the Negro</u>. Trenton: Africa World Press, Inc., 1998.

Wordsworth, William and Samuel Taylor Coleridge. <u>Lyrical Ballads, 1798: Wordsworth and Coleridge</u>.

London: Oxford University Press, 1970.

Zu-Bolton, Ahmos. "Interview/Conversation." June, 1999.

Quoted or Referenced Index

Adams, Hazard: 115, 116
Adler, Bill: 81, 161, 175, 182-183
"Ain't No Sunshine": 589
Albright, David: 90
Alexander, Margaret Walker: 491-493, 520, 602
Ali, Muhammad: 376, 379
Allen, Bonnie: 191, 242, 295
"America the Beautiful": 561
Amerson, Rich: 176
Anderson, Jolivette: 495
Aristotle: 552, 557
Askhari: 617-619
B, Michael: 476
Baldwin, James: 25, 181, 207, 239, 403, 404, 405, 487, 493, 496
Bamboozled: 566
Baraka, Amiri (LeRoi Jones): 6, 10, 12-13, 15, 20-21, 24, 33, 35, 106-107, 109, 125, 283, 291, 375, 379, 431-432, 580, 623
Baudelaire, Charles: 125-126
Bauval, Robert and Adrian Gilbert: 501-502
"Because You Know You're Young in Beauty Yet": 441
Bell, Al: 500
Belton, Steven and Katherine Harp: 82
Benjamin, Walter: 79, 88, 93, 94, 98, 99, 103
Bigger Thomas: 286, 588
Bland, Bobby "Blue" and B. B. King: 175
"Black Art": 431-432
"Black Art: Mute Matter Given Force and Function": 484
Black Bourgeoisie: 48
Black Boy: 354
Bluest Eye, The: 168
Boskamp, Mick: [quoted in Tony Mitchell article.] 105, 131, 142, 156, 161-162, 168, 181, 182, 189, 197, 201, 221, 354
Brave New World: 93, 513
Braxton, Charlie R.: 61

Bream, Jon: 238, 494, 500, 504
Brown, H. Rap: 211
Brown, James: 177, 623
Buggles, The: 86
Campbell, Tevin: 331
Charles, Ray: 223
Christian, Barbara: 67, 68, 87, 106, 107, 110, 204-205
Clinton, George: 567
Clapton, Eric: 30, 386-387
Coleman, Lisa: 109
Collins, Bootsy: 246
Color Purple, The: 404
"Come Go with Me": 177
Cook, Mercer and Steven Henderson: 140, 176, 623
Cooper, Barry Michael: 138
Cooper, Carol: 106, 170, 180, 194, 198, 220
Cornberg, David: 608-609
Courtly Love Poetry: 441
Crawford, Will: 623
Dadie, Bernard: 561-562
Dancing in September: 566
D'Angelo, Joe: 581-582
Dante: 366-367, 441
D'Arby, Terence Trent: 372, 483
Day, Morris: 374
Davis, Miles: 28, 90, 91, 98-99, 111-112, 176, 196, 389
Davis, Sammy Jr.: 470
Davis, Walter: 571
Dawkins, Diana: 34, 268, 348, 478, 499-503, 549-550, 555
DeCurtis, Anthony: 159, 370, 547, 548
Dickerson, Dez: 26, 585
Dickinson, Emily: 436
Diddley, Bo: 379
Douglass, Frederick: 543, 544, 560
Dramatics: 175-176
"Dry Your Tears Africa!": 561-562
Du Bois, W. E. B.: 189, 212, 466, 592
Durkee, Cutler: 392
Dylan, Bob: 623

E., Shelia: 248, 393
Ebiri, Bilge: 79-80, 269
Edrei, Mary: 28, 166
Electrifying Mojo: 100, 162, 383
Evers, Medgar: 520
Faber, Jim: 504
Farrakhan, Louis: 364, 567
Father MC: 531
Finn, Julio: 114, 115
Fiore, Raymond: 582
Fire Next Time, The: 493, 496
For Colored Girls Who Have Considered Suicide when the Rainbow Is Enuf: 495
"For Saundra": 264
Fowlie, Wallace: 119, 122, 124, 129, 131, 140, 142-143, 148-149, 152, 153-154, 155, 157, 158, 159
Frazier, E. Franklin: 48
From Mammies to Militants: 205
Fudger, Dave: 107, 153, 156, 161, 165, 166, 167, 168, 183, 187, 397
Funkadelic: 269, 574
Gates, Henry Louis and Nellie McKay: 11, 15, 29, 62, 264, 402, 466, 484-485, 491, 498, 543, 544, 575
Gaye, Marvin: 177, 188, 202-204, 237
George, Nelson: 16, 19, 34, 77
Giddings, Paula: 205
Giovanni, Nikki: 263-264
Giovanni's Room: 403
Goldberg, Michael: 374
golden parachute: 579
Graham, Lawrence Otis: 48
Graustark, Barbara: 12, 165, 179, 184, 224
Gundersen, Edna: 198, 504-505, 514, 521-522
Hamer, Fannie Lou: 590
Happy Feet: 264
Harold Melvin and the Blue Notes": 594
Harris, Trudier: 205
Hassan, Umar Bin: 620-621

Hawthorne, Nathaniel: 402
Hayes, Issac: 412
Hemingway, Ernest: 410
Hemings, Sally: 402
Hendrix, Jimi: 386, 387
"Hen Pecked": 175
Hidalgo, Luis: 111, 333
Hilburn, Robert: 20, 99, 116, 141, 153, 155, 161, 196, 214, 340, 425
Hill, Dave: 25, 33, 53, 54-55, 57-58, 69, 72, 83, 139, 172, 173, 180, 181-182, 183, 191, 192, 196, 197, 214, 216, 222, 224, 225, 226, 241-242, 247, 270, 305, 375, 385, 388, 389, 390, 391, 394, 412, 413, 423, 426
Hilliard, Asa: 488
"Hills like White Elephants": 410
Hoskyns, Barney: 106, 112-113, 165-166, 179, 218-219
"House Is not a Home, A": 523
Housequake.com: 577
Hughes, Langston: 15, 498, 625
Hurston, Zora Neale: 404, 436, 446-447, 531
Husney, Owen: 10, 51, 60-61, 63-64, 72
Huxley, Aldous: 93, 513
Ice Cube: 18
Ice T: 393
"I'm that Type of Guy": 531
Isis Papers, The: 426
Jackson, Jackie: 626
Jackson, Michael: 626
Jackson, Millie: 387
James, Rick: 386, 584
Jefferson, Thomas: 401-402
Jensen, Jeff: 586
Jimmy Jam: 498
Johnson, James Weldon: 11
Joyner, Tom: 587
Karenga, Maulana: 29, 484-485
Karlen, Neal: 21, 101-102, 102-103, 120, 121, 132, 137, 150, 156, 164-165, 166, 259, 277, 294, 332,

341, 376, 391, 553
Kashif: 63, 79, 160
Keats, John: 234
Kendricks, Eddie: 177
Killens, John Oliver: 491-493, 520
King, Don: 393
King, Martin Luther: 97
KISS: 431
Knyte, Andrew: 138
Kravitz, Lenny: 483
Kreis, Steven: 116, 119, 133, 134, 135, 136, 137, 140
LaBelle: 387
Leeds, Alan: 129-130, 162, 177, 192-193, 228, 243, 268, 280
Leeds, Eric: 102
Lessing, Doris: 106
"Let's Get it On": 177, 188, 202-204
Light, Allen: 352, 355, 356, 357, 361
L. L. Cool J: 531
Limbaugh, Rush: 469
Lindon, Amy: 185
Little Richard: 188, 199
Loder, Kurt: 356, 471, 564
M., Tony: 282
<u>Mack, The</u>: 600-601
"Mannish Boy": 379
McDaniels, Preselfannie: 606-607
McMillan, Terry: 404
McRoy, Ruth: 81-82
"Me and Mrs. Jones": 411
Mead, Margaret: 405
Medina, Tony: 604-605
Mellencamp, John Cougar: 509
Mistral, Gabriela: 532
Mitchell, Tony: 105, 131, 142, 156, 161-162, 168, 181, 182, 189, 197, 201, 221, 354
Miller, R. Baxter: 491-493, 520
<u>Modernism and Music: An Anthology of Sources</u>: 90
<u>Mojo, the Music Magazine</u>: 268

Moon, Chris: 83
Morrison, Toni: 168
"My Country 'tis of Thee (America)": 561
My Time with Prince: 26, 585
Narine, Dalton: 199
Narrative of the Life of Frederick Douglass: 543, 544
Native Son: 404
Neal, Larry: 623
"Negro Artist and the Racial Mountain, The": 498, 625
Nelson, John: 163-164
Nelson, Tyka: 162
Nilsen, Per: 33-34
N.W.A.: 626
Orion Mystery, The: 501-503
O'Reilly, Bill: 469
Our Kind of People: 48
Paradise Lost: 206
Parker, Ray Jr.: 530
Past Lives, Still Living: Traveling the Pathways to Freedom: 495
Paz, Octavio, 266, 532
Pendergrass, Teddy: 177, 188
Perry, Steve: 59, 60, 70, 629
Phillips, Karen: 76, 77
Phillips, Sam: 22, 627
Plato: 542, 552
Poe, Edgar Allen: 436
Price of the Ticket, The: 181, 405
Prince.org: 577
☥ Family, The: 34, 268, 348, 478, 499-503, 549-550, 555
Pryor, Richard: 588
Quennell, Peter: 111, 117, 118, 125, 128-129, 159
Questlove: 281, 291
Rap on Race, A: 405
Reagan, Ronald: 487
Real Sex: 431
"Respect Yourself": 594
Richards, Keith: 211
Richards, Paulette: 234

Robinson, Smokey: 623
Rockeymoore, Mark: 610-611
Rolling Stones: 210-211
Rosenberg, Donna: 266
Rowan, Carl T.: 37, 38
Ruffin, David: 177
Rush, Bobby: 175
Salaam, Kalamu ya: 144-145, 283, 284, 291, 292, 349, 400-401, 403, 492-493, 511, 527-528
Salewicz, Chris: 26, 153, 166, 168, 187, 195
Santana, Carlos: 469
Scarface: 600
Scarlet Letter: 402
"Serene Words": 532
"Sexual Healing": 177, 202-204, 237
Schwartz, Andy: 79, 85, 116-117, 165, 166, 167, 168, 553
Scott-Heron, Gil: 95-96
Shange, Ntozake: 495
Simonart, Serge: 399, 558
Sinclair, Tom: 159
"Sir Duke": 624
Sir Gawain and the Green Knight: 441
Sledge, Percy: 175
Smith, Chazz: 72, 73, 83-84
Songs in the Key of Life: 624, 625
Soul Food: 576
"So You Wanna Be an Avant-Garde Fan?": 571
Spangler, Earl: 37-39, 40-41, 42, 43, 44, 45-46, 47, 48-49, 49-50
Stanley, Paul: 431
Staples, Mavis: 102, 330
Staple Singers: 594
Stevenson, John Allen: 588-589
"Stormy Monday": 175
Straight out of Compton: 626
Superfly: 600
Sutherland, Steve: 107, 161, 397
Sweat, Keith: 175-176
Taylor, Kevin: 34

Temptations, The: 177
There Eyes Were Watching God: 404, 436, 531
Thompson-Cager, Chezia: 612-614
Thoreau, Henry David: 296-297
"Tight Rhymes, Phat Beats, and Loose Canons": 623
Toomer, Jean: 212
Toure': 77, 162, 338
Townsend, Pete: 387
"Treat them Like they Want to Be Treated": 531
Tucker, Ken: 172-173
Tupac: 413
"Turn out the Lights": 188
"Two Bodies": 266, 532
Up From Slavery: 475, 491
Uptown.com: 577
"Use Me": 589
"Vampire in the Mirror, A": 588-589
Vandross, Luther: 523
"Video Killed the Radio Star": 86
Waiting to Exhale: 404
"Wake Up Everybody": 594
Walker, Alice: 246-247, 404
Wall Street (film): 76, 81, 93
Walsh, Jim: 113-114, 551-552, 554-555
Ward, Jerry: 533, 567
Waring, Charles: 494
Washington, Booker T.: 475, 491
Waters, Muddy: 379
Watkins, Hollis: 59
Wayans, Damon: 64, 437, 469-470
Welsing, Francis Cress: 426
"We Raise de Wheat": 576
"What to a Slave Is the Fourth of July?": 560
Wheatley, Phyllis: 401-402
"When a Man Loves a Woman": 175
When and Where I Enter: 205
White, Barry: 209
Whitman, Walt: 296-297
Wideman, John Edgar: 62, 140

Wikipedia.org: 90, 579
Wilkie, Brian and James Hart: 296-297
Williams, Saul: 615-616
Willie, Pepe: 52, 58, 62-63, 64-65, 66, 70-71, 83, 91, 118-119
Wilson, Morris: 57, 68-69, 72
Withers, Bill: 589
"Woman Needs Love Just Like You Do, A": 530
Wonder, Stevie: 624, 625-626
Woodson, Carter G.: 457
Wright, Richard: 354, 404, 601-602
X, Malcolm: 493, 559-560
"Young Goodman Brown": 402
Zu-Bolton, Ahmos: 533

www.ingramcontent.com/pod-product-compliance
Lightning Source LLC
Chambersburg PA
CBHW021712300426
44114CB00009B/111